Taking SIDES

Clashing Views on Controversial Issues in American History
Volume II
Reconstruction to the Present

Seventh Edition

Taking SIDES

Clashing Views on Controversial Issues in American History
Volume II
Reconstruction to the Present

Seventh Edition

Edited, Selected, and with Introductions by

Larry Madaras
Howard Community College
and
James M. SoRelle
Baylor University

Dushkin/McGraw-Hill
A Division of The McGraw-Hill Companies

To Maggie and Cindy

Photo Acknowledgments

Part 1 Library of Congress
Part 2 AP/Wide World Photos
Part 3 National Archives
Part 4 Southern Christian Leadership Conference

Cover Art Acknowledgment

Charles Vitelli

Library of Congress Cataloging-in-Publication Data

Main entry under title:
 Taking sides: clashing views on controversial issues in American history, volume II, reconstruction to the present/edited, selected, and with introductions by Larry Madaras and James M. SoRelle.—7th ed.
 Includes bibliographical references and index.
 1. United States—History—1865–. I. Madaras, Larry, *comp.* II. SoRelle, James M., *comp.*

973

0-697-37533-1   1091-8833

Printed on Recycled Paper

PREFACE

The success of the past six editions of *Taking Sides: Clashing Views on Controversial Issues in American History* has encouraged us to remain faithful to its original objectives, methods, and format. Our aim has been to create an effective instrument to enhance classroom learning and to foster critical thinking. Historical facts presented in a vacuum are of little value to the educational process. For students, whose search for historical truth often concentrates on *when* something happened rather than on *why*, and on specific events rather than on the *significance* of those events, *Taking Sides* is designed to offer an interesting and valuable departure. The understanding that the reader arrives at based on the evidence that emerges from the clash of views encourages the reader to view history as an *interpretive* discipline, not one of rote memorization.

As in previous editions, the issues are arranged in chronological order and can be easily incorporated into any American history survey course. Each issue has an issue *introduction*, which sets the stage for the debate that follows in the pro and con selections and provides historical and methodological background to the problem that the issue examines. Each issue concludes with a *postscript*, which ties the readings together, briefly mentions alternative interpretations, and supplies detailed *suggestions for further reading* for the student who wishes to pursue the topics raised in the issue. Also, when applicable, Internet site addresses (URLs) have been provided in the postscripts, which should prove useful as starting points for further research.

Changes to this edition   In this edition we have continued our efforts to move beyond the traditionally ethnocentric and male-oriented focus of American history, both in terms of the issues and the authors selected to represent the clashing viewpoints. This edition depicts a society that benefited from the presence of Native Americans, African Americans, and women of various racial and ethnic origins. With this in mind, we present 10 entirely new issues: *Did William M. Tweed Corrupt Post–Civil War New York?* (Issue 2); *Did Late-Nineteenth-Century Immigrants Have to Leave Behind Their Old World Cultures to Come to America?* (Issue 4); *Was the Populist Party Prejudiced?* (Issue 5); *Did the Progressives Fail?* (Issue 7); *Were the 1920s an Era of Social and Cultural Rebellion?* (Issue 9); *Was Franklin Roosevelt a Reluctant Internationalist?* (Issue 11); *Were the 1950s America's "Happy Days"?* (Issue 13); *Did the Civil Rights Movement Improve Race Relations in the United States?* (Issue 14); *Did the Antiwar Movement Prolong War in Vietnam?* (Issue 15); and *Were the 1980s a Decade of Greed?* (Issue 17). In addition, either the YES or NO selections have been replaced in three issues to bring the debates up to date: *Did Booker T. Washington's Philosophy and Actions Betray the Interests of*

African Americans? (Issue 6); *Was Woodrow Wilson a Naive Idealist?* (Issue 8); and *Was the New Deal an Effective Answer to the Great Depression?* (Issue 10). Also, one of the issues retained from the previous edition has been changed so completely that it should be considered new: *Was It Necessary to Drop the Atomic Bomb to End World War II?* (Issue 12). In all, there are 25 new selections.

A word to the instructor An *Instructor's Manual With Test Questions* (multiple-choice and essay) is available through the publisher for the instructor using *Taking Sides* in the classroom. A general guidebook, *Using Taking Sides in the Classroom*, which discusses methods and techniques for integrating the pro-con approach into any classroom setting, is also available. An on-line version of *Using Taking Sides in the Classroom* and a correspondence service for Taking Sides adopters can be found at www.cybsol.com/usingtaking-sides/.

Taking Sides: Clashing Views on Controversial Issues in American History, Volume II is only one title in the Taking Sides series; the others are listed on the back cover. If you are interested in seeing the table of contents for any of the other titles, please visit the Taking Sides Web site at http://www.dushkin.com/takingsides/.

Acknowledgments Many individuals have contributed to the successful completion of this edition. We appreciate the evaluations submitted to Dushkin/McGraw-Hill by those who have used *Taking Sides* in the classroom. Special thanks to those who responded with specific suggestions for this edition:

Gary Best
University of Hawaii at Hilo

Mary Borg
University of Northern
   Colorado

Corlan A. Carlson
Whatcom Community
   College

William P. Dionisio
Sacramento City College

John Whitney Evans
College of St. Scholastica

Richard Jensen
University of Illinois–
   Chicago

Gordon Lam
Sierra College

Jon Nielson
Columbia College

James Revell
Rochester Institute of
   Technology

Neil Sapper
Amarillo College

H. Michael Tarver
McNeese State University

We are particularly indebted to Maggie Cullen, Cindy SoRelle, Barry A. Crouch, Virginia Kirk, Joseph and Helen Mitchell, and Jean Soto, who shared their ideas for changes, pointed us toward potentially useful historical works, and provided significant editorial assistance. Sandy Rohwein and Miriam Wilson (Howard Community College) performed indispensable typing duties connected with this project. Susan E. Myers in the library at Howard Community College provided essential help in acquiring books and articles on interlibrary loan. Finally, we are sincerely grateful for the commitment, encouragement, and patience provided over the years by David Dean, list manager for the Taking Sides series, David Brackley, developmental editor, and the entire staff of Dushkin/McGraw-Hill.

Larry Madaras
Howard Community College

James M. SoRelle
Baylor University

CONTENTS IN BRIEF

CONTENTS

Kenneth M. Stampp, a professor emeritus of history, argues that the period of Reconstruction after the Civil War produced many positive economic, political, and social outcomes. Professor of history Eric Foner maintains that radical rule was unsuccessful because it failed to secure civil, political, and economic rights for southern blacks.

Professor emeritus of history Alexander B. Callow, Jr., insists that by exercising a corrupting influence over the city and state government, as well as over key elements within the business community, William M. "Boss" Tweed and his infamous "ring" extracted enormous sums of ill-gotten money for their own benefit in post–Civil War New York. Professor of history Leo Hershkowitz portrays Tweed as a devoted public servant whose reputation as the symbol for urban political corruption is grossly undeserved.

Professor of history John Tipple argues that the power and greed of big businessmen of the late nineteenth century undermined the nation's traditional institutions and values. Professor of business history Alfred D. Chandler, Jr., concludes that American entrepreneurs were marketing innovators whose creation of great industrial corporations strengthened the country's economy.

Pulitzer Prize–winning historian Oscar Handlin asserts that immigrants to the United States in the late nineteenth century were alienated from the cultural traditions of the homelands they had left as well as from those of their adopted country. Rudolph J. Vecoli, director of the University of Minnesota Immigration and History Research Center, contends that the developed patterns of behavior and thought of Italian peasants did not change when they migrated to Chicago.

The late professor of history Richard Hofstadter (1916–1970) argues that Populist literature and rhetoric in the late nineteenth century created a conspiracy theory around the issues of industrialism and the "money question," which activated a virulent strain of nativism and anti-Semitism among these agrarian reformers. Professor of history Walter T. K. Nugent concludes that the Populists were neither conspiracy-minded nor hostile to foreigners in general or to Jews in particular; in fact, he argues, they were friendlier to immigrants and foreign institutions than their political opponents.

Professor of history Donald Spivey contends that Booker T. Washington alienated both students and faculty at Tuskegee Institute by establishing an authoritarian system that failed to provide an adequate academic curriculum to prepare students for the industrial workplace. Professor emeritus of history Louis R. Harlan portrays Washington as a political realist whose policies and actions were designed to benefit black society as a whole.

Professor of history Richard M. Abrams maintains that progressivism was a failure because it never seriously confronted the inequalities that still exist in American society. Professors of history Arthur S. Link and Richard L. McCormick argue that the Progressives were a diverse group of reformers who confronted and ameliorated the worst abuses that emerged in urban industrial America during the early 1900s.

Former national security adviser and political scholar Henry Kissinger characterizes President Woodrow Wilson as a high-minded idealist whose views made it difficult for later presidents to develop a logical foreign policy based on national self-interest. Professor of history Arthur S. Link contends that Wilson was a true realist who combined the principles of idealism and realism in the reforms he enacted.

History professor William E. Leuchtenburg argues that the growing secularization of American society, the demands by newly enfranchised women for economic equality and sexual liberation, and the hedonistic mood in the country in the 1920s produced a youth rebellion against the symbols of Victorian authority. Author David A. Shannon asserts that the social and cultural changes described by many as revolutionary were actually superficial elements whose significance to the 1920s has been exaggerated.

Professor of history Roger Biles contends that, in spite of its minimal reforms, the New Deal created a limited welfare state that implemented economic stabilizers to avert another depression. Professor of history Gary Dean Best argues that Roosevelt established an antibusiness environment with the creation of the New Deal regulatory programs, which retarded the nation's economic recovery from the Great Depression until World War II.

Diplomatic historian Robert A. Divine argues that even after France fell to Nazi Germany in June 1940, Franklin D. Roosevelt remained a reluctant internationalist who spoke belligerently but acted timidly because he sincerely hated war. Pulitzer Prize–winning historian Arthur M. Schlesinger, Jr., maintains that from a 1990s perspective, Roosevelt—not Stalin, Churchill, or anyone else—was the only wartime leader who saw clearly the direction and shape of the new world that the leaders were trying to create.

Professor of American history Robert James Maddox contends that the atomic bomb became the catalyst that forced the hard-liners in the Japanese army to accept the emperor's plea to surrender. Professor of history Barton J. Bernstein argues that the United States probably could have avoided the use of atomic bombs and still have ended the war by November 1945.

Professor of history and sociology Melvyn Dubofsky and professor of history Athan Theoharis argue that throughout the 1950s, the U.S. economy dominated much of the globe and created a period of unprecedented growth and prosperity for the percentage of the American population that made it into the middle class. Professor of history Douglas T. Miller and journalist Marion Nowak argue that the 1950s were an era of conformity in which Americans feared the bomb, communists, crime, and the loss of a national purpose.

Professor of history Robert Weisbrot describes the lasting achievements produced by the civil rights movement in the realm of school desegregation, the protection of voting rights for African Americans, and the deepening commitment to racial harmony. Political journalist Tom Wicker recognizes that legal segregation ended in the South in the 1960s but contends that in the 1970s and 1980s white animosity toward African American achievements drained momentum from the movement for true racial equality.

Author and editor Adam Garfinkle argues that the antiwar movement had little or no effect on major policy decisions about Vietnam and actually may have contributed to a patriotic backlash that helped Presidents Lyndon Johnson and Richard Nixon to continue the war. Professor of history Melvin Small argues that the antiwar movement had a significant impact on the Vietnam War policies of Johnson and Nixon.

According to professor of history Joan Hoff-Wilson, the Nixon presidency reorganized the executive branch and implemented a number of domestic reforms, despite its limited foreign policy successes and the Watergate scandal. Professor and political commentator Stanley I. Kutler argues that President Nixon was a crass, cynical, narrow-minded politician who unnecessarily prolonged the Vietnam War to ensure his reelection.

Political analyst Kevin Phillips argues that President Ronald Reagan's tax reform bills in the 1980s widened the income gap by decreasing the tax burden on the rich and increasing the taxes paid by the middle-income and poor classes. Conservative economist Alan Reynolds asserts that all income groups experienced significant gains in income during the 1980s.

INTRODUCTION

The Study of History

Larry Madaras
James M. SoRelle

In a pluralistic society such as ours, the study of history is bound to be a complex process. How an event is interpreted depends not only on the existing evidence but also on the perspective of the interpreter. Consequently, understanding history presupposes the evaluation of information, a task that often leads to conflicting conclusions. An understanding of history, then, requires the acceptance of the idea of historical relativism. Relativism means that redefinition of our past is always possible and desirable. History shifts, changes, and grows with new and different evidence and interpretations. As is the case with the law and even with medicine, beliefs that were unquestioned 100 or 200 years ago have been discredited or discarded since.

Relativism, then, encourages revisionism. There is a maxim that "the past must remain useful to the present." Historian Carl Becker argued that every generation should examine history for itself, thus ensuring constant scrutiny of our collective experience through new perspectives. History, consequently, does not remain static, in part because historians cannot avoid being influenced by the times in which they live. Almost all historians commit themselves to revising the views of other historians, synthesizing theories into macrointerpretations, or revising the revisionists.

SCHOOLS OF THOUGHT

Three predominant schools of thought have emerged in American history since the first graduate seminars in history were given at the Johns Hopkins University in Baltimore in the 1870s. The *progressive* school dominated the professional field in the first half of the twentieth century. Influenced by the reform currents of Populism, progressivism, and the New Deal, these historians explored the social and economic forces that energized America. The progressive scholars tended to view the past in terms of conflicts between groups, and they sympathized with the underdog.

The post–World War II period witnessed the emergence of a new group of historians who viewed the conflict thesis as overly simplistic. Writing against the backdrop of the cold war, these *neoconservative* or *consensus* historians argued that Americans possess a shared set of values and that the areas of agreement within the nation's basic democratic and capitalistic framework were more important than the areas of disagreement.

In the 1960s, however, the civil rights movement, women's liberation, and the student rebellion (with its condemnation of the war in Vietnam) fragmented the consensus of values upon which historians and social scientists of the 1950s centered their interpretations. This turmoil set the stage for the emergence of another group of scholars. *New Left* historians began to reinterpret the past once again. They emphasized the significance of conflict in American history, and they resurrected interest in those groups ignored by the consensus school. In addition, New Left historians critiqued the expansionist policies of the United States and emphasized the difficulties confronted by Native Americans, African Americans, women, and urban workers in gaining full citizenship status.

Progressive, consensus, and New Left history is still being written. The most recent generation of scholars, however, focuses upon social history. Their primary concern is to discover what the lives of "ordinary Americans" were really like. These new social historians employ previously overlooked court and church documents, house deeds and tax records, letters and diaries, photographs, and census data to reconstruct the everyday lives of average Americans. Some employ new methodologies, such as quantification (enhanced by advancing computer technology) and oral history, while others borrow from the disciplines of political science, economics, sociology, anthropology, and psychology for their historical investigations.

The proliferation of historical approaches, which are reflected in the issues debated in this book, has had mixed results. On the one hand, historians have become so specialized in their respective time periods and methodological styles that it is difficult to synthesize the recent scholarship into a comprehensive text for the general reader. On the other hand, historians know more about the American past than at any other time in history. They dare to ask new questions or ones that previously were considered to be germane only to scholars in other social sciences. Although there is little agreement about the answers to these questions, the methods employed and issues explored make the "new history" a very exciting field to study.

The topics that follow represent a variety of perspectives and approaches. Each of these controversial issues can be studied for its individual importance to American history. Taken as a group, they interact with one another to illustrate larger historical themes. When grouped thematically, the issues reveal continuing motifs in the development of American history.

ECONOMIC QUESTIONS

Issue 3 explores the dynamics of the modern American economy through investigations of the nineteenth-century entrepreneurs. It evaluates the contributions of post–Civil War entrepreneurial giants. Were these industrial leaders robber barons, as portrayed by contemporary critics and many history texts? John Tipple believes that industrialists like Cornelius Vanderbilt and John D. Rockefeller undermined American institutions and individualistic values by rendering them impotent in their pursuit of wealth. In contrast, Alfred D. Chandler, Jr., characterizes those businessmen as organizational and marketing innovators who created huge corporations that stimulated the rise of a national urban economy.

POLITICAL REFORMS AND THE STATUS QUO

Issue 2 assesses the nature of urban government in the late nineteenth century. Focusing on the activities of William M. "Boss" Tweed in post–Civil War New York City, Alexander B. Callow, Jr., discusses corrupting influences on city and state governments and on big businesses. Leo Hershkowitz presents a contrasting viewpoint, emphasizing Tweed's services and benefits to the city. He rejects Tweed's reputation for corruption, suggesting that it is undeserved.

The Progressive movement is examined in Issue 7. Richard M. Abrams attributes the failure of the movement to its limited scope. He maintains that it imposed a uniform set of values on a diverse people and did not address the inequalities that prevail in American society. Arthur S. Link and Richard L. McCormick, however, emphasize the reforms introduced by the Progressives to check the abuses of industrialization and urbanization during the early 1900s.

FROM DEPRESSION THROUGH PROSPERITY: 1930–1990

The Great Depression of the 1930s remains one of the most traumatic events in U.S. history. The characteristics of that decade are deeply etched in American folk memory, but the remedies that were applied to these social and economic ills—known collectively as the New Deal—are not easy to evaluate. In Issue 10, Roger Biles contends that the economic stabilizers created by New Deal programs prevented the recurrence of the Great Depression. Gary Dean Best, on the other hand, criticizes the New Deal from a 1990s conservative perspective. In his view, the Roosevelt administration prolonged the depression and retarded the recovery. Because New Deal agencies were antibusiness, they overregulated the economy and did not allow the free enterprise system to work out of the depression.

Issue 13 deals with the decade of the 1950s. Melvyn Dubofsky and Athan Theoharis stress the global superpower role of the United States and the prosperity of the middle class, which they feel made these years an era of happiness and optimism. Douglas T. Miller and Marion Nowak detect the underlying anxiety in the decade, with shadows of the cold war, communism, and the atomic bomb looming.

Because he was forced to resign the presidency to avoid impeachment proceedings resulting from his role in the Watergate scandal, President Richard Nixon remains a controversial political figure. How will Nixon, who died in the spring of 1994, be remembered? In Issue 16, Joan Hoff-Wilson downplays the significance of the Watergate scandal as well as foreign policy accomplishments in assessing Nixon's legacy. Instead, she argues, Nixon should be applauded for his domestic accomplishments, including reorganizing the executive branch of the federal government and implementing important civil rights, welfare, and economic planning programs. Stanley I. Kutler disagrees with these revisionist treatments of the former president, insisting that Nixon was a crass, cynical, narrow-minded politician who unnecessarily prolonged the Vietnam War to ensure his reelection and who implemented domestic reforms only to outflank his liberal opponents.

Following the economic upheavals of the 1970s, created by the Vietnam War and the oil crisis, President Ronald Reagan introduced economic policies based on supply-side economics. The success of these policies is the subject matter of Issue 17. Kevin Phillips focuses on the economic advantages that this approach brought to the wealthy. Alan Reynolds, on the other hand, uses statistics to show that all income groups experienced a rise in income levels during this decade.

THE OUTSIDERS: BLACKS, FARMERS, INTELLECTUALS, AND IMMIGRANTS

Perhaps no period of American history has been subject to more myth-making than the era of Reconstruction. In the first issue in the book, Kenneth M. Stampp argues that radical reconstruction after the Civil War succeeded economically, by consolidating the position of industrial capitalism; politically, by producing the most democratic governments the South had ever seen; and socially, by promoting ratification of the Fourteenth and Fifteenth Amendments, which gave African Americans the promise of equal rights. On the other hand, Eric Foner, while recognizing some of the accomplishments of the Reconstruction era, argues that it failed to secure civil, political, and economic rights for southern blacks or to establish the Republican Party as a permanent force in the South.

In the wake of industrialization during the late 1800s, the rapid pace of change created circumstances of hardship and loss to the agricultural community as well as to urban workers. To address these problems, farmers organized a collective movement that grew into the Populist Party in the 1890s. Issue 5 evaluates the Populist Party. Richard Hofstadter acknowledges the reformatory measures in the party platform but stresses the provincialism of the party and its mistrust of foreigners and its anti-Semitism. Walter T. K. Nugent rebuts this, emphasizing the party's open approach to foreigners and their institutions.

One of the most controversial figures in American history was the early-twentieth-century African American leader Booker T. Washington. Was Washington too accommodating toward white values and goals and too accepting of the political disfranchisement and social segregation that took away the basic freedoms that African Americans earned after their emancipation from slavery? In Issue 6, Donald Spivey argues the case against Washington's ideology and policies, while Louis R. Harlan maintains that there were two Washingtons. Harlan argues that Booker T. Washington, while publicly assuring whites that he accepted segregation, fought active and bitter battles behind the scenes to advance the political, economic, and educational opportunities for African Americans. Washington, then, was a political realist whose long-range goals of progress toward equality was a practical response to the climate of the times in which he lived.

The decade of the 1920s had a unique flavor. The role of intellectuals in protecting the values of the era is discussed in Issue 9. William E. Leuchtenburg views the era as one of social and cultural rebellion, whereas David A. Shannon sees these changes as superficial in comparison with the economic expansion that ushered in a culture of mass consumption.

Issue 14 evaluates the civil rights movement, which has brought many tangible opportunities to blacks and minorities, according to Robert Weisbrot. Tom Wicker, on the other hand, points out that racial equality has still not been achieved and that programs such as affirmative action have been the cause of bitterness and division among the races.

Massive immigration to the United States in the late nineteenth and early twentieth centuries introduced widespread changes in American society. Moreover, the presence of increasing numbers of immigrants from southern and eastern Europe, many of them Catholics and Jews, seemed to threaten native-born citizens, most of whom were Protestant and of northern and western European ancestry. Asian immigrants, mainly from China or Japan, added to nativist fears. In Issue 4, Oscar Handlin argues that the immigrants were alienated from their Old World cultures as they adjusted to an unfamiliar and often hostile environment. Rudolph J. Vecoli, on the other hand, contends that immigrant groups such as the Italian peasants retained their customs and traditions when they immigrated to Americans cities, such as Chicago.

THE UNITED STATES AND THE WORLD

As the United States developed a preeminent position in world affairs, the nation's politicians were forced to consider the proper relationship between their country and the rest of the world. To what extent, many asked, should the United States seek to expand its political, economic, or moral influence around the world? This was a particularly intriguing question for the Progressives of the early twentieth century, most of whom were more interested in domestic reforms than foreign policy.

One progressive president, Woodrow Wilson, spent the better part of his two terms in office addressing international problems, but scholars have reached no consensus regarding the effectiveness of his leadership. In Issue 8, Henry Kissinger maintains that President Wilson used World War I to enforce moral principles of international diplomacy, which made it difficult for the presidents who followed him to develop a coherent, well-reasoned foreign policy based upon the national interest. Arthur S. Link, however, views Wilson as a higher realist and true internationalist who understood much better than his narrow-minded nationalist opponents the new international role that the United States would play in world affairs.

The role of the United States in World War II is closely linked with President Franklin D. Roosevelt. In Issue 11, Robert A. Divine portrays Roosevelt as a leader whose words were tough but whose actions betrayed his hatred of war. Arthur M. Schlesinger, Jr., maintains that Roosevelt was the only wartime leader who foresaw the shape of the new, postwar world order.

The decision to drop the atomic bomb to end World War II, the subject of Issue 12, demonstrates how history affected one of the most important foreign policy decisions of the twentieth century. Could the United States have avoided the use of nuclear weapons? Robert James Maddox and Barton J. Bernstein present both sides of this issue.

No discussion of American foreign policy is complete without some consideration of the Vietnam War. In Issue 15, Adam Garfinkle and Melvin Small consider whether or not the antiwar movement prolonged the war in Vietnam.

CONCLUSION

The process of historical study should rely more on thinking than on memorizing data. Once the basics of who, what, when, and where are determined, historical thinking shifts to a higher gear. Analysis, comparison and contrast, evaluation, and explanation take command. These skills not only increase our knowledge of the past but they also provide general tools for the comprehension of all the topics about which human beings think.

The diversity of a pluralistic society, however, creates some obstacles to comprehending the past. The spectrum of differing opinions on any particular subject eliminates the possibility of quick and easy answers. In the final analysis, conclusions often are built through a synthesis of several different interpretations, but even then, they may be partial and tentative.

The study of history in a pluralistic society allows each citizen the opportunity to reach independent conclusions about the past. Since most, if not all, historical issues affect the present and future, understanding the past becomes necessary if society is to progress. Many of today's problems have a direct connection with the past. Additionally, other contemporary issues may lack obvious direct antecedents, but historical investigation can provide illuminating analogies. At first, it may appear confusing to read and to think about opposing historical views, but the survival of our democratic society depends on such critical thinking by acute and discerning minds.

PART 1

Reconstruction, Immigration, and the Industrial Revolution

*Deep and bitter wounds were left in the American nation
as a result of the Civil War. Reconstruction was a period of
further turmoil as the political institutions of the South were
redesigned.*

*Economic expansion and the seemingly unlimited resources
available in postbellum America offered great opportunity and
created new political, social, and economic challenges. Political
freedom and economic opportunity provided incentives for
immigration to America. The need for cheap labor to run the
machinery of the industrial revolution created an atmosphere for
potential exploitation that was intensified by the concentration
of wealth in the hands of a few capitalists. The labor movement
took root, with some elements calling for an overthrow of the
capitalist system, while others sought to establish political
power within the existing system. Strains began to develop
between immigrant and native-born workers as well as between
workers and owners.*

■ Was Reconstruction a Success?

■ Did William M. Tweed Corrupt Post–
   Civil War New York?

■ Were Nineteenth-Century Entrepreneurs
   Robber Barons?

■ Did Late-Nineteenth-Century Immigrants
   Have to Leave Behind Their Old
   World Cultures to Come to America?

ISSUE 1

Was Reconstruction a Success?

YES: Kenneth M. Stampp, from *The Era of Reconstruction, 1865–1877* (Alfred A. Knopf, 1965)

NO: Eric Foner, from *Reconstruction: America's Unfinished Revolution, 1863–1877* (Harper & Row, 1988)

ISSUE SUMMARY

YES: Kenneth M. Stampp, a professor emeritus of history, argues that the period of Reconstruction after the Civil War succeeded economically, by consolidating the position of industrial capitalism; politically, by producing the most democratic governments the South had ever seen; and socially, by promoting ratification of the Fourteenth and Fifteenth Amendments, which gave African Americans the promise of equal rights.

NO: Professor of history Eric Foner admits that radical rule produced a number of accomplishments, but he maintains that it failed to secure civil, political, and economic rights for southern blacks or to establish the Republican party as a permanent force in the South.

Given the complex political, economic, and social issues that America's leaders were forced to address in the post–Civil War years, it is not surprising that the era of Reconstruction (1865–1877) is shrouded in controversy. For the better part of the century following the war, historians typically characterized Reconstruction as a total failure that had proved detrimental to all Americans—northerners and southerners, whites and blacks. According to this traditional interpretation, a vengeful Congress, dominated by radical Republicans, imposed military rule upon the southern states. Carpetbaggers from the North, along with traitorous white scalawags and their black accomplices in the South, established coalition governments that rewrote state constitutions, raised taxes, looted state treasuries, and disenfranchised former Confederates while extending the ballot to the freedmen. This era finally ended in 1877, when courageous southern white Democrats successfully "redeemed" their region from "Negro rule" by toppling the Republican state governments.

This portrait of Reconstruction dominated the historical profession until the 1960s. One reason for this is that white historians (both northerners and southerners) who wrote about this period operated from two basic assumptions: (1) the South was perfectly capable of solving its own problems without federal government interference; and (2) the former slaves were intellectually inferior to whites and incapable of running a government (much less one in which some whites would be their subordinates). African American historians, such as W. E. B. Du Bois, wrote several essays and books that challenged this negative portrayal of Reconstruction, but their works were seldom taken seriously in the academic world and were rarely read by the general public. Still, these black historians foreshadowed the acceptance of revisionist interpretations of Reconstruction, which coincided with the successes of the civil rights movement (or "Second Reconstruction") in the 1960s.

Revisionist historians identified a number of accomplishments of the Republican state governments in the South and their supporters in Washington, D.C. For example, revisionists argued that the state constitutions written during Reconstruction were the most democratic documents that the South had seen up to that time. While taxes increased in the southern states, the revenues generated by these levies financed the rebuilding and expansion of the South's railroad network, the creation of a number of social service institutions, and the establishment of a public school system that benefited African Americans as well as whites. At the federal level, Reconstruction achieved the ratification of the Fourteenth and Fifteenth Amendments, which extended significant privileges of citizenship to African Americans, both North and South. Revisionists also placed the charges of corruption that were leveled by traditionalists against the Republican regimes in the South in a more appropriate context by insisting that political corruption was a *national* malady in the second half of the nineteenth century. Finally, revisionist historians sharply attacked the notion that African Americans dominated the reconstructed governments of the South. They pointed out that there were no black governors, only 2 black senators, and 15 black congressmen during this period. In no southern state did blacks control both houses of the legislature.

Kenneth M. Stampp's 1965 book *The Era of Reconstruction, 1865–1877* is a classic statement of the revisionist viewpoint. Published a century after the end of the Civil War, this work offered a more balanced appraisal of Reconstruction and, in fact, emphasized the successes of the period of Republican rule in the South. In the excerpt that follows, Stampp admits the shortcomings of radical rule but insists that the Republican state governments chalked up a number of positive accomplishments during Reconstruction.

More recently, a third group of historians, the postrevisionists, have challenged the validity of the term *radical* as applied to the Reconstruction era by both traditional and revisionist historians. Eric Foner's essay represents an example of this postrevisionist approach. Although he recognizes a number of positive accomplishments, Foner concludes that Reconstruction must be judged a failure, part of an "unfinished revolution" initiated at the close of the Civil War. A number of forces, says Foner, conspired to eradicate the idealistic goal of full freedom for African Americans and the more pragmatic desire to establish an effective presence in the South for the Republican party.

YES

Kenneth M. Stampp

THE ERA OF RECONSTRUCTION, 1865–1877

RADICAL RULE IN THE SOUTH

When Lord Bryce, in the 1880's, wrote *The American Commonwealth*, he commented at length on the southern state governments created under the radical plan of reconstruction. What he had to say about them was not remarkable for its originality, but a few passages are worth quoting to give the flavor of the approaching historical consensus. "Such a Saturnalia of robbery and jobbery has seldom been seen in any civilized country.... The position of these [radical] adventurers was like that of a Roman provincial governor in the latter days of the Republic.... [All] voting power lay with those who were wholly unfit for citizenship, and had no interest as taxpayers, in good government.... [Since] the legislatures were reckless and corrupt, the judges for the most part subservient, the Federal military officers bound to support what purported to be the constitutional authorities of the State, Congress distant and little inclined to listen to the complaints of those whom it distrusted as rebels, greed was unchecked and roguery unabashed." In drawing this unpleasant picture Lord Bryce anticipated the generalizations of the Dunningites, as did many others.

Each of the eleven states of the former Confederacy, during all or part of the decade between 1867 and 1877, fell under the control of the radical Republicans. Tennessee was the first to be captured by them—indeed, it never had a Johnson government—but it was also the first to be lost. Tennessee was "redeemed," as southern white Democrats liked to call their return to power, as early as 1869. The last three states to be redeemed were South Carolina, Florida, and Louisiana, where the radical regimes lasted until the spring of 1877....

The first step in the organization of new southern state governments, as required by the reconstruction acts, was the election of delegates to conventions to frame new state constitutions. Since these conventions were controlled by the radicals, since they were the first political bodies in the South to contain Negroes, white conservatives subjected them to violent denunciation. They contemptuously called them "black and tan conventions"; they described the delegates as "baboons, monkeys, mules," or "ragamuffins and jailbirds." The South Carolina convention, according to a local newspaper, was the "maddest, most infamous revolution in history."

Yet, the invectives notwithstanding, there was nothing mad and little revolutionary about the work of these conventions. In fact, one of the most significant observations to be made about them is that the delegates showed little interest in experimentation. For the most part the radicals wrote orthodox state constitutions, borrowing heavily from the previous constitutions and from those of other states. To find fault with the way these southern constitutions were drawn is to find fault with the way most new state constitutions have been drawn; to criticize their basic political structure is to criticize the basic political structure of all the states. They were neither original nor unique. There was no inclination to test, say, the unicameral legislature, or novel executive or judicial systems.

Nor did the conventions attempt radical experiments in the field of social or economic policy. Since land reform had been defeated in Congress, a few delegates tried to achieve it through state action. The South Carolina convention provided for the creation of a commission to purchase land for sale to Negroes. In Louisiana, some Negro delegates proposed that when planters sold their estates purchases of more than 150 acres be prohibited. One white scalawag suggested a double tax on uncultivated land. A few delegates in other states advocated various policies designed to force the breakup of large estates. But these and all other attacks upon landed property were easily defeated.

As for the freedmen, the new constitutions proclaimed the equality of all men by quoting or paraphrasing the Declaration of Independence. Negroes were given the same civil and political rights as white men. "The equality of all persons before the law," proclaimed the Arkansas constitution, "is recognized and shall ever remain inviolate; nor shall any citizen ever be deprived of any right, privilege, or immunity, nor exempted from any burden or duty, on account of race, color, or previous condition." But on the subject of the social relations of Negroes and whites, most of the radical constitutions were evasive. South Carolina provided that its public schools were to be open to all "without regard to race or color," but only the state university actually made an attempt at integration. The Louisiana constitution declared: "There shall be no separate schools or institutions of learning established exclusively for any race by the State of Louisiana." In New Orleans from 1871 to 1877 about one third of the public schools were integrated, and white resistance was remarkably mild; but elsewhere in Louisiana segregation was the rule. Outside of South Carolina and Louisiana the radicals made no explicit constitutional provision for social integration. The Mississippi convention first defeated a proposal that segregated schools be required, then defeated a proposal that they be prohibited; the result was that the new constitution ignored the issue altogether. The only reference to segregation in it was a vague statement that "the rights of all citizens to travel upon public conveyances shall not be infringed upon, nor in any manner abridged in this state." But whether or not this clause prohibited segregation in public transportation is far from clear.

Yet, though the new constitutions were essentially conservative documents, they did accomplish some modest reforms, most of which were long overdue. In general, they eliminated certain undemocratic features of the old constitutions, for example, the inequitable systems of legislative apportionment that had discriminated against the interior regions of Virginia, North Carolina, and South Carolina. In the states of the Southeast, many offices that had previously been appointive were now made elective, and county government was taken out of the hands of local oligarchies. The rights of women were enlarged, tax systems were made more equitable, penal codes were reformed, and the number of crimes punishable by death was reduced. Most of the constitutions provided for substantial improvements in the state systems of public education and in the facilities for the care of the physically and mentally handicapped and of the poor.

In South Carolina, according to the historians of reconstruction in that state, the radical convention was an orderly body which accomplished its work with reasonable dispatch. It produced a constitution "as good as any other constitution that state has ever had"—good enough to remain in force for nearly two decades after the white Democrats regained control. This was, in fact, the state's first really democratic constitution; for, in addition to removing distinctions based on race, it provided for manhood suffrage, abolished property qualifications for office-holding, gave the voters the power for the first time to select the governor and other state officers, and transferred the election of presidential electors from the legislature to the voters. Another important provision related to public education: unlike the previous constitution, "the

fundamental law of the state carried the obligation of universal education" and aimed at "the creation of a school system like that of Northern states." Other reforms included an extension of women's rights, adoption of the state's first divorce law, strengthening of the state's fiscal power, revision of the tax system, and modernization of the judiciary and of county government.

The responsible behavior of South Carolina's radical constitutional convention was in striking contrast to the angry and irresponsible criticism of the Democrats. Chiefly because of its provisions for racial equality, they ridiculed the new constitution as "the work of sixty-odd negroes, many of them ignorant and depraved, together with fifty white men, outcasts of Northern society, and Southern renegades, betrayers of their race and country." Specifically, the Democrats charged that manhood suffrage was designed to further the ambitions of "mean whites"; that Negro suffrage would bring ruin to the state; that the judicial reforms were "repugnant to our customs and habits of thought"; and that the public school requirements were "a fruitful source of peculant corruption." In spite of this fanciful criticism by a party whose chief appeal was to racial bigotry, the work of the radical convention was ratified by a majority of nearly three to one.

At the time that the new constitutions were ratified, elections were held for state officers and legislators. After the elections, when Congress approved of the constitutions, political power was transferred from the military to the new civil governments. Thus began the era of radical government in the South—an era which, according to tradition, produced some of the worst state administrations in American history. Some of the southern radical regimes earned their evil reputations, others did not; but viewed collectively, there was much in the record they made to justify severe criticism. To say that they were not always models of efficiency and integrity would be something of an understatement. "The great impediment of the Republican party in this state," wrote a Tennessee radical, "is the incompetence of its leaders.... After the war the loyal people in many counties had no competent men to be judges, lawyers or political leaders." Indeed, all of the radical governments suffered more or less from the incompetence of some, the dishonesty of a few, and above all the inexperience of most of the office-holders....

Meanwhile, the credit of some of the southern states was impaired as public debts mounted. In Florida the state debt increased from $524,000 in 1868 to $5,621,000 in 1874. In South Carolina a legislative committee reported that between 1868 and 1871 the state debt had increased from $5,403,000 to $15,768,000, but another committee insisted that it had increased to $29,159,000. By 1872 the debts of the eleven states of the former Confederacy had increased by approximately $132,000,000. The burden on taxpayers grew apace. Between 1860 and 1870 South Carolina's tax rate more than doubled, while property values declined by more than fifty per cent. In Tennessee a radical reported that during the first three years after the war taxes had increased sevenfold, though property had declined in value by one third. Throughout the South the tax burden was four times as great in 1870 as it had been in 1860. Such rates, complained many southern landholders, were confiscatory; and, indeed, taxes and other adversities of the postwar years forced some of them to sell all or part of their lands. Sympathy for South Carolina's planter aristocracy caused a northern conservative to ask: "When before did mankind behold the spectacle of a rich, high-spirited, cultivated, self-governed people suddenly cast down, bereft of their possessions, and put under the feet of the slaves they had held in bondage for centuries?"

High taxes, mounting debts, corruption, extravagance, and waste, however, do not constitute the complete record of the radical regimes. Moreover, to stop with a mere description of their misdeeds would be to leave all the crucial questions unanswered—to distort the picture and to view it without perspective. For example, if some of these governments contained an uncommonly large number of inexperienced or incompetent officeholders, if much of their support came from an untutored electorate, there was an obvious reason for this. Howard K. Beale, in a critique of various reconstruction legends, observed that the political rulers of the ante-bellum South "had fastened ignorance or inexperience on millions of whites as well as Negroes and that it was this ignorance and inexperience that caused trouble when Radicals were in power.... Wealthy Southerners... seldom recognized the need for general education of even the *white* masses." Even in 1865 the men who won control of the Johnson governments showed little disposition to adopt the needed reforms. In South Carolina the Johnsonians did almost nothing to establish a system of public education, and at the time that the radicals came to power only one eighth of the white children of school age were attending school. The Negroes, of course, had been ignored entirely. It was probably no coincidence that the radicals made their poorest record in South Carolina, the state which had done the least for education and whose prewar government had been the least democratic.

As for the corruption of the radical governments, this phenomenon can be understood only when it is related to the times and to conditions throughout the country. One must remember that the administrations of President Grant set the moral tone for American government at all levels, national, state, and local. The best-remembered episodes of the Grant era are its numerous scandals—the Crédit Mobilier and the Whiskey Ring being the most spectacular of them—involving members of Congress as well as men in high administration circles. There were, moreover, singularly corrupt Republican machines in control of various northern states, including Massachusetts, New York, and Pennsylvania. But corruption was not a phenomenon peculiar to Republicans of the Gilded Age, as the incredible operations of the so-called Tweed Ring in New York City will testify. Indeed, the thefts of public funds by this organization of white Tammany Democrats surpassed the total thefts in all the southern states combined....

Most of the debt increases in the southern states resulted not from the thefts and extravagance of radical legislators but from the grants and guarantees they gave to railroad promoters, among whom were always some native white Democrats. In Florida more than sixty per cent of the debt incurred by the radical regime was in the form of railroad guarantee bonds. In North Carolina the radical government, prodded by the carpetbagger Milton S. Littlefield, a skilled lobbyist, issued millions of dollars of railroad bonds. Among those who benefited were many of the state's "best

citizens," including George W. Swepson, a local business promoter and Democrat. Most of Alabama's reconstruction debt —$18,000,000 out of $20,500,000—was in the form of state bonds issued to subsidize railroad construction, for which the state obtained liens upon railroad property. When one measure for state aid was before the Alabama legislature, many Democrats were among the lobbyists working for its passage. Yet, complained a radical, the Democrats who expect to profit from the bill "will use the argument that the Republican party had a majority in the Legislature, and will falsely, but hopefully, charge it upon Republicans as a partisan crime against the state."

Indeed, all of the southern states, except Mississippi, used state credit to finance the rebuilding and expansion of their railroads, for private sources of credit were inadequate. This policy had been developed before the war; it was continued under the Johnsonians; and in some cases when the Democrats overthrew the radicals there was no decline in the state's generosity to the railroads. While the radicals controlled the southern legislatures, not only they but many members of the Democratic minority as well voted for railroad bond issues. According to an historian of reconstruction in Louisiana, "Such measures were supported by members of both parties, often introduced by Democrats, in every case supported by a large majority of Democrats in both houses." The subservience of many postwar southern legislatures to the demands of railroad and other business promoters is in some respects less shocking than pathetic. For it expressed a kind of blind faith shared by many Southerners of both parties that railroad building and industrialization would swiftly solve all of their section's problems. No price seemed too high for such a miracle.

In several states, for obviously partisan reasons, the actual increase in the size of the public debt was grossly exaggerated. In Mississippi, for example, there was a durable legend among white Democrats that the radicals had added $20,000,000 to the state debt, when, in fact, they added only $500,000. Mississippi radicals had guarded against extravagance by inserting a clause in the constitution of 1868 prohibiting the pledging of state funds to aid private corporations —a clause which the conservatives, incidentally, had opposed. In Alabama, apart from railroad bonds secured by railroad property, the radicals added only $2,500,000 to the state debt. They did not leave a debt of $30,000,000 as conservatives claimed. In most other states, when loans to the railroads are subtracted, the increases in state debts for which the radicals were responsible appear far less staggering.

As for taxes, one of the positive achievements of many of the radical governments was the adoption of more equitable tax systems which put a heavier burden upon the planters. Before the war the southern state governments had performed few public services and the tax burden on the landed class had been negligible; hence the vehement protests of the landholders were sometimes as much against radical tax policies as against the alleged waste of taxpayers' money. The restoration governments often brought with them a return to the old inequitable fiscal systems. In Mississippi the subsequent claim of the conservatives that they had reduced the tax burden the radicals had placed upon property holders was quite misleading. The conservatives did lower the state property tax, but, as a consequence, they found it necessary to shift various services and administrative burdens from the state to the counties. This led to an increase in the cost of county government, an increase in the rate of county taxes, and a net increase in total taxes, state and county, that Mississippi property holders had to pay.

As a matter of fact, taxes, government expenditures, and public debts were bound to increase in the southern states during the postwar years no matter who controlled them. For there was no way to escape the staggering job of physical reconstruction—the repair of public buildings, bridges, and roads— and costs had started to go up under the Johnson governments before the radicals came to power. So far from the expenditures of the reconstruction era being totally lost in waste and fraud, much of this physical reconstruction was accomplished while the radicals were in office. They expanded the state railroad systems, increased public services, and provided public school systems—in some states for the first time. Since schools and other public services were now provided for Negroes as well as for whites, a considerable increase in the cost of state government could hardly have been avoided. In Florida between 1869 and 1873 the number of children enrolled in the public schools trebled; in South Carolina between 1868 and 1876 the number increased from 30,000 to 123,000. The economies achieved by some of the restoration governments came at the expense of the schools and various state institutions such as hospitals for the insane. The southern propertied classes had always been reluctant to tax themselves to support education or state hospitals, and in many cases the budget-cutting of the conservatives simply strangled them.

Thus radical rule, in spite of its shortcomings, was by no means synonymous with incompetence and corruption; far too many carpetbagger, scalawag, and Negro politicians made creditable records to warrant such a generalization. Moreover, conditions were improving in the final years of reconstruction. In South Carolina the last radical administration, that of the carpetbagger Governor Daniel H. Chamberlain, was dedicated to reform; in Florida "the financial steadiness of the state government increased toward the end of Republican rule." In Mississippi the radicals made a remarkably good record. The first radical governor, James L. Alcorn, a scalawag, was a man of complete integrity; the second, Adelbert Ames, a carpetbagger, was honest, able, and sincerely devoted to protecting the rights of the Negroes. Mississippi radicals, according to Vernon L. Wharton, established a system of public education far better than any the state had known before; reorganized the state judiciary and adopted a new code of laws; renovated public buildings and constructed new ones, including state hospitals at Natchez and Vicksburg; and provided better state asylums for the blind, deaf, and dumb. The radicals, Wharton concludes, gave Mississippi "a government of greatly expanded functions at a cost that was low in comparison with that of almost any other state." No major political scandal occurred in Mississippi during the years of radical rule—indeed, it was the best governed state in the postwar South. Yet white conservatives attacked the radical regime in Mississippi as violently as they did in South Carolina, which suggests that their basic grievance was not corruption but race policy.

Finally, granting all their mistakes, the radical governments were by far the most democratic the South had ever known. They were the only governments in southern history to extend to Negroes complete civil and political equality, and to try to protect them in the enjoyment of the rights they were granted. The overthrow of these governments was hardly a victory for political democracy, for the conservatives who "redeemed" the South tried to relegate poor men, Negro and white, once more to political obscurity. Near the end of the nineteenth century another battle for political democracy would have to be waged; but this time it would be, for the most part, a more limited version—for whites only. As for the Negroes, they would have to struggle for another century to regain what they had won—and then lost—in the years of radical reconstruction....

TRIUMPH OF THE CONSERVATIVES

During the state and presidential elections of 1876, when violence broke out in South Carolina, Florida, and Louisiana, President Grant would do nothing more than issue a sanctimonious proclamation. Indeed, when the outcome of that election was in dispute, Republicans had to bargain hard with southern Democrats in order to secure the peaceful inauguration of Rutherford B. Hayes. In one last sectional compromise, that of 1877, the Republicans promised to remove the remaining federal troops in the South, to be fair to Southerners in the distribution of federal patronage, and to vote funds for a number of southern internal improvements. In return, southern Democrats agreed to acquiesce in the inauguration of Hayes and to deal fairly with the Negroes.

The Compromise of 1877 signified the final end of radical reconstruction, for with the removal of federal troops, the last of the radical regimes collapsed. Soon after his inauguration President Hayes made a goodwill tour of the South. Conservative Democratic leaders, such as Governor Wade Hampton of South Carolina, greeted him cordially and assured him that peace and racial harmony now reigned in the South. Hayes tried hard to believe it, because he hoped so much that it was true.

"What is the President's Southern policy?" asked ex-Governor Chamberlain of South Carolina. Judged by its results, "it consists in the abandonment of Southern Republicans, and especially the colored race, to the control and rule not only of the Democratic party, but of that class at the South which regarded slavery as a Divine Institution, which waged four years of destructive war for its perpetuation, which steadily opposed citizenship and suffrage for the negro—in a word, a class whose traditions, principles, and history are opposed to every step and feature of what Republicans call our national progress since 1860."

It was in the 1870's, then, and not in 1865, that the idealism of the antislavery crusade finally died. Along with the loss of the idealism that had been one of the prime motivating forces behind radical reconstruction, the practical considerations also lost their relevance. Whereas in 1865 the urban middle classes still regarded the agrarian South and West as a serious threat, by the 1870's their position was consolidated and their power supreme. By then the leaders of business enterprise had so far penetrated the Democratic party and had so much influence among the so-called "redeemers" of the South that they no longer equated Re-

publican political defeat with economic disaster. Samuel J. Tilden, the Democratic presidential candidate in 1876, was a wealthy, conservative New York corporation lawyer, thoroughly "sound" on monetary, banking, and fiscal policy, in no respect unfriendly to business interests. Whichever way the presidential election of 1876 had gone, these interests could hardly have lost. Grover Cleveland, the only Democrat elected President between James Buchanan before the Civil War and Woodrow Wilson in the twentieth century, was also "sound" and conservative on all the economic issues of his day.

As for the Republican party, it too felt more secure than it had before. In 1865 it was still uncertain whether this party, born of crisis, could survive in a reunited, peaceful Union in which the slavery issue was resolved. But by the 1870's the party was firmly established, had an efficient, powerful, amply endowed organization, and had the unswerving support of a mass of loyal voters. True, the Republicans lost the congressional elections of 1874 and almost lost the presidency in 1876, but this could be attributed to the depression and abnormal conditions. Normally, in order to exist as a major national party, Republicans no longer needed the votes of southern Negroes. The reason for this was that during and since the war they had won control of the Old Northwest, once a stronghold of agrarianism and copperheadism. Indeed, a significant chapter in the history of reconstruction is the political and economic reconstruction of this flourishing region. The Civil War, the identification of the Republican party with nationalism and patriotism, the veteran vote, the Homestead Act, and federal appropriations for internal improvements all helped to make the states of the Old Northwest Republican strongholds. Moreover, the westward advance of the industrial revolution —the growth of urban centers such as Cleveland, Detroit, and Chicago— identified powerful economic groups in the Old Northwest with the industrial interests of the Northeast.

How these western states voted in the eleven presidential elections between 1868 and 1908 is significant when it is remembered that they had consistently gone Democratic before the Civil War. In eight elections the Old Northwest went Republican unanimously. Of the seven states in this region, Indiana voted Democratic three times, Illinois and Wisconsin once, the rest never. Thus, with the Old Northwest made safe for the Republican party, the political motive for radical reconstruction vanished, and practical Republicans could afford to abandon the southern Negro. With the decline of the idealism and the disappearance of the realistic political and economic considerations that had supported it, radical reconstruction came to an end.

* * *

Viewing radical reconstruction with its three chief motivating forces in mind, are we to call it a success or a failure? Insofar as its purpose was to consolidate the position of American industrial capitalism, it was doubtless a striking success. During the last three decades of the nineteenth century, social and economic reformers subjected irresponsible business entrepreneurs to constant attack, but they won no significant victories. In fact, they met constant defeat, climaxed by the failure of the Populists in the 1890's. With William McKinley, the conservative son of an Ohio industrialist, installed in power in 1897, American capitalism rode

to the end of the nineteenth century with its power uncurbed and its supremacy not yet effectively challenged. Above all, the conservative Democratic leaders of the New South were no longer enemies but allies.

Politically, radical reconstruction was also a success. Even though Republicans failed in their effort to establish an effective and durable organization in the South, they nevertheless emerged from the era of reconstruction in a powerful position. Most of their subsequent political victories were narrow; sometimes they lost a congressional campaign. But until Wilson's election in 1912, only once, in 1892, did the Democrats win control of the presidency and both houses of Congress simultaneously. And if conservative Republican Congressmen counted almost no Southerners in their caucus, they found a large number of southern Democrats remarkably easy to work with. The coalition of northern Republicans and southern Dixiecrats, so powerful in recent Congresses, was an important fact of American political life as early as the 1880's. The coalition had to be an informal one and had to endure a great deal of partisan rhetoric, but it was real nonetheless.

Finally, we come to the idealistic aim of the radicals to make southern society more democratic, especially to make the emancipation of the Negroes something more than an empty gesture. In the short run this was their greatest failure. In the rural South the basic socioeconomic pattern was not destroyed, for share-cropping replaced the antebellum slave-plantation system. Most of the upper-class large landowners survived the ordeal of war and reconstruction, and the mass of Negroes remained a dependent, propertyless peasantry. After reconstruction, in spite of the Fourteenth and Fifteenth Amendments, the Negroes were denied equal civil and political rights. In 1883 the Supreme Court invalidated the Civil Rights Act of 1875; in 1894 Congress repealed the Force Acts; and in 1896 the Supreme Court sanctioned social segregation if Negroes were provided "equal" accommodations. Thus Negroes were denied federal protection, and by the end of the nineteenth century the Republican party had nearly forgotten them. In place of slavery a caste system reduced Negroes to an inferior type of citizenship; social segregation gave them inferior educational and recreational facilities; and a pattern of so-called "race etiquette" forced them to pay deference to all white men. Negroes, in short, were only half emancipated.

Still, no one could quite forget that the Fourteenth and Fifteenth Amendments were now part of the federal Constitution. As a result, Negroes could no longer be deprived of the right to vote, except by extralegal coercion or by some devious subterfuge. They could not be deprived of equal civil rights, except by deceit. They could not be segregated in public places, except by the spurious argument that this did not in fact deprive them of the equal protection of the laws. Thus Negroes were no longer denied equality by the plain language of the law, as they had been before radical reconstruction, but only by coercion, by subterfuge, by deceit, and by spurious legalisms. For a time, of course, the denial of equality was as effective one way as the other; but when it was sanctioned by the laws of the Johnson governments and approved by the federal government, there was no hope. When, however, state-imposed discrimination was, in effect, an evasion of the supreme law of the land, the odds, in the long run, were on the side of the Negro.

The Fourteenth and Fifteenth Amendments, which could have been adopted only under the conditions of radical reconstruction, make the blunders of that era, tragic though they were, dwindle into insignificance. For if it was worth four years of civil war to save the Union, it was worth a few years of radical reconstruction to give the American Negro the ultimate promise of equal civil and political rights.

NO

Eric Foner

THE RIVER HAS ITS BEND

Thus, in the words of W. E. B. Du Bois, "the slave went free; stood a brief moment in the sun; then moved back again toward slavery." The magnitude of the Redeemer counterrevolution underscored both the scope of the transformation Reconstruction had assayed and the consequences of its failure. To be sure, the era of emancipation and Republican rule did not lack enduring accomplishments. The tide of change rose and then receded, but it left behind an altered landscape. The freedmen's political and civil equality proved transitory, but the autonomous black family and a network of religious and social institutions survived the end of Reconstruction. Nor could the seeds of educational progress planted then be entirely uprooted. While wholly inadequate for pupils of both races, schooling under the Redeemers represented a distinct advance over the days when blacks were excluded altogether from a share in public services.

If blacks failed to achieve the economic independence envisioned in the aftermath of the Civil War, Reconstruction closed off even more oppressive alternatives than the Redeemers' New South. The post-Reconstruction labor system embodied neither a return to the closely supervised gang labor of antebellum days, nor the complete dispossession and immobilization of the black labor force and coercive apprenticeship systems envisioned by white Southerners in 1865 and 1866. Nor were blacks, as in twentieth-century South Africa, barred from citizenship, herded into labor reserves, or prohibited by law from moving from one part of the country to another. As illustrated by the small but growing number of black landowners, businessmen, and professionals, the doors of economic opportunity that had opened could never be completely closed. Without Reconstruction, moreover, it is difficult to imagine the establishment of a framework of legal rights enshrined in the Constitution that, while flagrantly violated after 1877, created a vehicle for future federal intervention in Southern affairs. As a result of this unprecedented redefinition of the American body politic, the South's racial system remained regional rather than national, an outcome of great importance when economic opportunities at last opened in the North.

From Eric Foner, *Reconstruction: America's Unfinished Revolution, 1863–1877* (Harper & Row, 1988). Copyright © 1988 by Eric Foner. Reprinted by permission of HarperCollins Publishers. Notes omitted.

Nonetheless, whether measured by the dreams inspired by emancipation or the more limited goals of securing blacks' rights as citizens and free laborers, and establishing an enduring Republican presence in the South, Reconstruction can only be judged a failure. Among the host of explanations for this outcome, a few seem especially significant. Events far beyond the control of Southern Republicans—the nature of the national credit and banking systems, the depression of the 1870s, the stagnation of world demand for cotton—severely limited the prospects for far-reaching economic change. The early rejection of federally sponsored land reform left in place a planter class far weaker and less affluent than before the war, but still able to bring its prestige and experience to bear against Reconstruction. Factionalism and corruption, although hardly confined to Southern Republicans, undermined their claim to legitimacy and made it difficult for them to respond effectively to attacks by resolute opponents. The failure to develop an effective long-term appeal to white voters made it increasingly difficult for Republicans to combat the racial politics of the Redeemers. None of these factors, however, would have proved decisive without the campaign of violence that turned the electoral tide in many parts of the South, and the weakening of Northern resolve, itself a consequence of social and political changes that undermined the free labor and egalitarian precepts at the heart of Reconstruction policy.

For historians, hindsight can be a treacherous ally. Enabling us to trace the hidden patterns of past events, it beguiles us with the mirage of inevitability, the assumption that different outcomes lay beyond the limits of the possible. Certainly, the history of other plantation societies offers little reason for optimism that emancipation could have given rise to a prosperous, egalitarian South, or even one that escaped a pattern of colonial underdevelopment. Nor do the prospects for the expansion of scalawag support —essential for Southern Republicanism's long-term survival—appear in retrospect to have been anything but bleak. Outside the mountains and other enclaves of wartime Unionism, the Civil War generation of white Southerners was always likely to view the Republican party as an alien embodiment of wartime defeat and black equality. And the nation lacked not simply the will but the modern bureaucratic machinery to oversee Southern affairs in any permanent way. Perhaps the remarkable thing about Reconstruction was not that it failed, but that it was attempted at all and survived as long as it did. Yet one can, I think, imagine alternative scenarios and modest successes: the Republican party establishing itself as a permanent fixture on the Southern landscape, the North summoning the resolve to insist that the Constitution must be respected. As the experiences of Readjuster Virginia and Populist-Republican North Carolina suggest, even Redemption did not entirely foreclose the possibility of biracial politics, thus raising the question of how Southern life might have been affected had Deep South blacks enjoyed genuine political freedoms when the Populist movement swept the white counties in the 1890s.

Here, however, we enter the realm of the purely speculative. What remains certain is that Reconstruction failed, and that for blacks its failure was a disaster whose magnitude cannot be obscured by the genuine accomplishments that did endure. For the nation as a whole, the collapse of Reconstruction was a tragedy that deeply affected the course of its future development. If racism contributed to the undoing of Reconstruction, by the same token Reconstruction's demise and the emergence of blacks as a disenfranchised class of dependent laborers greatly facilitated racism's further spread, until by the early twentieth century it had become more deeply embedded in the nation's culture and politics than at any time since the beginning of the antislavery crusade and perhaps in our entire history. The removal of a significant portion of the nation's laboring population from public life shifted the center of gravity of American politics to the right, complicating the tasks of reformers for generations to come. Long into the twentieth century, the South remained a one-party region under the control of a reactionary ruling elite who used the same violence and fraud that had helped defeat Reconstruction to stifle internal dissent. An enduring consequence of Reconstruction's failure, the Solid South helped define the contours of American politics and weaken the prospects not simply of change in racial matters but of progressive legislation in many other realms.

The men and women who had spearheaded the effort to remake Southern society scattered down innumerable byways after the end of Reconstruction. Some relied on federal patronage to earn a livelihood. The unfortunate Marshall Twitchell, armless after his near-murder in 1876, was appointed U.S. consul at Kingston, Ontario, where he died in 1905. Some fifty relatives and friends of the Louisiana Returning Board that had helped make Hayes President received positions at the New Orleans Custom House, and Stephen Packard was awarded the consulship at Liverpool—

compensation for surrendering his claim to the governorship. John Eaton, who coordinated freedmen's affairs for General Grant during the war and subsequently took an active role in Tennessee Reconstruction, served as federal commissioner of education from 1870 to 1886, and organized a public school system in Puerto Rico after the island's conquest in the Spanish-American War. Most carpetbaggers returned to the North, often finding there the financial success that had eluded them in the South. Davis Tillson, head of Georgia's Freedman's Bureau immediately after the war, earned a fortune in the Maine granite business. Former South Carolina Gov. Robert K. Scott returned to Napoleon, Ohio, where he became a successful real estate agent—"a most fitting occupation" in view of his involvement in land commission speculations. Less happy was the fate of his scalawag successor, Franklin J. Moses, Jr., who drifted north, served prison terms for petty crimes, and died in a Massachusetts rooming house in 1906.

Republican governors who had won reputations as moderates by courting white Democratic support and seeking to limit blacks' political influence found the Redeemer South remarkably forgiving. Henry C. Warmoth became a successful sugar planter and remained in Louisiana until his death in 1931. James L. Alcorn retired to his Mississippi plantation, "presiding over a Delta domain in a style befitting a prince" and holding various local offices. He remained a Republican, but told one Northern visitor that Democratic rule had produced "good fellowship" between the races. Even Rufus Bullock, who fled Georgia accused of every kind of venality, soon reentered Atlanta society, serving, among other things, as president of the city's chamber of commerce. Daniel H. Chamberlain left South Carolina in 1877 to launch a successful New York City law practice, but was well received on his numerous visits to the state. In retrospect, Chamberlain altered his opinion of Reconstruction: a "frightful experiment" that sought to "lift a backward or inferior race" to political equality, it had inevitably produced "shocking and unbearable misgovernment." "Governor Chamberlain," commented a Charleston newspaper, "has lived and learned."

Not all white Republicans, however, abandoned Reconstruction ideals. In 1890, a group of reformers, philanthropists, and religious leaders gathered at the Lake Mohonk Conference on the Negro Question, chaired by former President Hayes. Amid a chorus of advice that blacks eschew political involvement and concentrate on educational and economic progress and remedying their own character deficiencies, former North Carolina Judge Albion W. Tourgée, again living in the North, voiced the one discordant note. There was no "Negro problem," Tourgée observed, but rather a "white" one, since "the hate, the oppression, the injustice, are all on our side." The following year, Tourgée established the National Citizens' Rights Association, a short-lived forerunner of the National Association for the Advancement of Colored People, devoted to challenging the numerous injustices afflicting Southern blacks. Adelbert Ames, who left Mississippi in 1875 to join his father's Minnesota flour-milling business and who later settled in Massachusetts, continued to defend his Reconstruction record. In 1894 he chided Brown University President E. Benjamin Andrews for writing that Mississippi during his governorship had incurred a debt of $20 million. The actual figure, Ames pointed out, was less

than 3 percent of that amount, and he found it difficult to understand how Andrews had made "a $19,500,000 error in a $20,000,000 statement." Ames lived to his ninety-eighth year, never abandoning the conviction that "caste is the curse of the world." Another Mississippi carpetbagger, Massachusetts-born teacher and legislator Henry Warren, published his autobiography in 1914, still hoping that one day, "possibly in the present century," America would live up to the ideal of "equal political rights for all without regard to race."

For some, the Reconstruction experience became a springboard to lifetimes of social reform. The white voters of Winn Parish in Louisiana's hill country expressed their enduring radicalism by supporting the Populists in the 1890s, Socialism in 1912, and later their native son Huey Long. Among the female veterans of freedmen's education, Cornelia Hancock founded Philadelphia's Children's Aid Society, Abby May became prominent in the Massachusetts women's suffrage movement, Ellen Collins turned her attention to New York City housing reform, and Josephine Shaw Lowell became a supporter of the labor movement and principal founder of New York's Consumer League. Louis F. Post, a New Jersey-born carpetbagger who took stenographic notes for South Carolina's legislature in the early 1870s, became a follower of Henry George, attended the founding meeting of the NAACP, and as Woodrow Wilson's Assistant Secretary of Labor, sought to mitigate the 1919 Red Scare and prevent the deportation of foreign-born radicals. And Texas scalawag editor Albert Parsons became a nationally known Chicago labor reformer and anarchist, whose speeches drew comparisons between the plight of Southern blacks and Northern industrial workers, and between the aristocracy resting on slavery the Civil War had destroyed and the new oligarchy based on the exploitation of industrial labor it had helped to create. Having survived the perils of Texas Reconstruction, Parsons met his death on the Illinois gallows after being wrongfully convicted of complicity in the Haymarket bombing of 1886.

Like their white counterparts, many black veterans of Reconstruction survived on federal patronage after the coming of "home rule." P. B. S. Pinchback and Blanche K. Bruce held a series of such posts and later moved to Washington, D.C., where they entered the city's privileged black society. Richard T. Greener, during Reconstruction a professor at the University of South Carolina, combined a career in law, journalism, and education with various government appointments, including a stint as American commercial agent at Vladivostok. Long after the destruction of his low country political machine by disenfranchisement, Robert Smalls served as customs collector for the port of Beaufort, dying there in 1915. Mifflin Gibbs held positions ranging from register of Little Rock's land office to American consul at Madagascar. Other black leaders left the political arena entirely to devote themselves to religious and educational work, emigration projects, or personal advancement. Robert G. Fitzgerald continued to teach in North Carolina until his death in 1919; Edward Shaw of Memphis concentrated on activities among black Masons and the AME Church; Richard H. Cain served as president of a black college in Waco, Texas; and Francis L. Cardozo went on to become principal of a Washington, D.C., high school. Aaron A. Bradley, the mili-

tant spokesman for Georgia's lowcountry freedmen, helped publicize the Kansas Exodus and died in St. Louis in 1881, while Henry M. Turner, ordained an AME bishop in 1880, emerged as the late nineteenth century's most prominent advocate of black emigration to Africa. Former Atlanta councilman William Finch prospered as a tailor. Alabama Congressman Jeremiah Haralson engaged in coal mining in Colorado, where he was reported "killed by wild beasts."

Other Reconstruction leaders found, in the words of a black lawyer, that "the tallest tree... suffers most in a storm." Former South Carolina Congressman and Lieut. Gov. Alonzo J. Ransier died in poverty in 1882, having been employed during his last years as a night watchman at the Charleston Custom House and as a city street sweeper. Robert B. Elliott, the state's most brilliant political organizer, found himself "utterly unable to earn a living owing to the severe ostracism and mean prejudice of my political opponents." He died in 1884 after moving to New Orleans and struggling to survive as a lawyer. James T. Rapier died penniless in 1883, having dispersed his considerable wealth among black schools, churches, and emigration organizations. Most local leaders sank into obscurity, disappearing entirely from the historical record. Although some of their children achieved distinction, none of Reconstruction's black officials created a family political dynasty—one indication of how Redemption aborted the development of the South's black political leadership. If their descendants moved ahead, it was through business, the arts, or the professions. T. Thomas Fortune, editor of the New York *Age*, was the son of Florida officeholder Emanuel Fortune; Harlem Renaissance writer Jean Toomer, the grandson of Pinchback; renowned jazz pianist Fletcher Henderson, the grandson of an official who had served in South Carolina's constitutional convention and legislature.

By the turn of the century, as soldiers from North and South joined to take up the "white man's burden" in the Spanish-American War, Reconstruction was widely viewed as little more than a regrettable detour on the road to reunion. To the bulk of the white South, it had become axiomatic that Reconstruction had been a time of "savage tyranny" that "accomplished not one useful result, and left behind it, not one pleasant recollection." Black suffrage, wrote Joseph Le Conte, who had fled South Carolina for a professorship at the University of California to avoid teaching black students, was now seen by "all thoughtful men" as "the greatest political crime ever perpetrated by any people." In more sober language, many Northerners, including surviving architects of Congressional policy, concurred in these judgments. "Years of thinking and observation" had convinced O. O. Howard "that the restoration of their lands to the planters provided for [a] future better for the negroes." John Sherman's recollections recorded a similar change of heart: "After this long lapse of time I am convinced that Mr. Johnson's scheme of reorganization was wise and judicious.... It is unfortunate that it had not the sanction of Congress."

This rewriting of Reconstruction's history was accorded scholarly legitimacy —to its everlasting shame—by the nation's fraternity of professional historians. Early in the twentieth century a group of young Southern scholars gathered at Columbia University to study the Reconstruction era under the guidance of Professors John W. Burgess and William A. Dunning. Blacks, their mentors taught, were "children" utterly incapable of appreciating the freedom that had been thrust upon them. The North did "a monstrous thing" in granting them suffrage, for "a black skin means membership in a race of men which has never of itself succeeded in subjecting passion to reason, has never, therefore, created any civilization of any kind." No political order could survive in the South unless founded on the principle of racial inequality. The students' works on individual Southern states echoed these sentiments. Reconstruction, concluded the study of North Carolina, was an attempt by "selfish politicians, backed by the federal government... to Africanize the State and deprive the people through misrule and oppression of most that life held dear." The views of the Dunning School shaped historical writing for generations, and achieved wide popularity through D. W. Griffith's film *Birth of a Nation* (which glorified the Ku Klux Klan and had its premiere at the White House during Woodrow Wilson's Presidency), James Ford Rhodes's popular multivolume chronicle of the Civil War era, and the national best-seller *The Tragic Era* by Claude G. Bowers. Southern whites, wrote Bowers, "literally were put to the torture" by "emissaries of hate" who inflamed "the negroes' egotism" and even inspired "lustful assaults" by blacks upon white womanhood.

Few interpretations of history have had such far-reaching consequences as this image of Reconstruction. As Francis B. Simkins, a South Carolina-born historian, noted during the 1930s, "the alleged horrors of Reconstruction" did much to freeze the mind of the white South in unalterable opposition to outside pressures for social change and to any thought of breaching Democratic ascendancy, eliminating segregation, or restoring suffrage to disenfranchised blacks. They also justified Northern indifference to the nullification of the Fourteenth and Fifteenth Amendments. Apart from a few white dissenters like Simkins, it was left to black writers to challenge the prevailing orthodoxy. In the early years of this century, none did so more tirelessly than former Mississippi Congressman John R. Lynch, then living in Chicago, who published a series of devastating critiques of the racial biases and historical errors of Rhodes and Bowers. "I do not hesitate to assert," he wrote, "that the Southern Reconstruction Governments were the best governments those States ever had." In 1917, Lynch voiced the hope that "a fair, just, and impartial historian will, some day, write a history covering the Reconstruction period, [giving] the actual facts of what took place."

Only in the family traditions and collective folk memories of the black community did a different version of Reconstruction survive. Growing up in the 1920s, Pauli Murray was "never allowed to forget" that she walked in "proud shoes" because her grandfather, Robert G. Fitzgerald, had "fought for freedom" in the Union Army and then enlisted as a teacher in the "second war" against the powerlessness and ignorance inherited from slavery. When the Works Progress Administration sent agents into the black belt during the Great Depression to interview former slaves, they found Reconstruction remembered for its disappointments and betrayals, but also as a time of hope, possibility, and accomplishment. Bitterness still lingered over the federal government's failure to distribute land or protect blacks' civil and political rights. "The Yankees helped free us, so they say," declared eighty-one-year old former slave Thomas Hall, "but they let us be put back in slavery again." Yet coupled with this disillusionment were proud, vivid recollections of a time when "the colored used to hold office." Some pulled from their shelves dusty scrapbooks of clippings from Reconstruction newspapers; others could still recount the names of local black leaders. "They made pretty fair officers," remarked one elderly freedman; "I thought them was good times in the country," said another. Younger blacks spoke of being taught by their parents "about the old times, mostly about the Reconstruction, and the Ku Klux." "I know folks think the books tell the truth, but they shore don't," one eighty-eight-year old former slave told the WPA.

For some blacks, such memories helped to keep alive the aspirations of the Reconstruction era. "This here used to be a good county," said Arkansas freedman Boston Blackwell, "but I tell you it sure is tough now. I think it's wrong—exactly wrong that we can't vote now." "I does believe that the negro ought to be given more privileges in voting," echoed Taby Jones, born a slave in South Carolina in 1850, "because they went through the reconstruction period with banners flying." For others, Reconstruction inspired optimism that better times lay ahead. "The Bible says, 'What has been will be again'," said Alabama sharecropper Ned Cobb. Born in 1885, Cobb never cast a vote in his entire life, yet he never forgot that outsiders had once taken up the black cause—an indispensable source of hope for one conscious of his own weakness in the face of overwhelming and hostile local power. When radical Northerners ventured South in the 1930s to help organize black agricultural workers, Cobb seemed almost to have been waiting for them: "The whites came down to bring emancipation, and left before it was over.... Now they've come to finish the job." The legacy of Reconstruction affected the 1930s revival of black militancy in other ways as well. Two leaders of the Alabama Share Croppers Union, Ralph and Thomas Gray, claimed to be descended from a Reconstruction legislator. (Like many nineteenth-century predecessors, Ralph Gray paid with his life for challenging the South's social order—he was killed in a shootout with a posse while guarding a union meeting.)

Twenty more years elapsed before another generation of black Southerners launched the final challenge to the racial system of the New South. A few participants in the civil rights movement thought of themselves as following a path blazed after the Civil War. Discussing the reasons for his involvement, one black Mississippian spoke of the time when "a few Negroes was admitted into the government of the State of Mississippi and to the United States." Reconstruction's legacy was also evident in the actions of federal judge Frank Johnson, who fought a twelve-year battle for racial justice with Alabama Gov. George Wallace. Johnson hailed from Winston County, a center of Civil War Unionism, and his great-grandfather had served as a Republican sheriff during Reconstruction. By this time, however, the Reconstruction generation had passed from the scene and even within the black community, memories of the period had all but disappeared. Yet the institutions created or consolidated after the Civil War—the black family, school, and church—provided the base from which the modern civil rights revolution sprang. And for its legal strategy, the movement returned to the laws and amendments of Reconstruction.

"The river has its bend, and the longest road must terminate." Rev. Peter Randolph, a former slave, wrote these words as the dark night of injustice settled over the South. Nearly a century elapsed before the nation again attempted to come to terms with the implications of emancipation and the political and social agenda of Reconstruction. In many ways, it has yet to do so.

POSTSCRIPT

Was Reconstruction a Success?

In *Nothing But Freedom: Emancipation and Its Legacy* (Louisiana State University Press, 1984), Foner compares the treatment of American freedmen with those who were newly emancipated in Haiti and the British West Indies. Only in the United States, he claims, were the former slaves given voting and economic rights. Although these rights had been stripped away from the majority of black southerners by 1900, Reconstruction had, nevertheless, created a legacy of freedom that inspired succeeding generations of African Americans.

C. Vann Woodward, the dean of southern historians, is less sanguine about the potential for success presented by the Reconstruction proposals. Despite all the successes enumerated by the revisionists, Woodward concludes that the experiment failed. In "Reconstruction: A Counterfactual Playback," an essay in his thought-provoking *The Future of the Past* (Oxford University Press, 1988), Woodward argues that former slaves were as poorly treated in the United States as they were in other countries. He also believes that the confiscation of former plantations and the redistribution of land to the former slaves would have failed in the same way that the Homestead Act of 1862 failed to generate equal distribution of government lands to poor white settlers. Finally, Woodward claims that reformers who worked with African Americans during Reconstruction failed because their goals were out of touch with the realities of the late nineteenth century.

Thomas Holt's *Black Over White: Negro Political Leadership in South Carolina During Reconstruction* (University of Illinois Press, 1977) is representative of state and local studies that employ modern social science methodology to yield new perspectives. While critical of white Republican leaders, Holt (who is African American) also blames the failure of Reconstruction in South Carolina on freeborn mulatto politicians, whose background distanced them economically, socially, and culturally from the masses of freedmen. Consequently, these political leaders failed to develop a clear and unifying ideology to challenge white South Carolinians who wanted to restore white supremacy.

The study of the Reconstruction period benefits from an extensive bibliography. Traditional accounts of Reconstruction include William Archibald Dunning's *Reconstruction, Political and Economic, 1865–1877* (Harper & Brothers, 1907); Claude Bowers's *The Tragic Era: The Revolution After Lincoln* (Riverside Press, 1929); and E. Merton Coulter's *The South During Reconstruction, 1865–1877* (Louisiana State University Press, 1947), which is considered by many to be the last major work written from the Dunning (or traditional) point of view. Early revisionist views are presented in W. E. B. Du Bois, *Black Reconstruction in America: An Essay Toward a History of the Part Which*

Black Folk Played in the Attempt to Reconstruct Democracy in America, 1860–1880 (Harcourt, Brace, 1935), which is a Marxist analysis of Reconstruction, and John Hope Franklin, *Reconstruction: After the Civil War* (University of Chicago Press, 1961). Foner's *Reconstruction: America's Unfinished Revolution, 1863–1877* (Harper & Row, 1988) includes a complete bibliography on the subject. Briefer overviews are available in Forrest G. Wood, *The Era of Reconstruction, 1863–1877* (Harlan Davidson, 1975) and Michael Perman, *Emancipation and Reconstruction, 1862–1879* (Harlan Davidson, 1987). One well-written study of a specific episode from the Reconstruction years is Willie Lee Rose's *Rehearsal for Reconstruction: The Port Royal Experiment* (Bobbs-Merrill, 1964), which describes the failed effort at land reform in the sea islands of South Carolina. Richard Nelson Current's *Those Terrible Carpetbaggers: A Reinterpretation* (Oxford University Press, 1988) is a superb challenge to the traditional view of those much-maligned Reconstruction participants. Finally, for collections of interpretive essays on various aspects of the Reconstruction experience, see Staughton Lynd, ed., *Reconstruction* (Harper & Row, 1967); Seth M. Scheiner, ed., *Reconstruction: A Tragic Era?* (Holt, Rinehart & Winston, 1968); and Edwin C. Rozwenc, ed., *Reconstruction in the South*, 2d ed. (D. C. Heath, 1972).

ISSUE 2

Did William M. Tweed Corrupt Post–Civil War New York?

YES: Alexander B. Callow, Jr., from *The Tweed Ring* (Oxford University Press, 1966)

NO: Leo Hershkowitz, from *Tweed's New York: Another Look* (Anchor Press, 1977)

ISSUE SUMMARY

YES: Professor emeritus of history Alexander B. Callow, Jr., insists that by exercising a corrupting influence over the city and state government, as well as over key elements within the business community, William M. "Boss" Tweed and his infamous "ring" extracted enormous sums of ill-gotten money for their own benefit in post–Civil War New York.

NO: Professor of history Leo Hershkowitz portrays Tweed as a devoted public servant who championed New York City's interests during his 20-year career and whose reputation as the symbol for urban political corruption is grossly undeserved.

On the eve of the Civil War, the United States remained primarily a rural, agrarian nation. Of the country's 31 million inhabitants, 80 percent were characterized as "rural" dwellers by the United States Bureau of the Census; only 392 "urban" places (incorporated towns with 2,500 or more residents, or unincorporated areas with at least 2,500 people per square mile) dotted the national landscape; a mere nine U.S. cities contained populations in excess of 100,000. By 1920 the population of the United States had more than tripled, and for the first time in American history, a majority of those residents lived in cities. The number of places defined as "urban" had increased to 2,722, and 68 cities housed over 100,000 residents each.

After 1865 the growth of urban America was directly linked to the economic and technological changes that produced the country's industrial revolution, as well as to rapid immigration, which filled the nation's cities with what seemed to native-born Americans to be a multitude of foreigners from around the globe. Reflecting many of the characteristics of modern America, these industrial cities produced a number of problems for the people who lived in them—problems associated with fire and police protection, sanitation, utilities, and a wide range of social services. These coincided with increased concerns over employment opportunities and demands for transportation and housing improvements. Typically, municipal governments became the clearinghouses for such demands. They also became the targets for charges of corruption.

Political corruption is virtually synonymous with the post–Civil War era. Whether at the local, state, or national levels of government, and regardless of party affiliation, charges of corruption seemed commonplace. Nowhere did this appear to be more the case than in the realm of New York politics dominated by the Tammany Hall Democratic "machine" and its notorious "boss," William M. Tweed.

Born in New York City in 1823 to Irish immigrant parents, Tweed rose to political prominence by serving as alderman, congressman, and state senator. He developed a power base in local and state politics both during and immediately after the Civil War, and he controlled that base until reform initiatives by *The New York Times* and Samuel J. Tilden brought him down. He died in jail, serving a sentence for failing to audit claims against the city, in 1878.

Undoubtedly, James Lord Bryce had Tweed and the infamous "Tweed Ring" in mind when he depicted city government in the United States as a "conspicuous failure." But does Tweed deserve the charges of wrongdoing that have been heaped upon him? Did his activities run counter to the best interests of his constituents? Is it conceivable that this long-standing symbol of corruption in urban America has been unduly maligned? These questions are addressed in the selections that follow.

According to Alexander B. Callow, Jr., William Tweed's malefic reputation is well deserved. "Boss" Tweed, he says, perfected the art of political corruption by controlling three vital sources of graft: the city, the state, and the business community. Under Tweed's direction, the Tweed Ring extracted wealth from New York's city and state government by controlling the key legislative and financial agencies that awarded charters and franchises and were responsible for city improvements. The record of bribery and excessive charges for construction, says Callow, are incontrovertible, and Tweed used his political power to benefit personally from the graft collected.

Leo Hershkowitz, on the other hand, defends Tweed's reputation and insists that the "Boss's" image was fabricated by journalists, such as cartoonist Thomas Nast, to sell newspapers in New York. New York's diversity of peoples and interests, says Hershkowitz, made it impossible for one person to control the political realm to the extent that is attributed to Tweed. Hershkowitz points out that Tweed was never convicted on charges of graft or theft. He concludes that, in fact, the Tammany leader effectively represented the interests of New York residents by opening schools, building hospitals, paving streets, and providing a wide variety of other necessary services.

YES

Alexander B. Callow, Jr.

"HONEST" GRAFT

Post-Civil-War New York has been described as being encircled by a host of political rings, rings within rings, each depending on the other. There was the Gravel Ring, the Detective Ring, the Supervisors' Ring, the Courthouse Ring, the Albany Ring, the Street Commissioners' Ring, the Manure Ring, the Market Ring, and, consolidating and hovering above all, the Tweed Ring. And what was a political ring? It was the source of "magic wisdom" that made Tammany Hall a political power, said a big chief of the Tammany braves. Samuel Tilden, who almost became President of the United States on the claim he had smashed a "ring," said:

> The very definition of a "Ring" is that it encircles enough influential men in the organization of each party to control the action of both party machines; men who in public push to extremes the abstract ideas of their respective parties, while they secretly join their hands in schemes for personal power and profit.

Scholars and public alike have generally accepted Tilden's definition of the Tweed Ring. Why was it that later city bosses like [Richard] Croker had a "machine," while Tweed had a "Ring"—a word, as it were, with a more ominous ring, a political synonym for conspiracy, venality, and corruption? If the Tweed Ring's skills at organization have never been rightfully emphasized, its achievements in corruption certainly have, although large-scale graft existed before the emergence of the Tweed Ring, and continued after its downfall.

We shall probably never know exactly how much the Ring stole. Calculations have run as high as $300 million, which was probably too high, even for the Tweed Ring. The *New York Evening Post* estimated it at $59 million; the *Times* thought it was more like $75 million to $80 million....

Years after the fall of the Ring, Matthew J. O'Rourke, who had made a study of the Ring's plunders, estimated that if fraudulent bonds were included, the Ring probably stole about $200 million. Henry J. Taintor made the closest study. For six years he had been employed by the City to determine the amount of the Ring's graft. It cost the City over $73,000 to maintain Taintor's investigation, and for a moment during the Tweed Ring investigation in 1877

From Alexander B. Callow, Jr., *The Tweed Ring* (Oxford University Press, 1966). Copyright © 1966 by Alexander Callow. Reprinted by permission of Oxford University Press, Inc. Notes omitted.

there was the suspicion, later dispelled, that a dreadful irony had occurred: that Taintor, in investigating graft, had been tempted himself, and had padded his bills. At any rate, he testified his research showed that the Ring had stolen at least $60 million, but even this was not an accurate figure, he said, because he did not possess all the records. Whatever the figure, in order to maintain a political machine as well as to increase their personal fortune, the Tweed Ring's operation was on a gigantic scale.

There was three primary sources of graft: the city, the state, and the business community. In the city, the Ring's control of the key legislative and financial agencies, from the Supervisors and Aldermen to the Comptroller and Mayor, gave it command of New York's financial machinery and bountiful opportunity for graft. Every warrant, then, charged against the city treasury passed the Ring's scrutiny and was subject to its manipulation. Every scheme for city improvement, be they new streets, new buildings, new city parks, had to be financed from the city treasury, controlled by the Ring. The results were often graft, reflected in excessive charges and needless waste. Every charter and franchise for new businesses had to meet the approval of the city legislature and the Mayor, and many companies, therefore, had to pay the tribute of the bribe to get them passed. All the city's financial affairs, such as bond issues, tax-collecting, rentals on city properties, were vulnerable as sources of graft. In effect, there was a direct relationship between power and graft. The Ring's political influence was so extensive that one roadblock to graft, the check and balance system—pitting the upper house of the City legislature

against the lower house, and the Mayor as a check to the combined houses of the legislature—was simply nullified. When this happened, the city's financial operations became an open target.

This was largely true for the State legislature as well. Any check and balance between state and city, governor and legislature, was nullified. The Ring controlled the governor, John Hoffman; it controlled the powerful block of city Democrats in the State legislature. When he was elected State Senator in 1867 (and assumed office in 1868, when the Senate convened), Boss Tweed, as Chairman of the influential State Finance Committee, and as a member of the important Internal Affairs of Towns and Counties, Charitable and Religious, and Municipal Affairs committees, was in a commanding position to influence tax-levies, bond issues, and special projects for the city—all sources of graft. As the leader of the Black Horse Cavalry, a corrupt band of State legislators, he could control legislation leading to graft.

Not all the money came from the City and State treasury. The business community was an important source of profit, both as allies and victims. The Tweed Ring operated as lobby brokers for businessmen seeking to pass or kill legislation vital to their interests. Services rendered for the Erie Railroad, for example, brought in thousands of dollars. Businessmen provided large "kick-backs" in payment for receiving profitable contracts. The "cinch" bill, legislative extortion threatening business firms and individuals, was used extensively by the Ring through both the City and State legislatures.

Unlike the sly, sophisticated tactics of modern-day graft—the highly complicated dummy corporation, the undercover payoff via the "respectable" attorney—the Ring operated in a remarkably open and straightforward fashion. In effect, the shortest distance to the city treasury was a straight line. While the Ring used several methods for plunder, the largest share of the booty was gained by a method simple, direct, brazen, daring—and often sloppy. Every person who received a contract from the city, whether for supplies or for work on the city buildings and public works was instructed to alter his bills before submitting them for payment. At first the tribute was levied somewhat irregularly at 10 per cent, then it was raised to 55 per cent; in July 1869 it jumped to 60 per cent; and from November 1869 on, the tradesmen received 35 per cent and the Ring 65 per cent on all bills and warrants. When bills from contractors and tradesmen did not come in fast enough, Tweed ordered vouchers to be made out to imaginary firms and individuals. On large contracts, Tweed acted directly and got immediately to the point. When he was told that electric fire alarms would cost the city $60,000, he asked the contractor, "If we get you a contract for $450,000 will you give us $225,000?" No time was wasted. The contractor answered with a simple yes and got the contract. Nor did the Boss quibble over small sums. Once a merchant told Tweed that Comptroller [Richard B.] Connolly had refused to pay his bill. Only by "kicking-back" 20 per cent of the bill, would the merchant ever get paid. Tweed wrote Connolly: "For God's sake pay ——'s bill. He tells me you people ask 20 per cent. The whole d——d thing isn't but $1100. If you don't pay it, I will. Thine."

The division of the spoils varied: Tweed received from 10 to 25 per cent; Connolly from 10 to 20 per cent; [Peter B.] Sweeny 10 per cent; [A. Oakey] Hall 5 to 10 per cent. There was a percentage for the "sinking fund," and James Watson and W. E. Woodward shared 5 per cent. These last two, clerks of the gang, did the paper work and forging. "You must do just as Jimmy tells you, and you will get your money," was a well-known saying among Tweed Ring contractors.

James Watson, the Ring's bookkeeper, was City Auditor in Connolly's office. He first demonstrated his talents while a convict. In 1850 Watson was an agent for a prosperous firm which suddenly began to experience severe losses that Watson found inconvenient to explain. He fled to California. He was brought back to New York in irons and clapped in Ludlow Street jail. An active fellow with pleasant manners, he soon won the friendship of the warden. He took charge of the prison records and performed with such admirable efficiency, especially in calculations, that he was released, with the warden's help, and was appointed a collector in the Sheriff's office. He held that position under three Sheriffs. When the Tweed Ring was formed in 1866, he was made City Auditor, a position that paid a small salary. Four years later, he was worth anywhere from two to three million dollars. It was said that he was a simple man and lived in a curious state of "ostentatious modesty." He had only one luxury—fast trotting horses, a passion that later helped to ruin the Tweed Ring.

W. E. Woodward occupied a key post as clerk to the Supervisors; he helped to rig the percentages of the business that came through that office. At the time of the Aldermen's investigation of the Ring in 1877, the Aldermen were curious how a mere clerk could own a $150,000 home, the best home, in fact, in Norwalk, Connecticut. Asked how he could do this on a salary that never exceeded

$5000, Woodward gave a straightforward answer. "I used to take all I could get, and the Board of Supervisors were very liberal to me."

In the Comptroller's Office, Slippery Dick Connolly performed feats that justified his name, as his successor in 1871, the reformer, Andrew Green, confirmed when he found the treasury thoroughly sacked. As Comptroller, Connolly served the Ring three ways. He spent the money collected through the city's regular channels of revenue—taxes, rents from such city properties as markets, docks armories, etc. While some of the money was spent legitimately, a good deal of it was either embezzled or found its way into fraudulent contracts, excessive rents, or padded payrolls, a percentage of which was "kicked-back" into the Ring's coffers. However, only about a third of the city's money came from taxes or rents; the rest came from securities. Thus when a tax-levy of some $30 or more million was spent, usually at a brisk pace, Connolly's next job was to realize $30 to $50 millions more by issuing stocks and bonds.

Connolly performed this task like a financial conjuror. He created a litter of stocks and bonds raised for every conceivable project, ingenious in wording and intent. There were Accumulated Debt Bonds, Assessment Fund bonds, Croton Aqueduct Bonds, Croton Reservoir Bonds, Central Park Improvement Fund Stocks, City Improvement Stocks, Street Improvement Bonds, Fire Department Stocks, Tax Relief Bonds, Bridge Revenue Bonds, New Court House Stock. Repairs to the County Offices and Building Stocks, Dock Bonds, and bonds for the Soldiers' Relief Fund. The war chest to provide funds for padded payrolls, for example, was raised by the sale of appropriately named Riot Damages Indem-

nity Bonds. As a result of Connolly's various enterprises, the city groaned under a debt which increased by nearly $70 million from 1869 to 1871.

Finally, it was Connolly's responsibility to mask the Ring's fraudulent expenditures by slippery accounting techniques. In this, he was helped by the extensive power of the Ring which nullified an elaborate series of regulations established to prevent fraud. By state law, every warrant and claim drawn against the City must be itemized and accompanied by a signed affidavit certifying its authenticity. Before it could be cashed it must be thoroughly examined and signed by the Comptroller, City Auditor, the Board of Supervisors, and the Mayor. But since the Ring "owned" all these offices, it was relatively simple to rig a phony warrant and get the required signatures. Indeed, the Ring became so powerful that it owned its own bank, the Tenth National, to ensure the safe deposit of its booty. (Tweed, Connolly, Hall, James Ingersoll, and James Fisk, Jr., were the Tenth National's distinguished directors.) . . .

Added to all this was another lush source for graft. Connolly and his lieutenant James Watson were in a position to audit and pay off fictitious claims against the city. With logic, the New York City Council of Political Reform said: "In a sound fiscal system one officer *adjusts* claims and another *pays* them. From the weakness of human nature it is not deemed wise or prudent for the government of any great city or county to allow the *same* officer to adjust a claim *who* is to *pay* it; lest he may be tempted by a share of the money to conspire with the claimant and allow an unjust claim. But in our city, in 1868 and 1870, a *single* officer, the Comptroller, *adjusted* and *paid*, by adding so much to the permanent debt, $12,500,000 of claims!"

The Comptroller's office was also a point of frustration for those with legitimate claims against the city. They were kept waiting sometimes for years, before they could get their money. Subsequently, they often sold their claim to one of the Ring's agents for 50 or 60 cents on the dollar. Immediately after the transaction took place, the new owner was promptly paid. A clerk in Connolly's office, named Mike Moloney, was in charge of this branch of business.

> Moloney sits opposite the door by which his victims enter and watches for them with all the avidity that a spider might watch the approach of a fly. The moment an unlucky claimant makes his appearance Moloney jumps on his feet and steps forward to the counter to meet him. Bending forward he listens to the application of the victim, and then by a series of ominous shakes of his head, and "the oft-told tale" repeated in half-smothered whispers, he tries to convince the applicant that there is no prospect of him receiving his money for some time to come, and that, if he really needs it, he had better go over to City Hall and see Mr. Thomas Colligan. (The victim sees Mr. Colligan)... and comes out feeling much the same as if he had lost his pocketbook, while the genial Mr. Colligan pockets the "little difference," invites Moloney to dinner, and quietly divides the spoils while sipping Champagne or smoking a Havana.

It is difficult to know where to begin in dealing with the many specific schemes of the Tweed Ring. Perhaps it is best to begin with what E. L. Godkin once called "one of those neat and profitable little curiosities of fraud which the memory holds after graver things are forgotten."

In 1841, a man named Valentine, a clerk in the Common Council, persuaded the city to finance the publication of a city almanac which he would edit. Initially, it was a small volume of not quite 200 pages, which had a map of the city and a list of all persons associated with the government of New York City and their business and home addresses. Although the City Directory contained the same information, for some obscure reason the almanac seemed valuable. Down through the years, the almanac increased in bulkiness, and, more important, in cost to the taxpayers, until it became "a manual of folly, extravagance, and dishonesty." By 1865, *Valentine's Manual*, as it was called, had become a 879-page monument of costliness and superficiality. Among 141 pictures was a large, folding four-page lithograph, illustrating—"O precious gift to posterity!"—a facsimile of each Alderman's autograph. Expensive lithographs covered a number of vital subjects: a fur store built in 1820; a house that Valentine had once lived in; a grocery and tea store of ancient vintage; Tammany Hall as it looked in 1830; a Fifth Avenue billiard saloon; and a host of "portraits of undistinguished persons." Well over 400 pages were cluttered with extracts from old government documents, newspapers, and "memories." The cost of printing was $57,172.30; the number of copies printed, 10,000. A few copies found their way into secondhand bookstores, which paid two dollars apiece for them, $3.36 less than a copy cost the city. An outraged public opinion forced Mayor Hoffman to veto the resolution authorizing a similar expenditure for 1866. He found that Appleton's or Harper's would have published the same number of copies for $30,000 instead of $53,672. The Aldermen, however, overrode his veto....

The Tweed Ring created several companies which moved in to monopolize every phase of city printing as well as city advertising. One such firm was the New York Printing Company. Its expansion reflected all the gusto of American business enterprises. It began in a shabby little office on Centre Street, but almost at once business became so good that it absorbed three of the largest printing establishments in the city. The New York Printing Company was growing, said a newspaper, "but like other mushrooms it grows in the dark. It is spreading under the cover of night, and running its roots into the Treasury by deep underground passages." On a capital stock of $10,000 it paid a dividend of $50,000 to $75,000 to each of its stockholders. The city apparently liked its work, for during 1870–71 the firm obtained $260,283.81 of its business. All these amounts incorporated a 25 per cent tribute to the Ring. The company became so versatile in printing all kinds of material that the city paid it another $300,000 for printing in book form the records of New York City from 1675 to 1776. Nor did the firm confine its customers to the City and County. Insurance companies and steamboat and ferry companies were extremely vulnerable to a legislative bill which, in the public interest, could hurt them by regulating their activities and profits. Hence, they all received a notice that the New York Printing Company would be happy to do their printing.

The Tweed Ring composed the major stockholders of the Manufacturing Stationers' Company, which sold stationery supplies to city offices and schools. In 1870 the City and County paid it over $3 million. Among its many bills, there was this interesting one: for six reams of note paper, two dozen penholders, four ink bottles, one dozen sponges, and three dozen boxes of rubber bands, the city paid $10,000. James Parton singled out the Manufacturing Stationers' Company for its treachery.

We have before us a successful bid for supplying the city offices with stationery, in which we find the bidder offering to supply "blue folio post" at one cent per ream; "magnum bonum pens," at one cent per gross; "lead pencils," at one cent per dozen; "English sealing-wax," at one cent per pound; and eighty-three other articles of stationery, at the uniform price of one cent for the usual parcel. This was the "lowest bid," and it was, of course, the one accepted. It appeared, however, when the bill was presented for payment, that the particular kind of paper styled "blue folio post" had never been called for, nor any considerable quantity of the other articles proposed to be supplied for one cent. No one, strange to say, had ever wanted "magnum bonum" pens at one cent a gross, but in all the offices the cry had been for "Perry's extra fine," at three dollars. Scarcely any one had used "envelopes letter-size" at one cent per hundred but there had been countless calls for "envelopes note-size" at one cent each. Between the paper called "blue folio post," at one cent per ream, and paper called "foolscap extra ruled," at *five dollars and a half*, the difference was too slight to be perceived; but every one had used the foolscap. Of what avail are contracts, when the officials who award them, and the other officials who pay the bill, are in league with the contractor to steal the public money?

As the fictional Boss Blossom Brick said, "Official advertising is the Pain Killer of Politics." During the Civil War three men started an insignificant newspaper titled *The Transcript*. They were George Stout, "a journalist unknown to fame," Charles E. Wilbour, a court stenographer and "literary man, somewhat less unknown," and Cornelius Corson, "an employee in the City Hall, and not devoid of influence in that quarter." When Tweed, Connolly, and Sweeny became their partners, business, but not circulation, picked up. The Common Council (the Aldermen and Assistant Aldermen) ordered that a full list of all persons liable to serve in the army, amounting to some 50,000 names, should be printed in the *Transcript*. Later, thirty-five copies of the list were published in book-form, "though the bill was rendered for a large edition." From then on the *Transcript* enjoyed days of high prosperity. It published the major share of all "city advertising," which meant official records of the courts, and official statements and declarations, statistical reports, new ordinances, in effect, the facts and figures of city business. The rates were exorbitant enough to ensure a heady profit; for example, messages from the Mayor cost a dollar a line. A great deal of the advertisements came from Tweed's Department of Public Works, and from the Bureau of Assessments, where Richard Tweed was in control. Although the newspaper never sold more than a hundred copies, the city paid it $801,874 from 1869 to 1871 for publishing its official business and advertisements. The December 3, 1870, issue, for example, consisted of 504 pages. Advertisements were charged at a rate of 25 cents a line, higher than prevailing newspaper rates. It was estimated that the Ring received $68,000 in profits for that issue alone. The Christmas number for that year was a special: a double extra of 1000 pages, all advertisements, for which double rates were charged. It appeared to one newspaper that the Ring paid for its Christmas presents out of the public till. The profits, then, made by the three companies of the Ring which corralled city printing reached a grand total over a three-year period of $2,641,828.30, of which nine-tenths was pure profit.

As Boss Blossom Brick said, "Give the people plenty of taffy and the newspapers plenty of advertising—then help yourself to anything that's lying around loose." Funneling the taxpayers' dollars through the *Transcript* was a way to finance Tweed's mansion on Fifth Avenue and his palatial estate in Greenwich, Connecticut; but there was another method of using city advertising which ensured, for a few years at least, that gracious living could be enjoyed. The Tweed Ring found that the best way to protect itself against newspaper criticism was to distribute city advertising as a token of peace. It became a kind of hush money which bound the press to silence. Until the storm broke, in 1871, probably no New York political regime ever enjoyed less newspaper criticism than the Tweed Ring, and only when the evidence became painfully obvious and practically overwhelming did the press join the crusade against evil begun by the *New York Times* and *Harper's Weekly*. Before the storm, there had been some criticism, but it was spotty and half-hearted. The *Tribune* might thunder for a while, the *Sun* became nasty—as was its style—but a general grant of advertising had the same effect as placing alum on the tongue.

By law, the city corporation was limited to nine daily and eight weekly papers in which to advertise. But the Tweed Ring, with its usual disregard for procedure, extended delicious morsels of city advertising to twenty-six daily and forty-four weekly newspapers in the city alone, and seventeen weekly journals outside the city, making a total of eighty-seven organs. Probably no political regime in the history of New York City had exerted so much influence on the press....

Not content with the method of using advertising, the Ring also won the hearts of City Hall reporters by giving them $200 gifts at Christmas. This practice had started as early as 1862, under the administration of Mayor George Opdyke (who disapproved), but the Ring elaborated on the scheme. It also subsidized six to eight reporters on nearly all the city papers with fees of $2000 to $2500 to exercise the proper discretion when it came to writing about politics. There was the reward of patronage for the especially deserving: Stephen Hayes, on the *Herald* staff during the high days of the Ring, was rewarded with a sinecure in the Marine Court ($2500 a year), and Michael Kelly, also of the *Herald*, received positions in both the Fire Department and the Department of Public Works. Moreover, reporters from various newspapers of the country, from a Cleveland newspaper to the *Mobile Register*, were hired to write favorable notices of the Democratic administration in New York. And if a firm went too far and tried to print a pamphlet exposing the Ring, it might find its offices broken into by the Ring's men and the type altered to present a glowing account of the Ring's activities—as did the printing company of Stone, Jordan and Thomson.

At the time the Ring was breaking up, the City found itself confronted with claims amounting to over a million and a half dollars negotiated between newspapers and the Ring, some fraudulent and some not, for not all journals which received city advertising did so on the basis of a conspiracy with the Ring. But enough of them did to ensure the complacency and the apathy which seemed to grip many during the Ring's rule.

The Ring needed complacency and apathy when it came to operations behind the opening, widening, and improving of the city streets. With the city's enormous growth came a legitimate demand for new streets and the improvement of old ones. It became one of the Ring's most lucrative forms of graft. It was, indeed, a democratic form of graft—laborers got work; City Hall clerks were able to supplement their incomes; political debts were paid off in commissionerships, judges no longer had to rely entirely on their salaries; Ring members and friends prospered from the assessments involved and the excitement of "gambling" in real estate. As in the case of Recorder and Street Commissioner [John] Hackett, the key factor was the appointment of reliable Commissioners by the Ring judges, upon the suggestion of Corporation Counsel [John] O'Gorman. From then on a pattern emerged: Tammany favorites and members of the Ring's families constantly appeared as Commissioners; awards for damages were exorbitantly high; Commissioners charged "from ten to one hundred times as much as the law allowed" for their services and expenses, despite the fact that the Commissioners as employees of the city were disqualified by law from receiving any pay.

To "open" a new street did not mean to begin construction work. It was a legal term signifying that the land had been bought and was now officially "opened." Announcements of the transaction were published, and those property owners involved were invited to declare any objections to the Commissioners. The clerk drew up a report and the thing was done. Actually it usually amounted to a mere formality.

The cost for this activity under the Tweed Ring, however, would seem to indicate that an enormous amount of work went into it. What usually happened was that the surveyor reproduced a map of the street from maps made in 1811, when Manhattan island, except for a small area at its northern end, was surveyed so well that the maps were still adequate in post-Civil War New York. On the borders of the copy made by the surveyor, the clerk wrote the names of the owners of the lots on both sides of the street, copying his information from the tax books. Then the fun began. "The surveyor charges as though he had made original surveys and drawn original maps. The clerk charges as though his reports were the result of original searchers and researchers. The commissioners charge as though the opening had been the tardy fruit of actual negotiations." For the year ending in June 1866, it was estimated that the cost for "opening" twenty-five streets was $257,192.12. Of this cost, $4433 was charged for rent of an office, which ordinarily rented for $300 a year; "disbursements and postage-stamps" cost $950; and one surveyor's bill alone accounted for an astounding $54,000.

The Broadway widening "job" was a good example of the Ring in action. On May 17, 1869, the State legislature passed an act providing for the widening of Broadway between Thirty-fourth and Fifty-ninth streets, whereupon the Ring seized control of the legal machinery that decided assessments and damages to the property involved. With the friendly judge Albert Cardozo presiding, and two of the three Commissioners good Ring men, the Ring and a selected few began to buy property. Two of them paid $24,500

for a lot for which the Commissioners generously awarded them damages of $25,100. The new front was worth $10,000 more. Another lot sold for $27,500, but this payment was absorbed by a $30,355 award in damages. It was the resale value of the property, however, where the profit was made, and lots on Broadway were worth thousands. With tactics of this sort, the Ring managed to purchase some of the most valuable property in New York City.

With minor variations, the Broadway widening scheme was repeated in the Madison Avenue extension, the Church Street extension, the opening of Lexington Avenue through Stuyvesant Park, the Park Place widening, and the so-called "Fifth Avenue raid," where the Ring profited from the widening, extending, and "improvement" of that street. To one writer, who greatly exaggerated, it seemed that streets were opened "which no mortal had seen, no foot had trod; and they appeared only on the city map as spaces between imaginary lines leading from No-where to No-place." To a New York citizen in 1871 who examined the New York State *Senate Journal* of 1869, it might have seemed that the State legislature had gone No-where. On page 61 was an act entitled, "An act to afford relief against frauds and irregularities in assessments for local improvements in the city of New York."

Whether the source of graft was street openings, real estate speculation, city advertising, padded contractor's bills, juggled city records and bond issues fat with graft, a simple but imaginative profit on the City Directory, or a straightforward attack on the city treasury by supplying printing and stationery goods, the Tweed Ring explored the various paths to civic dishonesty. The roads to graft, however, were paved by the very interests the Ring exploited. The financial community, consumed in its own self-interests, stood to gain from the massive pump-priming in city improvements. The "open door" policy of state and city welfare deadened the voice of religious and philanthropic organizations; the newspapers, split by political partisanship and competitive self-interest, were softened by the morsels of political handouts; and the "people" were indifferent. The Tweed Ring thrived on the lack of civic conscience, and the result was graft.

NO

Leo Hershkowitz

TWEED'S NEW YORK: ANOTHER LOOK

MYTH

William M. Tweed, the notorious "Boss" Tweed, is one of the great myths of American history. His ugly features, small beady eyes, huge banana-like nose, vulturish expression and bloated body are the personification of big-city corruption. Thomas Nast, political propagandist and executioner of *Harper's Weekly*, has made them a triumph of the caricaturist art. Tweed's deeds, or rather misdeeds, as fashioned by historians and the like, are perhaps even better known. They have been told and retold in countless textbooks, monographs, biographies, articles, reminiscences, and have become an American epic whose proportions with each recounting become more fantastic, more shocking. Here are fables of monumental robberies of the New York City treasury, of fraud, deceit, treachery, of monstrous villainies, of carpets, furniture and of courthouses. Like fables, they are largely untrue, but like most legends, they perpetuate themselves and are renewed and enlarged with each telling.

The myth has become so much a part of history and Tweed such a convenient reference for the after-dinner speaker, pulp writer, or simply something to frighten little children with, that if there wasn't a Tweed, he would have to be invented, and he was.

Tweed is a fat, urban Jesse James without any saving graces. James is a western Robin Hood, a sort of criminal St. Francis. Tweed's patron saint is an eastern St. Tammany, refuge for the greedy, vulgar, corrupt—in short, consummate—politician. Tweed is the essence of urban rot, malodorous, the embodiment of all that is evil and cancerous in American municipal and political life. The monster lives. In a recent tax-evasion case, the prosecution charged a defendant with failure to report income allegedly obtained illegally. During the course of the trial, an enlarged Nast cartoon of "Boss Tweed" was produced to illustrate the similarity of crimes. The jury voted for conviction. Interestingly, the United States Court of Appeals reversed the verdict partly because the court felt use of the cartoon had prejudiced the jury. Eternally threatened plans to destroy the "Tweed Courthouse" (the name itself is an example of the myth) still standing behind New York's City Hall caused many New Yorkers to ask that the building be spared as a monument to graft and a reminder of the necessity of rooting out piggish politicians who take their slops at the public trough. Almost miraculously, the building, though supposedly built by corrupt politicians and contractors, is one of the finest examples of Italian Renaissance design in the country. It has not collapsed into a pile of plaster and sawdust, as critics predicted it would.

A popular cast-iron bank depicts an oily-faced tuxedoed figure, supposedly a banker, greedily swallowing the pennies of innocent children. What really "sells" the bank is calling it "Boss Tweed," even if one has nothing to do with the other. The myth is so salable and so deeply rooted that it is as American as "apple pie" or "Mother." A noted TV station produced a "documentary" on Tweed. When told that a mass of evidence exists that questions the "facts," representatives of the station offered an opinion, without pausing even to look at the material, that they wished all such records were destroyed. What price integrity as long as the legend lives, and it does so with abandon.

When political leaders think of New York, the vile image of Tweed taught them with their earliest history lessons returns to mind and appeals on behalf of the city fall on deaf ears. When Congress or the state legislature meet to debate New York's future, Tweed like some ghoulish specter rises up and beckons an end to discussion.

The myth is outrageously simple. Tweed was born in New York. Big, strong, ambitious and ruthless, he climbed out of the streets, and leaped like a snarling "Tammany Tiger" on unsuspecting citizens. Through fraud, deceit and intimidation, he was elected to various city

and state offices, and even served a term in Congress. Tweed yearned for bigger and better things. He met kindred souls whom he placed in strategic places as members of "The Ring" to pillage the city treasury, conquer the state and finally the nation. By using the simple device of padded or fictitious bills for items not delivered or not needed, millions were stolen. The county courthouse, the "Tweed Courthouse," became the symbol and center of the operation. Subservient members of "The Ring" were Peter B. ("Brains") Sweeny, city chamberlain; Richard B. ("Slippery Dick") Connolly, city comptroller; A. Oakey Hall ("The Elegant One"), mayor; and John T. ("Toots") Hoffman, mayor and governor. Hoffman would hopefully become President to serve Tweed better. An army of poor, unwashed and ignorant were also recruited. These were recent Irish and German immigrants, whose largely illegal votes were cheaply bought in return for jobs given away at City Hall or a turkey at Christmas. Judges were necessary to stay the hands of the law, so added to the conspiracy were George G. Barnard, John H. McCunn and Albert Cardozo. Misguided though willing contractors like Andrew Garvey, "Prince of Plasterers"; James H. Ingersoll, the "Chairmaker"; John Keyser, the "Plumber"; and numerous others were awarded contracts, but kicked back up to 75 per cent to Tweed and "The Ring." Tweed received the lion's or rather "Tiger's" share of perhaps 50 to 200 million dollars at a time when an average workman received two to three dollars a day.

The fable continues that this monumental looting was halted by courageous, honest men. There were Democrats like Samuel J. Tilden, who on the strength of his attacks against "The Ring" became governor and presidential candidate. Honest Republicans like George Jones, editor of the *Times*, combined to disgrace "The Ring" with the help of Nast and *Harper's Weekly*. Indictments were handed down against Tweed, who was found guilty and sentenced to the penitentiary. Finally, like most of the others of "The Ring," he fled the country. Recognized in Spain by a sailor, or someone or other who just happened to be an avid reader of *Harper's Weekly*—the myth is never clear on details—and was quite familiar with the Boss's features, he was returned to prison to die a lonely but deserved death, a lesson to evildoers.

With great delight, happy historians, political activists, popularizers, drooled over juicy tidbits like carpets and plumbing and people named Dummy and Cash, never bothering to look at dust-gathering records, or even those quite dust-free. It would seem that research would interfere with exorcising the devil or prevent the development of some interesting theories. One theory concerned the failure of adequate communication in an evolving, increasingly complicated metropolis. It was a lack of such communication as seen in a decentralized and chaotic government which explains the emergence of Tweed and the "Big Pay-off." Others see Tweed emerging from the schismatic web of Tammany politics to seize and consolidate power by "pulling wires," hiring professional toughs and modernizing control within Tammany.

Lord James Bryce, a hostile critic of American urban government, in his classic *American Commonwealth* found Tweed the end product of "rancid dangerous Democracy." The scornful Englishman felt that "The time was ripe, for the lowest class of voters, foreign and native, had now been thoroughly organized and knew themselves able to control the city."

This voting mob was ready to follow Tammany Hall, which he concluded "had become the Acropolis of the city; and he who could capture it might rule as tyrant." Bryce found Tweed's unscrupulousness matched by the crafty talents of others, creating a perfect blend of flagrant corruption. But the essential ingredient was democracy and failure to follow traditional leadership. It was such democracy which allowed a Falstaff-like Tweed to emerge as a hero; a "Portuguese Jew" like Albert Cardozo who was born in New York to "prostitute" his legal talents for party purposes; or a Fernando Wood, Tweed's predecessor in Tammany, to become a major figure from such small beginnings that he was "reported to have entered New York as the leg of an artificial elephant in a travelling show." Bryce thus denounced Tweed and a form of government that had little if any respect for birth or breeding, but rewarded the mean, the base-born for their audacity and treachery.

It all sounds so plausible, but does it help Tweed emerge from behind Thomas Nast's leering cartoons? The problem with Tweed and the myth is that it is all so much vapor and so little substance, and what has been written has not dispelled shadows; only deepened them. So little has been done to obtain even basic information about the man, and what is known is generally wrong. Perhaps never has so much nonsense been written about an individual.

A few questions to start. Was it possible for one man or even a group of men to plan such a vast swindle involving hundreds if not thousands of officials, clerks, laborers, contractors, and hope to succeed? If Tweed plotted such an operation which supposedly involved bribing the state legislature, coercing judges, muzzling the press, aborting the gossip of bank officers and city auditors, he must have been a genius, a Houdini, Machiavelli, Napoleon rolled into one. Such a mind surely would have withstood the trivial intrusion of a hundred brash reformers. Yet he was shaken from his lofty perch, tumbled into prison and hounded to death. All this was done without organized resistance and in literally the twinkling of an eye. Tweed had such "power" that he was thrown out of his party without a word spoken in his behalf, even before he was found guilty of anything. There was, except for counsel, no one to defend him, no congressman, senator, assemblyman, no one in authority. "The Ring" was so strongly forged that it shattered at the slightest pressure, its component parts flying about with no other thought than every man for himself. If "The Ring" was supposed to be a strong political or financial alliance well led and directed, then it like "Boss" Tweed was simply a figment of historical imagination, a pretty bit of caricature.

At no time did such a "Ring" dominate New York City politics, let alone the state or national scene. Supposed "Ring" members rarely had much to do with one another, socially or otherwise. Sweeny was a friend of Victor Hugo's, Hall aspired to make a mark in the theater, Tweed aspired to office, Connolly had Connolly. There was little to bind the so-called "Ring." Except by an accident of history that they served in various city posts at the same time, there is little to relate one with the other.

Even the dreaded "Tammany Tiger" was a paper one. Certainly in Tweed's day Tammany did not dominate New York politics. Perhaps it never did. The city was and is a complex, competitive system of diverse interest. It was then and is now too heterogeneous, too much made up of various groups, classes, outlooks, beliefs for any part or let alone one person to control. New Yorkers' cosmopolitanism and tolerance have a tragic price.

The city cannot send representatives to Washington or to Albany who can express the single-minded view of smaller, simpler communities. Its large immigrant population creates suspicion: is New York an American city? A rural backwater has more political clout than all of the city when it comes to power on national or state levels.

Partly this is in consequence of an age-old struggle between the city and the farm, and eternal tug of war between the city in its search for greater self-government and rural conservative interests who find New York a threat to themselves and their entrenched power. There were some deeply rooted animosities. Cities are not natural. God made the earth, trees, animals and man. Cities are man-made. Natural things are pure, innocent and obedient to order, while man is sinful, evil, disobedient, whose works like cities are suspect. There may be a Garden of Eden, but there is no City of Eden, only Sodom and Gomorrah. This kind of morality underlines economic and political selection. It is served by the Tweed myth, since the horrors of municipal corruption and Tammany bossism plainly demonstrate the impossibility of the city even governing itself. It is in a deeper sense an implied failure of man governing himself apart from some external power. As New York cannot be given greater home rule, it must even be more closely regulated and watched by the state; so too man must observe a higher authority.

To make matters worse, New York also destroys its political talent, its best lost in the heat of murderous combat. It was a rare aspirant indeed who could emerge from his trials to become a national figure of any permanence. Alexander Hamilton and Aaron Burr were testimony to this. De Witt Clinton and Edward Livingston were further examples of early casualties. By mid-nineteenth century, no New York City politician had any voice in national or state affairs. Fernando Wood, potentially a great politician and a champion of the city's interest against the state rural lobby, was destroyed by bitter intra-party fighting. William Tweed might have provided the city with a voice and he too was destroyed, but in such a way that the city too suffered in countless ways—not the least of which forever identified the metropolis as a spawning ground for corruption and filth. Why then pay it any attention? Why spend money on the sewers? Tweed was and is a convenient stick with which to beat the city over the head, preferably at regular intervals. In many ways, the tragedy of New York is that Tweed did not succeed, that a strong unified political force was not created, that the paper tiger was not real.

As for Tweed, there remain the stories. There is no evidence that he created the "Tammany Tiger" or ordered it to be used as his personal symbol. The clawing, snarling, toothed tiger was Nast's idea, part of the image he wished to create. It was plastered on Tweed and Tammany and sold. What politician would use such a symbol to win votes or influence people, except a madman or a cartoonist like Nast?

One of the universally accepted myths is that of Tweed's reactions to the July 1871 disclosures exposing "The Ring." He is supposed to have snarled like his tiger to a group of cowering reporters, reformers and the public at large, "What are you going to do about it?" Again, what politician, especially in this country, would make such an asinine statement, no matter how sure he was of his position? It was certainly not Tweed's style, and if he made "The Ring," he was not that stupid. In truth, the phrase was never used by Tweed, but invented by Nast as a caption for a June 10, 1871, cartoon a month before Tweed and "The Ring" made headlines. Reporters asked Tweed that question after the deluge and his troubles with the law. It was never Tweed's question. It was all "Boss," all Nast and all nonsense.

Tweed was no saint, but he was not the Nast creature. He was more a victim than a scoundrel or thief. Characteristically, Tweed was intensely loyal, warmhearted, outgoing, given to aiding the underdog and the underprivileged. But he was also gullible, naïve and easily fooled. If he were a real "boss," he should have been able, like Sweeny and others, to avoid inundating calamity. He was a good family man, and there simply is no scandal to report so far as his personal habits are concerned. Even his bitterest enemies could find nothing. He was not an intellectual, he was not at home with a Sweeny or an Oakey Hall, but found a close friendship with Jubilee Jim Fisk, the brilliant short-lived Roman candle and bon vivant.

Why then Tweed? First, he was what he was. In his prime, he reportedly weighed close to three hundred pounds. A "slim" Tweed would not be as inviting a target. Point one, for dieters. His features could be easily exaggerated by someone like Nast, and he was enough in the public eye for the *Times* and *Harper's*. He was ambitious, but not ruthless. He had money, but not enough to throw a scare into or buy off his opponents. He had power, but not enough to withstand attacks by newspapers, law, rivals and supposed friends.

Further, and much more importantly, he represented the interests of New York. He had established legislative programs which opened schools, hospitals, museums, programs tailored to meet the needs of a rapidly expanding constituency. His identification with the interests of the city was enough for the traditional rural-suburban leadership to seek his destruction. He provided a means for Republicans from President U.S. Grant on down to those in the local level to make people forget the corruptions in Republican circles, like the Whisky Ring, Indian Ring or Crédit Mobilier—all schemes to defraud millions from the government—but see instead the balloon-like figure of Tweed, Tammany and the defeat of Democratic opposition. National Democrats like Horatio Seymour and the inept "Sammy" Tilden could point to Tweed and gain cheers and votes for their efforts to "delouse" the party. If there ever was a scapegoat, its name was Tweed.

The Tweed story does not need exaggeration, lies, half-truths, rumors to make it interesting. It is in itself an incredible story. Debunking the myth is part of it, but there is much more. There are bigots like Nast, George T. Strong and others who saw in Tweed an outsider threatening their position by his supposedly championing the "drunken-ignorant Irish," the overly ambitious German-Jewish immigrants and those seeking to change the status quo. That

he sought to provide answers to the increasing complications of urban life did not help. Tweed never traveled in upper-class society. With all his apparent success, he was never able to wash away the tarnish of the Lower East Side. Moreover, there are some of the most incredible trials and abuses of the judicial process on record. There are hand-picked judges and juries, not as might be expected by Tweed, but by the prosecution. The misuse of grand jury indictments should become legendary.

Tweed was never tried for or found guilty of graft or theft, the crime Tweed stands accused of by history. He was convicted after some strange, improper, even illegal judicial proceedings, which were in many ways worse than anything Tweed supposedly committed, of a misdemeanor—failing to audit claims against the city. Hall was tried three times on the same charge and was not convicted. Connolly and Sweeny were never tried.

Tweed died in prison after having spent some four years there, and he would have remained longer but for his death—only one of these years was he in a penitentiary, on the misdemeanor conviction. The remaining years he spent in the county jail because he could not raise an exorbitant bail in a civil suit. The manipulation of the law by those sworn to uphold the law was a real crime. Then add the threatening, tampering with, and intimidation of witnesses, as well as the use of informers and agent provocateurs. Under these conditions, Snow White would have been hanged for loitering to commit prostitution.

The threat to individual liberty by an unbridled omnipresent legal system is rarely as clear as in the Tweed case. The innocent and guilty are too often given the same even-handed justice.

Couple this with yellow journalism and abuse of power by the press and Nast. Horace Greeley in his bid for the presidency in 1871 complained that he did not know whether he was running for that office or the penitentiary. Tweed was as much a victim of irresponsible journalism. Tweed, too, was "hot copy." He was also tried and convicted by newspapers in a too often repeated process in which rabid reporters and editors became judge and jury and headlines substitute for trial and district attorneys, while editors scratch each other's backs for the sake of publicity— where an indictment is often all that is necessary to make a point, sell papers and win votes....

EPILOGUE

And so Tweed passed into history to become the fabled legend. It was an undeserved fate. Except for Tweed's own very questionable "confession," there was really no evidence of a "Tweed Ring," no direct evidence of Tweed's thievery, no evidence, excepting the testimony of the informer contractors, of "wholesale" plunder by Tweed. What preceded is a story of political profiteering at the expense of Tweed, of vaulting personal ambitions fed on Tweed's carcass, of a conspiracy of self-justification of the corruption of law by the upholders of that law, of a venal irresponsible press and a citizenry delighting in the exorcism of witchery. If Tweed was involved then all those about him were equally guilty. He was never tried for theft. The only criminal trial that was held was for a misdemeanor of failing to audit, and this trial was held before a hand-picked judge and

jury at a time when Tweed-hunting was at its height.

Probably the "truth" about Tweed, "The Ring" and the "stolen" millions will never be known. It is possible to measure the difference between graft and profit? If Keyser charged so much for plastering, perhaps another could do the work for less, but would it be the same work, could it be done on time? How do you compare the cost of one carpet with that of another? Price is only one consideration. At one point, a decision has to be reached on any contract, no matter who is selected; there will always be someone who could have done it cheaper. Surely there were overcharges, but by how much? The throwing about of figures, 10, 30, 50, 200 million, is of no help. Is it possible to decide at what point profit becomes graft? It is difficult to answer these questions or work out an almost insoluble puzzle. In the end, the easiest solution is of course to blame Tweed, rather than examine financial records, vouchers, warrants. These were allowed to lie dormant silently collecting the dust of a century, in the end hopefully to disappear. How much easier to nail the "Elephant" to a wall or listen to the romanticism of history and the excesses of rhetoric created by Godkin, Bryce, Wingate, Lynch and so many others.

Tweed emerges as anything but a master thief. It was the contractors who willingly padded bills, never calling attention to any undue pressure upon them to do so; it was those lower-echelon agents in the city, especially Woodward and Watson, who were in direct liaison with the contractors, not Tweed. And lastly blame should be placed on the city and state. The former because it did not regulate expenditures properly and failed to pay its bills on time, a point brought up time and again by the contractors, and the latter because it interfered in city business; the city's welfare was subverted by state political interests. The Tweed story, or better the contractors' story, is about as good a reason for New York City home rule as can be offered.

Where did the legendary millions go? None of the contractors, with the possible exception of Garvey, had sizable sums of money, and even he wasn't to be compared to the "robber barons" like Morgan or Whitney or Rockefeller. These could sneeze out in a moment what purported to be the total Tweed plunder. What of Hall, Connolly, Sweeny, Hoffman? There is nothing to show they received any princely sums. No one connected with the so-called "Ring" set up a dynasty or retired to luxurious seclusion. Certainly not Tweed. If money was stolen, it held a Pharaoh's curse. Those who touched it did not enjoy it. So many died suddenly, so many died in dishonor and loneliness. None suffered as much as did William Magear Tweed and the City of New York.

Tweed spent some twenty years in public service. In the Fire Department, as alderman, member of the Board of Supervisors and Board of Education, member of Congress, state senator, commissioner of public works—it was a long list and resulted in a great deal of public good. He was instrumental in modernizing governmental and educational institutions, in developing needed reforms in public welfare programs, in incorporating schools, hospitals, establishing public baths, in preserving a site in Central Park for the Metropolitan Museum of Art, in widening Broadway, extending Prospect Park and removing fences from around public parks, establishing

Riverside Park and Drive, annexing the Bronx as a forerunner of the incorporation of Greater New York, in building the Brooklyn Bridge, in founding the Lenox Library. He was of considerable service during the Civil War. Tweed moved the city forward in so many ways and could have been, if he had not been destroyed, a progressive force in shaping the interests and destiny of a great city and its people.

Tweed's concepts about urbanization and accommodation while not philosophically formalized were years beyond their time. Twenty or thirty years later such programs were adopted by reformers and urban planners. Tweed was a pioneer spokesman for an emerging New York, one of the few that spoke for its interests, one of the very few that could have had his voice heard in Albany. Tweed grew with the city, his death was a tragedy for the future metropolis.

His life in the end was wasted, not so much by what he did, but by what was done to him, his work and the city being relegated to the garbage heap, both branded by the same indelible iron. He became a club with which to beat New York, really the ultimate goal of the blessed reformers.

It is time to seek a re-evaluation of Tweed and his time. If Tweed was not so bad, neither was the city. Old legends die hard, old ideas have deep roots, but hopefully some of the old legends will die and the deep roots wither away.

What was learned from the episode? Practically nothing. Politics, politicians, jurists and venal journalists certainly continued to ply their trade, spurred by their success, as in the past, with hardly a glance or hesitation, comforted in the downfall of the "Boss." The devil had been killed; would anyone bother to look at the judges or ask anyone else to do the Lord's work? Every once in a while, a bill is introduced in the Massachusetts legislature to have the Salem witches exonerated and declared non-witches. Some are. It might be time to have the New York state legislature and history provide a similar service for Tweed. Surely, there are other devils around to take his place. And a statue for Tweed? Yes, it would be his city alive and well.

POSTSCRIPT

Did William M. Tweed Corrupt Post–Civil War New York?

The opposing viewpoints of Callow and Hershkowitz regarding "Boss" Tweed's place in history is representative of a long-standing scholarly debate about the consequences of machine politics in the United States. James Bryce, *The American Commonwealth*, 2 vols. (Macmillan, 1888); Moisei Ostrogorski, *Democracy and the Organization of Political Parties* (1902; reprint, Anchor Books, 1964); and Ernest S. Griffith, *A History of American City Government: The Conspicuous Failure, 1870–1900* (National Civic League Press, 1974) present a litany of misdeeds associated with those who controlled municipal government.

Efforts to rehabilitate the sullied reputations of the machine politicians can be dated to the comments of Tammany Hall ward healer George Washington Plunkitt, whose turn-of-the-century observations included a subtle distinction between "honest" and "dishonest" graft.

There are several excellent urban history texts that devote space to the development of municipal government, including discussions of political machines, in the nineteenth century. Among these are David R. Goldfield and Blaine A. Brownell, *Urban America: From Downtown to No Town* (Houghton Mifflin, 1979); Howard P. Chudacoff and Judith E. Smith, *The Evolution of American Urban Society*, 3d ed. (Prentice Hall, 1981); and Charles N. Glaab and A. Theodore Brown, *A History of Urban America*, 3d ed. (Macmillan, 1983). Explorations of the life and work of other political bosses in this period include James A. Kehl, *Boss Rule in the Gilded Age: Matt Quay of Pennsylvania* (University of Pittsburgh Press, 1981); William A. Bullough, *The Blind Boss and His City: Christopher Augustine Buckley and Nineteenth-Century San Francisco* (University of California Press, 1979); and Zane L. Miller, *Boss Cox's Cincinnati: Urban Politics in the Progressive Era* (Oxford University Press, 1968). Scott Greer, ed., *Ethnics, Machines, and the American Future* (Harvard University Press, 1981) and Bruce M. Stave and Sondra Astor Stave, eds., *Urban Bosses, Machines, and Progressive Reformers*, 2d ed. (D. C. Heath, 1984) are excellent collections of essays on urban political machinery. Significant contributions to urban historiography in the late nineteenth century are Stephan Thernstrom, *Poverty and Progress: Social Mobility in the Nineteenth-Century City* (Harvard University Press, 1964) and Gunther Barth, *City People: The Rise of Modern City Culture in Nineteenth-Century America* (Oxford University Press, 1980).

More information on Tweed's role in Tammany Hall politics may be found at http://virtual-ny.com/ndc/Civilwar.html.

ISSUE 3

Were Nineteenth-Century Entrepreneurs Robber Barons?

YES: John Tipple, from "Big Businessmen and a New Economy," in H. Wayne Morgan, ed., *The Gilded Age* (Syracuse University Press, 1970)

NO: Alfred D. Chandler, Jr., from "The Beginnings of 'Big Business' in American Industry," *Business History Review* (Spring 1959)

ISSUE SUMMARY

YES: Professor of history John Tipple characterizes big businessmen of the late nineteenth century as destructive forces whose power and greed undermined the nation's traditional institutions and values.

NO: Professor of business history Alfred D. Chandler, Jr., concludes that American entrepreneurs were organizational and marketing innovators whose creation of great industrial corporations strengthened the country's economy by sparking the growth of a national urban market.

Between 1860 and 1914 the United States was transformed from a country of farms, small towns, and modest manufacturing concerns to a modern nation dominated by large cities and factories. During those years the population tripled, and the nation experienced astounding urban growth. A new proletariat emerged to provide the necessary labor for the country's developing factory system. Between the Civil War and World War I, the value of manufactured goods in the United States increased 12-fold, and the capital invested in industrial pursuits multiplied 22 times. In addition, the application of new machinery and scientific methods to agriculture produced abundant yields of wheat, corn, and other foodstuffs, despite the decline in the number of farmers.

Why did this industrial revolution occur in the United States during the last quarter of the nineteenth century? What factors contributed to the rapid pace of American industrialization? In answering these questions, historians often point to the first half of the 1800s and the significance of the "transportation revolution," which produced better roads, canals, and railroads to move people and goods more efficiently and cheaply from one point to another. Technological improvements such as the Bessemer process, refrigeration, electricity, and the telephone also made their mark in the nation's "Machine Age." Government cooperation with business, large-scale immigration from Europe and Asia, and the availability of foreign capital for industrial investments provided still other underpinnings for this industrial growth. Finally, American industrialization depended upon a number of individuals in the United States who were willing to organize and finance the nation's industrial base for the sake of anticipated profits. These, of course, were the entrepreneurs.

American public attitudes have reflected a schizophrenic quality as regards the activities of the industrial leaders of the late nineteenth century. Were these entrepreneurs "robber barons" who employed any means necessary to enrich themselves at the expense of their competitors? Or were they "captains of industry" whose shrewd and innovative leadership brought order out of industrial chaos and generated great fortunes that enriched the public welfare through the workings of various philanthropic agencies that these leaders established? Although the "robber baron" stereotype emerged as early as the 1870s, it probably gained its widest acceptance in the 1930s. In the midst of the Great Depression, as many critics were proclaiming the apparent failure of American capitalism, Matthew Josephson published *The Robber Barons* (1934), in which he bitterly condemned the ruthless and occasionally violent methods of industrialists such as John D. Rockefeller and Jay Gould. Since the 1930s, however, some historians, including Allan Nevins, Alfred D. Chandler, Jr., and Maury Klein, have sought to revise the negative assessments offered by earlier generations of scholars. In the hands of these "business historians," the late-nineteenth-century businessmen have become "industrial statesmen" who skillfully oversaw the process of raising the United States to a prominent position among the nations of the world. The following essays reveal the divergence of scholarly opinion as it applies to these American entrepreneurs.

John Tipple points out that the public antipathy expressed toward big businessmen like Rockefeller and Andrew Carnegie stemmed from their association with huge corporations whose existence challenged traditional American values. This adverse public opinion was well deserved, says Tipple, because the business magnates frequently behaved recklessly and unethically (if not illegally) in order to amass their great fortunes.

Alfred D. Chandler, Jr., on the other hand, sees the operations of the entrepreneurs as essential to the economic expansion of the country. These business executives, he concludes, developed innovative organizational and marketing strategies that promoted the growth of the nation's urban market economy.

YES   John Tipple

BIG BUSINESSMEN
AND A NEW ECONOMY

It is more than coincidence that the beginning of the Robber Baron legend, the portrayal of the big businessman as a warlike brigand cheating and plundering his way to millions, was contemporaneous with the inauguration of the corporation as the major instrument of business control in the United States. After the Civil War, the large corporation began to dominate the American economic scene. In those same years, Charles Francis Adams, Jr., launched his first assault against the "Erie robbers," and his brother, Henry Adams, warned of the day when great corporations, "swaying power such as has never in the world's history been trusted in the hands of mere private citizens," would be controlled by one man or combinations of men who would use these new leviathans to become masters of the nation.

Such dangerous potentialities were not recognizable prior to the Civil War because the majority of businesses operated as local enterprises, usually as individual proprietorships, partnerships, or as small closed corporations in which ownership and control were almost invariably synonymous. Under most circumstances, the power and influence of the businessman were limited to the immediate environs of operation and seldom extended beyond state boundaries. Equally important, there existed among most businessmen of prewar days a nearly universal desire and a practical necessity for community esteem. This governed their conduct, kept their ventures well within the limits of individual liability, and tended to restrain irresponsible profiteering. Antebellum criticisms of the businessman therefore were few and sporadic. Disapproval usually focused on the speculator or stock gambler, and was often inspired by an agrarian distrust of big-city ways.

The bloody struggles of the Civil War helped bring about revolutionary changes in economic and political life. War needs created almost insatiable demands for goods—arms, munitions, clothing—and offered some manufacturers unsurpassed opportunities to make fortunes. More important, the stimulus of massive military demands alerted entrepreneurs to new concepts of the power and possibilities of large-scale enterprise: "The great operations of war, the handling of large masses of men, the influence of discipline, the

From John Tipple, "Big Businessmen and a New Economy," in H. Wayne Morgan, ed., *The Gilded Age* (Syracuse University Press, 1970), pp. 13–22, 26–30. Copyright © 1970 by Syracuse University Press. Reprinted by permission. Notes omitted.

lavish expenditure of unprecedented sums of money, the immense financial operations, the possibilities of effective cooperation, were lessons not likely to be lost on men quick to receive and apply all new ideas." Though the war prevented general economic expansion, the new ideas were profitably applied to the peacetime economy.

With the rich resources of the trans-Mississippi West open to private exploitation, the businessman had singular opportunities to become wealthy. Before him spread an immense untapped continent whose riches were his virtually for the taking; new means to turn these resources to profitable account were at hand. A host of new inventions and discoveries, the application of science to industry, and improved methods of transportation and communication were ready to assist the businessman. But all these aids would have been valueless without effective means to put them to work. The practical agency to meet these unprecedented entrepreneurial demands on capital and management proved to be the corporation. The stockholding system provided immense capital beyond the reach of any individual, and the corporate hierarchy presented a feasible solution to the greatly augmented problems of management.

The corporation was no novelty. It had served political as well as economic purposes in seventeenth-century America; as an instrumentality of business its use antedated the discovery of this continent. Seldom before in American history, however, had the corporation been used on such a large scale. From a relatively passive creature of legalistic capitalism, it was transformed by fusion with techniques into a dynamic system spearheading economic expansion.

The impact of the newborn corporation on American society was almost cataclysmic. In the first few decades of its existence the modern corporate system enabled the nation to develop more wealth more rapidly than in any period since the discovery. But it also menaced hallowed economic theories and usages, threatening to ride like a great tidal wave over the traditional democratic social and political beliefs. Its size alone was sufficient to change fundamental social and economic relationships. Of the newly formed United States Steel Corporation an awed commentator wrote at the turn of the century: "It receives and expends more money every year than any but the very greatest of the world's national governments; its debt is larger than that of many of the lesser nations of Europe; it absolutely controls the destinies of a population nearly as large as that of Maryland or Nebraska, and indirectly influences twice that number." Moreover, this concentrated economic power normally gravitated into the hands of a few, raising up a corporate ruling class with great economic authority....

The dedicated businessman could make money on an unprecedented scale. Though John D. Rockefeller never quite became a billionaire, his fortune in 1892 reportedly amounted to $815,647,796.89. Andrew Carnegie did nearly as well. The profits from his industrial empire in the decade 1889 to 1899 averaged about $7,500,000 a year and, in 1900 alone, amounted to $40,000,000. In the following year he sold out his interest for several hundred million dollars. Such fortunes, exceptional even for those days, emphasized the wealth available to the big businessman. In 1892, two New York newspapers engaged in a heated contest to count the number of American millionaires, the

World uncovering 3,045 and the *Tribune* raising it to 4,047. Regardless of the exact total, millionaires were becoming fairly common. By 1900, for instance, the Senate alone counted twenty-five millionaires among its members, most of them the well-paid agents of big business—a notorious fact that led some suspicious folk to dub that august body the "Rich Man's Club" and the "House of Dollars."

This sudden leap of big businessmen into new positions of wealth and power caught the public eye. To Americans accustomed to thinking primarily of individuals, the big businessman stood out as the conspicuous symbol of corporate power—his popular image encompassing not only his personal attributes and failings but combining also the more amorphous and impersonal aspects of the business organization by which he had climbed to fortune. Just as the diminutive Andrew Carnegie came to represent the entire steel-making complex of men and decisions which bore his name, so the lean, ascetic John D. Rockefeller personified Standard Oil, and the prominent nose and rotund figure of J. P. Morgan signified the whole of Wall Street with its thousands of operators, its ethical flaws, and its business virtues.

Big businessmen were usually attacked not for personal failings, though they had them as well as the lion's share of wealth, but as the recognizable heads of large corporations. When Carnegie and Rockefeller gave up business careers and became private citizens, the rancor against them almost ceased. Instead of being censured for past actions, which had been widely and vehemently criticized, they were praised as benefactors and good citizens. Public castigation of the steel trust was shifted from "Little Andy" to the broader shoulders of Charles Schwab.

The odium of monopoly which had surrounded his father was inherited by John D. Rockefeller, Jr. Only as the active and directive heads of great corporations, and not as subordinates or members of a business elite, were big businessmen branded "Robber Barons" and indicted for alleged crimes against society.

If the big businessman was not resented as an individual but as a power symbol wielding the might of the great corporation, the provocative question arises of why there was such resentment against the corporation. The answer is that the large industrial corporation was an anomaly in nineteenth-century America. There was no place for it among existing institutions and no sanction for it in traditional American values....

What was to be done with such a monster? Either the corporation had to be made to conform to American institutions and principles or those institutions and principles had to be changed to accommodate the corporation. This was the dilemma first seriously confronted by Americans during the Gilded Age, and the issue that set off the great movement of introspection and reform which activated the American people for the next fifty years.

Most flagrantly apparent was the destructive effect of the large corporation upon free competition and equal opportunity. According to the accepted theory, which was a projection of the doctrines of liberal democracy into the economic sphere, the ideal economy—the only one, in fact, sanctioned by nature—was made up of freely competing individuals operating in a market unrestricted by man but fairly ruled by the inexorable forces of natural law. The ideal polity was achieved by bargaining among free and equal individuals under the benevolent eye of nature. It was assumed that, in economic affairs, impartial rivalry between individual entrepreneurs and free competition would automatically serve the best interests of society by preventing anyone from getting more than his fair share of the wealth.

In early nineteenth-century America, this self-regulating mechanism seemed to work. Where businesses and factories were small, prices and output, wages and profits, rose and fell according to supply and demand. Every man appeared to have equal opportunity to compete with every other man. Even after the war, the individual businessman was forced, in the interests of self-preservation, to observe the common rules of competition. Ordinarily his share of the market was too small to permit any attempt at price control unless he joined with others in a pool, a trade association, or another rudimentary price-fixing agreement. The average businessman eschewed trade agreements, not out of theoretical considerations, but for the practical reason that such coalitions did not work very well, often suffering from mutual distrust and the pursuit of centrifugal aims.

But what was true in a world of individual proprietors and workers was not necessarily correct for the corporation. It possessed greater unity of control and a larger share of the market and could either dictate prices or combine successfully with other corporations in monopolistic schemes. By bringing to bear superior economic force which to a great extent invalidated the tenets of the free market, the large organization put the big businessman in the favored position of operating in an economy dedicated to the idea of freely competing individuals, yet left him unhampered by the ordinary restrictions. Under such auspicious circumstances, he soon outdistanced unorganized rivals in the race for wealth.

This unfair advantage did not go unchallenged. As the earliest of the large corporations in the United States, the railroads were the first to come under concentrated attack. The immense extension of railways after 1865, and the crucial nature of their operations as common carriers, exposed their activities to public scrutiny and subjected their mistakes or misdeeds to considerable publicity. Popular resentment against the railroads in the early 1870's grew hottest in the farming states of the Midwest, but indignant reports from all over the country accused railroads of using monopoly power against equal opportunity.

A most frequent criticism, common to both East and West, was that railway superintendents and managers showed unreasonable favoritism by discriminating between persons and places, offering rate concessions to large shippers, charging more for short than long hauls, and giving preferential treatment to large corporations in the form of secret rebates and drawbacks. That these preferential rates might sometimes have been forced upon the railroads by pressure from business made little difference. The popular consensus was that this elaborate system of special rates denied the little man equal opportunity with the rich and influential, breaking the connection between individual merit and success. The ultimate effect extended further monopoly by preventing free competition among businesses where railway transportation was an important factor.

The Standard Oil Company seemed to be the outstanding example of a monopoly propagated in this manner, the charge being that the determining factor behind Rockefeller's spectacular conquest of the oil business had been this railway practice of secrecy and favoritism which had aided his company and ruined others. By collecting rebates on their own shipments and drawbacks on those of competitors, Standard had gained virtual control of oil transportation. It then could regulate the prices of crude oil, with the detrimental result, so Henry Demarest Lloyd charged, that by 1881, though the company produced only one-fiftieth of the nation's petroleum, Standard refined nine-tenths of the oil produced in the United States and dictated the price of all of it.

As the whipping boy among trusts, Standard undoubtedly got more than its share of criticism, yet by contemporary standards of competition, the corporation was fairly adjudged a monopoly. Through the testimony of H. H. Rogers, an executive of the company, The Hepburn Committee in 1879 was able to establish that 90 to 95 percent of all the refiners in the country acted in harmony with Standard Oil. In 1886, the monopolistic proclivities of the oil trust were attested to by the Cullom Committee:

> It is well understood in commercial circles that the Standard Oil Company brooks no competition; that its settled policy and firm determination is to crush out all who may be rash enough to enter the field against it; that it hesitates at nothing in the accomplishment of this purpose, in which it has been remarkably successful, and that it fitly represents the acme and perfection of corporate greed in its fullest development.

Similar convictions were expressed by a New York senate committee before which Rockefeller and other executives testified in 1888. Four years later, in 1892, the Supreme Court of Ohio declared that the object of the Standard Oil Company was "to establish a virtual monopoly of the business of producing petroleum, and of manufacturing, refining and dealing in it and all its products, throughout the entire country, and by which it might not merely control the production, but the price, at its pleasure."

These findings were reaffirmed by new investigations. In 1902, the United States Industrial Commission reported that Standard, through its control of pipe lines, practically fixed the price of crude oil. In 1907, the commissioner of corporations supported and amplified this conclusion. The company might fall short of an absolute monopoly, the commissioner pointed out, but its intentions were monopolistic. In 1911, the United States Supreme Court confirmed this allegation, observing that "no disinterested mind" could survey the history of the Standard Oil combination from 1870 onward "without being irresistibly driven to the conclusion that the very genius for commercial development and organization... soon begot an intent and purpose... to drive others from the field and to exclude them from their right to trade and thus accomplish the mastery which was the end in view."

Far from regarding the intricate system of business combination he had developed as a monster to be cured or destroyed, a big businessman such as Rockefeller looked proudly upon his creation as a marvel of beneficence, an extraordinary and distinctive expression of American genius. And Carnegie contended "not evil, but good" had come from the phenomenal development of the corporation. He and others pointed out that the world obtained goods and commodities of excellent quality at prices which earlier generations would have considered incredibly cheap. The poor enjoyed what the richest could never before have afforded.

The big businessman supported his actions as being entirely in keeping with the business requisites of the day. Rather than engaging in a conscious conspiracy to undermine equal opportunity, he had sought only the immediate and practical rewards of successful enterprise, rationalizing business conduct on the pragmatic level of profit and loss.

Instead of deliberately blocking free competition, big businessmen maintained that their actions were only natural responses to immutable law. Charles E. Perkins, president of the Chicago, Burlington and Quincy Railroad Company, denied deliberate misuses of power in establishing rates, and claimed that the price of railroad transportation, like all other prices, adjusted itself. Discriminatory practices were viewed as part of an inevitable conflict between buyer and seller, a necessary result of competition. The payment of rebates and drawbacks was simply one method of meeting the market. In answer to the accusation that the railroads had made "important discriminations" in favor of Standard Oil, an executive of that company replied: "It may be frankly stated at the outset that the Standard Oil Company has at all times within the limits of fairness and with due regard for the laws ought to secure the most advantageous freight rates and routes possible." Rockefeller went on record as saying that Standard had received rebates from the railroads prior to 1880, because it was simply the railroads' way of doing business. Each shipper made the best bargain he could, hoping to outdo his competitor.

Furthermore, Rockefeller claimed this traffic was more profitable to the railroads than to the Standard Oil Company, stating that whatever advantage the oil company gained was passed on in lower costs to the consumer. Just as his company later justified certain alleged misdemeanors as being typical of the sharp practices prevailing in the oil fields in the early days, so Rockefeller exonerated the whole system of rebates and drawbacks on the grounds that everybody was doing it, concluding cynically that those who objected on principle did so only because they were not benefiting from it.

Yet despite his public rationalizations, the big businessman's attitude toward competition was ambivalent. He lauded it as economic theory, but denied it in practical actions. Theoretically, there was no such thing as an absolute monopoly; there was always the threat of latent competition. Whenever a trust exacted too much, competitors would automatically appear. Competition as a natural law would survive the trusts. "It is here; we cannot evade it," declaimed Carnegie. "And while the law may be sometimes hard for the individual, it is best for the race, because it insures the survival of the fittest in every department."

In practical matters, however, the big businessman acted as if the law had long since become outmoded, if not extinct. Progressive opinion in the business world heralded the growing monopolistic trend as a sign of economic maturity. Increased concentration in capital and industry was defended as necessary and inevitable. Monopolistic practices in general were upheld in business circles on the grounds that they prevented disastrous competition. In the long run they benefited, rather than plundered, the public by maintaining reasonable rates and prices. "There seems to be a great readiness in the public mind to take alarm at these phenomena of growth, there might rather seem to be reason for public congratulation," announced Professor William Graham Sumner of Yale. "We want to be provided with things abundantly and cheaply; that means that we want increased economic power. All these enterprises are efforts to satisfy that want, and they promise to do it." Many big businessmen believed that, practically at least, the trust proved the superiority of combination over competition....

In condemning trusts as "dangerous to Republican institutions" and in branding corporate leaders as Robber Barons "opposed to free institutions and free commerce between the states as were the feudal barons of the middle ages," aroused Americans of the Gilded Age had clearly seized upon the major issue. They had somehow recognized that American society with its individualistic traditions was engaged in a life-and-death struggle with the organized forces of dissolution.

The once-welcome business and industrial concentration threatened the foundations of the nation. There was more individual power than ever, but those who wielded it were few and formidable. Charles Francis Adams, Jr., denounced these "modern potentates for the autocratic misuse of that power":

> The system of corporate life and corporate power, as applied to industrial development, is yet in its infancy.... It is a new power, for which our language contains no name. We know what aristocracy, autocracy, democracy are; but we have no word to express government by monied corporations.... It remains to be

seen what the next phase in this process of gradual development will be. History never quite repeats itself, and... the old familiar enemies may even now confront us, though arrayed in such a modern garb that no suspicion is excited.... As the Erie ring represents the combination of the corporation and the hired proletariat of a great city; as Vanderbilt embodies the autocratic power of Caesarism introduced into corporate life, and neither alone can obtain complete control of the government of the State, it, perhaps, only remains for the coming man to carry the combination of elements one step in advance, and put Caesarism at once in control of the corporation and of the proletariat, to bring our vaunted institutions within the rule of all historic precedent.

Yet the public already sensed that something had gone wrong with American institutions and values. With less understanding than Adams, they felt that somehow the old rules had been broken. Behind their growing animosity to the big businessman was the feeling that in some way he cheated his countrymen. The belief was becoming fairly common that extreme wealth was incompatible with honesty. "The great cities," Walt Whitman wrote in 1871, "reek with respectable as much as non-respectable robbery and scoundrelism." There were undoubtedly moral men of wealth, but many Americans agreed with Thomas A. Bland, who in *How to Grow Rich* suggested: "In all history, ancient and modern, the examples of men of honest lives and generous hearts who have become rich... is so rare as to be exceedingly exceptional, and even these have invariably profited largely... by the labor of others."

Very revealing in this regard was the portrayal of the big businessman in contemporary fiction. Socialist writers naturally depicted him as a "criminal of greed" or an "economic monster" who with other "business animals" preyed upon the life of the nation. Oddly enough, however, in an age when the corporation made unprecedented achievements in production and organization to the enrichment of countless people, when material success was widely favored as a legitimate goal, scarcely a single major novelist presented the big businessman as a hero or even in a favorable light. Except at the hands of a few hack writers, the business or industrial leader was consistently portrayed as powerful and capable, but nonetheless an enemy of American society. This may have reflected the bias of the aesthetic or creative temperament against the pragmatic money-maker, but the big businessman was in disfavor with most of American society.

In the popular mind, the vices of lying and stealing were legendarily associated with Wall Street. The big businessmen who dominated "the street" were regarded by some as the ethical counterparts of the pirate and buccaneer. By the simple devices of "stock-watering" or the issuance of fictitious securities not backed by capital assets, speculators were generally believed to have stolen millions of dollars from the American people. In the opinion of the more jaundiced, the men of Wall Street had barely escaped prison bars. "If the details of the great reorganization and trustification deals put through since 1885 could be laid bare," contended Thomas W. Lawson, a financier turned critic, "eight out of ten of our most successful stock-jobbing financiers would be in a fair way to get into State or federal prisons."

The iniquity of Wall Street was not merely legendary, but had firm basis in fact. Though not all speculators were swindlers nor all speculation gambling, only a small number of the stock exchange transactions were unquestionably of an investment character. The vast majority were virtually gambling. Many corporations, although offering huge blocks of stock to the public, issued only the vaguest and most ambiguous summary of assets and liabilities. While this was not iniquitous in itself, secrecy too often cloaked fraud.

The men at the top who had used the corporate device to make millions did not see it this way at all. They justified their millions on the ground that they had fairly earned it. Cornelius Vanderbilt, at the age of eighty-one, boasted that he had made a million dollars for every year of his life, but added that it had been worth "three times that to the people of the United States." Others shared his belief. In *The Railroad and the Farmer*, Edward Atkinson made practically the same statement, asserting that the gigantic fortune of the older Vanderbilt was but a small fraction of what the country gained from the development of the railway system under his genius. The Reverend Julian M. Sturtevant of Illinois College also envisioned the Vanderbilts and Astors of the world as "laborers of gigantic strength, and they must have their reward and compensation for the use of their capital." Carnegie maintained that great riches were no crime. "Under our present conditions the millionaire who toils on is the cheapest article which the community secures at the price it pays for him, namely, his shelter, clothing, and food."

Most Americans, however, did not so readily accept this evaluation. Some recognized that the big businessman in pursuing private ends had served national prosperity—the majority felt that he had taken extravagant profits entirely out of proportion to the economic services he had rendered. Rockefeller's millions were thought to be typical of the fortunes made by Robber Barons, representing "the relentless, aggressive, irresistible seizure of a particular opportunity, the magnitude of which... was due simply to the magnitude of the country and the immensity of the stream of its prosperous industrial life." The feeling was general that the great fortunes of all the big business magnates—Vanderbilt, Gould, Harriman, Stanford, Carnegie, Morgan, and the rest—represented special privilege which had enabled them to turn the abundant natural resources and multitudinous advantages offered by a growing nation into a private preserve for their own profit.

The public at large was not clearly aware of it, but the chief instrument of special privilege was the corporation. Though public franchises and political favoritism played a large part in the aggrandizement of the Robber Barons, in the money-making world of late nineteenth-century America special privilege invariably meant corporate privilege. The corporation enabled Vanderbilt to unify his railroads while making large speculative profits on the side. The same device made it possible for men like Rockefeller to create and combine private enterprises embodying new technological and financial techniques while diverting enormous profits to themselves. The corporation was the constructive power behind the building of the cross-country railroads, but it was also the destructive instrument used by Jay Gould, Tom Scott, Collis P. Huntington, and others to convert them into quick money-making machines with no regard for their obligations as public carriers.

The problem remained of establishing the relationship of big businessmen to the corporation. Judging by their conduct, they were not fully cognizant of the tremendous power placed in their hands by the corporation with single men controlling "thousands of men, tens of millions of revenue, and hundreds of millions of capital." Or they wilfully exerted this prodigious force for private benefit regardless of consequences to the nation or ideals. Unhappily, most of those labeled Robber Baron by their contemporaries fell into the latter category. Cornelius Vanderbilt held the law in contempt. Except where his own interests were involved, he had little regard for the consequences of his actions, manipulating and watering every corporate property he captured. One year after he took over the New York Central railroad, he increased the capitalization by $23,000,000, almost every cent of which represented inside profits for himself and friends. When admonished that some of his transactions were forbidden by law, he supposedly roared, "Law! What do I care about the law? Hain't I got the power?" He confirmed this attitude in testimony before the committee on railroads of the New York State Assembly in 1869. But Vanderbilt's methods were in no way exceptional. Most of the biggest businessmen made their millions in similar fashion. Twenty-four who because of notoriety and conspicuous power might be regarded as "typical" Robber Barons combined the role of promoter with that of entrepreneur. Stock manipulation along with corporate consolidation was probably the easiest way to wealth that ever existed in the United States. The exuberance with which promoters threw themselves into it proved that they were well aware of its golden possibilities.

As a consequence of these reckless corporate maneuverings, however, public opinion turned against the big businessman. While from a corporate point of view the conduct of the money-makers was often legal, although ethically dubious, the public often felt cheated. Puzzled and disenchanted by the way things had turned out, they questioned the way every millionaire got his money, and were quite ready to believe that a crime was behind every great fortune. While its exact nature escaped them, they felt they had been robbed. The classic statement of this feeling of outrage appeared in the Populist platform of 1892: "The fruits of the toil of millions are boldly stolen to build up colossal fortunes for a few, unprecedented in the history of mankind; and the possessors of these, in turn, despise the Republic and endanger liberty."

The inchoate charges were basically accurate: too much wealth was being selfishly appropriated by a few. By the irresponsible use of the corporation, essentially a supralegal abstraction above the traditional laws of the land, they were undermining individualistic institutions and values. Big businessmen like John D. Rockefeller were attacked as Robber Barons because they were correctly identified as destroyers, the insurgent vanguard of the corporate revolution.

NO

Alfred D. Chandler, Jr.

THE BEGINNINGS OF "BIG BUSINESS" IN AMERICAN INDUSTRY

Between the depression of the 1870's and the beginning of the twentieth century, American industry underwent a significant transformation. In the 1870's, the major industries serviced an agrarian economy. Except for a few companies equipping the rapidly expanding railroad network, the leading industrial firms processed agricultural products and provided farmers with food and clothing. These firms tended to be small, and bought their raw materials and sold their finished goods locally. Where they manufactured for a market more than a few miles away from the factory, they bought and sold through commissioned agents who handled the business of several other similar firms.

By the beginning of the twentieth century, many more companies were making producers' goods, to be used in industry rather than on the farm or by the ultimate consumer. Most of the major industries had become dominated by a few large enterprises. These great industrial corporations no longer purchased and sold through agents, but had their own nation-wide buying and marketing organizations. Many, primarily those in the extractive industries, had come to control their own raw materials. In other words, the business economy had become industrial. Major industries were dominated by a few firms that had become great, vertically integrated, centralized enterprises.

In the terms of the economist and sociologist a significant sector of American industry had become bureaucratic, in the sense that business decisions were made within large hierarchical structures. Externally, oligopoly was prevalent, the decision-makers being as much concerned with the actions of the few other large firms in the industry as with over-all changes in markets, sources of supplies, and technological improvements.

These basic changes came only after the railroads had created a national market. The railroad network, in turn, had grown swiftly primarily because of the near desperate requirements for efficient transportation created by the movement of population westward after 1815. Except for the

Excerpted from Alfred D. Chandler, Jr., "The Beginnings of 'Big Business' in American Industry," *Business History Review,* vol. 35 (Spring 1959). Copyright © 1959 by the President and Fellows of Harvard College. All rights reserved. Reprinted by permission of Harvard Business School. Notes omitted.

Atlantic seaboard between Boston and Washington, the construction of the American railroads was stimulated almost wholly by the demand for better transportation to move crops, to bring farmers supplies, and to open up new territories to commercial agriculture.

By greatly expanding the scope of the agrarian economy, the railroads quickened the growth of the older commercial centers, such as New York, Philadelphia, Cincinnati, Cleveland, and St. Louis, and helped create new cities like Chicago, Indianapolis, Atlanta, Kansas City, Dallas, and the Twin Cities. This rapid urban expansion intensified the demand for the products of the older consumer goods industries—particularly those which processed the crops of the farmer and planter into food, stimulants, and clothing.

At the same time, railroad construction developed the first large market in this country for producers' goods. Except for the making of relatively few textile machines, steamboat engines, and ordnance, the iron and nonferrous manufacturers had before 1850 concentrated on providing metals and simple tools for merchants and farmers. Even textile machinery was usually made by the cloth manufacturers themselves. However, by 1860, only a decade after beginning America's first major railroad construction boom, railroad companies had already replaced the blacksmiths as the primary market for iron products, and had become far and away the most important market for the heavy engineering industries. By then, too, the locomotive was competing with the Connecticut brass industry as a major consumer of copper. More than this, the railroads, with their huge capital outlay, their fixed operating costs, the large size of their labor and management force, and the technical complexity of their operations, pioneered in the new ways of oligopolistic competition and large-scale, professionalized, bureaucratized management.

The new nation-wide market created by the construction of the railroad network became an increasingly urban one. From 1850 on, if not before, urban areas were growing more rapidly than rural ones. In the four decades from 1840 to 1880 the proportion of urban population rose from 11 per cent to 28 per cent of the total population, or about 4 per cent a decade. In the two decades from 1880 to 1900 it grew from 28 per cent to 40 per cent or an increase of 6 per cent a decade. Was this new urban and national market, then, the primary stimulant for business innovation and change, and for the coming of big business to American industry?

CHANGES IN THE CONSUMERS' GOODS INDUSTRIES

The industries first to become dominated by great business enterprises were those making consumer goods, the majority of which were processed from products grown on the farm and sold in the urban markets. Consolidation and centralization in the consumers' goods industries were well under way by 1893. The unit that appeared was one which integrated within a single business organization the major economic processes: production or purchasing of raw materials, manufacturing, distribution, and finance.

Such vertically integrated organizations came in two quite different ways. Where the product tended to be somewhat new in kind and especially fitted for the urban market, its makers created their businesses by first building large marketing and then purchasing organizations. This technique appears to have been true of the manufacturers or distributors of fresh meat, cigarettes, high-grade flour, bananas, harvesters, sewing machines, and typewriters. Where the products were established staple items, horizontal combination tended to precede vertical integration. In the sugar, salt, leather, whiskey, glucose, starch, biscuit, kerosene, fertilizer, and rubber industries a large number of small manufacturers first combined into large business units and then created their marketing and buying organizations. For a number of reasons the makers of the newer types of products found the older outlets less satisfactory and felt more of a need for direct marketing than did the manufacturers of the long-established goods.

Integration via the Creation of Marketing Organization

The story of the changes and the possible reasons behind them can be more clearly understood by examining briefly the experience of a few innovating firms. First, consider the experience of companies that grew large through the creation of a nation-wide marketing and distributing organization. Here the story of Gustavus F. Swift and his brother Edwin is a significant one. Gustavus F. Swift, an Easterner, came relatively late to the Chicago meat-packing business. Possibly because he was from Massachusetts, he appreciated the potential market for fresh western meat in the eastern cities. For after the Civil War, Boston, New York, Philadelphia, and other cities were rapidly outrunning their local meat supply. At the same time, great herds of cattle were gathering on the western plains. Swift saw the possibilities of connecting the new market with the new source of supply by

the use of the refrigerated railroad car. In 1878, shortly after his first experimental shipment of refrigerated meat, he formed a partnership with his younger brother, Edwin, to market fresh western meat in the eastern cities.

For the next decade, Swift struggled hard to carry out his plans, the essence of which was the creation, during the 1880's, of the nation-wide distributing and marketing organization built around a network of branch houses. Each "house" had its storage plant and its own marketing organization. The latter included outlets in major towns and cities, often managed by Swift's own salaried representatives. In marketing the product, Swift had to break down, through advertising and other means, the prejudices against eating meat killed more than a thousand miles away and many weeks earlier. At the same time he had to combat boycotts of local butchers and the concerted efforts of the National Butchers' Protective Association to prevent the sale of his meat in the urban markets.

To make effective use of the branch house network, the company soon began to market products other than beef. The "full line" soon came to include lamb, mutton, pork, and, some time later, poultry, eggs, and dairy products. The growing distributing organization soon demanded an increase in supply. So between 1888 and 1892, the Swifts set up meat-packing establishments in Kansas City, Omaha, and St. Louis, and, after the depression of the 1890's, three more in St. Joseph, St. Paul, and Ft. Worth. At the same time, the company systematized the buying of its cattle and other products at the stockyards. In the 1890's, too, Swift began a concerted effort to make more profitable use of by-products.

Before the end of the 1890's, then, Swift had effectively fashioned a great, vertically integrated organization. The major departments—marketing, processing, purchasing, and accounting—were all tightly controlled from the central office in Chicago. A report of the Commissioner of Corporations published in 1905 makes clear the reason for such control:

> Differences in quality of animals and of their products are so great that the closest supervision of the Central Office is necessary to enforce the exercise of skill and sound judgement on the part of the agents who buy the stock, and the agents who sell the meat. With this object, the branches of the Selling and Accounting Department of those packing companies which have charge of the purchasing, killing, and dressing and selling of fresh meat, are organized in the most extensive and thorough manner. The Central Office is in constant telegraphic correspondence with the distributing houses, with a view to adjusting the supply of meat and the price as nearly as possible to the demand.

As this statement suggests, the other meat packers followed Swift's example. To compete effectively, Armour, Morris, Cudahy, and Schwarzschild & Sulzberger had to build up similar integrated organizations. Those that did not follow the Swift model were destined to remain small local companies. Thus by the middle of the 1890's, the meat-packing industry, with the rapid growth of these great vertically integrated firms had become oligopolistic (the "Big Five" had the major share of the market) and bureaucratic; each of the five had its many departments and several levels of management.

This story has parallels in other industries processing agricultural products. In tobacco, James B. Duke was the first to appreciate the growing market for the cigarette, a new product which was sold almost wholly in the cities. However, after he had applied machinery to the manufacture of cigarettes, production soon outran supply. Duke then concentrated on expanding the market through extensive advertising and the creation of a national and then world-wide selling organization. In 1884, he left Durham, North Carolina, for New York City, where he set up factories, sales, and administrative offices. New York was closer to his major urban markets, and was the more logical place to manage an international advertising campaign than Durham. While he was building his marketing department, Duke was also creating the network of warehouses and buyers in the tobacco-growing areas of the country.

In 1890, he merged his company with five smaller competitors in the cigarette business to form the American Tobacco Company. By 1895 the activities of these firms had been consolidated into the manufacturing, marketing, purchasing, and finance departments of the single operating structure Duke had earlier fashioned. Duke next undertook development of a full line by handling all types of smoking and chewing tobacco. By the end of the century, his company completely dominated the tobacco business. Only two other firms, R. J. Reynolds & Company and P. Lorillard & Company had been able to build up comparable vertically integrated organizations. When they merged with American Tobacco they continued to retain their separate operating organizations. When the 1911 antitrust decree split these and other units off from the American company, the tobacco industry had become, like the meat-packing business, oligopolistic, and its dominant firms bureaucratic.

What Duke and Swift did for their industries, James S. Bell of the Washburn-Crosby Company did during these same years in the making and selling of high-grade flour to the urban bakeries and housewives, and Andrew J. Preston achieved in growing, transporting, and selling another new product for the urban market, the banana. Like Swift and Duke, both these men made their major innovations in marketing, and then went on to create large-scale, departmentalized, vertically integrated structures.

The innovators in new consumer durables followed much the same pattern. Both Cyrus McCormick, pioneer harvester manufacturer, and William Clark, the business brains of the Singer Sewing Machine Company, first sold through commissioned agents. Clark soon discovered that salaried men, working out of branch offices, could more effectively and at less cost display, demonstrate, and service sewing machines than could the agents. Just as important, the branch offices were able to provide the customer with essential credit. McCormick, while retaining the dealer to handle the final sales, came to appreciate the need for a strong selling and distributing organization, with warehouses, servicing facilities, and a large salaried force, to stand behind the dealer. So in the years following the Civil War, both McCormick and Singer Sewing Machine Company concentrated on building up national and then world-wide marketing departments. As they purchased their raw materials from a few industrial companies rather than from a mass of farmers, their purchasing departments were smaller, and required less attention than those in the firms processing farmers' products. But the net result was the creation of a very similar type of organization.

Integration via Horizontal Combination

In those industries making more standard goods, the creation of marketing organizations usually followed large-scale combinations of a number of small manufacturing firms. For these small firms, the coming of the railroad had in many cases enlarged their markets but simultaneously brought them for the first time into competition with many other companies. Most of these firms appear to have expanded production in order to take advantage of the new markets. As a result, their industries became plagued with overproduction and excess capacity; that is, continued production at full capacity threatened to drop prices below the cost of production. So in the 1880's and early 1890's, many small manufacturers in the leather, sugar, salt, distilling and other corn products, linseed and cotton oil, biscuit, petroleum, fertilizer and rubber boot and glove industries, joined in large horizontal combinations.

In most of these industries, combination was followed by consolidation and vertical integration, and the pattern was comparatively consistent. First, the new combinations concentrated their manufacturing activities in locations more advantageously situated to meet the new growing urban demands. Next they systematized and standardized their manufacturing processes. Then, except in the case of sugar and corn products (glucose and starch), the combinations began to build large distributing and smaller purchasing departments. In so doing, many dropped their initial efforts to buy out competitors or to drive them out of business by price-cutting. Instead they concentrated on the creation of a more efficient flow from the producers of their raw materials to the ultimate consumer, and of the development and maintenance of markets through brand names and advertising. Since the large majority of these combinations began as regional groupings, most industries came to have more than one great firm. Only oil, sugar, and corn products remained long dominated by a single company. By World War I, partly because of the dissolutions under the Sherman Act, these industries had also become oligopolistic, and their leading firms vertically integrated.

Specific illustrations help to make these generalizations more precise. The best-known is the story of the oil industry, but equally illustrative is the experience of the leading distilling, baking, and rubber companies.

The first permanent combination in the whiskey industry came in 1887 when a large number of Midwestern distillers, operating more than 80 small plants, formed the Distillers' and Cattle Feeders' Trust. Like other trusts, it adopted the more satisfactory legal form of a holding company shortly after New Jersey in 1889 passed the general incorporation law for holding companies. The major efforts of the Distillers Company were, first, to concentrate production in a relatively few plants. By 1895 only 21 were operating. The managers maintained that the large volume per plant permitted by such concentration would mean lower costs, and also that the location of few plants more advantageously in relation to supply and marketing would still reduce expenses further. However, the company kept the price of whiskey up, and since the cost of setting up a distillery was small, it soon

had competition from small local plants. The company's answer was to purchase the new competitors and to cut prices. This strategy proved so expensive that the enterprise was unable to survive the depression of the 1890's.

Shortly before going into receivership in 1896, the Distillers Company had begun to think more about marketing. In 1895, it had planned to spend a million dollars to build up a distributing and selling organization in the Urban East—the company's largest market. In 1898, through the purchase of the Standard Distilling & Distributing Company and the Spirits Distributing Company, it did acquire a marketing organization based in New York City. In 1903, the marketing and manufacturing units were combined into a single operating organization under the direction of the Distillers Securities Company. At the same time, the company's president announced plans to concentrate on the development of brand names and specialties, particularly through advertising and packaging. By the early years of the twentieth century, then, the Distillers Company had become a vertically integrated, departmentalized, centralized operating organization, competing in the modern manner, more through advertising and product differentiation than price.

The experience of the biscuit industry is even more explicit. The National Biscuit Company came into being in 1898 as a merger of three regional combinations: The New York Biscuit Company formed in 1890, the American Biscuit and Manufacturing Company, and the United States Biscuit Company founded a little later. Its initial objective was to control price and production, but as in the case of the Distillers Company, this strategy proved too expensive. The

Annual Report for 1901 suggests why National Biscuit shifted its basic policies:

This Company is four years old and it may be of interest to shortly review its history.... When the company started, it was an aggregation of plants. It is now an organized business. When we look back over the four years, we find that a radical change has been wrought in our methods of business. In the past, the managers of large merchandising corporations have found it necessary, for success, to control or limit competition. So when this company started, it was thought that we must control competition, and that to do this we must either fight competition or buy it. The first meant a ruinous war of prices, and a great loss of profit; the second, a constantly increasing capitalization. Experience soon proved to us that, instead of bringing success, either of those courses, if persevered in, must bring disaster. This led us to reflect whether it was necessary to control competition.... we soon satisfied ourselves that within the Company itself we must look for success.

We turned our attention and bent our energies to improving the internal management of our business, to getting full benefit from purchasing our raw materials in large quantities, to economizing the expenses of manufacture, to systematizing and rendering more effective our selling department; and above all things and before all things to improve the quality of our goods and the condition in which they should reach the customer.

It became the settled policy of this Company to buy out no competition....

In concentrating on distribution, the company first changed its policy from selling in bulk to wholesalers to marketing small packages to retailers. It developed the various "Uneeda Biscuit" brands, which immediately became popular. "The next point," the same Annual Report continued, "was to reach the customer. Thinking we had something that the customer wanted, we had to advise the customer of its existence. We did this by extensive advertising." This new packaging and advertising not only quickly created a profitable business, but also required the building of a sizable marketing organization. Since flour could be quickly and easily purchased in quantity from large milling firms, the purchasing requirements were less complex, and so the company needed a smaller purchasing organization. On the other hand, it spent much energy after 1901 in improving plant layout and manufacturing processes in order to cut production costs and to improve and standardize quality. Throughout the first decade of its history, National Biscuit continued the policy of "centralizing" manufacturing operations, particularly in its great New York and Chicago plants.

In the rubber boot, shoe, and glove industries, the story is much the same. Expansion of manufacturing facilities and increasing competition as early as 1874, led to the formation, by several leading firms, of the Associated Rubber Shoe Companies—an organization for setting price and production schedules through its board of directors. This company continued until 1886. Its successor, the Rubber Boot and Shoe Company, which lasted only a year, attempted, besides controlling prices and production, to handle marketing, which had always been done by commissioned agents. After five years of uncontrolled competition, four of the five firms that had organized the selling company again combined, this time with the assistance of a large rubber importer, Charles A. Flint. The resulting United States Rubber Company came, by

1898, to control 75 per cent of the nation's rubber boot, shoe, and glove output.

At first the new company remained a decentralized holding company. Each constituent company retained its corporate identity with much freedom of action, including the purchasing of raw materials and the selling of finished products, which was done, as before, through jobbers. The central office's concern was primarily with controlling price and production schedules. Very soon, however, the company began, in the words of the 1896 Annual Report, a policy of "perfecting consolidation of purchasing, selling, and manufacturing." This was to be accomplished in four ways. First, as the 1895 Annual Report had pointed out, the managers agreed "so far as practicable, to consolidate the purchasing of all supplies of raw materials for the various manufactures into one single buying agency, believing that the purchase of large quantities of goods can be made at more advantageous figures than the buying of small isolated lots." The second new "general policy" was "to undertake to reduce the number of brands of goods manufactured, and to consolidate the manufacturing of the remaining brands in those factories which have demonstrated superior facilities for production or advantageous labor conditions. This course was for the purpose of utilizing the most efficient instruments of production and closing those that were inefficient and unprofitable." The third policy was to consolidate sales through the formation of a "Selling Department," which was to handle all goods made by the constituent companies in order to achieve "economy in the distribution expense." Selling was now to be handled by a central office in the New York City headquarters, with branch offices throughout the United States and Europe. Of the three great new departments, actually manufacturing was the slowest to be fully consolidated and centralized. Finally, the treasurer's office at headquarters began to obtain accurate data on profit and loss through the institution of uniform, centralized cost accounting.

Thus United States Rubber, National Biscuit, and the Distillers Securities Company soon came to have organizational structures paralleling those of Swift and American Tobacco. By the first decade of the twentieth century, the leading firms in many consumers' goods industries had become departmentalized and centralized. This was the organizational concomitant to vertical integration. Each major function, manufacturing, sales, purchasing, and finance, became managed by a single and separate department head, usually a vice president, who, assisted by a director or a manager, had full authority and responsibility for the activities of his unit. These departmental chiefs, with the president, coordinated and evaluated the work of the different functional units, and made policy for the company as a whole. In coordinating, appraising, and policy-making, the president and the vice presidents in charge of departments came to rely more and more on the accounting and statistical information, usually provided by the finance department, on costs, output, purchases, and sales....

CONCLUSION: THE BASIC INNOVATIONS

The middle of the first decade of the new century might be said to mark the end of an era. By 1903, the great merger movement was almost over, and by then the metals industries and those processing agricultural products had developed patterns of internal organization and external competition which were to remain. In those years, too, leading chemical, electrical, rubber, power machinery and implement companies had initiated their "full line" policy, and had instituted the earliest formal research and development departments created in this country. In this decade also, electricity was becoming for the first time a significant source of industrial power, and the automobile was just beginning to revolutionize American transportation. From 1903 on, the new generators of power and the new technologies appear to have become the dominant stimuli to innovation in American industry, and such innovations were primarily those which created new products and processes. Changes in organizational methods and marketing techniques were largely responses to technological advances.

This seems much less true of the changes during the 20 to 25 years before 1903. In that period, the basic innovations were more in the creation of new forms of organization and new ways of marketing. The great modern corporation, carrying on the major industrial processes, namely, purchasing, and often production of materials and parts, manufacturing, marketing, and finance —all within the same organizational structure —had its beginnings in that period. Such organizations hardly existed, outside of the railroads, before the 1880's. By 1900 they had become the basic business unit in American industry.

Each of these major processes became managed by a corporate department, and all were coordinated and supervised from a central office. Of the departments, marketing was the most significant. The creation of nation-wide distributing and selling organizations was the initial step in the growth of many larger consumer goods companies. Mergers in both the consumer and producer goods industries were almost always followed by the formation of a centralized sales department.

The consolidation of plants under a single manufacturing department usually accompanied or followed the formation of a national marketing organization. The creation of such a manufacturing department normally meant the concentration of production in fewer and larger plants, and such consolidation probably lowered unit costs and increased output per worker. The creation of such a department in turn led to the setting up of central traffic, purchasing, and often engineering organizations. Large-scale buying, more rational routing of raw materials and finished products, more systematic plant lay-out, and plant location in relation to materials and markets probably lowered costs still further. Certainly the creators of these organizations believed that it did. In the extractive and machinery industries integration went one step further. Here the motives for controlling raw materials or parts and components were defensive as well as designed to cut costs through providing a more efficient flow of materials from mine to market.

These great national industrial organizations required a large market to provide the volume necessary to support the increased overhead costs. Also, to be profitable, they needed careful coordination between the different functional departments. This coordination required a steady flow of accurate data on costs, sales, and on all purchasing, manufacturing, and marketing activities. As a result, the comptroller's office became an increasingly important department. In fact, one of the first moves after a combination by merger or purchase was to institute more effective and detailed accounting procedures. Also, the leading entrepreneurs of the period, men like Rockefeller, Carnegie, Swift, Duke, Preston, Clark, and the DuPonts, had to become, as had the railroad executives of an earlier generation, experts in reading and interpreting business statistics.

Consolidation and departmentalization meant that the leading industrial corporations became operating rather than holding companies, in the sense that the officers and managers of the companies were directly concerned with operating activities. In fact, of the 50 companies with the largest assets in 1909, only United States Steel, Amalgamated Copper, and one or two other copper companies remained purely holding companies. In most others, the central office included the heads of the major functional departments, usually the president, vice presidents, and sometimes a chairman of the board and one or two representatives of financial interests. These men made major policy and administrative decisions and evaluated the performance of the departments and the corporation as a whole. In the extractive industries a few companies, like Standard Oil (N.J.) and some of the metals companies, were partly holding and partly operating companies. At Standard Oil nearly all important decisions were made in the central headquarters, at 26 Broadway, which housed not only the presidents of the subsidiaries but the powerful policy formulating and coordinating committees. But in some of the metals companies, the subsidiaries producing and transporting raw materials retained a large degree of autonomy.

The coming of the large vertically integrated, centralized, functionally departmentalized industrial organization altered the internal and external situations in which and about which business decisions were made. Information about markets, supplies, and operating performance as well as suggestions for action often had to come up through the several levels of the departmental hierarchies, while decisions and suggestions based on this data had to be transmitted down the same ladder for implementation. Executives on each level became increasingly specialists in one function—in sales, production, purchasing, or finance —and most remained in one department and so handled one function only for the major part of their business careers. Only he who climbed to the very top of the departmental ladder had a chance to see his own company as a single operating unit. Where a company's markets, sources of raw materials, and manufacturing processes remained relatively stable, as was true in the metals industries and in those processing agricultural goods, the nature of the business executive's work became increasingly routine and administrative.

When the internal situation had become bureaucratic, the external one tended to be oligopolistic. Vertical integration by one manufacturer forced others to follow. Thus, in a very short time, many American industries became dominated by a few large firms, with the smaller ones handling local and more specialized aspects of the business. Occasionally industries like oil, tobacco, and sugar, came to be controlled by one company, but in most cases legal action by the federal government in the years after 1900 turned monopolistic industries into oligopolistic ones.

Costs, rather than interfirm competition, began to determine prices. With better information on costs, supplies, and market conditions, the companies were able to determine price quite accurately on the basis of the desired return on investment. The managers of the different major companies had little to gain by cutting prices below an acceptable profit margin. On the other hand, if one firm set its prices excessively high, the other firms could increase their share of the market by selling at a lower price and still maintain a profit. They would, however, rarely cut to the point where this margin was eliminated. As a result, after 1900, price leadership, price umbrellas, and other evidences of oligopolistic competition became common in many American industries. To increase their share of the market and to improve their profit position, the large corporations therefore concerned themselves less with price and concentrated more on obtaining new customers by advertising, brand names, and product differentiations; on cutting costs through further improvement and integration of the manufacturing, marketing, and buying processes; and on developing more diversified lines of products.

The coming of the large vertically integrated corporation changed more than just the practices of American industrialists and their industries. The effect on the merchant, particularly the wholesaler, and on the financier, especially the investment banker, has been suggested here. The relation between the growth of these great industrial units and the rise of labor unions has often been pointed out. Certainly the regulation of the large corporation became one of the major political issues of these years, and the devices created to carry out such a regulation were significant innovations in American constitutional, legal, and political institutions. But an examination of such effects is beyond the scope of this paper.

Reasons for the Basic Innovations

One question remains to be reviewed. Why did the vertically integrated corporation come when it did, and in the way it did? The creation by nearly all the large firms of nation-wide selling and distributing organizations indicates the importance of the national market. It was necessary that the market be an increasingly urban one. The city took the largest share of the goods manufactured by the processors of agricultural products. The city, too, with its demands for construction materials, lighting, heating and many other facilities, provided the major market for the metals and other producers' goods industries after railroad construction slowed. Without the rapidly growing urban market there would have been little need and little opportunity for the coming of big business in American industry. And such a market could hardly have existed before the completion of a nation-wide railroad network.

What other reasons might there have been for the swift growth of the great industrial corporation? What about foreign markets? In some industries, particularly oil, the overseas trade may have been an important factor. However, in most businesses the domestic customers took the lion's share of the output, and in nearly all of them the move abroad appears to have come after the creation of the large corporation, and after such corporations had fashioned their domestic marketing organization.

What about the investor looking for profitable investments, and the promoter seeking new promotions? Financiers and promoters certainly had an impact on the changes after 1897, but again they seem primarily to have taken advantage of what had already proved successful. The industrialists themselves, rather than the financiers, initiated most of the major changes in business organization. Availability of capital and cooperation with the financier figured much less prominently in these industrial combinations and consolidations than had been the case with the earlier construction of the railroads and with the financing of the Civil War.

What about technological changes? Actually, except for electricity, the major innovations in the metals industries seem to have come before or after the years under study here. Most of the technological improvements in the agricultural processing industries appear to have been made to meet the demands of the new urban market. The great technological innovations that accompanied the development of electricity, the internal combustion engine, and industrial chemistry did have their beginning in these years, and were, indeed, to have a fundamental impact on the American business economy. Yet this impact was not to be really felt until after 1900.

What about the entrepreneurial talent? Certainly the best-known entrepreneurs of this period were those who helped to create the large industrial corporation. If, as Joseph A. Schumpeter suggests, "The defining characteristic [of the entrepreneur and his function] is simply the doing of new things, and doing things that are already done, in a new way (innovation)," Rockefeller, Carnegie, Frick, Swift, Duke, McCormick, the DuPonts, the Guggenheims, Coffin of General Electric, Preston of United Fruit, and Clark of Singer Sewing Machine were all major innovators of their time. And their innovations were not in technology, but rather in organization and in marketing. "Doing a new thing" is, to Schumpeter, a "creative response" to a new situation, and the situation to which these innovators responded appears to have been the rise of the national urban market.

POSTSCRIPT

Were Nineteenth-Century Entrepreneurs Robber Barons?

Regardless of whether American entrepreneurs are regarded as "captains of industry" or "robber barons," there is no doubt that they constituted a powerful elite and were responsible for defining the character of society in the Gilded Age. For many Americans, these businessmen represented the logical culmination of the country's attachment to laissez-faire economics and rugged individualism. In fact, it was not unusual at all for the nation's leading industrialists to be depicted as the real-life models for the "rags-to-riches" theme epitomized in the self-help novels of Horatio Alger. Closer examination of the lives of most of these entrepreneurs, however, reveals the mythical dimensions of this American ideal. Simply put, the typical business executive of the late nineteenth century did not rise up from humble circumstances, a product of the American rural tradition or the immigrant experience, as frequently claimed. Rather, most of these big businessmen (Andrew Carnegie may have been an exception) were of Anglo-Saxon origin and reared in a city by middle-class parents. On Sundays, they attended an Episcopal or Congregational Protestant Church. According to one survey, over half the leaders had attended college at a time when even the pursuit of a high school education was considered unusual. In other words, instead of having to pull themselves up by their own bootstraps from the bottom of the social heap, these individuals usually started their climb to success at the middle of the ladder or higher.

The reader may be surprised to learn that in spite of the massive influx of immigrants from Asia and southern and eastern Europe in the years 1880 to 1924, today's leaders are remarkably similar in their social and economic backgrounds to their nineteenth-century counterparts. A 1972 study by Thomas Dye listing the top 4,000 decision makers in corporate, governmental, and public-interest sectors of American life revealed that 90 percent were affluent, white, Anglo-Saxon males. There were only two African Americans in the whole group; there were no Native Americans, Hispanics, or Japanese Americans, and very few recognizable Irish, Italians, or Jews.

A useful contextual framework for examining the role of the American entrepreneur can be found in Thomas C. Cochran and William Miller, *The Age of Enterprise: A Social History of Industrial America*, rev. ed. (Harper & Row, 1961) and Glenn Porter, *The Rise of Big Business, 1860–1910* (Harlan Davidson, 1973). Peter d'A. Jones, in his edited book *The Robber Barons Revisited* (D.C. Heath, 1968), has assembled an excellent collection of the major viewpoints on the "robber baron" thesis. For efforts to present the actions of the late-nineteenth-century businessmen in a favorable light, see Allan Nevins, *A Study in Power: John D. Rockefeller, Industrialist and Philanthropist*, 2 vols. (Scribner's, 1953); Harold Livesay, *Andrew Carnegie and the Rise of Big Business* (Little, Brown, 1975); and Maury Klein, *The Life and Legend of Jay Gould* (Johns Hopkins University Press, 1986). Robert Sobel's *The Entrepreneurs: Explorations Within the American Business Tradition* (Weybright & Talley, 1974) presents sympathetic sketches of the builders of often neglected industries of the nineteenth and twentieth centuries. For a critique of Matthew Josephson, one of the architects of the "robber baron" thesis, see Maury Klein, "A Robber Historian," *Forbes* (October 26, 1987).

The works of Alfred D. Chandler, Jr., are vital to the understanding of American industrialization. Chandler almost singlehandedly reshaped the way in which historians write about American corporations. Instead of arguing about the morality of nineteenth-century businessmen, he employed organizational theories of decision making borrowed from the sociologists and applied them to case studies of corporate America. See *Strategy and Structure: Chapters in the History of the American Industrial Enterprise* (MIT Press, 1962); *The Visible Hand: The Managerial Revolution in American Business* (Harvard University Press, 1977); and *Scale and Scope: The Dynamics of Industrial Capitalism* (Harvard University Press, 1990). Chandler's most important essays are collected in Thomas K. McCraw, ed., *The Essential Alfred Chandler: Essays Toward a Historical Theory of Big Business* (Harvard Business School Press, 1988). For an assessment of Chandler's approach and contributions, see Louis Galambos's "The Emerging Organizational Synthesis in Modern American History," *Business History Review* (Autumn 1970) and Thomas K. McCraw's "The Challenge of Alfred D. Chandler, Jr.: Retrospect and Prospect," *Reviews in American History* (March 1987).

ISSUE 4

Did Late-Nineteenth-Century Immigrants Have to Leave Behind Their Old World Cultures to Come to America?

YES: Oscar Handlin, from *The Uprooted: The Epic Story of the Great Migrations That Made the American People,* 2d ed. (Little, Brown, 1973)

NO: Rudolph J. Vecoli, from " 'Contadini' in Chicago: A Critique of 'The Uprooted,' " *The Journal of American History* (December 1964)

ISSUE SUMMARY

YES: Pulitzer Prize–winning historian Oscar Handlin asserts that immigrants to the United States in the late nineteenth century were alienated from the cultural traditions of the homelands they had left as well as from those of their adopted country.

NO: Rudolph J. Vecoli, director of the University of Minnesota Immigration and History Research Center, contends that in the Old World, Italian peasants lived in isolated rural cities and competed on small farms with one another to eke out a living, and that their developed patterns of behavior and thought did not change when they migrated to Chicago.

Immigration has been one of the most powerful forces shaping the development of the United States since at least the early seventeenth century. In fact, it should not be overlooked that even the ancestors of the country's Native American population were migrants to this "New World" some 37,000 years ago. There can be little doubt that the United States is a nation of immigrants.

The history of immigration to the United States can be organized into four major periods of activity: 1607–1830, 1830–1890, 1890–1924, and 1968 to the present. During the first period, the seventeenth and early eighteenth centuries, there was a growing number of European migrants who arrived in North America mostly from the British Isles, as well as several million Africans who were forced to migrate to colonial America as a consequence of the Atlantic slave trade. While increased numbers of non-English immigrants arrived in America in the eighteenth century, it was not until the nineteenth century that large numbers of immigrants from other northern and western European countries, as well as from China, arrived and created significant population diversity. Two European groups predominated during this second major period: as a result of the potato famine, large numbers of Irish Catholics emigrated in the 1850s; and, for a variety of religious, political, and economic reasons, so did many Germans. Chinese immigration increased, and these immigrants found work in low-paying service industries, such as laundries and restaurants, and as railroad construction workers.

The Industrial Revolution of the late nineteenth century sparked a third wave of immigration. Immigrants by the millions began pouring into the United States, attracted by the unskilled factory jobs that were becoming more abundant. Migration was encouraged by various companies whose agents distributed handbills throughout Europe advertising the ready availability of good-paying jobs in America. This phase of immigration, however, represented something of a departure from previous ones as most of these "new immigrants" came from southern and eastern Europe. This flood continued until World War I, after which mounting xenophobia culminated in the passage by Congress in 1924 of the National Origins Act, which restricted the number of immigrants into the country to 150,000 annually, and which placed quotas on the number of immigrants permitted from each foreign country.

In the aftermath of World War II, restrictions were eased for several groups, especially those who survived the Nazi death camps or who sought asylum in the United States in the wake of the aggressive movement into Eastern Europe by the Soviet Union. But restrictions against Asians and Africans were not lifted until the Immigration Reform Act of 1965, which set in motion a fourth phase of immigration history. In contrast to earlier migrations, the newest groups have come from countries in Latin America and Asia.

Efforts to curb immigration to the United States reflect an anxiety and ambivalence that many Americans have long held with regard to foreigners. Anxious to benefit from the labor of these newcomers but still hesitant to accept the immigrants as full-fledged citizens entitled to the same rights and privileges as native-born residents, Americans have on a number of occasions discovered that they had an "immigrant problem." Harsh anti-immigrant sentiment based on prejudicial attitudes toward race, ethnicity, or religion have periodically boiled over into violence and calls for legislation to restrict immigration.

What effect did these kinds of attitudes have on those who migrated to the United States in search of a life better than the one they experienced in their native lands? What happened to their Old World customs and traditions? How fully did immigrants assimilate into the new culture they encountered in the United States?

In the following readings, Oscar Handlin argues that the immigrants were uprooted from their Old World cultures as they attempted to adjust to an unfamiliar and often hostile environment in the United States. Rudolph J. Vecoli maintains that traits and customs developed in the Old World, where Italian peasants lived in isolated rural cities and competed on small farms with one another to eke out a living, were transferred intact when the peasants migrated to Chicago.

YES
Oscar Handlin

THE UPROOTED: THE EPIC STORY OF THE GREAT MIGRATIONS THAT MADE THE AMERICAN PEOPLE

Once I thought to write a history of the immigrants in America. Then I discovered that the immigrants *were* American history.

For almost fifteen years now, I have searched among the surviving records of the masses of men who peopled our country. As I worked, the conviction grew upon me that adequately to describe the course and effects of immigration involved no less a task than to set down the whole history of the United States. That is not a burden I can now assume.

My ambitions in this volume are more modest. I hope to seize upon a single strand woven into the fabric of our past, to understand that strand in its numerous ties and linkages with the rest; and perhaps, by revealing the nature of this part, to throw light upon the essence of the whole.

Choice of the strand about which this selection was written had particular significance for me, for it called for a radical reversal of perspective. I had written, as others had written, of the impact of the immigrant upon the society which received him, of the effect upon political, social, and economic institutions of the addition of some thirty-five million newcomers to the population of the United States in the century after 1820. It was not surprising that these aspects of the subject should have received earliest treatment. Towns that suddenly grew into cities and found themselves engulfed in slums, overwhelmed with problems of pauperism and relief; the governmental system that swiftly changed under the control of voters with new conceptions of politics—these drew immediate attention to the consequences of injecting alien elements into our society. These were practical problems in the face of which there was no forgetting the importance of immigration.

In retrospect too the effects of the movement of population upon the new continent were the most striking. The arrival of a labor force that permitted the expansion of industry without the pauperization of the native workers; the fact that costs of production could fall while the capacity to consume continued to grow; the remarkable fluidity of a social system in which each new group pushed upward the level of its predecessors—these were the phenomena that gave immigration a prominent role in the development of the United States.

In this work, however, I wished to regard the subject from an altogether different point of view. Immigration altered America. But it also altered the immigrants. And it is the effect upon the newcomers of their arduous transplantation that I have tried to study.

My theme is emigration as the central experience of a great many human beings. I shall touch upon broken homes, interruptions of a familiar life, separation from known surroundings, the becoming a foreigner and ceasing to belong. These are the aspects of alienation; and seen from the perspective of the individual received rather than of the receiving society, the history of immigration is a history of alienation and its consequences.

I have tried historically to trace the impact of separation, of the disruption in the lives and work of people who left one world to adjust to a new. These are the bleaker pages of our history. For the effect of the transfer was harsher upon the people than upon the society they entered.

The experience of these men on the move was more complex than that of eighteenth-century Negroes or of seventeenth-century Englishmen or of eleventh-century Normans. The participants in the earlier mass migrations had either wandered to unoccupied places, where they had only to adjust to new conditions of the physical environment, or they had gone under the well-defined conditions of conquering invader or imported slave.

It was the unique quality of the nineteenth-century immigration that the people who moved entered the life of the United States at a status equal to that of the older residents. So far as law and the formal institutions of the nation were concerned, the newcomers were one with those long settled in the New World. The immigrants could not impose their own ways upon society; but neither were they constrained to conform to those already established. To a significant degree, the newest Americans had a wide realm of choice.

Therein lay the broader meaning of their experience. Emigration took these people out of traditional, accustomed environments and replanted them in strange ground, among strangers, where strange manners prevailed. The customary modes of behavior were no longer adequate, for the problems of life were new and different. With old ties snapped, men faced the enormous compulsion of working out new relationships, new meanings to their lives, often under harsh and hostile circumstances.

The responses of these folk could not be easy, automatic, for emigration had stripped away the veneer that in more stable situations concealed the underlying nature of the social structure. Without the whole complex of institutions and social patterns which formerly guided their actions, these people became incapable of masking or evading decisions.

Under such circumstances, every act was crucial, the product of conscious weighing alternatives, never simple conformity to an habitual pattern. No man could escape choices that involved, day after day, an evaluation of his goals, of the meaning of his existence, and of the purpose of the social forms and institutions that surrounded him.

The immigrants lived in crisis because they were uprooted. In transplantation, while the old roots were sundered, before the new were established, the immigrants existed in an extreme situation. The shock, and the effects of the shock, persisted for many years; and their influence reached down to generations which themselves never paid the cost of crossing.

No one moves without sampling something of the immigrants' experience—mountaineers to Detroit, Okies to California, even men fixed in space but alienated from their culture by unpopular ideas or tastes. But the immigrants' alienation was more complete, more continuous, and more persistent. Understanding of their reactions in that exposed state may throw light on the problems of all those whom the modern world somehow uproots.

PEASANT ORIGINS

The immigrant movement started in the peasant heart of Europe. Ponderously balanced in a solid equilibrium for centuries, the old structure of an old society began to crumble at the opening of the modern era. One by one, rude shocks weakened the aged foundations until some climactic blow suddenly tumbled the whole into ruins. The mighty collapse left without homes millions of helpless, bewildered people. These were the army of emigrants.

The impact was so much the greater because there had earlier been an enormous stability in peasant society. A granite-like quality in the ancient ways of life had yielded only slowly to the forces of time. From the westernmost reaches of Europe, in Ireland, to Russia in the east, the peasant masses had maintained an imperturbable sameness; for fifteen centuries they were the backbone of a continent, unchanging while all about them radical changes again and again recast the civilization in which they lived.

Stability, the deep, cushiony ability to take blows, and yet to keep things as they were, came from the special place of these people on the land. The peasants were agriculturists; their livelihood sprang from the earth. Americans they met later would have called them "farmers," but that word had a different meaning in Europe. The bonds that held these men to their acres were not simply the personal ones of the husbandman who temporarily mixes his sweat with the soil. The ties were deeper, more intimate. For the peasant was part of a community and the community was held to the land as a whole.

Always, the start was the village. "I was born in such a village in such a parish"—so the peasant invariably began the account of himself. Thereby he indicated the importance of the village in his being; this was the fixed point by which he knew his position in the world and his relationship with all humanity.

The village was a place. It could be seen, it could be marked out in boundaries, pinned down on a map, described in all its physical attributes. Here was a road along which men and beasts would pass, reverence the saint's figure at the crossing. There was a church, larger or smaller, but larger than the other structures about it. The burial ground was not far away, and the smithy, the mill, perhaps an inn. There were so many houses of wood or thatch, and so built, scattered among the fields as in Ireland and Norway, or, as almost everywhere else, huddled together with their backs to the road. The fields were round about, located in terms of river, brook, rocks, or trees. All these could be perceived; the eye could grasp, the senses apprehend the feel, the sound, the smell, of them. These objects, real, authentic, true, could come back in memories, be summoned up to rouse the curiosity and stir the wonder of children born in distant lands.

Yet the village was still more. The aggregate of huts housed a community. Later, much later, and very far away, the Old Countrymen also had this in mind when they thought of the village. They spoke of relationships, of ties, of family, of kinship, of many rights and obligations. And these duties, privileges, connections, links, had each their special flavor, somehow a unique value, a meaning in terms of the life of the whole.

They would say then, if they considered it in looking backward, that the village was so much of their lives because the village *was* a whole. There were no loose, disorderly ends; everything was knotted into a firm relationship with every other thing. And all things had meaning in terms of their relatedness to the whole community.

In their daily affairs, these people took account of the relationships among themselves through a reckoning of degrees of kinship. The villagers regarded themselves as a clan connected within itself by ties of blood, more or less remote. That they did so may have been in recollection of the fact that the village was anciently the form the nomadic tribe took when it settled down to a stable agricultural existence. Or it may have been a reflection of the extent of intermarriage in a place where contact with outsiders was rare. In any case, considerations of kinship had heavy weight in the village, were among the most important determinants of men's actions.

But the ties of blood that were knotted into all the relationships of communal life were not merely sentimental. They were also functional; they determined or reflected the role of individuals in the society.

No man, for instance, could live alone in the village. Marriage was the normal expected state of all but the physically deformed. If death deprived a person of his marriage partner, all the forces of community pressure came into play to supply a new helpmate. For it was right and proper that each should have his household, his place in a family.

The family, being functional, varied somewhat to suit the order of local conditions. But always the unit revolved about the husband and wife. The man was head of the household and of its enterprises. He controlled all its goods, made the vital decisions that determined its well-being, had charge of the work in the fields, and was the source of authority and discipline within the home. His wife was mother, her domain the house and all that went on in and about it. She was concerned with the garden and the livestock, with domestic economy in its widest sense—the provision of food, shelter, and clothing for all. The children had each their task, as befitted their age and condition. Now they herded the cattle or assisted in the chores of cleaning and cookery; later they would labor by the side of mother and father, and prepare to set up families of their own. Other members too had their allotted and recognized roles. Grandparents, aunts and uncles, sometimes cousins up to the fourth degree with no establishments of their own, found a place and a job. The family felt the obligation of caring for all, but also knew that no one could expect food and a corner in which to sleep while doing nothing to earn it. In this respect such collateral relatives did not differ in condition from the hired servants, where they existed, who were also counted members of the family.

The family was then the operating economic unit. In a sense that was always recognized and respected, the land on which it worked was its own. The head of the household, it was true, held and controlled it; legally, no doubt, he had certain powers to waste or dispose of it. But he was subject to an overwhelming moral compulsion to keep it intact, in trust for those who lived from it and for their descendants who would take a place upon it.

The family's land was rarely marked out in a well-defined plot. The house, the garden, and the barnyard with its buildings were its own, but the bulk of agricultural lands were enmeshed in wide net of relationships that comprehended the whole community.

Once, it seems, the village had held and used all the land communally; until very recent times recognizable vestiges of that condition persisted. The pastures and meadows, the waste, the bogs and woodlands, existed for the use of all. It hardly mattered at first that the nobility or other interlopers asserted a claim to ownership. The peasants' rights to graze their cattle, to gather wood for building and peat for fire, in practice remained undisturbed. In some parts of Europe, even the arable lands rested in the hands of the whole village, redivided on occasions among its families according to their rights and condition.

Even where particular pieces of land were permanently held, it was rarely in such consolidated plots as the peasants might later see on American farms. A holding consisted rather of numerous tiny strips that patched the slopes of the countryside in a bewildering, variegated design. A Polish peasant, rich in land, could work his nine acres in forty different places.

Agriculture conformed to the pattern of landholding. By long usage, the fields almost everywhere were divided into thirds, a part for winter crops—wheat, rye; another for summer crops—barley, oats, and potatoes; and another to lie fallow. Since no man's lands were completely apart from his neighbor's there was no room for individuality in working the soil. Every family labored on its own and kept the fruits of its own labors. Yet all labor had to be directed toward the same ends, in the same way, at the same time.

Many important aspects of agriculture, moreover, were altogether communal. The pastures were open to all villagers; in the common fields, the boys tended the cattle together or a hired herdsman had their oversight. Women, working in groups at the wearisome indoor tasks, spinning or plucking cabbage leaves, could turn chores into festive occasions, lighten their labors with sociable gossip. The men were accustomed to give aid to each other, to lend or exchange as an expression of solidarity. After all, folk must live with each other.

So the peasants held together, lived together, together drew the stuff of life from an unwilling earth. Simple neighborliness, mutual assistance, were obligations inherent in the conditions of things, obligations which none could shirk without fear of cutting himself off from the whole. And that was the community, that the village—the capacity to do these things together, the relationships that regulated all....

DAILY BREAD

Let the peasant, now in America, confront his first problem; time enough if ever this is solved to turn to other matters.

How shall a man feed himself, find bread for his family? The condition of man is to till the soil; there is no other wholeness to his existence. True, in retrospect, life on the soil in the old home had not yielded a livelihood. But that was because there was not there soil enough. In consequence, the husbandmen, in their hundreds of thousands, have left their meager plots. They have now come to a New World where open land reaches away in acre after acre of inexhaustible plenty. Arrived, they are ready to work.

Yet only a few, a fortunate few, of these eager hands were destined ever to break the surface of the waiting earth. Among the multitudes that survived the crossing, there were now and then some who survived it intact enough in body and resources to get beyond the port of landing and through the interior cities of transit. Those who were finally able to establish themselves as the independent proprietors of farms of their own made up an even smaller number.

All the others were unable to escape from the cities. Decade after decade, as the Federal government made its count, the census revealed a substantial majority of the immigrants in the urban places; and the margin of that majority grew steadily larger. Always the percentage of the foreign-born who lived in the cities was much higher than that of the total population.

Yet the people who were to live the rest of their days amidst a world of steel and stone and brick were peasants. If they failed to reach the soil which had once been so much a part of their being, it was only because the town had somehow trapped them....

No wonder that the newcomer was somewhat incredulous when he finally learned that outside the city there were jobs, that his power to toil, here so little valued, elsewhere was urgently needed. Yet advertisements in the newspapers, chalked-up notices in the streets, told him it was indeed so. Was he then likely to quibble over terms, inquire closely as to conditions? At the intelligence bureaus, the employment offices whence all these benefits flowed, he was signed on, gathered up into a gang with others like him, and hurried along to his appointed task.

The jovial fellow who humored the men into agreement and who sealed the contract with a dram of the best was agent of a remarkable construction system that kept pace with the unparalleled expansion of the country through the nineteenth century. With no machines, with only pick, shovel, and sledge for tools, the boss and his gang contrived the numerous links that held the nation whole in these years. Out of their labors came first the chain of canals, and then an intricately meshed network of railroads—by 1910, more than 350,000 miles of them. And these tasks were hardly completed before bicycle riders and motorists began to call for and to get a paved highway system; 200,000 miles were already laid in 1910.

Engineers' estimates reckoned up the immense quantities of unskilled labor these projects would take; surveyors' reports revealed that the lines would run through unsettled or partly settled agricultural regions, places where no supply of such labor was available. To get the jobs done meant bringing in from outside the hands for the doing.

Thus the earliest immigrants find their calling. Desperate in the absence of alternative they leave behind wife and child and go to live the hard life of the construction camp. Exposed to the pitiless assaults of sun and snow and dusty winds, they work long hours, are paid low wages; in the lonely distances, away from all other beings, there is no arguing with a contractor who suddenly, arbitrarily lowers his rates. They may not complain of the degrading quarters—broken-down old freight cars of dilapidated shanties quickly thrown together. They can have nothing to say of the compulsion to buy food and supplies from the company's swindling store. To whom can they turn? It is not the railroad or canal that employs them; an intermediary, responsible to no one, battens off their misery.

In any case, until the laborers paid off the price of bringing them there and until they accumulated the fare to return, they were bound to submit to the unscrupulous exploitation of the boss. In many states, the money advanced to get the worker to the job was considered a debt, and the law condemned the unwitting immigrant to serve out his time for the contractor until the debt was cleared. Not until 1907 did the Federal government intervene to halt this practice as peonage.

Those who sampled the life of the construction gang were, therefore, not likely to wish to repeat the experience. For such men, it was a relief to discover, as time went on, that analogous opportunities were gradually opening up within the city itself. The increase of urban population strained existing housing and created a persistent demand for new construction that kept the building trades prosperous. Everywhere streets pushed out into the suburbs where farms had once been; men's muscles had to grade the ways, carry and fit the paving blocks. Each seaport dredged and improved its harbor, built imposing piers to accommodate the larger vessels of nineteenth-century commerce. Intricate systems of aqueducts, of gas pipes, of electric wires, of trolley tracks, supplied water and light and transportation for the new city millions.

Every one of these activities, which occupied the attention of a whole century, depended for its execution upon an ample fund of unskilled labor. The immigrants supplied that fund; and in doing so made for themselves a role that could have been occupied by no other element in American society—no other was so thoroughly deprived of the opportunity for choice. In sad succession, from 1830 to 1930, the Irish, the Bohemians, the Slovaks, the Hungarians, the Italians, and many other peoples less numerous took up for a period the service of the pick and shovel.

It was not likely that any among them, at the time, took much pride in their contribution to the nation. Nor was it likely that many individuals among them would long think such employment a satisfactory solution to the problem of finding a job. These tasks, were in their nature, intermittent and transitory; each project, once completed, left the laborers back where they started, face to face with the necessity of looking for another. Wages hung close to the cost of subsistence, never rose to a point that permitted a man to accumulate the stakes of a fresh start. At the end of a stint the worker was weaker and older, otherwise no different from what he was before. Meanwhile, from day to day he ran the risk of total calamity from illness or disabling injury.

Whatever elements of order appeared in this disorderly system came from the laborers themselves. With no prospect of security and so often incapable of protecting themselves against strange men or hostile events, the immigrants could look only to each other for assistance. Sometimes in the tired dusk of the close of a week's work they would stand by the track's edge against the rolling countryside and hear the clerk read off the notice of some new oppression: dismissals, lower rates, higher store charges. They would wait in the still air, stifle rage in the knowledge of their own impotence, and think to return acquiescent to the dark bunks of their degradation. Then one would speak, give words to their grievances, and be their leader. Sometimes they would watch the gaping ditch where the locks would be, see the line of aliens come up the slope to take their jobs, and one would yell, and urge them on, and lead them down to drive those others off. Or the quarrels would take some other form, rise from intoxication, from resentment at differences in language or manners.

Then men banded together in gangs and worked together under a leader. That was a way that seemed proper to those who had once been peasants. As the scale of hiring was enlarged and as the process became more complicated, management of the labor of the group fell entirely into the hands of the leader —"boss" he was usually called, but "padrone" by the Italians and Greeks. Ultimately he negotiated a single contract for the lot, assuming himself the expense of maintaining them, and retaining for himself a profit from the transaction. Before long, this means of organizing construction labor became so lucrative for the padrone that he turned into a species of subcontractor, built up new gangs on his own initiative, and often also recruited members from his countrymen abroad.

Guidance by the padrone had the virtue of shielding the laborer against the excesses of employers. It had also the advantage of a kind of security; at least there would always be something to eat, a place to sleep, and the company of understanding compatriots. But the padrone system had also this disadvantage, that it left the immigrant helpless against exploitation by the padrone himself. To their sorrow, the newcomers frequently learned that a leader in America was not bound by the patterns of obligation that were sacred in the Old World. Deception and dishonesty penetrated even these relationships and many men discovered that such attempts at self-help only worked into new forms of enslavement.

In no case could construction work, therefore, be ever more than a makeshift. Whether they went as individuals or in gangs, whether in the country or in the city, the peasants regarded this labor in the same light as they had viewed migratory labor in their European homes. This was an expedient taken up as a result of some immediate pressure. This was not a way of life, not a fitting use of man's power to toil, not a dependable source of daily bread. The quest for that, continuing, would take other turns.

In the beginning, the new-built canals served not only to carry the cargoes of commerce, but also to turn the wheels of industry. In those early decades, when manufacturing first became familiar to the American economy, the digging Irishmen often looked up with envy at the imposing new mills. But there was no room within those walls for such as they.

Pitched in small towns wherever the sources of water power happened to be, the factories were as inaccessible to the city-bound as the agricultural West. For the desperate, immobile immigrants in Boston and New York, Fall River and Paterson were as far away as Ohio and Illinois. And those who did manage somehow to get through to the industrial villages knew the likelihood was slight of being taken on by the superintendent or being received as an equal by the other workers.

In the 1820's and 1830's, factory employment was the province of groups relatively high in social status. North of Boston, the bulk of the labor force was made up of respectable young girls, many the daughters of neighborhood farmers, girls willing to work for a few years in anticipation of the marriageable young man. In souther New England the general practice was to employ whole families of artisans. Everywhere, paternalistic organization and the closely knit communal life of the boardinghouses did not allow the easy entrance of newcomers. The only immigrants who then found a place in industry were the few skilled operatives who had already mastered the craft in the Old Country and were hired for the sake of their skills.

The reservoir of unskilled peasant labor that mounted steadily higher in the cities did not long remain untapped, however. In the 1840's and 1850's came a succession of new inventions that enterprising men of capital used to transform the productive system of the United States. The older industries had disdained the immigrants; but the new ones, high in the risks of innovation and heavy initial investments, drew eagerly on this fund of workers ready to be exploited at attractively low wages. The manufacture of clothing, of machines, and of furniture flourished in the great commercial cities precisely where they could utilize freely the efforts of the newcomers, hire as many as they needed when necessary, lay off any surplus at will. A completely fluid labor supply set the ideal conditions for expansion.

Thereafter, whatever branch of the economy entered upon a period of rapid expansion did so with the aid of the same immigrant labor supply. At midcentury the immigrants went to dig in the mines that pockmarked the great coal and iron fields of Pennsylvania, first experienced Welshmen and Cornishmen, later raw Irishmen and Germans, and still later Slavs—a vague term that popularly took in Bohemians, Slovaks, Hungarians, and also Italians. These people spread with the spread of the fields, southward into West Virginia and westward to Illinois, in a burst of development from which impressive consequences followed.

The wealth of new power extracted from the earth, after 1870, set off a second revolution in American industry. Steam replaced water power. Iron replaced wood in the construction of machines. Factories became larger and more mechanized and the place of unskilled labor more prominent. On the payrolls of new enterprises, immigrant names were almost alone; and the newcomers now penetrated even into the older textile and shoe industries. The former peasants, first taken on for menial duties as janitors and sweepers, found themselves more often placed at machines as the processes of production were divided into ever simpler tasks open to the abilities of the unskilled.

By the end of the nineteenth century the national economy had been transformed. Immigrants then still did the burdensome jobs of commerce. They still toiled in construction and maintenance crews. But they had found a larger usefulness in the mines and factories. In the mill towns and industrial cities the availability of their labor had been instrumental in converting production from its old handicraft forms to the mechanized forms of power....

RELIGION AS A WAY OF LIFE

A man holds dear what little is left. When much is lost, there is no risking the remainder.

As his stable place in a whole universe slipped away from under him, the peasant come to America grasped convulsively at the familiar supports, pulled along with him the traditional bulwarks of his security. He did not learn until later that, wrenched out of context, these would no longer bear the weight of his needs.

Even in the Old World, these men's thoughts had led ineluctably to God. In the New, they were as certain to do so. The very process of adjusting immigrant ideas to the conditions of the United States made religion paramount as a way of life. When the natural world, the former context of the peasant ideas, faded behind the transatlantic horizon, the newcomers found themselves stripped to those religious institutions they could bring along with them. Well, the trolls and fairies will stay behind, but church and priest at very least will come.

The more thorough the separation from the other aspects of the old life, the greater was the hold of the religion that alone survived the transfer. Struggling against heavy odds to save something of the old ways, the immigrants directed into their faith the whole weight of their longing to be connected with the past.

As peasants at home, awed by the hazardous nature of the universe and by their own helplessness, these people had fled to religion as a refuge from the anguish of the world. Their view of their own lives had generated a body of conceptions and practices that intimately expressed their inmost emotions. It was not only that they held certain theological doctrines; but their beliefs were most closely enwrapped in the day-to-day events of their existence. The specific acts of being religious were the regular incidents of the village year. Their coming needed no forethought, indeed no consciousness. Their regularity was an aspect of the total order of the village. That was a feature of their attractiveness.

The peasants found also attractive the outward aspects of their religious institutions. The very formality of structure and organization had a meaning of consequence to them. They were all communicants of established churches, whether Roman Catholic, Lutheran, Anglican, or Orthodox. In some lands, where the monarch professed the same faith, to be "established" meant that the Church and State were closely united. That was true in Italy, Germany, Scandinavia, England, and Russia. But that link was not the essential element in establishment which also existed in countries such as Poland and Ireland, where Catholic peasants lived under non-Catholic rulers.

Recognition by the government and special treatment in law were only the surface indications of a deeper significance. To the peasants, establishment meant that their religion held a fixed, well-defined place in their society, that it was identified with the village, that it took in all those who belonged, all those who were not outcasts. Establishment in that sense gave these people a reassuring conviction that they belonged, were parts of a whole, insiders not outsiders.

The other attributes of establishment were appropriate also. About these churches was no confusing cloud of uncertainty. Their claim to men's allegiance rested on a solid basis of authority. It was not an individual choice that was involved in the process of belonging, but conformity. So, everyone else did. So it had been done year before year, generation before generation, as far back as the peasant could reckon... ever. The very rights and privileges of the Church, its lands and possessions, were evidence of its legitimacy and longevity. It was unthinkable not to be a member; it demanded a considerable feat of the imagination to conceive of what it would mean to be excluded, to draw down the censure of the entire community, to be barred from every social occasion.

There was no need to argue about these matters, to weigh alternatives, to consider. The Church gave no reasons for being, it was. Its communicants were within it not because they had rationally accepted its doctrines; they had faith because they were in it. Explanation in terms of reasonable propositions was superfluous; the Church was accepted as a mystery, which called for no explanation. These peasants felt the attractiveness of the demand on their faith as of the demand on their obedience to authority. Such, their own ideas had led them to believe, were the sources of certainty.

Village religion was, as a matter of course, conservative. Peasants and priests alike resisted change. They valued

in the Church its placid conviction of eternal and universal sameness, of continuity through the ages, of catholicity through Christendom. The very practices that stirred them now reached back to the earliest times. Here and in precisely this manner, generations of untold ancestors had worshiped. Dimly over the gap of years, fathers and sons engaged in a common communion, assured by the permanence of forms.

The peasants were certain of the fixity of their church in space as well as in time. This priest who ministered to them in this parish was not an isolated individual but one who had an established place in a great hierarchical structure that extended through society. Above the priest was a sequence of other dignitaries rising to loftier and loftier eminence to the one supereminent above all, pope or patriarch, king or emperor. When the retinue of the bishop pranced through the village, when that personage himself appeared attired in all the magnificence of his vestiture, when his distant countenance framed in the miter of his majesty looked down on the assembled community, then the people humbly in his presence were elevated through the dignity of his own imposing power. He had ordained the priest, stood guarantor of the efficacy of the parish rites, brought the village into communion with the whole world of true believers, made the peasant certain there was order in the Church and security of place for each soul within it.

Yet the grandeur of religion did not leave it aloof from its communicants. Splendid though it was in appearance, extensive and powerful in its compass, it was still close to the life of each man. The hierarchy that reached up to the most exalted also reached down to the most humble.

The Church was familiar to the peasants' day-to-day existence. Its outward forms and ceremonies were established in the round of the year. By long usage, each festival had a seasonal connotation through which, in the same celebration, were commingled the meanings of the distant Christian event and of the proximate changes in the immediate world of nature. All the acts of worship were embedded in a setting of which the landscape, the weather, and the sight of the heavens all were aspects. Each holiday thus had substance and individuality, a whole and entire character of its own. Its coming filled the whole place and the whole day, spread out from the church through the road where the procession passed to the blessed field around, extended on from the early service at the altar to the feat and the accompanying jubilation. Each occasion was thus local to the particular village, the possession of each participant, a part of his way of life. This the peasants had in mind when they hoped, most eagerly, to re-establish their religion in the New World.

It was not only the attractiveness of such elements of form that moved the immigrants to reconstruct their churches in America; it was also the substance embraced in those forms. These people were anxious that religion do and mean in the United States all that it had back there before the Atlantic crossing.

At home, worship had brought to the worshiper a pleasure that was aesthetic in nature. If in the new land he had the occasion, which he had rarely had in the old, to talk about the quality of that satisfaction, the peasant put the words of his description around specific impressions of the service—the stately manners, the inspiring liturgy, the magnificent furnishing. But such descriptions he knew were inadequate; for beyond the beauty that adhered to these things in their own right was a beauty of essence that grew out of their relationship to his own experience as a human being. Lacking the habit of introspection, the peasant could not set words to that satisfaction. He could only feel the lack of it.

How comforting were the ceremonial movements of the priest and how stirring his sermon—not at all a bickering argument but a be-gestured incantation! Here was not so much an effort to persuade man to be good as a reminder that he was bad, in effect magically to cleanse him. Indeed, magical qualities inhered in all the acts of worship. Touching on sin and the remission of sin, on evil and the warding-off of evil, these practices made sense in terms of peasant ideas.

In the rite before his eyes, the man could see that the world in which he lived was not whole, did not of itself justify itself. No. This was merely a dreary vestibule through which the Christian entered the life eternal that lay beyond the door of death. Long and narrow was the passage and bitter dark. With utmost striving was the crossing made, and little joy was in it. But there was a goal, and there would be an arrival. The bells that tolled at the culmination of each service would toll also at each soul's release, when the hard journey, over, would lead to its own compensation for the troubles of the way.

The promise of life to come, and the meaning of the life of the present, was consolation. At that expected future, retribution, rewarded good and punished evil, would make whole the order of mundane things, explain the lapses of justice, the incongruity of achievements, the neglect of merit in the existence of the peasant. To the congregation, devoutly silent under the plaster images, the monotonous chant affirmed over and over that the perspective of eternity would correct all the disturbing distortions in the perspective of today.

Faith brought the affirmation that man, though the creature of chance that appearances made him to be, was also actor in the great drama that had begun with the miracle of creation and would end in the miracle of redemption. For him, God had come to earth, had suffered, and had sacrificed Himself to save all humanity. That sacrifice, repeated at every mass, was the visible assurance of meaning in the universe.

The same sacrifice transfigured the communicants who shared the mystery. Wafers and wine, blood and flesh, united them in the togetherness of their common experience. Not only they within the village, but through the village to the uncounted numbers elsewhere, to their own ancestors in the churchyard who had also once shared, still shared. In the salving rite of Communion, there mingled with the satisfaction of the act itself the sentiments of village loyalty, the emotions of family love, and the awareness of fulfillment of the ideal of solidarity.

NO

Rudolph J. Vecoli

"CONTADINI" IN CHICAGO: A CRITIQUE OF "THE UPROOTED"

In *The Uprooted* Oscar Handlin attempted an overarching interpretation of European peasant society and of the adjustment of emigrants from that society to the American environment. This interpretation is open to criticism on the grounds that it fails to respect the unique cultural attributes of the many and varied ethnic groups which sent immigrants to the United States. Through an examination of the south Italians, both in their Old World setting and in Chicago, this article will indicate how Handlin's portrayal of the peasant as immigrant does violence to the character of the *contadini* (peasants) of the Mezzogiorno.

The idealized peasant village which Handlin depicts in *The Uprooted* did not exist in the southern Italy of the late nineteenth century. Handlin's village was an harmonious social entity in which the individual derived his identity and being from the community as a whole; the ethos of his village was one of solidarity communality, and neighborliness. The typical south Italian peasant, however, did not live in a small village, but in a "rural city" with a population of thousands or even tens of thousands. Seeking refuge from brigands and malaria, the *contadini* huddled together in these hill towns, living in stone dwellings under the most primitive conditions and each day descending the slopes to work in the fields below.

Nor were these towns simple communities of agriculturists, for their social structure included the gentry and middle class as well as the peasants. Feudalism died slowly in southern Italy, and vestiges of this archaic social order were still visible in the attitudes and customs of the various classes. While the great landowners had taken up residence in the capital cities, the lesser gentry constituted the social elite of the towns. Beneath it in the social hierarchy were the professional men, officials, merchants, and artisans; at the base were the *contadini* who comprised almost a distinct caste. The upper classes lorded over and exploited the peasants whom they regarded as less than human. Toward the upper classes, the *contadini* nourished a hatred which was veiled by the traditional forms of deference.

From Rudolph J. Vecoli, " 'Contadini' in Chicago: A Critique of 'The Uprooted,'" *The Journal of American History*, vol. 51, no. 3 (December 1964), pp. 404–471. Copyright © 1964 by The Organization of American Historians. Reprinted by permission. Notes omitted.

This is not to say that the south Italian peasants enjoyed a sense of solidarity either as a community or as a social class. Rather it was the family which provided the basis of peasant solidarity. Indeed, so exclusive was the demand for the family for the loyalty of its members that it precluded allegiance to other social institutions. This explains the paucity of voluntary associations among the peasantry. Each member of the family was expected to advance its welfare and to defend its honor, regardless of the consequences for outsiders. This singleminded attention to the interests of the family led one student of south Italian society to describe its ethos as one of "amoral familism."

While the strongest ties were within the nuclear unit, there existed among the members of the extended family a degree of trust, intimacy, and interdependence denied to all others. Only through the ritual kinship of *comparaggio* (godparenthood) could nonrelatives gain admittance to the family circle. The south Italian family was "father-dominated but mother-centered." The father as the head of the family enjoyed unquestioned authority over the household, but the mother provided the emotional focus for family life.

Among the various families of the *paese* (town), there were usually jealousies and feuds which frequently resulted in bloodshed. This atmosphere of hostility was revealed in the game of *passatella*, which Carlo Levi has described as "a peasant tournament of oratory, where interminable speeches reveal in veiled terms a vast amount of repressed rancor, hate, and rivalry." The sexual code of the Mezzogiorno was also expressive of the family pride of the south Italians. When violations occurred, family honor required that the seducer be punished. The south Italian was also bound by the tradition of personal vengeance, as in the Sicilian code of *omertá*. These cultural traits secured for southern Italy the distinction of having the highest rate of homicides in all of Europe at the turn of the century. Such antisocial behavior, however, has no place in Handlin's scheme of the peasant community.

If the south Italian peasant regarded his fellow townsman with less than brotherly feeling, he viewed with even greater suspicion the stranger—which included anyone not native to the town. The peasants knew nothing of patriotism for the Kingdom of Italy, or of class solidarity with other tillers of the soil; their sense of affinity did not extend beyond town boundaries. This attachment to their native village was termed *campanilismo*, a figure of speech suggesting that the world of the *contadini* was confined within the shadow cast by his town campanile. While this parochial attitude did not manifest itself in community spirit or activities, the sentiment of *campanilismo* did exert a powerful influence on the emigrants from southern Italy.

During the late nineteenth century, increasing population, agricultural depression, and oppressive taxes, combined with poor land to make life ever more difficult for the peasantry. Still, misery does not provide an adequate explanation of the great emigration which followed. For, while the peasants were equally impoverished, the rate of emigration varied widely from province to province. J. S. McDonald has suggested that the key to these differential rates lies in the differing systems of land tenure and in the contrasting sentiments of "individualism" and "solidarity" which they produced among the peasants. From Apulia and the interior of Sicily where large-scale agriculture prevailed and cultivators' associations were formed, there was little emigration. Elsewhere in the South, where the peasants as small proprietors and tenants competed with one another, emigration soared. Rather than practicing communal agriculture as did Handlin's peasants, these *contadini*, both as cultivators and emigrants, acted on the principle of economic individualism, pursuing family and self-interest.

Handlin's peasants have other characteristics which do not hold true for those of southern Italy. In the Mezzogiorno, manual labor—and especially tilling the soil—was considered degrading. There the peasants did not share the reverence of Handlin's peasants for the land; rather they were "accustomed to look with distrust and hate at the soil." No sentimental ties to the land deterred the south Italian peasants from becoming artisans, shopkeepers, or priests, if the opportunities presented themselves. Contrary to Handlin's peasants who meekly accepted their lowly status, the *contadini* were ambitious to advance the material and social position of their families. Emigration was one way of doing so. For the peasants in *The Uprooted* emigration was a desperate flight from disaster, but the south Italians viewed a sojourn in America as a means to acquire capital with which to purchase land, provide dowries for their daughters, and assist their sons to enter business or the professions.

If the design of peasant society described in *The Uprooted* is not adequate for southern Italy, neither is Handlin's description of the process of immigrant adjustment an accurate rendering of the experience of the *contadini*. For Handlin, "the history of immigration is a history of alienation and its consequences." In line with this theme, he emphasizes the isolation and loneliness of the immigrant, "the broken homes, interruptions of a familiar life, separation from known surroundings, the becoming a foreigner and ceasing to belong." While there is no desire here to belittle the hardships, fears, and anxieties to which the immigrant was subject, there are good reasons for contending that Handlin overstates the disorganizing effects of emigration and underestimates the tenacity with which the south Italian peasants at least clung to their traditional social forms and values.

Handlin, for example, dramatically pictures the immigrant ceasing to be a member of a solidarity community and being cast upon his own resources as an individual. But this description does not apply to the *contadini* who customarily emigrated as a group from a particular town, and, once in America, stuck together "like a swarm of bees from the same hive." After working a while, and having decided to remain in America, they would send for their wives, children, and other relatives. In this fashion, chains of emigration were established between certain towns of southern Italy and Chicago.

From 1880 on, the tide of emigration ran strongly from Italy to this midwestern metropolis where by 1920 the Italian population reached approximately 60,000. Of these, the *contadini* of the Mezzogiorno formed the preponderant element. Because of the sentiment of *campanilismo*, there emerged not one "Little Italy" but some seventeen larger and smaller colonies scattered about the city. Each group of townsmen clustered by itself, seeking, as Jane Addams observed, to fill "an entire tenement house with the people from one village." Within these settlements, the town groups maintained their distinct identities, practiced endogamy, and preserved their traditional folkways. Contrary to Handlin's dictum that the common experience of the immigrants was their inability to transplant the European village, one is struck by the degree to which the *contadini* succeeded in reconstructing their native towns in the heart of industrial Chicago. As an Italian journal commented:

> Emigrating, the Italian working class brings away with it from the mother country all the little world in which they were accustomed to live; a world of traditions, of beliefs, of customs, of ideals of their own. There is no reason to marvel then that in this great center of manufacturing and commercial activity of North America our colonies, though acclimating themselves in certain ways, conserve the customs of their *paesi* of origin.

If the south Italian immigrant retained a sense of belongingness with his fellow townsmen, the family continued to be the focus of his most intense loyalties. Among the male emigrants there were some who abandoned their families in Italy, but the many underwent harsh privations so that they might send money to their parents or wives. Reunited in Chicago the peasant family functioned much as it had at home; there appears to have been little of that confusion of roles depicted in *The Uprooted*. The husband's authority was not diminished, while the wife's subordinate position was not questioned. If dissension arose, it was when the children became somewhat "Americanized"; yet there are good reasons for believing that Handlin exaggerates the estrangement of the second generation from its immigrant parentage. Nor did the extended family disintegrate upon

emigration as is contended. An observation made with respect to the Sicilians in Chicago was generally true for the south Italians: "Intense family pride ... is the outstanding characteristic, and as the family unit not only includes those related by blood, but those related by ritual bonds as well (the *commare* and *compare*), and as intermarriage in the village groups is a common practice, this family pride becomes really a clan pride." The alliance of families of the town through intermarriage and godparenthood perpetuated a social organization based upon large kinship groups.

The south Italian peasants also brought with them to Chicago some of their less attractive customs. Many a new chapter of an ancient vendetta of Calabria or Sicily was written on the streets of this American city. The zealous protection of the family honor was often a cause of bloodshed. Emigration had not abrogated the duty of the south Italian to guard the chastity of his women. Without the mitigating quality of these "crimes of passion" were the depredations of the "Black Hand." After 1900 the practice of extorting money under threat of death became so common as to constitute a reign of terror in the Sicilian settlements. Both the Black Handlers and their victims were with few exceptions from the province of Palermo where the criminal element known collectively as the *mafia* had thrived for decades. The propensity for violence of the south Italians was not a symptom of social disorganization caused by emigration but a characteristic of their Old World culture. Here too the generalizations that the immigrant feared to have recourse to the peasant crimes of revenge, and that the immigrant was rarely involved in crime for profit, do not apply to the south Italians.

To speak of alienation as the essence of the immigrant experience is to ignore the persistence of traditional forms of group life. For the *contadino*, his family and his townsmen continued to provide a sense of belonging and to sanction his customary world-view and life-ways. Living "in," but not "of," the sprawling, dynamic city of Chicago, the south Italian was sheltered within his ethnic colony from the confusing complexity of American society.

While the acquisition of land was a significant motive for emigration, the south Italian peasants were not ones to dream, as did Handlin's, of possessing "endless acres" in America. Their goal was a small plot of ground in their native towns. If they failed to reach the American soil, it was not because, as Handlin puts it, "the town had somehow trapped them," but because they sought work which would pay ready wages. These peasants had no romantic illusions about farming; and despite urgings by railroad and land companies, reformers, and philanthropists to form agricultural colonies, the south Italians preferred to remain in the city.

Although Chicago experienced an extraordinary growth of manufacturing during the period of their emigration, few south Italians found employment in the city's industries. Great numbers of other recent immigrants worked in meatpacking and steelmaking, but it was uncommon to find an Italian name on the payroll of these enterprises. The absence of the *contadini* from these basic industries was due both to their aversion to this type of factory work and to discrimination against them by employers. For the great majority of the south Italian peasants "the stifling, brazen factories and the dark, stony pits" did not supplant "the warm living earth as the source of their daily bread." Diggers in the earth they had been and diggers in the earth they remained; only in America they dug with the pick and shovel rather than the mattock. In Chicago the Italian laborers quickly displaced the Irish in excavation and street work as they did on railroad construction jobs throughout the West.

The lot of the railroad workers was hard. Arriving at an unknown destination, they were sometimes attacked as "scabs," they found the wages and conditions of labor quite different from those promised, or it happened that they were put to work under armed guard and kept in a state of peonage. For twelve hours a day in all kinds of weather, the laborers dug and picked, lifted ties and rails, swung sledge hammers, under the constant goading of tyrannical foremen. Housed in filthy boxcars, eating wretched food, they endured this miserable existence for a wage which seldom exceeded $1.50 a day. Usually they suffered in silence, and by the most stern abstinence were able to save the greater part of their meager earnings. Yet it happened that conditions became intolerable, and the *paesani* (gangs were commonly composed of men from the same town) would resist the exactions of the "boss." These uprisings were more in the nature of peasants' revolts than of industrial strikes, and they generally ended badly for the *contadini*.

With the approach of winter the men returned to Chicago. While some continued on to Italy, the majority wintered in the city. Those with families in Chicago had households to return to; the others formed cooperative living groups. Thus they passed the winter months in idleness, much as they had in Italy. Railroad work was cyclical as well as seasonal. In times of depression emigration from Italy declined sharply; many of the Italian workers returned to their native towns to await the return of American prosperity. Those who remained were faced with long periods of unemployment; it was at these times, such as the decade of the 1890s, that the spectre of starvation stalked through the Italian quarters of Chicago.

Because the *contadini* were engaged in gang labor of a seasonal nature there developed an institution which was thought most typical of the Italian immigration: the padrone system. Bewildered by the tumult of the city, the newcomers sought out a townsman who could guide them in the ways of this strange land. Thus was created the padrone who made a business out of the ignorance and necessities of his countrymen. To the laborers, the padrone was banker, saloonkeeper, grocer, steamship agent, lodging-house keeper, and politician. But his most important function was that of employment agent.

While there were honest padrones, most appeared unable to resist the opportunities for graft. Although Handlin states that "the padrone had the virtue of shielding the laborer against the excesses of employers," the Italian padrones usually operated in collusion with the contractors. Often the padrones were shrewd, enterprising men who had risen from the ranks of the unskilled; many of them, however, were members of the gentry who sought to make an easy living by exploiting their peasant compatriots in America as they had in Italy. The padrone system should not be interpreted as evidence "that a leader in America was not bound by patterns of obligation that were sacred in the Old World"; rather, it was logical outcome of the economic individualism and "amoral familism" of south Italian society.

In their associational life the *contadini* also contradicted Handlin's assertion that the social patterns of the Old Country could not survive the ocean voyage. The marked incapacity of the south Italians for organizational activity was itself a result of the divisive attitudes which they had brought with them to America. Almost the only form of association among these immigrants was the mutual aid society. Since such societies were common in Italy by the 1870s, they can hardly be regarded as "spontaneously generated" by American conditions. Instead, the mutual aid society was a transplanted institution which was found to have especial utility for the immigrants. An Italian journalist observed: "If associations have been found useful in the *patria*, how much more they are in a strange land, where it is so much more necessary for the Italians to gather together, to fraternize, to help one another." Nowhere, however, was the spirit of *campanilismo* more in evidence than in these societies. An exasperated Italian patriot wrote: "Here the majority of the Italian societies are formed of individuals from the same town and more often from the same parish, others are not admitted. But are you or are you not Italians? And if you are, why do you exclude your brother who is born a few miles from your town?" As the number of these small societies multiplied (by 1912 there were some 400 of them in Chicago), various attempts were made to form them into a federation. Only the Sicilians, however, were able to achieve a degree of unity through two federations which enrolled several thousand members.

The sentiment of regionalism was also a major obstacle to the organizational unity of the Italians in Chicago. Rather than being allayed by emigration, this regional pride and jealousy was accentuated by the proximity of Abruzzese, Calabrians, Genoese, Sicilians, and other groups in the city. Each regional group regarded those from other regions with their strange dialects and customs not as fellow Italians, but as distinct and inferior ethnic types. Any proposal for cooperation among the Italians was sure to arouse these regional antipathies and to end in bitter recriminations. The experience of emigration did not create a sense of nationality among the Italians strong enough to submerge their parochialism. Unlike Handlin's immigrants who acquired "new modes of fellowship to replace the old ones destroyed by emigration," the South Italians confined themselves largely to the traditional ones of family and townsmen.

The quality of leadership of the mutual aid societies also prevented them from becoming agencies for the betterment of the *contadini*. These organizations, it was said, were often controlled by the "very worse [sic] element in the Italian colony," arrogant, selfish men, who founded societies not out of a sense of fraternity but to satisfy their ambition and vanity. The scope of their leadership was restricted to presiding despotically over the meetings, marching in full regalia at the head of the society, and gaining economic and political advantage through their influence over the members. If such a one were frustrated in his attempt to control a society, he would secede with his followers and found a new one. Thus even the townsmen were divided into opposing factions.

The function of the typical mutual aid society was as limited as was its sphere of membership. The member received relief in case of illness, an indemnity for his family in case of death, and a funeral celebrated with pomp and pageantry. The societies also sponsored an annual ball and picnic, and, most important of all, the feast of the local patron saint. This was the extent of society activities; any attempt to enlist support for philanthropic or civic projects was doomed to failure.

Since there was a surplus of doctors, lawyers, teachers, musicians, and classical scholars in southern Italy, an "intellectual proletariat" accompanied the peasants to America in search of fortune. Often, however, these educated immigrants found that America had no use for their talents, and to their chagrin they were reduced to performing manual labor. Their only hope of success was to gain the patronage of their lowly countrymen, but the sphere of colonial enterprise was very restricted. The sharp competition among the Italian bankers, doctors, journalists, and others engendered jealousies and rivalries. Thus this intelligentsia which might have been expected to provide tutelage and leadership to the humbler elements was itself rent by internecine conflict and expended its energies in polemics.

For the most part the upper-class immigrants generally regarded the peasants here as in Italy as boors and either exploited them or remained indifferent to their plight. These "respectable" Italians, however, were concerned with the growing prejudice against their nationality and wished to elevate its prestige among the Americans and other ethnic groups. As one means of doing this, they formed an association to suppress scavenging, organ-grinding, and begging as disgraceful to the Italian reputation. They simultaneously urged the workers to adopt American ways and to become patriotic Italians; but to these exhortations, the *contadino* replied: "It does not give me any bread whether the Italians have a good name in America or not. I am going back soon."

Well-to-do Italians were more liberal with advice than with good works. Compared with other nationalities in Chicago, the Italians were distinguished by their lack of philanthropic institutions. There was a substantial number of men of wealth among them, but as an Italian reformer commented: "It is strange that when a work depends exclusively on the wealthy of the colony, one can not hope for success. Evidently philanthropy is not the favored attribute of our rich." Indeed, there was no tradition of philanthropy among the gentry of southern Italy, and the "self-made" men did not recognize any responsibility outside the family. Projects were launched for an Italian hospital, an Italian school, an Italian charity society, an Italian institute to curb the padrone evil, and a White Hand Society to combat the Black Hand, but they all floundered in this morass of discord and disinterest. Clearly Handlin does not have the Italians in mind when he describes a growing spirit of benevolence as a product of immigrant life.

If there is one particular in which the *contadini* most strikingly refute Handlin's conception of the peasant it is in the place of religion in their lives. Handlin emphasizes the influence of Christian doctrine on the psychology of the peasantry, but throughout the Mezzogiorno, Christianity was only a thin veneer. Magic, not religion, pervaded their everyday existence; through the use of rituals, symbols, and charms, they sought to ward off evil spirits and to gain the favor of power-ful deities. To the peasants, God was a distant, unapproachable being, like the King, but the local saints and Madonnas were real personages whose power had been attested to by innumerable miracles. But in the devotions to their patron saints, the attitude of the peasants was less one of piety than of bargaining, making vows if certain requests were granted. For the Church, which they had known as an oppressive landlord, they had little reverence; and for the clergy, whom they knew to be immoral and greedy, they had little respect. They knew little of and cared less for the doctrines of the Church.

Nor was the influence of established religion on the south Italian peasants strengthened by emigration as Handlin asserts. American priests were scandalized by the indifference of the Italians to the Church. Even when Italian churches were provided by the Catholic hierarchy, the *contadini* seldom displayed any religious enthusiasm. As one missionary was told upon his arrival in an Italian colony: "We have no need of priests here, it would be better if you returned from whence you came." As in their native towns, the south Italian peasants for the most part went to church "to be christened, married or buried and that is about all."

Because they were said to be drifting into infidelity, the south Italians were also the object of much of the home mission work of the Protestant churches of Chicago. Drawing their ministry from Italian converts and Waldensians, these missions carried the Gospel to the *contadini*, who, however, revealed little inclination to become "true Christians." After several decades of missionary effort, the half dozen Italian Protestant churches counted their membership in the few hundreds. The suggestion that Italians were especially vulnerable to Protestant proselyting was not borne out in Chicago. For the *contadini*, neither Catholicism nor Protestantism became "paramount as a way of life."

According to Handlin, the immigrants found it "hard to believe that the whole world of spirits and demons had abandoned their familiar homes and come also across the Atlantic," but the *contadino* in America who carried a *corno* (a goat's horn of coral) to protect him from the evil eye harbored no such doubts. The grip of the supernatural on the minds of the peasants was not diminished by their ocean crossing. In the Italian settlements, sorcerers plied their magical trades on behalf of the ill, the lovelorn, the bewitched. As Alice Hamilton noted: "Without the help of these mysterious and powerful magicians they [the *contadini*] believe that they would be defenseless before terrors that the police and the doctor and even the priest cannot cope with." For this peasant folk, in Chicago as in Campania, the logic of medicine, law, or theology had no meaning; only magic provided an explanation of, and power over, the vagaries of life.

The persistence of Old World customs among the south Italians was perhaps best exemplified by the *feste* which were held in great number in Chicago. The cults of the saints and Madonnas had also survived the crossing, and the fellow townsmen had no doubt that their local divinities could perform miracles in Chicago as well as in the Old Country. Feast day celebrations were inspired not only by devotion to the saints and Madonnas; they were also an expression of nostalgia for the life left behind. The procession, the street fair, the crowds of townsmen, created the illusion of being once more back home; as one writer commented of a *festa*: "There in the midst of these Italians, with almost no Americans, it seemed to be truly a village of southern Italy." Despite efforts by "respectable" Italians and the Catholic clergy to discourage these colorful but unruly celebrations, the *contadini* would have their *feste*. After the prohibition of a *festa* by the Church was defied, a priest explained: "The feast is a custom of Sicily and survives despite denunciations from the altar. Wherever there is a colony of these people they have the festival, remaining deaf to the requests of the clergy." The south Italian peasants remained deaf to the entreaties of reformers and radicals as well as priests, for above all they wished to continue in the ways of their *paesi*.

The *contadini* of the Mezzogiorno thus came to terms with life in Chicago within the framework of their traditional pattern of thought and behavior. The social character of the south Italian peasant did not undergo a sea change, and the very nature of their adjustments to American society was dictated by their "Old World traits," which were not so much ballast to be jettisoned once they set foot on American soil. These traits and customs were the very bone and sinew of the south Italian character which proved very resistant to change even under the stress of emigration. Because it overemphasizes the power of environment and underestimates the toughness of culture heritage, Handlin's thesis does not comprehend the experience of the immigrants from southern Italy. The basic error of this thesis is that it subordinates historical complexity to the symmetrical pattern of a sociological theory. Rather than constructing ideal types of "the peasant" or "the immigrant," the historian of immigration must study the distinctive cultural character of each ethnic group and the manner in which this influenced its adjustments in the New World.

POSTSCRIPT

Did Late-Nineteenth-Century Immigrants Have to Leave Behind Their Old World Cultures to Come to America?

Handlin has been recognized as the most influential scholar on immigration history since his doctoral dissertation won the Dunning Prize when he was 26 years old. Published as *Boston's Immigrants: A Study in Acculturation* (Harvard University Press, 1941), this was the first study of immigration to integrate sociological concepts within a historical framework. A decade later, Handlin published *The Uprooted*, in which he combined the interdisciplinary framework with a personal narrative of the immigrants' history.

Handlin's book remains a classic though it was published nearly 50 years ago. Even at that time critics faulted Handlin for his lack of documentation, overgeneralization about the complex immigration experience, and the application of a sociological modernization model that downplayed the traditional values that accompanied the immigrants to the New World.

Vecoli was one of the earliest critics of Handlin's *The Uprooted*. Vecoli faults Handlin's major premises, denying that southern Italian peasants worked both their own individual plots and the communal lands of the small villages. Nor did these peasants accept a conservative class structure or the traditional religious practices of the Roman Catholic Church. Vecoli argues that many of these peasants lived in "rural cities," were extremely family-centered and individualistic, and isolated themselves from the political, economic, and church leaders in their communities.

John Bodnar's *The Transplanted: A History of Immigrants in Urban America* (Indiana University Press, 1986) is a basic summary of recent scholarship up to its date of publication. He takes issue with the Handlin thesis and supports the views of Vecoli and other historians who stress the continuity of values transmitted from the Old to the New World. Nora Faires has edited an informative "Roundtable on John Bodnar's *The Transplanted*," *Social Science History* (Fall 1988), which points out the directions in which modern scholarship is moving. James Paul Allen and Eugene James Turner have edited *We the People: An Atlas of America's Ethnic Diversity* (Macmillan, 1988), which contains wonderful charts and graphs about America's diverse population.

Two bibliographies worth consulting are Roger Daniels, "The Immigrant Experience in the Gilded Age," in Charles W. Calhoun, ed., *The Gilded Age: Essays on the Origins of Modern America* (S. R. Books, 1996) and Dirk Hoerder, "Changing Paradigms in Migration History: From 'to America' to World Wide Systems," *Canadian Review of American Studies* (Spring 1994).

PART 2

The Response to Industrialism: Reform and War

The mechanization of agriculture led to a surplus production of goods in the late nineteenth century. Farmers who specialized in cotton and wheat in the South and Midwest formed cooperatives, joined the third-party Populists, and pressured the state legislatures to pass laws regulating the shipping rates of the railroads. Many of the Populist attacks were directed at the bankers who controlled the nation's money supply and the middlemen who ran the grain exchange.

At the end of the nineteenth century, the African American population began fighting for civil rights, political power, and integration into society. Spokespeople for the blacks, such as Booker T. Washington, began to emerge, but their often unclear agendas frequently touched off controversy among both black people and white people.

With the growth of industry, urban problems became more acute. Improvements in water and sewerage, street cleaning, housing, mass transit, and fire and crime prevention developed slowly because the incredible population growth strained municipal services and urban governments had limited powers, which often fell under the control of political bosses. Historians disagree as to whether or not attempts to remedy these problems were successful.

The performance of America's 28th president, Woodrow Wilson, particularly his policies regarding the country's entrance into World War I, is also debated in this section.

- Was the Populist Party Prejudiced?

- Did Booker T. Washington's Philosophy and Actions Betray the Interests of African Americans?

- Did the Progressives Fail?

- Was Woodrow Wilson a Naive Idealist?

ISSUE 5

Was the Populist Party Prejudiced?

YES: Richard Hofstadter, from *The Age of Reform: From Bryan to F. D. R.* (Alfred A. Knopf, 1955)

NO: Walter T. K. Nugent, from *The Tolerant Populists: Kansas Populism and Nativism* (University of Chicago Press, 1963)

ISSUE SUMMARY

YES: The late professor of history Richard Hofstadter (1916–1970) argues that Populist literature and rhetoric in the late nineteenth century created a conspiracy theory around the issues of industrialism and the "money question," which activated a virulent strain of nativism and anti-Semitism among these agrarian reformers.

NO: Professor of history Walter T. K. Nugent's study of Kansas politics in the 1890s leads him to conclude that the Populists were neither conspiracy-minded nor hostile to foreigners in general or to Jews in particular; in fact, he argues, they were friendlier to immigrants and foreign institutions than their political opponents.

Industrialism produced significant changes and affected every major group in American society. Manufacturers and laborers obviously experienced the impact of these new forces, but industrial influences were felt beyond the confines of the nation's growing cities. Industrialism also altered the lives of rural Americans, who depended upon the soil for their livelihoods. Although they hoped to benefit from new markets and increased prosperity, the reality for most American farmers was greater poverty. After 1815 the independent, self-sufficient farmer began his retreat into American mythology in the wake of the relentless advance of commercial agriculture.

Between 1860 and 1900 American farmers confronted a steady downward spiral of agricultural prices, especially among major cash crops like wheat, corn, and cotton. Greater efficiency raised production levels, which in turn drove prices to lower levels. Meanwhile, farmers and their families had to purchase manufactured goods, many of which were inflated artificially in price by existing tariff schedules. Purchasing new land and better machinery to offset declining prices only compounded the problem and created a new one—the difficulty of repaying credit extended by the nation's banks. By 1890 many farmers were losing their lands to foreclosure and were being forced into tenancy or sharecropping; others abandoned the countryside for the city.

The independent yeoman farmer, once described by Thomas Jefferson as the backbone of the nation, seemed to be losing everything.

The discontent bred by these factors led American farmers to conclude that the best solution lay in organization. This was a momentous decision on the part of a group of citizens who for generations had expressed a commitment to individualism of the most rugged sort. But with industrialists forming managers' associations and urban workers pushing for the recognition of their unions, many farmers decided to follow suit. Initial attempts to form organizations resulted in the National Grange of the Patrons of Husbandry, essentially a social group, in the 1860s and the Alliance movement of the 1870s and 1880s. Finally, farmers attempted to organize an effective political movement in the 1890s, which culminated in the People's, or Populist, Party. The Populists mounted political opposition to the forces that threatened to make beggars of agricultural and urban workers alike, but with the defeat of William Jennings Bryan in the presidential election of 1896, Populism passed quickly from the scene. Nevertheless, many of the ideas and programs advanced by the People's Party were subsequently secured by reformers in the twentieth century.

Who were the Populists? How were their goals and ideology molded by the times in which they lived? As advocates of measures that would improve the status of the American farmer, how did the Populist Party react to the urban, industrial values that seemed to be dominating American society in the late nineteenth century? Did they display openly prejudicial attitudes toward certain groups, such as immigrants and Jews, who they associated in negative ways with the changes affecting them on a daily basis? These are some of the questions addressed in the selections that follow.

Richard Hofstadter commends the Populist Party for being the first to seriously attack the problems associated with industrialization and for being the first political movement to insist upon federal responsibility for the common good of American society. At the same time, Hofstadter claims, Populism was provincial, nativistic, nationalistic, and anti-Semitic. These characteristics, while exhibited largely in rhetorical terms, fostered among the Populists a conspiratorial intolerance of immigrants and other "strangers."

Walter T. K. Nugent offers a direct rebuttal of Hofstadter's analysis. Nugent's study of the Populist Party in Kansas leads him to the conclusion that the participants in this agrarian protest were not antagonistic toward foreigners and Jews and that, in fact, they were friendlier toward foreigners and foreign institutions than were their political opponents.

YES

Richard Hofstadter

THE FOLKLORE OF POPULISM

THE TWO NATIONS

For a generation after the Civil War, a time of great economic exploitation and waste, grave social corruption and ugliness, the dominant note in American political life was complacency. Although dissenting minorities were always present, they were submerged by the overwhelming realities of industrial growth and continental settlement. The agitation of the Populists, which brought back to American public life a capacity for effective political indignation, marks the beginning of the end of this epoch. In the short run the Populists did not get what they wanted, but they released the flow of protest and criticism that swept through American political affairs from the 1890's to the beginning of the first World War.

Where contemporary intellectuals gave the Populists a perfunctory and disdainful hearing, later historians have freely recognized their achievements and frequently overlooked their limitations....

There is indeed much that is good and usable in our Populist past. While the Populist tradition had defects that have been too much neglected, it does not follow that the virtues claimed for it are all fictitious. Populism was the first modern political movement of practical importance in the United States to insist that the federal government has some responsibility for the common weal; indeed, it was the first such movement to attack seriously the problems created by industrialism. The complaints and demands and prophetic denunciations of the Populists stirred the latent liberalism in many Americans and startled many conservatives into a new flexibility. Most of the "radical" reforms in the Populist program proved in later years to be either harmless or useful. In at least one important area of American life a few Populist leaders in the South attempted something profoundly radical and humane—to build a popular movement that would cut across the old barriers of race—until persistent use of the Negro bogy distracted their following. To discuss the broad ideology of the Populists does them some injustice, for it was in their concrete programs that they added most constructively to our political life, and in their more general picture of the world that they were most credulous and vulnerable. Moreover, any account of the fallibility of Populist thinking that does not acknowledge the stress and suffering out of which that thinking emerged will be seriously remiss. But anyone who enlarges our portrait of the Populist tradition is likely to bring out some unseen blemishes. In the books that have been written about the Populist movement, only passing mention has been made of its significant provincialism; little has been said of its relations with nativism and nationalism; nothing has been said of its tincture of anti-Semitism....

The utopia of the Populists was in the past, not the future. According to the agrarian myth, the health of the state was proportionate to the degree to which it was dominated by the agricultural class, and this assumption pointed to the superiority of an earlier age. The Populists looked backward with longing to the lost agrarian Eden, to the republican America of the early years of the nineteenth century in which there were few millionaires and, as they saw it, no beggars, when the laborer had excellent prospects and the farmer had abundance, when statesmen still responded to the mood of the people and there was no such thing as the money power. What they meant—though they did not express themselves in such terms—was that they would like to restore the conditions prevailing before the development of industrialism and the commercialization of agriculture. It should not be surprising that they inherited the traditions of Jacksonian democracy, that they revived the old Jacksonian cry: "Equal Rights for All, Special Privileges for None," or that most of the slogans of 1896 echoed the battle cries of 1836. General James B. Weaver,

the Populist candidate for the presidency in 1892, was an old Democrat and Free-Soiler, born during the days of Jackson's battle with the United States Bank, who drifted into the Greenback movement after a short spell as a Republican, and from there to Populism. His book, *A Call to Action*, published in 1892, drew up an indictment of the business corporation which reads like a Jacksonian polemic. Even in those hopeful early days of the People's Party, Weaver projected no grandiose plans for the future, but lamented the course of recent history, the growth of economic oppression, and the emergence of great contrasts of wealth and poverty, and called upon his readers to do "All in [their] power to arrest the alarming tendencies of our times."

Nature, as the agrarian tradition had it, was beneficent. The United States was abundantly endowed with rich land and rich resources, and the "natural" consequence of such an endowment should be the prosperity of the people. If the people failed to enjoy prosperity, it must be because of a harsh and arbitrary intrusion of human greed and error. "Hard times, then," said one popular writer, "as well as the bankruptcies, enforced idleness, starvation, and the crime, misery, and moral degradation growing out of conditions like the present, being unnatural, not in accordance with, or the result of any natural law, must be attributed to that kind of unwise and pernicious legislation which history proves to have produced similar results in all ages of the world. It is the mission of the age to correct these errors in human legislation, to adopt and establish policies and systems, in accord with, rather than in opposition to divine law." In assuming a lush natural order whose workings were being deranged by human laws, Populist writers were again drawing on the Jacksonian tradition, whose spokesmen also had pleaded for a proper obedience to "natural" laws as a prerequisite of social justice.

Somewhat akin to the notion of the beneficence of nature was the idea of a natural harmony of interests among the productive classes. To the Populist mind there was no fundamental conflict between the farmer and the worker, between the toiling people and the small businessman. While there might be corrupt individuals in any group, the underlying interests of the productive majority were the same; predatory behavior existed only because it was initiated and underwritten by a small parasitic minority in the highest places of power. As opposed to the idea that society consists of a number of different and frequently clashing interests—the social pluralism expressed, for instance, by Madison in the *Federalist*—the Populists adhered, less formally to be sure, but quite persistently, to a kind of social dualism: although they knew perfectly well that society was composed of a number of classes, for all practical purposes only one simple division need be considered. There were two nations. "It is a struggle," said Sockless Jerry Simpson, "between the robbers and the robbed." "There are but two sides in the conflict that is being waged in this country today," declared a Populist manifesto. "On the one side are the allied hosts of monopolies, the money power, great trusts and railroad corporations, who seek the enactment of laws to benefit them and impoverish the people. On the other are the farmers, laborers, merchants, and all other people who produce wealth and bear the burdens of taxation.... Between these two there is no middle ground." "On the one

side," said Bryan in his famous speech against the repeal of the Sherman Silver Purchase Act, "stand the corporate interests of the United States, the moneyed interests, aggregated wealth and capital, imperious, arrogant, compassionless.... On the other side stand an unnumbered throng, those who gave to the Democratic party a name and for whom it has assumed to speak." The people versus the interests, the public versus the plutocrats, the toiling multitude versus the money power—in various phrases this central antagonism was expressed. From this simple social classification it seemed to follow that once the techniques of misleading the people were exposed, victory over the money power ought to be easily accomplished, for in sheer numbers the people were overwhelming. "There is no power on earth that can defeat us," said General Weaver during the optimistic days of the campaign of 1892. "It is a fight between labor and capital, and labor is in the vast majority."

The problems that faced the Populists assumed a delusive simplicity: the victory over injustice, the solution for all social ills, was concentrated in the crusade against a single, relatively small but immensely strong interest, the money power. "With the destruction of the money power," said Senator [William] Peffer, "the death knell of gambling in grain and other commodities will be sounded; for the business of the worst men on earth will have been broken up, and the mainstay of the gamblers removed. It will be an easy matter, after the greater spoilsmen have been shorn of their power, to clip the wings of the little ones. Once get rid of the men who hold the country by the throat, the parasites can be easily removed." Since the old political parties were the primary means by which the people were kept wandering in the wilderness, the People's Party advocates insisted, only a new and independent political party could do this essential job. As the silver question became more prominent and the idea of a third party faded, the need for a monolithic solution became transmuted into another form: there was only one *issue* upon which the money power could really be beaten and this was the money issue. "When we have restored the money of the Constitution," said Bryan in his Cross of Gold speech, "all other necessary reforms will be possible; but ... until this is done there is no other reform that can be accomplished."

While the conditions of victory were thus made to appear simple, they did not always appear easy, and it would be misleading to imply that the tone of Populistic thinking was uniformly optimistic. Often, indeed, a deep-lying vein of anxiety showed through. The very sharpness of the struggle, as the Populists experienced it, the alleged absence of compromise solutions and of intermediate groups in the body politic, the brutality and desperation that were imputed to the plutocracy —all these suggested that failure of the people to win the final contest peacefully could result only in a total victory for the plutocrats and total extinction of democratic institutions, possibly after a period of bloodshed and anarchy. "We are nearing a serious crisis," declared Weaver. "If the present strained relations between wealth owners and wealth producers continue much longer they will ripen into frightful disaster. This universal discontent must be quickly interpreted and its causes removed." "We meet," said the Populist platform of 1892, "in the midst of a nation brought to the verge of moral, political, and material ruin. Corruption dominates the ballot-box, the Legislatures, the Congress, and touches even the ermine of the bench. The people are demoralized.... The newspapers are largely subsidized or muzzled, public opinion silenced, business prostrated, homes covered with mortgages, labor impoverished, and the land concentrating in the hands of the capitalists. The urban workmen are denied the right to organize for self-protection, imported pauperized labor beats down their wages, a hireling standing army, unrecognized by our laws, is established to shoot them down, and they are rapidly degenerating into European conditions. The fruits of the toil of millions are boldly stolen to build up colossal fortunes for a few, unprecedented in the history of mankind; and the possessors of these, in turn, despise the Republic and endanger liberty." Such conditions foreboded "the destruction of civilization, or the establishment of an absolute despotism."...

HISTORY AS CONSPIRACY

... There was something about the Populist imagination that loved the secret plot and the conspiratorial meeting. There was in fact a widespread Populist idea that all American history since the Civil War could be understood as a sustained conspiracy of the international money power.

... Wherever one turns in the Populist literature of the nineties one can find this conspiracy theory expressed. It is in the Populist newspapers, the proceedings of the silver conventions, the immense pamphlet literature broadcast by the American Bimetallic League, the Congressional debates over money; it is elaborated in such popular books as Mrs. S. E. V. Emery's *Seven Financial Conspiracies which have Enslaved the American Peo-*

ple or Gordon Clark's *Shylock: as Banker, Bondholder, Corruptionist, Conspirator.*

Mrs. Emery's book, first published in 1887, and dedicated to "the enslaved people of a dying republic," achieved great circulation, especially among the Kansas Populists. According to Mrs. Emery, the United States had been an economic Garden of Eden in the period before the Civil War. The fall of man had dated from the war itself, when "the money kings of Wall Street" determined that they could take advantage of the wartime necessities of their fellow men by manipulating the currency. "Controlling it, they could inflate or depress the business of the country at pleasure, they could send the warm life current through the channels of trade, dispensing peace, happiness, and prosperity, or they could check its flow, and completely paralyze the industries of the country." With this great power for good in their hands, the Wall Street men preferred to do evil. Lincoln's war policy of issuing greenbacks presented them with the dire threat of an adequate supply of currency. So the Shylocks gathered in convention and "perfected" a conspiracy to create a demand for their gold. The remainder of the book was a recital of a series of seven measures passed between 1862 and 1875 which were alleged to be a part of this continuing conspiracy, the total effect of which was to contract the currency of the country further and further until finally it squeezed the industry of the country like a hoop of steel.

Mrs. Emery's rhetoric left no doubt of the sustained purposefulness of this scheme—described as "villainous robbery," and as having been "secured through the most soulless strategy." She was most explicit about the so-called "crime of 1873," the demonetization of silver, giving a fairly full statement of the standard greenback-silverite myth concerning that event. As they had it, an agent of the Bank of England, Ernest Seyd by name, had come to the United States in 1872 with $500,000 with which he had bought enough support in Congress to secure the passage of the demonetization measure. This measure was supposed to have greatly increased the value of American four per cent bonds held by British capitalists by making it necessary to pay them in gold only. To it Mrs. Emery attributed the panic of 1873, its bankruptcies, and its train of human disasters: "Murder, insanity, suicide, divorce, drunkenness and all forms of immorality and crime have increased from that day to this in the most appalling ratio."

"Coin" Harvey, the author of the most popular single document of the whole currency controversy, *Coin's Financial School*, also published a novel, *A Tale of Two Nations*, in which the conspiracy theory of history was incorporated into a melodramatic tale. In this story the powerful English banker Baron Rothe plans to bring about the demonetization of silver in the United States, in part for his own aggrandizement but also to prevent the power of the United States from outstripping that of England. He persuades an American Senator (probably John Sherman, the *bête noire* of the silverites) to co-operate in using British gold in a campaign against silver. To be sure that the work is successful, he also sends to the United States a relative and ally, one Rogasner, who stalks through the story like the villains in the plays of Dion Boucicault, muttering to himself such remarks as "I am here to destroy the United States—Cornwallis could not have done more. For the wrongs and insults, for the glory of my own country, I will bury the knife deep into the heart of this nation." Against the plausibly drawn background of the corruption of the Grant administration, Rogasner proceeds to buy up the American Congress and suborn American professors of economics to testify for gold. He also falls in love with a proud American beauty, but his designs on her are foiled because she loves a handsome young silver Congressman from Nebraska who bears a striking resemblance to William Jennings Bryan!

One feature of the Populist conspiracy theory that has been generally overlooked is its frequent link with a kind of rhetorical anti-Semitism. The slight current of anti-Semitism that existed in the United States before the 1890's had been associated with problems of money and credit. During the closing years of the century it grew noticeably. While the jocose and rather heavy-handed anti-Semitism that can be found in Henry Adams's letters of the 1890's shows that this prejudice existed outside Populist literature, it was chiefly Populist writers who expressed that identification of the Jew with the usurer and the "international gold ring" which was the central theme of the American anti-Semitism of the age. The omnipresent symbol of Shylock can hardly be taken in itself as evidence of anti-Semitism, but the frequent references to the House of Rothschild make it clear that for many silverites the Jew was an organic part of the conspiracy theory of history. Coin Harvey's Baron Rothe was clearly meant to be Rothschild; his Rogasner (Ernest Seyd?) was a dark figure out of the coarsest anti-Semitic tradition. "You are very wise in your way," Rogasner is told at the climax of the tale, "the commercial way, inbred through generations. The politic, scheming, devious way, inbred through genera-

tions also." One of the cartoons in the effectively illustrated *Coin's Financial School* showed a map of the world dominated by the tentacles of an octopus at the site of the British Isles, labeled: "Rothschilds." In Populist demonology, anti-Semitism and Anglophobia went hand in hand.

The note of anti-Semitism was often sounded openly in the campaign for silver. A representative of the New Jersey Grange, for instance, did not hesitate to warn the members of the Second National Silver Convention of 1892 to watch out for political candidates who represented "Wall Street, and the Jews of Europe." Mary E. Lease described Grover Cleveland as "the agent of Jewish bankers and British gold." Donnelly represented the leader of the governing Council of plutocrats in *Caesar's Column*, one Prince Cabano, as a powerful Jew, born Jacob Isaacs; one of the triumvirate who lead the Brotherhood of Destruction is also an exiled Russian Jew, who flees from the apocalyptic carnage with a hundred million dollars which he intends to use to "revive the ancient splendors of the Jewish race, in the midst of the ruins of the world." One of the more elaborate documents of the conspiracy school traced the power of the Rothschilds over America to a transaction between Hugh McCulloch, Secretary of the Treasury under Lincoln and Johnson, and Baron James Rothschild. "The most direful part of this business between Rothschild and the United States Treasury was not the loss of money, even by hundreds of millions. It was the resignation of the country itself INTO THE HANDS OF ENGLAND, as England had long been resigned into the hands of HER Jews."

Such rhetoric, which became common currency in the movement, later passed beyond Populism into the larger stream of political protest. By the time the campaign of 1896 arrived, an Associated Press reporter noticed as "one of the striking things" about the Populist convention at St. Louis "the extraordinary hatred of the Jewish race. It is not impossible to go into any hotel in the city without hearing the most bitter denunciation of the Jews as a class and of the particular Jews who happen to have prospered in the world." This report may have been somewhat overdone, but the identification of the silver cause with anti-Semitism did become close enough for Bryan to have to pause in the midst of his campaign to explain to the Jewish Democrats of Chicago that in denouncing the policies of the Rothschilds he and his silver friends were "not attacking a race; we are attacking greed and avarice which know no race or religion."

It would be easy to misstate the character of Populist anti-Semitism or to exaggerate its intensity. For Populist anti-Semitism was entirely verbal. It was a mode of expression, a rhetorical style, not a tactic or a program. It did not lead to exclusion laws, much less to riots or pogroms. There were, after all, relatively few Jews in the United States in the late 1880's and early 1890's, most of them remote from the areas of Populist strength. It is one thing, however, to say that this prejudice did not go beyond a certain symbolic usage, quite another to say that a people's choice of symbols is of no significance. Populist anti-Semitism does have its importance—chiefly as a symptom of a certain ominous credulity in the Populist mind. It is not too much to say that the Greenback-Populist tradition activated most of what we have of modern popular anti-Semitism in the United States. From Thaddeus Stevens and Coin Harvey to Father Coughlin,

and from Brooks and Henry Adams to Ezra Pound, there has been a curiously persistent linkage between anti-Semitism and money and credit obsessions. A full history of modern anti-Semitism in the United States would reveal, I believe, its substantial Populist lineage, but it may be sufficient to point out here that neither the informal connection between Bryan and the Klan in the twenties nor Thomas E. Watson's conduct in the Leo Frank case were altogether fortuitous. And Henry Ford's notorious anti-Semitism of the 1920's, along with his hatred of "Wall Street," were the foibles of a Michigan farm boy who had been liberally exposed to Populist notions.

THE SPIRIT MILITANT

The conspiratorial theory and the associated Anglophobic and Judophobic feelings were part of a larger complex of fear and suspicion of the stranger that haunted, and still tragically haunts, the nativist American mind. This feeling, though hardly confined to Populists and Bryanites, was none the less exhibited by them in a particularly virulent form. Everyone remote and alien was distrusted and hated—even Americans, if they happened to be city people. The old agrarian conception of the city as the home of moral corruption reached a new pitch. Chicago was bad; New York, which housed the Wall Street bankers, was farther away and worse; London was still farther away and still worse. This traditional distrust grew stronger as the cities grew larger, and as they were filled with immigrant aliens. As early as 1885 the Kansas preacher Josiah Strong had published *Our Country*, a book widely read in the West, in which the cities were discussed as a great problem of the future, much as though they were some kind of monstrous malignant growths on the body politic. Hamlin Garland recalled that when he first visited Chicago, in the late 1880's, having never seen a town larger than Rockford, Illinois, he naturally assumed that it swarmed with thieves. "If the city is miles across," he wondered, "how am I to get from the railway station to my hotel without being assaulted?" While such extreme fears could be quieted by some contact with the city, others were actually confirmed—especially when the farmers were confronted with city prices. Nativist prejudices were equally aroused by immigration, for which urban manufacturers, with their insatiable demand for labor, were blamed. "We have become the world's melting pot," wrote Thomas E. Watson. "The scum of creation has been dumped on us. Some of our principal cities are more foreign than American. The most dangerous and corrupting hordes of the Old World have invaded us. The vice and crime which they have planted in our midst are sickening and terrifying. What brought these Goths and Vandals to our shores? The manufacturers are mainly to blame. They wanted cheap labor: and they didn't care a curse how much harm to our future might be the consequence of their heartless policy." . . .

As we review these aspects of Populist emotion, an odd parallel obtrudes itself. Where else in American thought during this period do we find this militancy and nationalism, these apocalyptic forebodings and drafts of world-political strategies, this hatred of big businessmen, bankers, and trusts, these fears of immigrants and urban workmen, even this occasional toying with anti-Semitic rhetoric? We find them, curi-

ously enough, most conspicuous among a group of men who are in all obvious respects the antithesis of the Populists. During the late 1880's and the '90's there emerged in the eastern United States a small imperialist elite representing, in general, the same type that had once been Mugwumps, whose spokesmen were such solid and respectable gentlemen as Henry and Brooks Adams, Theodore Roosevelt, Henry Cabot Lodge, John Hay, and Albert J. Beveridge. While the silverites were raging openly and earnestly against the bankers and the Jews, Brooks and Henry Adams were expressing in their sardonic and morosely cynical private correspondence the same feelings, and acknowledging with bemused irony their kinship at this point with the mob. While Populist Congressmen and newspapers called for war with England or Spain, Roosevelt and Lodge did the same, and while Mrs. Lease projected her grandiose schemes of world partition and tropical colonization, men like Roosevelt, Lodge, Beveridge, and Mahan projected more realistic plans for the conquest of markets and the annexation of territory. While Populist readers were pondering over Donnelly's apocalyptic fantasies, Brooks and Henry Adams were also bemoaning the approaching end of their type of civilization, and even the characteristically optimistic T. R. could share at moments in "Brooks Adams' gloomiest anticipations of our gold-ridden, capitalist-bestridden, usurer-mastered future." Not long after Mrs. Lease wrote that "we need a Napoleon in the industrial world who, by agitation and education, will lead the people to a realizing sense of their condition and the remedies," Roosevelt and Brooks Adams talked about the threat of the eight-hour movement and the danger that the country would be "enslaved" by the organizers of the trusts, and played with the idea that Roosevelt might eventually lead "some great outburst of the emotional classes which should at least temporarily crush the Economic Man."

Not only were the gentlemen of this imperialist elite better read and better fed than the Populists, but they despised them. This strange convergence of unlike social elements on similar ideas has its explanation, I believe, in this: both the imperialist elite and the Populists had been bypassed and humiliated by the advance of industrialism, and both were rebelling against the domination of the country by industrial and financial capitalists. The gentlemen wanted the power and status they felt due them, which had been taken away from their class and type by the *arriviste* manufacturers and railroaders and the all-too-potent banking houses. The Populists wanted a restoration of agrarian profits and popular government. Both elements found themselves impotent and deprived in an industrial culture and balked by a common enemy. On innumerable matters they disagreed, but both were strongly nationalistic, and amid the despairs and anxieties of the nineties both became ready for war if that would unseat or even embarrass the moneyed powers, or better still if it would topple the established political structure and open new opportunities for the leaders of disinherited farmers or for ambitious gentlemen. But if there seems to be in this situation any suggestion of a forerunner or analogue of modern authoritarian movements, it should by no means be exaggerated. The age was more innocent and more fortunate than ours, and by comparison with the grimmer realities of the twentieth century many of the events of the nineties take on a comic-opera quality. What came in the end was only a small war and a quick victory; when the farmers and the gentlemen finally did coalesce in politics, they produced only the genial reforms of Progressivism; and the man on the white horse turned out to be just a graduate of the Harvard boxing squad, equipped with an immense bag of platitudes, and quite willing to play the democratic game.

NO   Walter T. K. Nugent

THE TOLERANT POPULISTS: KANSAS POPULISM AND NATIVISM

Although a sizable body of literature appeared during the 1950's that asserted that the Populists were deeply hostile to things non-American, the Kansas story does not support those assertions. In fact, it supports something more like the opposite of each of the outstanding points of criticism.

The Populists have been accused of nativism, both of a personal kind and of an ideological kind; instead, they were friendlier and more receptive to foreign persons and foreign institutions than the average of their contemporary political opponents. They have been accused of "conspiracy-mindedness"; for them, however, tangible fact quite eclipsed neurotic fiction. They have been accused of anti-Semitism, both personal and ideological; instead they consistently got along well with their Jewish neighbors and consistently refrained from extending their dislike of certain financiers, who happened to be Jews, to Jews in general. They have been accused of chauvinism and jingoism, especially with reference to the Spanish-American War; instead, such lukewarm support as they gave collectively to Cuban intervention was based on quite different grounds, and as a group they strongly opposed the imperialism that the war engendered. Finally, they have been accused of selling out their vaunted reform principles by seeking political fusion with the Democratic party, especially in 1896, and thus of revealing a neurotic instability; but instead, fusion was for them a legitimate means to the accomplishment of real, if limited, reform. In the case of Kansas, the largest of the wheat-belt Populist states, the five principal criticisms of Populism voiced by recent writers not only do not square with the facts, but should be replaced with a viewpoint so much in contrast as to be practically the opposite. Briefly put, this viewpoint is as follows.

Populism in Kansas was a political response to economic distress. From the early days of the Farmers' Alliance, the progenitor of the People's party, to about 1892, relief of economic difficulty was virtually the sole reason for the party's existence; after 1892 this purpose was alloyed to some degree with the desire of the party to perpetuate itself as a political organism. In both periods, however, economic difficulties remained the party's chief reason for being,

From Walter T. K. Nugent, *The Tolerant Populists: Kansas Populism and Nativism* (University of Chicago Press, 1963). Copyright © 1963 by University of Chicago Press. Reprinted by permission. Notes omitted.

and relief of them its main objective. Populism called for the enactment of a set of legislative reforms by state and federal governments and accepted the extension of governmental power involved in such enactment. In its most complete and ideal form, the Populist program appeared in the national party platform of 1892, the "Omaha Platform," but this platform bore no more nor less relation to the practical operations of the party than platforms usually do. In Kansas the People's party placed its emphasis consistently on the three questions of land, money, and transportation, which were the issues causing greatest distress in that particular state. Since monetary reform seemed to have the broadest political appeal of all the reforms called for in the Populist program, it received more stress than the rest of the program at the time (1894–97) when the party seemed to have its best chance of succeeding.

As Populism followed the ways of practical party politics in the program that it offered and in the issues it chose to stress, it took a practical approach to its sources of support as well. Economic distress cut across lines of religion, of nationality origins, of race, of previous political affiliation, even of occupation and of wealth and status. To so great an extent was this the case that it is not even accurate to say that the Populists accepted or sought the support of third-party men, Republicans, Democrats, immigrants of many kinds, organized labor, city dwellers, and others, to broaden their agriculturalist base. For these groups were in and of Populism from the beginning. The job of the party leaders was therefore not so much to attract new groups but to be sure that the party program appealed to each of those groups already there and to spread the Populist message to further individual members of the existing coalition, of which the lowest common denominator was a desire for one or more specific economic reforms.

As a result, large numbers of every politically consequential foreign-born group then in Kansas, with the exception of the Mennonites, became active Populists. Party leaders received this support warmly and eagerly, except for one or two occasions: the 1894 state convention and probably the one of 1890. At those times, certain influential leaders supported the non-economic issues of women's suffrage and prohibition so vocally that they led the party to take positions unacceptable to many foreign-born groups. Even here, however, the attitude of these leaders to the foreign-born was one of indifference not of hostility. The fact of the matter seems to be, to judge by statements made by the delegates on the floor of the 1894 convention, that many Populists were simply unconcerned with ethnic groups or foreign matters; they were neither favorable nor hostile, except when they thought they might justifiably appeal to ethnic bloc votes or when they cited examples of enlightened foreign institutions to document their own reform program. To the great majority of Populists, in 1894 and at other times, foreignness and certainly Jewishness were simply not affective categories. For practical political reasons, among others, the Populists expressed themselves favorably toward foreign groups, either abroad or close at hand. This was certainly true of the fusionists; it was true of the non-fusionists except when women's suffrage and prohibition got in the way; it was even true, at times, of the Middle-of-the-Road group, which combined an antibanker (including English, Anglo-Jewish, and Wall Street banker) rhetoric with some benevolence toward immigrants as individuals.

Many leading Populists were in fact first or second generation immigrants. In the 1890's the Populists surpassed the Republicans in the proportion of their state legislators who were foreign-born. Foreign-born Populists abounded among county-level officeholders, county committeemen, precinct workers, and delegates to county, district, and state political conventions. Wherever an ethnic group existed, there existed as well its Populist voters and Populist leaders, with the exception of the Mennonites, who were undeviatingly Republican. The Populists, however, had immigrant blocs of their own, especially on the frequent occasions of county and state-level fusion with the Democrats. The party organization appealed to foreign-language groups with pamphlets, newspapers, and campaign speakers. They presented much the same arguments to their polyglot audience as the party was making to the English-speaking voters. The only difference was in window dressing, such as testimonials from Prince Bismarck and from German political economists in support of silver coinage. At their 1894 state convention, and prior and subsequently in their newspapers, the Populists forthrightly condemned the American Protective Association, the most influential and widespread nativist organization since the Know-Nothings.

On three contemporaneous issues relating directly to immigrants, the Populists took positions that might seem at first glance to have been nativistic, but in each case their attitude to the immigrant was neutral or favorable. When they attacked "alien" landholding, they were at-

tacking landlordism, not the immigrant small landholder. When they called for an end to contract or "pauper labor" immigration, they clearly excepted "worthwhile" or "sturdy" immigrants and based their position on labor competition, not on racism. When their congressmen supported the Lodge-McCall literacy test to restrict immigration, they apparently did so as the only practical way to enact the bill's riders, which would have lessened labor competition, and almost never expressed approval of the philosophy of superior and inferior, desirable or undesirable, races put forward by [Henry Cabot] Lodge and the Immigration Restriction League. In each of these three instances the Populists based their actions on reasonable economic grounds, if not especially perceptive or laudable ones. Their aim was to attract the political support of organized labor, of tenant farmers, and very likely of Irish-Americans.

The rhetoric of Populism was highly charged with nationalism, but it was a nineteenth-century kind of nationalism that did not include the nativistic or anti-Semitic characteristics of some twentieth-century right-wing nationalists. Only two foreign groups fell under the censure of any considerable number of Populists. This censure was a consequence of two issues firmly rooted in economic realities and in neither case did they grow out of or were they extended to racial or nativistic antagonism. The two groups were English or Anglo-Jewish financiers and English or Anglo-Irish landlords, respectively responsible in part for money stringency and for large landholding. Many Populists feared that the trend toward tighter money and tighter land would continue unchecked unless these two groups, *and their American or Gentile associates*, were stopped. In both cases the antipathy of the Populists clearly extended to all malevolent financiers, monopolists, and land barons, whether English or American, whether Jew or Gentile, whether native or alien. For the Populists, or many of them, to have laid their troubles at the door of a mixed group of English, Anglo-Jewish, and American capitalists may have been naïve and simplistic, but the point is that the common denominator of their hostility was not nativism or anti-Semitism but distrust and dislike of a truly unsympathetic economic class. In some cases their anti-English attitude transcended this economic base, since the economic problem meshed so well with the rather widespread anti-English attitude shared by many nineteenth-century Americans as part of the American Revolutionary tradition. But the English people escaped the censure placed upon certain financially powerful Englishmen, and Jewish financiers escaped any blame whatever as Jews, although a few of them, as investment bankers, shared the criticisms heaped by the Populists, or rather, some of their more outspoken rhetoricians, upon the wickedness of powerful financial interests in general. This was certainly the case with the terms "Shylock" and "Rothschild," which appeared with some frequency in Populist literature but which were cachets not of Jewish conspiracy but of oppressive finance.

So far did Populist expressions of friendliness to Jews as individuals, in Kansas and elsewhere, to Jews as a group, to English immigrants, to English institutions such as co-operatives and public ownership of utilities, outweigh the expressions that might be construed with effort as Anglophobic or anti-Semitic, and so specious are the grounds upon which the Populists have been accused of Anglophobia, anti-Semitism, or nativism, that these accusations must simply fall without support. There is an exception that proves the rule. A handful of Populists sometimes let their antipathies include "racial characteristics" of these two groups, especially the English, and thereby they evidenced irrationality and prejudice. They were atypical. Many, in fact nearly all, of these Populists were attached to the Middle-of-the-Road Populist splinter group in 1894 and 1896. This group attempted to overthrow the recognized state leadership, whose reform credentials were at least as old and respectable as the dissidents'; it was in all probability subsidized by the Republican state organization; and it received the support of less than 1 per cent of the rank and file at the polls in 1896 and of the Populist press.

In what, then, did their nationalism consist? It is difficult to answer such a question, because to accuse such a pragmatic, anti-intellectual people as these agrarians of having possessed "concepts" or "ideas," much more a "system," is itself a distortion. They did, however, possess felt attitudes that were forced into words to form the rhetoric of their speeches and editorials. Needless to say, the scribes and leaders of Populism came closer than anyone else to expressing these views in logical form, subject, of course, to political exigencies. But it can be assumed that their rhetoric must have been congenial to the rank and file— otherwise they would have been unable to attract and to hold that rank and file. Nonetheless, the rhetoric is undoubtedly more radical, more logically organized, and much more explicit than the views of the mass of the party. In their rhetoric, Populist nationalism consisted of a feeling that the United States was a different *kind* of political society from any that had ever existed before and therefore more worth preserving than any previous one. America was not just another nation-state but an embodiment of certain ideals. It was the embodiment of democratic republicanism: a society where the people rule, where the governed consent to their governors, where the rights of life, liberty, and property are protected because this very protection is the object of their own self-government. It was the embodiment, too, of economic democracy: where resources wanted only honest labor to be translated into the reality of abundance, where opportunity was equal, where the distribution of the nation's wealth was equitable. It was the antithesis of Europe and Europe's corruption, decadence, parasitical upper classes, stagnation, and economic and political oppression. It was a place, in short, where the people rule for themselves and for the protection of their natural rights. Or, at least, so it should have been.

Yet who were the people? The answer is already implied. The people were those who believed in the ideals of democratic republicanism, of economic democracy, and of freedom from European conditions of life. The people were those who actively sought the preservation of those ideals. They were those who labored by their own hands, who had equal opportunities to labor and to accumulate, who used the resources of the United States to produce their own and the nation's wealth. They were those who created wealth rather than those who manipulated wealth already produced. Very often this legitimate wealth-producing activity was defined by the Populists as agricultural and laboring activity; those who farmed or labored were by definition the real people. This corresponded

conveniently both to what might roughly be called the Jeffersonian-Jacksonian tradition and to the actual political bases of the People's party's support. Translated into the rhetoric of a political campaign, it often meant emphasizing "the producing classes" or the common bonds of "the farming and laboring people."

The conscious derivation for all of this was the American Revolution, and secondarily, the War of 1812. These struggles successfully created a nation embodying this set of ideals. Such conscious roots made it easy, of course, for some Populists to look upon the machinations of English financiers as a third and final attempt by England to subjugate America. It was primarily through the American Revolution that a nation of, by, and for the people was created and through it that all that was wrong with Europe and Britain was left behind.

Consequently, it was up to the people—often implying the farmers and laborers—to see to it that this nation, this unique society, did not perish from the earth. Who threatened its extinction? Certainly not the refugee from European misery, at least so long as he, too, believed in American republicanism and opportunity. In this unique kind of nation the doors were open to those who wished legitimately to share its benefits. The goods of this nation were not to be shut up inside for the exclusive use of those already there but rather to beckon as to a flourishing haven those who wished to escape the oppression of a decadent Europe. The nation, was, in Lincoln's words, a last, best hope of earth. The immigrant was to show his good faith in these ideals by becoming a citizen and remaining permanently (as the Populists' alien land law provided) and by not attempting to destroy the opportunity of individuals already possessing it (as Populist demands for an end to "pauper labor" immigration showed). For an immigrant to take away the job of an American laborer was unnecessary anyway, since opportunity and America were virtually synonymous.

The "worthwhile" or "sturdy" immigrant was not, then, the enemy of American nationality. In fact, he seemed to justify the Populist approach to American nationality—certainly he did in the case of immigrant agricultural colonies in Kansas, which had been very successful—and he was therefore quite welcome. But who then *was* the enemy? To most Populists who thought about the matter beyond their immediate economic distress—and by no means all of them thought through their views of American nationalism with anything like the completeness that this sketch might imply—the enemy lay in certain recently emergent opportunities for malevolence. America was shifting from a predominantly rural and agricultural nation to one predominantly urban and industrial. This shift was in no way evil in itself. Populist spokesmen such as Senators [William Alfred] Peffer and [William A.] Harris had expressly denied any hope of turning back the clock, and if they were not absolutely delighted with a process that seemed to be toppling the farmers and their allies from political and economic predominance (if indeed they had ever possessed it), they were determined to live with such a trend. What is more, they were determined to see that these changes should benefit all the people and not just a few; that they should take place in such ways as to guarantee democratic republicanism and economic democracy. The majority of them therefore accepted industrialization but

condemned monopoly, accepted banking and finance but condemned usury and financial sleight of hand, welcomed accumulation but condemned economic feudalism, welcomed enterprise but condemned speculation. It was not industry and urbanism that oppressed them, they thought, but their abuse.

For most Populists these considerations identified the enemy well enough. An appealing program, aimed conveniently at the relief of immediate distress as well as at the placing of new trends within the old ideals, could be constructed without further ado. A rhetoric quickly emerged that concerned itself with attacking landlordism, transportation monopoly, and money shortages, and this rhetoric remained the basic vehicle of Populist ideas from start to finish. In a minority of cases, however, it seemed convenient to personalize the enemy, and in doing so, some Populists passed the bounds of precise statement. At times, American financiers and monopolists such as the Belmonts, Morgans, and Vanderbilts, English financiers such as the Rothschilds, American and English land and mortgage loan companies, and prominent American statesmen such as Sherman, McKinley, and Cleveland, together seemed to form a common and inimical class dedicated to the people's overthrow. Ever since the Civil War this group seemed to have conspired to bring about the economic destruction of the farmers and their allies. This minority of Populists thereby dealt with the money question in terms of a "money power." Yet even they nearly all used the term "conspiracy" in a general sense to mean the common attitudes of an entrenched and powerful minority, and only a tiny proportion meant by the term an explicit conspiratorial agreement, as when they referred to Ernest Seyd and the "Hazzard Circular" of the sixties and seventies. But most Populists did not voice this line, a fact more remarkable if one grants that rhetoric tends to be more radical than the general feeling of its political following. This "conspiracy" was, in addition, a financial one and not a Jewish or English one. To look at a close-knit community of interest and to see in the mind's eye a conspiracy is not necessarily great irrationality but rather a lack of factual knowledge about the competitive methods of late nineteenth-century capitalism. In antibanker, antimonopoly, or anticapitalist statements formed fairly frequent themes in Populist rhetoric, populists of every hue made it clear that it was usury, irresponsible economic power, and minority rule that they were opposing and not the industrial revolution, urbanism, or capitalism and banking as such. The abuse of new trends, not the trends themselves, had driven them, they felt, from their once uncontested eminence. Now they wanted to regain that eminence and accepted the fact that it could never again be theirs alone. If agrarian class predominance was over and done with, plutocratic class predominance should be scuttled before it progressed any further. Then economic democracy would be reborn.

The Populist view of American nationality, with its stress on democratic republicanism and economic democracy, was therefore intended to be at once majoritarian, individualistic, and humanitarian. That it was a nationalism naïvely humanitarian rather than aggressive appeared very clearly in the Populists' approach to the Cuban insurrection and the Spanish-American War. They sympathized deeply with the insurgent Cubans and viewed their uprising as a struggle for freedom and democracy much like the American uprising of the 1770's. In Kansas this sympathy expressed itself in a moral support for the insurrectionists that sprang from a confident view of their own moral righteousness. Nonetheless, the Populist press and Populist congressmen held back from armed intervention, took a cautious attitude to the blowing up of the *Maine*, restrained themselves from anything more vigorous than sympathetic gestures toward the Cubans in spite of the Spanish "despotism" and "Weylerism" they believed the Cubans to be suffering, and in unison with their Democratic neighbors hoped that war could be avoided. This was very close to the Republican position also. When war came, they supported it as everyone else did, but until then their humanitarian sympathy for the Cubans was checked by the fear that a war beginning with Cuban intervention could only benefit large financial interests. The Kansas Republicans' coolness toward Cuban intervention resulted mainly from the caution that McKinley maintained into April, 1898, and the desire of the Kansas Republicans to support their own administration. The Populists avoided the Republicans' scornful references to Cuban or Spanish racial inferiority and far more frequently than the Republicans took a humanitarian view of the matter. In Kansas the Populists were not violent jingoes. Furthermore, unlike the Republicans in their area, and other people elsewhere, the official Populist position on the question of American imperial expansion for commercial or military purposes, which arose after Dewey's victory in Manila Bay, was to join the Democrats in opposing expansion and in demanding that the United States leave the Philippines and other potential colonies alone. They were interested in the spread of American democratic ideals, in the overthrow of Spanish oppression of Cuba, if this could be done without the commitment of American armed forces, but not at all in American conquest or colonization. Populism in Kansas apparently lost many adherents because of this stand, but it remained the official party position nevertheless.

It is worth noting that Populist opposition to imperialism was much more firmly expressed than Populist sympathy to the Cuban insurrectionists, because the Democratic party was also much less firm on the latter question than on the former. As a matter of fact, official Populist rhetoric was tailored to fit the political exigencies involved in getting along with the Democrats not only on the war and imperialism issues but on most other questions as well. Political fusion with the Democrats on all levels marked Kansas Populism very strongly, and to some writers, fusion has meant that the Populists lacked any real dedication to the principles they so vigorously espoused. But the Populist movement chose political means to accomplish its program of economic reform; it was a political party, not a pressure group or an ideological front; for better or worse it therefore bound itself to use partisan methods. If one looks no further than the Omaha platform of 1892 to find out what Populism stood for and then observes that many planks in that platform were soft-pedaled in 1892 and later for the sake of fusion and political success, one might assume that Populist devotion to reform principles was a sham. But this is a superficial view. Fusion was the only apparent way to achieve any reforms, any accomplishment of any principles at all, and the degree to which the People's party was willing to fuse with the Democrats in Kansas

was the degree to which it possessed political common sense. The identification of fusion with dedication to principle, rather than with a sellout, comes into even greater relief as soon as one recalls the shabby story of the Middle-of-the-Road Populists, those self-styled simon-pure reformers who almost certainly connived at the defeat of the reform party with the local Republican organization. The prevalence of fusion sentiment indicates as well the willingness of the Populists to seek out and accept the support of the foreign-born blocs that ordinarily made their political home in the Democratic party. It also indicates their pragmatic approach to political action, their willingness to use an obvious means at hand to achieve legitimate political ends, and their flexibility, which stood in such contrast to the rigidity of the Middle-of-the-Road Populists.

The political horse sense that provided them with their receptivity to fusion was a natural outgrowth of the immediacy of the distress from which their movement sprang. It accounted, too, for the apparent anomaly of a radical program based on conservative ideals. For the Populists of Kansas were not a collection of rag-tag calamity howlers, ne'er-do-wells, and third-party malcontents, as William Allen White and others have suggested, but a large body of people of diverse occupational, wealth-holding, and status levels. As a group they were hardly distinguishable from their Republican neighbors, except for a probably higher mortgage indebtedness, and their greater degree of political and economic awareness. The great majority could be called "middle class," and they were interested in preserving what they considered to be their middle-class American ideals and substance. These were being threatened, they felt, not by the facts of industrialism and urbanism but by their existing *shape*. To change that shape, they settled upon the device of a political party.

Their view of the future was one in which many wrongs would have to be righted, many present trends would have to be redirected to conform to old ideals, for that future to become acceptable. Yet they were confident that this would happen. In several ways they were confused, ill-informed, and behind the times. They were unaware of urban problems, for example, and they never understood that money reform was basically a solution only to agricultural problems, if indeed to them, and not a solution for growing monopoly or for inequities of wealth distribution. Yet if this is true, it is true as well to acquit them of nativism, anti-Semitism, conspiracy-mindedness, jingoism, lack of principle, and of living in some neurotic agrarian dream world. They were bound together not by common neuroses but by common indebtedness, common price squeezes, common democratic and humanitarian ideals, and common wrath at the infringement of them. From this wrath rose the Farmers' Alliance, and from the Alliance their ultimate instrument of protest, the People's party. The Populists were far too concerned with land, money, and transportation, and also, later on, with the mechanics of winning and keeping public office, to have much time to worry about whether their ideals were mythical or their anxieties neurotic. Tight money and foreclosure sales were the products of nobody's imagination. Even in their rhetoric they were too busy preaching positive reforms in a depression to be concerned with racism or anti-Semitism or agrarian Arcadias; and in their practical political activities, they took all the help they could get.

The Populists were liberal nationalists bringing to radical social changes a radical response. By such means they meant to re-assert what they considered to be the fundamental ideals upon which their society had previously depended —in their view of history—and must continue to depend—in their view of political philosophy. They undertook this task in the Kansas of the 1890's, with its particular kind of social structure, its particular distribution of wealth and income, its specific economic conditions, and its peculiar laws and traditions. These particularities form the limits of historical analogy, and they give no grounds for making the Populists the gawky ancestors of Father Coughlin or of Senator Joseph R. McCarthy. They make it very difficult to call the Populists the descendants of the Jeffersonians and Jacksonians or the precursors of Progressivism or the New Deal, although with these movements the Populists shared a considerable body of ideals. They make it unrealistic even to equate the Kansas Populists with Populists of other regions or other states.

This particular set of facts, however, allows the Populists of Kansas to be judged on their own grounds. The verdict is very simple. They were people who were seeking the solution of concrete economic distress through the instrumentality of a political party. By this means they would not only help themselves but they would redirect, not reverse, the unsatisfactory trends of their time to correspond with the ideals of the past. This involved profoundly the political co-operation of the foreign-born, and it involved a deep respect and receptivity for non-American institutions and ideas.

POSTSCRIPT

Was the Populist Party Prejudiced?

Hofstadter's thesis was the first major challenge to the favorable interpretation of the Populists presented in John D. Hicks, *The Populist Revolt: A History of the Farmers' Alliance and the People's Party* (University of Minnesota Press, 1931). This critique was extended by Victor C. Ferkiss, a political scientist. In "Populist Influences in American Fascism," *Western Political Quarterly* (June 1957), Ferkiss argued that the Populist movement was not based upon egalitarian goals of human freedom. In fact, he concluded, by encouraging majority rule over governmental institutions, the Populists committed themselves to a "plebiscitary democracy" very similar to that proposed for Germany by Adolf Hitler.

In addition to Hicks's work cited above, the origins of the farmers' revolt of the late nineteenth century are explored in D. Sven Nordin, *Rich Harvest: A History of the Grange, 1867–1900* (University Press of Mississippi, 1974); Robert C. McMath, Jr., *Populist Vanguard: A History of the Southern Farmers' Alliance* (University of North Carolina Press, 1975); Michael Schwartz, *Radical Protest and Social Structure: The Southern Farmers' Alliance and Cotton Tenancy, 1880–1890* (Academic, 1976); Stephen Hahn, *The Roots of Southern Populism: Yeoman Farmers and the Transformation of the Georgia Upcountry, 1850–1890* (Oxford University Press, 1983); and Donna Barnes, *Farmers in Rebellion: The Rise and Fall of the Southern Farmers' Alliance and People's Party in Texas* (University of Texas Press, 1984).

Agricultural History (April 1965) has published the results of a symposium on Populism in the form of essays by several revisionists and their critics. Interested students should also consult two historiographical collections: Theodore Saloutos, ed., *Populism: Reaction or Reform?* (Holt, Rinehart & Winston, 1968) and William F. Holmes, ed., *American Populism* (D. C. Heath, 1994). Norman Pollack offers a valuable collection of primary sources in *The Populist Mind* (Bobbs-Merrill, 1967), and he provides favorable evaluations of the Populists in *The Populist Response to Industrial America: Midwestern Populist Thought* (Harvard University Press, 1962) and *The Just Polity: Populism, Law, and Human Welfare* (University of Illinois Press, 1987). Lawrence Goodwyn's *Democratic Promise: The Populist Moment in America* (Oxford University Press, 1976) is a sensitive portrait that depicts Populism as a cooperative "people's movement" whose supporters espoused true egalitarianism. Bruce Palmer, in *"Man Over Money": The Southern Populist Critique of American Capitalism* (University of North Carolina Press, 1980), offers divergent views of some of the themes developed by Goodwyn. More recently, Gene Clanton's *Populism: The Humane Preference in America, 1890–1900* (Twayne, 1991) and Robert C.

McMath, Jr.'s *American Populism: A Social History, 1877–1898* (Hill & Wang, 1993) offer surveys of the entire Populist movement.

The relationship between African Americans and southern white Populists was enormously complex. C. Vann Woodward's classic biography *Tom Watson: Agrarian Rebel* (Oxford University Press, 1938) and Lawrence Goodwyn's "Populist Dreams and Negro Rights: East Texas as a Case Study," *American Historical Review* (December 1971) emphasize the success of black-white coalitions. Gerald H. Gaither, in *Blacks and the Populist Revolt: Ballots and Bigotry in the "New South"* (University of Alabama Press, 1977), challenges the optimistic biracial portrayals by Woodward and Goodwyn. Gregg Cantrell, *Kenneth and John B. Rayner and the Limits of Southern Dissent* (University of Illinois Press, 1993) represents one of the few biographical studies of a black Populist leader.

Robert F. Durden, *The Climax of Populism: The Election of 1896* (University of Kentucky Press, 1966) and Paul W. Glad, *McKinley, Bryan, and the People* (J. B. Lippincott, 1964) are competent studies of the Populists' electoral defeat. William Jennings Bryan's involvement in Populist goals is covered in Glad, *The Trumpet Soundeth: William Jennings Bryan and His Democracy, 1896–1912* (University of Nebraska Press, 1960) and in the early chapters of Robert W. Cherny, *A Righteous Cause: The Life of William Jennings Bryan* (Little, Brown, 1985). Finally, for an intriguing argument, see Henry M. Littlefield, "The Wizard of Oz: Parable of Populism," *American Quarterly* (Spring 1964).

ISSUE 6

Did Booker T. Washington's Philosophy and Actions Betray the Interests of African Americans?

YES: Donald Spivey, from *Schooling for the New Slavery: Black Industrial Education, 1868–1915* (Greenwood Press, 1978)

NO: Louis R. Harlan, from "Booker T. Washington and the Politics of Accommodation," in John Hope Franklin and August Meier, eds., *Black Leaders of the Twentieth Century* (University of Illinois Press, 1982)

ISSUE SUMMARY

YES: Professor of history Donald Spivey contends that Booker T. Washington alienated both students and faculty at Tuskegee Institute by establishing an authoritarian system that failed to provide an adequate academic curriculum to prepare students for the industrial workplace.

NO: Professor emeritus of history Louis R. Harlan portrays Washington as a political realist who had the same long-range goals of progress toward equality as his black critics and whose policies and actions were designed to benefit black society as a whole.

In the late nineteenth and early twentieth centuries, most black Americans' lives were characterized by increased inequality and powerlessness. Although the Thirteenth Amendment had fueled a partial social revolution by emancipating approximately 4 million southern slaves, the efforts of the Fourteenth and Fifteenth Amendments to provide all African Americans with the protections and privileges of full citizenship had been undermined by the United States Supreme Court.

Seventy-five percent of all African Americans resided in rural areas by 1910. Ninety percent lived in the South, where they suffered from abuses associated with the sharecropping and crop-lien systems, political disfranchisement, and antagonistic race relations, which often boiled over into acts of violence, including race riots and lynchings. Black southerners who moved north in the decades preceding World War I to escape the ravages of racism instead discovered a society in which the color line was drawn more rigidly to limit black opportunities. Residential segregation led to the emergence of racial ghettos. Jim Crow also affected northern education, and competition for jobs produced frequent clashes between black and white workers. By the early twentieth century, then, most African Americans endured a second-class citizenship reinforced by segregation laws (both customary and legal) in the "age of Jim Crow."

Prior to 1895 the foremost spokesman for the nation's African American population was former slave and abolitionist Frederick Douglass, whose crusade for blacks emphasized the importance of civil rights, political power, and immediate integration. August Meier has called Douglass "the greatest living symbol of the protest tradition during the 1880s and 1890s." At the time of Douglass's death in 1895, however, this tradition was largely replaced by the emergence of Booker T. Washington. Born into slavery in Virginia in 1856, Washington became the most prominent black spokesman in the United States as a result of a speech delivered in the year of Douglass's death at the Cotton States Exposition in Atlanta, Georgia. Known as the "Atlanta Compromise," this address, with its conciliatory tone, found favor among whites and gave Washington, who was president of the Tuskegee Institute in Alabama, a reputation as a "responsible" spokesman for black America.

What did Booker T. Washington really want for African Americans? Did his programs realistically address the difficulties confronted by blacks in a society where the doctrine of white supremacy was prominent? Is it fair to describe Washington simply as a conservative whose accommodationist philosophy betrayed his own people? Did the "Sage of Tuskegee" consistently adhere to his publicly stated philosophy of patience, self-help, and economic advancement?

One of the earliest and most outspoken critics of Washington's program was his contemporary, W. E. B. Du Bois. In a famous essay in *The Souls of Black Folk* (1903), Du Bois levels an assault upon Washington's narrow educational philosophy for blacks and his apparent acceptance of segregation. By submitting to disfranchisement and segregation, Du Bois charges, Washington had become an apologist for racial injustice in the United States. He also claims that Washington's national prominence was bought at the expense of black interests throughout the nation.

In the first of the following selections, Donald Spivey offers a more recent interpretation that follows the critical assessment of Du Bois. He portrays Booker T. Washington as an authoritarian "overseer" who imposed a militaristic system at Tuskegee and who alienated students and faculty at Tuskegee by insisting upon a program that not only subordinated political, social, and civil rights to economic goals but also failed to provide the training necessary to allow students to become capable, skilled artisans.

In the second selection, Louis R. Harlan argues that Washington understood the reality of southern race relations and knew what he was capable of accomplishing without endangering his leadership position, which was largely controlled by whites. He was, then, a consummate politician—master of the art of the possible in turn-of-the-century race relations—who shared with his black critics most of the same long-range goals for racial equality.

YES

Donald Spivey

SHINE, BOOKER, SHINE: THE BLACK
OVERSEER OF TUSKEGEE

Perhaps Paulo Freire had Booker T. Washington in mind when he wrote in his classic study on education, "The oppressed have been destroyed precisely because their situation has reduced them to things. In order to regain their humanity they must cease to be things and fight as men.... They cannot enter the struggle as objects in order later to become men." To Booker T. Washington the sensible thing for blacks to do was to fashion a coalition with whites in power to make themselves indispensable "objects" to the prosperity of the nation. His conception of the proper course for blacks rested upon the blacks' own exploitability. He believed that the profit motive dictated American thought and action. Those who proved themselves antagonistic would remain powerless or be annihilated; those who proved themselves of value would be rewarded. Thus, he contended that social, political, and civil rights were secondary issues for blacks—subordinate to and dependent upon the race's economic importance. This philosophy of uplift through submission drew heated criticism from many black leaders. What is not a familiar story is that in his championing of these ideas, Washington alienated many of his Tuskegee students and faculty members and never gained the full support of the white South....

Like the good overseer, and like his mentor, Samuel Chapman Armstrong, [the founder of Hampton Institute's industrial education program,] Booker T. sought to make his students superb laborers, that is, totally reliable. He criticized Tuskegee students who showed any signs of being unreliable. "Young men come here [Tuskegee Institute] and want to work at this industry or that, for a while, and then get tired and want to change to something else." To be a good worker, Washington professed, one must understand "the Importance of Being Reliable."

Booker Washington worked diligently to please the dominant white society, to make his blacks "the best labor in the world." He watched his students' every move. He was a stickler for precision and detail. The Founder emphasized such things to the Tuskegee student body and teachers as the proper

From Donald Spivey, *Schooling for the New Slavery: Black Industrial Education, 1868–1915* (Greenwood Press, 1978). Copyright © 1978 by Donald Spivey. Reprinted by permission of Greenwood Press, Westport, CT. Notes omitted.

positioning of brooms. Washington sent a notice to three department heads: "Will you kindly see that all brooms in your department are kept on their proper end. I notice that this is not done now." One faculty member responded on top of the Founder's memo: "This must be a mistake." It was not. Booker Washington demanded that everyone, including Mrs. Washington, place and store brooms with the brush end up.

The Founder placed every aspect of the student's life at Tuskegee under a strict regime of rules and regulations. Committees were formed that conducted daily examinations of the students' rooms and personal belongings. Careful attention was given to whether or not all had toothbrushes. One committee reported that it had noted some "absence of tooth brushes and tooth mugs." The Founder received other reports on the toothbrush situation. "There is a very large number of students that use the tooth brush only to adorn the washstand," one of Washington's student informers reported.

The slightest trace of dirt or grime was call for alarm and disciplinary action at Tuskegee. A committee appointed to inspect one of the dorms noted, "The wood work needs scrubbing and dusting thoroughly." The committee also reported that beds were not properly made in military fashion and some of the linen needed ironing and was improperly folded. Students who left their beds unmade were often punished by not receiving dinner.

When Tuskegee students did dine, they did so under stringent rules and regulations. Talking during meals was permitted only at precise intervals designated by the ringing of bells....

The list of regulations ended with Rule Number 15: "For the violation of the above rules you will be severely punished."

Naturally, students sometimes fell short of the mark. Captain Austin, a stickler for detail, noted that student discipline during meals needed improvement. And no detail escaped his military eye: "Students continue to eat after bell rings and this together with the noise made by the knives and forks tinkling against the plates make it very difficult to hear the adjutant read the notices." In Austin's report to Booker Washington, which contained dining violations, he stated that the men students had become "careless in dress." He complained also about the behavior of women students in the dining hall. "The girls," Austin reported, "are exceedingly boisterous and rough when rising from their tables."

Search and seizure comprised part of the everyday life at Tuskegee. Men and women alike were searched for liquor, obscene materials, or anything else that in some way might contribute to the breakdown of rules or affect the school's "reputation." Searching of students' rooms and personal belongings became official policy at Tuskegee in 1906, when it was written into the School Code.

Booker Washington gave the students' social life the closest scrutiny. The institute forbade male and female students from associating after classes. The woman students received constant reminders from the Dean of Women to remain "moral and pure." This same advice was given to the men students by the Commandant of Cadets. Separate walkways across campus were designated for male and female to guarantee the two kept separated. Male students were forbidden to walk around or near the girls' dormitory after dusk. This was done, as one school official put it, to "prevent the promiscuous mingling of boys and girls."

Washington was working to make Tuskegee students into the type of blacks that the white South relished. Their training was primarily in "how to behave" rather than in how to become skilled tradesmen. To be a skilled craftsman requires proficiency in mathematical and verbal skills. The school's curriculum, however, was industrial almost to the total exclusion of the academic. What academic studies that did exist were secondary and often optional. That the school would commit itself to this type of program was clear from the staff that Washington employed at the school. Most of the faculty members were Hampton graduates, and they knew more about discipline than trades.

The *Southern Workman* reported that Hampton graduates held most of the key posts at Tuskegee Institute, noting the fact that the school's principal was "Hampton's most distinguished graduate." Washington issued a directive in 1908 to his departmental heads in which he stated that he wanted the school to "employ each year a reasonable number of Hampton graduates." He added that he "did not want the number of Hampton graduates decreased on the teaching force at Tuskegee."

The Founder was not completely close-minded in hiring personnel for teaching positions at Tuskegee, but instructors he hired from academic institutions often failed to fit well into his educational scheme because he subordinated every aspect of Tuskegee's educational program to the industrial schooling idea of producing tractable blacks. Blacks from academic universities like Howard, Fisk,

and Atlanta were employed at the school. Roscoe Conkling Bruce, a product of Harvard University who headed the so-called academic curriculum at Tuskegee, found that the institute's commitment to preparing students as common laborers was total. Bruce thought that perhaps some of the students might be material for professional careers. He complained about educating students "chiefly in accordance with the demands for labor."

Another thorn in Washington's side was a young instructor in the academic department named Leslie P. Hill, who had been hired by Bruce. Hill obviously failed to adjust to the second-class status of academic studies at Tuskegee. He initiated innovative approaches to his teaching of educational theory, history, and philosophy. However, the Founder regarded Hill as hostile to the educational philosophy of the school. Washington, in his explanation for firing Hill, remarked that the young Harvard graduate seemed to feel that the methods employed at Tuskegee were "either wrong or dangerous."

If he had many of the school's instructors in mind, Hill was absolutely right. Higher education at Tuskegee was a sad joke. Hill recognized that the general atmosphere discouraged serious effort among the industrial faculty. He noted that courses lacked outlines, instructors failed to use facilities properly, and that many of them lacked the competence to teach the skills for which they were hired.

Roscoe Bruce found the entire Tuskegee situation quite perplexing. He understood that Tuskegee was an industrial school—a fact, Bruce remarked, that he was "often reminded of." But he said that he failed to see how students who received little to no academic training would be able to carry on up-to-date craft positions. He wrote to the principal, "You see, the truth is that the carpenter is not taught enough mathematics, the machinist enough physics, or the farmer enough chemistry for the purpose of his particular work." Bruce also found it discouraging that there was no distinction made in the school's curriculum between those students who were going to be teachers and the ones "who plan to make horseshoes or to paint houses."

Washington conceded that some difficulties existed with the industrial idea of education, but that he had said so in his book, *Up From Slavery.*

> I told those who doubted the wisdom of the plan [industrial education] that I knew our first buildings would not be so comfortable or so complete in their finish as buildings erected by the experienced hands of outside workmen, but that in the teaching of civilization, self-help, and self-reliance, the erection of the buildings by the students themselves would more than compensate for any lack of comfort or fine finish.

His point, no doubt, was that problems are to be expected but they will be solved in time.

Regardless of what Booker T. said, Tuskegee was not preparing its students to take their place as skilled artisans in the industrial world. The school maintained a general policy of allowing students to graduate without even having finished a trade course. One report indicated that some positions calling for manual skills had become open to blacks in the South and that the opportunities for the Tuskegee graduates were "greater than ever," but that the students were not properly prepared for these jobs.

Roscoe C. Bruce reported to Washington on another separate occasion in which he complained that upon visiting the Girls' Laundry Department he was struck by the lack of any real skills training. Bruce said that the students did not seem to be receiving instruction in the art of the task but in fact simply performed menial chores.

W. T. B. Williams of the General Education Board conducted a survey of Tuskegee in 1906 and concluded that the student who completed the course of studies had what might be equivalent to a ninth grade education in the public school system. He considered there to be a general lack of training and preparation at the school. In addition, said Williams, "the majority of the students are barely able to read the Bible." He said in conclusion, "Considering the elementary nature of much of this work and the maturity of the students, the daily requirements seem pretty light."

The lack of quality in instruction and academic training at Tuskegee drove Roscoe Bruce to resign in 1906. Washington replaced him with J. R. E. Lee, who fit well into the Tuskegee idea. But Lee's own correspondence reveals the lack of serious academic or skills education at the school. Lee noted that the students who had attended one or two years of education at the general education schools, such as Fisk or Atlanta, were able to go immediately to the senior ranks at Tuskegee. Lee admitted that the work required of students at those schools was "far above the work required here [at Tuskegee]."

The lack of a positive, achievement-oriented atmosphere at Tuskegee had a negative effect on students and teachers. In 1912, one Tuskegee instructor openly admitted that the students they produced were ill-equipped to pursue a skilled occupation in industry. He thought that perhaps the problem lay with the teachers. He begged that they "give more time and attention" to their duties.

Instructors, on the other hand, blamed the problem on the students. Teachers in the industrial classes claimed that the students lacked the necessary attitude to become tradesmen, that they took their assignments lightly and performed them poorly. The instructor in basic construction and design accused the students of not following floor plans and of being sloppy and lazy in the performance of their tasks.

However, the teachers seemed more preoccupied with social matters than with correcting their students' deficiencies. "The young women teachers engage in frivolities hardly in keeping with their calling," W. T. B. Williams reported. "They are good women but not seriously concerned about the work in hand. They seem to give far more attention to dress rather than to almost anything else...."

The female instructors were not alone. The men could stand on their own in terms of being frivolous. They repeatedly hosted gala social outings. One example was the going away party for Booker T. Washington, Jr., given in his honor by the faculty men. It was an elaborate and extravagant affair with orchestra, "seating arrangements patterned after that in the Cabinet Room of the White House," and dinner crowned with "Fried Chicken, Booker T. Washington, Jr. Style."

After a visit to Tuskegee in 1904, Robert Curtis Ogden commented on the "peculiar" social attitude of the school's faculty. He and his other white companions had been guests of honor at a faculty-hosted concert of classical music. Ogden, commenting later to Booker Washington about the concert, said that he believed his guests appreciated the entertainment, but that they would have enjoyed seeing more of the teachers and students at work rather than watching their hosts do their "level best to be like white folks and not natural."

Tuskegee's faculty was imitative of whites, but they were black and not the omnipotent authority symbol that, for example, Hampton's all-white staff was to its students. Tuskegee students, justifiably, found faults with the faculty, the education they received, and the conditions of campus life. They voiced their displeasure. The class in agricultural science at Tuskegee was taught by the renowned George Washington Carver, and he could not escape the growing discontent among students. One student complained that he had come to Tuskegee to learn the most advanced techniques in farming from George Washington Carver but found that the professor seemed to be more interested in producing "hired hands." The student remarked that overall he felt that he was "not receiving progressive instruction."

In addition, students challenged the strict discipline of the school in subtle ways. Julio Despaigne, Washington's key informant in the dorms, reported, "The students have the habit of making their beds at the morning good for when the inspector comes that he can find it well, and in the afternoon they disorder them and put clean and dirty clothes on them."

The rebellion of the students against the oppressive social restrictions of the institute manifested itself in different subtle ways. Some students began skipping chapel to meet with members of the opposite sex. Others volunteered for duties that held a high likelihood of putting them in contact with the opposite sex; a favorite assignment among male and female students was night duty at the school's hospital. Those fortunate enough to draw that duty were on their honor not to fraternize. The administration, however, soon found out the hospital was being used as a place for social carousing. Walter McFadden and Katie Paterson received an official reprimand from the administration "for questionable socializing while on night duty together at the hospital."

Some male students placed latches on their doors to keep night inspectors from entering while they, allegedly, broke school rules. This was met with quick action on the part of the administration. The Executive Council decided that because of

> the misconduct, gambling and so forth, which is indulged in on the part of certain young men who place night latches on their doors and lock themselves into their rooms from teachers' and officers' attempts to get into the room and who jump out of the windows before they can be detected in their mischief: because of this it has been found necessary to remove all the night latches from the doors.

The women students of the laundry class asserted themselves against unfair practices. They could not understand why they should be paid less than their labor was worth. They objected to the hard work with low pay. The young women said that they had the work of both students and teachers to do including that of the summer teachers and that on one occasion they had remained until five o'clock on Saturday evening in order to supply the boys with their week's laundry. "We hope you will not think of us as complainers," they closed in their letter to Booker Washington, "but, simply as children striving to perform their duty; and, at the same time receive some recompense in return. We are asking for higher wages. May we have it?" The Founder's answer was to appoint a committee to investigate their complaint, with the quiet result that nothing ever came of it.

The students' discontent gradually gave way to outright hostility against the school. Students stole from the institution, broke windows, wrecked dormitories, defaced walls, and on several occasions debased the school chapel. Some tried to avoid school and work by pretending to be ill. The institute's physician reported to Booker Washington, "I wish you also to bear in mind that a large number of the students who come to the hospital are not calling because they are ill, but are simply giving way to some imaginary ills, or else taking advantage of the easy method of losing an hour or two from work." One student spoke bluntly to Washington about the feeling among many of the students that to be successful at the school it was required to become "slaves of you [Mr. Washington] and Tuskegee." A group of native-born African students, accused of challenging the authority of one of their instructors and later brought before Washington for discipline, criticized the education they were receiving at Tuskegee and the attitude of teachers, including the Founder himself, who they said "acted as a master ordering his slaves." They concluded: "We do not intend no longer to remain in your institution...."

Students openly rebelled against the school's disciplinary practices. Charles H. Washington, a member of the senior class, considered the prying eyes of the faculty into every aspect of the individual student's private life to be too much for him. He told a faculty member point-blank to pass on the word that they "are to cease meddling with his affairs."

During the last ten years of Washington's reign at Tuskegee, from 1905 to his death in 1915, faculty members alluded to a growing student hostility against them. They became fearful for their personal safety, believing that students were carrying weapons and ready to use them. The situation at Tuskegee became more tense with the passing of each day. Students acted discourteously to instructors in and out of class. A group of faculty members reported to Washington that pupils had become so rebellious that they "never felt safe in appearing before the students."

In the tradition of the overseer whose position is dependent upon his ability to keep those under his charge in line, Washington met student discontent each step of the way with a tightening of rules and regulations. But student unrest continued. The result was that discipline at Tuskegee during the latter part of his administration approached absurdity. Students were suspended for talking without permission, failing to dress according to standards, or even for "failing to take a napkin to the dining hall." Young men students were chastised for "putting their hands in their pockets," and failing to obey that rule, the administration sought to offer "such inducements as will make them do so."

That the punishment students received outweighed the offense is clearly indicated in the case of Lewis Smith, whom a fellow student accused of "over indiscrete conduct with Emma Penny of the same class." Smith, a senior and slated to graduate as class salutatorian, was brought before the administration for allegedly attempting to hug and kiss Miss Penny. Although he denied the charges and his testimony was substantiated by a fellow classmate, the administration saw fit to punish Smith. He was denied the distinction of graduating as class salutatorian.

Smith was lucky. He could have been suspended or expelled—favorite disciplinary measures during the latter years of Booker T.'s rule over Tuskegee Institute. A case in point is the 1912 flag incident. A few members of the senior class of that year decided to celebrate by flying their class flag over Tompkins Hall. They made the unpardonable mistake, however, of not obtaining the administration's permission. School officials considered the students' act a conspiracy against the institute's authority, an "organized movement on the part of some of the members of the senior class... and that this was not carried out on the spur of the moment." The accused students begged for mercy and swore that they acted out of no intent to challenge school authority or embarrass the administration. One of the accused vowed they would rather have had their "heads severed from their bodies" than to do anything against Tuskegee. The young men were suspended.

The slightest infraction on the part of the student, or even suspicion of having broken a rule, was reason enough for the Washington administration to notify parents. This had near disastrous results in the case of Charles Bell, a senior who was brought before the administration on the suspicion of having engaged in "sexual misconduct" with a young woman named Varner of the same class. Both denied the charges. There was no eyewitness testimony or other "proof" that Bell and Varner had done anything wrong, except the fact that they were often seen together. The administration, nevertheless, passed its suspicions on to

Miss Varner's father. He showed up later on campus with his gun, saying that he would shoot Bell on sight. Bell was forced to leave the institute until the situation quieted.

When Tuskegee students did pose a real threat to the sovereignty of Booker Washington, he showed no mercy. In 1903, a group of Tuskegee students launched a strike against the school. The material on the strike, and it is extremely sketchy, does indicate that the participants objected to the entire Tuskegee order of things. They wanted more academic training, better instruction, more opportunity to learn trades, and an easing of rules and regulations. Washington's response was undiluted: "No concessions."

In an official but insubstantial report on the strike to the school's white financial backers, Booker T. contended that a few malcontents had occupied one of the school's buildings, thinking that this was the way to be heard. The students were not upset with the institute, he said, "nor were they in opposition to any industrial work," but "objected to being required to devote too much time to both industrial work and studies with too little time for preparation." The strike apparently ended as quickly as it had begun once the administration served notice that all those who failed to return to work immediately would be expelled.

Those who obtained an "education" at Tuskegee did so in accordance with the industrial schooling idea and under the watchful eyes of Booker Taliaferro Washington. Student dissatisfaction did nothing to change the Founder's mind about the rightness of the type of educational philosophy he professed and protected. His administration practiced a stiff brand of discipline that it never backed down from. But students, on occasion, contin-ued to try and voice their complaints. Perhaps it is understandable, then, why the Washington administration felt it might be necessary to establish a "guard house" for the purpose of confining its student incorrigibles. It did just that in 1912.

Booker T.'s educational practices were based on his desire to please whites and gain their support. The Founder worked to make whites more a part of the school's operations. He invited them to visit the institute on every occasion. He believed that the school's annual commencement exercises afforded an excellent opportunity to win goodwill from the local whites. "I think it would be well for you to spend a week in Montgomery among the white and colored people," Washington advised a fellow faculty member. "I am very anxious that in addition to the colored people we have a large representative class of whites to attend Commencement." In fact, the Founder considered paying the fares of white visitors to the commencement exercises. The school advertised the commencement of 1904 in the *Tuskegee News*.

Washington did everything possible to bring in more local white support. When Washington received advice from a "reliable source" that if he kept the number of Jews down in attendance at commencement, more local whites would probably come, he responded: "Of course I do not want to keep the Jews away, but I think it would be a good plan to increase the number of Gentiles if possible."

The Founder received unsolicited advice on how to gain more local and national support. One Northerner wrote him suggesting that the school would gain more support if it devoted itself exclusively to the production of domestic servants. The writer suggested that the program should stress "cooking, waiting on table, cleaning silver and washing windows, sewing, dusting, washing and ironing."

In his response, Washington made it clear that Tuskegee did this and more:

At this institution we give training in every line of domestic work, hence any girl who finishes our course should be able to perform any of the usual duties connected with a servant's life, but one of the most important things to be accomplished for the colored people now is the getting of them to have correct ideas concerning labor, that is to get them to feel that all classes of labor, whether of the head or hand, are dignified. This lesson I think Tuskegee, in connection with Hampton, has been successful in teaching the race.

And, like Hampton, Tuskegee aimed to do more than serve as an agency to place individual domestics. Washington in conclusion said that the most economical thing to be done was to send out a set of people not only trained in hand but thoroughly equipped in mind and heart so that they themselves could go out and start smaller centers or training schools.

He believed that it would be of greater service to the whole country "if we can train at Tuskegee one girl who could go out and start a domestic training school in Atlanta, Baltimore, or elsewhere, than we would be doing by trying to put servants directly into individual houses which would be a never ending task." ...

Booker T. Washington never intentionally did anything to upset or anger Southern whites. He repledged his love for the South and his obedience to its traditions in *My Larger Education*, published four years before his death. The Founder said in that work, "I understand thoroughly the prejudices, the customs, the traditions of the South—and, strange as it may seem to those who do not wholly understand the situation, I love the South." The philosophy of "uplift" for blacks that he preached across the nation and taught at Tuskegee Institute was in accordance with that love and the prevailing racial, economic order. His role was like that of the black overseer during slavery who, given the position of authority over his fellow slaves, worked diligently to keep intact the very system under which they both were enslaved.

NO

Louis R. Harlan

BOOKER T. WASHINGTON AND THE POLITICS OF ACCOMMODATION

It is ironic that Booker T. Washington, the most powerful black American of his time and perhaps of all time, should be the black leader whose claim to the title is most often dismissed by the lay public. Blacks often question his legitimacy because of the role that favor by whites played in Washington's assumption of power, and whites often remember him only as an educator or, confusing him with George Washington Carver, as "that great Negro scientist." This irony is something that Washington will have to live with in history, for he himself deliberately created the ambiguity about his role and purposes that has haunted his image. And yet, Washington was a genuine black leader, with a substantial black following and with virtually the same long-range goals for Afro-Americans as his rivals. This presentation is concerned with Washington's social philosophy, such as it was, but it also addresses his methods of leadership, both his Delphic public utterances that meant one thing to whites and another to blacks and his adroit private movements through the brier patch of American race relations. It does not try to solve the ultimate riddle of his character.

Washington's own view of himself was that he was the Negro of the hour, whose career and racial program epitomized what blacks needed to maintain themselves against white encroachments and to make progress toward equality in America. The facts of his life certainly fitted his self-image. He was the last of the major black leaders to be born in slavery, on a small farm in western Virginia in 1856. Growing up during the Reconstruction era in West Virginia, he believed that one of the lessons he learned was that the Reconstruction experiment in racial democracy failed because it began at the wrong end, emphasizing political means and civil rights acts rather than economic means and self-determination. Washington learned this lesson not so much through experiences as a child worker in the salt works and coal mines as by what he was taught as a houseboy for the leading family of Malden, West Virginia, and later as a student at Hampton Institute in Virginia. Hampton

From Louis R. Harlan, "Booker T. Washington and the Politics of Accommodation," in John Hope Franklin and August Meier, eds., *Black Leaders of the Twentieth Century* (University of Illinois Press, 1982). Copyright © 1982 by the Board of Trustees of the University of Illinois. Reprinted by permission of the author and University of Illinois Press.

applied the missionary method to black education and made its peace with the white South.

After teaching school in his home town, Washington briefly studied in a Baptist seminary and in a lawyer's office. But he soon abandoned these alternative careers, perhaps sensing that disfranchisement and the secularization of society would weaken these occupations as bases for racial leadership. He returned to Hampton Institute as a teacher for two years and then founded Tuskegee Normal and Industrial Institute in Alabama in 1881. Over the next quarter of a century, using Hampton's methods but with greater emphasis on the skilled trades, Washington built up Tuskegee Institute to be an equal of Hampton.

Washington's bid for leadership went beyond education and institution-building, however. Symbolic of his fresh approach to black-white relations was a speech he gave in 1895 before a commercial exposition, known as the Atlanta Compromise Address, and his autobiography, *Up from Slavery* (1901). As Washington saw it, blacks were toiling upward from slavery by their own efforts into the American middle class and needed chiefly social peace to continue in this steady social evolution. Thus, in the Atlanta Compromise he sought to disarm the white South by declaring agitation of the social equality question "the merest folly" and proclaiming that in "purely social" matters "we can be as separate as the fingers, yet one as the hand in all things essential to mutual progress." These concessions came to haunt Washington as southerners used segregation as a means of systematizing discrimination, and northerners followed suit. And they did not stop at the "purely social."

Washington's concessions to the white South, however, were only half of a bargain. In return for downgrading civil and political rights in the black list of priorities, Washington asked whites to place no barriers to black economic advancement and even to become partners of their black neighbors "in all things essential to mutual progress." Washington saw his own role as the axis between the races, the only leader who could negotiate and keep the peace by holding extremists on both sides in check. He was always conscious that his unique influence could be destroyed in an instant of self-indulgent flamboyance.

Washington sought to influence whites, but he never forgot that it was the blacks that he undertook to lead. He offered blacks not the empty promises of the demagogue but a solid program of economic and educational progress through struggle. It was less important "just now," he said, for a black person to seek admission to an opera house than to have the money for the ticket. Mediating diplomacy with whites was only half of Washington's strategy; the other half was black solidarity, mutual aid, and institution-building. He thought outspoken complaint against injustice was necessary but insufficient, and he thought factional dissent among black leaders was self-defeating and should be suppressed

Washington brought to his role as a black leader the talents and outlook of a machine boss. He made Tuskegee Institute the largest and best-supported black educational institution of his day, and it spawned a large network of other industrial schools. Tuskegee's educational function is an important and debatable subject, of course, but the central concern here is Washington's use of the school as the base of operations of what came to be known as the Tuskegee Machine. It was an all-black school with an all-black faculty at a time when most black colleges were still run by white missionaries. Tuskegee taught self-determination. It also taught trades designed for economic independence in a region dominated by sharecrop agriculture. At the same time, by verbal juggling tricks, Washington convinced the southern whites that Tuskegee was not educating black youth away from the farms. Tuskegee also functioned as a model black community, not only by acquainting its students with a middle-class way of life, but by buying up the surrounding farmland and selling it at low rates of interest to create a community of small landowners and homeowners. The Institute became larger than the town.

Washington built a regional constituency of farmers, artisans, country teachers, and small businessmen; he expanded the Tuskegee Machine nationwide after the Atlanta Compromise seemed acceptable to blacks all over the country, even by many who later denounced it. His first northern black ally was T. Thomas Fortune, editor of the militant and influential New York *Age* and founder of the Afro-American Council, the leading forum of black thought at the time. Washington was not a member, but he usually spoke at the annual meetings, and his lieutenants so tightly controlled the council that it never passed an action or resolution not in Washington's interest. Seeking more direct allies, Washington founded in 1900 the National Negro Business League, of which he was president for life. The league was important not so much for what it did for black business, which was little, but because the local branch of the league was a stronghold of Washington men in every substantial black population center.

Other classes of influential blacks did not agree with Washington's stated philosophy but were beholden to him for the favors he did them or offered to do for them. He was not called the Wizard for nothing. White philanthropists who approved of him for their own reasons gave him the money to help black colleges by providing for a Carnegie library here, a dormitory there. Through Washington Andrew Carnegie alone gave buildings to twenty-nine black schools. Not only college administrators owed him for favors, but so did church leaders, YMCA directors and many others. Though never much of a joiner, he became a power in the Baptist church, and he schemed through lieutenants to control the secret black fraternal orders and make his friends the high potentates of the Pythians, Odd Fellows, and so on. Like any boss, he turned every favor into a bond of obligation.

It was in politics, however, that Washington built the most elaborate tentacle of the octopus-like Tuskegee Machine. In politics as in everything else, Washington cultivated ambiguity. He downgraded politics as a solution of black problems, did not recommend politics to the ambitious young black man, and never held office. But when Theodore Roosevelt became president in 1901 and asked for Washington's advice on black and southern appointments, Washington consented with alacrity. He became the chief black adviser of both Presidents Roosevelt and William Howard Taft. He failed in his efforts to liberalize Republican policy on voting rights, lynching, and racial discrimination, however, and relations between the Republican party and black voters reached a low ebb.

In patronage politics, however, Washington found his opportunity. For a man who minimized the importance of politics, Washington devoted an inordinate amount of his time and tremendous energy to securing federal jobs for his machine lieutenants. These men played a certain role in the politics of the period, but their first obligation was to the Tuskegean. Washington advised the presidents to replace the old venal officeholding class of blacks with men who had proven themselves in the independent world of business, but in practice it took only loyalty to Washington to cleanse miraculously an old-time political hack.

Washington also used high political office in the North to win the loyalty of key figures in the legal profession whose ideology and natural bent were usually in the direction of more outspoken protest. A notable example was William H. Lewis of Boston, a graduate of Amherst College and Harvard University Law School, who had been an outspoken critic of Washington. President Roosevelt had long admired Lewis's all-American prowess on the football field as much as his professional attainments, and when Washington began talking of raising the quality of the black civil service, Roosevelt brought up Lewis. Washington was skeptical, but as soon as possible he met with Lewis and made a deal with him. As Lewis wrote, there were "many things about which we might differ, but that we had the same aims and the same end in view." Lewis became, with Washington's blessing, the assistant U.S. district attorney in Boston, and a few years later Taft appointed him assistant attorney general of the United States, the highest appointive federal post held by a black man up to that time—and for decades afterward.

In another sphere also Washington spread the web of his Tuskegee Machine over the several hundred black weekly newspapers and half-dozen magazines through which the black community communicated with itself. W. E. B. Du Bois tried in 1903 to prove that Washington's "hush money" controlled the black press through subsidies and outright ownership. Challenged, Du Bois could not prove his case, but when Washington's papers were opened forty years later, they revealed the essential accuracy of the charge. The question of how *much* control is complicated, however, by the willing complicity of the editors in this domination. The editors were themselves small businessmen who generally agreed with Washington's economic orientation and the conventional wisdom of a commercial age. Furthermore, Washington's small subsidies, except in a few instances, were only a minor part of the operating funds of these newspapers.

Washington's outright critics and enemies were called "radicals" because they challenged Washington's conservatism and bossism, though their tactics of verbal protest would seem moderate indeed to a later generation of activists. They were the college-educated blacks, engaged in professional pursuits, and proud of their membership in an elite class—what one of them called the Talented Tenth. The strongholds of the radicals were the northern cities and southern black colleges. They stood for full political and civil rights, liberal education, free expression, and aspiration. They dreamed of a better world and believed Booker T. Washington was a menace to its achievement.

The first to challenge Washington and all his works was a young Harvard graduate, William Monroe Trotter, who founded in 1900 a newspaper, the Boston *Guardian*. Trotter not only differed with the Tuskegean on every conceivable subject but engaged in personal abuse. He spoke of Washington's "crime of race ridicule and belittlement." He called him Pope Washington, The Black Boss, the Benedict Arnold of the Negro race, the Exploiter of Exploiters, the Great Traitor, and the Great Divider. In reporting a speech by Washington in Boston in 1902 Trotter described him thus: "His features were harsh in the extreme. His vast leonine jaws into which vast mastiff-like rows of teeth were set clinched together like a vise. His forehead shot up to a great cone; his chin was massive and square; his eyes were dull and absolutely characterless, and with a glance that would leave you uneasy and restless during the night if you had failed to report to the police such a man around before you went to bed." That this yellow journalism was far from an accurate description of Washington's modest and reassuring appearance was beside the point. In Trotter's vendetta against Washington no charge, true or false, was too big or too petty to use.

Trotter seized the chance to confront Washington directly when the black leader spoke at a Boston church in 1903 under sponsorship of the local branch of the National Negro Business League. Trotter stood on a chair to interrupt Washington's speech with nine questions that were actually challenges. Quoting from a Washington speech, for example, Trotter asked: "When you said: 'It was not so important whether the Negro was in the inferior car as whether there was in that car a superior man not a beast,' did you not minimize the outrage of the insulting Jim-crow car discrimination and justify it by the 'bestiality' of the Negro?" The final provocative question was: "Are the rope and the torch all the race is to get under your leadership?"

The police moved through the crowd to arrest Trotter for disorderly conduct, and Washington proceeded with his speech as though nothing had happened, but Trotter had achieved his purpose. The incident appeared next day in all the newspapers as the Boston Riot, penetrating Washington's news screen to show that not all blacks approved of Washington's leadership. Washington publicly ignored the affair, but his Boston lieutenants made a martyr of Trotter by vigorous prosecution of his case, forcing him to serve thirty days in jail.

Perhaps the most important effect of the Boston Riot was that it forced Du Bois, the leading black intellectual and now the leading civil rights champion of his generation, off the fence. A Harvard Ph.D. with German university training, Du Bois was never even considered for tenure in any leading American university, and in 1903 he was a professor at Atlanta University. In *The Souls of Black Folk*, published before the Boston Riot, he had criticized Washington in a searching but moderate way, in no way comparable with Trotter's cry that the emperor had no clothes. Believing that Trotter was being victimized, Du Bois wrote Trotter a private letter of sympathy, which Trotter promptly published, and this started Du Bois's movement out of academe into the arena of racial politics.

Washington has a chance in January 1904 to heal the wounds of dissidence that the Boston Riot has opened. With the consent and cooperation of Du Bois, Washington convened the Carnegie Hall Conference, a three-day secret meeting of about thirty black leaders, excluding Trotter. But Washington with his penchant for bossism torpedoed his own effort at rapprochement by packing the meeting with his own lieutenants to such a degree that Du Bois and his adherents resigned from the organization that was created at the conference.

The following year, Du Bois and Trotter formed their own organization, the Niagara Movement, dedicated to "persistent manly agitation" for civil rights, voting rights, job opportunities, equal educational opportunities, and human rights in general. The Niagara Movement is an important link in the historical development of the civil rights movement, but here we are concerned with its role in the minority-group leadership struggle with Washington. This small band of intellectuals, hurling their manifestos, was no match for the political skill and marshaled power of the Wizard of Tuskegee. They themselves limited their membership to the small black professional class, insisted on an ideological "likemindedness" that few could achieve, and had no white allies. By contrast, Washington had a broader base and a commoner touch. Though Washington proposed the leadership of another elite class, the black businessmen, he kept in close touch with the black masses and directed his program to their immediate needs. Furthermore, he fished for allies wherever he could find them, among whites and even among the professional men who would ordinarily be expected in the Niagara Movement. He cared little about the ideology of a lieutenant, as long as the man did what Washington wanted done.

The Niagara Movement called Washington, in effect, a puppet of the whites, who thrust him into prominence because he did not challenge their wrongdoing. According to the Niagarites, Washington needed to mollify the whites in be-

half of his school to such an extent that he was rendered unfit for black leadership, that instead of leadership he gave them cowardice and apology. Furthermore, his critics charged that Washington was a half-educated southerner whose control over black affairs was stifling an emergent black educated elite, the Talented Tenth, the logical leaders. Because of his own class orientation he was trying to change the social position of blacks through the acquisitive propensities and the leadership of businessmen instead of through political and civil rights agitation, which the Niagara men saw as the need of the hour. Extremists among them called Washington an instrument of white indirect rule, like the slave drivers of the old days. Even the moderate Kelly Miller of Howard University observed in 1903 that Washington was "not a leader of the people's own choosing." Though they might accept his gifts, said Miller, "few thoughtful colored men espouse what passes as Mr. Washington's policy without apology or reserve."

Washington dismissed his black critics by questioning their motives, their claim to superior wisdom, and—the politician's ultimate argument—their numbers. Washington understood, if his critics did not, that his leadership of the black community largely depended on his recognition by whites as the black leader. If he did not meet some minimal standards of satisfactoriness to whites, another Washington would be created. He obviously could not lead the whites; he could not even divide the whites. He could only, in a limited way, exploit the class divisions that whites created among themselves. He could work in the cracks of their social structure, move like Brer Rabbit through the brier patch, and thus outwit the more numerous and powerful whites.

While Washington recognized the centrality of black-white relations in his efforts to lead blacks, he was severely restricted by the historical context of his leadership. It was an age of polarization of black and white. The overheated atmosphere of the South at the turn of the century resembled that of a crisis center on the eve of war. Lynching became a more than weekly occurrence; discrimination and humiliation of blacks were constant and pervasive and bred a whole literature and behavioral science of self-justification. Race riots terrorized blacks in many cities, and not only in the South. It would have required not courage but foolhardiness for Washington, standing with both feet in Alabama, to have challenged this raging white aggression openly and directly. Even unqualified verbal protest would have brought him little support from either southern blacks or white well-wishers. Du Bois took higher ground and perhaps a better vision of the future when he urged forthright protest against every white injustice, on the assumption that whites were rational beings and would respond dialectically to black protest. But few white racists of the early twentieth century cared anything for the facts. And when Du Bois in his Atlanta years undertook to implement his protest with action, he was driven to the negative means of refusing to pay his poll tax or refusing to ride segregated streetcars and elevators.

Instead of either confronting all of white America or admitting that his Faustian bargain for leadership had created a systemic weakness in his program, Washington simply met each day as it came, pragmatically, seeking what white allies he could against avowed white enemies. A serious fault of this policy was that Washington usually appealed for white support on a basis of a vaguely conceived mutual interest rather than on ideological agreement. For example, in both the South and the North Washington allied himself with the white upper class against the masses. In the South he joined with the planter class and when possible with the coal barons and railroad officials against the populists and other small white farmer groups who seemed to him to harbor the most virulent anti-black attitudes born of labor competition. Similarly, in the North, Washington admired and bargained with the big business class. The bigger the businessman, the more Washington admired him, as the avatar and arbiter of American society. At the pinnacle in his measure of men were the industrialists Carnegie, John D. Rockefeller, and Henry H. Rogers and the merchant princes Robert C. Ogden and Julius Rosenwald. To be fair to Washington, he appreciated their philanthropic generosity at least as much as he admired their worldly success, but his lips were sealed against criticism of even the more rapacious and ungenerous members of the business elite.

Washington made constructive use of his philanthropic allies to aid not only Tuskegee but black education and black society as a whole. He guided the generous impulse of a Quaker millionairess into the Anna T. Jeanes Foundation to improve the teaching in black public schools. He persuaded the Jewish philanthropist Julius Rosenwald to begin a program that lasted for decades for building more adequate black schoolhouses all over the South. Washington's influence on Carnegie, Rockefeller, Jacob Schiff, and other rich men also transcended immediate Tuskegee interests to endow other black institutions. In short, Washington did play a role in educational statesmanship. There were limits, however, to his power to advance black interests through philanthropy. When his northern benefactors became involved in the Southern Education Board to improve the southern public school systems, for example, he worked repeatedly but without success to get this board to redress the imbalance of public expenditures or even to halt the rapid increase of discrimination against black schools and black children. He had to shrug off his failure and get from these so-called philanthropists whatever they were willing to give.

Having committed himself to the business elite, Washington took a dim view of the leaders of the working class. Immigrants represented to him, as to many blacks, labor competitors; Jews were the exception here, as he held them up to ambitious blacks as models of the work-ethic and group solidarity. He claimed in his autobiography that his disillusionment with labor unions went back to his youthful membership in the Knights of Labor and stemmed from observation of their disruption of the natural laws of economics. In his heyday, however, which was also the age of Samuel Gompers, Washington's anti-union attitudes were explained by the widespread exclusion of blacks from membership in many unions and hence from employment in many trades. There is no evidence that Washington ever actively supported black strikebreaking, but his refusal to intervene in behalf of all-white unions is understandable. It was more often white employees rather than employers who excluded blacks,

or so Washington believed. He worked hard to introduce black labor into the non-union, white-only cotton mills in the South, even to the extent of interesting northern capitalists in investing in black cotton mills and similar enterprises.

Washington was a conservative by just about any measure. Though he flourished in the Progressive era it was not he, but his opponents who were the men of good hope, full of reform proposals and faith in the common man. Washington's vision of the common man included the southern poor white full of rancor against blacks, the foreign-born anarchist ready to pull down the temple of American business, and the black sharecropper unqualified by education or economic freedom for the ballot. Though Washington opposed the grandfather clause and every other southern device to exclude the black man from voting solely on account of his color, Washington did not favor universal suffrage. He believed in literacy and property tests, fairly enforced. He was no democrat. And he did not believe in woman suffrage, either.

In his eagerness to establish common ground with whites, that is, with some whites, Washington overstepped his purpose in public speeches by telling chicken-thief, mule, and other dialect stories intended to appeal to white stereotypes of blacks, and he occasionally spoke of the Afro-American as "a child race." No doubt his intent was to disarm his listeners, and before mixed audiences he often alternately addressed the two groups, reassuring whites that blacks should cooperate with their white neighbors in all constructive efforts, but saying to blacks that in their cooperation there should be "no unmanly cowering or stooping." At the cost of some forcefulness of presentation, Washington did have a remarkable capacity to convince whites as well as blacks that he not only understood them but agreed with them. It is one of Washington's intangible qualities as a black leader that he could influence, if not lead, so many whites. The agreement that whites sensed in him was more in his manner than in his program or goals, which always included human rights as well as material advancement for blacks.

In his constant effort to influence public opinion, Washington relied on the uncertain instruments of the press and the public platform. A flood of books and articles appeared over his name, largely written by his private secretary and a stable of ghostwriters, because he was too busy to do much writing. His ghostwriters were able and faithful, but they could not put new words or new ideas out over his signature, so for the crucial twenty years after 1895, Washington's writings showed no fresh creativity or real response to events, only a steady flood of platitudes. Washington's speeches generally suffered from an opposite handicap, that he was the only one who could deliver them. But he was too busy making two or three speeches a day to write a new one for each occasion, so the audiences rather than the speeches changed. But everywhere he went, North, South, or West, he drew large crowds ready to hear or rehear his platitudes.

Washington did try to change his world by other means. Some forms of racial injustice, such as lynching, disfranchisement, and unequal facilities in education and transportation, Washington dealt with publicly and directly. Early in his career as a leader he tried to sidestep the lynching question by saying that, deplorable though it was, he was too busy working for the education of black youth to divide his energies by dealing with other public questions. Friends and critics alike sharply told him that if he proposed to be a leader of blacks, he was going to have to deal with this subject. So he began an annual letter on lynching that he sent to all the southern white dailies, and he made Tuskegee Institute the center of statistical and news information on lynching. He always took a moderate tone, deplored rape and crime by blacks, but always denied that the crime blacks committed was either the cause of or justification for the crime of lynching. He tried to make up for his moderation by persistence, factual accuracy, and persuasive logic. Disfranchisement of black voters swept through the South from Texas to Virginia during Washington's day. He publicly protested in letters to the constitutional conventions and legislatures in Alabama, Georgia, and Louisiana and aided similar efforts in several other states. He failed to stop lynching, to prevent the loss of voting rights, and to clean up the Jim Crow cars or bring about even minimal standards of fairness in the public schools. But he did try.

As for social segregation, Washington abided by southern customs while in the South but forthrightly declared it unreasonable for white southerners to dictate his behavior outside of the South. His celebrated dinner at the White House in 1901, therefore, though it caused consternation and protest among white southerners, was consistent with his lifetime practice. Tuskegee Institute underwent an elaborate ritual of segregation with every white visitor, but the man who came to dinner at the White House, had tea with the queen of England, and attended hundreds of banquets and private meals with whites outside the South certainly never internalized the attitudes of the segregators.

What Washington could not do publicly to achieve equal rights, he sought to accomplish secretly. He spent four years in cooperation with the Afro-American Council on a court case to test the constitutionality of the Louisiana grandfather clause, providing funds from his own pocket and from northern white liberal friends. In his own state of Alabama, Washington secretly directed the efforts of his personal lawyer to carry two grandfather-clause cases all the way to the U.S. Supreme Court, where they were lost on technicalities. He took the extra precaution of using code names in all the correspondence on the Alabama cases. Through private pressure on railroad officials and congressmen, Washington tried to bring about improvement in the Jim Crow cars and railroad waiting rooms. He had more success in the Dan Rogers case, which overturned a criminal verdict against a black man because blacks were excluded from the jury. He also secretly collaborated with two southern white attorneys to defend Alonzo Bailey, a farm laborer held in peonage for debt; the outcome here was also successful, for the Alabama peonage law was declared unconstitutional. These and other secret actions were certainly not enough to tear down the legal structure of white supremacy, but they show that Washington's role in Afro-American history was not always that of the accommodationist "heavy." He was working, at several levels and in imaginative ways, and always with vigor, toward goals similar to those of his critics. If his methods did not work, the same could be said of theirs. And he did not take these civil rights actions as a means of answering criticism, because he kept his part in the court cases a se-

cret except to a handful of confidants, a secret not revealed until his papers were opened to historians in recent decades.

There was another, uglier side of Washington's secret behavior, however—his ruthless spying and sabotage against his leading black critics. Washington never articulated a justification for these actions, perhaps because, being secret, they did not require defense. And yet Washington and Emmett Scott left the evidence of his secret machinations undestroyed in his papers, apparently in the faith that history would vindicate him when all the facts were known. Then, too, Washington was not given to explaining himself....

Espionage became an important instrument of Washington's black leadership—or bossism—a few days before the Boston Riot in 1903, when he hired a young black man, Melvin J. Chisum, to infiltrate the inner councils of Trotter's anti-Washington organization in Boston. Chisum later spied on the Niagara Movement's Brooklyn branch, arranged to bribe an opposition newspaper editor in Washington, D.C., and reported these and other clandestine actions to the Wizard on a part bench in New York City. Washington also used Pinkerton detectives and other paid and unpaid secret agents on a variety of errands, to infiltrate the inner councils of the Niagara Movement, to repress newspaper reporting of Niagara meetings, to find out if Trotter's wife worked as a domestic, to research the tax records of Atlanta to get evidence that Du Bois, a champion of black political action, had not paid his poll tax. When a young black magazine editor, J. Max Barber, began to criticize him, Washington tried to muzzle Barber through his publisher and advertisers, then hounded Barber not only out of his magazine but out of job after job until Barber retired from race work to become a dentist. Even the white liberals who joined with the Niagara Movement to form the interracial National Association for the Advancement of Colored People in 1909 were not immune from Washington's secret attacks. Washington arranged with the racially biased New York newspaper reporters to cover—in a sensational fashion —a dinner meeting of the Cosmopolitan Club, an interracial social group to which a number of NAACP leaders belonged. Even they never guessed that Washington had done this in collusion with white racists.

The Booker T. Washington who emerges into the light of history from his private papers is a complex, Faustian character quite different from the paragon of self-uplift and Christian forbearance that Washington projected in his autobiography. On the other hand, there is little evidence for and much evidence against the charge of some of his contemporaries that he was simply an accommodationist who bargained away his race's birthright for a mess of pottage. Nor does he fit some historians' single-factor explanations of his career: that he offered "education for the new slavery," that he was a proto-black-nationalist, that he was or must have been psychologically crippled by the constraints and guilt feelings of his social role.

Washington's complexity should not be overstressed, however, for the more we know about anybody the more complex that person seems. And through the complexity of Washington's life, its busyness and its multiple levels, two main themes stand out, his true belief in his program for black progress and his great skill in and appetite for politics,

broadly defined, serving both his goals and his personal power.

First, let us look closely at Washington's industrial education and small business program. It may have been anachronistic preparation for the age of mass production and corporate gigantism then coming into being, but it had considerable social realism for a black population which was, until long after Washington's death, predominantly rural and southern. Furthermore, it was well attuned to the growth and changing character of black business in his day. Increasingly, the nineteenth-century black businesses catering to white clients surrendered predominance to ghetto businesses such as banks, insurance companies, undertakers, and barbers catering to black customers. These new businessmen, with a vested interest in black solidarity, were the backbone of Washington's National Negro Business League. Washington clearly found congenial the prospect of an elite class of self-made businessmen as leaders and models for the struggling masses. There was also room for the Talented Tenth of professional men in the Tuskegee Machine, however. Washington welcomed every college-educated recruit he could secure. Directly or through agents, he was the largest employer in the country of black college graduates.

Second, let us consider Washington as a powerful politician. Though he warned young men away from politics as a dead-end career, what distinguished Washington's career was not his rather conventional goals, which in public or private he shared with almost every other black spokesman, but his consummate political skill, his wheeling and dealing....

Du Bois spent much of his long life puzzling over the phenomenon of

Washington, a man who did not seem to have an abstraction about him. But toward the end of his life, in 1954 in an oral history memoir at Columbia University, Du Bois said of his old rival dead almost forty years: "Oh, Washington was a politician. He was a man who believed that we should get what we could get." Du Bois, who himself found the political part of his race work the least agreeable, went on to say of Washington: "It wasn't a matter of ideals or anything of that sort.... With everybody that Washington met, he evidently had the idea: 'Now, what's your racket? What are you out for?'" Du Bois was a shrewd observer, but what he saw in Washington as a lack—of ideals, of principles, of vision—was his great and almost unique gift as a black political leader. Washington could almost immediately, intuitively, and without formal questioning see through the masks and intellectual superstructure of men to the mainsprings of their behavior. Then he imaginatively sought to bend their purposes to his own. Du Bois said that Washington had no faith in white people but that he was very popular among them because, whenever he met a white man, he listened to him until he figured out what that man wanted him to say, and then as soon as possible he said it. Washington did not always get his way, of course, but he always understood, as his more doctrinaire critics did not, that politics was the art of the possible. What was surprising about Washington was the number and diversity of those he enlisted in his coalition.

Washington's program was not consensus politics, for he always sought change, and there was always vocal opposition to him on both sides that he never tried to mollify. Denounced on the one hand by the Niagara Movement and the NAACP for not protesting enough, he was also distrusted and denounced by white supremacists for bringing the wooden horse within the walls of Troy. All of the racist demagogues of his time—Benjamin Tillman, James Vardaman, Theodore Bilbo, Thomas Dixon, and J. Thomas Heflin, to name a few—called Washington their insidious enemy. One descriptive label for Washington might be centrist coalition politics. The Tuskegee Machine had the middle and undecided majority of white and black people behind it. Washington was a rallying point for the southern moderates, the northern publicists and makers of opinion, and the thousands who read his autobiography or crowded into halls to hear him. Among blacks he had the businessmen solidly behind him, and even, as August Meier has shown, a majority of the Talented Tenth of professional men, so great was his power to reward and punish, to make or break careers. He had access to the wellsprings of philanthropy, political preferment, and other white sources of black opportunity. For blacks at the bottom of the ladder, Washington's program offered education, a self-help formula, and, importantly for a group demoralized by the white aggression of that period, a social philosophy that gave dignity and purpose to lives of daily toil.

It could be said with some justification that the Tuskegee Machine was a stationary machine, that it went nowhere. Because the machine was held together by the glue of self-interest, Washington was frequently disappointed by the inadequate response of his allies. The southern upper class did not effectively resist disfranchisement as he had hoped and never gave blacks the equal economic chance that he considered an integral part of the Atlanta Compromise. Washington's philanthropist-friends never stood up for equal opportunity in public education. Black businessmen frequently found their own vested interest in a captive market rather than a more open society. And Washington himself often took the view that whatever was good for Tuskegee and himself was good for the Negro.

To the charge that he accomplished nothing, it can only be imagined what Washington would have answered, since he did not have the years of hindsight and self-justification that some of his critics enjoyed. He would probably have stressed how much worse the southern racial reaction would have been without his coalition of moderates, his soothing syrup, and his practical message to blacks of self-improvement and progress along the lines of least resistance. Washington's power over his following, and hence his power to bring about change, have probably been exaggerated. It was the breadth rather than the depth of his coalition that was unique. Perhaps one Booker T. Washington was enough. But even today, in a very different society, Washington's autobiography is still in print. It still has some impalpable power to bridge the racial gap, to move new readers to take the first steps across the color line. Many of his ideas of self-help and racial solidarity still have currency in the black community. But he was an important leader because, like Frederick Douglass before him and Martin Luther King after him, he had the program and strategy and skill to influence the behavior of not only the Afro-American one-tenth, but the white nine-tenths of the American people. He was a political realist.

POSTSCRIPT

Did Booker T. Washington's Philosophy and Actions Betray the Interests of African Americans?

Discussions of race relations in the late-nineteenth- and early-twentieth-century United States invariably focus upon the ascendancy of Booker T. Washington, his apparent accommodation to existing patterns of racial segregation, and the conflicting traditions within black thought, epitomized by the clash between Washington and Du Bois. Seldom, however, is attention given to black nationalist thought in the "age of Booker T. Washington."

Black nationalism, centered on the concept of racial solidarity, has been a persistent theme in African American history, and it reached one of its most important stages of development between 1880 and 1920. In the late 1800s Henry McNeal Turner and Edward Wilmot Blyden encouraged greater interest in the repatriation of black Americans to Africa, especially Liberia. This goal continued into the twentieth century and culminated in the "Back-to-Africa" program of Marcus Garvey and his Universal Negro Improvement Association. Interestingly, Booker T. Washington also exhibited nationalist sentiment by encouraging blacks to withdraw from white society, develop their own institutions and businesses, and engage in economic and moral uplift. Washington's nationalism concentrated on economic self-help and manifested itself in 1900 with the establishment of the National Negro Business League.

A thorough assessment of the protest and accommodationist views of black Americans is presented in August Meier, *Negro Thought in America, 1800–1915* (University of Michigan Press, 1963). Rayford Logan, in *The Betrayal of the Negro: From Rutherford B. Hayes to Woodrow Wilson* (Macmillan, 1965), describes the last quarter of the nineteenth century as "the nadir" for black life. By far the best studies of Booker T. Washington are two volumes by Louis R. Harlan: *Booker T. Washington: The Making of a Black Leader, 1856–1901* (Oxford University Press, 1972) and *Booker T. Washington: The Wizard of Tuskegee, 1901–1915* (Oxford University Press, 1983). In addition, Harlan has edited the 13-volume *Booker T. Washington Papers* (University of Illinois Press, 1972–1984). For assessments of two of Booker T. Washington's harshest critics, see David Levering Lewis, *W. E. B. Du Bois: Biography of a Race, 1868–1919* (Henry Holt, 1993), the first of a projected two-volume study, and Stephen R. Fox, *The Guardian of Boston: William Monroe Trotter* (Atheneum, 1970). John H. Bracey, Jr., August Meier, and Elliott Rudwick, in *Black Nationalism in America* (Bobbs-Merrill, 1970), provide an invaluable collection of documents pertaining to black nationalism. See also Edwin S. Redkey, *Black Exodus: Black Nationalist and Back-to-Africa Movements, 1890–1910* (Yale University Press, 1969) and Hollis R. Lynch, *Edward Wilmot Blyden: Pan-Negro Patriot, 1832–1912* (Oxford University Press, 1967). Diverse views of Marcus Garvey, who credited Booker T. Washington with inspiring him to seek a leadership role on behalf of African Americans, are found in Edmund David Cronon, *Black Moses: The Story of Marcus Garvey and the Universal Negro Improvement Association* (University of Wisconsin Press, 1955); Tony Martin, *Race First: The Ideological and Organizational Struggles of Marcus Garvey and the UNIA* (Greenwood Press, 1976); and Judith Stein, *The World of Marcus Garvey: Race and Class in Modern Society* (Louisiana State University Press, 1986). Some of Garvey's own writings are collected in Amy Jacques-Garvey, ed., *Philosophy and Opinions of Marcus Garvey* (1925; reprint, Atheneum, 1969).

Race relations in the late nineteenth century are explored in C. Vann Woodward, *The Strange Career of Jim Crow* (Oxford University Press, 1966), a volume that sparked a lively historiographical debate concerning the origins of segregation. Of the numerous challenges to the Woodward thesis that a full-blown pattern of racial segregation did not emerge until 1890, Howard N. Rabinowitz's *Race Relations in the Urban South, 1865–1890* (Oxford University Press, 1978) is one of the most insightful. In addition, a number of monographs that have appeared over the past three decades explore the development of an African American presence in the nation's major cities. Among the best of these urban studies are Gilbert Osofsky, *Harlem: The Making of a Ghetto: Negro New York, 1890–1930* (Harper & Row, 1966); Allan H. Spear, *Black Chicago: The Making of a Negro Ghetto, 1890–1920* (University of Chicago Press, 1967); Kenneth L. Kusmer, *A Ghetto Takes Shape: Black Cleveland, 1870–1930* (University of Illinois Press, 1976); and George C. Wright, *Life Behind a Veil: Blacks in Louisville, Kentucky, 1865–1930* (Louisiana State University Press, 1985).

ISSUE 7

Did the Progressives Fail?

YES: Richard M. Abrams, from "The Failure of Progressivism," in Richard Abrams and Lawrence Levine, eds., *The Shaping of the Twentieth Century,* 2d ed. (Little, Brown, 1971)

NO: Arthur S. Link and Richard L. McCormick, from *Progressivism* (Harlan Davidson, 1983)

ISSUE SUMMARY

YES: Professor of history Richard M. Abrams maintains that progressivism was a failure because it tried to impose a uniform set of values upon a culturally diverse people and never seriously confronted the inequalities that still exist in American society.

NO: Professors of history Arthur S. Link and Richard L. McCormick argue that the Progressives were a diverse group of reformers who confronted and ameliorated the worst abuses that emerged in urban industrial America during the early 1900s.

Progressivism is a word used by historians to define the reform currents in the years between the end of the Spanish-American War and America's entrance into the Great War in Europe in 1917. The so-called Progressive movement had been in operation for over a decade before the label was first used in the 1919 electoral campaigns. Former president Theodore Roosevelt ran as a third-party candidate in the 1912 election on the Progressive party ticket, but in truth the party had no real organization outside of the imposing figure of Theodore Roosevelt. Therefore, as a label, "progressivism" was rarely used as a term of self-identification for its supporters. Even after 1912, it was more frequently used by journalists and historians to distinguish the reformers of the period from socialists and old-fashioned conservatives.

The 1890s was a crucial decade for many Americans. From 1893 until almost the turn of the century, the nation went through a terrible economic depression. With the forces of industrialization, urbanization, and immigration wreaking havoc upon the traditional political, social, and economic structures of American life, changes were demanded. The reformers responded in a variety of ways. The proponents of good government believed that democracy was threatened because the cities were ruled by corrupt political machines while the state legislatures were dominated by corporate interests. The cure was to purify democracy and place government directly in the hands of the people through such devices as the initiative, referendum, recall, and the direct election of local school board officials, judges, and U.S. senators.

Social justice proponents saw the problem from a different perspective. Settlement workers moved into cities and tried to change the urban environment. They pushed for sanitation improvements, tenement house reforms, factory inspection laws, regulation of the hours and wages of women, and the abolition of child labor.

A third group of reformers considered the major problem to be the trusts. They argued for controls over the power of big business and for the preservation of the free enterprise system. Progressives disagreed on whether the issue was size or conduct and on whether the remedy was trust-busting or the regulation of big business. But none could deny the basic question: How was the relationship between big business and the U.S. government to be defined?

How successful was the Progressive movement? What triggered the reform impulse? Who were its leaders? How much support did it attract? More important, did the laws that resulted from the various movements fulfill the intentions of its leaders and supporters?

In the following selections, Richard M. Abrams performs a real service in distinguishing the Progressives from other reformers of the era, such as the Populists, the Socialists, the mainstream labor unions, and the corporate reorganization movement. According to Abrams, the Progressive movement failed because it tried to impose a uniform set of middle-class Protestant moral values upon a nation that was growing more culturally diverse, and because the reformers supported movements that brought about no actual changes or only superficial ones at best. The real inequalities in American society, says Abrams, were never addressed.

In contrast, Arthur S. Link and Richard L. McCormick view progressivism from the point of view of the reformers and rank it as a qualified success. They survey the criticisms of the movement made by historians since the 1950s and generally find them unconvincing. They believe that the Progressives made the first real attempts to change the destructive direction in which modern urban-industrial society was moving.

YES

Richard M. Abrams

THE FAILURE OF PROGRESSIVISM

Our first task is definitional, because clearly it would be possible to beg the whole question of "failure" by means of semantical niceties. I have no intention of being caught in that kind of critics' trap. I hope to establish that there was a distinctive major reform movement that took place during most of the first two decades of this century, that it had a mostly coherent set of characteristics and long-term objectives, and that, measured by its own criteria—not criteria I should wish, through hindsight and preference, to impose on it—it fell drastically short of its chief goals.

One can, of course, define a reform movement so broadly that merely to acknowledge that we are where we are and that we enjoy some advantages over where we were would be to prove the "success" of the movement. In many respects, Arthur Link does this sort of thing, both in his and William B. Catton's popular textbook, *American Epoch*, and in his article, "What Happened to the Progressive Movement in the 1920's?" In the latter, Link defines "progressivism" as a movement that "began convulsively in the 1890's and waxed and waned afterward to our own time, to insure the survival of democracy in the United States by the enlargement of governmental power to control and offset the power of private economic groups over the nation's institutions and life." Such a definition may be useful to classify data gathered to show the liberal sources of the enlargement of governmental power since the 1890's; but such data would not be finely classified enough to tell us much about the *non*liberal sources of governmental power (which were numerous and important), about the distinctive styles of different generations of reformers concerned with a liberal society, or even about vital distinctions among divergent reform groups in the era that contemporaries and the conventional historical wisdom have designed as progressive....

Now, without going any further into the problem of historians' definitions which are too broad or too narrow—there is no space here for such an effort —I shall attempt a definition of my own, beginning with the problem that contemporaries set themselves to solve and that gave the era its cognomen, "progressive." That problem was *progress*—or more specifically, how American society was to continue to enjoy the fruits of material progress without

From Richard M. Abrams, "The Failure of Progressivism," in Richard Abrams and Lawrence Levine, eds., *The Shaping of the Twentieth Century*, 2d ed. (Little, Brown, 1971). Copyright © 1971 by Richard M. Abrams. Reprinted by permission of the author.

the accompanying assault upon human dignity and the erosion of the conventional values and moral assumptions on which the social order appeared to rest....

To put it briefly and yet more specifically, a very large body of men and women entered into reform activities at the end of the nineteenth century to translate "the national credo" (as Henry May calls it) into a general program for social action. Their actions, according to Richard Hofstadter, were "founded upon the indigenous Yankee-Protestant political tradition [that] assumed and demanded the constant disinterested activity of the citizen in public affairs, argued that political life ought to be run, to a greater degree than it was, in accordance with general principles and abstract laws apart from and superior to personal needs, and expressed a common feeling that government should be in good part an effort to moralize the lives of individuals while economic life should be intimately related to the stimulation and development of individual character."

The most consistently important reform impulse, among *many* reform impulses, during the progressive era grew directly from these considerations. It is this reform thrust that we should properly call "the progressive movement." We should distinguish it carefully from reform movements in the era committed primarily to other considerations.

The progressive movement drew its strength from the old mugwump reform impulse, civil service reform, female emancipationists, prohibitionists, the social gospel, the settlement-house movement, some national expansionists, some world peace advocates, conservation advocates, technical efficiency experts, and a wide variety of intellectuals who helped cut through the stifling, obstructionist smokescreen of systematized ignorance. It gained powerful allies from many disadvantaged business interests that appealed to politics to redress unfavorable trade positions; from some ascendant business interests seeking institutional protection; from publishers who discovered the promotional value of exposés; and from politicians-on-the-make who sought issues with which to dislodge long-lived incumbents from their place. Objectively it focused on or expressed (1) a concern for responsive, honest, and efficient government, on the local and state levels especially; (2) recognition of the obligations of society—particularly of an affluent society—to its underprivileged; (3) a desire for more rational use of the nation's resources and economic energies; (4) a rejection, on at least intellectual grounds, of certain social principles that had long obstructed social remedies for what had traditionally been regarded as irremediable evils, such as poverty; and, above all, (5) a concern for the maintenance or restoration of a consensus on what conventionally had been regarded as *fixed moral* principles. "The first and central faith in the national credo," writes Professor May, "was, as it always had been, the reality, certainty, and eternity of moral values.... A few thought and said that ultimate values and goals were unnecessary, but in most cases this meant that they believed so deeply in a consensus on these matters that they could not imagine a serious challenge." Progressives shared this faith with most of the rest of the country, but they also conceived of themselves, with a grand sense of stewardship, as its heralds, and its agents.

The progressive movement was (and is) distinguishable from other contemporary reform movements not only by its devotion to social conditions regarded, by those within it as well as by much of the generality, as *normative*, but also by its definition of what forces threatened that order. More specifically, progressivism directed its shafts at five principal enemies, each in its own way representing reform:

1. The *socialist reform movement*—because, despite socialism's usually praiseworthy concern for human dignity, it represented the subordination of the rights of private property and of individualistic options to objectives that often explicitly threatened common religious beliefs and conventional standards of justice and excellence.

2. The corporate reorganization of American business, which I should call *the corporate reform movement* (its consequence has, after all, been called "the corporate revolution")—because it challenged the traditional relationship of ownership and control of private property, because it represented a shift from production to profits in the entrepreneurial definition of efficiency, because it threatened the proprietary small-business character of the American social structure, because it had already demonstrated a capacity for highly concentrated and socially irresponsible power, and because it sanctioned practices that strained the limits of conventionality and even legality.

3. *The labor union movement*—because despite the virtues of unionized labor as a source of countervailing force against the corporations and as a basis for a more orderly labor force, unionism (like corporate capitalism and socialism) suggested a reduction of individualistic options (at least for wage-earners and especially for small employers), and a demand for a partnership with business management in the decision-making process by a class that convention excluded from such a role.

4. *Agrarian radicalism*, and populism in particular—because it, too, represented (at least in appearance) the insurgency of a class conventionally believed to be properly excluded from a policy-making role in the society, a class graphically represented by the "Pitchfork" Bens and "Sockless" Jerrys, the "Cyclone" Davises and "Alfalfa" Bills, the wool hat brigade and the rednecks.

5. *The ethnic movement*—the demand for specific political and social recognition of ethnic or ex-national affiliations—because accession to the demand meant acknowledgment of the fragmentation of American society as well as a retreat from official standards of integrity, honesty, and efficiency in government in favor of standards based on personal loyalty, partisanship, and sectarian provincialism.

Probably no two progressives opposed all of these forces with equal animus, and most had a noteworthy sympathy for one or more of them....

So much for what progressivism was not. Let me sum it up by noting that what it rejected and sought to oppose necessarily says much about what it was—perhaps even more than can be ascertained by the more direct approach.

My thesis is that progressivism failed. It failed in what it—or what those who shaped it—conceived to be its principal objective. And that was, over and above everything else, to restore or maintain the conventional consensus on a particular view of the universe, a particular set of values, and a particular constellation of behavioral modes in the country's commerce, its industry, its social relations, and its politics. Such a view, such values, such modes were challenged by the influx of diverse religious and ethnic elements into the nation's social and intellectual stream, by the overwhelming economic success and power of the corporate form of business organization, by the subordination of the work-ethic bound up within the old proprietary and craft enterprise system, and by the increasing centrality of a growing proportion of low-income, unskilled, wage-earning classes in the nation's economy and social structure. Ironically, the *coup de grâce* would be struck by the emergence of a philosophical and scientific rationale for the existence of cultural diversity within a single social system, a rationale that largely grew out of the very intellectual ferment to which progressivism so substantially contributed.

Progressivism sought to save the old view, and the old values and modes, by educating the immigrants and the poor so as to facilitate their acceptance of and absorption into the Anglo-American mode of life, or by excluding the "unassimilable" altogether; by instituting antitrust legislation or, at the least, by imposing regulations upon corporate practices in order to preserve a minimal base for small proprietary business enterprise; by making legislative accommodations to the newly important wage-earning classes —accommodations that might provide some measure of wealth and income redistribution, on-the-job safety, occupational security, and the like—so as to fore-

stall a forcible transfer of policy-making power away from the groups that had conventionally exercised that power; and by broadening the political selection process, through direct elections, direct nominations, and direct legislation, in order to reduce tensions caused unnecessarily by excessively narrow and provincial cliques of policy-makers. When the economic and political reforms failed to restore the consensus by giving the previously unprivileged an ostensible stake in it, progressive energies turned increasingly toward using the force of the state to proscribe or restrict specifically opprobrious modes of social behavior, such as gaming habits, drinking habits, sexual habits, and Sabbatarian habits. In the ultimate resort, with the proliferation of sedition and criminal syndicalist laws, it sought to constrict political discourse itself. And (except perhaps for the disintegration of the socialist movement) *that* failed, too.

One measure of progressivism's failure lies in the xenophobic racism that reappeared on a large scale even by 1910. In many parts of the country, for example, in the far west and the south, racism and nativism had been fully blended with reform movements even at the height of progressive activities there. The alleged threats of "coolie labor" to American living standards, and of "venal" immigrant and Negro voting to republican institutions generally, underlay the alliance of racism and reform in this period. By and large, however, for the early progressive era the alliance was conspicuous only in the south and on the west coast. By 1910, signs of heightening ethnic animosities, most notably anti-Catholicism, began appearing in other areas of the country as well. As John Higham has written, "It is hard to explain the rebirth of anti-

Catholic ferment [at this time] except as an outlet for expectations which progressivism raised and then failed to fulfill." The failure here was in part the inability of reform to deliver a meaningful share of the social surplus to the groups left out of the general national progress, and in part the inability of reform to achieve its objective of assimilation and consensus.

The growing ethnic animus, moreover, operated to compound the difficulty of achieving assimilation. By the second decade of the century, the objects of the antagonism were beginning to adopt a frankly assertive posture. The World War, and the ethnic cleavages it accentuated and aggravated, represented only the final blow to the assimilationist idea; "hyphenate" tendencies had already been growing during the years before 1914. It had only been in 1905 that the Louisville-born and secular-minded Louis Brandeis had branded as "disloyal" all who "keep alive" their differences of origin or religion. By 1912, by now a victim of anti-Semitism and aware of a rising hostility toward Jews in the country, Brandeis had become an active Zionist; before a Jewish audience in 1913, he remarked how "practical experience" had convinced him that "to be good Americans, we must be better Jews, and to be better Jews, we must become Zionists."

Similarly, American Negroes also began to adopt a more aggressive public stance after having been subdued for more than a decade by antiblack violence and the accommodationist tactics suggested in 1895 by Booker T. Washington. As early as 1905, many black leaders had broken with Washington in founding the Niagara Movement for a more vigorous assertion of Negro demands for equality. But most historians seem to agree that it was probably the Springfield race riot of 1908 that ended illusions that black people could gain an equitable share in the rewards of American culture by accommodationist or assimilationist methods. The organization of the NAACP in 1909 gave substantive force for the first time to the three-year-old Niagara Movement. The year 1915 symbolically concluded the demise of accommodationism. That year, the Negro-baiting movie, "The Birth of a Nation," played to massive, enthusiastic audiences that included notably the president of the United States and the chief justice of the Supreme Court; the KKK was revived; and Booker T. Washington died. The next year, black nationalist Marcus Garvey arrived in New York from Jamaica.

Meanwhile, scientific knowledge about race and culture was undergoing a crucial revision. At least in small part stimulated by a keen self-consciousness of his own "outsider" status in American culture, the German-Jewish immigrant Franz Boas was pioneering in the new anthropological concept of "cultures," based on the idea that human behavioral traits are conditioned by historical traditions. The new view of culture was in time to undermine completely the prevailing evolutionary view that ethnic differences must mean racial inequality. The significance of Boas's work after 1910, and that of his students A. L. Kroeber and Clyde Kluckhohn in particular, rests on the fact that the racist thought of the progressive era had founded its intellectual rationale on the monistic, evolutionary view of culture; and indeed much of the progressives' anxiety over the threatened demise of "the American culture" had been founded on that view.

Other intellectual developments as well had for a long time been whittling away at the notion that American society had to stand or fall on the unimpaired coherence of its cultural consensus. Yet the new work in anthropology, law, philosophy, physics, psychology, and literature only unwittingly undermined that assumption. Rather, it was only as the ethnic hostilities grew, and especially as the power of the state came increasingly to be invoked against dissenting groups whose ethnic "peculiarities" provided an excuse for repression, that the new intelligence came to be developed. "The world has thought that it must have its culture and its political unity coincide," wrote Randolph Bourne in 1916 while chauvinism, nativism, and antiradicalism were mounting; now it was seeing that cultural diversity might yet be the salvation of the liberal society—that it might even serve to provide the necessary countervailing force to the power of the state that private property had once served (in the schema of Locke, Harrington, and Smith) before the interests of private property became so highly concentrated and so well blended with the state itself.

The telltale sign of progressivism's failure was the violent crusade against dissent that took place in the closing years of the Wilson administration. It is too easy to ascribe the literal hysteria of the postwar years to the dislocations of the War alone. Incidents of violent repression of labor and radical activities had been growing remarkably, often in step with xenophobic outbreaks, for several years before America's intervention in the War. To quote Professor Higham once more. "The seemingly unpropitious circumstances under which antiradicalism and anti-Catholicism came to life [after 1910] make their renewal a subject of moment." It seems clear that they both arose out of the sources of the reform ferment

itself. When reform failed to enlarge the consensus, or to make it more relevant to the needs of the still disadvantaged and disaffected, and when in fact reform seemed to be encouraging more radical challenges to the social order, the old anxieties of the 1890's returned.

The postwar hysteria represented a reaction to a confluence of anxiety-laden developments, including the high cost of living, the physical and social dislocations of war mobilization and the recruitment of women and Negroes into war production jobs in the big northern cities, the Bolshevik Revolution, a series of labor strikes, and a flood of radical literature that exaggerated the capabilities of radical action. "One Hundred Per Cent Americanism" seemed the only effective way of meeting all these challenges at once. As Stanley Coben has written, making use of recent psychological studies and anthropological work on cultural "revitalization movements": "Citizens who joined the crusade for one hundred per cent Americanism sought, primarily, a unifying force which would halt the apparent disintegration of their culture. . . . The slight evidence of danger from radical organizations aroused such wild fear only because Americans had already encountered other threats to cultural stability."

Now, certainly during the progressive era a lot of reform legislation was passed, much that contributed genuinely to a more liberal society, though more that contributed to the more absolutistic moral objectives of progressivism. Progressivism indeed had real, lasting effects for the blunting of the sharper edges of self-interest in American life, and for the reduction of the harsher cruelties suffered by the society's underprivileged. These achievements deserve emphasis, not least because they derived directly from the progressive habit of looking to standards of conventional morality and human decency for the solution of diverse social conflicts. But the deeper nature of the problem confronting American society required more than the invocation of conventional standards; the conventions themselves were at stake, especially as they bore upon the allocation of privileges and rewards. Because most of the progressives never confronted that problem, in a way their efforts were doomed to failure.

In sum, the overall effect of the period's legislation is not so impressive. For example, all the popular government measures put together have not conspicuously raised the quality of American political life. Direct nominations and elections have tended to make political campaigns so expensive as to reduce the number of eligible candidates for public office to (1) the independently wealthy; (2) the ideologues, especially on the right, who can raise the needed campaign money from independently wealthy ideologues like themselves, or from the organizations set up to promote a particular ideology; and (3) party hacks who pay off their debt to the party treasury by whistle-stopping and chicken dinner speeches. Direct legislation through the Initiative and Referendum device has made cities and states prey to the best-financed and -organized special-interest group pressures, as have so-called nonpartisan elections. Which is not to say that things are worse than before, but only that they are not conspicuously better. The popular government measures did have the effect of shaking up the established political organizations of the day, and that may well have been their only real purpose.

But as Arthur Link has said, in his text, *The American Epoch*, the popular government measures "were merely instruments to facilitate the capture of political machinery.... They must be judged for what they accomplished or failed to accomplish on the higher level of substantive reform." Without disparaging the long list of reform measures that passed during the progressive era, the question remains whether all the "substantive reforms" together accomplished what the progressives wanted them to accomplish.

Certain social and economic advantages were indeed shuffled about, but this must be regarded as a short-term achievement for special groups at best. Certain commercial interests, for example, achieved greater political leverage in railroad policy-making than they had had in 1900 through measures such as the Hepburn and Mann-Elkins Acts— though it was not until the 1940's that any real change occurred in the general rate structure, as some broad regional interests had been demanding at the beginning of the century. Warehouse, farm credits, and land-bank acts gave the diminishing numbers of farm owners enhanced opportunities to mortgage their property, and some business groups had persuaded the federal government to use national revenues to educate farmers on how to increase their productivity (Smith-Lever Act, 1914); but most farmers remained as dependent as ever upon forces beyond their control—the bankers, the middlemen, the international market. The FTC, and the Tariff Commission established in 1916, extended the principle of using government agencies to adjudicate intra-industrial conflicts ostensibly in the national interest, but these agencies would develop a lamentable tendency of deferring to and even confirming rather than moderating the power of each industry's dominant interests. The

Federal Reserve Act made the currency more flexible, and that certainly made more sense than the old system, as even the bankers agreed. But depositers would be as prey to defaulting banks as they had been in the days of the Pharaoh—bank deposit insurance somehow was "socialism" to even the best of men in this generation. And despite Woodrow Wilson's brave promise to end the banker's stifling hold on innovative small business, one searches in vain for some provision in the FRA designed specifically to encourage small or new businesses. In fact, the only constraints on the bankers' power that emerged from the era came primarily from the ability of the larger corporations to finance their own expansion out of capital surpluses they had accumulated from extortionate profits during the War.

A major change almost occurred during the war years when organized labor and the principle of collective bargaining received official recognition and a handful of labor leaders was taken, temporarily, into policy-making councils (e.g., in the War Labor Board). But actually, as already indicated, such a development, if it had been made permanent, would have represented a defeat, not a triumph, for progressivism. The progressives may have fought for improved labor conditions, but they jealously fought against the enlargement of union power. It was no aberration that once the need for wartime productive efficiency evaporated, leading progressives such as A. Mitchell Palmer, Miles Poindexter, and Woodrow Wilson himself helped civic and employer organizations to bludgeon the labor movement into disunity and docility. (It is possible, I suppose, to argue that such progressives were simply inconsistent, but if we understand progressivism in the

terms I have outlined above I think the consistency is more evident.) Nevertheless, a double irony is worth noting with respect to progressivism's objectives and the wartime labor developments. On the one hand, the progressives' hostility to labor unions defeated their own objectives of (1) counterbalancing the power of collectivized capital (i.e., corporations), and (2) enhancing workers' share of the nation's wealth. On the other hand, under wartime duress, the progressives did grant concessions to organized labor (e.g., the Adamson Eight-Hour Railway Labor Act, as well as the WLB) that would later serve as precedents for the very "collectivization" of the economic situation that they were dedicated to oppose.

Meanwhile, the distribution of advantages in the society did not change much at all. In some cases, from the progressive reformers' viewpoint at least, it may even have changed for the worse. According to the figures of the National Industrial Conference Board, even income was as badly distributed at the end of the era as before. In 1921, the highest 10 percent of income recipients received 38 percent of total personal income, and that figure was only 34 percent in 1910. (Since the share of the top 5 percent of income recipients probably declined in the 1910–20 period, the figures for the top 10 percent group suggest a certain improvement in income distribution at the top. But the fact that the share of the lowest 60 percent also declined in that period, from 35 percent to 30 percent, confirms the view that no meaningful improvement can be shown.) Maldistribution was to grow worse until after 1929.

American farmers on the whole and in particular seemed to suffer increasing disadvantages. Farm life was one of the institutional bulwarks of the mode of life the progressives ostensibly cherished. "The farmer who owns his land," averred Gifford Pinchot, "is still the backbone of the Nation; and one of the things we want most is more of him, . . . [for] he is the first of home-makers." If only in the sense that there were relatively fewer farmers in the total population at the end of the progressive era, one would have to say farm life in the United States had suffered. But, moreover, fewer owned their own farms. The number of farm tenants increased by 21 percent from 1900 to 1920; 38.1 percent of all farm operators in 1921 were tenants; and the figures look even worse when one notices that tenancy *declined* in the most *impoverished* areas during this period, suggesting that the family farm was surviving mostly in the more marginal agricultural areas. Finally, although agriculture had enjoyed some of its most prosperous years in history in the 1910–20 period, the 21 percent of the nation's gainfully employed who were in agriculture in 1919 (a peak year) earned only 16 percent of the national income.

While progressivism failed to restore vitality to American farming, it failed also to stop the vigorous ascendancy of corporate capitalism, the most conspicuous challenge to conventional values and modes that the society faced at the beginning of the era. The corporation had drastically undermined the very basis of the traditional rationale that had supported the nation's freewheeling system of resource allocation and had underwritten the permissiveness of the laws governing economic activities in the nineteenth century. The new capitalism by-passed the privately-owned proprietary firm, it featured a separation of ownership and control, it subordinated the profit motive to varied and variable other objectives such as empire-building, and, in many of the techniques developed by financial brokers and investment bankers, it appeared to create a great gulf between the making of money and the producing of useful goods and services. Through a remarkable series of judicial sophistries, this nonconventional form of business enterprise had become, in law, a *person*, and had won privileges and liberties once entrusted only to men, who were presumed to be conditioned and restrained by the moral qualities that inhere in human nature. Although gaining legal dispensations from an obliging Supreme Court, the corporation could claim no theoretical legitimacy beyond the fact of its power and its apparent inextricable entanglement in the business order that had produced America's seemingly unbounded material success.

Although much has been written about the supposed continuing vitality of small proprietary business enterprise in the United States, there is no gainsaying the continued ascendancy of the big corporation nor the fact that it still lacks legitimation. The fact that in the last sixty years the number of small proprietary businesses has grown at a rate that slightly exceeds the rate of population growth says little about the character of small business enterprise today as compared with that of the era of the American industrial revolution; it does nothing to disparage the apprehensions expressed in the antitrust campaigns of the progressives. To focus on the vast numbers of automobile dealers and gasoline service station owners, for example, is to miss completely their truly humble dependence upon the very few giant automobile and oil companies, a foretold dependence that was the very point of progressives' anticorporation, antitrust sentiments. The progressive movement must indeed be credited with placing real restraints upon monopolistic tendencies in the United States, for most statistics indicate that at least until the 1950's business concentration showed no substantial increase from the turn of the century (though it may be pertinent to note that concentration ratios did increase significantly in the decade immediately following the progressive era). But the statistics of concentration remain impressive—just as they were when John Moody wrote *The Truth About the Trusts* in 1904 and Louis Brandeis followed it with *Other People's Money* in 1914. That two hundred corporations (many of them interrelated) held almost one-quarter of all business assets, and more than 40 percent of all corporate assets in the country in 1948; that the fifty largest manufacturing corporations held 35 percent of all industrial assets in 1948, and 38 percent by 1962; and that a mere twenty-eight corporations or one one-thousandth of a percentage of all nonfinancial firms in 1956 employed 10 percent of all those employed in the nonfinancial industries, should be sufficient statistical support for the apprehensions of the progressive era —*just as it is testimony to the failure of the progressive movement to achieve anything substantial to alter the situation.*

Perhaps the crowning failure of progressivism was the American role in World War I. It is true that many progressives opposed America's intervention, but it is also true that a great many more supported it. The failure in progressivism lies not in the decision to intervene but in the futility of intervention measured by progressive expectations.

NO

Arthur S. Link and
Richard L. McCormick

PROGRESSIVISM IN HISTORY

Convulsive reform movements swept across the American landscape from the 1890s to 1917. Angry farmers demanded better prices for their products, regulation of the railroads, and the destruction of what they thought was the evil power of bankers, middlemen, and corrupt politicians. Urban residents crusaded for better city services and more efficient municipal government. Members of various professions, such as social workers and doctors, tried to improve the dangerous and unhealthy conditions in which many people lived and worked. Businessmen, too, lobbied incessantly for goals which they defined as reform. Never before had the people of the United States engaged in so many diverse movements for the improvement of their political system, economy, and communities. By around 1910, many of these crusading men and women were calling themselves progressives. Ever since, historians have used the term *progressivism* to describe the many reform movements of the early twentieth century.

Yet in the goals they sought and the remedies they tried, the reformers were a varied and contradictory lot. Some progressives wanted to increase the political influence and control of ordinary people, while other progressives wanted to concentrate authority in experts. Many reformers tried to curtail the growth of large corporations; others accepted bigness in industry on account of its supposed economic benefits. Some progressives were genuinely concerned about the welfare of the "new" immigrants from southern and eastern Europe; other progressives sought, sometimes frantically, to "Americanize" the newcomers or to keep them out altogether. In general, progressives sought to improve the conditions of life and labor and to create as much social stability as possible. But each group of progressives had its own definitions of improvement and stability. In the face of such diversity, one historian, Peter G. Filene, has even argued that what has been called the progressive movement never existed as a historical phenomenon ("An Obituary for 'The Progressive Movement,'" *American Quarterly*, 1970).

Certainly there was no *unified* movement, but, like most students of the period, we consider progressivism to have been a real, vital, and significant

From Arthur S. Link and Richard L. McCormick, *Progressivism* (Harlan Davidson, 1983), pp. 1–3, 8–10, 21–25, 113–118. Copyright © 1983 by Harlan Davidson, Inc. Reprinted by permission.

phenomenon, one which contemporaries recognized and talked and fought about. Properly conceptualized, progressivism provides a useful framework for the history of the United States in the late nineteenth and early twentieth centuries.

One source of confusion and controversy about progressives and progressivism is the words themselves. They are often used judgmentally to describe people and changes which historians have deemed to be "good," "enlightened," and "farsighted." The progressives themselves naturally intended the words to convey such positive qualities, but we should not accept their usage uncritically. It might be better to avoid the terms progressive and progressivism altogether, but they are too deeply embedded in the language of contemporaries and historians to be ignored. Besides, we think that the terms have real meaning. In this book the words will be used neutrally, without any implicit judgment about the value of reform.

In the broadest sense, progressivism was the way in which a whole generation of Americans defined themselves politically and responded to the nation's problems at the turn of the century. The progressives made the first comprehensive efforts to grapple with the ills of a modern urban-industrial society. Hence the record of their achievements and failures has considerable relevance for our own time.

WHO WERE THE PROGRESSIVES?

Ever since the early twentieth century, people have argued about who the progressives were and what they stood for. This may seem to be a strange topic of debate, but it really is not. Progressivism engaged many different groups of Americans, and each group of progressives naturally considered themselves to be the key reformers and thought that their own programs were the most important ones. Not surprisingly, historians ever since have had trouble agreeing on who really shaped progressivism and its goals. Scholars who have written about the period have variously identified farmers, the old middle classes, professionals, businessmen, and urban immigrants and ethnic groups as the core group of progressives. But these historians have succeeded in identifying *their* reformers only by defining progressivism narrowly, by excluding other reformers and reforms when they do not fall within some specific definition, and by resorting to such vague, catch-all adjectives as "middle class." ...

The advocates of the middle-class view might reply that they intended to study the leaders of reform, not its supporters, to identify and describe the men and women who imparted the dominant character to progressivism, not its mass base. The study of leadership is surely a valid subject in its own right and is particularly useful for an understanding of progressivism. But too much focus on leadership conceals more than it discloses about early twentieth-century reform. The dynamics of progressivism were crucially generated by ordinary people—by the sometimes frenzied mass supporters of progressive leaders, by rank-and-file voters willing to trust a reform candidate. The chronology of progressivism can be traced by events which aroused large numbers of people —a sensational muckraking article, an outrageous political scandal, an eye-opening legislative investigation, or a tragic social calamity. Events such as these gave reform its rhythm and its power.

Progressivism cannot be understood without seeing how the masses of Americans perceived and responded to such events. Widely circulated magazines gave people everywhere the sordid facts of corruption and carried the clamor for reform into every city, village, and county. State and national election campaigns enabled progressive candidates to trumpet their programs. Almost no literate person in the United States in, say, 1906 could have been unaware that ten-year-old children worked through the night in dangerous factories, or that many United States senators served big business. Progressivism was the only reform movement ever experienced by the whole American nation. Its national appeal and mass base vastly exceeded that of Jacksonian reform. And progressivism's dependence on the people for its objectives and timing has no comparison in the executive-dominated New Deal of Franklin D. Roosevelt or the Great Society of Lyndon B. Johnson. Wars and depressions had previously engaged the whole nation, but never reform. And so we are back to the problem of how to explain and define the outpouring of progressive reform which excited and involved so many different kinds of people.

A little more than a decade ago, Buenker and Thelen recognized the immense diversity of progressivism and suggested ways in which to reorient the study of early twentieth-century reform. Buenker observed that divergent groups often came together on one issue and then changed alliances on the next ("The Progressive Era: A Search for a Synthesis," *Mid-America*, 1969). Indeed, different reformers sometimes favored the same measure for distinctive, even opposite, reasons. Progressivism could be understood only in the light of these shifting coalitions. Thelen, in his study of Wisconsin's legislature, also emphasized the importance of cooperation between different reform groups. "The basic riddle in Progressivism," he concluded, "is not what drove groups apart but what made them seek common cause."

There is a great deal of wisdom in these articles, particularly in their recognition of the diversity of progressivism and in the concept of shifting coalitions of reformers. A two-pronged approach is necessary to carry forward this way of looking at early twentieth-century reform. First, we should study, not an imaginary unified progressive movement, but individual reforms and give particular attention to the goals of their diverse supporters, the public rationales given for them, and the results which they achieved. Second, we should try to identify the features which were more or less common to different progressive reforms.

The first task—distinguishing the goals of a reform from its rhetoric and its results—is more difficult than it might appear to be. Older interpretations of progressivism implicitly assumed that the rhetoric explained the goals and that, if a proposed reform became law, the results fulfilled the intentions behind it. Neither assumption is a sound one: purposes, rationale, and results are three different things. Samuel P. Hays' influential article, "The Politics of Reform in Municipal Government in the Progressive Era" (*Pacific Northwest Quarterly*, 1964), exposed the fallacy of automatically equating the democratic rhetoric of the reformers with their true purposes. The two may have coincided, but the historian has to demonstrate that fact, not take it for granted. The unexamined identification of either intentions or rhetoric with results is also invalid, although it is still a common feature of the scholarship on progressivism. Only within the last decade have historians begun to examine the actual achievements of the reformers. To carry out this first task, in the following... we will distinguish between the goals and rhetoric of individual reforms and will discuss the results of reform whenever the current literature permits. To do so is to observe the ironies, complexities, and disappointments of progressivism.

The second task—that of identifying the common characteristics of progressivism—is even more difficult than the first but is an essential base on which to build an understanding of progressivism. The rest of this chapter focuses on identifying such characteristics. The place to begin that effort is the origins of progressivism....

THE CHARACTER AND SPIRIT OF PROGRESSIVISM

Progressivism was characterized, in the first place, by a distinctive set of attitudes toward industrialism. By the turn of the century, the overwhelming majority of Americans had accepted the permanence of large-scale industrial, commercial, and financial enterprises and of the wage and factory systems. The progressives shared this attitude. Most were not socialists, and they undertook reform, not to dismantle modern economic institutions, but rather to ameliorate and improve the conditions of industrial life. Yet progressivism was infused with a deep outrage against the worst consequences of industrialism. Outpourings of anger at corporate wrongdoing and of hatred for industry's callous pursuit of profit frequently punctuated the course of reform in the early twentieth century. Indeed, antibusiness emotion was a prime mover of progressivism. That the acceptance of industrialism *and* the outrage against it were intrinsic to early twentieth-century reform does not mean that progressivism was mindless or that it has to be considered indefinable. But it does suggest that there was a powerful irony in progressivism: reforms which gained support from a people angry with the oppressive aspects of industrialism also assisted the same persons to accommodate to it, albeit to an industrialism which was to some degree socially responsible.

The progressives' ameliorative reforms also reflected their faith in progress—in mankind's ability, through purposeful action, to improve the environment and the conditions of life. The late nineteenth-century dissidents had not lacked this faith, but their espousal of panaceas bespoke a deep pessimism: "Unless this one great change is made, things will get worse." Progressive reforms were grounded on a broader assumption. In particular, reforms could protect the people hurt by industrialization, and make the environment more humane. For intellectuals of the era, the achievement of such goals meant that they had to meet Herbert Spencer head on and confute his absolute "truths." Progressive thinkers, led by Lester Frank Ward, Richard T. Ely, and, most important, John Dewey, demolished social Darwinism with what Goldman has called "reform Darwinism." They asserted that human adaptation to the environment did not interfere with the evolutionary process, but was, rather, part and parcel of the law of natural change. Progressive intellectuals and their popularizers produced a vast literature to condemn laissez faire and to promote the concept of the active state.

To improve the environment meant, above all, to intervene in economic and social affairs in order to control natural forces and impose a measure of order upon them. This belief in interventionism was a third component of progressivism. It was visible in almost every reform of the era, from the supervision of business to the prohibition of alcohol (John W. Chambers II, *The Tyranny of Change: America in the Progressive Era, 1900–1917*, 1980). Interventionism could be both private and public. Given their choice, most progressives preferred to work noncoercively through voluntary organizations for economic and social changes. However, as time passed, it became evident that most progressive reforms could be achieved only by legislation and public control. Such an extension of public authority made many progressives uneasy, and few of them went so far as Herbert Croly in glorifying the state in his *The Promise of American Life* (1909) and *Progressive Democracy* (1914). Even so, the intervention necessary for their reforms inevitably propelled progressives toward an advocacy of the use of governmental power. A familiar scenario during the period was one in which progressives called upon public authorities to assume responsibility for interventions which voluntary organizations had begun.

The foregoing describes the basic characteristics of progressivism but says little about its ideals. Progressivism was inspired by two bodies of belief and knowledge—evangelical Protestantism and the natural and social sciences. These sources of reform may appear at first glance antagonistic to one another. Actually, they were complementary, and each imparted distinctive qualities to progressivism.

Ever since the religious revivals from about 1820 to 1840, evangelical Protestantism had spurred reform in the United States. Basic to the reform mentality was an all-consuming urge to purge the world of sin, such as the sins of slavery and intemperance, against which nineteenth-century reformers had crusaded. Now the progressives carried the struggle into the modern citadels of sin—the teeming cities of the nation. No one can read their writings and speeches without being struck by the fact that many of them believed that it was their Christian duty to right the wrongs created by the processes of industrialization. Such belief was the motive force behind the Social Gospel, a movement which swept through the Protestant churches in the 1890s and 1900s. Its goal was to align churches, frankly and aggressively, on the side of the downtrodden, the poor, and working people—in other words, to make Christianity relevant to this world, not the next. It is difficult to measure the influence of the Social Gospel, but it seared the consciences of millions of Americans, particularly in urban areas. And it triumphed in the organization in 1908 of the Federal Council of Churches of Christ in America, with its platform which condemned exploitative capitalism and proclaimed the right of workers to organize and to enjoy a decent standard of living. Observers at the Progressive party's national convention of 1912 should not have been surprised to hear the delegates sing, spontaneously and emotionally, the Christian call to arms, "Onward, Christian Solders!"

The faith which inspired the singing of "Onward, Christian Soldiers!" had significant implications for progressive reforms. Progressives used moralistic appeals to make people feel the awful weight of wrong in the world and to exhort them to accept personal responsibility for its eradication. The resultant reforms could be generous in spirit, but they could also seem intolerant to the people who were "reformed." Progressivism sometimes seemed to envision life in a small town Protestant community or an urban drawing room—a vision sharply different from that of Catholic or Jewish immigrants. Not every progressive shared the evangelical ethos, much less its intolerance, but few of the era's reforms were untouched by the spirit and techniques of Protestant revivalism.

Science also had a pervasive impact on the methods and objectives of progressivism. Many leading reformers were specialists in the new disciplines of statistics, economics, sociology, and psychology. These new social scientists set out to gather data on human behavior as it actually was and to discover the laws which governed it. Since social scientists accepted environmentalist and interventionist assumptions implicitly, they believed that knowledge of natural laws would make it possible to devise and apply solutions to improve the human condition. This faith underpinned the optimism of most progressives and predetermined the methods used by almost all reformers of the time: investigation of the facts and application of social-science knowledge to their analysis; entrusting trained experts to decide what should be done; and, finally, mandating government to execute reform.

These methods may have been rational, but they were also compatible with progressive moralism. In its formative period, American social science was heavily infused with ethical concerns. An essential purpose of statistics, economics, sociology, and psychology was to improve and uplift. Leading practitioners of these disciplines, for example, Richard T. Ely, an economist at the University of Wisconsin, were often in the vanguard of the Social Gospel. Progressives blended science and religion into a view of human behavior which was unique to their generation, which had grown up in an age of revivals and come to maturity at the birth of social science.

All of progressivism's distinctive features found expression in muckraking—the literary spearhead of early twentieth-century reform. Through the medium of such new ten-cent magazines as *McClure's, Everybody's* and *Cosmopolitan*, the muckrakers exposed every dark aspect and corner of American life. Nothing escaped the probe of writers such as Ida M. Tarbell, Lincoln Steffens, Ray Stannard Baker, and Burton J. Hendrick— not big business, politics, prostitution, race relations, or even the churches. Behind the exposés of the muckrakers lay the progressive attitude toward industrialism: it was here to stay, but many of its aspects seemed to be deplorable. These could be improved, however, if only people became aware of conditions and determined to ameliorate them. To bring about such awareness, the muckrakers appealed to their readers' consciences. Steffens' famous series, published in book form as *The Shame of the Cities* in 1904, was frankly intended to make people feel guilty for the corruption which riddled their cities. The muckrakers also used the social scientists' method of careful and painstaking gathering of data—and with devastating effects. The investigative function—which was later largely taken over by governmental agencies—proved absolutely vital to educating and arousing Americans.

All progressive crusades shared the spirit and used the techniques discussed here, but they did so to different degrees and in different ways. Some voiced a greater willingness to accept industrialism and even to extol its potential benefits; others expressed more strongly the outrage against its darker aspects. Some intervened through voluntary organizations; others relied on government to achieve changes. Each reform reflected a distinctive balance between the claims of Protestant moralism and of scientific rationalism. Progressives fought among themselves over these questions even while they set to the common task of applying their new methods and ideas to the problems of a modern society....

In this analysis we have frequently pointed to the differences between the rhetoric, intentions, and results of progressive reform. The failure of reform always to fulfill the expectations of its advocates was not, of course, unique to the progressive era. Jacksonian reform, Reconstruction, and the New Deal all exhibited similar ironies and disappointments. In each case, the clash between reformers with divergent purposes, the inability to predict how given methods of reform would work in practice, and the ultimate waning of popular zeal for change all contributed to the disjuncture of rationale, purpose, and achievement. Yet the gap between these things seems more obvious in the progressive era because so many diverse movements for reform took place in a brief span of time and were accompanied by resounding rhetoric and by high expectations for the improvement of the American social and political environment. The effort to change so many things all at once, and the grandiose claims made for the moral and material betterment which would result, meant that disappointments were bound to occur.

Yet even the great number of reforms and the uncommonly high expectations for them cannot fully account for the consistent gaps which we have observed between the stated purposes, real intentions, and actual results of progressivism. Several additional factors, intrinsic to the nature of early twentieth-century reform, help to explain the ironies and contradictions.

One of these was the progressives' confident reliance on modern methods of reform. Heirs of recent advances in natural science and social science, they enthusiastically devised and applied new techniques to improve American government and society. Their methods often worked; on the other hand, progressive programs often simply did not prove capable of accomplishing what had been expected of them. This was not necessarily the reformers' fault. They hopefully used untried methods even while they lacked a science of society which was capable of solving all the great problems which they attacked. At the same time, the progressives' scientific methods made it possible to know just how far short of success their programs had sometimes fallen. The evidence of their failures thus was more visible than in any previous era of reform. To the progressives' credit, they usually published that evidence—for contemporaries and historians alike to see.

A second aspect of early twentieth-century reform which helps to account for the gaps between aims and achievements was the deep ambivalence of the progressives about industrialism and its consequences. Individual reformers were divided, and so was their movement as a whole. Compared to many Americans of the late 1800s, the progressives fundamentally accepted an industrial society and sought mainly to control and ameliorate it. Even reformers who were intellectually committed to socialist ideas often acted the part of reformers, not radicals.

Yet progressivism was infused and vitalized, as we have seen, by people truly angry with their industrial society. Few of them wanted to tear down the modern institutions of business and commerce, but their anger was real, their moralism was genuine, and their passions were essential to the reforms of their time.

The reform movement never resolved this ambivalence about industrialism. Much of its rhetoric and popular passion pointed in one direction—toward some form of social democracy—while its leaders and their programs went in another. Often the result was confusion and bitterness. Reforms frequently did not measure up to popular, antibusiness expectations, indeed, never were expected to do so by those who designed and implemented them. Even conservative, ameliorative reformers like Theodore Roosevelt often used radical rhetoric. In doing so, they misled their followers and contributed to the ironies of progressivism.

Perhaps most significant, progressives failed to achieve all their goals because, despite their efforts, they never fully came to terms with the divisions and conflicts in American society. Again and again, they acknowledged the existence of social disharmony more fully and frankly than had nineteenth-century Americans. Nearly every social and economic reform of the era was predicated on the progressive recognition that diverse cultural and occupational groups had conflicting interests, and that the responsibility for mitigating and adjusting those differences lay with the whole society, usually the government. Such recognition was one of the progressives' most significant achievements. Indeed, it stands among the most important accomplishments of liberal reform in all of American history. For, by frankly acknowledging the existence of social disharmony, the progressives committed the twentieth-century United States to recognizing—and to lessening—the inevitable conflicts of a heterogeneous industrial society.

Yet the significance of the progressives' recognition of diversity was compromised by the methods and institutions which they adopted to diminish or eliminate social and economic conflict. Expert administrative government turned out to be less neutral than the progressives believed that it would be. No scientific reform could be any more impartial than the experts who gathered the data or than the bureaucrats who implemented the programs. In practice, as we have seen, administrative government often succumbed to the domination of special interests.

It would be pointless to blame the progressives for the failure of their new methods and programs to eradicate all the conflicts of an industrial society, but it is perhaps fair to ask why the progressives adopted measures which tended to disguise and obscure economic and social conflict almost as soon as they had uncovered it. For one thing, they honestly believed in the almost unlimited potentialities of science and administration. Our late twentieth-century skepticism of these wonders should not blind us to the faith with which the progressives embraced them and imbued them with what now seem magical properties. For another, the progressives were reformers, not radicals. It was one thing to recognize the existence of economic and social conflict, but quite another thing to admit that it was permanent. By and large, these men and women were personally and ideologically inclined to believe that the American society was, in the final analysis, harmonious, and that such conflicts as did exist could be resolved. Finally, the class and cultural backgrounds of the leading progressives often made them insensitive to lower-class immigrant Americans and their cultures. Attempts to reduce divisions sometimes came down to imposing middle-class Protestant ways on the urban masses. In consequence, the progressives never fulfilled their hope of eliminating social conflict. Reformers of the early twentieth century saw the problem more fully than had their predecessors, but they nonetheless tended to consider conflicts resolved when, in fact, they only had been papered over. Later twentieth-century Americans have also frequently deceived themselves in this way.

Thus progressivism inevitably fell short of its rhetoric and intentions. Lest this seem an unfairly critical evaluation, it is important to recall how terribly ambitious were the stated aims and true goals of the reformers. They missed some of their marks because they sought to do so much. And, despite all their shortcomings, they accomplished an enormous part of what they set out to achieve.

Progressivism brought major innovations to almost every facet of public and private life in the United States. The political and governmental systems particularly felt the effects of reform. Indeed, the nature of political participation and the uses to which it was put went through transitions as momentous as those of any era in American history. These developments were complex, as we have seen, and it is no easy matter to sort out who

was helped and who was hurt by each of them or by the entire body of reforms. At the very least, the political changes of the progressive era significantly accommodated American public life to an urban-industrial society. On balance, the polity probably emerged neither more nor less democratic than before, but it did become better suited to address, or at least recognize, the questions and problems which arose from the cities and factories of the nation. After the progressive era, just as before, wealthier elements in American society had a disproportionate share of political power, but we can hardly conclude that this was the fault of the progressives.

The personal and social life of the American people was also deeply affected by progressivism. Like the era's political changes, the economic and social reforms of the early twentieth century were enormously complicated and are difficult to summarize without doing violence to their diversity. In the broadest sense, the progressives sought to mitigate the injustice and the disorder of a society now dominated by its industries and cities. Usually, as we have observed, the quests for social justice and social control were extricably bound together in the reformers' programs, with each group of progressives having different interpretations of these dual ends. Justice sometimes took second place to control. However, before one judges the reformers too harshly for that, it is well to remember how bad urban social conditions were in the late nineteenth century and the odds against which the reformers fought. It is also well to remember that they often succeeded in mitigating the harshness of urban-industrial life.

The problems with which the progressives struggled have, by and large, continued to challenge Americans ever since. And, although the assumptions and techniques of progressivism no longer command the confidence with early twentieth-century Americans had in them, no equally comprehensive body of reforms has ever been adopted in their place. Throughout this study, we have criticized the progressives for having too much faith in their untried methods. Yet if this was a failing, it was also a source of strength, one now missing from reform in America. For the essence of progressivism lay in the hopefulness and optimism which the reformers brought to the tasks of applying science and administration to the high moral purposes in which they believed. The historical record of their aims and achievements leaves no doubt that there were many men and women in the United States in the early 1900s who were not afraid to confront the problems of a modern industrial society with vigor, imagination, and hope. They of course failed to solve all those problems, but no other generation of Americans has done conspicuously better in addressing the political, economic, and social conditions which it faced.

POSTSCRIPT

Did the Progressives Fail?

In spite of their differences, both interpretations make concessions to their respective critics. Link and McCormick, for example, admit that the intended reforms did not necessarily produce the desired results. Furthermore, the authors concede that many reformers were insensitive to the cultural values of the lower classes and attempted to impose middle-class Protestant ways on the urban masses. Nevertheless, Link and McCormick argue that in spite of the failure to curb the growth of big business, the progressive reforms did ameliorate the worst abuses of the new urban industrial society. Although the Progressives failed to solve all the major problems of their times, they did set the agenda that still challenges the reformers of the 1990s.

Abrams also makes a concession to his critics when he admits that "progressivism had real lasting effects for the blunting of the sharper edges of self-interest in American life, and for the reduction of the harsher cruelties suffered by the society's underprivileged." Yet the thrust of his argument is that the progressive reformers accomplished little of value. While Abrams probably agrees with Link and McCormick that the Progressives were the first group to confront the problems of modern America, he considers their intended reforms inadequate by their very nature. Because the reformers never really challenged the inequalities brought about by the rise of the industrial state, maintains Abrams, the same problems have persisted to the present day.

Historians have generally been sympathetic to the aims and achievements of the progressive historians. Many, like Charles Beard and Frederick Jackson Turner, came from the Midwest and lived in model progressive states like Wisconsin. Their view of history was based on a conflict between groups competing for power, so it was easy for them to portray progressivism as a struggle between the people and entrenched interests.

It was not until after World War II that a more complex view of progressivism emerged. Richard Hofstadter's *Age of Reform* (Alfred A. Knopf, 1955) was exceptionally critical of the reformist view of history as well as of the reformers in general. Born of Jewish immigrant parents and raised in cities in New York, the Columbia University professor argued that progressivism was a moral crusade undertaken by WASP families in an effort to restore older Protestant and individualistic values and to regain political power and status. Both Hofstadter's "status revolution" theory of progressivism and his profile of the typical Progressive have been heavily criticized by historians. Nevertheless, he changed the dimensions of the debate and made progressivism appear to be a much more complex issue than had previously been thought.

Most of the writing on progressivism for the past 20 years has centered around the "organizational" model. Writers of this school have stressed the role of the "expert" and the ideals of scientific management as basic to an understanding of the Progressive Era. This fascination with how the city manager plan worked in Dayton or railroad regulation in Wisconsin or the public schools laws in New York City makes sense to a 1990s generation surrounded by bureaucracies on all sides. Two books that deserve careful reading are Robert Wiebe's *The Search for Order, 1877–1920* (Hill & Wang, 1967) and the wonderful collection of essays by Samuel P. Hayes, *American Political History as Social Analysis* (Knoxville, 1980), which brings together two decades' worth of articles from diverse journals that were seminal in exploring ethnocultural approaches to politics within the organizational model.

In a highly influential article written for the *American Quarterly* in the spring of 1970, Professor Peter G. Filene proclaimed "An Obituary for the 'Progressive Movement.'" After an extensive review of the literature, Filene concluded that since historians cannot agree on its programs, values, geographical location, members, and supporters, there was no such thing as a Progressive movement. Few historians were as bold as Filene and wrote progressivism out of the pantheon of American reform movements. But he put the proponents of the early-twentieth-century reform movement on the defensive. Students who want to see how professional historians directly confronted Filene in their refusal to attend the funeral of the Progressive movement should read the essays by John D. Buenker, John C. Burnham, and Robert M. Crunden in *Progressivism* (Schenkman, 1977).

Three works provide an indispensable review of the literature of progressivism in the 1980s. Link and McCormick's *Progressivism* (Harlan Davidson, 1983) deserves to be read in its entirety for its comprehensive yet concise coverage. More scholarly but still readable are the essays on the new political history in Richard L. McCormick, *The Party Period and Public Policy: American Politics from the Age of Jackson to the Progressive Era* (Oxford University Press, 1986). The more advanced student should consult Daniel T. Rodgers, "In Search of Progressivism," *Reviews in American History* (December 1982). While admitting that Progressives shared no common creed or values, Rodgers nevertheless feels that they were able "to articulate their discontents and their social visions" around three distinct clusters of ideas: "The first was the rhetoric of antimonopolism, the second was an emphasis on social bonds and the social nature of human beings, and the third was the language of social efficiency."

ISSUE 8

Was Woodrow Wilson a Naive Idealist?

YES: Henry Kissinger, from *Diplomacy* (Simon & Schuster, 1994)

NO: Arthur S. Link, from "The Higher Realism of Woodrow Wilson," *Journal of Presbyterian History* (March 1963)

ISSUE SUMMARY

YES: Former national security adviser and political scholar Henry Kissinger characterizes President Woodrow Wilson as a high-minded idealist whose views made it difficult for later presidents to develop a logical foreign policy based on national self-interest.

NO: Professor of history Arthur S. Link contends that Wilson was a true realist who combined the principles of idealism and realism in the reforms he enacted as president of Princeton University, governor of New Jersey, and president of the United States.

Historians have dealt with Woodrow Wilson rather strangely. The presidential polls conducted by historian Arthur M. Schlesinger, Jr., in 1948 and 1962, as well as the 1983 Murray-Blessing poll, ranked Wilson among the top 10 presidents. Historian William G. Carleton considers him the greatest twentieth-century president, only two notches below Thomas Jefferson and Abraham Lincoln. Yet among his biographers, Wilson, for the most part, has been treated ungenerously. They carp at him for being naive, overly idealistic, too inflexible, rigid, uncompromising, formal, stiff, unkind, disloyal to friends, overcompromising, oratorical, preachy, messianic, and moralistic. It appears that, like many of his contemporaries, Wilson's biographers respect the man but do not like the person.

Why has Wilson been treated with a nagging pettiness by historians? Perhaps the reasons have to do with Wilson's own introspective personality and his lack of formal political experience. He was, along with Jefferson and, to some extent, Theodore Roosevelt, our most intellectual president. He spent nearly 20 years as a history and political science teacher and scholar at Bryn Mawr College, Wesleyan University, and Princeton University, his alma mater. While his multivolume *History of the United States* now appears dated as it gathers dust on musty library shelves, Wilson's Ph.D. dissertation on congressional government, which he wrote as a graduate student at Johns Hopkins University, remains a classic statement of the weakness of leadership in the American constitutional system.

In addition to working many years as a college professor, Wilson served a short stint as a lawyer and spent eight distinguished years as president of Princeton University, which he turned into one of the outstanding universities in the country. He introduced the preceptorial system, widely used today, which supplemented course lectures with discussion conferences led by young instructors, and he took the lead in reorganizing the university's curriculum.

Historians agree that no president, with the exception of Franklin Roosevelt and perhaps Ronald Reagan, performed the ceremonial role of the presidency as well as Wilson. His speeches rang with oratorical brilliance and substance. No wonder he abandoned the practice of Jefferson and his successors by delivering the president's annual State of the Union Address to Congress in person rather than in writing.

During his first four years, Wilson also fashioned an ambitious legislative program. Wilson's "New Freedom" pulled together conservative and progressive, rural and urban, and southern and northern Democrats. This coalition passed measures such as the Underwood/Simmons Tariff Act, the first bill to significantly lower tariff rates since the Civil War, and the Owens/Keating Child Labor Act. It was through Wilson's adroit maneuvering that the Federal Reserve System was established. This banking measure, the most significant in U.S. history, established a major federal agency, which regulates the money supply in the country to this day. Finally, President Wilson revealed his flexibility when he abandoned his initial policy of rigid and indiscriminate trust-busting for one of regulating big business, through the creation of the Federal Trade Commission.

It is in his roles as commander in chief and chief diplomat that Woodrow Wilson has received the greatest criticism. In the following selections, Henry Kissinger argues that because Wilson believed that America was a morally superior nation, his intermingling of power and principle made it difficult for future presidents to develop a foreign policy based on a coherent outline of national interest. Arthur S. Link asserts that Wilson was a true realist who combined the principles of idealism and realism in the reforms that he enacted throughout his professional career.

YES

Henry Kissinger

THE HINGE: THEODORE ROOSEVELT
OR WOODROW WILSON

Until early in this century, the isolationist tendency prevailed in American foreign policy. Then, two factors projected America into world affairs: its rapidly expanding power, and the gradual collapse of the international system centered on Europe. Two watershed presidencies marked this progression: Theodore Roosevelt's and Woodrow Wilson's. These men held the reins of government when world affairs were drawing a reluctant nation into their vortex. Both recognized that America had a crucial role to play in world affairs though they justified its emergence from isolation with opposite philosophies.

Roosevelt was a sophisticated analyst of the balance of power. He insisted on an international role for America because its national interest demanded it, and because a global balance of power was inconceivable to him without American participation. For Wilson, the justification of America's international role was messianic: America had an obligation, not to the balance of power, but to spread its principles throughout the world. During the Wilson Administration, America emerged as a key player in world affairs, proclaiming principles which, while reflecting the truisms of American thought, nonetheless marked a revolutionary departure for Old World diplomats. These principles held that peace depends on the spread of democracy, that states should be judged by the same ethical criteria as individuals, and that the national interest consists of adhering to a universal system of law.

To hardened veterans of a European diplomacy based on the balance of power, Wilson's views about the ultimately moral foundations of foreign policy appeared strange, even hypocritical. Yet Wilsonianism has survived while history has bypassed the reservations of his contemporaries. Wilson was the originator of the vision of a universal world organization, the League of Nations, which would keep the peace through collective security rather than alliances. Though Wilson could not convince his own country of its merit, the idea lived on. It is above all to the drumbeat of Wilsonian idealism that American foreign policy has marched since his watershed presidency, and continues to march to this day.

From Henry Kissinger, *Diplomacy* (Simon & Schuster, 1994). Copyright © 1994 by Henry Kissinger. Reprinted by permission of Simon & Schuster, Inc. Notes omitted.

America's singular approach to international affairs did not develop all at once, or as the consequence of a solitary inspiration. In the early years of the Republic, American foreign policy was in fact a sophisticated reflection of the American national interest, which was, simply, to fortify the new nation's independence. Since no European country was capable of posing an actual threat so long as it had to contend with rivals, the Founding Fathers showed themselves quite ready to manipulate the despised balance of power when it suited their needs; indeed, they could be extraordinarily skillful at maneuvering between France and Great Britain not only to preserve America's independence but to enlarge its frontiers. Because they really wanted neither side to win a decisive victory in the wars of the French Revolution, they declared neutrality. Jefferson defined the Napoleonic Wars as a contest between the tyrant on the land (France) and the tyrant of the ocean (England)—in other words, the parties in the European struggle were morally equivalent. Practicing an early form of nonalignment, the new nation discovered the benefit of neutrality as a bargaining tool, just as many an emerging nation has since.

At the same time, the United States did not carry its rejection of Old World ways to the point of forgoing territorial expansion. On the contrary, from the very beginning, the United States pursued expansion in the Americas with extraordinary singleness of purpose. After 1794, a series of treaties settled the borders with Canada and Florida in America's favor, opened the Mississippi River to American trade, and began to establish an American commercial interest in the British West Indies. This culminated in the Louisiana Purchase of 1803, which brought to the young country a huge, undefined territory west of the Mississippi River from France along with claims to Spanish territory in Florida and Texas— the foundation from which to develop into a great power....

Though in fact the British Royal Navy protected America from depredations by European powers, American leaders did not perceive Great Britain as their country's protector. Throughout the nineteenth century, Great Britain was considered the greatest challenge to American interests, and the Royal Navy the most serious strategic threat. No wonder that, when America began to flex its muscles, it sought to expel Great Britain's influence from the Western Hemisphere, invoking the Monroe Doctrine which Great Britain had been so instrumental in encouraging.

... By 1902, Great Britain had abandoned its claim to a major role in Central America.

Supreme in the Western Hemisphere, the United States began to enter the wider arena of international affairs. America had grown into a world power almost despite itself. Expanding across the continent, it had established its preeminence all around its shores while insisting that it had no wish to conduct the foreign policy of a Great Power. At the end of the process, America found itself commanding the sort of power which made it a major international factor, no matter what its preferences. America's leaders might continue to insist that its basic foreign policy was to serve as a "beacon" for the rest of mankind, but there could be no denying that some of them were also becoming aware that America's power entitled it to be heard on the issues of the day, and that it did not need to wait until all of mankind had become democratic to make itself a part of the international system.

No one articulated this reasoning more trenchantly than Theodore Roosevelt. He was the first president to insist that it was America's duty to make its influence felt globally, and to relate America to the world in terms of a concept of national interest. Like his predecessors, Roosevelt was convinced of America's beneficent role in the world. But unlike them, Roosevelt held that America had real foreign policy interests that went far beyond its interest in remaining unentangled. Roosevelt started from the premise that the United States was a power like any other, not a singular incarnation of virtue. If its interests collided with those of other countries, America had the obligation to draw on its strength to prevail. ...

For Roosevelt, muscular diplomacy in the Western Hemisphere was part of America's new global role. The two oceans were no longer wide enough to insulate America from the rest of the world. The United States had to become an actor on the international stage. Roosevelt said as much in a 1902 message to the Congress: "More and more, the increasing interdependence and complexity of international political and economic relations render it incumbent on all civilized and orderly powers to insist on the proper policing of the world."

Roosevelt commands a unique historical position in America's approach to international relations. No other president defined America's world role so completely in terms of national interest, or identified the national interest so comprehensively with the balance of power. Roosevelt shared the view of his countrymen, that America was the best hope for the world. But unlike most of them, he did not believe that it could preserve the peace or fulfill its destiny simply by practicing civic virtues. In his perception of the nature of world order, he was much closer to Palmerston or Disraeli than to Thomas Jefferson.

A great president must be an educator, bridging the gap between his people's future and its experience. Roosevelt taught an especially stern doctrine for a people brought up in the belief that peace is the normal condition among nations, that there is no difference between personal and public morality, and that America was safely insulated from the upheavals affecting the rest of the world. For Roosevelt rebutted each of these propositions. To him, international life meant struggle, and Darwin's theory of the survival of the fittest was a better guide to history than personal morality. In Roosevelt's view, the meek inherited the earth only if they were strong. To Roosevelt, America was not a cause but a great power—potentially the greatest. He hoped to be the president destined to usher his nation onto the world scene so that it might shape the twentieth century in the way Great Britain had dominated the nineteenth—as a country of vast strengths which had enlisted itself, with moderation and wisdom, to work on behalf of stability, peace, and progress.

... In a world regulated by power, Roosevelt believed that the natural order of things was reflected in the concept of "spheres of influence," which assigned preponderant influence over large regions to specific powers, for example, to the United States in the Western Hemisphere or to Great Britain on the Indian subcontinent. In 1908, Roosevelt acquiesced to the Japanese occupation of Korea because, to his way of thinking, Japanese-Korean relations had to be determined by the relative power of each country, not by the provisions of a treaty or by international law....

With Roosevelt holding such European-style views, it was not surprising that he approached the global balance of power with a sophistication matched by no other American president and approached only by Richard Nixon. Roosevelt at first saw no need to engage America in the specifics of the European balance of power because he considered it more or less self-regulating. But he left little doubt that, if such a judgment were to prove wrong, he would urge America to engage itself to re-establish the equilibrium. Roosevelt gradually came to see Germany as a threat to the European balance and began to identify America's national interest with those of Great Britain and France....

In one of history's ironies, America did in the end fulfill the leading role Roosevelt had envisioned for it, and within Roosevelt's lifetime, but it did so on behalf of principles Roosevelt derided, and under the guidance of a president whom Roosevelt despised. Woodrow Wilson was the embodiment of the tradition of American exceptionalism, and originated what would become the dominant intellectual school of American foreign policy—a school whose precepts Roosevelt considered at best irrelevant and at worst inimical to America's long-range interests....

Wilson's was an astonishing achievement. Rejecting power politics, he knew how to move the American people. An academic who arrived in politics relatively late, he was elected due to a split in the Republican Party between Taft and Roosevelt. Wilson grasped that America's instinctive isolationism could be overcome only by an appeal to its be-lief in the exceptional nature of its ideals. Step by step, he took an isolationist country into war, after he had first demonstrated his Administration's devotion to peace by a passionate advocacy of neutrality. And he did so while abjuring any selfish national interests, and by affirming that America sought no other benefit than vindication of its principles.

In Wilson's first State of the Union Address, on December 2, 1913, he laid down the outline of what later came to be known as Wilsonianism. Universal law and not equilibrium, national trustworthiness and not national self-assertion were, in Wilson's view, the foundations of international order. Recommending the ratification of several treaties of arbitration, Wilson argued that binding arbitration, not force, should become the method for resolving international disputes:

> There is only one possible standard by which to determine controversies between the United States and other nations, and that is compounded of these two elements: Our own honor and our obligations to the peace of the world. A test so compounded ought easily to be made to govern both the establishment of new treaty obligations and the interpretation of those already assumed....

America's influence, in Wilson's view, depended on its unselfishness; it had to preserve itself so that, in the end, it could step forward as a credible arbiter between the warring parties. Roosevelt had asserted that the war in Europe, and especially a German victory, would ultimately threaten American security. Wilson maintained that America was essentially disinterested, hence should emerge as mediator. Because of America's faith in values higher than the balance of power, the war in Europe now afforded it an extraordinary opportunity to proselytize for a new and better approach to international affairs.

Roosevelt ridiculed such ideas and accused Wilson of pandering to isolationist sentiments to help his re-election in 1916. In fact, the thrust of Wilson's policy was quite the opposite of isolationism. What Wilson was proclaiming was not America's withdrawal from the world but the universal applicability of its values and, in time, America's commitment to spreading them. Wilson restated what had become the conventional American wisdom since Jefferson, but put it in the service of a crusading ideology:

- America's special mission transcends day-to-day diplomacy and obliges it to serve as a beacon of liberty for the rest of mankind.

- The foreign policies of democracies are morally superior because the people are inherently peace-loving.

- Foreign policy should reflect the same moral standards as personal ethics.

- The state has no right to claim a separate morality for itself.

Wilson endowed these assertions of American moral exceptionalism with a universal dimension:

> Dread of the power of any other nation we are incapable of. We are not jealous of rivalry in the fields of commerce or of any other peaceful achievement. We mean to live our own lives as we will; but we mean also to let live. We are, indeed, a true friend to all the nations of the world, because we threaten none, covet the possessions of none, desire the overthrow of none.

No other nation has ever rested its claim to international leadership on its altruism. All other nations have sought to be judged by the compatibility of their national interests with those of other societies. Yet, from Woodrow Wilson through George Bush, American presidents have invoked their country's unselfishness as the crucial attribute of its leadership role. Neither Wilson nor his later disciples, through the present, have been willing to face the fact that, to foreign leaders imbued with less elevated maxims, America's claim to altruism evokes a certain aura of unpredictability; whereas the national interest can be calculated, altruism depends on the definition of its practitioner.

To Wilson, however, the altruistic nature of American society was proof of divine favor:

> It was as if in the Providence of God a continent had been kept unused and waiting for a peaceful people who loved liberty and the rights of men more than they loved anything else, to come and set up an unselfish commonwealth.

The claim that American goals represented providential dispensation implied a global role for America that would prove far more sweeping than any Roosevelt had ever imagined. For he had wanted no more than to improve the balance of power and to invest America's role in it with the importance commensurate with its growing strength. In Roosevelt's conception, America would have been one nation among many—more powerful than most and part of an elite group of great powers—but still subject to the historic ground rules of equilibrium.

Wilson moved America onto a plane entirely remote from such considerations.

Disdaining the balance of power, he insisted that America's role was "not to prove... our selfishness, but our greatness." If that was true, America had no right to hoard its values for itself. As early as 1915, Wilson put forward the unprecedented doctrine that the security of America was inseparable from the security of *all* the rest of mankind. This implied that it was henceforth America's duty to oppose aggression *everywhere:*

> ... because we demand unmolested development and the undisturbed government of our own lives upon our own principles of right and liberty, we resent, from whatever quarter it may come, the aggression we ourselves will not practice. We insist upon security in prosecuting our self-chosen lines of national development. We do more than that. We demand it also for others. We do not confine our enthusiasm for individual liberty and free national development to the incidents and movements of affairs which affect only ourselves. We feel it wherever there is a people that tries to walk in these difficult paths of independence and right.

Envisioning America as a beneficent global policeman, this foreshadowed the containment policy, which would be developed after the Second World War....

Germany's announcement of unrestricted submarine warfare and its sinking of the *Lusitania* became the proximate cause of America's declaration of war. But Wilson did not justify America's entry into the war on the grounds of specific grievances. National interests were irrelevant; Belgium's violation and the balance of power had nothing to do with it. Rather, the war had a moral foundation, whose primary objective was a new and more just international order. "It is a fear-

ful thing," Wilson reflected in the speech asking for a declaration of war,

> to lead this great peaceful people into war, into the most terrible and disastrous of all wars, civilization itself seeming to be in the balance. But right is more precious than peace, and we shall fight for the things which we have always carried nearest our hearts, for democracy, for the right of those who submit to authority to have a voice in their own governments, for the rights and liberties of small nations, for a universal dominion of right by such a concert of free, peoples as shall bring peace and safety to all nations and make the world itself at last free.

In a war on behalf of such principles, there could be no compromise. Total victory was the only valid goal. Roosevelt would almost certainly have expressed America's war aims in political and strategic terms; Wilson, flaunting American disinterest, defined America's war aims in entirely moral categories. In Wilson's view, the war was not the consequence of clashing national interests pursued without restraint, but of Germany's unprovoked assault on the international order. More specifically, the true culprit was not the German nation, but the German Emperor himself....

Wilson's historic achievement lies in his recognition that Americans cannot sustain major international engagements that are not justified by their moral faith. His downfall was in treating the tragedies of history as aberrations, or as due to the shortsightedness and the evil of individual leaders, and in his rejection of any objective basis for peace other than the force of public opinion and the worldwide spread of democratic institutions. In the process, he would ask the nations of Europe to undertake something for which they were neither philosophically nor historically prepared, and right after a war which had drained them of substance.

For 300 years, the European nations had based their world order on a balancing of national interests, and their foreign policies on a quest for security, treating every additional benefit as a bonus. Wilson asked the nations of Europe to base their foreign policy on moral convictions, leaving security to result incidentally, if at all. But Europe had no conceptual apparatus for such a disinterested policy, and it still remained to be seen whether America, having just emerged from a century of isolation, could sustain the permanent involvement in international affairs that Wilson's theories implied.

Wilson's appearance on the scene was a watershed for America, one of those rare examples of a leader who fundamentally alters the course of his country's history. Had Roosevelt or his ideas prevailed in 1912, the question of war aims would have been based on an inquiry into the nature of American national interest. Roosevelt would have rested America's entry into the war on the proposition—which he in fact advanced—that, unless America joined the Triple Entente, the Central Powers would win the war and, sooner or later, pose a threat to American security.

The American national interest, so defined, would, over time, have led America to adopt a global policy comparable to Great Britain's toward Continental Europe. For three centuries, British leaders had operated from the assumption that, if Europe's resources were marshaled by a single dominant power, that country would then have the resources to challenge Great Britain's command of the seas, and thus threaten its independence. Geopolitically, the United States, also an island off the shores of Eurasia, should, by the same reasoning, have felt obliged to resist the domination of Europe or Asia by any one power and, even more, the control of *both* continents by the *same* power. In these terms, it should have been the extent of Germany's geopolitical reach and not its moral transgressions that provided the principal *casus belli*.

However, such an Old World approach ran counter to the wellspring of American emotions being tapped by Wilson—as it does to this day. Not even Roosevelt could have managed the power politics he advocated, though he died convinced that he could have. At any rate, Roosevelt was no longer the president, and Wilson had made it clear, even before America entered the war, that he would resist any attempt to base the postwar order on established principles of international politics.

Wilson saw the causes of the war not only in the wickedness of the German leadership but in the European balance-of-power system as well. On January 22, 1917, he attacked the international order which had preceded the war as a system of "organized rivalries":

> The question upon which the whole future peace and policy of the world depends is this: Is the present war a struggle for a just and secure peace, or only for a new balance of power? ... There must be, not a balance of power, but a community of power; not organized rivalries, but an organized common peace.

What Wilson meant by "community of power" was an entirely new concept that later became known as "collective security" (though William Gladstone in Great Britain had put forward a stillborn variation of it in the course of 1880). Convinced that all the nations of the world had an equal interest in peace and would therefore unite to punish those who disturbed it, Wilson proposed to defend the international order by the moral consensus of the peace-loving:

... this age is an age... which rejects the standards of national selfishness that once governed the counsels of nations and demands that they shall give way to a new order of things in which the only questions will be: "Is it right?" "Is it just?" "Is it in the interest of mankind?"

To institutionalize this consensus, Wilson put forward the League of Nations, a quintessentially American institution. Under the auspices of this world organization, power would yield to morality and the force of arms to the dictates of public opinion. Wilson kept emphasizing that, had the public been adequately informed, the war would never have occurred—ignoring the passionate demonstrations of joy and relief which had greeted the onset of war in *all* capitals, including those of democratic Great Britain and France. If the new theory was to work, in Wilson's view, at least two changes in international governance had to take place: first, the spread of democratic governments throughout the world, and, next, the elaboration of a "new and more wholesome diplomacy" based on "the same high code of honor that we demand of individuals."

In 1918, Wilson stated as a requirement of peace the hitherto unheard-of and breathtakingly ambitious goal of "the destruction of every arbitrary power anywhere that can separately, secretly and of its single choice disturb the peace of the world; or, if it cannot be presently destroyed, at the least its reduction to

virtual impotence." A League of Nations so composed and animated by such attitudes would resolve crises without war, Wilson told the Peace Conference on February 14, 1919:

... throughout this instrument [the League Covenant] we are depending primarily and chiefly upon one great force, and that is the moral force of the public opinion of the world—the cleansing and clarifying and compelling influences of publicity... so that those things that are destroyed by the light may be properly destroyed by the overwhelming light of the universal expression of the condemnation of the world.

The preservation of peace would no longer spring from the traditional calculus of power but from worldwide consensus backed up by a policing mechanism. A universal grouping of largely democratic nations would act as the "trustee of peace," and replace the old balance-of-power and alliance systems.

Such exalted sentiments had never before been put forward by any nation, let alone been implemented. Nevertheless, in the hands of American idealism they were turned into the common currency of national thinking on foreign policy. Every American president since Wilson has advanced variations of Wilson's theme. Domestic debates have more often dealt with the failure to fulfill Wilson's ideals (soon so commonplace that they were no longer even identified with him) than with whether they were in fact lending adequate guidance in meeting the occasionally brutal challenges of a turbulent world. For three generations, critics have savaged Wilson's analysis and conclusions; and yet, in all this time, Wilson's principles have remained the bedrock of American foreign-policy thinking.

And yet Wilson's intermingling of power and principle also set the stage for decades of ambivalence as the American conscience tried to reconcile its principles with its necessities. The basic premise of collective security was that all nations would view every threat to security in the same way *and* be prepared to run the same risks in resisting it. Not only had nothing like it ever actually occurred, nothing like it was destined to occur in the entire history of both the League of Nations and the United Nations. Only when a threat is truly overwhelming and genuinely affects all, or most, societies is such a consensus possible—as it was during the two world wars and, on a regional basis, in the Cold War. But in the vast majority of cases—and in nearly all of the difficult ones—the nations of the world tend to disagree either about the nature of the threat or about the type of sacrifice they are prepared to make to meet it. This was the case from Italy's aggressions against Abyssinia in 1935 to the Bosnian crisis in 1992. And when it has been a matter of achieving positive objectives or remedying perceived injustices, global consensus has proved even more difficult to achieve. Ironically, in the post–Cold War world, which has no overwhelming ideological or military threat and which pays more lip service to democracy than has any previous era, these difficulties have only increased.

Wilsonianism also accentuated another latent split in American thought on international affairs. Did America have any security interests it needed to defend regardless of the methods by which they were challenged? Or should America resist only changes which could fairly be described as illegal? Was it the fact or the method of international

transformation that concerned America? Did America reject the principles of geopolitics altogether? Or did they need to be reinterpreted through the filter of American values? And if these should clash, which would prevail?

The implication of Wilsonianism has been that America resisted, above all, the method of change, and that it had no strategic interests worth defending if they were threatened by apparently legal methods. As late as the Gulf War, President Bush insisted that he was not so much defending vital oil supplies as resisting the principle of aggression. And during the Cold War, some of the domestic American debate concerned the question whether America, with all its failings, had a moral right to organize resistance to the Moscow threat.

Theodore Roosevelt would have had no doubt as to the answer to these questions. To assume that nations would perceive threats identically or be prepared to react to them uniformly represented a denial of everything he had ever stood for. Nor could he envision any world organization to which victim and aggressor could comfortably belong at the same time. In November 1918, he wrote in a letter:

> I am for such a League provided we don't expect too much from it.... I am not willing to play the part which even Aesop held up to derision when he wrote of how the wolves and the sheep agreed to disarm, and how the sheep as a guarantee of good faith sent away the watchdogs, and were then forthwith eaten by the wolves.

The following month, he wrote this to Senator Knox of Pennsylvania:

> The League of Nations may do a little good, but the more pompous it is and

the more it pretends to do, the less it will really accomplish. The talk about it has a grimly humorous suggestion of the talk about the Holy Alliance a hundred years ago, which had as its main purpose the perpetual maintenance of peace. The Czar Alexander by the way, was the President Wilson of this particular movement a century ago.

In Roosevelt's estimation, only mystics, dreamers, and intellectuals held the view that peace was man's natural condition and that it could be maintained by disinterested consensus. To him, peace was inherently fragile and could be preserved only by eternal vigilance, by the arms of the strong, and by alliances among the like-minded.

But Roosevelt lived either a century too late or a century too early. His approach to international affairs died with him in 1919; no significant school of American thought on foreign policy has invoked him since. On the other hand, it is surely the measure of Wilson's intellectual triumph that even Richard Nixon, whose foreign policy in fact embodied many of Roosevelt's precepts, considered himself above all a disciple of Wilson's internationalism, and hung a portrait of the wartime president in the Cabinet Room.

The League of Nations failed to take hold in America because the country was not yet ready for so global a role. Nevertheless, Wilson's intellectual victory proved more seminal than any political triumph could have been. For, whenever America has faced the task of constructing a new world order, it has returned in one way or another to Woodrow Wilson's precepts. At the end of World War II, it helped build the United Nations on the same principles as those of the League, hoping to found peace on a concord of the victors. When this hope died, America waged the Cold War not as a conflict between two superpowers but as a moral struggle for democracy. When communism collapsed, the Wilsonian idea that the road to peace lay in collective security, coupled with the worldwide spread of democratic institutions, was adopted by administrations of both major American political parties.

In Wilsonianism was incarnate the central drama of America on the world stage: America's ideology has, in a sense, been revolutionary while, domestically, Americans have considered themselves satisfied with the *status quo*. Tending to turn foreign-policy issues into a struggle between good and evil, Americans have generally felt ill at ease with compromise, as they have with partial or inconclusive outcomes. The fact that America has shied away from seeking vast geopolitical transformations has often associated it with defense of the territorial, and sometimes the political, *status quo*. Trusting in the rule of law, it has found it difficult to reconcile its faith in peaceful change with the historical fact that almost all significant changes in history have involved violence and upheaval.

America found that it would have to implement its ideals in a world less blessed than its own and in concert with states possessed of narrower margins of survival, more limited objectives, and far less self-confidence. And yet America has persevered. The postwar world became largely America's creation, so that, in the end, it did come to play the role Wilson had envisioned for it—as a beacon to follow, and a hope to attain.

NO

Arthur S. Link

THE HIGHER REALISM OF
WOODROW WILSON

On March 4, 1913, a gaunt man walked to the stands outside the east front of the Capitol in Washington to take the oath of office as twenty-eighth President of the United States. Although his face was somber with a sense of high seriousness, it radiated strength and determination, and there was thrilling power in his voice as he summoned the American people to the tasks of national reconstruction. Eight years later, in 1921, he assisted in the rituals inaugurating his successor, Warren G. Harding. Now he was broken in body, and his drawn face reflected the pain that had come from his recent repudiation at the hands of the people during the election of 1920.

He was Woodrow Wilson, born in Staunton, Virginia, on December 28, 1856, reared in Presbyterian manses in Georgia and the Carolinas, educated at Davidson College in North Carolina and Princeton University, trained in the study of law at the University of Virginia, and prepared for a career in teaching and scholarship at The Johns Hopkins University. He had taught successively from 1885 to 1902 at Bryn Mawr College in Pennsylvania, Wesleyan University in Connecticut, and Princeton, and had served as president of the latter institution from 1902 to 1910. Plunging into the troubled sea of politics in 1910, he had won the Governorship of New Jersey and gone on with almost irresistible power to capture the Presidency in 1912. Then he had guided the destinies of the American people from 1913 to 1921 and helped to direct the destinies of the world during eight of the most critical years of the modern epoch.

I am happy to come before this particular audience in this venerable city to talk about the man who has been the subject of my main thought and work for twenty years. I must confess at the outset that I have prepared this paper with a definite purpose in mind. It is neither to praise Woodrow Wilson nor to bury him. The record of his contribution has its own integrity, and what little I could say would neither add to nor detract from it. It is not to bring you any new view of President Wilson, for I doubt that I could say anything really new about him at this point. My purpose is, rather, to attempt to pull together a number of thoughts and convictions that have been coursing through my

From Arthur S. Link, "The Higher Realism of Woodrow Wilson," *Journal of Presbyterian History*, vol. 41 (March 1963). Copyright © 1963 by The Presbyterian Historical Society. Reprinted by permission of The Department of History of the Presbyterian Church. Notes omitted.

mind during the past few years; in brief, to clarify my own conclusions about the subject of my life's work.

I have felt impelled to this undertaking in part by many conversations with English and German historians which have challenged my own emerging view of President Wilson. My experiences during a year abroad in 1958–1959 have brought home the fact that Europeans on the whole still view Wilson very much as many of them viewed him forty years ago at the end of the Paris Peace Conference and the great struggle in the United States over ratification of the Treaty of Versailles. This European image is, I think it is fair to say, one of a well-intentioned idealist, a man good by ordinary Christian standards, but essentially a destructive force in modern history because he was visionary, unrealistic, provincial, and ignorant of European problems; he was also zealous and messianic in conceit but devoid of either practical knowledge or the humility to follow others better informed than he. I do not think that this is an essentially unfair statement of the European point of view. It was, of course, the image of John Maynard Keynes, Georges Clemenceau, and most of the thoughtful European public at the end of the Peace Conference. It is the view still largely held by English, French, and German scholars alike if for different reasons.

I have felt impelled to my subject not only by recent forceful reminders of the strong survival of the old European image of President Wilson, but also by the emergence in our own country during the past few years of a new school of historical critics, and by their work in constructing an image of President Wilson that is remarkably like the older European one.

Calling themselves realists, and drawing their inspiration from the distinguished diplomat-historian George Kennan, and the Austrian-trained authority in international relations Hans J. Morgenthau, now at the University of Chicago, these new American critics have found Wilson wanting because he did not think in terms of strategy, bases, and armed power, but dwelt too much in ethereal realms.

Are the old European and new American critics right, I have asked myself over and over during the past few years. Is this the image that I also see, the Wilson that I know? Were the Austrians right in thinking that his irresponsible preaching of a slogan, "self-determination," was primarily responsible for the destruction of the Hapsburg Empire? Were the Germans right in holding him responsible for what they regarded as the monstrous betrayal of Versailles? Were the French right in thinking that he prevented the imposition of the only kind of peace settlement upon Germany that could endure? Were the English and new American critics near the truth when they portrayed him as a tragic figure irrelevant in the modern world?

I must confess that I have sometimes been tempted to agree. No one who has ever given any serious attention to President Wilson's life could fail to agree that he was *primarily* a Christian idealist. By this I mean a man who almost always tended to judge policies on a basis of whether they were right by Christian standards, not whether they brought immediate material or strategic advantage. I mean also a man whose foreign policies were motivated by the assumption that a nation as much as an individual should live according to the law of Christian love, and by a positive repudiation of the assumptions of the classical "realists" about international behavior.

No one who has given serious study to Wilson's career, moreover, could fail to agree that there is at least an appearance of reality about the old European and new American image. Wilson was not merely an idealist, but a crusading idealist. An orator of enormous eloquence and power, he was also a phrase-maker who more than once fell victim to the magic of his own words. In international relations he did not give undue weight to material forces or base his policies upon the assumption that nations must always act selfishly. At times he did seem to give the appearance of believing that he was a kind of messiah divinely appointed to deliver Europe from the cruel tyranny of history.

I have myself made all these criticisms and others more elaborately in my own writings. But they have never really satisfied me and do not satisfy me now. I do not think that they add up to an historical image that is accurate. Indeed, I cannot escape the conclusion that they altogether miss the main point and meaning of President Wilson's career.

The point, in my opinion, and the theme of this paper, is that among all the major statesmen and thoughtful critics of his age, President Wilson was in fact the supreme realist, and that because this is true, what he stood for and fought to accomplish has large meaning for our own generation.

This is, to be sure, a very broad, perhaps even an audacious, statement, one that does not mean very much unless we are careful to define our terms. A realist, I take it, is one who faces life and its situations without illusions; in short, one who can see realities or truth through the fog of delusion that normally shrouds the earthbound individual. If the European and American critics of President Wilson who thought mainly in strategic and material terms, who measured national power by army divisions and naval bases, and the like, if *they* were realists, then President Wilson was a realist of a different sort. Sheerly for purposes of convenience, let us call his view of the national and international situations with which he had to cope a "higher realism," higher because more perceptive, more in accord with ultimate reality, more likely to win the long-run moral approval of societies professing allegiance to the common Western, humane, Christian traditions.

We still have not passed beyond the statement of a thesis and a definition of elementary terminology. There now remains the much more important task of seeing to what degree the evidence of Wilson's career supports my generalization. We obviously do not have time to review all the important events of Wilson's long and active career here. On the other hand, we cannot concentrate our attention on one aspect without running the risks of distortion. President Wilson actually had three separate public careers—as university president and educational statesman, as a domestic leader concerned almost exclusively with problems of political and economic reconstruction in the United States, and, finally, as a world statesman who attempted to give leadership in a movement for the reconstruction of the international community. He made large and seemingly different contributions in each field. And yet we must try to view his career and labors as a whole, for he was fundamentally the same man throughout. His "higher realism" was no less a force in his leadership at home than abroad.

It was evident in a striking way in the first contributions that he made as a public leader, as president of Princeton University from 1902 to 1910. There were first the things that he did and tried to do for Princeton: his introduction of a systematic and meaningful course of undergraduate study, and his positive repudiation of a conference, method of instruction to supplement the lecture system; and his proposal for the reorganization of undergraduate social life in order to elevate the intellectual climate of the university. By such plans and by his own inspiration, he not only transformed Princeton but also helped to transform higher education in the United States.

And yet Wilson made his greatest contributions in the field of education more by the things that he fought for than by what he did. For one thing, he stood for standards and academic integrity. For another, he had an exalted concept of the university and college and the role that they should play in preparing men and women for the nation's service because they were dedicated to the cause of truth and the intellectual enrichment of mankind. Finally, during an era of increasing specialization and degradation of undergraduate curricula by the introduction of all sorts of so-called useful programs of study, Wilson never ceased to remind fellow teaches and administrators that their first job was to help perpetuate the cultural traditions upon which Western civilization rested, not to teach students how to make money.

Who, we are entitled to ask, were the true "realists" in educational policy? Were they the alleged realists of Wilson's time, the sincere devotees of the new so-called progressive concepts and faddists, who were then beginning their long attack upon traditional studies and destroying the unity of university curricula? To ask the question is almost to answer it. The entire drive in American higher education during the past twenty years toward recovery of standards and unity in curricula and against the vulgarization that followed the widespread introduction of so-called useful courses of study— this entire movement, so full of promise, is testimony to the higher realism of Wilson's leadership in the academic world.

It was the same, I would suggest, with Wilson's leadership during his second career as Governor of New Jersey from 1911 to 1913 and President of the United States afterward. He came to political leadership at one of the most critical junctures in American history, at the high tide of what American historians call the progressive movement. For more than a quarter of a century the American people had been in revolt in city, state, and nation against corruption and venality among officeholders, irresponsibility on all levels of government, and, above all, the emergence and spread of great aggregations of economic power among railroads, banks, corporations, and so on, which were uncontrolled and often repudiated any responsibility to the people as a whole. This revolt was at the point of culmination at the very time that Wilson was catapulted into political life in 1910, and because this was true the American people were now confronted with certain choices that would determine their future political system and the role that government would hereafter play in making fundamental economic decisions.

There was, first, the choice concerning the reconstruction of the American political system. Some so-called realists of the time argued cogently from the facts that the very concept and structure of representative government were fatally defective, and that the answer lay either in direct democracy or in concentration of political power in fewer hands. "Realists" on the other side, eager to preserve a status quo that benefited their own economic interests, argued just as convincingly that the American constitutional system, with its diffusion and separation of powers, was the most nearly perfect form of government on earth.

There was, secondly, the choice concerning the role that government should play in economic life. At the one extreme were the "realists" who, talking in terms of immutable economic law, defended traditional American policies of *laissez faire* in an effort to protect their privileged position. At the other extreme were "realists" with a greater popular appeal—men who demanded a sweeping extension of the power of government to bridle all hitherto uncontrolled economic interests. Some of these were socialists, ready to abandon capitalism in the major sectors of the economy altogether. Others were progressives who believed in capitalism but argued that it had reached a permanent phase of semimonopolistic maturity in the United States and could be saved only by instituting sweeping and rigorous public controls over all important areas of national economic life.

It was Woodrow Wilson's privilege to play a decisive role in the determination of these choices. To the "realists" who had despaired of representative government in the cities and states he replied more by example than by precept—by giving a spectacular example of responsible leadership in action as Governor of New Jersey. By making representative government work on the local level he, along with a company of other leaders at the time, guaranteed its survival. To the "realists" (and he had earlier been among them) who had proclaimed the incapacity of the Presidential-Congressional system to cope with the great problems of national administration, Wilson responded, both by reasoned word and striking deed, by transforming that system and demonstrating that it had immensely greater capacities than the so-called realists had thought. He did this by transforming the office of President from that of an aloof presiding official into incomparably the most powerful force in the American constitutional system—the force that gave unity and direction not only to the other branches of the federal government but to public opinion as well. This, we can now see, was the "higher realism" of a man who well understood the weaknesses of the American institutional structure but who knew the fundamental strength of the American democracy far better than most so-called realists of his time.

I think that it is also fair to say that President Wilson demonstrated the same kind of long-run wisdom, or "higher realism," in leading the American people to adoption of new policies for the regulation of economic life. He rejected the arguments both of defenders of the status quo and of proponents of violent change as being unsound in principle and unacceptable to the majority of the people. And he (along with his supporters in Congress) instituted a series of measures to impose a large measure of public direction and control, but also to balance private initiative with public regulation in order to stimulate the enormous latent competitive energies of the people. In short, he laid the solid foundations of the present mixed American system of political economy, which, to the amazement and bafflement of many Europeans, works so curiously and so well. Viewing the subsequent development of the American economy within the framework erected by President Wilson and his colleagues, I think that we would have to conclude that Wilson's solution was the only "realistic" one that could have been adopted. It saved American capitalism by making it socially responsible and hence acceptable to the people, without, however, impeding the forces that are essential for growth in the capitalistic system.

I am sure that in talking about Wilson's "higher realism" in meeting domestic challenges, I have simply been saying things and making judgments with which virtually every historian of the United States would readily agree. It is precisely this "higher realism" that has entitled Wilson to rank, by the agreement of American historians, among the four or five successful Presidents in our history. In talking about Wilson's policies and contributions in the realm of foreign affairs, I am, I know, on more controversial ground. Wilson was magnificently prepared for leadership in internal affairs by long study of American history and institutions. He had little if any preparation for leadership in the world at large; indeed, at the outset of his tenure in the White House he had no serious interest in foreign affairs. At the outset and later he made mistakes that still seriously impair his record. Even so, I cannot but conclude that President Wilson on the whole showed the same kind of wisdom and long-range vision and understanding, in short, "higher realism," in his third career as international statesman as he had already revealed in his first two careers at home.

This, I know, is a big statement, and I would like to preface it with a few generalizations about Wilson's thought and character as a diplomat in order to lay foundations for some later observations.

The first is the most obvious and the one with which most historians would agree, namely, that President Wilson was, as I have already said, above all an idealist in the conduct of foreign affairs, one who subordinated immediate goals and material interests to what he considered to be superior ethical standards and moral purposes. His idealism was perhaps best revealed in his thinking about the purposes that the United States should serve in the world. The mission of America, he said over and over and sincerely believed, was not a mission of aggrandizement of material power but one of service to mankind. It was a mission of peace, of sacrifice, of leading the nations into a new international community organized to achieve right ends.

Secondly, all of Wilson's thinking about international relations was conditioned, in general, by a loathing for war and, in particular, by a conviction that physical force should never be used to achieve selfish and material aims.

Thirdly, Wilson was actually in many ways "realistic," even by conventional standards, in his thinking about the methods in the conduct of foreign relations. For example, he used armed force in the classic way to achieve certain diplomatic objectives in Mexico and the Caribbean. He understood the meaning of the term "balance of power." He was keenly aware of the relevance of material interests and had few illusions about the fundamental bases of international behavior. It is, one must say, the sheerest nonsense to talk about him as an impractical idealist and visionary.

Fourthly, while admitting that there were times when a nation had no recourse but to use armed force in international disputes, and while using force himself on behalf of the American government on certain occasions, President Wilson never permitted war's neuroses and fascinations either to derange his reason or to obscure the political objectives for which force was being used. Hence he was never the victim of that greatest twentieth-century delusion, that it is necessary to win wars even at the risk of losing everything for which wars are fought.

This is a very imperfect characterization of the thought and character of Wilson the diplomatist, but it may help us to understand his policies during the greatest tragedy of the modern epoch and the event that raised the gravest challenges to his leadership—the First World War. It was for Wilson a period with three distinct stages—the period of American neutrality, from August, 1914 to April 1917; the period of American belligerency, from April, 1917 to November, 1918; and the period of peace-making, from November, 1918 to June, 1919. The challenges of each period were different, but he met them all, on the whole, with the same "higher realism" that had characterized his leadership at home.

His policies during the first period can best be briefly described by saying that from the outbreak of the war in Europe to the beginning of the German unlimited submarine campaign in early 1917, President Wilson tried as hard as any man could have done to be neutral, to make the necessary accommodations to the exercise of belligerent power, and to engage in stern defense of American rights only when they could not, because fundamental human principles were involved, be compromised.

Some of the recent American "realists" have joined the older English and French critics in charging Wilson with impractical idealism precisely because he did follow such a course—because he did not rally the American people to preparation for what they have said was an inevitable participation; because he conducted long and patient negotiations to avoid a break with Germany; because he did not undertake large and early measures of assistance to the Allies and thus help to shorten the duration of Europe's agony; because he refused throughout the period of American neutrality even to align the American people and their government morally on the Allied side.

Looking back upon the final outcome, as we are entitled to do, we well might wonder who the true realists were during this period. So-called "realists," or President Wilson, who in an almost uncanny way kept himself immune from the emotional hysterias and passions that seized other men; who believed that the causes of the war were so complex and remote that it was impossible to assess the blame; who, overborne by the tragedy of the event, fought desperately to preserve American neutrality so that he could perform the healing task of reconciliation once the nations of Europe had come to some sense; who believed that an enduring peace could come only through a "peace without victory," a "peace between equals"? Who were the deluded men who had lost sight of reality? The European leaders who thought that they could win decisive victories on the battlefields and on or under the seas, and who thought that they could impose their nations' wills upon other great peoples? Or Wilson, who thought that they were momentarily mad?

The climactic confrontation, the supreme reckoning between so-called realists and the alleged impractical idealist, came once the United States had been forced into the conflict and Germany was defeated. It did not occur earlier, because the British and French leaders had refused to permit it to occur before the Armistice was safely signed. But it could not then be long postponed, for the Allied leaders had matured their plans, and President Wilson had meanwhile formed a peace program of his own and announced it to the world in the Fourteen Points address and other speeches.

There is no need to review the turbulent events of the Paris Peace Conference here. They are familiar enough, to begin with; but a detailed account of them now would obscure my larger purpose —to look back upon the Paris settlement and, while looking back, to attempt to see who the true realists were.

The supreme task of the victors at Paris in 1919 was, obviously, to work out a peace settlement and reconstruct an international order that could endure. It had to be a peace that could survive the ebbing of passions and hatreds that consumed Europe in 1919. It had to be a peace that could survive because it could command the approval of the German people. Above all, it had to be the kind of settlement that would endure because it could retain the long-run support of the American and English peoples, even of the French people. The necessity of constructing this kind of settlement was, as we can now see clearly, the supreme reality of peace-making in 1919. We must, therefore, judge men and measures at the Paris Conference according to whether they met this test or not.

By this criterion I do not see how any fair historian can but conclude that the so-called realists at Paris—the dedicated if cynical Clemenceau, concerned only about the destruction of the ancient foe and the future security of France; the well-intentioned Lloyd George, who had given so many hostages to war passions at home and to the Commonwealths that he was no longer a free man; and the Italians, Sonnino and Orlando, eager only for spoils—how could they be called anything other than sublime irrationalists and dreamers? Theirs was a dream, a nightmare, of unreality. Given the task of reconstructing Europe and preventing a future war, they would have responded by attempting to perpetuate the division of Europe and by making a new war almost inevitable.

On the other side and standing usually in solidarity if splendid isolation was the alleged impractical idealist fighting for the only kind of a settlement that had any chance of survival—for a peace of reconciliation, for disarmament by victors as well as vanquished, against annexations and indemnities, and for a new international organization that would include former enemy states as active members from the beginning. Over and over he warned that this was the only kind of peace that would prove acceptable to the American people in the short run and to the moral opinion of the world in the long run, in short, the only kind of settlement that could endure. It should require little reference to events that followed the Paris Conference to demonstrate the "higher realism" of President Wilson's views.

If proof is needed on specific points, one could cite, for example, Wilson's point of view on the problem of reparations. Over and over he insisted, and with a steadfast consistency, that reparations should be compensation for specific willful damage only, not indemnity; that the Germans should not be saddled with a debt that was heavier than they could carry; and that there should be a time limit to the obligation that the German nation should be forced to assume. What the Allied leaders demanded and finally obtained is well-known to any student of modern history. What the realistic solution of this problem was is now too obvious for comment. Or, as a second example, one might cite Wilson's attitude toward the Russian Revolution—how he saw the deeply rooted causes of that cataclysm and the futility of any Western effort to suppress it by military force; and how the realism of his attitude contrasted to the egregious folly of so-called realists who thought that it lay within their power to change the course of Russian history.

The result of the clash between European so-called realism and Wilsonian so-called idealism was of course the Treaty of Versailles, that compromise that violated the terms of the agreement by which the Germans had stopped fighting, and made a mockery of some of the principal planks in the American President's peace program. Why, it is fair to ask, did President Wilson permit such a peace to be made and sign the treaty embodying it? The answer, I submit, is that it was "higher realism" that drove him to this difficult decision. Having won many of the things for which he had been fighting, at least partially, he had to give as well as to take, for he could not impose his will entirely upon his colleagues. He signed the Versailles treaty in the conviction that the passage of time and the treaty's new creation, the League of Nations, would almost certainly operate to rectify what

he knew were the grievous mistakes of the Peace Conference. He signed the Versailles treaty, in short, because he believed that it was the best settlement possible in the circumstances of 1919.

What President Wilson hoped would occur did of course in large part take place during the 1920's and early 1930's, even though alleged realists in the United States combined with authentic visionaries to repudiate Wilson's work and prevent their government from playing the role of mediating leadership within the League of Nations of which Wilson had dreamed. The great tragedy of the postwar period was not that the Versailles treaty was imperfect. It was that the forces of reconciliation could not operate rapidly enough without American leadership in the League, that France and Great Britain had neither the will nor the strength to defend the treaty alone during the 1930's and, above all, that the German people submitted to demonic forces that promised a speedy rectification of all the injustices of Versailles. But this is precisely what President Wilson, in another flash of "higher realism," predicted would occur if the so-called realists, both in the United States and in Europe, continued to have their way.

That is the age-old question, whether the so-called realists or the higher realists shall have their way in determination of national and international policies. President Wilson survives a more powerful force in history than when he lived because he gave us the supreme demonstration in the twentieth century of higher realism in statesmanship.

This, obviously, was no accident. Woodrow Wilson's "higher realism" was the product of insight and wisdom informed by active Christian faith. He was not, fundamentally, a moralist, as he so often seemed to be, but a man who lived in faith, trying to be guided by the Holy Spirit in meeting the complex problems of a changing nation and world. Using one of his own metaphors we can say that the light of heaven gleamed upon his sword. His percepts and ideals will be relevant so long as democracy endures, so long as men seek after a new international community organized for peace and the advancement of mankind.

POSTSCRIPT

Was Woodrow Wilson a Naive Idealist?

Kissinger is particularly well suited to write a history of diplomacy. At Harvard University he received a Ph.D. in political science and wrote a dissertation that was subsequently published as *A World Restored: Metternich, Castlereagh and the Problems of Peace, 1812–1822* (Houghton Mifflin, 1973). In it he admired how the major nations restored the balance of power in Europe once Napoleon was defeated. As President Richard Nixon's chief assistant for national security affairs and later as Nixon's and then President Gerald Ford's secretary of state in the 1970s, Kissinger became one of the nation's most active, visible, and controversial diplomats. He applied the "realistic" approach that he had previously written about to American foreign policy.

As an exponent of realism, Kissinger excoriates Wilson's handling of America's entrance into World War I and the subsequent negotiations of the peace treaty at Versailles. According to Kissinger, Wilson was reflective of an excessive moralism and naivete, which Americans hold about the world even today. Rejecting the fact that the United States had a basic national interest in preserving the balance of power in Europe, Wilson told the American people that they were entering the war to "bring peace and safety to all nations and make the world itself at last free." Kissinger believes that Theodore Roosevelt, the realist, had a firmer handle on foreign policy than did Wilson, the idealist. But in the long run, Wilsonianism triumphed and has influenced every modern-day president's foreign policy.

Kissinger's critique of Wilson is similar to the realist critique of traditional American foreign policy put forth during the height of the cold war in the 1950s by journalist Walter Lippman and by political scientists Hans Morgenthau and Robert Endicott Osgood. George F. Kennan, another realist diplomat, advanced a similar criticism about what he called the "legalistic-moralistic" streak that could be found in American foreign policy; see *American Diplomacy, 1900–1950* (Mentor Books, 1951).

Scholars have criticized the realist approach to Wilson for a number of reasons. Some say that it is "unrealistic" to expect an American president to ask for a declaration of war to defend abstract principles such as the balance of power or our national interest. Presidents and other elected officials must have a moral reason if they expect the American public to support a foreign war in which American servicemen might be killed.

Many recent historians agree with David F. Trask that Wilson developed realistic and clearly articulated goals and coordinated his larger diplomatic aims with the use of force better than any other wartime U.S. president. See "Woodrow Wilson and the Reconciliation of Force and Diplomacy, 1917–

1918," *Naval War College Review* (January/February 1975). John Milton Cooper, Jr., in *The Warrior and the Priest: Woodrow Wilson and Theodore Roosevelt* (Harvard University Press, 1984), presents Wilson as the realist and Theodore Roosevelt as the idealist, thereby reversing the dichotomy presented by Kennan and the other realists.

Link, a world-renowned scholar, has spent a half-century editing *The Papers of Woodrow Wilson* and writing books and articles about Wilson's life. Link's earliest writings on Wilson in the 1950s were informed by the realist perspective and criticized "the unreal quality of some of Wilson's thought and policy" and his rigidity in dealing with people who disagreed with him.

Though still mildly critical, Link warmed to his subject and criticizes both Wilson's European critics and many current biographers who view Wilson as a well-intentioned man with naive ideals. In the article reprinted here and in his later writings, Link argues that, more than his contemporaries, Wilson was the supreme realist who grappled with the major educational, political reform, and foreign policy issues of his times. The reforms he advocated as university president, state governor, and president of the United States were brought about only because of Wilson's ability to pursue his goals to their limits until it became necessary to make compromises. Link's analysis, however, raises some serious questions about Wilson's political skills.

Thomas Bailey, in *Woodrow Wilson and the Lost Peace* (MacMillan, 1944) and *Woodrow Wilson and the Great Betrayal* (Macmillan, 1945), which are summarized in "Woodrow Wilson Wouldn't Yield," *American Heritage* (June 1957), argues that Wilson should have ordered his senators to vote for a treaty with reservation. But Link has argued elsewhere that Wilson was a man ahead of his times. The American public was not willing to assume the international obligations inherent in being a world power. Link's earliest views on Wilson are summarized in his lectures on *Wilson the Diplomatist* (Johns Hopkins University Press, 1956). In 1979 Harlan Davidson published Link's most recent thoughts on *Woodrow Wilson: Revolution, War and Peace*.

Books continue to proliferate about Wilson. Critical from a realistic perspective are Jan Willem Schulte Nordholt, *Woodrow Wilson: A Life for World Peace* (University of California Press, 1991) and Lloyd E. Ambrosius, *Wilsonian Statecraft: Theory and Practice of Liberal Internationalism During World War I* (Scholarly Resources Books, 1991).

Books sympathetic to Wilson include Arthur Walworth, *Wilson and His Peacemakers: American Diplomacy at the Paris Peace Conference* (W. W. Norton, 1986) and Kendrick A. Clements, *The Presidency of Woodrow Wilson* (University Press of Kansas, 1992). See also the biography by August Heckscher, *Woodrow Wilson* (Scribners, 1991), and Thomas J. Knock, *To End All Wars: Woodrow Wilson and the Quest for a New World Order* (Oxford University Press, 1992).

PART 3

From Prosperity Through World War II

The 1920s are often portrayed as a hedonistic interlude for everyone between the Progressive and New Deal reform eras. Tensions arose between the values of the nation's rural past and the new social and moral values of modern America. The onset of a more activist federal government accelerated with the Great Depression. With more than one-quarter of the workforce unemployed, Franklin D. Roosevelt was elected on a promise to give Americans a "new deal." World War II short-circuited these plans and introduced people throughout the world to the anxious realities of the atomic age.

- Were the 1920s an Era of Social and Cultural Rebellion?

- Was the New Deal an Effective Answer to the Great Depression?

- Was Franklin Roosevelt a Reluctant Internationalist?

- Was It Necessary to Drop the Atomic Bomb to End World War II?

ISSUE 9

Were the 1920s an Era of Social and Cultural Rebellion?

YES: William E. Leuchtenburg, from *The Perils of Prosperity, 1914–32* (University of Chicago Press, 1958)

NO: David A. Shannon, from *Between the Wars: America, 1919–1941* (Houghton Mifflin, 1965)

ISSUE SUMMARY

YES: History professor William E. Leuchtenburg attributes the social and cultural rebellion of the 1920s to the growing secularization of American society, the demands by newly enfranchised women for economic equality and sexual liberation, and the hedonistic mood in the country, which produced a youth rebellion against the symbols of Victorian authority.

NO: Author David A. Shannon asserts that the social and cultural changes described by many as revolutionary were actually superficial elements whose significance to the 1920s has been exaggerated; the real catalysts were the monumental processes that expanded the American economy by ushering in prosperity through the creation of a mass consumer culture.

Americans have never been shy about attaching labels to their history, and frequently they do so to characterize particular years or decades in their distant or recent past. It is doubtful, however, that any period in our nation's history has received as many catchy appellations as has the decade of the 1920s. Described at various times as "the Jazz Age," "the Roaring Twenties," "the dry decade," "the prosperity decade," "the age of normalcy," and simply "the New Era," these are years that obviously have captured the imagination of the American public, including the chroniclers of the nation's past.

In 1920 the Great War was over, and President Woodrow Wilson received the Nobel Peace Prize despite his failure to persuade the Senate to adopt the Covenant of the League of Nations. The "Red Scare" culminated in the Palmer raids conducted by the Justice Department, which came to an embarrassingly fruitless halt, and Republican Warren Harding won a landslide victory in the campaign for the presidency. In this election, women, buoyed by the ratification of the Nineteenth Amendment, exercised their suffrage rights for the first time in national politics. In Pittsburgh, Pennsylvania, the advent of the radio age was symbolized by the broadcast of election results by KDKA, the nation's first commercial radio station. F. Scott Fitzgerald and Sinclair

Lewis each published their first important novels and thereby helped to usher in the most significant American literary renaissance since the early nineteenth century.

During the next nine years, Americans witnessed a number of amazing events: the rise and fall of the Ku Klux Klan; the trial, conviction, and execution of anarchists Nicola Sacco and Bartolomeo Vanzetti on murder charges and the subsequent legislative restrictions on immigration into the United States; the continuation of Prohibition laws and the emergence of the illicit manufacture and trade of alcohol controlled by mob bosses like Alphonse "Scarface Al" Capone; battles over the teaching of evolution in the schools, epitomized by the rhetorical clashes between William Jennings Bryan and Clarence Darrow during the Scopes trial in Dayton, Tennessee; the Harding scandals; "talking" motion pictures; and, in 1929, the collapse of the New York Stock Exchange, symbolizing the beginning of the Great Depression and bringing a startling end to the euphoric claims of business prosperity that had dominated the decade.

For many historians the 1920s marked an era of change in the United States, from international involvement and war to isolationism and peace, from the feverish reform of the Progressive Era to the conservative political retrenchment of Republican ascendancy, from the entrenched values of Victorian America to the cultural rebellion identified with the proliferation of "flivvers," "flappers," and hip flasks. In 1931 Frederick Lewis Allen focused on these changes in his popular account of the decade, *Only Yesterday*. In a chapter entitled "The Revolution of Morals and Manners," Allen established a widely accepted image of the 1920s as a period of significant social and cultural rebellion. The selections that follow evaluate the validity of these perceptions.

William E. Leuchtenburg subscribes to Allen's view that the morals and manners of Americans underwent a revolutionary change in the 1920s. According to Leuchtenburg, religious sanctions dissolved in the face of growing secularization and reduced stability of the family. The "new woman" of the decade, politically empowered by the Nineteenth Amendment, rebelled against traditional domestic roles ascribed to her and demanded sexual and economic freedom. Young Americans, in particular, participated in a self-indulgent hedonism that challenged the authority of traditional social and cultural institutions.

David A. Shannon insists that the crucial changes for most Americans in the 1920s were economic, not social or cultural. The prosperity of an expanding industrial economy, with its increased productivity, per capita income, and readily available consumer goods, was the most significant change in the post–World War I United States. The emergence of the "mass man," not the "flapper," therefore, was of greatest consequence to most Americans in the decade.

YES

William E. Leuchtenburg

THE REVOLUTION IN MORALS

The disintegration of traditional American values—so sharply recorded by novelists and artists—was reflected in a change in manners and morals that shook American society to its depths. The growing secularization of the country greatly weakened religious sanctions. People lost their fear of Hell and at the same time had less interest in Heaven; they made more demands for material fulfillment on Earth. The "status revolution" of the turn of the century undercut the authority of the men who had set America's moral standards: the professional classes, especially ministers, lawyers, and teachers; the rural gentry; the farmers; the urban patricians. The new urban minorities and *arriviste* businessmen were frequently not equipped—not even aware of the need either to support old standards or to create new ones. Most important, the authority of the family, gradually eroded over several centuries, had been sharply lessened by the rise of the city. "Never in recent generations," wrote Freda Kirchwey, "have human beings so floundered about outside the ropes of social and religious sanctions."

When Nora, the feminist heroine of *A Doll's House* (1879) by the Norwegian playwright Henrik Ibsen, walked out into the night, she launched against male-dominated society a rebellion that has not ended yet. The "new woman" revolted against masculine possessiveness, against "overevaluation" of women "as love objects," against being treated, at worst, as a species of property. The new woman wanted the same freedom of movement that men had and the same economic and political rights. By the end of the 1920's she had come a long way. Before the war, a lady did not set foot in a saloon; after the war, she entered a speakeasy as thoughtlessly as she would go into a railroad station. In 1904, a woman was arrested for smoking on Fifth Avenue; in 1929, railroads dropped their regulation against women smoking in dining cars. In the business and political worlds, women competed with men; in marriage, they moved toward a contractual role. Once ignorant of financial matters, they moved rapidly toward the point where they would be the chief property-holders of the country. Sexual independence was merely the most sensational aspect of the generally altered status of women.

From William E. Leuchtenburg, *The Perils of Prosperity, 1914–32* (University of Chicago Press, 1958). Copyright © 1958 by University of Chicago Press. Reprinted by permission.

In 1870, there were only a few women secretaries in the entire country; by the time of World War I, two million women worked in business offices, typing the letters and keeping the records of corporations and countinghouses in every city in the nation. During the war, when mobilization created a shortage of labor, women moved into jobs they had never held before. They made grenades, ran elevators, polished locomotives, collected streetcar fares, and even drilled with rifles. In the years after the war, women flew airplanes, trapped beaver, drove taxis, ran telegraph lines, worked as deep-sea divers and steeplejacks, and hunted tigers in the jungle; women stevedores heaved cargoes on the waterfront, while other women conducted orchestras, ran baseball teams, and drilled oil wells. By 1930, more than ten million women held jobs. Nothing did more to emancipate them. Single women moved into their own apartments, and wives, who now frequently took jobs, gained the freedom of movement and choice that went along with leaving home.

After nearly a century of agitation, women won the suffrage in 1920 with the adoption of the Nineteenth Amendment. The American suffragettes modeled themselves on their British counterparts, who blew up bridges, hurled bombs, and burned churches, activities previously regarded as the exclusive privilege of Irish rebels. Using less violent methods, American women had greater success, and the adoption of the suffrage amendment climaxed a long debate in which suffragettes argued that the advent of the women's vote would initiate a new era of universal peace and benevolence, while their enemies forecast a disintegration of American society. (The chief result of women's suffrage, [H. L.] Mencken predicted, would be that adultery would replace boozing as the favorite pastime of politicians.)

As it turned out, women's suffrage had few consequences, good or evil. Millions of women voted (although never in the same proportion as men), women were elected to public office (several gained seats in Congress by the end of the 1920's), but the new electorate caused scarcely a ripple in American political life. Women like Jane Addams made great contributions, but it would be difficult to demonstrate that they accomplished any more after they had the vote than before. It was widely believed, although never proved, that women cast a "dry" vote for Hoover in 1928 and that women were likely to be more moved than men to cast a "moral-issue" vote. Otherwise, the earth spun around much as it had before.

The extreme feminists argued that women were equal to men, and even more so. "Call on God, my dear," Mrs. Belmont is alleged to have told a despondent young suffragette. "She will help you." Female chauvinists wanted not merely sexual equality but, insofar as possible, to dispense with sexuality altogether, because they conceived of sexual intercourse as essentially humiliating to women. "Man is the only animal using this function out of season," protested Charlotte Perkins Gilman. "Excessive indulgence in sex-waste has imperiled the life of the race." Chanting slogans like "Come out of the kitchen" and "Never darn a sock," feminist leaders rebelled against the age-old household roles of women; before long, even a woman contented with her familiar role felt called on to apologize that she was "just a housewife."

In Dorothy Canfield Fisher's The Home-Maker (1924), the process is taken to its logical conclusion: a woman who has been a failure as a mother succeeds in business while her husband, a failure in business, stays at home and makes a success of raising children. The literature of the time reflects the growing male sense of alarm, notably in D. H. Lawrence's morbid fear that he would be absorbed and devoured by woman but even more in a new American character represented by the destructive Nina Leeds of O'Neill's *Strange Interlude* (1928), the husband-exploiting title figure of George Kelly's *Craig's Wife* (1926), and the possessive "son-devouring tigress" of Sidney Howard's *The Silver Cord* (1927).

The new freedom for women greatly increased the instability of the family. By the turn of the century, women were demanding more of marriage than they ever had before and were increasingly unwilling to continue alliances in which they were miserable. For at least a century, the family had been losing many of its original social and economic functions; the state, the factory, the school, and even mass amusements robbed the family of functions it once had. The more that social usefulness was taken away from the family, the more marriage came to depend on the personalities of the individuals involved, and, since many Americans of both sexes entered marriage with unreasonable expectations, this proved a slender reed. In 1914, the number of divorces reached 100,000 for the first time; in 1929, over 205,000 couples were divorced in a single year. The increase in divorce probably meant less an increase in marital unhappiness than a refusal to go on with marriages which would earlier have been tolerated.

As the family lost its other social functions, the chief test of a good family became how well it developed the personalities of the children, and parents, distrustful both of their own instincts and of tribal lore, eagerly sought out expert advice to avoid the opprobrium of having raised unhappy children. Dr. John B. Watson published the first edition of *Behaviorism* in 1914, but it was not until its third edition in 1925 that behaviorism—the idea that man was nothing but a machine responding to stimuli—took the country by storm. Since man was only a machine, environment alone was significant in determining both man's character and the nature of his society. "Give me a dozen healthy infants, well-formed, and my own specified world to bring them up in," declared Watson, "and I'll guarantee to take any one at random and train him to become any specialist I might select—doctor, lawyer, artist, merchant-chief, and yes, even beggarman and thief, regardless of his talents, tendencies, abilities, vocations and race of his ancestor." Watson's theories had the greatest impact on child-rearing; the Department of Labor incorporated behaviorist assumptions in its pamphlet *Infant and Child Care*, which, with emphasis on rigid scheduling of a baby's activities, became the government's leading best seller. Watson predicted that the time would come when it would be just as bad manners to show affection to one's mother or father as to come to the table with dirty hands. To inculcate the proper attitudes at an early age, Watson warned parents, "Never hug and kiss them, never let them sit in your lap."

Great as Watson's influence was, it could not hold a candle to that of Sigmund Freud. Before the war, Freud's name was known, outside of medical circles, only to a coterie of intellectuals. He had been referred to in the United States as early as 1895 by Dr. Robert

Edes, but, a decade later, only a few well-informed medical men knew his name. By 1908, Dr. A. A. Brill, who had studied at Jung's Clinic of Psychiatry in Zurich, was won to Freudian theory and undertook the major task of translating Freud's work. In 1909, when Freud journeyed to the United States to give a series of lectures at Clark University, he was amazed that "even in prudish America" his work was so well known. The following year, Brill published the first of his translations of Freud, *Three Contributions to a Theory of Sex* (previously available only in the German *Drei Adhandlungen zur Sexual-Theorie*), and in 1913, Brill, at the invitation of the precocious Walter Lippmann, explained Freud to a group of American intellectuals gathered at Mabel Dodge's salon....

In the years after the war, psychology became a national mania. Books appeared on the *Psychology of Golf*, the *Psychology of the Poet Shelley*, and the *Psychology of Selling Life Insurance*. People talked knowingly of "libido," "defense mechanism," and "fixation," confused the subconscious with the unconscious, repression with suppression, and dealt with the tortuously difficult theories of Freud and of psychoanalysis as though they were simple ideas readily grasped after a few moments' explanation. One article explained solemnly that the immense popularity of the song "Yes, We Have No Bananas" was the result of a national inferiority complex. Psychiatrist Karl Menninger found himself badgered at parties to perform analyses of the personalities of guests as though he were a fortune teller. "When I refuse," he explained, "my questioners often show me how the thing is done." Neophytes were able to read books like *Psychoanalysis by Mail* and *Psychoanalysis Self-Applied*, while the Sears, Roebuck catalogue offered *Ten Thousand Dreams Interpreted* and *Sex Problems Solved*. Like the automobile, Freud was brought within the reach of everyone.

Freud's popularity had an inevitable effect on the "revolution in morals." It was assumed that he was arguing that unless you freely expressed your libido and gave outlet to your sex energy, you would damage your health; by the distortion of his work, a scientific imprimatur was given to self-indulgence. By a similar but more understandable misinterpretation, it was believed that Freud was denying the reality of love; his name was invoked in support of the dehumanization of sex. "I'm hipped on Freud and all that," observed a Scott Fitzgerald heroine, "but it's rotten that every bit of *real* love in the world is ninety-nine percent passion and one little soupçon of jealousy."

What only the initiate understood was that although Freud did emphasize the strong power of unconscious motivation, psychiatry was aimed not at stressing the irrational or at licensing indulgence but at making it possible for man to use his rational powers to control unconscious forces. Freud taught that the most "irrational" act had meaning. Psychiatrists used Freud's theories to enable men to control their emotions through a clearer understanding of their irrational impulses. The vast popularity of Freud in America, which was to move the center of psychiatry from Vienna to Park Avenue, alarmed many psychoanalysts. They realized that the popularity had been achieved less through an understanding of Freud than through a belief that he shared the American conviction that every man had the right not merely to pursue happiness but to possess it.

This distortion had a number of unfortunate results, not least of which was the disappointment patients experienced when they came to realize that progress could be made only when self-indulgent fantasies were surrendered; but its ultimate effect was good. In Europe, psychiatry followed a course of near-fatalism in treating mental illness; in the more optimistic and more expectant American environment, psychiatry made greater gains and received far greater public support.

Freudian theories had a great impact on American writers, in part because they suggested new techniques for the exploration of human motivation, in part because they gave postwar intellectuals an invaluable weapon against the older standards. In some works the use of Freud was explicit; in others, as in the novels of Sherwood Anderson, where the influence of Freud seems obvious, there was apparently no conscious use of Freud at all. Eugene O'Neill turned to Freudian themes in his ambitious *Strange Interlude* (1928) as well as in his *Desire Under the Elms* (1924) and *Mourning Becomes Electra* (1931). Freud's greatest impact on the form of the novel was in the "stream-of-consciousness" technique, although its most important exponent, the Irish novelist James Joyce, was more directly influenced by Jung than by Freud. Stream of consciousness was employed in America most notably in William Faulkner's *The Sound and the Fury* (1929) and in the works of the novelist and poet Conrad Aiken. "I decided very early," Aiken recalled, "that Freud, and his co-workers and rivals and followers, were making the most important contribution of the century to the understanding of man and his consciousness; accordingly I made it my business to learn as much from them as I could." ...

In the attempt to work out a new standard of relations between men and women, Americans in the 1920's became obsessed with the subject of sex. Some novelists wrote of little else, in particular James Branch Cabell, whose *Jurgen* (1919), actually a curiously unerotic novel despite its absorption with the subject, was praised for its "phallic candour." Radio singers crooned songs like "Hot Lips," "Baby Face," "I Need Lovin'," and "Burning Kisses." Magazines like *Paris Nights*, *Flapper Experiences*, and *Snappy Stories* covered newsstands. The newspaperman Frank Kent returned from a tour of the country in 1925 with the conviction that "between the magazines and the movies a lot of these little towns seem literally saturated with sex." Advertising, once pristine, began the transition which, as one writer remarked, was to transmute soap from a cleansing agent to an aphrodisiac and to suggest "that every woman buying a pair of stockings is aiming for an assignation, or at the very least for a rescue via a fire-ladder."

Absorption with sex was the life's blood of the newspaper tabloid. Developed by Lord Northcliffe in England, the tabloid first appeared in America with the founding of the New York *Daily News* in 1919. As a picture newspaper like the *Sketch* and the *Mirror* in England, the *News* caught on immediately; within five years it had the largest circulation of any newspaper in New York. Hearst followed with the *New York Daily Mirror*, a slavish imitation of the *News*, and in 1924 Bernarr MacFadden demonstrated how far salacious sensationalism could be carried with the *New York Evening Graphic*. The New York tabloids soon had their imitators in other cities. Although the tabloids won millions of readers, they did not cut into the circulation of the established newspapers; they found a new, semiliterate market.

Not even the tabloids exploited sex with the zeal of Hollywood; it was the movies which created the American love goddess. When the "vamp," Theda Bara, appeared in *The Blue Flame* in 1920, crowds mobbed theaters in eastern cities to get in. Movie producers found that films like *The Sheik* drew large audiences, while *Sentimental Tommy* or epics like *America* played to empty houses. When it was apparent that sex was infinitely more profitable than the prewar sentimental-patriotic fustian, the country got a steady diet of movies like *Up in Mabel's Room,* *Her Purchase Price,* and *A Shocking Night.* (Cecil B. De Mille changed the title of Sir James Barrie's *The Admirable Crichton* into *Male and Female.)* Clara Bow was featured as the "It" girl, and no one had to be told what "it" was. The only ones in Hollywood with "it," explained the novelist Elinor Glyn, were "Rex, the wild stallion, actor Tony Moreno, the Ambassador Hotel doorman and Clara Bow." Movie ads promised kisses "where heart, and soul, and sense in concert move, and the blood is lava, and the pulse a blaze."

Threatened by censorship bills in thirty-six states, the industry made a gesture toward reforming itself. Following the model of organized baseball, which had made Judge Kenesaw Mountain Landis its "czar" after the Chicago Black Sox scandal of 1919, the movie industry hired Harding's Postmaster-General, Will Hays, to be the "Judge Landis of the movies." All the Hays Office succeeded in doing in the 1920's was to add hypocrisy to sex by insisting on false moralizations and the "moral" ending. Movie ads continued to entice patrons with "brilliant men, beautiful jazz babies, champagne baths, midnight revels, petting parties in the purple dawn, all ending in one terrific smashing climax that makes you gasp."

Taboos about sex discussion were lifted; women talked freely about inhibitions and "sex starvation." Speech became bolder, and men and women told one another off-color stories that a short while before would have been reserved for the Pullman smoker. Novelists and playwrights spoke with a new bluntness; in Hemingway's *The Sun Also Rises* (1926), the word "bitch" recurs frequently. The woman who once was shocked by everything now prided herself, observed a writer in *Harper's,* on the fact that nothing at all shocked her; "immunity to the sensation of 'recoil with painful astonishment' is the mark of our civilization."

Parental control of sex was greatly lessened; the chaperone vanished at dances, and there was no room for a duenna in the rumble seat of an automobile. The bachelor girl had her own latchkey. Girls petted, and when they did not pet, they necked, and no one was certain of the exact difference; Lloyd Morris observed: "The word 'neck' ceased to be a noun; abruptly became a verb; immediately lost all anatomical precision." At one conference in the Midwest, eight hundred college girls met to discuss petting, to deal with searching questions like What do nice girls do? and How far should you go? "Whether or not they pet," said one writer, "they hesitate to have anyone believe that they do not." The consensus of the delegates was: "Learn temperance in petting, not abstinence."

Victorian dance forms like the waltz yielded to the fast-stepping Charleston, the Black Bottom, or slow fox trots in which, to the syncopated rhythms of the jazz band, there was a "maximum of motion in the minimum of space." Jazz made its way northward from the bordellos of New Orleans to the dance halls of Chicago during these years, crossed the ocean to Paris (where it was instantly taken up as a uniquely American contribution to music), and created its own folk heroes in the lyrical Bix Beiderbecke and the dynamic Louis Armstrong who, legend has it, once played two hundred different choruses of "Sweet Sue." The tango and the fox trot hit the country before the war, but it was not until the 1920's that the more voluptuous and the more frenetic dance crazes swept the nation. Moralists like Bishop Cannon protested that the new dances brought "the bodies of men and women in unusual relations to each other"; but by the end of the period the fox trot was as popular and the saxophones wailed as loudly at the high-school dances of the Bishop's Methodist parishioners as in the dance halls of New York and Los Angeles.

What did it all add up to? Lord Birkenhead, the British Lord High Chancellor, observed in 1928: "The proportion of frail to virtuous women is probably constant throughout the ages in any civilization." Perhaps, but the meager evidence suggests otherwise. There appears to have been an increase in promiscuity, especially in sexual experience before marriage for middle-class women; there was probably an increase in extramarital experience as well. With effective contraceptive techniques widely used, the fear of pregnancy was greatly lessened. ("The veriest schoolgirl today knows as much as the midwife of 1885," wrote Mencken.) At the same time, quite

possibly as a consequence, a great many brothels lost their customers and had to close their doors, while itinerant workers in the same field disappeared from the sidewalks. The degree of sexual experimentation in the 1920's has certainly been exaggerated, but there is a good deal to bear out Alexander Pope's aphorism that "every woman is at heart a rake."

Not only the American woman but the American girl was reputed to be freer with her sexual favors than she had ever been before, although serious periodicals published learned debates over whether this was fact or fiction. The flapper had as many defenders as accusers on this score, but no one doubted that every campus had its Jezebels. Smith College girls in New York, noted Malcolm Cowley, modeled themselves on Hemingway's Lady Brett. Certainly, girls were less reticent than they bad been before the war. "One hears it said," lamented a Southern Baptist periodical, "that the girls are actually tempting the boys more than the boys do the girls, by their dress and conversation." They dressed more freely; they wore bathing suits which revealed more than had ever been revealed before. At dances, corsets were checked in cloakrooms; then even this pretense was abandoned. Above all, they were out for a good time. "None of the Victorian mothers," wrote F. Scott Fitzgerald in *This Side of Paradise*, "had any idea how casually their daughters were accustomed to be kissed."

Although Fitzgerald reported that the ideal flapper was "lovely and expensive and about nineteen," the flapper appeared bent on playing down her femininity and emphasizing her boyishness. She used the most ingenious devices to conceal the fact that she had breasts. Even the nudes at the Folies Bergères were flatchested and were picked for that reason, and in England, women wore the "Eton crop" and bound their chests with wide strips of ribbon to achieve a "boyish bust." The flapper wore dresses that suggested she had no hips at all; her waistline moved steadily southward. As one writer recalled, "Women not only lost their waists; they sat on them." She dieted recklessly in an effort to remove unwanted protuberances. Girls, noted Dr. Charles F. Pabst, were attempting to become "pathologically thin." "A strikingly sad example of improper dieting," he said, "was the case of a shapely motion-picture actress, who became a nervous wreck and blasted her career by restricting herself to tomatoes, spinach and orange juice." The flapper bobbed her hair and dyed it raven black. She concealed everything feminine but her matchstick legs. In 1919 her skirt was six inches above the ground; by 1927 it had edged about to her knees. The well-accoutered flapper wore a tight felt hat, two strings of beads, bangles on her wrists, flesh-colored stockings rolled below the knees, and unbuckled galoshes. Ironically, the more she adopted mannish styles, the more she painted her face, daubing her cheeks with two circles of rouge and her lips with "kissproof" lipstick; cosmetics became the chief way of distinguishing feminine members of the race.

The vogue of the flapper was only the most obvious instance of the new American cult of youth. "It is the glory of the present age that in it one can be young," Randolph Bourne wrote in 1913. In every age, youth has a sense of a separate destiny, of experiencing what no one has ever experienced before, but it may be doubted that there was ever a time in American history when youth had such a special sense of

importance as in the years after World War I. There was a break between generations like a geological fault; young men who had fought in the trenches felt that they knew a reality their elders could not even imagine. Young girls no longer consciously modeled themselves on their mothers, whose experience seemed unusable in the 1920's.

Instead of youth modeling itself on age, age imitated youth. Scott Fitzgerald, looking back on the years of which he was the chief chronicler, recalled: "May one offer in exhibit the year 1922! That was the peak of the younger generation, for though the Jazz Age continued, it became less and less an affair of youth. The sequel was a children's party taken over by elders." "Oh, yes, we are collegiate" was the theme song of a generation yearning for the irresponsible, idealized days of youth. Everyone wanted to be young. Mrs. Gertrude Atherton's *Black Oxen* (1923) described how grandmothers might be rejuvenated through a glandular operation and once more stir up young men. It was the young girl who started the flapper ideal; it was her mother who kept it going.

Americans in the 1920's, at least on the surface, were less sinridden and more self-indulgent than they had ever been before. They broke the Sabbath apparently without compunction, missing the morning sermon to play golf, driving into the country in the afternoon instead of sitting stiffly in the parlor. The mood of the country was hedonistic; Omar Khayyam's quatrains took the colleges by storm. The ideal of hedonism was living for the moment, and if one can isolate a single spirit which permeated every segment of society in the postwar years, it was the obliteration of time.

Abandoning the notion of saving income or goods or capital over time, the country insisted on immediate consumption, a demand which became institutionalized in the installment plan. The President's Research Committee on Social Trends noted "the new attitude towards hardship as a thing to be avoided by living in the here and now, utilizing installment credit and other devices to telescope the future into the present." Songs became obsolescent almost as soon as they appeared, and people prided themselves not on remembering the old songs but on knowing the latest. The imitation of youth by age was an effort to telescope the years, while youth itself tried to escape the inexorability of time. One of the younger generation, replying to its critics, observed: "The trouble with them is that they can't seem to realize that we are busy, that what pleasure we snatch must be incidental and feverishly hurried. We have to make the most of our time.... We must gather rose-buds while we may."

In the magazine *Secession*, a group of intellectuals, including Hart Crane, Kay Boyle, and Elliot Paul, signed a "Proclamation" declaring "Time is a tyranny to be abolished." Gertrude Stein's concept of a "continuous present" effaced not merely history and tradition but any sense of "time." "The future," she declared, "is not important any more." In Italy, the Futurists had cast out Petrarch and Dante and rejected harmony and sentiment; their present-mindedness had a direct impact on Ezra Pound, who found their chief spokesman, Marinetti, "thoroughly simpatico." The characters in the novels of the day, particularly those of Scott Fitzgerald, lived only for the moment, while Edna St. Vincent Millay penned the theme of the generation in "My candle burns at both ends." The

spirit of hedonism of the decade, wrote Edmund Wilson, was "letting oneself be carried along by the mad hilarity and heartbreak of jazz, living only for the excitement of the evening."

The obliteration of time carried with it a conscious assault on the authority of history. The Dada movement, which developed in the war years in Zurich, adopted as its motto: "Je ne veux même pas savoir s'il y a eu des hommes avant moi" ("I do not wish even to know whether there have been men before me"). More remarkably, the very men who were the spokesmen for history and tradition led the onslaught; in this, Henry Ford and Charles Beard were one. Ford's interest in history was actually an anti-history. He took cottages in which Noah Webster and Patrick Henry had once lived and moved them to Dearborn, Michigan, where they had no meaning. He sentimentalized and pillaged the past, but he had no respect for it. "History is more or less the bunk," he said. "We want to live in the present, and the only history that is worth a tinker's dam is the history we make today." As early as 1907, the historians Charles Beard and James Harvey Robinson had deliberately attempted to subordinate the past to the present with the aim of enabling the reader "to catch up with his own times; ... to know what was the attitude of Leo XIII toward the Social Democrats even if he has forgotten that of Innocent III toward the Albigenses." Beard's emphasis on current history had its counterpart in Veblen's dislike for dead languages, Holmes's skepticism about the value of learning as a guide in jurisprudence, and Dewey's emphasis on the functional in education.

The revolution in morals routed the worst of Victorian sentimentality and false modesty. It mitigated the harsh moral judgments of rural Protestantism, and it all but wiped out the awful combination of sanctimoniousness and lewdness which enabled Anthony Comstock to defame Bernard Shaw as "this Irish smut-dealer" and which allowed Teddy Roosevelt, with unconscious humor, to denounce the Mexican bandit Villa as a "murderer and a bigamist." It greatly extended the range of choice; "the conduct of life," wrote Joseph Wood Krutch, had been made "more thrillingly difficult." Yet, at the same time, it raised baffling problems of the relations between husband and wife, parent and child, and, in itself, provided no ready guides to con-

duct. The hedonism of the period was less a solution than a pathological symptom of what Walter Lippmann called a "vast dissolution of ancient habits," and it rarely proved as satisfying as people hoped. "Sons and daughters of the puritans, the artists and writers and utopians who flocked to Greenwich Village to find a frank and free life for the emotions and senses, felt at their backs the icy breath of the monster they were escaping," wrote Joseph Freeman. "Because they could not abandon themselves to pleasure without a sense of guilt, they exaggerated the importance of pleasure, idealized it and even sanctified it."

NO

David A. Shannon

AMERICAN SOCIETY AND CULTURE IN THE 1920'S

Journalists, scenario writers, even professional historians (usually a rather solemn bunch) who normally make a serious effort to deal with the problems that confront society and individuals in their relations with one another are prone to get a little giddy when they approach the social and cultural history of the 1920's and prattle joyously but aimlessly about "the jazz age." To judge from some accounts, Americans did little else from 1920 until 1929 but make millions in the stock market, dance the Charleston and the Black Bottom, dodge gangster bullets, wear raccoon coats, and carry hip flasks. "Flapper," "saxophone," "bathtub gin," and "speakeasy" are the key words in this special genre of popular historical writing, and the interpretation of the era, usually only implied, is that America went on a hedonistic binge for approximately a decade. Obviously, such a characterization of an epoch is shallow and exaggerated once one thinks about it critically and looks into the epoch more searchingly, but that style of social history for the postwar decade persists and thrives.

Probably the great change in the conditions of society and the mood of the people after 1929 is the root cause of this curious historiographical aberration. The grimness, despair, and drabness of America in the 1930's probably prompted writers to look back at the previous decade with a kind of nostalgia for a more carefree existence and led them to look too fondly and too long at what were actually superficialities. An extraordinarily skillful popular historian, Frederick Lewis Allen, set the style with his *Only Yesterday*, which appeared in 1931, a gray year indeed. The book was a delight to read and still is, and Allen's feat was all the more remarkable for having done it so soon after the fact. A careful reading of *Only Yesterday* reveals that Allen was often concerned with more than the superficialities of the 1920's, but he nevertheless put an unusual emphasis upon the bizarre and transitory aspects of the 1920's that contrasted sharply with the 1930's.

The thesis of this [essay] is not to declaim that there were no flappers, no saxophones, no jazz age. The [essay] will suggest that there were other aspects of the 1920's . . . that are more useful to examine if we wish to understand the era and the way that it helped to shape our own contemporary society. In other words, the flappers were not a myth, but we will do well to look beyond the flappers, which have already been written about more than sufficiently.

PROSPERITY AND ECONOMIC CHANGE

Prosperity was a basic fact of the 1920's, one that shaped and conditioned many aspects of life outside the economic realm. A generally expanding economy underlay a generally expansive view about life, as happened again in the generation after World War II. To say that the economy was healthy would be to ignore the almost fatal illness that struck it low in 1929, but it was clearly prosperous.

The path of the economy even during its boom years was not entirely smooth, however. Although relatively brief, the postwar depression that hit in mid-1920 was as steep and as sudden as any the American economy had ever experienced. The year 1921 was a hard one. Unemployment went up to 4,750,000, and national income was down 28 per cent from the previous year. Farm prices were far too low to enable most farmers to meet their costs of production. But in 1922 the economy came back strong, and by the end of the year it was buzzing along in better shape than it had been when the depression hit. There were minor dips in the business cycle in 1924 and 1927, but they were not serious.

Besides cyclical fluctuations there were other blemishes on prosperity's record. Some economic activities did not share in the general prosperity. Agriculture never really recovered from the postwar depression, and low farm prices were the root of farmer discontent that manifested itself in McNary-Haugenism. Some industries were in bad shape throughout the period. The world market for textiles declined when women's styles changed. A dress in 1928 required less than one-half the material that a seamstress needed to make a dress in 1918. Furthermore, many clothes in the 1920's were made of synthetic fibers. Rayon became very popular. Consequently the textile industry was unable to pay wages consistent with the rising standard of living. The industry continued its long-range shift of operations from New England to the South, particularly to the southern Appalachians, where wage rates were lower. Coal was another sick industry. As home owners shifted gradually to other fuels for space heating and as automobiles and trucks gradually displaced the railroads, once a major market for coal, the total coal market shrank slightly. There was approximately 10 per cent less coal mined at the end of the decade than there had been at the beginning. New mining technology enabled mine operators to get along with a smaller labor force. Almost one fourth of the nation's coal miners at work in 1923 were out of the pits by 1929, and since most miners lived in isolated communities where there were almost no other employment opportunities, the economic hardship in the mining towns was acute. Even employed miners worked at hourly wage rates that were 14 per cent lower in 1929 than they had been in 1923.

But despite cyclical downswings and generally depressed conditions in agriculture, textiles, and coal, prosperity was strong. One has only to look at the statistics. Real per-capita income increased almost one third from 1919 to 1929. (Real per-capita income is total national income divided by population and adjusted for price changes.) The mythical average person—not worker, but all people, men, women, and children—received $716 in 1929. In 1919 he had received just $543, measured in 1929 dollars. Manufacturing industries increased their output by almost two thirds, but because of a tremendous increase in labor productivity due to technological advances there were actually fewer people engaged in manufacturing in 1929 than there had been in 1919. A large number of these displaced production workers went into service industries, where many of the jobs were "white collar." Furthermore, there was a shift in the nature of industrial production that tended to improve the lot of the consumer. Since the early days of American industry a large part of production had been capital goods, that is, products that were used to produce further wealth rather than be consumed by the people. Much American production, for example, had gone into building a vast railroad network, the biggest and most intricate rail system that any nation in the world had found it necessary to develop. The number of miles of railroad track began actually to decrease slightly after 1920. When any industrial economy matures it reaches a point at which a significantly higher proportion of production may go to consumer goods, and the American economy reached this level in the postwar decade. This is not to say that capital production ceased, which would have been calamitous for long-range growth —indeed, it even increased in absolute terms—but a larger proportion of annual production was in the form of articles that ordinary people could use, such as washing machines, radios, and motor cars. The number of such durable consumer goods in use was small compared to what it would be by midcentury, but

still more people than ever before enjoyed their convenience. In fact, because of increased national production, relatively stable price levels, and increased production of consumer goods, most Americans lived better in the 1920's than ever before.

To a considerable degree the prosperity of the 1920's was due to the vast expansion of a few relatively new industries and to increased construction, much of which was actually due to the new industries. Road building, for example, was a major enterprise during the decade, and the roads were necessary because of the relatively new automobile industry.

In 1915, soon after Henry Ford developed the Model T, there were about 2.5 million cars on the roads of America. By 1920 there were over 9 million and the industry's growth had only started. By 1925 there were nearly 20 million cars registered, and in 1929 there were 26.5 million. In that last year of the boom the industry produced 5,622,000 motor vehicles. Ford had made the big break-through with his mass-produced, inexpensive Model T, but later decisions of the industry similarly broadened the market. In 1923 the major car manufacturers abandoned open cars except for a few sports models and concentrated on closed vehicles. Many a family that had resisted getting one of the older and colder models succumbed to the lure of relatively comfortable transportation. The auto industry also soon discovered that to tap a really mass market it had to develop a credit system. It developed an auto financing system which remains largely the same today. By 1925 over two thirds of the new cars purchased each year were bought on credit. Installment buying, which became general in other fields as well, did not increase the purchasing power of any given family income. In fact, it reduced it by as much as the interest charges amounted to. But it did greatly stimulate new car purchases, and the purchases had a stimulating effect upon the economy in general.

The auto industry statistics were impressive. In 1929 automobiles accounted for over one eighth of the total dollar value of all manufacturing in the nation. Over 7 per cent of all wage earners engaged in manufacturing worked for automobile companies. The industry took 15 per cent of national steel production. When one considers the effect that auto production had on the manufacture and distribution of tires, oil and gasoline, and glass it has been estimated that the industry provided jobs for about 3.7 million workers, roughly one tenth of the non-agricultural labor force.

Motor vehicles were the most spectacular new industry, but chemicals and electric appliances also had a very large growth. Before World War I the American chemical industry had been rather small, unable to compete with German firms for most items. The war shut off German imports and the federal government confiscated German patents and sold them to domestic corporations. By the end of the 1920's the American chemical industry had grown roughly 50 per cent larger than it had been before the outbreak of the war in Europe. The electric appliance industry became economically significant as more and more American homes gained access to electric power. In 1912 roughly one sixth of America's families had electricity in their homes; by 1927 almost two thirds of them had electric power. The first use that families put the new power to was lighting, but they quickly began to use it to lighten their work. By 1925, 80 per cent of the homes with electricity had electric irons, 37 per cent had vacuum cleaners, and 25 per cent had washing machines. Most families continued to use ice for food storage. Radio was intimately connected with the electric industry, although especially in the early 1920's many of the sets manufactured were operated by storage batteries, big things that weighed over twenty-five pounds and were nothing like the dry cells that power today's transistor radios. The home radio industry was altogether new. The first commercial radio station was KDKA, operated by the Westinghouse Electric Company from East Pittsburgh, in 1920. By 1924 there were over five hundred commercial radio stations. By 1929 sales of radios amounted to over $400 million and roughly two fifths of the families of America owned one. Without these new industries, which were based primarily upon new inventions or improved technology, it is doubtful if the 1920's would have been any more prosperous than the prewar period.

Trade unions usually increase in membership strength during periods of prosperity. More workers are employed, thereby increasing trade-union potential, and employers, optimistic about the prospect of profits, usually want labor stability and are willing to make concessions to unions in order to prevent disruption of production. But trade unions in the 1920's departed from this general rule; they actually decreased in membership and influence during the decade. Total union membership in 1920 was roughly five million; by the end of the decade it had declined to about three and one-half million.

There were three main reasons for failure of trade unions in the 1920's: a strong counterattack against them by employers, in which government cooperated; cautious and complacent union leadership; and widespread lack of interest in unions among unorganized workers. During the postwar depression, an opportune time, many employers engaged in a fierce and somewhat successful anti-union drive. Their campaign was for the open shop, which they called "the American plan" in an effort to associate unionism with un-Americanism. (In an open shop no employee is under any compulsion to join a union. If a union exists in the shop, nonmembers receive whatever wages and hours union members have, which puts the union at a disadvantage in getting new members. In a closed shop the employer agrees to hire only union members. In a union shop the employer hires as he chooses but the employees must join the union.) The open-shop campaign was strong even in some industries where unionism had been well established, such as printing and building construction. Some building contractors were under pressure to break unions. The president of the Bethlehem Steel Company announced in late 1920 that his firm would not sell steel to contractors in New York and Philadelphia who consented to keep their established closed-shop policy. Also in the 1920's employers embarked upon a program to extend what came to be called welfare capitalism. A rather nebulous concept, welfare capitalism ran the gamut from employee stock-purchase plans (usually nonvoting stock) to athletic and social programs for employees and better toilets and locker rooms. Welfare capitalism programs tended to make employees identify their welfare with the company rather than a union and to remove some of the annoyances that sometimes erupt into union-management conflict.

Despite the intensity of the employers' attack it is likely that more vigorous and imaginative union leadership would have enabled the unions to hold their own. Samuel Gompers, the primary founder of the American Federation of Labor and its president for all but one year of its existence during his lifetime, was seventy years old in 1920, hardened in his approach to unionism, and lacking in the vigor which he had displayed at the beginning of the century. William Green, successor to the AFL presidency after Gompers' death in 1924, was depressingly cautious and almost completely without imagination. Whatever forward motion the labor movement made from Green's accession to the AFL presidency in 1924 to his death in the 1950's was made despite Green rather than because of him. The fundamental difficulty in union leadership from World War I until the early 1930's was that the AFL had no real interest in getting the unorganized into unions except for those in skilled trades. Not until labor leaders eager to organize unskilled workers in basic industry came to the fore in the 1930's did the unions get off the ground. There was one major exception that proved the generalization: in the needle trades David Dubinsky and Sidney Hillman adopted new techniques and ideas. Their innovations were successful, and their organizations thrived while the rest of labor stagnated and shriveled.

Many workers in basic industry in the 1920's were apathetic or hostile to unionism, not only because of their employers' attitudes and the failure of union leadership to excite them but because they lived better than ever they had before and because they had formed their social ideas in a preindustrial society. There is no question but that most industrial workers were better off materially in the 1920's than they had been earlier. Real wages (the relationship of money wages to the cost of living) in 1919 were at 105 on a scale in which 1914 was 100. By 1928 the figure stood at 132, a truly significant increase. Many an industrial worker's social ideas and assumptions earned him the unionist's contemptuous term "company man." Especially in the new industries like autos and electric appliances a large part of the labor force was composed of men who had begun their lives in small towns or on the farm, where there had been no big employers and where the terms of work were laid down by the employer on a take-it-or-leave-it basis or settled by each individual employee bargaining with the employer. Individualistic social attitudes formed in a rural society were difficult to shake, even when a man lived the anything but individualistic life of a city worker on a production line, the employee of a vast and complex corporation. It took the depression of the next decade to shock many workers from a rural background into modifying their views about the relationship of capital and labor sufficiently to join a union and make it a countervailing power to the corporation.

There are no statistics that reveal precisely how many industrial workers in the 1920's were originally from urban areas, but the population statistics reveal a vast growth of the cities during the decade. Many rural counties continued to grow, but urban counties grew much more rapidly. The general pattern of migration was from the farm or small town to the small city of the same region and thence to a big city, often out of the region. The biggest growths were in New York City, the industrial cities on or near the Great Lakes, the San Francisco area,

and Los Angeles. California tended to draw its new population from the West and the Midwest. New York's growth came from all over the nation, but the bulk of it came from the East and the Southeast. The burgeoning cities of the Midwest grew from rural-to-urban movement within the region and from migration from the South.

Great numbers of the migrants from the South were Negro. Negro migration to the North first became numerically significant during World War I. In 1910 more than 90 per cent of the Negroes of the United States lived in states that had been slave areas in 1860. The census of that year showed only 850,000 Negroes living outside the South. The census of 1920 showed 1,400,000 in the North and West, most of them having migrated after 1917. The movement continued, even expanded, during the 1920's. In the 1930 census, 2,300,000 Negroes were living outside the South. The day was rapidly coming when the typical American Negro would not be a southern sharecropper but a northern or western urban wage earner.

This movement from rural to urban areas, for both Negroes and whites, came about for essentially economic reasons. Agriculture languished; industry flourished. Economic conditions pushed people off the farms and out of the small towns; better economic conditions in the cities pulled them into population clusters.

THE EFFECTS OF AFFLUENCE

America in the 1920's was a relatively affluent society. Affluence made it possible for Americans to change significantly the way they lived, to buy a car and a radio, to go to movies, to improve their schools and send their children to school for more years than they themselves had attended. These effects of affluence in turn had their own effects, some of them very far-reaching.

Foreign visitors to the United States in the late 1920's who had not seen the nation for a decade or two were impressed most of all by the numbers of automobiles they saw and the changes that the automobile had wrought in society. In 1929 there were between one fifth and one sixth as many cars in the United States as there were people, a far higher proportion than that of any other country except Canada. It was physically possible for everyone in America to be rolling on automobile wheels simultaneously, and in some of the traffic jams of summer weekends it appeared that the nation had actually tried to perform the feat.

Any attempt to enumerate all the effects of widespread automobile ownership would bog down in superficial relationships, but some of the major effects are evident. The very appearance of the country changed. Merchants and manufacturers could not resist trying to profit from the captive audiences that traveled the main highways and erected billboards on the land that only a few generations back had been a wilderness. Short-order restaurants and gasoline stations lined the roads approaching towns and cities. Tourist cabins, the predecessors of motels, clustered around the main points of tourist interest. Towns and cities began their sprawl into the countryside as the automobile enabled workers to live a great distance from their employment. Cities such as Los Angeles, which experienced most of their growth after the coming of the automobile age, tended not to have the central business area traditional in older American and European cities.

The social effects of the automobile have been the subject of a great deal of speculation. Many observers have asserted that the car changed courtship patterns by making young people more mobile and removing them from the supervision of their elders. Certainly every community by the end of the 1920's had a secluded area known as "lovers' lane" where cars parked on summer nights, but this whole theory of changed courtship patterns tends to underestimate the ingenuity of young people of the pre-automobile age. "Lovers' lanes" once had buggies parked beside them, and because of the superiority of horse intelligence to that of an automobile a buggy driver could pay less attention to his driving than could a car driver. Still, there are other, more important, and better documented social effects of the automobile.

By the end of the 1920's thousands of families took long vacation trips by car and quite obviously the American public knew more of its nation's geography at first hand than had earlier and less mobile generations. In 1904 a Chicago lawyer made a trip by auto from New York to San Francisco, and his trip was so unusual that he wrote a book about his experiences. By 1929, however, families that had taken such trips found it difficult even to interest their neighbors in their tales of travel.

Perhaps one of the most far-reaching changes brought by the automobile, or the bus, was the change in rural schools. Before the day of cars each rural township operated a grade school, some of them through grade six, more often through grade eight. Most of these rural schools had one room and one teacher. Despite the sentimental nostalgia of some people in a later age, these schools did not offer good education. The teachers were poorly prepared; most of them had not been to college at all. With a room full of children of various sizes and ages, most teachers were able to do little more than maintain a degree of discipline. The products of these schools were ill equipped for living anywhere but on the farm and were not particularly well educated even for that. The school bus made consolidated rural schools possible, and farm youngsters of high-school age for the first time began to go beyond the eighth grade in significant numbers. Many of the new consolidated rural schools were a long way from being ideal educational institutions, but they were clearly an improvement over the ungraded one-room school. At last, rural children were receiving substantially the same kind of education as urban children.

Indeed, the automobile and the radio tended to blur the distinction between rural and urban life. The farmer went to town for his entertainment (usually the movies) and listened to the same radio programs as the city dweller. His children attended schools like those in urban centers. He read a city newspaper. The farmer frequently even took a job in the city, at least for part of the year, and continued to live on the land. Because of the generally depressed conditions of agriculture during the 1920's and the greater amount of capital necessary to begin profitable farming that came as a result of farm mechanization, most of the farmer's children became wage earners in town or city. There still remained a great difference in the ways of life of the small town and the big city, but no longer, except in the most primitive, poorest, and most isolated parts of the nation, did the farmer live significantly differently from the small-town dweller.

Affluence changed the education of the city youngster just as it and the automobile had changed rural schooling. The greatest change was in the number of students in high school. High-school enrollments in 1920 totaled 2.2 million; by 1930 almost exactly twice as many students were in the nation's secondary schools. An increase in the population was part of the reason for the increased enrollments, but more important was an increase in the percentage of high-school-age boys and girls who went on past the eighth grade. In 1930 roughly one half of the population between the ages of fourteen and eighteen was in school.

The main reason why more young people stayed in school instead of dropping out to go to work was that their families, for the first time, could afford to continue without the youngsters' wages. Failure to recognize the fact that children's wages were needed at home was the chief flaw in the reasoning of earlier opponents of child labor. In the first Wilson administration reformers had put a law through Congress prohibiting child labor, and the Supreme Court had in 1918 declared the act unconstitutional. The reformers then set about amending the Constitution, getting an amendment through Congress but never getting it ratified by a sufficient number of states. Enforcement of compulsory school-attendance laws in the 1920's (usually to age fifteen or sixteen) succeeded in accomplishing most of what the reformers had desired, but not even the school laws could be enforced well when public opinion opposed them. When employers wanted to hire children, when parents wanted children to go to work to help on the family income, and when the children themselves wanted to leave school—and this was the situation in many of the textile towns of the Appalachian South throughout the decade —truant officers were unable really to enforce the law. But the attendance laws were enforced where public opinion supported them. Affluence rather than law kept children in school and off the labor market. By 1929 most urban young people at least started to high school. Finishing high school became almost universal in the middle classes, and most of the children from working-class homes finished high school if they had at least average academic ability.

The great number of high-school students had a profound effect on the nature of the high school. At one time, secondary education had been primarily preparation for the college and university. Now in the 1920's the high schools were filled with young people who had no intention whatsoever of going on to college. Furthermore, many of the students lacked the intelligence or the desire or both to cope with the conventional high-school curriculum of literature, mathematics, science, and foreign language. A number of educators argued that trigonometry and Latin did not have much relevance for students who were going to stop their formal education after high school to go to work and that the schools should provide these young people with other training. Many schools never solved the problem in a satisfactory manner; most of them watered down the conventional curriculum to accommodate the new kind of student and created vocational courses which often had little more relevance than did Latin. But despite educational deficiencies—and we must not assume that the secondary schools of the era before World War I were paragons of intellectual virtue —increasing numbers of young people insisted upon a high-school education and they probably profited from their high-school years.

Colleges and universities also were swollen during the 1920's, their enrollments increasing from about 600,000 in 1920 (larger than usual with soldiers returning from World War I) to about 1,200,000 in 1930. The greatest increase in college enrollments came in the vocational fields, teacher preparation, engineering, and business administration. Undergraduate schools of business were something new in higher education, but it was not surprising that in the business civilization of the 1920's hundreds of young men studied such vocational subjects as salesmanship and advertising....

By 1929 the typical American had become a mass man. He worked for a huge industrial corporation; he bought mass-produced articles made by the large corporation; he more than likely lived in an apartment house or in a small residence that differed little from thousands of others; he read a mass newspaper; he at tended Metro-Goldwyn-Mayer movies and listened to national radio programs; he avidly followed the athletic exploits of Babe Ruth and Red Grange—and, wondrously, he voted for Herbert Hoover because the Great Engineer praised "rugged individualism." He was the new mass man of the New Era and all seemed rosy. But he and the New Era were soon to receive a jolt of unprecedented force and power.

POSTSCRIPT

Were the 1920s an Era of Social and Cultural Rebellion?

The degree to which one views the 1920s as a rebellious decade may very well depend on the extent to which World War I is interpreted as a watershed event in American history. How much did American society in the 1920s differ from its prewar counterpart? The argument for change is widespread. For example, Henry May has characterized the years from 1912 to 1917 as marking "the end of American innocence." Similarly, the literary and artistic members of the "lost generation" were certain that the war had created a much different world from the one they had occupied previously. A different political climate seemed to exist in the 1920s in which a business-oriented conservatism deflated the momentum for reform that had dominated the first two decades of the twentieth century. An excellent collection of essays that explores this issue is John Braeman, Robert H. Bremner, and David Brody, eds., *Change and Continuity in Twentieth Century America: The 1920s* (Ohio State University Press, 1968).

There are a number of important overviews of the 1920s that treat the topics raised by Leuchtenburg and Shannon. Among the more useful ones are John D. Hicks, *Republican Ascendancy, 1921–1933* (Harper & Row, 1960), a volume in The New American Nation series; Roderick Nash, *The Nervous Generation: American Thought, 1917–1930* (Rand McNally, 1970); and Paul Carter, *The Twenties in America*, 2d ed. (Harlan Davidson, 1975).

The economic history of the decade is discussed in George Soule, *Prosperity Decade: From War to Depression, 1917–1929* (Holt, Rinehart & Winston, 1947); Peter Fearon, *War, Prosperity, and Depression* (University of Kansas Press, 1987); and John Kenneth Galbraith, *The Great Crash, 1929*, rev. ed. (Houghton Mifflin, 1989).

The status of women in the decade after suffrage receives general treatment in William H. Chafe, *The Paradox of Change: American Women in the Twentieth Century* (Oxford University Press, 1991) and, more thoroughly, in Dorothy M. Brown, *Setting a Course: American Women in the 1920s* (Twayne, 1987). Discussions of feminism in the 1920s are competently presented in William L. O'Neill, *Everyone Was Brave: The Rise and Fall of Feminism in America* (University of Illinois Press, 1973).

Race is also the focal point of several studies of the Harlem Renaissance. The best of these works include Nathan Irvin Huggins, *Harlem Renaissance* (Oxford University Press, 1971); David Levering Lewis, *When Harlem Was in Vogue* (Alfred A. Knopf, 1981); and Cary D. Wintz, *Black Culture and the Harlem Renaissance* (Rice University Press, 1988).

ISSUE 10

Was the New Deal an Effective Answer to the Great Depression?

YES: Roger Biles, from *A New Deal for the American People* (Northern Illinois University Press, 1991)

NO: Gary Dean Best, from *Pride, Prejudice, and Politics: Roosevelt Versus Recovery, 1933–1938* (Praeger, 1991)

ISSUE SUMMARY

YES: Professor of history Roger Biles contends that, in spite of its minimal reforms and nonrevolutionary programs, the New Deal created a limited welfare state that implemented economic stabilizers to avert another depression.

NO: Professor of history Gary Dean Best argues that Roosevelt established an antibusiness environment with the creation of the New Deal regulatory programs, which retarded the nation's economic recovery from the Great Depression until World War II.

The catastrophe triggered by the 1929 Wall Street debacle crippled the American economy, deflated the optimistic future most Americans assumed to be their birthright, and ripped apart the values by which the country's businesses, farms, and governments were run. In the 1920s the whirlwind of a boom economy had sucked people into its vortex. During the next decade, the inertia of the Great Depression stifled their attempts to make ends meet.

The world depression of the 1930s began in the United States, which is where some of the most serious effects were felt. The United States had suffered periodic economic setbacks—in 1873, 1893, 1907, and 1920—but those slumps had been limited and temporary. The omnipotence of American productivity, the ebullient American spirit, and the self-deluding thought "it can't happen here" blocked out any consideration of an economic collapse that might devastate the capitalist economy and threaten U.S. democratic government.

All aspects of American society trembled from successive jolts; there were 4 million unemployed people in 1930 and 9 million more by 1932. Those who had not lost their jobs took pay cuts or worked for scrip. Charitable organizations attempted to provide for millions of homeless and hungry people, but their resources were not adequate. There was no security for those whose savings were lost forever when banks failed or stocks declined. Manufacturing halted, industry shut down, and farmers destroyed wheat, corn, and milk rather than sell them at a loss. Worse, there were millions of homeless Americans—refugees from the cities roaming the nation on freight trains, victims of the drought of the Dust Bowl seeking a new life farther west, and hobo children estranged from their parents. Physicians reported increased cases of malnutrition. Some people plundered grocery stores to avoid starvation.

Business and government leaders alike seemed immobilized by the economic giant that had fallen to its knees. "In other periods of depression there has always been hope, but as I look about, I now see nothing to give ground for hope—nothing of man," said former president Calvin Coolidge on New Year's Day 1933. Herbert Hoover, the incumbent president at the start of the Great Depression, attempted some relief programs. However, they were ineffective, considering the magnitude of the unemployment, hunger, and distress. Nor did Hoover's initiatives recognize the need for serious changes in the relationship between the federal government and society or for any modification of its relationship with individual Americans.

As governor of New York, Franklin D. Roosevelt (who was elected president in 1932) had introduced some relief measures, such as industrial welfare and a comprehensive system of unemployment remedies, to alleviate the social and economic problems facing the citizens of the state. Yet his campaign did little to reassure his critics that he was more than a "Little Lord Fauntleroy" rich boy who wanted to be the president. In light of later developments, Roosevelt may have been the only presidential candidate to deliver more programs than he actually promised.

In the following selections, Roger Biles argues that in spite of its minimal reforms and nonrevolutionary programs, the New Deal created a limited welfare state that implemented economic stabilizers to avert another depression. Conservative historian Gary Dean Best is highly critical of Roosevelt's pragmatic approach to solving the depression. Roosevelt established an antibusiness environment, maintains Best, when he created a host of New Deal regulatory programs whose long-range effect was to retard the nation's economic recovery until World War II.

YES

Roger Biles

A NEW DEAL FOR THE
AMERICAN PEOPLE

At the close of the Hundred Days, Franklin D. Roosevelt said, "All of the proposals and all of the legislation since the fourth day of March have not been just a collection of haphazard schemes, but rather the orderly component parts of a connected and logical whole." Yet the president later described his approach quite differently. "Take a method and try it. If it fails admit it frankly and try another. But above all, try something." The impetus for New Deal legislation came from a variety of sources, and Roosevelt relied heavily at various times on an ideologically diverse group of aides and allies. His initiatives reflected the contributions of, among others, Robert Wagner, Rexford Tugwell, Raymond Moley, George Norris, Robert LaFollette, Henry Morgenthau, Marriner Eccles, Felix Frankfurter, Henry Wallace, Harry Hopkins, and Eleanor Roosevelt. An initial emphasis on recovery for agriculture and industry gave way within two years to a broader-based program for social reform; entente with the business community yielded to populist rhetoric and a more ambiguous economic program. Roosevelt suffered the opprobrium of both the conservatives, who vilified "that man" in the White House who was leading the country down the sordid road to socialism, and the radicals, who saw the Hyde Park aristocrat as a confidence man peddling piecemeal reform to forestall capitalism's demise. Out of so many contradictory and confusing circumstances, how does one make sense of the five years of legislative reform known as the New Deal? And what has been its impact on a half century of American life?

A better understanding begins with the recognition that little of the New Deal was new, including the use of federal power to effect change. Nor, for all of Roosevelt's famed willingness to experiment, did New Deal programs usually originate from vernal ideas. Governmental aid to increase farmers' income, pro-pounded in the late nineteenth century by the Populists, surfaced in Woodrow Wilson's farm credit acts. The prolonged debates over McNary-Haugenism in the 1920s kept the issue alive, and Herbert Hoover's Agricultural Marketing Act set the stage for further federal involvement. Centralized economic planning, as embodied in the National Industrial Recovery

Act, flowed directly from the experiences of Wilson's War Industries Board; not surprisingly, Roosevelt chose Hugh Johnson, a veteran of the board, to head the National Recovery Administration. Well established in England and Germany before the First World War, social insurance appeared in a handful of states—notably Wisconsin—before the federal government became involved. Similarly, New Deal labor reform took its cues from the path-breaking work of state legislatures. Virtually alone in its originality, compensatory fiscal policy seemed revolutionary in the 1930s. Significantly, however, Roosevelt embraced deficit spending quite late after other disappointing economic policies and never to the extent Keynesian economists advised. Congress and the public supported the New Deal, in part, because of its origins in successful initiatives attempted earlier under different conditions.

Innovative or not, the New Deal dearly failed to restore economic prosperity. As late as 1938 unemployment stood at 19.1 percent and two years later at 14.6 percent. Only the Second World War, which generated massive industrial production, put the majority of the American people back to work. To be sure, partial economic recovery occurred. From a high of 13 million unemployed in 1933, the number under Roosevelt's administration fell to 11.4 million in 1934, 10.6 million in 1935, and 9 million in 1936. Farm income and manufacturing wages also rose, and as limited as these achievements may seem in retrospect, they provided sustenance for millions of people and hope for many more. Yet Roosevelt's resistance to Keynesian formulas for pump priming placed immutable barriers in the way of recovery that only war could demolish. At a time calling for drastic inflationary methods,

Roosevelt introduced programs effecting the opposite result. The NRA restricted production, elevated prices, and reduced purchasing power, all of which were deflationary in effect. The Social Security Act's payroll taxes took money from consumers and out of circulation. The federal government's $4.43 billion deficit in fiscal year 1936, impressive as it seemed, was not so much greater than Hoover's $2.6 billion shortfall during his last year in office. As economist Robert Lekachman noted, "The 'great spender' was in his heart a true descendant of thrifty Dutch Calvinist forebears." It is not certain that the application of Keynesian formulas would have sufficed by the mid-1930s to restore prosperity, but the president's cautious deflationary policies clearly retarded recovery.

Although New Deal economic policies came up short in the 1930s, they implanted several "stabilizers" that have been more successful in averting another such depression. The Securities and Exchange Act of 1934 established government supervision of the stock market, and the Wheeler-Rayburn Act allowed the Securities and Exchange Commission to do the same with public utilities. Severely embroiled in controversy when adopted, these measures have become mainstays of the American financial system. The Glass-Steagall Banking Act forced the separation of commercial and investment banking and broadened the powers of the Federal Reserve Board to change interest rates and limit loans for speculation. The creation of the Federal Deposit Insurance Corporation (FDIC) increased government supervision of state banks and significantly lowered the number of bank failures. Such safeguards restored confidence in the discredited banking system and established a firm economic foundation that performed well for decades thereafter.

The New Deal was also responsible for numerous other notable changes in American life. Section 7(a) of the NIRA, the Wagner Act, and the Fair Labor Standards Act transformed the relationship between workers and business and breathed life into a troubled labor movement on the verge of total extinction. In the space of a decade government laws eliminated sweatshops, severely curtailed child labor, and established enforceable standards for hours, wages, and working conditions. Further, federal action eliminated the vast majority of company towns in such industries as coal mining. Although Robert Wagner and Frances Perkins dragged Roosevelt into labor's corner, the New Deal made the unions a dynamic force in American society. Moreover, as Nelson Lichtenstein has noted, "by giving so much of the working class an institutional voice, the union movement provided one of the main political bulwarks of the Roosevelt Democratic party and became part of the social bedrock in which the New Deal welfare state was anchored."

Roosevelt's avowed goal of "cradle-to-grave" security for the American people proved elusive, but his administration achieved unprecedented advances in the field of social welfare. In 1938 the president told Congress: "Government has a final responsibility for the well-being of its citizenship. If private co-operative endeavor fails to provide work for willing hands and relief for the unfortunate, those suffering hardship from no fault of their own have a right to call upon the Government for aid; and a government worthy of its name must make fitting response." The New Deal's safety net included low-cost housing; old-age pensions; unemployment insurance; and aid for dependent mothers and children, the disabled, the blind, and public health services. Sometimes disappointing because of limiting eligibility requirements and low benefit levels, these social welfare programs nevertheless firmly established the principle that the government had an obligation to assist the needy. As one scholar wrote of the New Deal, "More progress was made in public welfare and relief than in the three hundred years after this country was first settled."

More and more government programs, inevitably resulting in an enlarged administrative apparatus and requiring additional revenue, added up to a much greater role for the national government in American life. Coming at a time when the only Washington bureaucracy most of the people encountered with any frequency was the U.S. Postal Service, the change seemed all the more remarkable. Although many New Deal programs were temporary emergency measures, others lingered long after the return of prosperity. Suddenly, the national government was supporting farmers, monitoring the economy, operating a welfare system, subsidizing housing, adjudicating labor disputes, managing natural resources, and providing electricity to a growing number of consumers. "What Roosevelt did in a period of a little over 12 years was to change the form of government," argued journalist Richard L. Strout. "Washington had been largely run by big business, by Wall Street. He brought the government to Washington." Not surprisingly, popular attitudes toward government also changed. No longer willing to accept economic deprivation and social dislocation as the vagaries of an uncertain existence, Americans tolerated—indeed, came to expect—the national government's involvement in the problems of everyday life. No longer did "government" mean just "city hall."

The operation of the national government changed as well. For one thing, Roosevelt's strong leadership expanded presidential power, contributing to what historian Arthur Schlesinger, Jr., called the "imperial presidency." Whereas Americans had in previous years instinctively looked first to Capitol Hill, after Roosevelt the White House took center stage in Washington. At the same time, Congress and the president looked at the nation differently. Traditionally attentive only to one group (big business), policymakers in Washington began responding to other constituencies such as labor, farmers, the unemployed, the aged, and to a lesser extent, women, blacks, and other disadvantaged groups. This new "broker state" became more accessible and acted on a growing number of problems, but equity did not always result. The ablest, richest, and most experienced groups fared best during the New Deal. NRA codes favored big business, and AAA benefits aided large landholders; blacks received relief and government jobs but not to the extent their circumstances merited. The long-term result, according to historian John Braeman, has been "a balkanized political system in which private interests scramble, largely successfully, to harness governmental authority and/or draw upon the public treasury to advance their private agendas."

Another legacy of the New Deal has been the Roosevelt revolution in politics. Urbanization and immigration changed the American electorate, and a new generation of voters who resided in the cities during the Great Depression opted for Franklin D. Roosevelt and his party. Before the 1930s the Democrats of the northern big-city machines and the solid South uneasily coexisted and surrendered primacy to the unified Republican party. The New Deal coalition that elected Roosevelt united behind common economic interests. Both urban northerners and rural southerners, as well as blacks, women, and ethnic immigrants, found common cause in government action to shield them from an economic system gone haywire. By the end of the decade the increasing importance of the urban North in the Democratic party had already become apparent. After the economy recovered from the disastrous depression, members of the Roosevelt coalition shared fewer compelling interests. Beginning in the 1960s, tensions mounted within the party as such issues as race, patriotism, and abortion loomed larger. Even so, the Roosevelt coalition retained enough commitment to New Deal principles to keep the Democrats the nation's majority party into the 1980s.

Yet for all the alterations in politics, government, and the economy, the New Deal fell far short of a revolution. The two-party system survived intact, and neither fascism, which attracted so many followers in European states suffering from the same international depression, nor communism attracted much of a following in the United States. Vital government institutions functioned without interruption and if the balance of powers shifted, the national branches of government maintained an essential equilibrium. The economy remained capitalistic; free enterprise and private ownership, not socialism, emerged from the 1930s. A limited welfare state changed the meld of the public and private but left them separate. Roosevelt could be likened to the British conservative Edmund Burke, who advocated measured change to offset drastic alterations—"reform to preserve." The New Deal's great achievement was the application of just enough change to preserve the American political economy.

Indications of Roosevelt's restraint emerged from the very beginning of the New Deal. Rather than assume extraordinary executive powers as Abraham Lincoln had done in the 1861 crisis, the president called Congress into special session. Whatever changes ensued would come through normal governmental activity. Roosevelt declined to assume direct control of the economy, leaving the nation's resources in the hands of private enterprise. Resisting the blandishments of radicals calling for the nationalization of the banks, he provided the means for their rehabilitation and ignored the call for national health insurance and federal contributions to Social Security retirement benefits. The creation of such regulatory agencies as the SEC confirmed his intention to revitalize rather than remake economic institutions. Repeatedly during his presidency, Roosevelt responded to congressional pressure to enact bolder reforms, as in the case of the National Labor Relations Act, the Wagner-Steagall Housing Act, and the FDIC. The administration forwarded the NIRA only after Senator Hugo Black's recovery bill mandating 30-hour workweeks seemed on the verge of passage.

As impressive as New Deal relief and social welfare programs were, they never went as far as conditions demanded or many liberals recommended. Fluctuating congressional appropriations, oscillating economic conditions, and Roosevelt's own hesitancy to do too much violence to the federal budget left Harry Hopkins, Harold Ickes, and others only partially equipped to meet the staggering need. The president justified the creation of the costly WPA in 1935 by "ending this business of relief." Unskilled workers, who constituted the greatest number of WPA employees, obtained but 60 to 80 percent of the minimal family income as determined by the government. Roosevelt and Hopkins continued to emphasize work at less than existing wage scales so that the WPA or PWA never competed with free labor, and they allowed local authorities to modify pay rates. They also continued to make the critical distinction between the "deserving" and "undeserving" poor, making sure that government aided only the former. The New Deal never challenged the values underlying this distinction, instead seeking to provide for the growing number of "deserving" poor created by the Great Depression. Government assumed an expanded role in caring for the disadvantaged, but not at variance with existing societal norms regarding social welfare.

The New Deal effected no substantial redistribution of income. The Wealth Tax Act of 1935 (the famous soak-the-rich tax) produced scant revenue and affected very few taxpayers. Tax alterations in 1936 and 1937 imposed no additional burdens on the rich; the 1938 and 1939 tax laws actually removed a few. By the end of the 1930s less than 5 percent of Americans paid income taxes, and the share of taxes taken from personal and corporate income levies fell below the amount raised in the 1920s. The great change in American taxation policy came during World War II, when the number of income tax payers grew to 74 percent of the population. In 1942 Treasury Secretary Henry Morgenthau noted that "for the first time in our history, the income tax is becoming a people's tax." This the New Deal declined to do.

Finally, the increased importance of the national government exerted remarkably little influence on local institutions. The New Deal seldom dictated and almost always deferred to state and local governments—encouraging, cajoling, bargaining, and wheedling to bring parochial interests in line with national objectives. As Harry Hopkins discovered, governors and mayors angled to obtain as many federal dollars as possible for their constituents but with no strings attached. Community control and local autonomy, conditions thought to be central to American democracy, remained strong, and Roosevelt understood the need for firm ties with politicians at all levels. In his study of the New Deal's impact on federalism, James T. Patterson concludes: "For all the supposed power of the New Deal, it was unable to impose all its guidelines on the autonomous forty-eight states.... What could the Roosevelt administration have done to ensure a more profound and lasting impression on state policy and politics? Very little."

Liberal New Dealers longed for more sweeping change and lamented their inability to goad the president into additional action. They envisioned a wholesale purge of the Democratic party and the creation of a new organization embodying fully the principles of liberalism. They could not abide Roosevelt's toleration of the political conservatives and unethical bosses who composed part of the New Deal coalition. They sought racial equality, constraints upon the southern landholding class, and federal intrusion to curb the power of urban real estate interests on behalf of the inveterate poor.

Yet to do these things would be to attempt changes well beyond the desires of most Americans. People pursuing remunerative jobs and the economic security of the middle class approved of government aiding the victims of an unfortunate economic crisis but had no interest in an economic system that would limit opportunity. The fear that the New Deal would lead to such thoroughgoing change explains the seemingly irrational hatred of Roosevelt by the economic elite. But, as historian Barry Karl has noted, "it was characteristic of Roosevelt's presidency that he never went as far as his detractors feared or his followers hoped."

The New Deal achieved much that was good and left much undone. Roosevelt's programs were defined by the confluence of forces that circumscribed his admittedly limited reform agenda—hostile judiciary; powerful congressional opponents, some of whom entered into alliances of convenience with New Dealers and some of whom awaited the opportunity to build on their opposition; the political impotence of much of the populace; the pugnacious independence of local and state authorities; the strength of people's attachment to traditional values and institutions; and the basic conservatism of American culture. Obeisance to local custom and the decision to avoid tampering with the fabric of American society allowed much injustice to survive while shortchanging blacks, women, small farmers, and the "unworthy" poor. Those who criticized Franklin Roosevelt for an unwillingness to challenge racial, economic, and gender inequality misunderstood either the nature of his electoral mandate or the difference between reform and revolution—or both.

If the New Deal preserved more than it changed, that is understandable in a society whose people have consistently chosen freedom over equality. Americans traditionally have eschewed expanded government, no matter how efficiently managed or honestly administered, that imposed restraints on personal success— even though such limitations redressed legitimate grievances or righted imbalances. Parity, most Americans believed, should not be purchased with the loss of liberty. But although the American dream has always entailed individual success with a minimum of state interference, the profound shock of capitalism's near demise in the 1930s undermined numerous previously unquestioned beliefs. The inability of capitalism's "invisible hand" to stabilize the market and the failure of the private sector to restore prosperity enhanced the consideration of stronger executive leadership and centralized planning. Yet with the collapse of democratic governments and their replacement by totalitarian regimes, Americans were keenly sensitive to any threats to liberty. New Deal programs, frequently path breaking in their delivery of federal resources outside normal channels, also retained a strong commitment to local government and community control while promising only temporary disruptions prior to the return of economic stability. Reconciling the necessary authority at the federal level to meet nationwide crises with the local autonomy desirable to safeguard freedom has always been one of the salient challenges to American democracy. Even after New Deal refinements, the search for the proper balance continues.

NO

Gary Dean Best

PRIDE, PREJUDICE AND POLITICS: ROOSEVELT VERSUS RECOVERY, 1933–1938

This book had its genesis in the fact that I have for a long time felt uncomfortable with the standard works written about Franklin Delano Roosevelt and the New Deal, and with the influence those works have exerted on others writing about and teaching U.S. history. Although I approach the subject from a very different perspective, Paul K. Conkin's preface to the second edition of *The New Deal* (1975) expressed many of my own misgivings about writings on the subject. Conkin wrote that "pervading even the most scholarly revelations was a monotonous, often almost reflexive, and in my estimation a very smug or superficial valuative perspective—approval, even glowing approval, of most enduring New Deal policies, or at least of the underlying goals that a sympathetic observer could always find behind policies and programs."

Studies of the New Deal such as Conkin described seemed to me to be examples of a genre relatively rare in U.S. historiography—that of "court histories."...

But, like most historians teaching courses dealing with the Roosevelt period, I was captive to the published works unless I was willing and able to devote the time to pursue extensive research in the period myself. After some years that became possible, and this book is the result.

My principal problem with Roosevelt and the New Deal was not over his specific reforms or his social programs, but with the failure of the United States to recover from the depression during the eight peacetime years that he and his policies governed the nation. I consider that failure tragic, not only for the 14.6 percent of the labor force that remained unemployed as late as 1940, and for the millions of others who subsisted on government welfare because of the prolonged depression, but also because of the image that the depression-plagued United States projected to the world at a crucial time in international affairs. In the late 1930s and early 1940s, when U.S. economic strength might have given pause to potential aggressors in the world, our economic weakness furnished encouragement to them instead.

From the standpoint, then, not only of our domestic history, but also of the tragic events and results of World War II, it has seemed to me that Roosevelt's failure to generate economic recovery during this critical period deserved more attention than historians have given it.

Most historians of the New Deal period leave the impression that the failure of the United States to recover during those eight years resulted from Roosevelt's unwillingness to embrace Keynesian spending. According to this thesis, recovery came during World War II because the war at last forced Roosevelt to spend at the level required all along for recovery. This, however, seemed to me more an advocacy of Keynes' theories by the historians involved than an explanation for the U.S. failure to recover during those years. Great Britain, for example, managed to recover by the late 1930s without recourse to deficit spending. By that time the United States was, by contrast, near the bottom of the list of industrial nations as measured in progress toward recovery, with most others having reached the predepression levels and many having exceeded them. The recovered countries represented a variety of economic systems, from state ownership to private enterprise. The common denominator in their success was not a reliance on deficit spending, but rather the stimulus they furnished to industrial enterprise.

What went wrong in the United States? Simplistic answers such as the reference to Keynesianism seemed to me only a means of avoiding a real answer to the question. A wise president, entering the White House in the midst of a crippling depression, should do everything possible to stimulate enterprise. In a free economy, economic recovery means *business* recovery. It follows, therefore, that a wise chief executive should do everything possible to create the conditions and psychology most conducive to business recovery —to encourage business to expand production, and lenders and investors to furnish the financing and capital that are required. An administration seeking economic recovery will do as little as possible that might inhibit recovery, will weigh all its actions with the necessity for economic recovery in mind, and will consult with competent business and financial leaders, as well as economists, to determine the best policies to follow. Such a president will seek to promote cooperation between the federal government and business, rather than conflict, and will seek to introduce as much consistency and stability as possible into government economic policies so that businessmen and investors can plan ahead. While obviously the destitute must be cared for, ultimately the most humane contribution a liberal government can make to the victims of a depression is the restoration of prosperity and the reemployment of the idle in genuine jobs.

In measuring the Roosevelt policies and programs during the New Deal years against such standards, I was struck by the air of unreality that hung over Washington in general and the White House in particular during this period. Business and financial leaders who questioned the wisdom of New Deal policies were disregarded and deprecated because of their "greed" and "self-interest," while economists and business academicians who persisted in calling attention to the collision between New Deal policies and simple economic realities were dismissed for their "orthodoxy." As one "orthodox" economist pointed out early in the New Deal years,

> economic realism... insists that policies aiming to promote recovery will, in fact, retard recovery if and where they fail to take into account correctly of stubborn facts in the existing economic situation and of the arithmetic of business as it must be carried out in the economic situation we are trying to revive. The antithesis of this economic realism is the vaguely hopeful or optimistic idealism in the field of economic policy, as such, which feels that good intentions, enough cleverness, and the right appeal to the emotions of the people ought to insure good results in spite of inconvenient facts.

Those "inconvenient facts" dogged the New Deal throughout these years, only to be stubbornly resisted by a president whose pride, prejudices, and politics would rarely permit an accommodation with them.

Most studies of the New Deal years approach the period largely from the perspective of the New Dealers themselves. Critics and opponents of Roosevelt's policies and programs are given scant attention in such works except to point up the "reactionary" and "unenlightened" opposition with which Roosevelt was forced to contend in seeking to provide Americans with "a more abundant life." The few studies that have concentrated on critics and opponents of the New Deal in the business community have been by unsympathetic historians who have tended to distort the opposition to fit the caricature drawn by the New Dealers, so that they offer little to explain the impact of Roosevelt's policies in delaying recovery from the depression.

The issue of *why* businessmen and bankers were so critical of the New Deal has been for too long swept under the rug, together with the question of *how* Roosevelt and his advisers could possibly expect to produce an economic recovery while a state of war existed between his administration and the employers and investors who, alone, could produce such a recovery. Even a Keynesian response to economic depression is ultimately dependent on the positive reactions of businessmen and investors for its success, as Keynes well knew, and those reactions were not likely to be as widespread as necessary under such a state of warfare between government and business. Businessmen, bankers, and investors may have been "greedy" and "self-interested." They may have been guilty of wrong perceptions and unfounded fears. But they are also the ones, in a free economy, upon whose decisions and actions economic recovery must depend. To understand their opposition to the New Deal requires an immersion in the public and private comments of critics of Roosevelt's policies. The degree and nature of business, banking, and investor concern about the direction and consequences of New Deal policies can be gleaned from the hundreds of banking and business periodicals representative of every branch of U.S. business and finance in the 1930s, and from the letters and diaries of the New Deal's business and other critics during the decade.

* * *

Statistics are useful in understanding the history of any period, but particularly periods of economic growth or depression. Statistics for the Roosevelt years may easily be found in *Historical Statistics of the United States* published by the Bureau of the Census, U.S. Department of Commerce (1975). Some of the trauma of the depression years may be inferred from the fact that the population of the United States grew by over 17 million between 1920 and 1930, but by only about half of that (8.9 million) between 1930 and 1940.

Historical Statistics gives the figures ... for unemployment, 1929–1940. These figures are, however, only estimates. The federal government did not monitor the number of unemployed during those years. Even so, these figures are shocking, indicating as they do that even after the war had begun in Europe, with the increased orders that it provided for U.S. mines, factories, and farms, unemployment remained at 14.6 percent.

One characteristic of the depression, to which attention was frequently called during the Roosevelt years, was the contrast between its effects on the durable goods and consumer goods industries. Between 1929 and 1933, expenditures on personal durable goods dropped by nearly 50 percent, and in 1938 they were still nearly 25 percent below the 1929 figures. Producers' durable goods suffered even more, failing by nearly two-thirds between 1929 and 1933, and remaining more than 50 percent below the 1929 figure in 1938. At the same time, expenditures on nondurable, or consumer, goods showed much less effect. Between 1929 and 1933 they fell only about 14.5 percent, and by 1938 they exceeded the 1929 level. These figures indicate that the worst effects of the depression, and resultant unemployment, were being felt in the durable goods industries. Roosevelt's policies, however, served mainly to stimulate the consumer goods industries where the depression and unemployment were far less seriously felt.

One consequence of Roosevelt's policies can be seen in the U.S. balance of trade during the New Deal years. By a variety of devices, Roosevelt drove up the prices of U.S. industrial and agricultural products, making it difficult for these goods to compete in the world market, and opening U.S. markets to cheaper foreign products.... With the exception of a $41 million deficit in 1888, these were the only deficits in U.S. trade for a century, from the 1870s to the 1970s.

... [W]hile suicides during the Roosevelt years remained about the same as during the Hoover years, the death rate by "accidental falls" increased significantly. In fact, according to *Historical Statistics*, the death rate by "accidental falls" was higher in the period 1934–1938 than at any other time between 1910 and 1970 (the years for which figures are given).

Interestingly, the number of persons arrested grew steadily during the depression years. In 1938 nearly twice as many (554,000) were arrested as in 1932 (278,000), and the number continued to increase until 1941. And, while the number of telephones declined after 1930 and did not regain the 1930 level until 1939, the number of households with radios increased steadily during the depression years. And Americans continued to travel. Even in the lowest year, 1933, 300,000 Americans visited foreign countries (down from 517,000 in 1929), while the number visiting national parks, monuments, and such, steadily increased during the depression—in 1938 nearly five times as many (16,331,000) did so as in 1929 (3,248,000).

Comparisons of the recovery of the United States with that of other nations may be found in the volumes of the League of Nations' *World Economic Survey* for the depression years. [A] table (from the volume of 1938/39) shows comparisons of unemployment rates. From this it can be seen that in 1929 the United States had the lowest unemployment rate of the countries listed; by 1932 the United States was midway on the list, with seven nations reporting higher unemployment rates and seven reporting lower unemployment. By mid-1938, however, after over five years of the New Deal, only three nations had higher unemployment rates, while twelve had lower unemployment. The United States, then, had lost ground in comparison with the other nations between 1932 and 1938.

The *World Economic Survey* for 1937/38 compared the levels of industrial production for 23 nations in 1937, expressed as a percentage of their industrial production in 1929.... It must be remembered that the figures for the United States reflect the level of industrial production reached just before the collapse of the economy later that year. Of the 22 other nations listed, 19 showed a higher rate of recovery in industrial production than the United States, while only 3 lagged behind. One of these, France, had followed policies similar to those of the New Deal in the United States. As the *World Economic Survey* put it, both the Roosevelt administration and the Blum government in France had "adopted far-reaching social and economic policies which combined recovery measures with measures of social reform." It added: "The consequent doubt regarding the prospects of profit and the uneasy relations between business-men and the Government have in the opinion of many, been an important factor in delaying recovery," and the two countries had, "unlike the United Kingdom and Germany," failed to "regain the 1929 level of employment and production." The *World Economic Survey* the following year (1939) pointed out that industrial production in the United States

had fallen from the 92.2 to 65 by June 1938, and hovered between 77 and 85 throughout 1939. Thus, by the end of 1938 the U.S. record was even sorrier than revealed by the [data].

* * *

Every survey of American historians consistently finds Franklin Delano Roosevelt ranked as one of this nation's greatest presidents. Certainly, exposure to even a sampling of the literature on Roosevelt and the New Deal can lead one to no other conclusion. Conventional wisdom has it that Roosevelt was an opportune choice to lead the United States through the midst of the Great Depression, that his cheerful and buoyant disposition uplifted the American spirit in the midst of despair and perhaps even forestalled a radical change in the direction of American politics toward the right or the left. Roosevelt's landslide reelection victory in 1936, and the congressional successes in 1934, are cited as evidence of the popularity of both the president and the New Deal among the American people. Polls by both Gallup and the Democratic National Committee early in the 1936 campaign, however, give a very different picture, and suggest that the electoral victories can be as accurately accounted for in terms of the vast outpourings of federal money in 1934 and 1936, and the inability or unwillingness of Landon to offer a genuine alternative to the New Deal in the latter year. To this must be added the fact that after early 1936 two of the most unpopular New Deal programs—the NRA and the AAA—had been removed as issues by the Supreme Court.

Conventional wisdom, in fact, suffers many setbacks when the Roosevelt years are examined from any other perspective than through a pro-New Deal Prism

—from the banking crisis of 1933 and the first inaugural address, through the reasons for the renewed downturn in 1937, to the end of the New Deal in 1937–1938. The American present has been ill-served by the inaccurate picture that has too often been presented of this chapter in the American past by biographers and historians. Roosevelt's achievements in alleviating the hardship of the depression are deservedly well known, his responsibility for prolonging the hardship is not. His role in providing long-overdue and sorely needed social and economic legislation is in every high school American history textbook, but the costs for the United States of his eight-year-long war against business recovery are mentioned in none.

Such textbooks (and those in college, too) frequently contain a chapter on the Great Depression, followed by one on the New Deal, the implication being that somewhere early in the second of the chapters the depression was ended by Roosevelt's policies. Only careful reading reveals that despite Roosevelt's immense labors to feed the unemployed, only modest recovery from the lowest depths of the depression was attained before the outbreak of World War II. Roosevelt, readers are told, was too old-fashioned, too conservative, to embrace the massive compensatory spending and unbalanced budgets that might have produced a Keynesian recovery sooner. But World War II, the books tell us, made such spending necessary and the recovery that might have occurred earlier was at last achieved.

Generations of Americans have been brought up on this version of the New Deal years. Other presidential administrations have been reevaluated over the years, and have risen or fallen in grace as

a result, but not the Roosevelt administration. The conventional wisdom concerning the Roosevelt administration remains the product of the "court historians," assessments of the New Deal period that could not have been better written by the New Dealers themselves. The facts, however, are considerably at variance with this conventional wisdom concerning the course of the depression, the reasons for the delay of recovery, and the causes of the recovery when it came, finally, during World War II.

From the uncertainty among businessmen and investors about the new president-elect that aborted a promising upturn in the fall of 1932, to the panic over the prospect of inflationary policies that was a major factor in the banking crisis that virtually paralyzed the nation's economy by the date of his inauguration, Roosevelt's entry into the White House was not an auspicious beginning toward recovery. The prejudices that were to guide the policies and programs of the New Deal for the next six years were revealed in Roosevelt's inaugural address, although the message was largely overlooked until it had become more apparent in the actions of the administration later. It was an attitude of hostility toward business and finance, of contempt for the profit motive of capitalism, and of willingness to foment class antagonism for political benefit. This was not an attitude that was conducive to business recovery, and the programs and policies that would flow from those prejudices would prove, in fact, to be destructive of the possibility of recovery.

There followed the "hundred days," when Roosevelt rammed through Congress a variety of legislation that only depressed business confidence more. The new laws were served up on attractive platters, with tempting descriptions —truth in securities, aid for the farmer, industrial self-regulation—but when the covers were removed the contents were neither attractive nor did they match the labels. By broad grants of power to the executive branch of the government, the legislation passed regulation of the U.S. economy into the hands of New Dealers whose aim was not to promote recovery but to carry out their own agendas for radical change of the economic system even at the expense of delaying recovery. Thus, truth in securities turned to paralysis of the securities markets, aid for the farmer became a war against profits by processors of agricultural goods, and industrial self-regulation became government control and labor-management strife. International economic cooperation as a device for ending the depression was abandoned for an isolationist approach, and throughout 1933 the threat of inflation added further uncertainty for businessmen and investors.

The grant of such unprecedented peacetime authority to an American president aroused concern, but these after all were only "emergency" powers, to be given up once recovery was on its way. Or were they? Gradually the evidence accumulated that the Tugwells and the Brandeisians intended to institutionalize the "emergency" powers as permanent features of American economic life. By the end of 1933, opposition to the New Deal was already sizable. Business alternated between the paralysis of uncertainty and a modest "recovery" born of purchases and production inspired by fear of higher costs owing to inflation and the effects of the AAA and NRA. The implementation of the latter two agencies in the fall of 1933 brought a renewed downturn that improved only slightly during the winter and spring. A renewed legislative onslaught by the New Deal in the 1934 congress, combined with labor strife encouraged by the provisions of the NIRA, brought a new collapse of the economy in the fall of 1934, which lowered economic indices once again to near the lowest levels they had reached in the depression.

The pattern had been established. The war against business and finance was under way, and there would be neither retreat nor cessation. Roosevelt's pride and prejudices, and the perceived political advantages to be gained from the war, dictated that his administration must ever be on the offensive and never in retreat. But the administration suffered defeats, nevertheless, and embarrassment. The Supreme Court proved a formidable foe, striking down both the NRA and the AAA. Dire predictions from the administration about the implications for the economy of the loss of the NRA proved embarrassing when the economy began to show gradual improvement after its departure. But defeat did not mean retreat. Under the goading of Felix Frankfurter and his disciples, Roosevelt became even more extreme in his verbal and legislative assault against business. Their attempts to cooperate with the Roosevelt administration having been spurned, businessmen and bankers awakened to the existence of the war being waged upon them and moved into opposition. Roosevelt gloried in their opposition and escalated the war against them in the 1936 reelection campaign.

Reelected in 1936 on a tidal wave of government spending, and against a lackluster Republican campaigner who offered no alternative to the New Deal, Roosevelt appeared at the apogee of his power and prestige. His triumph was, however, to be short-lived, despite an enhanced Democratic majority in Congress. A combination of factors was about to bring the New Deal war against business to a stalemate and eventual retreat. One of these was his ill-advised attempt to pack the Supreme Court with subservient justices, which aroused so much opposition even in his own party that he lost control of the Democrat-controlled Congress. More important, perhaps, was the growing economic crisis that the Roosevelt administration faced in 1937, largely as a result of its own past policies. The massive spending of 1936, including the payment of the veterans' bonus, had generated a speculative recovery during that year from concern about inflationary consequences. Fears of a "boom" were increased as a result of the millions of dollars in dividends, bonuses, and pay raises dispensed by businesses late in 1936 as a result of the undistributed profits tax. The pay raises, especially, were passed on in the form of higher prices, as were the social security taxes that were imposed on businesses beginning with 1937. Labor disturbances, encouraged by the Wagner Labor Act and the Roosevelt alliance with John L. Lewis' Congress of Industrial Organizations in the 1936 campaign, added further to the wage-price spiral that threatened as 1937 unfolded. Massive liquidations of low-interest government bonds, and sagging prices of the bonds, fueled concern among bankers and economists, and within the Treasury, that a "boom" would imperil the credit of the federal government and the solvency of the nation's banks whose portfolios consisted mainly of low-interest government bonds.

In considering the two principal options for cooling the "boom"—raising interest rates or cutting federal spending—the Roosevelt administration chose to move toward a balanced budget. It was a cruel dilemma that the New Dealers faced. All knew that the economy had not yet recovered from the depression, yet they were faced with the necessity to apply brakes to an economy that was becoming overheated as a consequence of their policies. Moreover, the reduction in consumer purchasing power caused by the cuts in federal spending was occurring at the same time that purchasing power was already being eroded as a result of the higher prices that worried the administration. Private industry, it should have been obvious, could not "take up the slack," since the Roosevelt administration had done nothing to prepare for the transition from government to private spending that John Maynard Keynes and others had warned them was necessary. The New Dealers had been far too busy waging war against business to allow it the opportunity to prepare for any such transition.

In fact, far from confronting the emergency of 1937 by making long-overdue attempts to cooperate with business in generating recovery, Roosevelt was busy pressing a new legislative assault against them. Denied passage of his legislative package by Congress during its regular 1937 session, Roosevelt called a special session for November despite evidence that the economy had begun a new downturn. Even the collapse of the stockmarket, within days after his announcement of the special session, and the growing unemployment that soon followed, did not deter Roosevelt from his determination to drive the legislative assault through it. With the nation in the grips of a full-blown economic collapse, Roosevelt offered nothing to the special session but the package of antibusiness legislation it had turned down in the regular session. Once again he was rebuffed by Congress. The nation drifted, its economic indices falling, with its president unwilling to admit the severity of the situation or unable to come to grips with what it said about the bankruptcy of the New Deal policies and programs.

By early 1938, Roosevelt was faced with problems similar to those he had faced when he first entered the White House five years earlier, but without the political capital he had possessed earlier. In 1933 the Hoover administration could be blamed for the depression. In 1938 the American people blamed the Roosevelt administration for retarding recovery. Five years of failure could not be brushed aside. Five years of warfare against business and disregard of criticism and offers of cooperation had converted supporters of 1933 into cynics or opponents by 1938. Even now, however, pride, prejudice, and politics dominated Roosevelt, making it impossible for him to extend the needed olive branch to business. The best that he could offer in 1938 was a renewal of federal spending and more of the same New Deal that had brought the nation renewed misery. In the 1938 congressional session he continued to press for passage of the antibusiness legislation that had been rejected by both sessions of 1937.

But Congress was no longer the pliant body it had been in 1933, and in the 1938 congressional elections the people's reaction was registered when the Republicans gained 81 new seats in the House and 8 in the Senate—far more than even the most optimistic Republican had predicted. If the message was lost on Roosevelt, it was obvious to some in his administration, notably his new Secretary of Commerce Harry Hopkins and his Secretary of the Treasury Henry Morgenthau. Two of the earliest business-baiters in the circle of Roosevelt advisers, they now recognized the bankruptcy of that course and the necessity for the administration to at last strive for recovery by removing the obstacles to normal and profitable business operation that the New Deal had erected. This was not what Roosevelt wanted to hear, nor was it what his Frankfurter disciples wanted him to hear. These latter knew, as Hopkins and Morgenthau had learned earlier, just which Rooseveltian buttons could be pushed to trigger his antibusiness prejudices and spite. A battle raged within the New Deal between the Frankfurter radicals and the "new conservatives," Hopkins and Morgenthau, amid growing public suspicion that the former were not interested in economic recovery.

It was not a fair battle. Hopkins and Morgenthau knew how to play the game, including use of the press, and had too many allies. They did not hesitate to talk bluntly to Roosevelt, perhaps the bluntest talk he had heard since the death of Louis McHenry Howe. Moreover, Roosevelt could afford the loss of a Corcoran and/or a Cohen, against whom there was already a great deal of congressional opposition, but a break with both Hopkins and Morgenthau would have been devastating for an administration already on the defensive. Gradually the Frankfurter radicals moved into eclipse, along with their policies, to be replaced increasingly by recovery and preparedness advocates, including many from the business and financial world.

Conventional wisdom has it that the massive government spending of World War II finally brought a Keynesian recovery from the depression. Of more significance, in comparisons of the prewar and wartime economic policies of the Roosevelt administration, is the fact that the war against business that characterized the former was abandoned in the latter. Both the attitude and policies of the Roosevelt administration toward business during the New Deal years were reversed when the president found new, foreign enemies to engage his attention and energies. Antibusiness advisers were replaced by businessmen, pro-labor policies became pro-business policies, cooperation replaced confrontation in relations between the federal government and business, and even the increased spending of the war years "trickled down" rather than "bubbling up." Probably no American president since, perhaps, Thomas Jefferson ever so thoroughly repudiated the early policies of his administration as Roosevelt did between 1939 and 1942. This, and not the emphasis on spending alone, is the lesson that needs to be learned from Roosevelt's experience with the depression, and of the legacy of the New Deal economic policies.

The judgment of historians concerning Roosevelt's presidential stature is curiously at odds with that of contemporary observers. One wonders how scholars of the Roosevelt presidency are able so blithely to ignore the negative assessments of journalists, for example, of the stature of Raymond Clapper, Walter Lippmann, Dorothy Thompson, and Arthur Krock, to name only a few. Can their observations concerning Roosevelt's pettiness and spitefulness, their criticism of the obstacles to recovery created by his anticapitalist bias, and their genuine concern over his apparent grasp for dictatorial power be dismissed so cavalierly? Is there any other example in U.S. history of an incumbent president running for reelection against the open op-

position of the two previous nominees of his own party? Will a public opinion poll ever again find 45 percent of its respondents foreseeing the likelihood of dictatorship arising from a president's policies? Will a future president ever act in such a fashion that the question will again even suggest itself to a pollster? One certainly hopes not.

Perhaps the positive assessment of Roosevelt by American historians rests upon a perceived liberalism of his administration. If so, one must wonder at their definition of liberalism. Surely a president who would pit class against class for political purposes, who was fundamentally hostile to the very basis of a free economy, who believed that his ends could justify very illiberal means, who was intolerant of criticism and critics, and who grasped for dictatorial power does not merit description as a liberal. Nor are the results of the Gallup poll mentioned above consistent with the actions of a liberal president. If the perception is based on Roosevelt's support for the less fortunate "one-third" of the nation, and his program of social legislation, then historians need to be reminded that such actions do not, in themselves, add up to liberalism, they having been used by an assortment of political realists and demagogues—of the left and the right—to gain and hold power.

There were certainly positive contributions under the New Deal, but they may not have outweighed the negative aspects of the period. The weight of the negative aspects would, moreover, have been much heavier except for the existence of a free and alert press, and for the actions of the Supreme Court and Congress in nullifying, modifying, and rejecting many of the New Deal measures. When one examines the full range of New Deal proposals and considers the implications of their passage in the original form, the outline emerges of a form of government alien to any definition of liberalism except that of the New Dealers themselves. Historians need to weigh more thoroughly and objectively the implications for the United States if Roosevelt's programs had been fully implemented. They need also to assess the costs in human misery of the delay in recovery, and of reduced U.S. influence abroad at a critical time in world affairs owing to its economic prostration. We can only speculate concerning the possible alteration of events from 1937 onward had the United States faced the world with the economic strength and military potential it might have displayed had wiser economic policies prevailed from 1933 to 1938. There is, in short, much about Roosevelt and the New Deal that historians need to reevaluate.

POSTSCRIPT

Was the New Deal an Effective Answer to the Great Depression?

Both Biles and Best agree that the New Deal concentrated a tremendous amount of power in the executive branch of the government. They also acknowledge that it was World War II—not the New Deal's reform programs —that pulled the United States out of the depression.

But the two writers disagree with each other in their assumptions and assessments of the New Deal. Biles argues that the New Deal was a non-revolution compared to the economic and political changes taking place in communist Russia, fascist Italy, and Nazi Germany. The New Deal, in his view, was not so new. The Wilson administration had imposed strong governmental controls during World War I, and a number of the farm, business, and collective utility projects had been suggested and passed in different versions during the Harding, Coolidge, and Hoover presidencies.

Best's major failing is his inability to view the human side of the New Deal. By concentrating on the strengths and weaknesses of a business recovery, he seems to forget that the New Deal was much more than the sum total of a number of economic statistics. Since that time, people have come to expect the national government to manage the economy responsibly.

The most influential earliest books by historians on the New Deal were highly sympathetic and written from the perspective of Washington D.C. A well-written, partisan, and never-to-be-completed history is Arthur M. Schlesinger, Jr.'s volumes on *The Age of Roosevelt,* which consists of *The Crisis of the Older Order, 1919–1933* (1957), *The Coming of the New Deal* (1959), and *The Politics of Upheaval* (1960), all published by Houghton Mifflin. The best one-volume history of the New Deal from this perspective remains William E. Leuchtenburg's *Franklin D. Roosevelt and the New Deal* (Harper & Row, 1963). In a retrospective written 50 years later, "The Achievement of the New Deal," Leuchtenburg chides left-wing critics of the New Deal who blame Roosevelt for not ending racial segregation or hard-core poverty. Both Leuchtenburg and Biles remind us of what the New Deal accomplished, not what it failed to do. This essay, along with other important interpretative essays that the author wrote over many years, can be found in Leuchtenburg's *The FDR Years: On Roosevelt and His Legacy* (Columbia University Press, 1995).

John Braeman has written two bibliographical essays that critically analyze some of the major specialized works written in the 1970s and 1980s. See "The New Deal and the Broker State: A Review of the Recent Scholarly Literature," *Business History Review* (vol. 46, 1971) and "The New Deal: The Collapse of the Liberal Consensus," *Canadian Review of American Studies*

(Summer 1989), which reviews a dozen or so books and concludes that, in the long-term, the New Deal brought about "a balkanized political system in which private interests scramble, barely successfully, to harass governmental authority and/or draw upon the public treasury to advance their private agendas."

Comprehensive syntheses and bibliographies can be found in Robert S. McElvaine, *The Great Depression: America, 1929–1941* (Times Books, 1984) and Anthony J. Badger, *The New Deal: The Depression Years, 1933–1940* (Farrar, Straus & Giroux, 1989). For a convenient reproduction of approximately 150 of "the most important" articles on all aspects of the New Deal, see *The Great Depression and the New Deal* (Garland Publishing, 1990), edited by Melvyn Dubofsky and Stephen Burnwood.

Liberal criticisms of the New Deal can be found in the first volume of James MacGregor Burns's political biography *Roosevelt: The Lion and the Fox* (Harcourt Brace, 1956), a work so elegantly written that 40 years later the many other biographies pale in comparison. Burns believes that Roosevelt retarded the recovery and created a recession in 1937 when he attempted to balance the budget. Alan Brinkley, in *The End of Reform: New Deal Liberalism in Recession and War* (Alfred A. Knopf, 1995), a study of the much-neglected years 1937–1945, argues that Roosevelt and his advisers gave up on trying to redistribute income by centralized planning and concentrated on encouraging production in hopes that a rising tide would lift all boats. James Q. Wilson attacks Brinkley with conservative arguments similar to those of Best in "Liberal Ghosts," *The New Republic* (May 22, 1995).

Radical criticisms of the New Deal and its legacy became common in the 1960s. A good starting point is Howard Zinn, ed., *New Deal Thought* (Bobbs-Merrill, 1966). Two of the most sophisticated New Left criticisms are Barton J. Bernstein, *The New Deal: The Conservative Achievements of Liberal Reform* (Pantheon Books, 1967) and Paul K. Conklin, *The New Deal*, 2d ed. (Harlan Davidson, 1975). Steve Fraser and Gary Gerstle edited a series of social and economic essays, which they present in *The Rise and Fall of the New Deal Order, 1930–1980* (Princeton University Press, 1989).

Contemporary left-wing critics are dissected in Arthur M. Schlesinger, Jr.'s *The Politics of Upheaval, vol. 3* (Houghton Mifflin, 1960), but the standard work is now Alan Brinkley's overview *Voices of Protest: Huey Long, Father Coughlin and the Great Depression* (Alfred A. Knopf, 1982).

The celebration of Roosevelt's 100th birthday in 1982 and the 50th anniversary of the New Deal in 1983 inspired a number of conferences and the subsequent publication of the papers. Among the most important are Harvard Sitkoff, ed., *Fifty Years Later: The New Deal Evaluated* (Alfred A. Knopf, 1985); Wilbur J. Cohen, ed., *The Roosevelt New Deal: A Program Assessment Fifty Years After* (Lyndon B. Johnson School of Public Affairs, 1986); and Herbert D. Rosenbaum and Elizabeth Barteline, eds., *Franklin D. Roosevelt: The Man, the Myth, the Era, 1882–1945* (Greenwood Press, 1987).

ISSUE 11

Was Franklin Roosevelt a Reluctant Internationalist?

YES: Robert A. Divine, from *Roosevelt and World War II* (Johns Hopkins University Press, 1969)

NO: Arthur M. Schlesinger, Jr., from "The Man of the Century," *American Heritage* (May/June 1994)

ISSUE SUMMARY

YES: Diplomatic historian Robert A. Divine argues that even after France fell to Nazi Germany in June 1940, Franklin D. Roosevelt remained a reluctant internationalist who spoke belligerently but acted timidly because he sincerely hated war.

NO: Pulitzer Prize–winning historian Arthur M. Schlesinger, Jr., maintains that from a 1990s perspective, Roosevelt—not Stalin, Churchill, or anyone else—was the only wartime leader who saw clearly the direction and shape of the new world that the leaders were trying to create.

By the end of World War I the United States had become the world's most powerful nation. Because of its loans to the Allies during the war and its growing international trade in agricultural products, manufactured goods, and armaments, the United States became a creditor nation for the first time in its history. Militarily, the United States had become the world's dominant power.

In order to prevent the reoccurrence of another world war, the United States initiated a series of arms limitation conferences. The most successful conference took place in Washington, D.C., in 1921. In spite of its participation in world trade and its attempts to restore financial solvency in Europe, however, the United States followed a policy that Professor Thomas Paterson has called "independent internationalism." For example, the United States refused to ratify the Treaty of Versailles because by doing so it would have to become a member of the League of Nations. In 1928 the United States and France, along with just about every other nation in the world, signed the Kellogg-Briand Pact outlawing war as an instrument of national policy. But none of the agreements signed by the United States in the 1920s had any enforcement provisions that would have bound the nation to share security responsibilities in Europe or Asia or to punish violators.

The Great Depression of the 1930s destroyed the balance of power in Europe and Asia. When Japan attacked China's province of Manchuria in 1931 it violated the Kellogg-Briand Pact and the Nine-Power Treaty signed at the Washington conference. Meanwhile, events took an ugly turn in Europe. Five weeks before Franklin Roosevelt became president, Adolf Hitler was installed as chancellor of Germany. Hitler hated democracy and communism, but most of all he despised Jews. In 1936 his soldiers marched into the Rhineland and continued making annexations until 1939, when he overran Poland. England and France had no recourse but to declare war. A little more than 20 years after World War I ended, World War II began.

How did the United States respond to the aggressive actions of Germany and Japan? Most of the American public agreed that the drive for profits in the arms industry was one (though not the only one) of the major causes of America's entrance into World War I. Therefore, the American public concluded that they should isolate themselves from the political turmoil in the rest of the world.

President Franklin Roosevelt himself took a nationalist approach, preferring to concentrate on his own domestic New Deal solutions. The Johnson Act of 1934 specified that governments that defaulted on war debt payments to the United States were not permitted to borrow from private American citizens or firms. Congress also passed three Neutrality Acts from 1935 to 1937 that were designed to keep the country from repeating the mistakes that dragged the United States into World War I.

When World War II broke out in September 1939, the cash-and-carry provision of the permanent Neutrality Law had expired the previous May. Roosevelt failed to revise the neutrality laws in the spring and summer of 1939, but in November, after the European war began, he convinced Congress to repeal the arms embargo. Now England and France could purchase munitions from the United States—still on a cash-and-carry basis—to aid their fight against the Nazis.

Did Roosevelt acquiesce in neutrality legislation that he did not like during his first six years in office because he had to concentrate on his domestic reforms? Or did he follow a policy of appeasement, like his English and French counterparts did, at the Munich Conference of 1938? Were there other alternatives?

In the following selections, Robert A. Divine argues that until 1938 Roosevelt was a sincere isolationist like most of the American public because he truly hated war. He remained a reluctant internationalist who spoke belligerently but acted timidly until he was reelected for a third term in 1940. Arthur M. Schlesinger, Jr., argues that Roosevelt saw the dangers of Nazism sooner than his contemporaries did and that he also understood better than anyone the direction and shape of the new world that the Allies were trying to create.

YES   Robert A. Divine

ROOSEVELT AND WORLD WAR II

[B]y the end of 1938, Roosevelt was no longer the confirmed isolationist he had been earlier in the decade. The brutal conquests by Italy, Japan, and Germany had aroused him to their ultimate threat to the United States. But he was still haunted by the fear of war that he voiced so often and so eloquently. His political opponents and subsequent historians have too readily dismissed his constant reiteration of the horrors of war as a politician's gesture toward public opinion. I contend that he was acting out of a deep and sincere belief when he declared that he hated war, and it was precisely this intense conviction that prevented him from embracing an interventionist foreign policy in the late 1930's. In the Munich crisis, he reveals himself in painful transition from the isolationist of the mid-1930's who wanted peace at almost any price to the reluctant internationalist of the early 1940's who leads his country into war in order to preserve its security.

No aspect of Roosevelt's foreign policy has been more controversial than his role in American entry into World War II. Although much of the discussion centers on the events leading to Pearl Harbor, I do not intend to enter into that labyrinth. The careful and well-researched studies by Herbert Feis, Roberta Wohlstetter, and Paul Schroeder demonstrate that while the administration made many errors in judgment, Roosevelt did not deliberately expose the fleet to a Japanese attack at Pearl Harbor in order to enter the war in Europe by a back door in the Pacific. This revisionist charge has already received far more attention than it deserves and has distracted historians from more significant issues.

What is more intriguing is the nature of Roosevelt's policy toward the war in Europe. There are a number of tantalizing questions that historians have not answered satisfactorily. Why was Roosevelt so devious and indirect in his policy toward the European conflict? When, if ever, did F.D.R. decide that the United States would have to enter the war in Europe to protect its own security? And finally, would Roosevelt have asked Congress for a declaration of war against Germany if Japan had not attacked Pearl Harbor?

In the months that followed the Munich Conference, President Roosevelt gradually realized that appeasement had served only to postpone, not to prevent, a major European war. In January, 1939, he sought to impart this fact in his annual message to Congress. He warned the representatives and senators that "philosophies of force" were loose in the world that threatened "the tenets of faith and humanity" on which the American way of life was founded. "The world has grown so small and weapons of attack so swift," the President declared, "that no nation can be safe" when aggression occurs anywhere on earth. He went on to say that the United States had "rightly" decided not to intervene militarily to prevent acts of aggression abroad and then added, somewhat cryptically, "There are many methods short of war, but stronger and more effective than mere words, of bringing home to aggressor governments the aggregate sentiments of our own people." Roosevelt did not spell out these "methods short of war," but he did criticize the existing neutrality legislation, which be suggested had the effect of encouraging aggressor nations. "We have learned," he continued, "that when we deliberately try to legislate neutrality, our neutrality laws may operate unevenly and unfairly—may actually give aid to an aggressor and deny it to the victim. The instinct of self-preservation should warn us that we ought not to let that happen any more."

Most commentators interpreted the President's speech as a call to Congress to revise the existing neutrality legislation, and in particular the arms embargo. Yet for the next two months, Roosevelt procrastinated. Finally, after Hitler's armies overran the remainder of Czechoslovakia in mid-March, Senator Key Pittman came forward with an administration proposal to repeal the arms embargo and permit American citizens to trade with nations at war on a cash-and-carry basis. The Pittman bill obviously favored England and France, since if these nations were at war with Nazi Germany, they alone would possess the sea power and financial resources to secure arms and supplies from a neutral United States. At the same time, the cash-and-carry restrictions would guard against the loss of American lives and property on the high seas and thus minimize the risk of American involvement.

Although the Pittman bill seemed to be a perfect expression of Roosevelt's desire to bolster the European democracies yet not commit the United States, the President scrupulously avoided any public endorsement in the spring of 1939. His own political stock was at an all-time low as a result of the court-packing dispute, a sharp economic recession, and an unsuccessful effort to purge dissident Democrats in the 1938 primaries. By May, Roosevelt's silence and Pittman's inept handling had led to a deadlock in the Senate. The President then turned to the House of Representatives, meeting with the leaders of the lower chamber on May 19 and telling them that passage of the cash-and-carry measure was necessary to prevent the outbreak of war in Europe. Yet despite this display of concern, Roosevelt refused to take the issue to the people, asking instead that Cordell Hull champion neutrality revision. The presidential silence proved fatal. In late June, a rebellious House of Representatives voted to retain the arms embargo and thus sabotage the administration's effort to align the United States with Britain and France.

Belatedly, Roosevelt decided to intervene. He asked the Senate Foreign Relations Committee to reconsider the Pittman bill, but in early July the Committee rebuffed the President by voting

12 to 11 to postpone action until the next session of Congress. Roosevelt was furious. He prepared a draft of a public statement in which he denounced congressional isolationists "who scream from the housetops that this nation is being led into a world war" as individuals who "deserve only the utmost contempt and pity of the American people." Hull finally persuaded him not to release this inflammatory statement. Instead, Roosevelt invited a small bipartisan group of senators to meet with him and Cordell Hull at the White House. The senators listened politely while the President and Secretary of State warned of the imminence of war in Europe and the urgent need of the United States to do something to prevent it. Senator William Borah, a leading Republican isolationist, then stunned Roosevelt and Hull by announcing categorically that there would be no war in Europe in the near future, that he had access to information from abroad that was far more reliable than the cables arriving daily at the State Department. When the other senators expressed their belief that Congress was not in the mood to revise the Neutrality Act, the meeting broke up. In a press release the next day, Roosevelt stated that the administration would accept the verdict of Congress, but he made it clear that he and Hull still believed that its failure to revise the neutrality legislation "would weaken the leadership of the United States... in the event of a new crisis in Europe." In a press conference three days later, Roosevelt was even blunter, accusing the Republicans of depriving him of the only chance he had to prevent the outbreak of war in Europe.

When the German invasion of Poland on September 1, 1939, touched off World War II, Roosevelt immediately proclaimed American neutrality and put the arms embargo and other restrictions into effect. In a radio talk to the American people on the evening of September 3, he voiced his determination to keep the country out of the conflict. "We seek to keep war from our firesides," he declared, "by keeping war from coming to the Americas." Though he deliberately refrained from asking the people to remain neutral in thought as Wilson had done in 1914, he closed by reiterating his personal hatred of war and pledging that, "as long as it remains within my power to prevent, there will be no blackout of peace in the United States."

President Roosevelt did not give up his quest for revision of the Neutrality Act, however. After a careful telephone canvass indicated that a majority of the Senate would now support repeal of the arms embargo, the President called Congress into special session. On September 21, Roosevelt urged the senators and representatives to repeal the arms embargo and thereby return to the traditional American adherence to international law. Calling Jefferson's embargo and the neutrality legislation of the 1930's the sole exceptions to this historic policy, he argued that the removal of the arms embargo was a way to insure that the United States would not be involved in the European conflict, and he promised that the government would also insist that American citizens and American ships be barred from entering the war zones. Denying that repeal was a step toward war, Roosevelt asserted that his proposal "offers far greater safeguards than we now possess or have ever possessed to protect American lives and property from danger.... There lies the road to peace." He then closed by declaring that America must stand aloof from the conflict so that it could preserve the culture of Western Europe. "Fate seems now to compel us to assume the task of helping to maintain in the western world a citadel wherein that civilization may be kept alive," he concluded.

It was an amazing speech. No less than four times the President declared that his policy was aimed at keeping the United States out of the war. Yet the whole intent of arms embargo repeal was to permit England and France to purchase arms and munitions from the United States. By basing his appeal on a return to international law and a desire to keep out of the war, Roosevelt was deliberately misleading the American people. The result was a long and essentially irrelevant debate in Congress over the administration bill to repeal the arms embargo and to place all trade with belligerents on a cash-and-carry basis. Advocates of the bill followed the President's cue, repeatedly denying that the legislation was aimed at helping Britain and France and insisting that the sole motive was to preserve American neutrality. Isolationist opponents quite logically asked, if the purpose was to insure neutrality, why did not the administration simply retain the arms embargo and add cash-and-carry for all other trade with countries at war. With heavy majorities already lined up in both houses, administration spokesmen refused to answer this query. They infuriated the isolationists by repeating with parrot-like precision the party line that the substitution of cash-and-carry for the arms embargo would keep the nation out of war.

The result was an overwhelming victory for Roosevelt. In late October the Senate, thought to be the center of isolationist strength, voted for the administration bill by more than two

to one; in early November the House concurred after a closer ballot. Now Britain and France could purchase from the United States anything they needed for their war effort, including guns, tanks, and airplanes, provided only that they paid cash and carried away these supplies in their own ships.

Roosevelt expressed his thoughts most clearly in a letter to William Allen White a month later. "Things move with such terrific speed, these days," he wrote, "that it really is essential to us to think in broader terms and, in effect, to warn the American people that they, too, should think of possible ultimate results in Europe.... Therefore, my sage old friend, my problem is to get the American people to think of conceivable consequences without scaring the American people into thinking that they are going to be dragged into this war." In 1939, Roosevelt evidently decided that candor was still too risky, and thus he chose to pursue devious tactics in aligning the United States indirectly on the side of England and France.

The blitzkrieg that Adolf Hitler launched in Europe in the spring of 1940 aroused Americans to their danger in a way that Roosevelt never could. Norway and Denmark fell in April, and then on May 10 Germany launched an offensive thrust through the low countries into northern France that drove Holland and Belgium out of the war in less than a week and forced the British into a humiliating retreat from the continent at Dunkirk before the month was over. The sense of physical security from foreign danger that the United States had enjoyed for over a century was shattered in a matter of days. The debate over policy would continue, but from May, 1940, on, virtually all Americans recognized that the

German victories in Europe imperiled the United States....

In early June, the news from Europe became even worse. As he sat in his White House study one evening reading the latest dispatches, Roosevelt remarked to his wife, "All bad, all bad." He realized that a vigorous defense program was not enough—that American security depended on the successful resistance of England and France to German aggression. As Hitler's armies swept toward Paris and Mussolini moved his troops toward the exposed French frontier on the Mediterranean, Roosevelt sought to throw American influence into the balance. On June 10, he was scheduled to deliver a commencement speech at the University of Virginia in Charlottesville. Going over the State Department draft, he stiffened the language, telling a diplomat who called at the White House that morning that his speech would be a "'tough' one—one in which the issue between the democracies and the Fascist powers would be drawn as never before." News that Italy had attacked France reached the President just before he boarded the train to Charlottesville and reinforced his determination to speak out boldly.

Addressing the graduates that evening, President Roosevelt condemned the concept of isolationism that he himself had held so strongly only a few years before. He termed the idea that the United States could exist as a lone island of peace in a world of brute force "a delusion." "Such an island," he declared, "represents to me and to the overwhelming majority of Americans today a helpless nightmare of a people without freedom—the nightmare of a people lodged in prison, handcuffed, hungry, and fed through the bars from day to day by the contemptuous, unpitying masters of other continents." In clear and unambiguous words, he declared that his sympathies lay wholly on the side of "those nations that are giving their life blood in combat" against Fascist aggression. Then, in his most significant policy statement, he announced that his administration would follow a twofold course of increasing the American defense effort and extending to England and France "the material resources of this nation."

The Charlottesville speech marks a decisive turn in Roosevelt's policy. At the time, most commentators focused on one dramatic sentence, written in at the last moment, in which he condemned the Italian attack on France by saying, "the hand that held the dagger has struck it into the back of its neighbor." But far more important was the President's pledge to defend American security by giving all-out aid to England and France. By promising to share American supplies with these two belligerents, Roosevelt was gambling that they could successfully contain Germany on the European continent and thus end the threat to American security. Given the German military advantages, the risks were enormous. If Roosevelt diverted a large portion of the nation's limited supply of weapons to England and France and then they surrendered to Hitler, the President would be responsible for leaving this country unprepared to meet a future German onslaught.

At the same time, the President's admirers have read too much into the Charlottesville speech. Basil Rauch argues that the speech ended America's status as a neutral. Robert Sherwood goes even further, claiming that at Charlottesville Roosevelt committed the United States "to the assumption of responsibility for nothing less than the leadership of the world."

Samuel Rosenman is more moderate, labeling this address as "the beginning of all-out aid to the democracies," but noting that it stopped short of war. But is it even accurate to say that the speech signified all-out aid short of war? An examination of Roosevelt's subsequent steps to help France and England reveals that the President was still extremely reluctant to do anything that would directly involve the United States in the European conflict.

The French quickly discovered the limitations of the President's new policy. Heartened by Roosevelt's words at Charlottesville, Paul Reynaud, the French Premier, immediately tried to secure American military intervention to save his country. In a personal appeal to Roosevelt on June 14, Reynaud asked him to send American troops as well as American supplies in France's hour of greatest need. The next day, the President replied. The United States admired the stubborn and heroic French resistance to German aggression, Roosevelt wrote, and he promised to do all he could to increase the flow of arms and munitions to France. But there he drew the line. "I know that you will understand that these statements carry with them no implication of military commitments," the President concluded. "Only the Congress can make such commitments." On June 17, the French, now fully aware that American military involvement was out of the question, surrendered to Germany.

The British, left waging the fight alone against Germany, also discovered that Roosevelt's actions failed to live up to the promise of his words. On May 15, five days after he replaced Neville Chamberlain as Prime Minister, Winston Churchill sent an urgent message to President Roosevelt. Churchill eloquently expressed his determination to fight Hitler to the bit-ter end, but he warned that Britain had to have extensive aid from the United States. Above all else, England needed forty or fifty American destroyers to protect the Atlantic supply line from German submarine attacks. Churchill pointed out that England had lost thirty-two destroyers since the war began, and she needed most of her remaining sixty-eight in home waters to guard against a German invasion. "We must ask, therefore," Churchill concluded, "as a matter of life or death, to be reinforced with these destroyers."

Despite the urgency of the British request, Roosevelt procrastinated. On June 5, the President told Secretary of the Interior Harold Ickes that it would require an act of Congress to transfer the destroyers to Great Britain. Even pressure from several other cabinet members, including Henry Morgenthau and the two new Republicans Roosevelt appointed in June, Secretary of War Henry Stimson and Secretary of the Navy Frank Knox, failed to move Roosevelt. His reluctance was increased when Congress decreed on June 28 that the President could not transfer any warships to a belligerent until the Chief of Naval Operations certified that they were "not essential to the defense of the United States."

Roosevelt's inaction caused deep concern among members of the Committee to Defend America by Aiding the Allies, the pro-British pressure group headed by William Allen White. A few of the more interventionist members of White's committee developed the idea in mid-July of arranging a trade whereby the United States would give Britain the needed destroyers in return for the right to build naval and air bases on British islands in the Western Hemisphere. On August 1, a three-man delegation called at the

White House to present this idea to the President, who received it noncommittally. Lord Lothian, the British ambassador, had suggested as far back as May 24 that England grant the United States the rights for bases on Newfoundland, Bermuda, and Trinidad, and in July, in talks with Secretary of the Navy Frank Knox, Lothian linked the possibility of these bases with the transfer of destroyers. Knox liked the idea, but he could not act without the President's consent. And Roosevelt remained deaf to all pleas, including one by Churchill on July 21 in which the British Prime Minister said, "Mr. President, with great respect I must tell you that in the long history of the world this is a thing to do NOW."

Churchill's appeal and the possibility of justifying the transfer of the destroyers as a trade for bases evidently persuaded Roosevelt to act. On August 2, when Frank Knox raised the issue in a cabinet meeting, Roosevelt approved the idea of giving Britain the destroyers in return for the right to build bases on British islands in the Atlantic and Caribbean, and, in addition, in return for a British pledge to send its fleet to the New World if Germany defeated England. Roosevelt still believed that the destroyer transfer would require an act of Congress, and the cabinet advised him to secure the support of Wendell Willkie, the Republican candidate for the presidency in the forthcoming campaign, to insure favorable Congressional action. Through William Allen White, who acted as an intermediary, Roosevelt received word that while Willkie refused to work actively to line up Republican support in Congress, he did agree not to make the destroyer deal a campaign issue.

Roosevelt called his advisers together on August 13 to make a final decision.

With the help of Morgenthau, Knox, Stimson, and Undersecretary of State Sumner Welles, Roosevelt drafted a cable to Churchill proposing the transfer of fifty destroyers in return for eight bases and a private pledge in regard to the British fleet. The next day a joyous Churchill cabled back his acceptance of these terms, saying that "each destroyer you can spare to us is measured in rubies." But Churchill realized that the deal meant more than just help at sea. "The moral value of this fresh aid from your Government and your people at this critical time," he cabled the President, "will be very great and widely felt."

It took two more weeks to work out the details of the transaction, and during that period a group of distinguished international lawyers convinced the Attorney General that the administration could transfer the destroyers without the approval of Congress. One final hitch developed when Churchill insisted that the bases be considered free gifts from the British; Roosevelt finally agreed that two of the sites would be gifts, but that the remaining six would have to be considered a *quid pro quo* for the destroyers. On September 3, the President made the transaction public in a message to Congress in which he bore down heavily on the advantages to be gained by the United States. Barely mentioning the transfer of the destroyers, the President called the acquisition of eight naval and air bases stretching in an arc from Newfoundland to British Guiana "an epochal and far-reaching act of preparation for continental defense in the face of grave danger." Searching desperately for a historical precedent, Roosevelt described the trade as "the most important action in the reinforcement of our national defense that has been taken since the Louisiana Purchase."

What is most striking about the destroyer-for-bases deal is the caution and reluctance with which the President acted. In June he announced a policy of all-out aid to Britain, yet he delayed for nearly four months after receiving Churchill's desperate plea for destroyers. He acted only after interventionists had created strong public support, only after the transfer could be disguised as an act in support of the American defense program, only after the leader of the opposition party had agreed not to challenge him politically on this issue, and only after his legal advisers found a way to bypass Congress. What may have appeared on the surface to be a bold and courageous act by the President was in reality a carefully calculated and virtually foolproof maneuver.

It would be easy to dismiss the destroyer-for-bases deal as just another example of Roosevelt's tendency to permit political expediency to dictate his foreign policy. Certainly Roosevelt acted in this case with a careful eye on the political realities. This was an election year, and he was not going to hand Wendell Willkie and the Republicans a ready-made issue. But I believe that Roosevelt's hesitation and caution stem as much from his own uncertainty as from political calculation. He realized that the gift of vessels of war to a belligerent was a serious departure from traditional neutrality, and one that might well give Germany the grounds on which to declare war against the United States. He wanted to give England all-out aid short of war, but he was not at all sure that this step would not be an act of war. Only when he convinced himself that the destroyer-for-bases deal could be

construed as a step to defend the nation's security did he give his consent. Thus his rather extravagant public defense of his action was not just a political move to quiet isolationist critics; rather it was his own deeply felt rationalization for a policy step of great importance that undoubtedly moved the United States closer to participation in the European conflict.

Perhaps even more significant is the pattern that emerges from this review of Roosevelt's policy in the spring and summer of 1940, for it is one that recurs again and again in his conduct of foreign policy. Confronted by a major crisis, he makes a bold and forthright call at Charlottesville for a policy of all-out aid short of war. But then, having pleased the interventionists with his rhetoric, he immediately retreats, turning down the French appeal for intervention and delaying on the British plea for destroyers, thus reassuring his isolationist critics. Then, as a consensus begins to form, he finally enters into the destroyer-for-bases deal and thus redeems the pledge he had made months before at Charlottesville. Like a child playing a game of giant steps, Roosevelt moved two steps forward and one back before he took the giant step ahead. Movement in a straight and unbroken line seems to have been alien to his nature—he could not go forward until he had tested the ground, studied all the reactions, and weighed all the risks....

After his triumphant election to a third term, Roosevelt relaxed on a Caribbean cruise. But after only a week, a navy seaplane arrived with an urgent dispatch from Winston Churchill. The Prime Minister gave a lengthy and bleak description of the situation in Europe and then informed the President that England was rapidly running out of money for continued purchases of American goods. "The moment approaches when we shall no longer be able to pay cash for shipping and other supplies," Churchill wrote, concluding with the confident assertion that Roosevelt would find "ways and means" to continue the flow of munitions and goods across the Atlantic.

When the President returned to Washington in mid-December, he called in the press, and in his breeziest and most informal manner began to outline the British dilemma and his solution to it. His advisers were working on several plans, he said, but the one that interested him most was simply to lend or lease to England the supplies she needed, in the belief that "the best defense of Great Britain is the best defense of the United States." Saying that he wanted to get rid of the dollar sign, Roosevelt compared his scheme to the idea of lending a garden hose to a neighbor whose house was on fire. When the fire is out, the neighbor either returns the hose or, if it is damaged, replaces it with a new one. So it would be, Roosevelt concluded, with the munitions the United States would provide Britain in the war against Nazi Germany.

In a fireside chat to the American people a few days later, Roosevelt justified this lend-lease concept on grounds of national security. Asserting that Hitler aimed not just at victory in Europe but at world domination, Roosevelt repeated his belief that the United States was in grave peril. If England fell, he declared, "all of us in the Americas would be living at the point of a gun." He admitted that the transfer of arms and munitions to Britain risked American involvement in the conflict, but he argued that "there is far less chance of the United States getting into war if we do all we can now

to support the nations defending themselves against attack by the Axis than if we acquiesce in their defeat, submit tamely to an Axis victory, and wait our turn to be the object of attack in another war later on." He declared that he had no intention of sending American troops to Europe; his sole purpose was to "keep war away from our country and our people." Then, in a famous phrase, he called upon the United States to become "the great arsenal of democracy."

Congress deliberated over the lend-lease bill for the next two months, and a strong consensus soon emerged in favor of the measure. Leading Republicans, including Wendell Willkie, endorsed the bill, and most opponents objected only to the leasing provision, suggesting instead an outright loan to Britain. The House acted quickly, approving lend-lease by nearly 100 votes in February; the Senate took longer but finally gave its approval by a margin of almost two to one in early March. After the President signed the legislation into law, Congress granted an initial appropriation of seven billion dollars to guarantee the continued flow of vital war supplies to Great Britain.

Roosevelt had thus taken another giant step forward, and this time without any hesitation. His election victory made him bolder than usual, and Churchill's candid plea had convinced him that speed was essential. The granting of lend-lease aid was very nearly an act of war, for it gave Britain unrestricted access to America's enormous industrial resources. But the President felt with great sincerity that this policy would lead not to American involvement but to a British victory that alone could keep the nation out of war....

In the six months preceding Pearl Harbor, Franklin Roosevelt moved slowly but steadily toward war with Germany.

On July 7, he announced that he had sent 4,000 American marines to Iceland to prevent that strategic island from falling into German hands. Secretary of War Stimson, though pleased with this action, expressed disappointment over the President's insistence on describing it solely as a measure of hemispheric self-defense. Iceland was the key to defending the supply route across the Atlantic, and Stimson believed that the President should have frankly told Congress that the United States was occupying the island to insure the delivery of goods to Britain.

Once American forces landed in Iceland, Roosevelt authorized the Navy to convoy American ships supplying the marines on the island. In addition, he at first approved a naval operations plan which permitted British ships to join these convoys and thus receive an American escort halfway across the Atlantic, but in late July he reversed himself, ordering the Navy to restrict its convoys to American and Icelandic vessels. In August, at the famous Atlantic Conference with Churchill, Roosevelt once again committed himself to the principle of convoying British ships halfway across the Atlantic, but he failed to give the necessary order to the Navy after his return to Washington.

Roosevelt's hesitancy and indecision finally ended in early September when a German submarine fired a torpedo at the American destroyer *Greer.* Though subsequent reports revealed that the *Greer* had been following the U-boat for more than three hours and had been broadcasting its position to nearby British naval units, Roosevelt interpreted this incident as a clear-cut case of German aggression. In a press release on September 5, he called the attack on the *Greer* deliberate, and on the same day he told Samuel Rosenman to begin drafting a statement that would express his determination "to use any means necessary to get the goods to England." Rosenman and Harry Hopkins prepared a strongly worded speech, and after a few revisions the President delivered it over a worldwide radio network on the evening of September 11.

In biting phrases, Roosevelt lashed out against Hitler and Nazi Germany. He described the attack on the *Greer* as part of a concerted German effort to "acquire absolute control and domination of the seas for themselves." Such control, he warned, would lead inevitably to a Nazi effort to dominate the Western Hemisphere and "create a permanent world system based on force, terror, and murder." The attack on the *Greer* was an act of piracy, Roosevelt declared; German submarines had become the "rattlesnakes of the Atlantic." Then, implying but never openly saying that American ships would shoot German submarines on sight, Roosevelt declared that henceforth the United States Navy would escort "all merchant ships—not only American ships but ships of any flag—engaged in commerce in our defensive waters."

Contemporary observers and many historians labeled this the "shoot-on-sight" speech, seeing its significance primarily in the orders to American naval officers to fire at German submarines in the western Atlantic. "The undeclared war" speech would be a better label, for its real importance was that Roosevelt had finally made a firm decision on the convoy issue on which he had been hedging ever since the passage of lend-lease by Congress. Branding the Germans as "pirates" and their U-boats as "rattlesnakes" distracted the American people from the fact that the President was now putting into practice the policy of convoying British ships halfway across the ocean, and thereby assuming a significant share of the responsibility for the Battle of the Atlantic. The immediate effect was to permit the British to transfer forty destroyers from the western Atlantic to the submarine-infested waters surrounding the British Isles. In the long run, the President's decision meant war with Germany, since from this time forward there would inevitably be more and more U-boat attacks on American destroyers, increasingly heavy loss of life, and a direct challenge to the nation's honor and prestige. Only Hitler's reluctance to engage in war with the United States while he was still absorbed in the assault on Russia prevented an immediate outbreak of hostilities.

With the convoy issue now resolved, Roosevelt moved to revise the Neutrality Act. In mid-October he asked the House to permit the arming of American merchant ships with deck guns, and then later in the month he urged the Senate to remove the "carry" provision of the law so that American merchantmen could take supplies all the way across the Atlantic to British ports. When a German submarine torpedoed the destroyer *Kearney* near Iceland, Roosevelt seized on the incident to speed up action in Congress.

"America has been attacked," the President declared in a speech on October 27. "The U.S.S. *Kearney* is not just a Navy ship. She belongs to every man, woman, and child in this Nation." Describing Nazi efforts at infiltration in South America, the President bluntly charged that Germany was bent on the conquest of "the United States itself." Then, coming very close to a call for war, he asserted,

"The forward march of Hitlerism can be stopped—and it will be stopped. Very simply and very bluntly—we are pledged to pull our own oar in the destruction of Hitlerism." Although he called only for the revision of the Neutrality Act, the tone of the entire address was one of unrelieved belligerency, culminating in the following peroration: "Today in the face of this newest and greatest challenge, we Americans have cleared our decks and taken our battle stations. We stand ready in the defense of our Nation and the faith of our fathers to do what God has given us the power to see as our full duty."

Two weeks later, by quite slim majorities, Congress removed nearly all restrictions on American commerce from the Neutrality Act. For the first time since the war began in 1939, American merchant vessels could carry supplies all the way across the Atlantic to British ports. The significance of this action was obscured by the Japanese attack on Pearl Harbor which triggered American entry into the war in December and gave rise to the subsequent charge that Roosevelt led the nation into the conflict via the back door. Revision of the Neutrality Act was bound to lead to war with Germany within a matter of months. Hitler could be forbearing when it was only a question of American escort vessels operating in the western Atlantic. He could not have permitted American ships to carry a major portion of lend-lease supplies to Britain without giving up the Battle of the Atlantic. With the German offensive halting before Leningrad and Moscow in December, Hitler would have been compelled to order his submarine commanders to torpedo American ships as the only effective way to hold Britain in check. And once Germany began sinking American ships regularly, Roosevelt would have had to ask Congress for a declaration of war.

The crucial question, of course, is why Roosevelt chose such an oblique policy which left the decision for peace or war in the hands of Hitler. His apologists, notably Robert Sherwood and Basil Rauch, insist that he had no choice. The isolationists were so powerful that the President could not lay the issue squarely before Congress and ask for a declaration of war. If he had, writes Basil Rauch, he would have "invited a prolonged, bitter, and divisive debate" and thereby have risked a defeat which would have discredited the administration and turned the nation back to isolationism. Sherwood sadly agrees, saying, "He had no more tricks left. The hat from which he had pulled so many rabbits was empty. The President of the United States was now the creature of circumstance which must be shaped not by his own will or his own ingenuity but by the unpredictable determination of his enemies."

In part this was true, but these sympathetic historians fail to point out that Roosevelt was the prisoner of his own policies. He had told the nation time and time again that it was not necessary for the United States to enter the war. He had propounded the doctrine that America could achieve Hitler's downfall simply by giving all-out aid to England. He had repeatedly denied that his measures would lead the nation to war. In essence, he had foreclosed to himself the possibility of going directly to the people and bluntly stating that the United States must enter the war as the only way to guarantee the nation's security. All he could do was edge the country closer and closer, leaving the ultimate decision to Germany and Japan.

We will never know at what point Roosevelt decided in his own mind that it was essential that the United States enter the war. His own personal hatred of war was deep and genuine, and it was this conviction that set him apart from men like Stimson and Morgenthau, who decided that American participation was necessary as early as the spring of 1941. William Langer and Everett Gleason believe that Roosevelt realized by the fall of 1941 that there was no other way to defeat Hitler, but they conclude that, even so, he thought the American military contribution could be limited to naval and air support and not include the dispatch of an American army to the European battlefields.

It is quite possible that Roosevelt never fully committed himself to American involvement prior to Pearl Harbor. His hesitancy was not just a catering to isolationist strength but a reflection of his own inner uncertainty. Recognizing that Hitler threatened the security of the United States, he took a series of steps which brought the nation to the brink of war, but his own revulsion at the thought of plunging his country into the most devastating conflict in history held him back until the Japanese attack left him no choice.

NO
Arthur M. Schlesinger, Jr.

THE MAN OF THE CENTURY

After half a century it is hard to approach Franklin D. Roosevelt except through a minefield of clichés. Theories of FDR, running the gamut from artlessness to mystification, have long paraded before our eyes. There is his famous response to the newspaperman who asked him for his philosophy: "Philosophy? I am a Christian and a Democrat—that's all"; there is Robert E. Sherwood's equally famous warning about "Roosevelt's heavily forested interior"; and we weakly conclude that both things were probably true.

FDR's Presidency has commanded the attention of eminent historians at home and abroad for fifty years or more. Yet no consensus emerges, especially in the field of foreign affairs. Scholars at one time or another have portrayed him at every point across a broad spectrum: as an isolationist, as an internationalist, as an appeaser, as a warmonger, as an impulsive decision maker, as an incorrigible vacillator, as the savior of capitalism, as a closet socialist, as a Machiavellian intriguer plotting to embroil his country in foreign wars, as a Machiavellian intriguer avoiding war in order to let other nations bear the brunt of the fighting, as a gullible dreamer who thought he could charm Stalin into postwar collaboration and ended by selling Eastern Europe down the river into slavery, as a tight-fisted creditor sending Britain down the road toward bankruptcy as a crafty imperialist serving the interests of American capitalist hegemony, as a high-minded prophet whose vision shaped the world's future. Will the real FDR please stand up?

Two relatively recent books illustrate the chronically unsettled state of FDR historiography—and the continuing vitality of the FDR debate. In *Wind Over Sand (1988)* Frederick W. Marks III finds a presidential record marked by ignorance, superficiality, inconsistency, random prejudice, erratic impulse, a man out of his depth, not waving but drowning, practicing a diplomacy as insubstantial and fleeting as wind blowing over sand. In *The Juggler* (1991), Warren F. Kimball finds a record marked by intelligent understanding of world forces, astute maneuver, and a remarkable consistency of purpose, a farsighted statesman facing dilemmas that defied quick or easy solutions. One-third of each book is given over to endnotes and bibliography, which suggests that each portrait is based on meticulous research. Yet the two historians arrive at diametrically opposite conclusions.

So the debate goes on. Someone should write a book entitled *FDR: For and Against,* modeled on Pieter Geyl's *Napoleon: For and Against.* "It is impossible," the great Dutch historian observed, "that two historians, especially two historians living in different periods, should see any historical personality in the same light. The greater the political importance of a historical character, the more impossible this is." History, Geyl (rightly) concluded, is an "argument without end."

I suppose we must accept that human beings are in the last analysis beyond analysis. In the case of FDR, no one can be really sure what was going on in that affable, welcoming, reserved, elusive, teasing, spontaneous, calculating, cold, warm, humorous, devious, mendacious, manipulative, petty, magnanimous, superficially casual, ultimately decent, highly camouflaged, finally impenetrable mind. Still, if we can't as historians puzzle out what he *was,* we surely must as historians try to make sense out of what he *did.* If his personality escapes us, his policies must have some sort of pattern.

What Roosevelt wrote (or Sam Rosenman wrote for him) in the introduction to the first volume of his *Public Papers* about his record as governor of New York goes, I believe, for his foreign policy too: "Those who seek inconsistencies will find them. There were inconsistencies of methods, inconsistencies caused by ceaseless efforts to find ways to solve problems for the future as well as for the present. There were inconsistencies born of insufficient knowledge. There were inconsistencies springing from the need of

experimentation. But through them all, I trust that there also will be found a consistency and continuity of broad purpose."

Now purpose can be very broad indeed. To say that a statesman is in favor of peace, freedom, and security does not narrow things down very much. Meaning resides in the details, and in FDR's case the details often contradict each other. If I may invoke still another cliché, FDR's foreign policy seems to fit Churchill's description of the Soviet Union: "a riddle wrapped in a mystery inside an enigma." However, we too often forget what Churchill said next: "But perhaps there is a key. That key is Russian national interest." German domination of Eastern Europe, Churchill continued, "would be contrary to the historic life-interests of Russia." Here, I suggest, may be the key to FDR, the figure in his carpet: his sense of the historic life-interests of the United States.

Of course, "national interest" narrows things down only a little. No one, except a utopian or a millennialist, is against the national interest. In a world of nation-states the assumption that governments will pursue their own interests gives order and predictability to international affairs. As George Washington said, "no nation is to be trusted farther than it is bound by [its] interest." The problem is the substance one pours into national interest. In our own time, for example, Lyndon Johnson and Dean Rusk thought our national interest required us to fight in Vietnam; William Fulbright, Walter Lippmann, Hans Morgenthau thought our national interest required us to pull out of Vietnam. The phrase by itself settles no arguments.

* * *

How did FDR conceive the historic life-interests of the United States? His conception emerged from his own long, if scattered, education in world affairs. It should not be forgotten that he arrived in the White House with an unusual amount of international experience. He was born into a cosmopolitan family. His father knew Europe well and as a young man had marched with Garibaldi. His elder half-brother had served in American legations in London and Vienna. His mother's family had been in the China trade; his mother herself had lived in Hong Kong as a little girl. As FDR reminded Henry Morgenthau in 1934, "I have a background of a little over a century in Chinese affairs."

FDR himself made his first trip to Europe at the age of three and went there every summer from his ninth to his fourteenth year. As a child he learned French and German. As a lifelong stamp collector he knew the world's geography and politics. By the time he was elected President, he had made thirteen trips across the Atlantic and had spent almost three years of his life in Europe. "I started... with a good deal of interest in foreign affairs," he told a press conference in 1939, "because both branches of my family have been mixed up in foreign affairs for a good many generations, the affairs of Europe and the affairs of the Far East."

Now much of his knowledge was social and superficial. Nor is international experience in any case a guarantee of international wisdom or even of continuing international concern. The other American politician of the time who rivaled FDR in exposure to the great world was, oddly, Herbert Hoover. Hoover was a mining engineer in Australia at twenty-three, a capitalist in the Chinese Empire at twenty-five, a promoter in the City of London at twenty-seven. In the years from his Stanford graduation to the Great War, he spent more time in the British Empire than he did in the United States. During and after the war he supervised relief activities in Belgium and in Eastern Europe. Keynes called him the only man to emerge from the Paris Peace Conference with an enhanced reputation.

* * *

Both Hoover and Roosevelt came of age when the United States was coming a world power. Both saw more of that world than most of their American contemporaries. But international experience led them to opposite conclusions. What Hoover saw abroad soured him on foreigners. He took away from Paris an indignant conviction of an impassable gap between his virtuous homeland and the European snake pit. Nearly twenty years passed before he could bring himself to set foot again on the despised continent. He loathed Europe and its nationalist passions and hatreds. "With a vicious rhythm," he said in 1940, "these malign forces seem to drive [European] nations like the Gadarene swine over the precipice of war." The less America had to do with so degenerate a place, the Quaker Hoover felt, the better.

The patrician Roosevelt was far more at home in the great world. Moreover, his political genealogy instilled in him the conviction that the United States must at last take its rightful place among the powers. In horse breeder's parlance, FDR was by Woodrow Wilson out of Theodore Roosevelt. These two remarkable Presidents taught FDR that the United States was irrevocably a world power and poured substance into his conception of America's historic life-interests.

FDR greatly admired TR, deserted the Democratic party to cast his first presidential vote for him, married his niece, and proudly succeeded in 1913 to the office TR had occupied fifteen years earlier, Assistant Secretary of the Navy. From TR and from that eminent friend of both Roosevelts, Admiral Mahan, young Roosevelt learned the strategic necessities of international relations. He learned how to distinguish between vital and peripheral interests. He learned why the national interest required the maintenance of balances of power in areas that, if controlled by a single power, could threaten the United States. He learned what the defense of vital interests might require in terms of ships and arms and men and production and resources. His experience in Wilson's Navy Department during the First World War consolidated these lessons.

But he also learned new things from Wilson, among them that it was not enough to send young men to die and kill because of the thrill of battle or because of war's morally redemptive qualities or even because of the need to restore the balance of power. The awful sacrifices of modern war demanded nobler objectives. The carnage on the Western Front converted FDR to Wilson's vision of a world beyond war, beyond national interest, beyond balances of power, a world not of secret diplomacy and antagonistic military alliances but of an organized common peace, founded on democracy, self-determination, and the collective restraint of aggression.

* * *

Theodore Roosevelt had taught FDR geopolitics. Woodrow Wilson now gave him a larger international purpose in which the principles of power had a strong but secondary role. FDR's two mentors detested each other. But they joined to construct the framework within which FDR, who cherished them both, approached foreign affairs for the rest of his life.

As the Democratic vice presidential candidate in 1920, he roamed the country pleading for the League of Nations. Throughout the twenties he warned against political isolationism and economic protectionism. America would commit a grievous wrong, he said, if it were "to go backwards towards an old Chinese Wall policy of isolationism." Trade wars, he said, were "symptoms of economic insanity." But such sentiments could not overcome the disillusion and disgust with which Americans in the 1920s contemplated world troubles. As President Hoover told the Italian foreign minister in 1931, the deterioration of Europe had led to such "despair . . . on the part of the ordinary American citizen [that] now he just wanted to keep out of the whole business."

Depression intensified the isolationist withdrawal. Against the national mood, the new President brought to the White House in 1933 an international outlook based, I would judge, on four principles. One was TR's commitment to the preservation of the balance of world power. Another was Wilson's vision of concerted international action to prevent or punish aggression. The third principle argued that lasting peace required the free flow of trade among nations. The fourth was that in a democracy foreign policy must rest on popular consent. In the isolationist climate of the 1930s, this fourth principle compromised and sometimes undermined the first three.

Diplomatic historians are occasionally tempted to overrate the amount of time Presidents spend in thinking about foreign policy In fact, from Jackson to FDR, domestic affairs have always been, with a few fleeting exceptions—perhaps Polk, McKinley, Wilson—the presidential priority. This was powerfully the case at the start for FDR. Given the collapse of the economy and the anguish of unemployment, given the absence of obvious remedy and the consequent need for social experiment, the surprise is how much time and energy FDR did devote to foreign affairs in these early years.

He gave time to foreign policy because of his acute conviction that Germany and Japan were, or were about to be, on the rampage and that unchecked aggression would ultimately threaten vital interests of the United States. He packed the State Department and embassies abroad with unregenerate Wilsonians. When he appointed Cordell Hull Secretary, he knew what he was getting; his brain trusters, absorbed in problems at hand, had warned him against international folly. But there they were, Wilsonians all: Hull, Norman Davis, Sumner Welles, William Phillips, Francis B. Sayre, Walton Moore, Breckinridge Long, Josephus Daniels, W. E. Dodd, Robert W. Bingham, Claude Bowers, Joseph E. Davies. Isolationists like Raymond Moley did not last long at State.

* * *

Roosevelt's early excursions into foreign policy were necessarily intermittent, however, and in his own rather distracting personal style. Economic diplomacy he confided to Hull, except when Hull's free-trade obsessions threatened New Deal recovery programs, as at the London Economic Conference of 1933. He liked, when he found the time, to handle the political side of things himself. He relished meetings with foreign leaders and found himself in advance of most of them in his forebodings about Germany and Japan. He invited his ambassadors, especially his political appointees, to write directly to him, and nearly all took advantage of the invitation.

His diplomatic style had its capricious aspects. FDR understood what admirals and generals were up to, and he understood the voice of prophetic statesmanship. But he never fully appreciated the professional diplomat and looked with some disdain on the career Foreign Service as made up of tea drinkers remote from the realities of American life. His approach to foreign policy, while firmly grounded in geopolitics and soaring easily into the higher idealism, always lacked something at the middle level.

At the heart of Roosevelt's style in foreign affairs was a certain incorrigible amateurism. His off-the-cuff improvisations, his airy tendency to throw out half-baked ideas, caused others to underrate his continuity of purpose and used to drive the British especially wild, as minutes scribbled on Foreign Office dispatches make abundantly clear. This amateurism had its good points. It could be a source of boldness and creativity in a field populated by cautious and conventional people. But it also encouraged superficiality and dilettantism.

The national mood, however, remained FDR's greatest problem. Any U.S. contribution to the deterrence of aggression depended on giving the government power to distinguish between aggressors and their victims. He asked Congress for this authority, first in cooperating with League of Nations sanctions in 1933, later in connection with American neutrality statutes. Fearing that aid to one side would eventually involve the nation in war, Congress regularly turned him down. By rejecting policies that would support victims against aggressors, Congress effectively nullified the ability of the United States to throw its weight in the scales against aggressors.

Roosevelt, regarding the New Deal as more vital for the moment than foreign policy and needing the support of isolationists for his domestic program, accepted what he could not change in congressional roll calls. But he did hope to change public opinion and began a long labor of popular education with his annual message in January 1936 and its condemnation of "autocratic institutions that beget slavery at home and aggression abroad."

It is evident that I am not persuaded by the school of historians that sees Roosevelt as embarked until 1940 on a mission of appeasement, designed to redress German grievances and lure the Nazi regime into a constructive role in a reordered Europe. The evidence provided by private conversations as well as by public pronouncements is far too consistent and too weighty to permit the theory that Roosevelt had illusions about coexistence with Hitler. Timing and maneuver were essential, and on occasion he tacked back and forth like the small-boat sailor that Gaddis Smith reminds us he was. Thus, before positioning the United States for entry into war, he wanted to make absolutely sure there was no prospect of negotiated peace: hence his interest in 1939–40 in

people like James D. Mooney and William Rhodes Davis and hence the Sumner Welles mission. But his basic course seems pretty clear: one way or another to rid the world of Hitler.

I am even less persuaded by the school that sees Roosevelt as a President who rushed the nation to war because he feared German and Japanese economic competition. America "began to go to war against the Axis in the Western Hemisphere," the revisionist William Appleman Williams tells us, because Germany was invading U.S. markets in Latin America. The Open Door cult recognizes no geopolitical concerns in Washington about German bases in the Western Hemisphere. Oddly, the revisionists accept geopolitics as an O.K. motive for the Soviet Union but deny it to the United States. In their view American foreign policy can never be aimed at strategic security but must forever be driven by the lust of American business for foreign markets.

* * *

In the United States, of course, as any student of American history knows, economic growth has been based primarily on the home market, not on foreign markets, and the preferred policy of American capitalists, even after 1920, when the United States became a creditor nation, was protection of the home market, not freedom of trade. Recall Fordney-McCumber and Smoot-Hawley. The preference of American business for high tariffs was equally true in depression. When FDR proposed his reciprocal trade agreements program in 1934, the American business community, instead of welcoming reciprocal trade as a way of penetrating foreign markets, denounced the whole idea. Senator Vandenberg even called the bill "Fascist in its philosophy, Fascist in its objectives." A grand total of two Republicans voted for reciprocal trade in the House, three in the Senate.

The "corporatism" thesis provides a more sophisticated version of the economic interpretation. No doubt we have become a society of large organizations, and no doubt an associational society generates a certain momentum toward coordination. But the idea that exporters, importers, Wall Street, Main Street, trade unionists, and farmers form a consensus on foreign policy and impose that consensus on the national government is hard to sustain.

It is particularly irrelevant to the Roosevelt period. If Roosevelt was the compliant instrument of capitalist expansion, as the Open Door ideologies claim, or of corporate hegemony, as the corporatism thesis implies, why did the leaders of American corporate capitalism oppose him so viciously? Business leaders vied with one another in their hatred of "that man in the White House." The family of J. P. Morgan used to warn visitors against mentioning Roosevelt's name lest fury raise Morgan's blood pressure to the danger point. When Averell Harriman, one of that rare breed, a pro-New Deal businessman, appeared on Wall Street, old friends cut him dead. The theory that Roosevelt pursued a foreign policy dictated by the same corporate crowd that fought him domestically and smeared him personally belongs, it seems to me, in the same library with the historiography of Oliver Stone.

* * *

What was at stake, as FDR saw it, was not corporate profits or Latin American markets but the security of the United States and the future of democracy. Basking as we do today in the glow of democratic triumph, we forget how desperate the democratic cause appeared half a century ago. The Great War had apparently proved that democracy could not produce peace; the Great Depression that it could not produce prosperity. By the 1930s contempt for democracy was widespread among elites and masses alike: contempt for parliamentary methods, for government by discussion, for freedoms of expression and opposition, for bourgeois individualism, for pragmatic muddling through. Discipline, order, efficiency, and all-encompassing ideology were the talismans of the day. Communism and fascism had their acute doctrinal differences, but their structural similarities—a single leader, a single party, a single body of infallible dogma, a single mass of obedient followers—meant that each in the end had more in common with the other than with democracy, as Hitler and Stalin acknowledged in August 1939.

The choice in the 1930s seemed bleak: either political democracy with economic chaos or economic planning with political tyranny Roosevelt's distinctive contribution was to reject this either/or choice. The point of the New Deal was to chart and vindicate a middle way between laissez-faire and totalitarianism. When the biographer Emil Ludwig asked FDR to define his "political motive," Roosevelt replied, "My desire to obviate revolution.... I work in a contrary sense to Rome and Moscow."

Accepting renomination in 1936, FDR spoke of people under economic stress in other lands who had sold their heritage of freedom for the illusion of a living. "Only our success," he continued, "can stir their ancient hope. They begin to know that here in America we are waging a great and successful war. It is not alone a war against want and destitution and economic demoralization. It is more than that: it is a war for the survival of democracy. We are fighting to save a great and precious form of government for ourselves and for the world."

Many people around the world thought it a futile fight. Let us not underestimate the readiness by 1940 of Europeans, including leading politicians and intellectuals, to come to terms with a Hitler-dominated Europe. Even some Americans thought the downfall of democracy inevitable. As Nazi divisions stormed that spring across Scandinavia, the Low Countries, and France, the fainthearted saw totalitarianism, in the title of a poisonous little book published in the summer by Anne Morrow Lindbergh, a book that by December 1940 had rushed through seven American printings, as "the wave of the future." While her husband, the famous aviator, predicted Nazi victory and opposed American aid to Britain, the gentle Mrs. Lindbergh lamented "the beautiful things... lost in the dying of an age," saw totalitarianism as democracy's predestined successor, a "new, and perhaps even ultimately good, conception of humanity trying to come to birth," discounted the evils of Hitlerism and Stalinism as merely "scum on the wave of the future," and concluded that "the wave of the future is coming and there is no fighting it." For a while Mrs. Lindbergh seemed to be right. Fifty years ago there were only twelve democracies left on the planet.

Roosevelt, however, believed in fighting the wave of the future. He still labored under domestic constraints. The American people were predominantly against Hitler. But they were also, and for a while more strongly, against war. I believe that

FDR himself, unlike the hawks of 1941 —Stimson, Morgenthau, Hopkins, Ickes, Knox—was in no hurry to enter the European conflict. He remembered what Wilson had told him when he himself had been a young hawk a quarter-century before: that a President could commit no greater mistake than to take a divided country into war. He also no doubt wanted to minimize American casualties and to avoid braking political promises. But probably by the autumn of 1941 FDR had finally come to believe that American participation was necessary if Hitler was to be beaten. An increasing number of Americans were reaching the same conclusion. Pearl Harbor in any case united the country, and Hitler then solved another of FDR's problems by declaring war on the United States.

We accepted war in 1941, as we had done in 1917, in part because, as Theodore Roosevelt had written in 1910, if Britain ever failed to preserve the European balance of power, "the United States would be obliged to get in... in order to restore the balance." But restoration of the balance of power did not seem in 1941, any more than it had in 1917, sufficient reason to send young men to kill and die. In 1941 FDR provided higher and nobler aims by resurrecting the Wilsonian vision in the Four Freedoms and the Atlantic Charter and by proceeding, while the war was on, to lay the foundations for the postwar reconstruction of the world along Wilsonian lines.

I assume that it will not be necessary to linger with a theory that had brief currency in the immediate postwar years, the theory that Roosevelt's great failing was his subordination of political to military objectives, shoving long-term considerations aside in the narrow interest of victory. FDR was in fact the most political of politicians, political in every reflex and to his fingertips—and just as political in war as he had been in peace. As a virtuoso politician he perfectly understood that there could be no better cloak for the pursuit of political objectives in wartime than the claim of total absorption in winning the war. He had plenty of political objectives all the same.

The war, he believed, would lead to historic transformations around the world. "Roosevelt," Harriman recalled, "enjoyed thinking aloud on the tremendous changes he saw ahead—the end of colonial empires and the rise of newly independent nations across the sweep of Africa and Asia." FDR told Churchill, "A new period has opened in the world's history, and you will have to adjust yourself to it." He tried to persuade the British to leave India and to stop the French from returning to Indochina, and he pressed the idea of UN trusteeships as the means of dismantling empires and preparing colonies for independence.

* * *

Soviet Russia, he saw would emerge as a major power. FDR has suffered much criticism in supposedly thinking he could charm Stalin into post-war collaboration. Perhaps FDR was not so naive after all in concentrating on Stalin. The Soviet dictator was hardly the helpless prisoner of Marxist-Leninist ideology. He saw himself not as a disciple of Marx and Lenin but as their fellow prophet. Only Stalin had the power to rewrite the Soviet approach to world affairs; after all, he had already rewritten Soviet ideology and Soviet history. FDR was surely right in seeing Stalin as the only lever capable of overturning the Leninist doctrine of irrevocable hostility between capitalism and communism. As Walter Lippmann once observed, Roosevelt was too cynical to think he could charm Stalin. "He distrusted everybody. What he thought he could do was to outwit Stalin, which is quite a different thing."

Roosevelt failed to save Eastern Europe from communism, but that could not have been achieved by diplomatic methods alone. With the Red Army in control of Eastern Europe and a war still to be won against Japan, there was not much the West could do to prevent Stalin's working his will in countries adjacent to the Soviet Union. But Roosevelt at Yalta persuaded Stalin to sign American-drafted Declarations on Liberated Europe and on Poland—declarations that laid down standards by which the world subsequently measured Stalin's behavior in Eastern Europe and found it wanting. And FDR had prepared a fallback position in case things went wrong: not only tests that, if Stalin failed to meet them, would justify a change in policy but also a great army, a network of overseas bases, plans for peacetime universal military training, and the Anglo-American monopoly of the atomic bomb.

In the longer run Roosevelt anticipated that time would bring a narrowing of differences between democratic and Communist societies. He once told Sumner Welles that marking American democracy as one hundred and Soviet communism as zero, the American system, as it moved away from laissez-faire, might eventually reach sixty, and the Soviet system, as it moved toward democracy, might eventually reach forty. The theory of convergence provoked much derision in the Cold War years. Perhaps it looks better now.

So perhaps does his idea of making China one of the Four Policemen of the peace. Churchill, with his scorn for "the pigtails," dismissed Roosevelt's insistence on China as the "Great American Illusion." But Roosevelt was not really deluded. As he said at Teheran, he wanted China there "not because he did not realize the weakness of China at present, but he was thinking farther into the future." At Malta he told Churchill that it would take "three generations of education and training... before China could become a serious factor." Today, two generations later, much rests on involving China in the global web of international institutions.

As for the United States, a great concern in the war years was that the country might revert to isolationism after the war just as it had done a quarter-century before—a vivid memory for FDR's generation. Contemplating Republican gains in the 1942 midterm election, Cordell Hull told Henry Wallace that the country was "going in exactly the same steps it followed in 1918." FDR himself said privately, "Anybody who thinks that isolationism is dead in this country is crazy."

He regarded American membership in a permanent international organization, in Charles Bohlen's words, as "the only device that could keep the United States from slipping back into isolationism." And true to the Wilsonian vision, he saw such an organization even more significantly as the only device that could keep the world from slipping back into war. He proposed the Declaration of the United Nations three weeks after Pearl Harbor, and by 1944 he was grappling with the problem that had defeated Wilson: how to reconcile peace enforcement by an international organization with the American Constitution. For international peace enforcement requires armed force ready to act swiftly on the command of the organization, while the Constitution requires (or, in better days, required) the consent of Congress before American troops can be sent into combat against a sovereign state. Roosevelt probably had confidence that the special agreements provided for in Article 43 of the UN Charter would strike a balance between the UN's need for prompt action and Congress's need to retain its war-making power and that the great-power veto would further protect American interests.

* * *

He moved in other ways to accustom the American people to a larger international role—and at the same time to assure American predominance in the postwar world. By the end of 1944 he had sponsored a series of international conferences designed to plan vital aspects of the future. These conferences, held mostly at American initiative and dominated mostly by American agendas, offered the postwar blueprints for international organization (Dumbarton Oaks), for world finance, trade, and development (Bretton Woods), for food and agriculture (Hot Springs), for relief and rehabilitation (Washington), for civil aviation (Chicago). In his sweeping and sometimes grandiose asides, FDR envisaged plans for regional development with environmental protection in the Middle East and elsewhere, and his Office of the Coordinator for Inter-American Affairs pioneered economic and technical assistance to developing countries. Upon his death in 1945 FDR left an imaginative and comprehensive framework for American leadership in making a better world—an interesting achievement for a President who was supposed to subordinate political to military goals.

New times bring new perspectives. In the harsh light of the Cold War some of FDR's policies and expectations were condemned as naive or absurd or otherwise misguided. The end of the Cold War may cast those policies and expectations in a somewhat different light.

FDR's purpose, I take it, was to find ways to safeguard the historic life-interests of the Republic—national security at home and a democratic environment abroad—in a world undergoing vast and fundamental transformations. This required policies based on a grasp of the currents of history and directed to the protection of U.S. interests and to the promotion of democracy elsewhere. From the vantage point of 1994, FDR met this challenge fairly well.

Take a look at the Atlantic Charter fifty years after. Is not the world therein outlined by Roosevelt and Churchill at last coming to pass? Consider the goals of August 1941—"the right of all peoples to choose the form of government under which they will live," equal access "to the trade and to the raw materials of the world," "improved labor standards, economic advancement and social security," assurance that all "may live their lives in freedom from fear and want," relief from "the crushing burden of armaments," establishment of a community of nations. Is this not the agenda on which most nations today are at last agreed?

Does not most of the world now aspire to FDR's Four Freedoms? Has not what used to be the Soviet Union carried its movement toward the West even more rapidly than FDR dared contemplate? Has not China emerged as the "serious factor" FDR predicted? Did not the Yalta accords call for precisely the democratic freedoms to which Eastern Europe aspires today? Has not the UN, at last liberated by the end of the Cold War to pursue the goals of the founders, achieved new salience as the world's best hope for peace and cooperation?

Consider the world of 1994. It is manifestly not Adolf Hitler's world. The thousand-year Reich turned out to have a brief and bloody run of a dozen years. It is manifestly not Joseph Stalin's world. That world disintegrated before our eyes, rather like the Deacon's one-hoss shay. Nor is it Winston Churchill's world. Empire and its glories have long since vanished into the past.

*   *   *

The world we live in today is Franklin Roosevelt's world. Of the figures who, for good or for evil, bestrode the narrow world half a century ago, he would be the least surprised by the shape of things at the end of the century. Far more than the rest, he possessed what William James called a "sense of futurity." For all his manifold foibles, flaws, follies, and there was a sufficiency of all of those, FDR deserves supreme credit as the twentieth-century statesman who saw most deeply into the grand movements of history.

POSTSCRIPT

Was Franklin Roosevelt a Reluctant Internationalist?

Divine is a well-known diplomatic historian who has written numerous books on World War II diplomacy and military policies. Divine takes issue with many historians like Herbert Feis, Basil Rauch, and playwright Robert Sherwood, who believe that Roosevelt was a true internationalist. He makes the case that Roosevelt sincerely abhorred war and held strong isolationist views until the Munich crisis in September 1938.

But Divine may have underestimated the importance of politics in the presidential election year of 1940, when both candidates were strongly courting the isolationist vote in their campaigns. Roosevelt, in particular, was running for an unprecedented third term and was fearful that any hint that American soldiers may be sent to fight overseas could cost him the election.

Schlesinger portrays Roosevelt's diplomacy in a broader and more favorable light than Divine does. Admitting that no contemporary of Roosevelt, much less a historian, has been able to penetrate the mind of this very complex individual, Schlesinger nevertheless believes that of all the allied leaders, only Roosevelt saw the big picture before, during, and after World War II. Schlesinger believes that the world of today greatly resembles the vision projected by Roosevelt over 50 years ago. Fascism was eliminated from Italy, Germany, and Japan as a result of World War II. Communism collapsed in Eastern Europe and Russia in 1989. Countries all over the world struggle to achieve what Roosevelt and Churchill outlined when they signed the Atlantic Charter in the summer of 1941.

The bibliography on America's entrance into World War II is enormous and continues to grow. The best and most accessible short text and comprehensive bibliography is Justin D. Doeneke and John E. Wiltz, *From Isolation to War, 1931–1941,* 2d ed. (Harlan Davidson, 1991), a publication in *The American History Series,* which contains 30 volumes written by specialists summarizing the most recent scholarship and interpretations. See also J. Garry Clifford, "Both Ends of the Telescope: New Perspectives on FDR and American Entry into World War II," *Diplomatic History* (Spring 1989) and two articles in Gerald K. Haines and J. Samuel Walker, eds., *American Foreign Relations: A Historiographical Review* (Greenwood Press, 1981): Ernest C. Bolt, Jr.'s "Isolation, Expansionism and Peace: American Foreign Policy Between the Wars" and Gerald K. Haines's "Roads to War: United States Foreign Policy, 1931–1941."

ISSUE 12

Was It Necessary to Drop the Atomic Bomb to End World War II?

YES: Robert James Maddox, from "The Biggest Decision: Why We Had to Drop the Atomic Bomb," *American Heritage* (May/June 1995)

NO: Barton J. Bernstein, from "The Atomic Bombings Reconsidered," *Foreign Affairs* (January/February 1995)

ISSUE SUMMARY

YES: Professor of American history Robert James Maddox contends that the atomic bomb became the catalyst that forced the hard-liners in the Japanese army to accept the emperor's plea to surrender, thus avoiding a costly, bloody invasion of the Japanese mainland.

NO: Professor of history Barton J. Bernstein argues that the United States probably could have avoided both a landed invasion of the Japanese mainland and the use of atomic bombs and still have ended the war by November 1945.

America's development of the atomic bomb began in 1939 when a small group of scientists led by well-known physicist Albert Einstein called President Franklin D. Roosevelt's attention to the enormous potential uses of atomic energy for military purposes. In his letter, Einstein warned Roosevelt that Nazi Germany was already experimenting in this area. The program to develop the bomb, which began very modestly in October 1939, soon expanded into the $2 billion Manhattan Project, which combined the talents and energies of scientists (many of whom were Jewish refugees from Hitler's Nazi Germany) from universities and research laboratories across the country. The Manhattan Project was the beginning of the famed military-industrial-university complex that we take for granted today.

Part of the difficulty in reconstructing the decision to drop the atomic bomb lies in the rapidity with which events moved in the spring of 1945. On May 7, 1945, Germany surrendered. Almost a month earlier the world was stunned by the death of FDR, who was succeeded by Harry Truman, a former U.S. senator who was chosen as a compromise vice-presidential candidate in 1944. The man from Missouri had never been a confidant of Roosevelt. Truman did not even learn of the existence of the Manhattan Project until 12 days after he became president, at which time Secretary of War Henry L. Stimson advised him of a "highly secret matter" that would have a "decisive" effect upon America's postwar foreign policy.

Because Truman was unsure of his options for using the bomb, he approved Stimson's suggestion that a special committee of high-level political, military, and scientific policymakers be appointed to consider the major issues. The committee recommended unanimously that "the bomb should be used against Japan as soon as possible . . . against a military target surrounded by other buildings . . . without prior warning of the nature of the weapon."

A number of scientists disagreed with this report. They recommended that the weapon be tested on a desert island before representatives of the United Nations and that an ultimatum be sent to Japan warning of the destructive power of the bomb. These young scientists suggested that the bomb be used if the Japanese rejected the warning, and only "if sanction of the United Nations (and of public opinion at home) were obtained."

A second scientific committee created by Stimson rejected both the test demonstration and warning alternatives. This panel felt that if the bomb failed to work during the demonstration, there would be political repercussions both at home and abroad.

Thus, by the middle of June 1945, the civilian leaders were unanimous that the atomic bomb should be used. During the Potsdam Conference in July, Truman learned that the bomb had been successfully tested in New Mexico. The big three—Truman, Atlee, and Stalin—issued a warning to Japan to surrender or suffer prompt and utter destruction. When the Japanese equivocated in their response, the Americans replied by dropping an atomic bomb on Hiroshima on August 6, which killed 100,000 people, and a second bomb on August 9, which leveled the city of Nagasaki. During this time the emperor pleaded with the Japanese military to end the war. On August 14 the Japanese accepted the terms of surrender with the condition that the emperor not be treated as a war criminal.

Was it necessary to drop the atomic bombs on Japan in order to end the war? In the following selections, two viewpoints are advanced. Robert James Maddox, a long-time critic of cold war revisionist history, argues that Truman believed that the use of the atomic bomb would shorten the war and save lives, particularly American ones. Maddox also asserts that the bombings at Hiroshima and Nagasaki allowed the emperor to successfully plead with army hard-liners to end the war. Barton J. Bernstein agrees that military considerations were paramount in Truman's mind. But he also suggests that Truman viewed the bomb as a bonus that could pressure the Russians to modify their hard line toward the Eastern European countries. Furthermore, he contends that alternatives to the bomb should have been tried because they could have rendered unnecessary an invasion of the Japanese mainland or the dropping of any atomic bombs.

YES

Robert James Maddox

THE BIGGEST DECISION: WHY WE HAD TO DROP THE ATOMIC BOMB

On the morning of August 6, 1945, the American B-29 *Enola Gay* dropped an atomic bomb on the Japanese city of Hiroshima. Three days later another B-29, *Bock's Car*, released one over Nagasaki. Both caused enormous casualties and physical destruction. These two cataclysmic events have preyed upon the American conscience ever since. The furor over the Smithsonian Institution's *Enola Gay* exhibit and over the mushroom-cloud postage stamp (in 1994) are merely the most obvious examples. Harry S. Truman and other officials claimed that the bombs caused Japan to surrender, thereby avoiding a bloody invasion. Critics have accused them of at best failing to explore alternatives, at worst of using the bombs primarily to make the Soviet Union "more manageable" rather than to defeat a Japan they knew already was on the verge of capitulation.

* * *

By any rational calculation Japan was a beaten nation by the summer of 1945. Conventional bombing had reduced many of its cities to rubble, blockade had strangled its importation of vitally needed materials, and its navy had sustained such heavy losses as to be powerless to interfere with the invasion everyone knew was coming. By late June advancing American forces had completed the conquest of Okinawa, which lay only 350 miles from the southernmost Japanese home island of Kyushu. They now stood poised for the final onslaught.

Rational calculations did not determine Japan's position. Although a peace faction within the government wished to end the war—provided certain conditions were met—militants were prepared to fight on regardless of consequences. They claimed to welcome an invasion of the home islands, promising to inflict such hideous casualties that the United States would retreat from its announced policy of unconditional surrender. The militarists held effective power over the government and were capable of defying the emperor, as they had in the past, on the ground that his civilian advisers were misleading him.

Okinawa provided a preview of what invasion of the home islands would entail. Since April 1 the Japanese had fought with a ferocity that mocked any notion that their will to resist was eroding. They had inflicted nearly 50,000 casualties on the invaders, many resulting from the first large-scale use of kamikazes. They also had dispatched the superbattleship *Yamato* on a suicide mission to Okinawa, where, after attacking American ships offshore, it was to plunge ashore to become a huge, doomed steel fortress. *Yamato* was sunk shortly after leaving port, but its mission symbolized Japan's willingness to sacrifice everything in an apparently hopeless cause.

The Japanese could be expected to defend their sacred homeland with even greater fervor, and kamikazes flying at short range promised to be even more devastating than at Okinawa. The Japanese had more than 2,000,000 troops in the home islands, were training millions of irregulars, and for some time had been conserving aircraft that might have been used to protect Japanese cities against American bombers.

Reports from Tokyo indicated that Japan meant to fight the war to a finish. On June 8 an imperial conference adopted "The Fundamental Policy to Be Followed Henceforth in the Conduct of the War," which pledged to "prosecute the war to the bitter end in order to uphold the national polity, protect the imperial land, and accomplish the objectives for which we went to war." Truman had no reason to believe that the proclamation meant anything other than what it said.

Against this background, while fighting on Okinawa still continued, the President had his naval chief of staff, Adm. William D. Leahy, notify the Joint Chiefs of Staff (JCS) and the Secretaries of War

and Navy that a meeting would be held at the White House on June 18. The night before the conference Truman wrote in his diary that "I have to decide Japanese strategy—shall we invade Japan proper or shall we bomb and blockade? That is my hardest decision to date. But I'll make it when I have all the facts."

* * *

Truman met with the chiefs at three-thirty in the afternoon. Present were Army Chief of Staff Gen. George C. Marshall, Army Air Force's Gen. Ira C. Eaker (sitting in for the Army Air Force's chief of staff, Henry H. Arnold, who was on an inspection tour of installations in the Pacific), Navy Chief of Staff Adm. Ernest J. King, Leahy (also a member of the JCS), Secretary of the Navy James Forrestal, Secretary of War Henry L. Stimson, and Assistant Secretary of War John J. McCloy. Truman opened the meeting, then asked Marshall for his views. Marshall was the dominant figure on the JCS. He was Truman's most trusted military adviser, as he had been President Franklin D. Roosevelt's.

Marshall reported that the chiefs, supported by the Pacific commanders Gen. Douglas MacArthur and Adm. Chester W. Nimitz, agreed that an invasion of Kyushu "appears to be the least costly worthwhile operation following Okinawa." Lodgment in Kyushu, he said, was necessary to make blockade and bombardment more effective and to serve as a staging area for the invasion of Japan's main island of Honshu. The chiefs recommended a target date of November 1 for the first phase, code-named Olympic, because delay would give the Japanese more time to prepare and because bad weather might postpone the invasion "and hence the end of the war" for up to six months. Marshall said that in his opinion, Olympic was "the only course to pursue." The chiefs also proposed that Operation Cornet be launched against Honshu on March 1, 1946.

* * *

Leahy's memorandum calling the meeting had asked for casualty projections which that invasion might be expected to produce. Marshall stated that campaigns in the Pacific had been so diverse "it is considered wrong" to make total estimates. All he would say was that casualties during the first thirty days on Kyushu should not exceed those sustained in taking Luzon in the Philippines —31,000 men killed, wounded, or missing in action. "It is a grim fact," Marshall said, "that there is not an easy, bloodless way to victory in war." Leahy estimated a higher casualty rate similar to Okinawa, and King guessed somewhere in between.

King and Eaker, speaking for the Navy and the Army Air Forces respectively, endorsed Marshall's proposals. King said that he had become convinced that Kyushu was "the key to the success of any siege operations." He recommended that "we should do Kyushu now" and begin preparations for invading Honshu. Eaker "agreed completely" with Marshall. He said he had just received a message from Arnold also expressing "complete agreement." Air Force plans called for the use of forty groups of heavy bombers, which "could not be deployed without the use of airfields on Kyushu." Stimson and Forrestal concurred.

Truman summed up. He considered "the Kyushu plan all right from the military standpoint" and directed the chiefs to "go ahead with it." He said he "had hoped that there was a possibility

of preventing an Okinawa from one end of Japan to the other," but "he was clear on the situation now" and was "quite sure" the chiefs should proceed with the plan. Just before the meeting adjourned, McCloy raised the possibility of avoiding an invasion by warning the Japanese that the United States would employ atomic weapons if there were no surrender. The ensuing discussion was inconclusive because the first test was a month away and no one could be sure the weapons would work.

In his memoirs Truman claimed that using atomic bombs prevented an invasion that would have cost 500,000 American lives. Other officials mentioned the same or even higher figures. Critics have assailed such statements as gross exaggerations designed to forestall scrutiny of Truman's real motives. They have given wide publicity to a report prepared by the Joint War Plans Committee (JWPC) for the chiefs' meeting with Truman. The committee estimated that the invasion of Kyushu, followed by that of Honshu, as the chiefs proposed, would cost approximately 40,000 dead, 150,000 wounded, and 3,500 missing in action for a total of 193,500 casualties.

That those responsible for a decision should exaggerate the consequences of alternatives is commonplace. Some who cite the JWPC report profess to see more sinister motives, insisting that such "low" casualty projections call into question the very idea that atomic bombs were used to avoid heavy losses. By discrediting that justification as a cover-up, they seek to bolster their contention that the bombs really were used to permit the employment of "atomic diplomacy" against the Soviet Union.

The notion that 193,500 anticipated casualties were too insignificant to have caused Truman to resort to atomic bombs might seem bizarre to anyone other than an academic, but let it pass. Those who have cited the JWPC report in countless op-ed pieces in newspapers and in magazine articles have created a myth by omitting key considerations: First, the report itself is studded with qualifications that casualties "are not subject to accurate estimate" and that the projection "is admittedly only an educated guess." Second, the figures never were conveyed to Truman. They were excised at high military echelons, which is why Marshall cited only estimates for the first thirty days on Kyushu. And indeed, subsequent Japanese troop buildups on Kyushu rendered the JWPC estimates totally irrelevent by the time the first atomic bomb was dropped.

* * *

Another myth that has attained wide attention is that at least several of Truman's top military advisers later informed him that using atomic bombs against Japan would be militarily unnecessary or immoral, or both. There is no persuasive evidence that any of them did so. None of the Joint Chiefs ever made such a claim, although one inventive author has tried to make it appear that Leahy did by braiding together several unrelated passages from the admiral's memoirs. Actually, two days after Hiroshima, Truman told aides that Leahy had "said up to the last that it wouldn't go off."

Neither MacArthur nor Nimitz ever communicated to Truman any change of mind about the need for invasion or expressed reservations about using the bombs. When first informed about their imminent use only days before Hiroshima, MacArthur responded with a lecture on the future of atomic warfare and even after Hiroshima strongly recommended that the invasion go forward. Nimitz, from whose jurisdiction the atomic strikes would be launched, was notified in early 1945. "This sounds fine," he told the courier, "but this is only February. Can't we get one sooner?" Nimitz later would join Air Force generals Carl D. Spaatz, Nathan Twining, and Curtis LeMay in recommending that a third bomb be dropped on Tokyo.

Only Dwight D. Eisenhower later claimed to have remonstrated against the use of the bomb. In his *Crusade in Europe*, published in 1948, he wrote that when Secretary Stimson informed him during the Potsdam Conference of plans to use the bomb, he replied that he hoped "we would never have to use such a thing against any enemy," because he did not want the United States to be the first to use such a weapon. He added, "My views were merely personal and immediate reactions; they were not based on any analysis of the subject."

Eisenhower's recollections grew more colorful as the years went on. A later account of his meeting with Stimson had it taking place at Ike's headquarters in Frankfurt on the very day news arrived of the successful atomic test in New Mexico. "We'd had a nice evening at headquarters in Germany," he remembered. Then, after dinner, "Stimson got this cable saying that the bomb had been perfected and was ready to be dropped. The cable was in code... 'the lamb is born' or some damn thing like that." In this version Eisenhower claimed to have protested vehemently that "the Japanese were ready to surrender and it wasn't necessary to hit them with that awful thing." "Well," Eisenhower concluded, "the old gentleman got furious."

* * *

The best that can be said about Eisenhower's memory is that it had become flawed by the passage of time. Stimson was in Potsdam and Eisenhower in Frankfurt on July 16, when word came of the successful test. Aside from a brief conversation at a flag-raising ceremony in Berlin on July 20, the only other time they met was at Ike's headquarters on July 27. By then orders already had been sent to the Pacific to use the bombs if Japan had not yet surrendered. Notes made by one of Stimson's aides indicate that there was a discussion of atomic bombs, but there is no mention of any protest on Eisenhower's part. Even if there had been, two factors must be kept in mind. Eisenhower had commanded Allied forces in Europe, and his opinion on how close Japan was to surrender would have carried no special weight. More important, Stimson left for home immediately after the meeting and could not have personally conveyed Ike's sentiments to the President, who did not return to Washington until after Hiroshima.

On July 8 the Combined Intelligence Committee submitted to the American and British Combined Chiefs of Staff a report entitled "Estimate of the Enemy Situation." The committee predicted that as Japan's position continued to deteriorate, it might "make a serious effort to use the USSR [then a neutral] as a mediator in ending the war." Tokyo also would put out "intermittent peace feelers" to "weaken the determination of the United Nations to fight to the bitter end, or to create inter-allied dissension." While the Japanese people would be willing to make large concessions to end the war, "For a surrender to be acceptable to the Japanese army, it would be necessary for the military leaders to believe that it would not entail discrediting warrior tradition and that it would permit the ultimate resurgence of a military Japan."

Small wonder that American officials remained unimpressed when Japan proceeded to do exactly what the committee predicted. On July 12 Japanese Foreign Minister Shigenori Togo instructed Ambassador Naotaki Sato in Moscow to inform the Soviets that the emperor wished to send a personal envoy, Prince Fuminaro Konoye, in an attempt "to restore peace with all possible speed." Although he realized Konoye could not reach Moscow before the Soviet leader Joseph Stalin and Foreign Minister V. M. Molotov left to attend a Big Three meeting scheduled to begin in Potsdam on the fifteenth, Togo sought to have negotiations begin as soon as they returned.

American officials had long since been able to read Japanese diplomatic traffic through a process known as the MAGIC intercepts. Army intelligence (G-2) prepared for General Marshall its interpretation of Togo's message the next day. The report listed several possible constructions, the most probable being that the Japanese "governing clique" was making a coordinated effort to "stave off defeat" through Soviet intervention and an "appeal to war weariness in the United States." The report added that Undersecretary of State Joseph C. Grew, who had spent ten years in Japan as ambassador, "agrees with these conclusions."

Some have claimed that Togo's overture to the Soviet Union, together with attempts by some minor Japanese officials in Switzerland and other neutral countries to get peace talks started through the Office of Strategic Services (OSS), constituted clear evidence that the Japanese were near surrender. Their sole prerequisite was retention of their sacred emperor, whose unique cultural/religious status within the Japanese polity they would not compromise. If only the United States had extended assurances about the emperor, according to this view, much bloodshed and the atomic bombs would have been unnecessary.

A careful reading of the MAGIC intercepts of subsequent exchanges between Togo and Sato provides no evidence that retention of the emperor was the sole obstacle to peace. What they show instead is that the Japanese Foreign Office was trying to cut a deal through the Soviet Union that would have permitted Japan to retain its political system and its prewar empire intact. Even the most lenient American official could not have countenanced such a settlement.

* * *

Togo on July 17 informed Sato that "we are not asking the Russians' mediation in *anything like unconditional surrender* [emphasis added]." During the following weeks Sato pleaded with his superiors to abandon hope of Soviet intercession and to approach the United States directly to find out what peace terms would be offered. "There is... no alternative but immediate unconditional surrender," he cabled on July 31, and he bluntly informed Togo that "your way of looking at things and the actual situation in the Eastern Area may be seen to be absolutely contradictory." The Foreign Ministry ignored his pleas and continued to seek Soviet help even after Hiroshima.

"Peace feelers" by Japanese officials abroad seemed no more promising from the American point of view. Although several of the consular personnel and military attachés engaged in these activities claimed important connections at home, none produced verification. Had the Japanese government sought only an assurance about the emperor, all it had to do was grant one of these men authority to begin talks through the OSS. Its failure to do so led American officials to assume that those involved were either well-meaning individuals acting alone or that they were being orchestrated by Tokyo. Grew characterized such "peace feelers" as "familiar weapons of psychological warfare" designed to "divide the Allies."

Some American officials, such as Stimson and Grew, nonetheless wanted to signal the Japanese that they might retain the emperorship in the form of a constitutional monarchy. Such an assurance might remove the last stumbling block to surrender, if not when it was issued, then later. Only an imperial rescript would bring about an orderly surrender, they argued, without which Japanese forces would fight to the last man regardless of what the government in Tokyo did. Besides, the emperor could serve as a stabilizing factor during the transition to peacetime.

There were many arguments against an American initiative. Some opposed retaining such an undemocratic institution on principle and because they feared it might later serve as a rallying point for future militarism. Should that happen, as one assistant Secretary of State put it, "those lives already spent will have been sacrificed in vain, and lives will be lost again in the future." Japanese hardliners were certain to exploit an overture as evidence that losses sustained at Okinawa had weakened American resolve and to argue that continued resistance would bring further concessions. Stalin, who earlier had told an American envoy that he favored abolishing the emperorship because the ineffectual Hirohito might be succeeded by "an energetic and vigorous figure who could cause trouble," was just as certain to interpret it as a treacherous effort to end the war before the Soviets could share in the spoils.

There were domestic considerations as well. Roosevelt had announced the unconditional surrender policy in early 1943, and it since had become a slogan of the war. He also had advocated that peoples everywhere should have the right to choose their own form of government, and Truman had publicly pledged to carry out his predecessor's legacies. For him to have formally *guaranteed* continuance of the emperorship, as opposed to merely accepting it on American terms pending free elections, as he later did, would have constituted a blatant repudiation of his own promises.

Nor was that all. Regardless of the emperor's actual role in Japanese aggression, which is still debated, much wartime propaganda had encouraged Americans to regard Hirohito as no less a war criminal than Adolf Hitler or Benito Mussolini. Although Truman said on several occasions that he had no objection to retaining the emperor, he understandably refused to make the first move. The ultimatum he issued from Potsdam on July 26 did not refer specifically to the emperorship. All it said was that occupation forces would be removed after "a peaceful and responsible" government had been established according to the "freely expressed will of the Japanese people." When the Japanese rejected the ultimatum rather than at last inquire whether they might retain the emperor, Truman permitted the plans for using the bombs to go forward.

Reliance on MAGIC intercepts and the "peace feelers" to gauge how near Japan was to surrender is misleading in any case. The army, not the Foreign Office, controlled the situation. Intercepts of Japanese military communications, designated ULTRA, provided no reason to believe the army was even considering surrender. Japanese Imperial Headquarters had correctly guessed that the next operation after Okinawa would be Kyushu and was making every effort to bolster its defenses there.

General Marshall reported on July 24 that there were "approximately 500,000 troops in Kyushu" and that more were on the way. ULTRA identified new units arriving almost daily. MacArthur's G-2 reported on July 29 that "this threatening development, if not checked, may grow to a point where we attack on a ratio of one (1) to one (1) which is not the recipe for victory." By the time the first atomic bomb fell, ULTRA indicated that there were 560,000 troops in southern Kyushu (the actual figure was closer to 900,000), and projections for November 1 placed the number at 680,000. A report, for medical purposes, of July 31 estimated that total battle and non-battle casualties might run as high as 394,859 *for the Kyushu operation alone.* This figure did not include those men expected to be killed outright, for obviously they would require no medical attention. Marshall regarded Japanese defenses as so formidable that even after Hiroshima he asked MacArthur to consider alternate landing sites and began contemplating the use of atomic bombs as tactical weapons to support the invasion.

The thirty-day casualty projection of 31,000 Marshall had given Truman at the June 18 strategy meeting had become meaningless. It had been based on the assumption that the Japanese had about 350,000 defenders in Kyushu and that naval and air interdiction would preclude significant reinforcement. But the Japanese buildup since that time meant that the defenders would have nearly twice the number of troops available by "X-day" than earlier assumed. The assertion that apprehensions about casualties are insufficient to explain Truman's use of the bombs, therefore, cannot be taken seriously. On the contrary, as Winston Churchill wrote after a conversation with him at Potsdam, Truman was tormented by "the terrible responsibilities that rested upon him in regard to the unlimited effusions of American blood."

* * *

Some historians have argued that while the first bomb *might* have been required to achieve Japanese surrender, dropping the second constituted a needless barbarism. The record shows otherwise. American officials believed more than one bomb would be necessary because they assumed Japanese hard-liners would minimize the first explosion or attempt to explain it away as some sort of natural catastrophe, precisely what they did. The Japanese minister of war, for instance, at first refused even to admit that the Hiroshima bomb was atomic. A few hours after Nagasaki he told the cabinet that "the Americans appeared to have one hundred atomic bombs... they could drop three per day. The next target might well be Tokyo."

Even after both bombs had fallen and Russia entered the war, Japanese militants insisted on such lenient peace terms that moderates knew there was no sense even transmitting them to the United States. Hirohito had to intervene personally on two occasions during the

next few days to induce hard-liners to abandon their conditions and to accept the American stipulation that the emperor's authority "shall be subject to the Supreme Commander of the Allied Powers." That the militarists would have accepted such a settlement before the bombs is farfetched, to say the least.

Some writers have argued that the cumulative effects of battlefield defeats, conventional bombing, and naval blockade already had defeated Japan. Even without extending assurances about the emperor, all the United States had to do was wait. The most frequently cited basis for this contention is the *United States Strategic Bombing Survey*, published in 1946, which stated that Japan would have surrendered by November 1 "even if the atomic bombs had not been dropped, even if Russia had not entered the war, and even if no invasion had been planned or contemplated." Recent scholarship by the historian Robert R Newman and others has demonstrated that the survey was "cooked" by those who prepared it to arrive at such a conclusion. No matter. This or any other document based on information available only after the war ended is irrelevant with regard to what Truman could have known at the time.

* * *

What often goes unremarked is that when the bombs were dropped, fighting was still going on in the Philippines, China, and elsewhere. Every day that the war continued thousands of prisoners of war had to live and die in abysmal conditions, and there were rumors that the Japanese intended to slaughter them if the homeland was invaded. Truman was Commander in Chief of the American armed forces, and he had a duty to the men under his command not shared by those sitting in moral judgment decades later. Available evidence points to the conclusion that he acted for the reason he said he did: to end a bloody war that would have become far bloodier had invasion proved necessary. One can only imagine what would have happened if tens of thousands of American boys had died or been wounded on Japanese soil and then it had become known that Truman had chosen not to use weapons that might have ended the war months sooner.

NO

Barton J. Bernstein

THE ATOMIC BOMBINGS
RECONSIDERED

THE QUESTIONS AMERICA SHOULD ASK

Fifty Years Ago, during a three-day period in August 1945, the United States dropped two atomic bombs on Japan, killing more than 115,000 people and possibly as many as 250,000, and injuring at least another 100,000. In the aftermath of the war, the bombings raised both ethical and historical questions about why and how they were used. Would they have been used on Germany? Why were cities targeted so that so many civilians would be killed? Were there likely alternative ways to end the war speedily and avoid the Allies' scheduled November 1, 1945, invasion of Kyushu?

Such questions often fail to recognize that, before Hiroshima and Nagasaki, the use of the A-bomb did not raise profound moral issues for policymakers. The weapon was conceived in a race with Germany, and it undoubtedly would have been used against Germany had the bomb been ready much sooner. During the war, the target shifted to Japan. And during World War II's brutal course, civilians in cities had already become targets. The grim Axis bombing record is well known. Masses of noncombatants were also intentionally killed in the later stages of the American air war against Germany; that tactic was developed further in 1945 with the firebombing of Japanese cities. Such mass bombing constituted a transformation of morality, repudiating President Franklin D. Roosevelt's prewar pleas that the warring nations avoid bombing cities to spare civilian lives. Thus, by 1945, American leaders were not seeking to avoid the use of the A-bomb on Japan. But the evidence from current archival research shows that by pursuing alternative tactics instead, they probably could still have obviated the dreaded invasion and ended the war by November.

SHIFTING FROM GERMANY TO JAPAN

In 1941, urged by émigré and American scientists, President Roosevelt initiated the atomic bomb project—soon code-named the Manhattan Project

From Barton J. Bernstein, "The Atomic Bombings Reconsidered," *Foreign Affairs* (January/February 1995). Copyright © 1995 by The Council on Foreign Relations, Inc. Reprinted by permission.

—amid what was believed to be a desperate race with Hitler's Germany for the bomb. At the beginning, Roosevelt and his chief aides assumed that the A-bomb was a legitimate weapon that would be used first against Nazi Germany. They also decided that the bomb project should be kept secret from the Soviet Union, even after the Soviets became a wartime ally, because the bomb might well give the United States future leverage against the Soviets.

By mid-1944, the landscape of the war had changed. Roosevelt and his top advisers knew that the likely target would now be Japan, for the war with Germany would undoubtedly end well before the A-bomb was expected to be ready, around the spring of 1945. In a secret September 1944 memorandum at Hyde Park, Roosevelt and British Prime Minister Winston Churchill ratifed the shift from Germany to Japan. Their phrasing suggested that, for the moment anyway, they might have had some slight doubts about actually using the bomb, for they agreed that "it might *perhaps*, after mature consideration, be used against the Japanese" (my emphasis).

Four days later, mulling over matters aloud with a visiting British diplomat and chief U.S. science adviser Vannevar Bush, Roosevelt briefly wondered whether the A-bomb should be dropped on Japan or whether it should be demonstrated in America, presumably with Japanese observers, and then used as a threat. His speculative notion seemed so unimportant and so contrary to the project's long-standing operating assumptions that Bush actually forgot about it when he prepared a memo of the meeting. He only recalled the president's remarks a day later and then added a brief paragraph to another memorandum.

Put in context alongside the dominant assumption that the bomb would be used against the enemy, the significance of F.D.R.'s occasional doubts is precisely that they were so occasional—expressed twice in almost four years. All of F.D.R.'s advisers who knew about the bomb always unquestioningly assumed that it would be used. Indeed, their memoranda frequently spoke of after it is used or "when it is used," and never "if it is used." By about mid-1944, most had comfortably concluded that the target would be Japan.

The bomb's assumed legitimacy as a war weapon was ratified bureaucratically in September 1944 when General Leslie Groves, the director of the Manhattan Project, had the air force create a special group—the 509th Composite Group with 1,750 men—to begin practicing to drop atomic bombs. So dominant was the assumption that the bomb would be used against Japan that only one high-ranking Washington official, Undersecretary of War Robert Patterson, even questioned this notion after V-E Day. He wondered whether the defeat of Germany on May 8, 1945, might alter the plans for dropping the bomb on Japan. It would not.

THE ASSUMPTION OF USE

The Manhattan Project, costing nearly $2 billion, had been kept secret from most cabinet members and nearly all of Congress. Secretary of War Henry L. Stimson, a trusted Republican, and General George C. Marshall, the equally respected army chief of staff disclosed the project to only a few congressional leaders. They smuggled the necessary appropriations into the War Department budget without the knowledge—much less the scrutiny—of most congressmen, including most members of the key appropriations committees. A conception of the national interest agreed upon by a few men from the executive and legislative branches had revised the normal appropriations process.

In March 1944, when a Democratic senator heading a special investigating committee wanted to pry into this expensive project, Stimson peevishly described him in his diary as "a nuisance and pretty untrustworthy... He talks smoothly but acts meanly." That man was Senator Harry S. Truman. Marshall persuaded him not to investigate the project, and thus Truman did not learn any more than that it involved a new weapon until he was suddenly thrust into the presidency on April 12, 1945.

In early 1945, James E. Byrnes, then F.D.R.'s "assistant president" for domestic affairs and a savvy Democratic politician, began to suspect that the Manhattan Project was a boondoggle. "If [it] proves a failure," he warned Roosevelt, "it will be subjected to relentless investigation and criticism." Byrnes' doubts were soon overcome by Stimson and Marshall. A secret War Department report, with some hyperbole, summarized the situation: "If the project succeeds, there won't be any investigation. If it doesn't, they won't investigate anything else."

Had Roosevelt lived, such lurking political pressures might have powerfully confirmed his intention to use the weapon on the enemy—an assumption he had already made. How else could he have justified spending roughly $2 billion, diverting scarce materials from other war enterprises that might have been even more useful, and bypassing Congress? In a nation still unprepared to trust scientists, the Manhattan Project could have seemed a gigantic waste if its value were not dramatically demonstrated by the use of the atomic bomb.

Truman, inheriting the project and trusting both Marshall and Stimson, would be even more vulnerable to such political pressures. And, like F.D.R., the new president easily assumed that the bomb should and would be used. Truman never questioned that assumption. Bureaucratic developments set in motion before he entered the White House reinforced his belief And his aides, many inherited from the Roosevelt administration, shared the same faith.

PICKING TARGETS

Groves, eager to retain control of the atomic project, received Marshall's permission in early spring 1945 to select targets for the new weapon. Groves and his associates had long recognized that they were considering a weapon of a new magnitude, possibly equivalent to the "normal bombs carried by [at least] 2,500 bombers." And they had come to assume that the A-bomb would be "detonated well above ground, relying primarily on blast effect to do material damage, [so that even with] minimum probable efficiency, there will be the maximum number of structures (dwellings and factories) damaged beyond repair."

On April 27, the Target Committee, composed of Groves, army air force men like General Lauris Norstad, and scientists including the great mathematician John Von Neumann, met for the first time to discuss how and where in Japan to drop the bomb. They did not want to risk wasting the precious weapon, and decided that it must be dropped visually and not by radar, despite the poor weather conditions in Japan during the summer, when the bomb would be ready.

Good targets were not plentiful. The air force, they knew, "was systematically bombing out the following cities with the prime purpose... of not leaving one stone lying on another: Tokyo, Yokohama, Nagoya, Osaka, Kyoto, Kobe, Yawata, and Nagasaki... The air force is operating primarily to laying [sic] waste all the main Japanese cities ... Their existing procedure is to bomb the hell out of Tokyo."

By early 1945, World War II—especially in the Pacific—had become virtually total war. The firebombing of Dresden had helped set a precedent for the U.S. air force, supported by the American people, to intentionally kill mass numbers of Japanese citizens. The earlier moral insistence on noncombatant immunity crumbled during the savage war. In Tokyo, during March 9–10, a U.S. air attack killed about 80,000 Japanese civilians. American B-29s dropped napalm on the city's heavily populated areas to produce uncontrollable firestorms. It may even have been easier to conduct this new warfare outside Europe and against Japan because its people seemed like "yellow subhumans" to many rank-and-file American citizens and many of their leaders.

In this new moral context, with mass killings of an enemy's civilians even seeming desirable, the committee agreed to choose "large urban areas of not less than three miles in diameter existing in the larger populated areas" as A-bomb targets. The April 27 discussion focused on four cities: Hiroshima, which, as "the largest untouched target not on the 21st Bomber Command priority list," warranted serious consideration; Yawata, known for its steel industry; Yokohama; and Tokyo, "a possibility [though] now practically all bombed and burned out and... practically rubble with only the palace grounds left standing." They decided that other areas warranted more consideration: Tokyo Bay, Kawasaki, Yokohama, Nagoya, Osaka, Kobe, Kyoto, Hiroshima, Kure, Yawata, Kokura, Shimonoseki, Yamaguchi, Kumamoto, Fukuoka, Nagasaki, and Sasebo.

The choice of targets would depend partly on how the bomb would do its deadly work—the balance of blast, heat, and radiation. At their second set of meetings, during May 11–12, physicist J. Robert Oppenheimer, director of the Los Alamos laboratory, stressed that the bomb material itself was lethal enough for perhaps a billion deadly doses and that the weapon would give off lethal radioactivity. The bomb, set to explode in the air, would deposit "a large fraction of either the initial active material or the radioactive products in the immediate vicinity of the target; but the radiation... will, of course, have an effect on exposed personnel in the target area." It was unclear, he acknowledged, what would happen to most of the radioactive material: it could stay for hours as a cloud above the place of detonation or, if the bomb exploded during rain or in high humidity and thus caused rain, "most of the active material will be brought down in the vicinity of the target area." Oppenheimer's report left unclear whether a substantial proportion or only a small fraction of the population might die from radiation. So far as the skimpy records reveal, no member of the Target Committee chose to dwell on this matter. They probably assumed that the bomb blast would claim most of its victims before the radiation could do its deadly work.

In considering targets, they discussed the possibility of bombing the emperor's palace in Tokyo and "agreed that we should not recommend it but that any action for this bombing should come from authorities on military policy." They decided to gather information on the effectiveness of using the bomb on the palace.

The Target Committee selected their four top targets: Kyoto, Hiroshima, Yokohama, and Kokura Arsenal, with the implication that Niigata, a city farther away from the air force 509th group's Tinian base, might be held in reserve as a fifth. Kyoto, the ancient former capital and shrine city, with a population of about a million, was the most attractive target to the committee. "From the psychological point of view," the committee minutes note, "there is the advantage that Kyoto is an intellectual center for Japan and [thus] the people there are more apt to appreciate the significance of such a weapon." The implication was that those in Kyoto who survived the A-bombing and saw the horror would be believed elsewhere in Japan.

Of central importance, the group stressed that the bomb should be used as a terror weapon—to produce "the greatest psychological effect against Japan" and to make the world, and the U.S.S.R. in particular, aware that America possessed this new power. The death and destruction would not only intimidate the surviving Japanese into pushing for surrender, but, as a bonus, cow other nations, notably the Soviet Union. In short, America could speed the ending of the war and by the same act help shape the postwar world.

By the committee's third meeting, two weeks later, on May 28, they had pinned down matters. They chose as their targets (in order) Kyoto, Hiroshima, and Niigata, and decided to aim for the center of each city. They agreed that aiming for industrial areas would be a mistake because such targets were small, spread on the cities' fringes, and quite dispersed. They also knew that bombing was imprecise enough that the bomb might easily miss its mark by a fifth of a mile, and they wanted to be sure that the weapon would show its power and not be wasted.

The committee understood that the three target cities would be removed from the air force's regular target list, reserving them for the A-bomb. But, the members were informed, "with the current and prospective rate of... bombings, it is expected to complete strategic bombing of Japan by 1 Jan 46 so availability of future [A-bomb] targets will be a problem." In short, Japan was being bombed out.

THE RATIFICATION OF TERROR BOMBING

On May 28, 1945, physicist Arthur H. Compton, a Nobel laureate and member of a special scientific panel advising the high-level Interim Committee newly appointed to recommend policy about the bomb, raised profound moral and political questions about how the atomic bomb would be used. "It introduces the question of mass slaughter, really for the first time in history," he wrote. "It carries with it the question of possible radioactive poison over the area bombed. Essentially, the question of the use... of the new weapon carries much more serious implications than the introduction of poison gas."

Compton's concern received some independent support from General Marshall, who told Secretary Stimson on May 29 that the A-bomb should first be used not against civilians but against military installations—perhaps a naval base—and then possibly against large manufacturing areas after the civilians had received ample warnings to flee. Marshall feared "the opprobrium which might follow from an ill considered employment of such force." A graduate of Virginia Military Institute and a trained soldier, Marshall struggled to retain the older code of not *intentionally* killing civilians. The concerns of Compton the scientist and Marshall the general, their values so rooted in an earlier conception of war that sought to spare noncombatants, soon gave way to the sense of exigency, the desire to use the bomb on people, and the unwillingness or inability of anyone near the top in Washington to plead forcefully for maintaining this older morality.

On May 31, 1945, the Interim Committee, composed of Stimson, Bush, Harvard President James Conant, physicist and educator Karl T. Compton, Secretary of State designate James E. Byrnes, and a few other notables, discussed the A-bomb. Opening this meeting, Stimson, the aged secretary of war who had agonized over the recent shift toward mass bombing of civilians, described the atomic bomb as representing "a new relationship of man to the universe. This discovery might be compared to the discoveries of the Copernican theory and the laws of gravity, but far more important than these in its effects on the lives of men."

Meeting, as they were, some six weeks before the first nuclear test at Alamogordo, they were still unsure of the power of this new weapon. Oppenheimer told the group that it would have an explosive force of between 2,000 and 20,000 tons of TNT. Its visual effect would be tremendous. "It would be accompanied by a brilliant luminescence which would rise to a height of 10,000 to 20,000 feet," Oppenheimer reported. "The neutron effect [radiation] would be dangerous to life for a radius of at least two-thirds of a mile." He estimated that 20,000 Japanese would be killed.

According to the committee minutes, the group discussed "various types of targets and the effects to be produced." Stimson "expressed the conclusion, on which there was general agreement, that we could not give the Japanese any warning; that we could not concentrate on a civilian area; but that we should seek to make a profound psychological impression on as many of the inhabitants as possible. At the suggestion of Dr. Conant, the secretary agreed that the most desirable target would be a vital war plant employing a large number of workers and closely surrounded by workers' houses."

Directed by Stimson, the committee was actually endorsing terror bombing—but somewhat uneasily. They would not focus exclusively on a military target (the older morality), as Marshall had recently proposed, nor fully on civilians (the emerging morality). They managed to achieve their purpose—terror bombing—without bluntly acknowledging it to themselves. All knew that families—women, children, and, even in the daytime, during the bomb attack, some workers—dwelled in "workers' houses."

At the committee's morning or afternoon session, or at lunch, or possibly at all three times—different members later presented differing recollections—the notion of a noncombat demonstration of the A-bomb came up. The issue of how to use the bomb was not even on Stimson's agenda, nor was it part of the formal mandate of the Interim Committee, but he may have showed passing interest in the subject of a noncombat demonstration. They soon rejected it. It was deemed too risky for various reasons: the bomb might not work, the Japanese air force might interfere with the bomber, the A-bomb might not adequately impress the Japanese militarists, or the bomb might incinerate any Allied POWs whom the Japanese might place in the area.

The discussion on May 31 had focused substantially on *how* to use the bomb against Japan. At one point some of the members had considered trying several A-bomb strikes at the same time and presumably on the same city. Groves opposed this notion, partly on the grounds that "the effect would not be sufficiently distinct from our regular air force bombing program." Like the others, he was counting on the dramatic effect of a single bomb, delivered by a single plane, killing many thousands. It was not new for the air force to kill so many Japanese, but this method would be new. And the use of the new weapon would carry, as stressed by American proclamations in early August, the likelihood of more nuclear attacks on Japanese cities—a continuing "rain of ruin."

Two weeks after the Interim Committee meeting, on June 16, after émigré physicists James Franck and Leo Szilard and some colleagues from the Manhattan Project's Chicago laboratory raised moral and political questions about the surprise use of the bomb on Japan, a special four-member scientific advisory committee disposed of the matter of a noncombat demonstration. The group was composed of physicists Arthur Compton, J. Robert Oppenheimer, Enrico Fermi, and Ernest O. Lawrence. By one report, Lawrence was the last of the four to give up hope for a noncombat demonstration. Oppenheimer, who spoke on the issue in 1954 and was not then controverted by the other three men, recalled that the subject of a noncombat demonstration was not the most important matter dealt with during the group's busy weekend meeting and thus did not receive much attention. On June 16, the four scientists concluded: "We can propose no technical demonstration likely to bring an end to the war; we see no acceptable alternative to direct military use."

At that time, as some members of the scientific panel later grudgingly acknowledged, they knew little about the situation in Japan, the power of the militarists there, the timid efforts by the peace forces there to move toward a settlement, the date of the likely American invasion of Kyushu, and the power of the still untested A-bomb. "We didn't know beans about the military situation," Oppenheimer later remarked pungently.

But even different counsel by the scientific advisers probably could not have reversed the course of events. The bomb had been devised to be used, the project cost about $2 billion, and Truman and Byrnes, the president's key political aide, had no desire to avoid its use. Nor did Stimson. They even had additional reasons for wanting to use it: the bomb might *also* intimidate the Soviets and render them tractable in the postwar period.

Stimson emphasized this theme in a secret memorandum to Truman on April 25: "If the problem of the proper use of this weapon can be solved, we should then have the opportunity to bring the world into a pattern in which the peace of the world and our civilization can be saved." Concern about the bomb and its relationship to the Soviet Union dominated Stimson's thinking in the spring and summer of 1945. And Truman and Byrnes, perhaps partly under Stimson's tutelage, came to stress the same hopes for the bomb.

THE AGONIES OF KILLING CIVILIANS

During 1945, Stimson found himself presiding, with agony, over an air force that killed hundreds of thousands of Japanese civilians. Usually, he preferred not to face these ugly facts, but sought refuge in the notion that the air force was actually engaged in precision bombing and that somehow this precision bombing was going awry. Caught between an older morality that opposed the intentional killing of noncombatants and a newer one that stressed virtually total war, Stimson could neither fully face the facts nor fully escape them. He was not a hypocrite but a man trapped in ambivalence.

Stimson discussed the problem with Truman on June 6. Stimson stressed that he was worried about the air force's mass bombing, but that it was hard to restrict it. In his diary, Stimson recorded: "I told him I was anxious about this feature of the war for two reasons: first, because I did not want to have the United States get the reputation of outdoing Hitler in atrocities; and second, I was a little fearful that before we could get ready the air force might have Japan so thoroughly bombed out that the new weapon would not have a fair background to show its strength." According to Stimson, Truman "laughed and said he understood."

Unable to reestablish the old morality and wanting the benefits for America of the new, Stimson proved decisive—even obdurate—on a comparatively small matter: removing Kyoto from Groves' target list of cities. It was not that Stimson was trying to save Kyoto's citizens; rather, he was seeking to save its relics, lest the Japanese become embittered and later side with the Soviets. As Stimson explained in his diary entry of July 24: "The bitterness which would be caused by such a wanton act might make it impossible during the long post-war period to reconcile the Japanese to us in that area rather than to the Russians. It might thus . . . be the means of preventing what our policy demanded, namely, a sympathetic Japan to the United States in case there should be any aggression by Russia in Manchuria."

Truman, backing Stimson on this matter, insisted privately that the A-bombs would be used only on military targets. Apparently the president wished not to recognize the inevitable—that a weapon of such great power would necessarily kill many civilians. At Potsdam on July 25, Truman received glowing reports of the vast destruction achieved by the Alamogordo blast and lavishly recorded the details in his diary: a crater of 1,200 feet in diameter, a steel tower destroyed a half mile away, men knocked over six miles away. "We have discovered," he wrote in his diary, "the most terrible bomb in the history of the world. It may be the fire destruction prophesied." But when he approved the final list of A-bomb targets, with Nagasaki and Kokura substituted for Kyoto, he could write in his diary, "I have told Sec. of War . . . Stimson to use it so that military objectives and soldiers and sailors are the target and not women and children. Even if the Japs are savages, ruthless, merciless, and fanatic . . . [t]he target will be a purely military one." Truman may have been engaging in self-deception to make the mass deaths of civilians acceptable.

Neither Hiroshima nor Nagasaki was a "purely military" target, but the official press releases, cast well before the atomic bombings, glided over this matter. Hiroshima, for example, was described simply as "an important Japanese army base." The press releases were drafted by men who knew that those cities had been chosen partly to dramatize the killing of noncombatants.

On August 10, the day after the Nagasaki bombing, when Truman realized the magnitude of the mass killing and the Japanese offered a conditional surrender requiring continuation of the emperor, the president told his cabinet that he did not want to kill any more women and children. Rejecting demands to drop more atomic bombs on Japan, he hoped not to use them again. After two atomic bombings, the horror of mass death had forcefully hit the president, and he was willing to return partway to the older morality—civilians might be protected from A-bombs. But he continued to sanction the heavy conventional bombing of Japan's cities, with the deadly toll that napalm, incendiaries, and other bombs produced. Between August 10 and August 14—the war's last day, on which about 1,000 American planes bombed Japanese cities, some delivering their deadly cargo after Japan announced its surrender—the United States probably killed more than 15,000 Japanese.

THE ROADS NOT TAKEN

Before August 10, Truman and his associates had not sought to avoid the use of the atomic bomb. As a result, they had easily dismissed the possibility of a noncombat demonstration. Indeed, the post-Hiroshima pleas of Japan's military leaders for a final glorious battle suggest that such a demonstration probably would not have produced a speedy surrender. And American leaders also did not pursue other alternatives: modifying their unconditional surrender demand by guaranteeing the maintenance of the emperor, awaiting the Soviet entry into the war, or simply pursuing heavy conventional bombing of the cities amid the strangling naval blockade.

Truman and Byrnes did not believe that a modification of the unconditional surrender formula would produce a speedy surrender. They thought that guaranteeing to maintain the emperor would prompt an angry backlash from Americans who regarded Hirohito as a war criminal, and feared that this concession might embolden the Japanese militarists to expect more concessions and thus prolong the war. As a result, the president and his secretary of state easily rejected Stimson's pleas for a guarantee of the emperor.

Similarly, most American leaders did not believe that the Soviet entry into the Pacific war would make a decisive difference and greatly speed Japan's surrender. Generally, they believed that the U.S.S.R.'s entry would help end the war—ideally, before the massive invasion of Kyushu. They anticipated Moscow's intervention in mid-August, but the Soviets moved up their schedule to August 8, probably because of the Hiroshima bombing, and the Soviet entry did play an important role in producing Japan's surrender on August 14. Soviet entry without the A-bomb *might* have produced Japan's surrender before November.

The American aim was to avoid, if possible, the November 1 invasion, which would involve about 767,000 troops, at a possible cost of 31,000 casualties in the first 30 days and a total estimated American death toll of about 25,000. And American leaders certainly wanted to avoid the second part of the invasion plan, an assault on the Tokyo plain, scheduled for around March 1, 1946, with an estimated 15,000–21,000 more Americans dead. In the spring and summer of 1945, no American leader believed—as some later falsely claimed —that they planned to use the A-bomb to save half a million Americans. But, given the patriotic calculus of the time, there was no hesitation about using A-bombs to kill many Japanese in order to save the 25,000–46,000 Americans who might otherwise have died in the invasions. Put bluntly— Japanese life— including civilian life—was cheap, and some American leaders, like many rank-and-file citizens, may well have savored the prospect of punishing the Japanese with the A-bomb.

Truman, Byrnes, and the other leaders did not have to be reminded of the danger of a political backlash in America if they did not use the bomb and the invasions became necessary. Even if they had wished to avoid its use—and they did not—the fear of later public outrage spurred by the weeping parents and loved ones of dead American boys might well have forced American leaders to drop the A-bomb on Japan.

No one in official Washington expected that one or two atomic bombs would end the war quickly. They expected to use at least a third, and probably more. And until the day after Nagasaki, there had never been in their thinking a choice between atomic bombs and conventional bombs, but a selection of both —using mass bombing to compel surrender. Atomic bombs and conventional bombs were viewed as supplements to,

not substitutes for, one another. Heavy conventional bombing of Japan's cities would probably have killed hundreds of thousands in the next few months, and might have produced the desired surrender before November 1.

Taken together, some of these alternatives—promising to retain the Japanese monarchy, awaiting the Soviets' entry, and even more conventional bombing— very probably could have ended the war before the dreaded invasion. Still, the evidence—to borrow a phrase from F.D.R. —is somewhat "iffy," and no one who looks at the intransigence of the Japanese militarists should have full confidence in those other strategies. But we may well regret that these alternatives were not pursued and that there was not an effort to avoid the use of the first A-bomb—and certainly the second.

Whatever one thinks about the necessity of the first A-bomb, the second— dropped on Nagasaki on August 9—was almost certainly unnecessary. It was used because the original order directed the air force to drop bombs "as made ready" and, even after the Hiroshima bombing, no one in Washington anticipated an imminent Japanese surrender. Evidence now available about developments in the Japanese government—most notably the emperor's then-secret decision shortly before the Nagasaki bombing to seek peace—makes it clear that the second bomb could undoubtedly have been avoided. At least 35,000 Japanese and possibly almost twice that number, as well as several thousand Koreans, died unnecessarily in Nagasaki.

Administration leaders did not seek to avoid the use of the A-bomb. They even believed that its military use might produce a powerful bonus: the intimidation of the Soviets, rendering them, as

Byrnes said, "more manageable," espe-cially in Eastern Europe. Although that was not the dominant purpose for us-ing the weapon, it certainly was a strong confirming one. Had Truman and his as-sociates, like the dissenting scientists at Chicago, foreseen that the A-bombing of Japan would make the Soviets intransi-gent rather than tractable, perhaps Amer-ican leaders would have questioned their decision. But precisely because Ameri-can leaders expected that the bombings would also compel the Soviet Union to loosen its policy in Eastern Europe, there was no incentive to question their inten-tion to use the atomic bomb. Even if they had, the decision would probably have been the same. In a powerful sense, the atomic bombings represented the imple-mentation of an assumption—one that Truman comfortably inherited from Roo-sevelt. Hiroshima was an easy decision for Truman.

THE REDEFINITION OF MORALITY

Only years later, as government archives opened, wartime hatreds faded, and sen-sibilities changed, would Americans be-gin seriously to question whether the atomic bombings were necessary, desir-able, and moral. Building on the postwar memoirs of Admiral William Leahy and General Dwight D. Eisenhower, among others, doubts began to emerge about the use of the atomic bombs against Japan. As the years passed, Americans learned that the bombs, according to high-level American military estimates in June and July 1945, probably could not have saved a half million American lives in the invasions, as Truman sometimes con-tended after Nagasaki, but would have saved fewer than 50,000. Americans also came slowly to recognize the barbarity of

World War II, especially the mass killings by bombing civilians. It was that redef-inition of morality that made Hiroshima and Nagasaki possible and ushered in the atomic age in a frightening way.

That redefinition of morality was a product of World War II, which included such barbarities as Germany's systematic murder of six million Jews and Japan's rape of Nanking. While the worst atrocities were perpetrated by the Axis, all the major nation-states sliced away at the moral code—often to the applause of their leaders and citizens alike. By 1945 there were few moral restraints left in what had become virtually a total war. Even F.D.R.'s prewar concern for sparing enemy civilians had fallen by the wayside. In that new moral climate, any nation that had the A-bomb would probably have used it against enemy peoples. British leaders as well as Joseph Stalin endorsed the act. Germany's and Japan's leaders surely would have used it against cities. America was not morally unique—just technologically exceptional. Only it had the bomb, and so only it used it.

To understand this historical context does not require that American citizens or others should approve of it. But it does require that they recognize that pre- and post-Hiroshima dissent was rare in 1945. Indeed, few then asked why the United States used the atomic bomb on Japan. But had the bomb not been used, many more, including numerous outraged American citizens, would have bitterly asked that question of the Truman administration.

In 1945, most Americans shared the feelings that Truman privately expressed a few days after the Hiroshima and Nagasaki bombings when he justified the weapons' use in a letter to the Federal

Council of Churches of Christ. "I was greatly disturbed over the unwarranted attack by the Japanese on Pearl Harbor and their murder of our prisoners of war," the president wrote. "The only language they seem to understand is the one we have been using to bombard them. When you have to deal with a beast you have to treat him as a beast."

POSTSCRIPT

Was It Necessary to Drop the Atomic Bomb to End World War II?

Maddox makes a compelling case for the military circumstances surrounding the decision to drop the atomic bomb on Japan. The Americans had suffered 50,000 casualties in the capture of the island of Okinawa in the spring of 1945. This was considered a preview of the impending invasion of Japan. Maddox points out that estimates of casualties were mere guesswork at a given time and that Army Chief of Staff George C. Marshall himself increased these numbers considerably when he realized that the Japanese were stationing hundreds of thousands of troops on their main islands.

In the plethora of books and articles published in 1995 on the 50th anniversary of the dropping of the atomic bomb, Maddox's *Weapons for Victory: The Hiroshima Decision Fifty Years Later* (University of Missouri Press, 1995) stands out in its defense of the military reasons why Truman dropped the bomb. A long review essay by Donald Kagan on "Why America Dropped the Bomb," *Commentary* (September 1995) and "Letters from Readers" in the December 1995 issue thank Maddox and make similar points.

Although he is a revisionist, Bernstein often disagrees with a number of revisionist premises. He sees Truman not as reversing the policies of Roosevelt but as carrying them out to their logical conclusion. Bernstein also believes that Truman made his decision based primarily on military considerations. Unlike Maddox, however, he sees the bomb as a diplomatic bonus that Truman's secretary of state, Jimmy Byrnes, thought might make the Russians more manageable in Eastern Europe.

Bernstein's essay "The Atomic Bomb and American Foreign Policy, 1941–1945: A Historiographic Controversy," *Peace and Change* (Spring 1974) analyzes all the major works published between 1945 and 1973. He was also a key adviser in the controversy over the Smithsonian's *Enola Gay* script commemorating the 50th anniversary of the use of the A-bomb. The American Legion pressured the Smithsonian to cancel the exhibit because of its moderate revisionist tone.

Two collections of articles are worth examining: Philip Nobile, ed., *The Bombing of Hiroshima and Nagasaki, Judgment at the Smithsonian: The Uncensored Script of the Smithsonian's 50th Anniversary Exhibit of the Enola Gay* (Marlowe, 1995) and Michael J. Hogan, ed., *Hiroshima as History and Memory* (Cambridge University Press, 1996).

To review documents on the decision to use atomic bombs on Hiroshima and Nagasaki, see `http://www.peak.org/~danneng/decision/decision.html`.

PART 4

The Cold War and Beyond

The United States emerged from World War II in a position of global responsibility and power, but the struggle between the United States and the Soviet Union, which began near the end of the war, dominated U.S. foreign policy for more than 40 years. Since the war, many events have brought about numerous changes, both in the United States and in the world. The 1950s ushered in growth and prosperity. The civil rights movement resulted in many positive political and economic changes for middle-class blacks. The war in Vietnam still influences U.S. policymakers today. This section includes an issue on President Nixon, who played a major role in the political life of the country and whose legacy continues to be debated, and concludes with a review of the 1980s.

- Were the 1950s America's "Happy Days"?

- Did the Civil Rights Movement Improve Race Relations in the United States?

- Did the Antiwar Movement Prolong War in Vietnam?

- Will History Forgive Richard Nixon?

- Were the 1980s a Decade of Greed?

ISSUE 13

Were the 1950s America's "Happy Days"?

YES: Melvyn Dubofsky and Athan Theoharis, from *Imperial Democracy: The United States Since 1945,* 2d ed. (Prentice Hall, 1988)

NO: Douglas T. Miller and Marion Nowak, from *The Fifties: The Way We Really Were* (Doubleday, 1977)

ISSUE SUMMARY

YES: Professor of history and sociology Melvyn Dubofsky and professor of history Athan Theoharis argue that throughout the 1950s, the U.S. economy dominated much of the globe and created a period of unprecedented growth and prosperity for the percentage of the American population that made it into the middle class.

NO: Professor of history Douglas T. Miller and journalist Marion Nowak argue that the nostalgia craze, which re-creates the 1950s as a sweet, simple, golden age of harmony, masks the fact that the decade was an era of conformity in which Americans feared the bomb, communists, crime, and the loss of a national purpose.

Since the mid-1970s, Americans have used the 1950s as the standard by which all future successes and failures are measured. Cable television replays old shows espousing the family values that Americans most admire. But what were the 1950s really like? Was the period truly America's "Happy Days"?

Most people agree that America in the 1950s became, in the words of economist John Kenneth Gailbraith, *The Affluent Society* (Houghton Mifflin, 1958). Because the United States was physically untouched during World War II, it was instrumental in rebuilding the economies of the major noncommunist countries in Europe and Asia through the use of the Marshall Plan, Point Four Program, and other foreign aid programs.

At home the expected postwar recession and depression never occurred. Controlling inflation while stabilizing employment became the primary concerns of the economists. During the war American workers had built up over $140 billion in savings. Hungry for consumer goods they had been unable to acquire in the years from 1942 through the middle of 1945, Americans went on a massive consumer buying spree—one that has continued to the present day.

There were, however, some disturbing economic trends in the 1950s. Poverty was still widespread among many nonwhite groups and the displaced coal miners in Appalachia. Large corporations were buying up smaller ones, and individual farms were coming under the control of agribusiness. Income inequality also increased: In 1949 the top 1 percent of the population owned 19 percent of the nation's wealth; by 1960 they owned 33 percent.

If the rich got richer, so too did millions of other Americans. As Michael W. Schuger points out in his article "The 1950s: A Retrospective View," *Nebraska History* (Spring 1996), "Average family income, which was $3,000 in 1947, increased dramatically to $5,400 in 1959. The gross national product increased from $318 billion in 1950 to $440 billion in 1960. Between 1945 and 1960 the real earning power of the average wage earner increased by 22 percent."

In spite of this pleasant lifestyle, America became an anxiety-ridden society in the 1950s. World War II ended in the defeat of fascism, but a cold war developed against America's former ally the Soviet Union, which seemed bent on spreading communism not only throughout Eastern Europe but also across the entire world. The United States extended economic and military assistance to Greece and Turkey in 1947 and two years later formed the first peacetime alliance in history—the North Atlantic Treaty Organization—in order to contain the spread of communism. Although Western Europe stood fast, leaks sprang up in other parts of the world.

Crime, corruption, and communism seemed rampant in the 1950s. The news was spread by television. In 1946 there were only 7 television sets in the entire country; by 1960 they numbered over 50 million. Politicians filled the void on daytime television with an endless parade of hearings. Juvenile delinquency, it was argued, resulted from a moral breakdown in the home and community. Comic books and rock and roll music were held to be the culprits, and the city council of Jersey City solved the problem by banning rock and roll music at all school dances. Meanwhile, Senator Joseph McCarthy continued his search for communists in the government but overreached himself when he bullied high-level military officials in his senatorial investigation of the army in 1954. Eisenhower's powerful chief of staff, Sherman Adams, resigned amidst allegations that he received gifts from a contractor. The government panicked when the Russians launched the earth-orbiting *Sputnik I* satellite into space in October 1957. Could Ivan read better than Johnny? Had America lost its moral leadership and prestige in the eyes of the world, as two government reports indicated in 1960?

In the first of the following selections, Melvyn Dubofsky and Athan Theoharis argue that throughout the 1950s, the United States dominated much of the world's economy. At home the country experienced a period of unprecedented growth and prosperity for nearly two-thirds of the population, which made it into the middle class. In the second selection, Douglas T. Miller and Marion Novak assert that the decade was an era dominated by the need to conform and feelings of fear about the bomb, communists, crime, and the loss of a national purpose.

YES

**Melvyn Dubofsky and
Athan Theoharis**

IMPERIAL DEMOCRACY: THE UNITED STATES SINCE 1945

ECONOMIC GROWTH AND A CONSUMER SOCIETY

Throughout the 1950s the United States economy dominated much of the globe. Though less dependent on foreign trade for economic growth than most other industrial nations, the relatively small percentages of United States domestic production and capital that entered international trade had an enormous impact on the economies of smaller, less productive nations. Despite the fact that America's gross national product expanded relatively more slowly than other rapidly industrializing societies, the United States' productive base was so immense that between 1949 and 1960 absolute real GNP increased from $206 billion to over $500 billion, a rise of nearly 150 percent. Such economic power, especially in relation to weaker, less industrialized societies, allowed the United States to set the terms of trade. Thus American corporations during the 1950s purchased raw materials cheaply and sold manufactured goods dearly. As America grew wealthier, raw material-producing nations in Latin America, Africa, and Asia became relatively poorer....

The New Growth Industries

During the 1950s some of the old standbys of industrial America—railroads, coal mining, textiles, and shoe manufacturing—continued a decline that had begun in the 1920s. Railroad freight traffic fell steadily before the inroads of highway trucking, and passengers discarded long-distance trains in favor of more rapid air or cheaper bus transportation. By the end of the 1960s nearly the entire rail network in the Northeast, including the giant Penn-Central, had gone bankrupt. Coal found itself unable to compete with oil, natural gas, nuclear power, and water power; the nearly 600,000 miners employed at the end of World War II had fallen to about 100,000 by 1970. Cotton and woolen manufacture succumbed to synthetic fibers and domestic production to cheaper foreign manufactures. The shoe industry wrote an equally sorry chapter. Endicott-Johnson, the world's largest shoe manufacturer, had

From Melvyn Dubofsky and Athan Theoharis, *Imperial Democracy: The United States Since 1945*, 2d ed. (Prentice Hall, 1988). Copyright © 1988 by Prentice Hall, Inc., Upper Saddle River, NJ. Reprinted by permission. Notes omitted.

employed about 28,000 production workers in its New York Southern Tier factories in the late 1940s; by 1970 the production force had dipped below 4,000, the company began to dismantle its mills, and it even purchased shoes from Rumania for sale in its American retail outlets. Such instances of economic decline caused permanent depression in many New England towns and Appalachian coal patches. Again in the 1950s, as in the 1920s, economic sores festered on a generally healthy economic body.

If parts of New England and Appalachia declined economically, other regions of the nation prospered as never before. Wherever chemicals, business machines, electronics, and computers were manufactured the economy boomed, for these were the postwar growth industries par excellence. They were the new industries fit for survival in a "new society." Their economic growth based on technological and scientific advances, electronic-chemical firms stressed research and development programs (almost half of which were financed by the federal government), hired thousands of new graduates from the nation's universities, and served as the employers for a technocratic-scientific elite.

E. I. DuPont de Nemours & Co., Dow, and Monsanto prospered by manufacturing the synthetic goods that increasingly transformed the United States into a plastic society. Women wore their nylon stockings, people cooked on their Teflon pots and pans, men donned Dacron suits and Orlon shirts, and cars rolled on synthetic tires. Electronics, the child of wartime technological innovations, transistorized the postwar world. As tiny transistors replaced bulky tubes, teenagers walked everywhere holding the ubiquitous portable radio, and homebodies carried small TVs from room to room and house to patio. It was a society in which stereophonic sound replaced high fidelity phonographs only to be displaced in turn by quadraphonic sound. The electronics industry promised to turn every home into a private concert hall; indeed, some new houses were built with sound systems wired into every room. And electric eyes now opened and shut garage doors.

Meantime, automation and its associated business machines produced still greater profits and affected the economy more substantially than plastics and electronics. What Ford and General Electric symbolized in the 1920s, IBM and Xerox personified in post-World War II America. Ever since the industrial revolution, machinery had been replacing human labor in manufacturing. But where humans once operated the new machines, in the postwar era of automation such companies as IBM produced machines that controlled themselves as well as other machines. Automation, based on the same simple feedback principle that operated home thermostats, controlled steel strip mills, auto assembly lines, and entire petrochemical complexes. Computers, the next stage in the process of automation and first introduced commercially in 1950, had the ability to remember, sort materials, and make decisions; computers could also write poetry, compose music, play chess, and simulate strategy in a football game. So varied were the computer's uses that they were utilized by hotel chains, insurance companies, banks, airlines, and even universities (by the 1960s college students were identified by their IBM numbers) to simplify increasingly complex paper transactions. Where automation once threatened only blue-collar industrial workers, it now endangered the job security of millions of white-collar clerks. Even politicians, eager to predict beforehand the results of elections, worshipped at the shrine of the high-speed mainframe computer....

One reason for the success of the new growth industries was their close link to the Department of Defense, postwar America's largest single business contractor. The Pentagon supplied a lavish market for electronic and chemical manufacturers, as its deadly nuclear missiles with their elaborate guidance systems relied on synthetics, transistorized modules, and advanced computers. Even the more mundane hardware used by infantry, artillery, and nonnuclear aircraft depended heavily on electronic components and computerized guidance. NASA too provided an economic bonanza for the world of electronics. Without transistors, computers, and chemical fuels, there would have been no flight in space, no man on the moon. Between government contracts and consumer demand for household appliances (household use of electricity tripled in the 1950s), the growth industries prospered enormously.

American agriculture changed as well in the postwar era. Farming became a big business. Agricultural productivity rose more rapidly than demand for foodstuffs for most of the first two postwar decades, forcing millions of smaller farmers off the land; and large farmers prospered as a result of government subsidy programs and their own efficiency. Because production rose so rapidly, prices for agricultural goods declined, and profits could be made only by lowering unit costs of production through intensive application of fertilizers, use of costly new farm machinery, and introduction of sophisticated managerial techniques. Smaller farms simply lacked the resources and the capital to purchase fertilizer, acquire new machinery, and hire costly managerial experts. They also lacked enough land to make the use of expensive new machinery profitable or to join the soil bank, a program intended to promote soil conservation by paying farmers cash subsidies to let some of their land lie fallow. In other words, because most federal farm programs and subsidies were directly proportional to farm size and productivity, large farmers received proportionately more benefits than small farmers. The beneficiaries of federal largesse, the big farmers also possessed the land, capital, and knowledge necessary to grow food and fibers most efficiently. Consequently the percentage of owner-operated farms rose, and the size of the typical farm increased substantially. Cotton production shifted away from the South, where it remained profitable only on the extremely large plantation, to the immense corporate, irrigated farms of Texas, Arizona, and southern California. Farming in such prosperous agricultural states as California, Arizona, and Florida was justly labeled "agribusiness." In some cases industrial corporations, Tenneco among others, purchased large farms....

Affluence and Consumption

The stability of the American political and economic system as well as the absence of working-class discontent and militancy flowed from the successful creation of a mass consumer society. The car in every garage and chicken in every pot which Hoover and the Republicans had promised Americans in 1928 arrived in the 1950s. And now it also included beefsteaks, color television, stereophonic sound, and suburban split-levels.

Mass consumption depended on constantly rising real wage levels, a condition the United States economy sustained between 1945 and 1960. By 1956 the real income of the average American was more than 50 percent greater than it had been in 1929, and by 1960 it was 35 percent higher than it had been in the last year of World War II.

How typical Americans spent their increased earnings was determined as much by external factors as by intrinsic, real personal needs. Indeed, the larger the income an individual earned the more choice he or she had in its disposal. As growing numbers of citizens satisfied their need for food and shelter, the manufacturers of attractive but nonessential goods competed lustily for the consumer's dollar.

To sell the autos, refrigerators, dishwashers, stereo sets, and other appliances that rolled off production lines, manufacturers resorted to Madison Avenue and intensive advertising. Between 1946 and 1957 expenditures on advertising increased by almost 300 percent, rising to over $10 billion annually. Not only did the money devoted to advertising rise significantly, but the lords of Madison Avenue also developed more sophisticated selling tactics. Successful advertising was complicated when consumers had to select from among breakfast cereals and cars that differed neither in price nor utility and also had to be convinced to buy products never before manufactured. Employing all the tools of normal (and abnormal) psychology, advertisers alerted consumers to the psychic benefits of larger cars, sweeter-smelling underarms, striped toothpaste, and Marlboro—the man's cigarette. Brighter teeth, Madison Avenue implied, guaranteed every wallflower a desirable husband, and

the cigarillo won every man a buxom and accommodating female. Able to allocate money and talent to the one-minute television spot, advertisers bombarded viewers with irresistible commercials. Madison Avenue sales campaigns got such good results in the marketplace that in time many candidates for public office substituted the one-minute television spot for the half-hour platform speech. By the 1960s, Madison Avenue sold presidents as well as Pontiacs, congressmen as well as Cadillacs.

More than advertising was required to create the postwar consumer society. Regardless of the reality of rising wages, millions of citizens still lacked income sufficient to satisfy their demand for goods. A 1950 Census Bureau survey of over 7,000 families, for example, showed that 60 percent have earnings of $4,000 or less spent more than they earned. Even those workers whose incomes exceeded their current expenses seldom had a margin of savings adequate to sustain the cash purchase of such costly durables as autos and large home appliances. Only by borrowing money on the assumption that higher future earnings would render repayment painless could most citizens satisfy their desire for cars and dishwashers.

As advertising stimulated the demand for consumer goods, the nation's financial institutions financed their purchase. Between 1946 and 1957, private indebtedness increased by 360 percent—in contrast, total public debt rose by only 11 percent and the federal debt actually declined. More remarkable still was the rise in consumer installment indebtedness; the estimated annual installment credit outstanding soared from just over $4 billion in 1946 to over $34 billion in 1957. Automobile installment credit alone rose from under $1 billion to in excess of $15 billion. The propensity to buy now and pay later made the cash registers ring. Detroit produced over five million new cars in 1949 and in the peak year of 1955 sold nearly eight million autos, a record unsurpassed until the late 1960s.

For those individuals whose earnings rose annually, consumer credit and installment buying provided a relatively easy means to achieve rapid material affluence. But for those Americans whose income failed to rise, or rose only haltingly, installment buying became more an economic trap than an avenue to comfort. Unable to save sufficient cash to underwrite their purchases, these unfortunate consumers frequently failed to earn enough to pay the interest as well as the principal on their installment contract. In some cases, credit costs effectively increased the original purchase price by one third or more.

The consumption craze took many shapes in the 1950s. Such economists as Walt W. Rostow suggested that when men and women in America's "high mass consumption society" satisfied their desire for cars and appliances, they invested surplus income in babies. Whatever the precise cause no one could doubt that a population explosion took place from 1945 through the 1950s. Medical science and improved nutrition lengthened life spans, and the multiple (three or more) child household became commonplace. The public philosophy of the 1950s, as proclaimed by psychologists, TV comedians, preachers, and politicians, sanctified the home and woman's place in it. The ideal female married young and well, bore a large brood, and remained home to create the perfect environment for keeping the American family together. The sanctification of the family and the ide-

alization of the woman as mother and homemaker further promoted the growth of a consumer society. Larger families required bigger houses with more appliances to simplify "mom's" work and increased purchases to provide for the children. Before long many one-car families would become two-, three-, and in rare instances even four-car households.

If affluence enabled many Americans to enjoy unsurpassed material comforts, millions of citizens still struggled to make ends meet. If new recruits joined the "jet set" and flew to vacations in Rio, Biarritz, and Monaco, many workers, like the Bronx couple that *New York Times* reporter A. H. Raskin investigated, who lived half an hour by subway from Times Square, saw "less of Great White Way than the average farmer from Pumpkin Corners." John K. Galbraith lamented in *The Affluent Society* the ubiquity of public squalor amidst America's opulence and hinted at the persistence of poverty. Nonetheless, regardless of how unequally and inequitably the fruits of affluence were distributed, many of those Americans who did not share fully still felt themselves more comfortable in the 1950s than they had been in the 1930s and more fortunate than non-Americans. As Raskin's Bronx worker remarked: "We're a lot better off than we would be anywhere else in the world. We may not get everything we want, but at least we can choose what to do with our money. In other countries they don't even have a choice. No matter how bad things are, we're better off than they are."

The Triumph of the Suburbs
The emergence of an affluent mass consumer society saw the reassertion of a pattern of residential mobility and settlement that had been retarded by depres-

sion and war. In the 1950s, as also had happened in the 1920s, millions of citizens deserted the cities for the suburbs. Except in the South and Southwest where urban population continued to grow as a result of the annexation of adjacent land, the bulk of metropolitan population growth occurred in the suburbs. By 1960 in most northern metropolises, suburban residents outnumbered central city occupants, and as people fled the urban core, so, too, did businesses, trades, and professions. The "Miracle Mile" in Manhasset on Long Island's North Shore brought Fifth Avenue to the suburbs, just as similar suburban shopping centers elsewhere attracted downtown's most prestigious retailers to new locations with ample parking space and affluent consumers.

Suburban development stimulated a housing boom of unprecedented dimensions. As of 1960, one fourth of all the housing in the nation had been constructed in the previous decade, during which annual new-housing starts regularly exceeded the growth of new households. In the 1950s, for the first time in history, more Americans owned their homes, albeit usually with heavy mortgages, than rented dwelling space.

The reasons for this exodus to suburbia might have remained constant from the 1920s to the 1950s; after 1945, however, the opportunity to flee the city had expanded significantly. The desire for a private home with a lawn and garden in a suburban arcadia had long been an integral aspect of popular culture. The economic costs and occupational impracticality of suburban life, however, had put it beyond the reach of most Americans. All this changed in the postwar world, as federal credit and highway policies, technological innovations, and a mass consumer society reshaped metropolitan America.

In the postwar world, as automobile ownership became general, Americans had been liberated from dependence on mass public transit. The possession of a private car snapped the link that hitherto had connected the individual's home to his place of work via public transit. Through federal and state highway programs funded by fuel taxes, limited access highways were constructed that linked new suburbs and older central cities. The prospect of smooth, unimpeded traffic flow on safe, modern highways and in private cars led passengers to abandon subways, trolleys, and buses and to move from the city to the suburbs. Americans were now free to reside wherever their incomes allowed, and suburbia was also opening up to a wider range of incomes.

Federal policies enlarged the suburban housing market by providing generous mortgage loans to World War II veterans and by insuring the mortgages marketed by private lending agencies. The self-amortizing mortgage, whereby the homeowner paid back his original loan at a fixed monthly rate (comparable to rent) over a 20- to 30-year-term, became the common means to home ownership. Federal tax policy also stimulated suburban expansion, for citizens received a generous income tax deduction for the interest charges and real estate taxes paid on their homes. The availability of long-term credit and the inducement of tax advantages drew well-to-do middle-class Americans to suburbia. Working-class citizens needed a further inducement, the chance to purchase a home within their means. Here the firm of Arthur Levitt and Sons provided one solution, doing for the housing market what Ford had done for autos. Just as Ford offered a basic car in a single color at a low price, Levitt sold a standardized dwelling unit in one color —white—at a price within the reach of thousands of working-class Americans. His original "little boxes" constructed in the first Levittown in central Long Island soon had counterparts in New Jersey and Pennsylvania.

Suburbia in general and Levittown in particular occasioned a new image of American society, one consonant with the concept of a mass consumer public. Suburbia, in the words of social critic and planner Lewis Mumford, offered the prospect of

> a multitude of uniform, identifiable houses, lined up inflexibly, at uniform distances, on uniform roads, in a treeless communal waste, inhabited by people of the same class, the same income, the same age group, witnessing the same television performances, eating the same tasteless pre-fabricated foods, from the same freezers, conforming in every outward and inward respect to a common mold.

In the "little boxes made of ticky tacky," about which Pete Seeger sang, lived William F. Whyte's "organization men" who in their haste to adjust smoothly to their fellow junior executives became as undifferentiated as the houses in which they dwelled.

Critics of suburbia mounted a contradictory attack against the emerging character of national life. On the one hand, they charged suburban residents with uniformity, dullness, and unthinking accommodation to neighborhood mores. On the other hand, they indicted suburbanites, as did John Keats in *The Crack in the Picture Window*, for alcoholism, adultery (wife-swapping was said to be the fa-

vorite indoor suburban sport), and juvenile delinquency. Whatever the substance of the criticism, it seemed to miss the mark, for suburban growth proceeded unabated.

In fact most social criticism portrayed a fictional suburbia, not its reality. By the late 1950s American suburbs contained as many differences as similarities; there was no single ideal-type suburban community. Communities of upwardly mobile young executives who preferred accommodation to conflict, uniformity to individualism, such as William F. Whyte located in Chicago's environs, did exist. So, too, did communities of wealthy senior executives and rentiers, whose incomes and security enabled them to experiment with architecture and engage in eccentric behavior. At the other end of the suburban spectrum, one could find working-class developments whose residents had moved from the city but had scarcely altered their life style; they still voted Democratic, preferred baseball to ballet, and the company of relatives to that of neighbors. Even the allegedly undifferentiated, standardized world of Levittown contained, as the sociologist Herbert Gans discovered, a universe of strikingly individualized homes. Levittowners wasted no time in applying personal touches and preferences to the standardized homes and creating a society in which, according to Gans, they felt very much at home and comfortable....

MASS CULTURE AND ITS CRITICS

The affluence of the 1950s and 1960s laid the basis for what came to be known as "mass culture." Never before had so much music, drama, and literature been accessible to so many people as a result of fundamental changes in the presentation of entertainment and enlightenment. Television, the long-playing record, improved sound-reproduction equipment, and paperback books brought a plethora of cultural forms within reach of the great mass of Americans.

Once again, as had happened during the 1920s, Americans celebrated their exceptional prosperity. A new hedonism symbolized by oversized, overpowered cars crammed with options and adorned outside with two-tone color patterns, vinyl tops, and fins captivated consumers. Americans relished a culture of consume, enjoy, and dispose. We were, in the words of the historian David Potter, "people of plenty."

Not everyone, to be sure, joined in the American celebration. Some critics raised questions about the quality of life. Whereas once left-wing intellectuals had lamented the ubiquity of poverty and exploitation, they now bewailed a consumer society in which shoppers had become as indistinguishable from each other as the merchandise they purchased.

A few critical voices cried out in the wilderness. The industrial sociologist William F. Whyte portrayed in scholarly detail the culture of the prototypical success story of the 1950s, the rising young corporate executive, the hero of best-selling novelist Sloan Wilson's *The Man in the Gray Flannel Suit*. Whyte showed these young executives as insecure, status-driven people who lived transitorily in suburban developments housing only their own kind, and as "organization men" who molded their personalities to suit the corporate image. The radical and idiosyncratic scholar C. Wright Mills discerned a bleak future in his 1951 book, *White Collar*. He described a society of men and women who worked without autonomy or direction, who strived only for status, and who lived as dependent beings, not free citizens. In *White Collar*, one glimpsed an American mass potentially susceptible to producing fascism, as their Italian and German likes had in the 1920s and 1930s.

David Riesman, the premier critic of mass society, early on diagnosed the new American disease in *The Lonely Crowd* (1950). Americans once, he wrote, had been an inner-directed people, men and women who could distinguish right from wrong, who could chart their own directions and goals in life. Now, Americans had become an other-directed people, who lacked their own internal moral compasses. The great mass of postwar Americans lost themselves in a "lonely crowd" to which they looked for values and personal decisions. The independent democratic citizen had become a cypher in the clutches on an anonymous mass society.

Such tendencies toward mass society caused a minority of Americans to worry that the nation had lost its sense of purpose amidst a flood of consumer goods. They wondered if mass society could rise above the level of a car dealer's showroom.

But the great mass of Americans shared no such worries. Those who could consumed as never before, and those who could not aspired to do the same....

The Culture of Consensus

The hard edges of the Cold War and the tensions of McCarthyism had been softened in the United Sates of the late 1950s by the smiles, platitudes, and tranquility of the Eisenhower era. It was a time to consume, to achieve, and to celebrate.

Intellectuals and writers who for much of the twentieth century had been at war with a materialistic, bourgeois America now also joined the celebration. *Partisan Review*, a literary intellectual journal which had served at the end of the 1930s as a voice for non-Stalinist Marxists, in the 1950s sponsored a symposium entitled "Our Country and Our Culture." In it one contributor declared, "For the first time in the history of the modern intellectual, America is not to be conceived of as a priori the vulgarest and stupidest nation of the world."

Indeed, the America of the 1950s was a country in which private foundations generously subsidized free-lance intellectuals and many of those same intellectuals gladly served such government agencies as the Central Intelligence Agency through the Congress for Cultural Freedom. Cultural anticommunism united intellectuals, trade unionists, and such socialists as Norman Thomas in a common front with corporate executives and federal officials.

What had happened to American intellectuals and social critics was aptly caught in the substance and title of *Commentary* editor Norman Podhoretz's 1968 autobiography. The son of Jewish-immigrant parents, himself born and bred in the Brownsville, Brooklyn, ghetto, Podhoretz had made his way to Columbia University and from there to the apex of the New York literary intellectual universe. His journey through life was surely, as he titled it, a case of *Making It* in America.

Formal academic works reflected a similar influence. Where once history books stressed have-nots versus haves, farmers versus bankers, section versus section, and city versus country, in the 1950s they spoke of consensus and shared values. David Potter perceived abundance as the single most influential factor in the American experience, and he entitled his interpretive history of America *People of Plenty*. In 1956 Richard Hofstadter won the Pulitzer Prize for a study, *The Age of Reform*, which emphasized the relative absence of class conflict, the priority of status over class, and the basic American commitment to private property, the profit motive, and capitalist institutions.

Economists, too, saw social harmony and material abundance as the new reality. In their view, the Keynesian economic revolution had given them the tools to fine tune the economy in order to maintain full employment and price stability. Students no longer had to look to classical economics or its Marxist repudiation for solutions to contemporary problems.

None celebrated America's success more lustily than political scientists and sociologists. Both academic groups saw democracy, especially in America, as a completed, successful experiment. Full democratic rights were in place, all adults had basic citizenship, and all were formally legal before the law. No single, unified group ruled or dominated society to the detriment of others. Instead, a variety of equally balanced interest groups competed with each other for public favors and influence with the state, which acted as an honest broker among them. This system came to be known as pluralism to distinguish it from authoritarianism and totalitarianism.

According to the political sociologists, pluralism was not a belief system comparable to socialism, communism, or fascism. It was rather a simple practice of balancing harmoniously competing claims and rights in an affluent, democratic society, which had, as the sociologist Seymour Martin Lipset claimed in his book *Political Man*, abolished all class politics based on irreconcilable "isms." Indeed, as Daniel Bell proclaimed in a collection of essays published in 1960, the United States had seen *The End of Ideology*. One essay in the collection analyzed trade unionism as "The Capitalism of the Proletariat," and another, "Crime as an American Way of Life," dissected criminal activities as an ethnic version of "making it." The passions which had generated mass socialist parties, the Bolshevik Revolution, fascism in Italy, and nazism in Germany, Bell proclaimed as dead. The new generation, he wrote, "finds itself... within a framework of political society that has rejected... the old apocalyptic and chiliastic visions."

John F. Kennedy's election as president symbolized the marriage of "new generation" intellectuals to the power of the American state. The new president invited Robert Frost to read a poem at the inauguration. The historian Arthur Schlesinger, Jr., served as White House scholar-in-residence; the economic historian Walt W. Rostow acted as a foreign-policy planner; the economist John Kenneth Galbraith went to India as ambassador; and the historians Samuel Eliot Morison and Henry Steele Commager sang the praises of "Camelot" on the Potomac.

Not that voices of dissent and criticism were silent in the 1950s. Not at all. The *New Republic* and *Nation* magazines maintained their long traditions of left-liberal social and political commentary. In the 1950s a group of anti-Stalinist Social Democrats founded *Dissent*, a journal which tried to keep alive in America the perspectives associated with Western European labor and social democratic parties. For the more orthodox on the left, there was always *Monthly Review*, in which Paul Baran and Paul Sweezy subjected contemporary American and world developments to the scrutiny of Marxist economics and theory. But in the 1950s and early 1960s their audiences were relatively small and their sometimes strident criticism of affluent America no more than tiny voices in the wilderness.

It was this reality that led C. Wright Mills to cry out as early as 1951 that "political expression is banalized, political theory is barren administrative detail, history is made behind men's backs."

In reality, the affluent mass culture of the 1950s that bred a quiet generation of organization men lost in the void of a "lonely crowd" was more ephemeral than it first appeared. Indeed it was shot through with unseen cracks and flaws. John Kenneth Galbraith may have bemoaned the widespread public squalor amidst the private affluence; for more than 30 million Americans even affluence was beyond reach. Rural life decayed apace, urban ghettos spread and festered, nonwhite Americans remained at best second-class citizens and at worst the hapless victims of social and economic discrimination, and most wage workers, regardless of skin color, endured as objects of external authority. Wealth and poverty, the ideal of equality versus the reality of inequality, and authority against freedom remained inextricably at war in affluent America. During the 1960s, the social tinder represented by poverty and racialism ignited in the form of urban race riots and the impassioned militancy of the New Left and the radical feminist movements.

Before then, however, the presidency of Dwight David Eisenhower made affluence and harmony appear to be the rule. Unprecedented economic growth, rising real incomes, and the new mass culture promoted by television laid the foundation for the relative quiescence of the Eisenhower era. Eisenhower's ability to dampen old political feuds, to legitimate the New Deal "revolution" as he castigated overgrown government and "creeping socialism," his success at softening the harsher aspects of the Cold War, and his taming of the worst excesses of McCarthyism reinforced the aura of complacency associated with the 1950s. Ike's mid-American, small-town origins, his wide, winning grin, and his placidity assured most Americans that all was well at home and abroad.

NO

**Douglas T. Miller and
Marion Nowak**

THE FIFTIES: THE WAY WE REALLY WERE

Hula hoops, bunny hops, 3-D movies. Davy Crockett coonskins, chloro-
phyll toothpaste, 22 collegians stuffed into a phone booth. Edsels and tail-
finned Cadillacs. Greasy duck's-ass hairdos, leather jackets, souped-up hot
rods, dragging, cruising, mooning. Like crazy, man, dig? Kefauver hearings,
Howdy Doody, Kukla, Fran and Ollie, Bridey Murphy, Charles Van Doren,
Francis Gary Powers. *The Catcher in the Rye, The Power of Positive Thinking;
Howl, On the Road.* Patti Page, Pat Boone, Vic Damone; Little Richard, Chuck
Berry, Elvis Presley; The Platters, The Clovers, The Drifters; Bill Haley and the
Comets, Danny and the Juniors. Mantle, Mays, Marciano. Pink shirts, gray
flannels, white bucks. I LIKE IKE.

THE FABULOUS FIFTIES!—or so 1970s nostalgia would lead one to believe. A 1972 issue of *Newsweek*, complete with Marilyn Monroe cover, explored this phenomenon under the heading "Yearning for the Fifties: The
Good Old Days." "It was a simple decade," *Newsweek* writers recalled, "when
hip was hep, good was boss." That same year *Life* magazine reminisced about
"The Nifty Fifties"—"it's been barely a dozen years since the '50s ended and
yet here we are again, awash in the trappings of that sunnier time."

This wistful view of the fifties first became evident about 1971 and 1972. It
quickly exploded into a national craze that still pervades the popular images
of the mid-century era. Numerous examples of fifties nostalgia exist in the
seventies. It was the theme of movies like *American Graffiti, The Last Picture
Show, Let the Good Times Roll,* and *The Way We Were.* Television shows "Happy
Days" and "Laverne and Shirley" recreated an idyllic fifties world of youth
and innocence. The TV show "M*A*S*H" even managed to make people a
little homesick for the Korean War. By February 1976, the fifties rock-and-
roll parody *Grease* began its fifth season. It had become Broadway's longest
running show by far, and this despite the fact that it never had name stars,
hit songs, or a high budget.

Popular music in this post-Beatles period also saw a major revival of
fifties rock. By the mid-seventies Elvis Presley, Chuck Berry, Rick Nelson,
Fats Domino, Little Richard, and Bill Haley again were drawing mass audi-

ences. Record companies were reissuing fifties hits on special golden-oldies LPs, and many radio stations were devoting several hours daily to an oldies format. The fifties musical revival spawned contemporary groups such as Sha-Na-Na, Flash Cadillac and the Continental Kids, and Vince Vance and the Valiants. These groups not only sang the oldies, they also revived the greaser look. Vince Vance even got himself arrested while attempting to steal an Edsel hubcap. Nightclubs too have cashed in on nostalgia. Across the country, clubs have featured old music and special trivia nights with questions such as "Who played James Dean's girlfriend in *Rebel Without a Cause*?"

Another sign of the fifties fad has been in clothing. Leather motorcycle jackets, picture sweaters, pedal pushers, pleated skirts, and strapless evening dresses have been hot items in the last few years. In 1973, Monique, the New York *Daily News* fashion reporter, announced: "the feeling of the fifties that will rule a large part of the fashion next fall is already apparent." A year earlier Cyrinda Foxe, a Marilyn Monroe look-alike modeling a dress from a fifties collection, claimed that "people just go crazy when I walk down the street! The fifties were so much sexier."

What does all this nostalgia mean? Periods of intense longing for an earlier era indicate that people are discontented with the present. Excessive, sentimental nostalgia generally occurs during times of perceived crisis. Such has been the case in the seventies. The rise of the fifties enthusiasm coincided with widespread disillusionment and a growing conservatism. For many people the 1950s came to symbolize a golden age of innocence and simplicity, an era supposedly unruffled by riots, racial violence,

Vietnam, Watergate, assassinations. People numbed by the traumas of the sixties and seventies, desiring to forget the horrors of presidential crime, soaring prices, Cambodian bombings, Kent State, My Lai, the Manson case, the Chicago Convention, the murder of two Kennedy's, Martin Luther King, and Malcolm X, yearned for a quieter time. As a Cleveland oldies-but-goodies disc jockey put it, "my audience wants to forget its problems and return to—or at least recall—those happy high-school times—the prom, no wars, no riots, no protests, the convertibles and the drive-in." Another DJ even saw the fifties music revival as a way to bridge the generation gap. "I get the feeling that through this music some of the kids are finding a back-door way of getting together with their parents." Nostalgia, then, is a pleasant distraction. One imagines the past, and so overlooks the present.

Additionally, since we live in a society that prizes youth over age, there is a natural tendency for nostalgia on the part of the aging generation. For those who grew up in the fifties, the happy images of that decade are a positive reassurance —a reclaiming of fading youth. Then too in the mid-seventies the general realization that energy, prosperity, and growth are not limitless undoubtedly makes Americans a more retrospective, nostalgic people. We may die tomorrow, but we wish to remember it as a good world while it lasted.

But whatever the reasons for the fifties revival, the image of that decade conveyed by current nostalgia is badly distorted. The artifacts of the fifties are sill with us. The facts are less clear. Looking back on that period, people today see it as a time of fun and innocence, a soda-shop world with youth as its only participants. They recall Bo Diddley and Buddy Holly, but ignore Joe McCarthy and John Foster Dulles. Nostalgia is highly selective. No one is staging a House Un-American Activities Committee revival, or longing for the good old days of nuclear brinksmanship and the deadly H-bomb tests.

Certainly, there was some fun in the fifties—the Coasters' songs, Lenny Bruce's nightclub routines, Sid Caesar's TV antics. But in retrospect it was essentially a humorless decade, one in which comic Mort Sahl could raise national ire by cracking a single J. Edgar Hoover joke. Much of what strikes observers as quaint now—Nixon's Checkers speech, Norman Vincent Peale's homilies, or tail-finned Cadillacs—were grotesque realities at the time. It was more an era of fear than fun. The bomb, communists, spies, and Sputnik all scared Americans. And fear bred repression both of the blatant McCarthyite type and the more subtle, pervasive, and personal daily pressures to conform.

Astute social critics have found the fifties anything but the good old days. To the late Paul Goodman it was an "extraordinarily senseless and unnatural" time. American society, in his words, was "a Closed Room with a Rat Race as the center of fascination, powerfully energized by fear of being outcasts." To Michael Harrington the decade "was a moral disaster, an amusing waste of life." Norman Mailer bluntly described the fifties as "one of the worst decades in the history of man." ...

"Meet the Typical American," announced a 1954 *Reader's Digest* article. "The average American male stands five feet nine inches tall, weighs 158 pounds, prefers brunettes, baseball, beefsteak and French fried potatoes, and thinks the abil-

ity to run a home smoothly and efficiently is the most important quality in a wife." The average American woman, the article continued, "is five feet four, weighs 132, can't stand an unshaven face." This typical female preferred marriage to a career. As the average weights of men and women might suggest, many Americans were on the heavy side. The prevalent styles encouraged this. Women in pleated skirts falling a few inches below the knees were expected to be shapely in a plump sort of way. Bikinis were largely limited to the girlie magazines. But big breasts, symbols of motherhood, were definitely in vogue. For men, excess flab was easily concealed beneath baggy pleated pants, suits and shirts that did not follow body lines, boxer shorts and bathing trunks, Bermudas with knee-length socks. So in this decade of suburban prosperity, many people carried paunches as if they were symbols of success.

The goals of these "average" Americans were not radical. What George Meany said of organized labor in the mid-fifties would have applied to most groups: "We do not seek to recast American society. We do seek an ever-rising standard of living by which we mean not only more money but more leisure and a richer cultural life."

Leisure and culture—Americans took to these as never before. About one sixth of all personal income was spent on leisure pursuits. In record force people painted-by-numbers, drank, gardened, watched TV, traveled, listened to music, hunted and fished, read *Reader's Digest* condensed books. Doing-it-oneself became a national fad. Everything from home permanents to boat building had millions of amateur practitioners. In 1954 it was reported that 70 per cent of all wallpaper bought was hung by novices, while some 11 million weekend carpenters drilled, sawed, and sanded some 180 square miles of plywood with their 25 million power tools. In California, the Pan Pacific Do-It-Yourself Show even exhibited separate pieces of fur that could be assembled into a do-it-yourself mink coat. For persons of a more sedentary nature, American industry produced quantities of amusing junk—cigarette lighters that played "Smoke Gets in Your Eyes," whisky-flavored toothpaste, mink-trimmed clothespins, Venus toothpicks, Jayne Mansfield hot-water bottles.

Americans could do just about anything. Or so at least they were told in hundreds of books purportedly revealing the secrets of how to make love, how to tap one's secret source of strength, how to mix a good martini, how to get thin or fat, how to be popular, powerful, famous, rich.

But it was *Culture* that American boosters boasted of most. "Once in a great while a society explodes in a flood of new ideas, new tastes, new standards," claimed Fenton Turck in a 1952 *Reader's Digest* article. "A fresh and exciting age emerges, alive with expanding opportunities. Today's Americans are living in one of these extraordinary periods." Turck talked of a great flowering of culture. As evidence of this he cited such things as increased attendance at concerts, opera, and theater. Art museums, opera companies, and symphony orchestras all multiplied in the fifties, as did the sale of quality paperbacks and classical records.

Culture had status appeal and an increased portion of the population had both the leisure and money to dabble in it. Perhaps the apogee of the era's culture boom was reached in April 1960, when the Parke-Bernet Galleries held a huge art auction to benefit the Museum of Modern Art. The New York City auction room was linked via closed-circuit TV to similar rooms in Chicago, Dallas, and Los Angeles. The auction was a great success; an Utrillo went to a Dallas millionaire for $20,000, A Cézanne to a New York collector for $200,000. Bidding on a Hans Hartung had reached the $10,000 level before anyone noticed it was hung upside down. "We're ready for our renaissance," claimed poet Louis Untermeyer at mid-decade. "Westward the course of culture!"

In addition to celebrating American culture and living standards, many people saw the United States in the middle of the twentieth century as having a peculiar and providential mission. "We are living in one of the great watershed periods of history," asserted Democratic presidential nominee Adlai Stevenson in the 1952 campaign. This era "may well fix the pattern of civilization for many generations to come. God has set for us an awesome mission: nothing less than the leadership of the free world." The editors of *Fortune* felt the same. "There come times in the history of every people," they wrote, "when destiny knocks on their door with an iron insistence." In American history, as they read it, destiny had so knocked three times: "Once when we faced the seemingly impossible odds of British power to gain our independence: once at Fort Sumter, when we faced the bloody task of preserving our union: and it is knocking today [1951].... Our outlook is the same as it was at the time of the Revolution, and again at the time of the Civil War: the shape of things to come depends on us: our moral decision, our wisdom, our vision, and our will."

That America would succeed in fulfilling its God-given mission few doubted. The future was bright. "Our spiritual road map," predicted philosopher Morris Ernst, "will carry the direction pointers: 1976—This Way—Energy, Leisure, Full Rich Life."

Yet despite the varied and frequent versions of "America the Beautiful," doubts and anxieties were also present. The fifties was a time of tensions and insecurities. Early in the decade the usually optimistic Norman Vincent Peale spoke of an "epidemic of fear and worry" in the United States. "All doctors," he declared, "are having cases of illness which are brought on directly by fear, and aggravated by worry and a feeling of insecurity." For some Americans the greatest anxieties stemmed from the cold war. "Our nation," warned a late-fifties civil defense pamphlet, "is in a grim struggle for national survival and the preservation of freedom in the world." And of course there was the constant threat of nuclear destruction which left people, in the words of one mid-fifties observer, "in a state of suspension, waiting to see whether the Bomb is going to fall or not."

For other people, the speed of social and economic change generated uncertainties and cast doubts on old certitudes. The new prosperity and changing lifestyles, while materially benefiting many, caused insecurities. Traditional ethnic neighborhoods were breaking down as newly prosperous people fled to suburbia. Yet this very mobility created rootlessness. Many people simply discovered that abundance was not enough. In any case Americans became quite self-critical and made best sellers of books telling them of their shortcomings.

In this light, some of the most important social and cultural phenomena of the fifties are more understandable. The overwhelming emphasis on the family gave people a sense of place and personal identity. The massive return to religion provided individuals with a sense of security; it reassured them that the traditional moral verities were still valid. Sustained and successful attacks against progressive education were another manifestation of the search for traditional, absolute values. So too was the intellectual emphasis on consensus. Historians, sociologist, and other social scientists played down conflict and instead stressed the harmonious and enduring nature of American democratic values. Blacks and other nonwhites, who did not share equally in America's bounty, were assured by the white media that they never had it so good. Generally speaking, neither racial nor economic classes were recognized. Critics of this celebrated consensus, whether from right or left, tended to be treated as psychological deviants suffering from such cliché ills as status anxiety or authoritarian personality. Nonconformists and rebels were subject to harsh conformist pressures. No wonder then that bipartisan banality flourished. Both major political parties clung tenaciously to the same center, maintaining the status quo while mouthing provincial Protestant platitudes and preparing for Armageddon....

If one were attempting a precise periodization, the fifties could well be divided into three parts: 1948–53, 1954–57, 1958–60. These three periods might then be labeled "The Age of Fear," "The Era of Conservative Consensus," and "The Time of National Reassessment."

The Age of Fear: The post-World War II era really begins around 1948. By then the nation had essentially adjusted to a peacetime economy; depression had not recurred and people were coming to believe in the possibility of perpetual prosperity. At the same time, the cold war had become a debilitating reality. A chronology of terror began unfolding. In 1948 a communist coup was successful in Czechoslovakia and the Soviets blockaded western access to Berlin. That same year in the United States, talk of treason and communist infiltration became commonplace, especially after a former New Deal State Department official, Alger Hiss, was accused by Whittaker Chambers of having passed secrets to the Russians. The following year, 1949, the Soviets exploded their first atomic bomb and Mao Tse-tung's communist forces were victorious in China. Early in 1950 President Harry S. Truman announced plans to begin development of a hydrogen bomb (it was perfected by 1952); Senator Joseph McCarthy added the loudest voice to the already sizable outcry of anticommunist witch hunters. Nineteen fifty also saw the conviction of Alger Hiss for perjury, the arrest and trial of Ethel and Julius Rosenberg as atomic spies (they were executed in 1953), the outbreak of the Korean War, and Senator Estes Kefauver's televised criminal investigations that dramatically revealed the extent and power of organized crime.

Such events shocked and frightened people, and the last years of Truman's presidency proved a trying time—a period of suspicions, accusations, loyalty oaths, loathings, extreme chauvinistic Americanism. Republicans, attempting to regain power, were not averse to charging the Democrats with being "soft on communism," though in reality both parties were excessively anticommunist. Tensions raised by Korean fighting, supposed communist infiltration, spy trials, loyalty investigations, inflation, crime, and the bomb reached near hysteric proportions in the early fifties. Dissent was suppressed, conformity demanded. With the exception of a few legitimate espionage cases, none of which really endangered national security, *most victims of the anti-red mania were guilty of little more than holding unpopular opinions.* Not only the national government, but thousands of local communities as well felt obliged to search out and destroy suspected subversive views. Teachers, government workers, entertainers, and many others were dismissed. Textbooks were censored and libraries closed.

Yet such fear and repression, plus prosperity, also made Americans seem united under a national faith. Seeing the world in dualistic terms of good versus evil, people celebrated the United States as the bastion of freedom, democracy, and "people's capitalism." Intellectuals defended America and searched for enduring consensual values of the country's past and present. A noncritical conservative consensus emerged offering hope and reassurance during this age of fear. The widespread emphasis on religion and the family gave further solace. The combined anxiety and hope of this period is well illustrated in the title of a 1950 song— "Jesus Is God's Atomic Bomb."

The Era of Conservative Consensus: The conservative consensus and celebration of America continued into the mid-fifties, and fortunately for national nerves the fears and anxieties began to ebb. Several factors contributed to this: the death of Stalin and the end of the Korean War in 1953; the downfall of Senator McCarthy in 1954; The Geneva summit conference with the Soviets in 1955; the lack of new spy sensations after 1950; continued prosperity; and, above all, the election of Eisenhower to the presidency.

When Ike was first elected in 1952, one Pennsylvania housewife remarked: "It's like America has come home." And so it seemed to millions. While politics traditionally means conflict, Ike appeared to people as above politics. He was the heroic general come to unite the nation in peace and prosperity as he had defended it earlier in war. Democratic presidents Roosevelt and Truman had for 20 years emphasized a politics of class strife and crisis. With Eisenhower came the appearance at least of a politics of unity and classlessness. His boyish grin and downhome homely face, his simple sincere platitudes about home, mother, and heaven, his circumlocutions when difficult issues came up, all these things endeared him to millions and made him a symbol, not of party, but of national consensus. Americans, tired of constant crises and the hysteria of the age of fear, found in Ike a symbol of hope and confidence.

And so, by the mid-fifties there came a brief happy moment—the quintessential fifties—prosperous, stable, bland, religious, moral, patriotic, conservative, domestic, buttoned-down. Huge tail-finned cars sold in record numbers, *The Power of Positive Thinking* and *The Man in the Gray Flannel Suit* sat atop the best-seller lists, and the "Spirit of Geneva" seemed to diffuse itself over the globe. Domestically no problem appeared more pressing than the specter of juvenile delinquency, though in reality young people overwhelmingly accepted the values of their elders and dedicated themselves to the bourgeois goals of security, sociabil-

ity, domesticity. They went steady, married young, had lots of children, lived the conforming life of "togetherness."

Crises still existed. Poverty, racism, sexism, and militarism all threatened America. But Eisenhower and most citizens tried to ignore such ills. The sting seemed gone from the times, and a cheerful nation overwhelmingly re-elected Eisenhower in 1956. Just before that election, David Riesman and Stewart Alsop visited a new suburb south of Chicago to poll voters. They found people vague about politics but liking Ike. "Most of the people we spoke to were young housewives, often interrupted in their midday television program...." They were educated but complacent. "As one looked over that flat Illinois prairie at all the signs of prosperity," generalized Riesman, "it was not hard to see why these people were so bland politically and responded to the same qualities in Ike.... These people were not self-made men who remembered their struggles against hardship but, rather, a society-made generation who could not believe society would let them down...." These were the model fifties figures —suburbanized, bureaucratized, smug, secure.

The Time of National Reassessment: Eisenhower's second term quickly revealed how precarious the mid-fifties plateau of repose actually was. Even before that new term began, America's foreign relations suffered major setbacks. Just prior to the 1956 elections, fighting broke out in Egypt and Hungary. In late October, Anglo-French-Israeli forces invaded the Suez region of Egypt in an attempt to regain the canal which Egyptian leader Gamal Abdel Nasser earlier had nationalized. Third World anticolonial resentment and threatened Soviet intervention convinced the Eisenhower administration that the invasion must be ended. America pressured Britain, France, and Israel to withdraw. They did so. However, these nations' humiliation embittered them toward the United States. Western unity seemed seriously weakened. During these same tense days of late October and early November 1956, the Soviet Union, taking advantage of the dissent among the Western powers, harshly crushed an anticommunist uprising in Hungary that had broken out only a week before the Suez war. For a few weeks the world hovered on the brink of nuclear war. And while both crises were over at about the same time as Eisenhower's November re-election, they greatly intensified international tensions. Suez and Hungary clearly revealed the 1955 Geneva summit to be only a temporary thaw in the cold war.

Less than a year later, the domestic tranquillity of the mid-fifties was also disrupted. In September 1957, American racism was shockingly unveiled when the school-integration issue reached crisis proportions in Little Rock. Eisenhower, who was not sympathetic to the civil rights movement, reluctantly was forced to send troops into that city to insure compliance with the Supreme Court's 1954 desegregation decision. But the ugly scenes in front of Central High School laid bare for Americans and the world this nation's deep-seated racial tensions.

Then a month later in October 1957, the Soviets launched Sputnik I, the world's first earth-orbiting satellite. Americans were profoundly shocked. National self-confidence seemed shattered in the light of this demonstrated Soviet superiority in space science. Calls for an expanded arms race accelerated. American afflu-

ence, once the nation's pride, now was blamed for enfeebling the populace. Progressive education, which had been on the defensive throughout the decade, was quickly demolished as people demanded intellectual discipline with more emphasis on science, mathematics, and language.

Sputnik clearly struck the major blow against mid-fifties tranquillity. But other developments in the last three years of Eisenhower's presidency added to American doubts and increased the national penchant for soul-searching. At about the same time as the Soviet space successes, the American economy began to slump. By the spring of 1958, a major recession existed; unemployment had climbed to 7.7 per cent of the total labor force, the highest rate since 1941. That same year congressional committees disclosed conflict-of-interest violations by presidential appointees and charges of influence-peddling by Vice-President Nixon's former campaign manager. Even Ike's closest, most trusted and influential adviser, Sherman Adams, was dismissed for taking bribes. Adams, it was revealed, had accepted expensive gifts from Bernard Goldfine, a wealthy businessman with cases pending before the government. On tour in Latin America that year, Nixon was spat upon, jeered, and stoned. A year later, Charles Van Doren, a handsome young instructor from Columbia University, scion of an eminent literary family, revealed to investigators that the brilliance he had displayed in winning vast sums on a TV quiz show was fake. The show had been rigged. At about the same time famed disc jockey Alan Freed, the self-appointed father of rock and roll, became involved in a payola scandal. Among other revelations were exposés of widespread cheating in schools and of a group of New York cops working for a burglary ring.

By May 1960, when the Soviets announced that Francis Gary Powers had been shot down in a U-2 spy plane over Russian territory, the American propensity for critical self-evaluation had become obsessive. A presidential Commission on National Goals, which Eisenhower had established after Sputnik, produced a ponderous report, *Goals for Americans.* The Rockefeller Brothers Fund issued their own version, *Prospect for America. Life, Look,* the New York *Times* and other mass-circulation publications featured articles and whole issues discussing national purpose and the future role of America. Leading social and political writers began turning out books with titles like *American the Vincible* and *What Ivan Knows and Johnny Doesn't.*

Much of the national debate focused on dissatisfaction with the quality of American life. Conformity and materialism, critics argued, had dulled Americans into a complacent averageness. "Our goal has become a life of amiable sloth," complained *Time* editor Thomas Griffith in 1959. "We are in danger of becoming a vibrating and mediocre people." "Looking at some of the institutions we nourish and defend," Robert Heilbroner noted, early in 1960, "it would not be difficult to maintain that our society is an immense stamping press for the careless production of underdeveloped and malformed human beings, and that, whatever it may claim to be, it is not a society fundamentally concerned with moral issues, with serious purposes, or with human dignity." Such laments swelled into a national chorus of self-reproach as Americans once more showed themselves to be an anxious, self-conscious people.

Yet there remained an underlying note of hope in this intramural abuse. Most doubters viewed their disparagements as enterprises of self-correction. "America the Beautiful" would soar once more if only we could speed up economic growth, put a man on the moon, develop a more flexible military establishment, rekindle a spirit of national self-sacrifice, and so on and so on. John F. Kennedy's 1960 campaign epitomized the schizophrenic national mood of doubt and hope. In this, many others concurred. Walter Lippmann stated in July 1960, "We're at the end of something that is petering out and aging and about finished." He was not unhappy about this; rather he sensed that a new and better day was coming. Arthur Schlesinger, Jr., already active with Kennedy people, also lamented the late fifties but foretold "a new epoch" of "vitality," "identity," and "new values... straining for expression and for release."

The fifties, then, is not a neat single unit. The decade began with terror and affluence uniting a people under a national faith. The mid-fifties, desperately tired of crises, continued that faith in a more casual and relaxed manner. Yet by 1960, that mask of faith was drawn aside to reveal a changing face: regretful, doubting, yet also looking in hope to a rebirth.

POSTSCRIPT

Were the 1950s America's "Happy Days"?

The period after World War II was one of both affluence and anxiety for most Americans. Dubofsky and Theoharis emphasize the affluent side. The American economy not only brought prosperity to its increasing white-collar and stable blue-collar workers at home; it also revived the economies of the Western European nations and noncommunist Asian countries. The increased wealth of the American worker in the 1950s brought about a consumption craze. Installment buying for automobiles and appliances and single-family homes purchased with long-term mortgages, financed in many cases at low interest rates by the government on behalf of the veterans, were the order of the day.

There were cracks in the economy, to be sure. Dubofsky and Theoharis point out that most nonwhites, especially blacks and Hispanics, did not share in the general prosperity. Some of "the old standbys of industrial America—railroads, coal mining, textiles, and shoe manufacturing—continued a decline that had begun in the 1920s." Labor union membership in general dropped, and individual farms fell into the hands of agribusinesses. Finally, many poor people, especially those with incomes under $4,000 per year, were spending more than they earned.

Miller and Nowak focus on the negative side mentioned in passing by Dubofsky and Theoharis. They point out that in a society "that prizes youth over age," there is a tendency on the part of the older generation to re-create through television, movies, and books a nostalgic past that never really existed. Americans, say Miller and Nowak, lost their motives and became anxious as they moved to their "little boxes" in the suburbs. They became overweight, were obsessed with their status, and were afraid of communists who might overthrow the American government.

Both readings can be criticized for giving an unbalanced assessment of the 1950s. Dubofsky mentions the cracks in the affluent society. Blacks would push their demands for school desegregation, which the Supreme Court ordered in the *Brown v. Board of Education of Topeka, Kansas* decisions of 1954 and 1955, and demonstrate successfully for political and legal equality in the 1960s.

There is an enormous bibliography on the 1950s. A recent sympathetic overview is Michael W. Schuyler, "The 1950s: A Retrospective View," *Nebraska History* (Spring 1996), which summarizes the major social and economic currents of the 1950s. Also supportive of the absence of extremes is Stephen J. Whitfield's "The 1950s: The Era of No Hard Feelings," *South Atlantic Quarterly* (Summer 1975). Alan Ehrenhalt's "Learning from the Fifties," *Wilson*

Quarterly (Summer 1995) is a brilliant case study of Chicago, Illinois, that points out the high price some people in the 1950s paid to enjoy the good life. The starting point for the critical cultural studies of television, film, and literature is Guile McGregor, "Domestic Blitz: A Revisionist History of the Fifties," *American Studies* (Spring 1993).

There are a number of excellent monographs on the 1950s. Eric F. Goldman, *The Crucial Decade and After: America, 1945–1960* (Random House, 1960) remains a great read and pushes the view that Americans had developed "a broad concern about the public issues of the day."

In a class by themselves are Paul A. Carter's *Another Part of the Fifties* (Columbia University Press, 1983) and journalist David Halberstam's *The Fifties* (Willard Books, 1993), a book that is eminently readable in its portraits of 1950s heroes like Charles Van Doren, Marlon Brando, and Bill Russell. Some of the same material is covered from a more conservative viewpoint by Jeffrey Hart, ed., *When the Going Was Good: Life in the Fifties* (Crown Publishers, 1982).

President Dwight D. Eisenhower dominated the politics of the 1950s in the same way that one of his predecessors, Franklin D. Roosevelt, did the depression decade and World War II. In the 1950s the public loved Eisenhower, but the intellectuals did not. Early assessments of him as an ineffectual, old man who let his staff make the decisions can be found in Dean Alberton's collection of articles *Eisenhower as President* (Hill & Wang, 1963). Revisionists who have researched through the private papers and diaries of the president and his staff have concluded that he really was in charge. See Fred I. Greenstein, *The Hidden Hand Presidency* (Johns Hopkins University Press, 1994). Past revisionist arguments that he was in charge but fumbled anyway are assessed in the chapter entitled "Vicissitudes of Presidential Reputations: Eisenhower," in Arthur M. Schlesinger, Jr., *The Cycles of American History* (Houghton Mifflin, 1986). A major biography that is sympathetic to its subject remains Stephen A. Ambrose's *Eisenhower: Soldier and President* (Simon & Schuster, 1990).

Other worthy books on a variety of 1950s topics include Thomas C. Reeves, ed., *McCarthyism*, 3rd ed. (Robert E. Krieger, 1989); Harold G. Vatter, *The U.S. Economy in the 1950s* (University of Chicago Press, 1985); James Gilbert, *A Cycle of Outrage: America's Reaction to the Juvenile Age* (Oxford University Press, 1986); and Karal A. Marling, ms*As Seen on TV: The Visual Culture of Everyday Life in the 1950s* (Harvard University Press, 1994).

ISSUE 14

Did the Civil Rights Movement Improve Race Relations in the United States?

YES: Robert Weisbrot, from *Freedom Bound: A History of America's Civil Rights Movement* (Plume Books, 1990)

NO: Tom Wicker, from *Tragic Failure: Racial Integration in America* (William Morrow, 1996)

ISSUE SUMMARY

YES: Professor of history Robert Weisbrot describes the lasting achievements produced by the civil rights movement in the realm of school desegregation, access to public accommodations, the protection of voting rights for African Americans, and the deepening commitment to racial harmony.

NO: Political journalist Tom Wicker recognizes that legal segregation ended in the South in the 1960s but contends that in the 1970s and 1980s enthusiasm for racial integration waned as white animosity toward African American achievements drained momentum from the movement for true racial equality.

On a steamy August day in 1963, Martin Luther King, Jr., mounted a podium constructed in front of the Lincoln Memorial in Washington, D.C., and, in the studied cadence of a preacher, delivered his famous "I Have a Dream" speech. For many Americans, black and white, King's speech represented the symbolic climax of the civil rights movement. The Civil Rights Act of 1964 and the Voting Rights Act of 1965 were merely denouements.

There were other symbolic events at the March on Washington in addition to King's electrifying oration. The call for the march had been issued by A. Philip Randolph, a long-time civil rights activist, who had threatened in 1941 to stage a similar protest march to bring attention to the economic inequality suffered by African Americans. Randolph's presence at the head of the march reflected a realization of *his* dream. Moreover, several of the speakers that day paid homage to W. E. B. Du Bois, the godfather of the twentieth-century black protest movement in the United States, who had died the previous day (at the age of 95) in Ghana, West Africa, an embittered exile from the land of his birth. For decades, African Americans had endured an enforced second-class citizenship. But in the 1940s and 1950s, following constitutional victories spearheaded by the National Association for the Advancement of Colored People (NAACP) in the areas of housing, voting, and education, black Americans awakened to the possibilities for change in their status. These victories coincided with the rise of independent nations in Africa, led by black leaders such as Kwame Nkrumah, and this fostered pride in the African homeland among many black Americans. Finally, the nonviolent direct action movement, pioneered by interracial organizations such as the Congress of Racial Equality (CORE) and individuals like Randolph, King, Ella Baker, James Farmer, and Fannie Lou Hamer, issued a clarion call to African Americans and their white supporters that full equality was around the corner.

Despite these idealistic predictions of the future, King's vision of a color-blind society, liberated from the harsh realities of prejudice and discrimination, faced serious barriers after the mid-1960s. King's desegregation campaigns had little impact on the economic plight of many African Americans, a point made consistently by Malcolm X prior to his assassination in 1965. The rise of black nationalism produced fissures within the leading civil rights organizations and alienated many whites who had committed their time and money to fostering interracial harmony. Following King's death in 1968, the federal government made efforts to enforce school integration and to legislate affirmative action programs. This fueled controversy that manifested itself in a conservative white backlash against much of the racial progress that had occurred during the previous generation. By the 1990s, in the midst of debates over hiring quotas and the Rodney King affair, to say nothing of the racial implications of the sensationalist media attention devoted to the criminal and civil prosecutions of O. J. Simpson, serious questions could be raised concerning the long-term success of the civil rights movement.

In the first of the following selections, Robert Weisbrot acknowledges the illusory nature of many of the movement's hopes for racial progress and admits that the United States remains a race-conscious society. Nevertheless, he credits the nonviolent direct action campaigns of the 1950s and 1960s with sharply reducing the levels of ignorance, fear, and hate that are the products of the nation's racial heritage. Moreover, he recognizes a substantial record of achievement that includes the desegregation of schools and places of public accommodation, the protection of voting rights, and a severe weakening of the legal and social standing once accorded racism in America.

For Tom Wicker, the civil rights glass is half empty. In the second selection, he argues that, despite legal victories over segregation in the South during the 1960s, recent decades have witnessed a retrenchment campaign abetted by both major political parties and stimulated by white fears that black gains during the civil rights era were achieved at the expense of whites. Consequently, in the long run the civil rights movement failed to bring either racial equality or racial harmony to the United States.

YES
Robert Weisbrot

THE SHIFTING POLITICS OF RACE

Lagging progress toward equality led blacks in the 1970s to propose new, bolder answers to the riddle of "all deliberate speed." Instead of seeking merely to punish overt acts of discrimination, some civil rights spokesmen urged the government to guarantee fair representation of blacks in schools, jobs, and other areas of society. This strategy, pursued mainly through a sympathetic judiciary, broadened the concept of equal opportunity and the frontiers of federal regulation. Yet the idea of race-conscious and at times preferential treatment of blacks, even to remedy past injustice, strained the civil rights coalition and brought further backlash in an age of prolonged liberal eclipse....

THE RECEDING CIVIL RIGHTS VISION

It is now clear that the more expansive hopes for civil rights progress were markedly inflated. Residential segregation, seen in the persistence of inner-city black ghettos and lily-white suburbs, has easily survived federal fiats against housing discrimination. De facto segregation of churches, social centers, and private schools also remains routine, suggesting that in important respects the society's newfound emphasis on interracial harmony has been more rhetorical than real. Wealth, too, is largely segregated along racial lines; the median family income of blacks is barely half that of whites, and blacks are three times as likely to be poor. As for black political power, it is still embryonic with regard to national office holding and access to the circles that make foreign and domestic policy. In all, the roots of racial inequality have proved too deeply embedded in centuries of American history to be washed away by a decade's liberal reform.

Race relations have changed at a glacial pace in much of the rural South, where only the hardiest civil rights activists could weather the repressive social climate. Southern whites understandably regard black militancy as an urban malady, for only in the cities have blacks developed an independent business and professional class able to lead sustained protests. In many outlying towns, where whites monopolize credit and own the farms and textile mills that provide crucial jobs, the etiquette of racial deference persists.

Unwritten rules of segregation in small Southern communities still have the force of law. Harassment and occasional beatings discourage blacks from approaching the polls on election day, whatever the language of federal statutes. Blacks also know to avoid restaurants where they will draw stares instead of service, hotels that will always be "fully booked," and golf courses where management sand traps will foil their bids for access. Even white physicians who treat persons of both races commonly route their patients into separate waiting rooms with pre-1960 firmness. Here progress in race relations often comes in rudimentary concessions to black dignity, as in the recent removal of a chain-link fence dividing black and white plots in a Georgia county cemetery. Until that headline-making decision, black funeral processions had entered the cemetery through a back gate.

Challenges to old racial mores can bring spiraling retaliation. In Ludowici, Georgia, where students picked separate white and black homecoming queens until 1984, an argument in the high school lunchroom over interracial dating degenerated into an interracial brawl. Discipline was swift and selective: several students were expelled, all of them black. After local black leaders protested, hooded Klansmen visited the town, and within hours the home of a civil rights activist was burned to the ground. Fire marshals blamed faulty wiring, but Joseph Lowery of the Southern Christian Leadership Conference thought it absurd to deny the real problem: faulty white racial attitudes. The former SNCC [Student Nonviolent Coordinating Committee] worker Charles Sherrod observed, "Those people who shot at us, and blew up churches and all that 20 years ago, they haven't gone anywhere. The attitudes are still there. Their behavior has changed because we have got a little power. They won't do anything they can't get away with."

Few officials anywhere in the South still defy civil rights laws openly, for events in the 1960s showed the futility of shrill racist posturing. Softer sabotage, however, still limits the impact of federal guarantees. After passage of the Voting Rights Act in 1965, whites generally acquiesced in the registration of blacks but devised ways to undermine the new electorate. Testimony in 1982 before the Senate Judiciary Committee revealed that nearly half the counties of Alabama, Georgia, Louisiana, and South Carolina had disregarded the act's "preclearance" requirement by changing electoral laws—often for transparent racial reasons—without first obtaining federal approval. Cities with large black populations imported white voters by annexing adjacent suburbs, and cities with a few predominantly black areas discarded district elections for at-large voting. Legislators have also excluded black voters from communities through redistricting schemes of rare cartographic cunning. The understaffed Justice Department has trailed such infractions at a discouraging distance. An amendment to the North Carolina constitution, designed to gerrymander away the influence of new black voters, escaped challenge from federal attorneys until 1981, fourteen years after it was illegally implemented.

Outside the South racism treads more softly but still sequesters most blacks in ghettos. Blacks formed 6 percent of the suburban population in 1980 (up from 5 percent in 1970), and even this figure was inflated by spillover into older, industrial suburbs that white flight turned into segregated enclaves. Federal studies show pervasive discrimination by white realtors and residents, resulting in hundreds of census tracts in New York, Cleveland, and other metropolitan areas that contain no nonwhites. Nor is housing bias entirely covert. Obscene phone calls, curses, threats, firebombings, and rocks and bricks crashing through windows are among the dozens of incidents that each year impart a rough frontier quality to black settlement in white neighborhoods. Such experiences confirm that the open-housing legislation of the 1960s has meant little beside the resolve of whites to maintain property values and "ethnic purity" in their communities.

Racial violence and harassment, a central target of civil rights protest, still occurs daily in every region of the country. The Justice Department conservatively recorded a rise in racist attacks from 99 in 1980 to 276 in 1986; the count by individual cities is more extensive. New York City's police department charted an increase in bias-related clashes from four a week to ten a week in early 1987. Chicago reported 240 episodes of racially motivated violence and harassment in 1986, an increase for the third consecutive year. The spark is often no more than the presence of a black person in a store, on the street, in a new home. For dejected white students at the University of Massachusetts at Amherst, the defeat of the Boston Red Sox in the 1986 World Series was enough reason to beat a black New York Mets fan unconscious and injure several others. Several months earlier, at Howard Beach, New York, three black "outsiders" fled an attack by eleven whites; one of the blacks, twenty-three-year-old Michael Griffith, was killed when he ran onto a parkway of speeding cars in his attempt to escape a beating. Kevin Nesmith, a black student at the Citadel Military School, in Charleston, South Carolina, resigned after whites in Klan robes burst into his room at two in the morning shouting racial slurs and hazing him. Something akin to a freedom ride befell black students returning from Newton North High School to their homes in Boston when whites smashed the bus windows with stones and a tire iron. These and other recent episodes do not approach the systematic, officially sanctioned terror against blacks that once scarred American history. They nonetheless point to the continued difficulty blacks face in securing basic civil rights.

Police each year kill dozens of blacks, including children. Defenders of police conduct stress the extreme danger facing officers in some ghetto neighborhoods, their need to use deadly force on occasion to survive, and their able protection of blacks, notably during civil rights marches that have drawn white hecklers. Still, cases abound of unprovoked, cold-blooded police shootings of ghetto residents that almost invariably go unpunished.

The criminal justice system is less blatantly harsh toward blacks than in the past, but patterns of punishment still appear skewed by racial prejudice. Blacks average longer prison terms than whites for the same offense and are the primary victims of capital punishment. Criminals of any race, moreover, are treated more severely for victimizing whites. In 1987 a case that challenged the death penalty as being tainted, in practice, by racial bias showed that in Georgia, even after accounting for 230 other factors, killers of white persons were four times more likely to be executed than killers of blacks. Despite corroborating evidence of prejudice in meting out capital punishment, the Supreme Court narrowly upheld the death penalty. The majority opinion asserted, in language shades removed from *Plessy v. Ferguson*, that the treatment of black and white prisoners was admittedly different but not discriminatory.

* * *

Failure to include blacks fully in the nation's prosperity is the most glaring limitation of the movement for racial justice. In the South two-thirds of all black workers, compared with one-third of all whites, hold low-income jobs. The national economy today relegates more than half of all black workers to menial jobs, perpetuates a black underclass of deepening antisocial bent, and confines even educated blacks to the margins of wealth and opportunity. These problems can be traced to various causes—racial differences in family structure, education, and job experience among them—but they are also rooted in both past and persistent discrimination.

Title VII of the 1964 Civil Rights Act did not end bias in employment but drove it behind closed office doors. Managers commonly assigned blacks to dead-end jobs, minimized their executive role, scrutinized them more harshly than comparably trained whites, and excluded them from the after-hours fraternizing that can advance careers. In 1982 only one in thirty black men (compared with one in ten whites) filled management or administrative jobs, reflecting a ten-year increase so minute that it was probably a matter of statistical error. No black headed a corporation in *Fortune* magazine's top 1,000, and few had risen above the level of vice-president in any major firm. Tokenism thus became more intricate in the era of affirmative action, permitting a greater minority presence in the office but seldom in the conference suites where deals, promotions, and salaries are decided.

An aura of the closed medieval guild still surrounds craft unions, which have countered civil rights laws with subtler means of racial exclusion. One AFL-CIO union, representing New York City's electrical contractors, avoided punishment for racist practices by devising an "outreach training program" for minorities in 1971. Over a decade later state investigators charged that the program required black and Hispanic trainees to work eleven years before they could reach class A journeyman status, compared with five years for white apprentices. Nonwhite trainees were also taught a curriculum separate from that of whites, with obsolete textbooks and without the fifth year of classroom instruction needed to pass the union exam and obtain work at journeymen's wages. Many other AFL-CIO locals have also been exposed for turning affirmative action programs into a permanent racial obstacle course for minorities....

A RECORD OF CHANGE

Like other reform movements the crusade for racial justice inevitably fell short of the utopian goals that sustained it. Still, if America's civil rights movement is judged by the distance it traveled rather than by barriers yet to be crossed, a record of substantial achievement unfolds. In communities throughout the South, "whites only" signs that had stood for generations suddenly came down from hotels, rest rooms, theaters, and other facilities. Blacks and whites seldom mingle socially at home, but they are apt to lunch together at fast-food shops that once drew blacks only for sit-ins. Integration extends equally to Southern workers, whether at diner counters or in the high-rise office buildings that now afford every Southern city a skyline.

School desegregation also quickened its pace and by the mid-1970's had become fact as well as law in over 80 percent of all Southern public schools. Swelling private school enrollments have tarnished but not substantially reversed this achievement. A privileged 5 to 10 percent of all Southern white children may find shelter from the *Brown* [v. Board of Education of Topeka, Kansas (1954)] verdict at private academies; but the words "massive resistance" have virtually disappeared from the region's political vocabulary.

Hate groups once flourished without strong federal restraint, but the civil rights movement has curbed the Ku Klux Klan and other extremist threats. Beginning in 1964 the FBI infiltrated the Klan so thoroughly that by 1965 perhaps one in five members was an informant. During the 1980s, amid a rise in racial assaults, synagogue bombings, and armed robberies to bankroll fringe groups, the federal government mounted the largest campaign against organized subversion since World War II. In 1987, members of the Florida Realm of the United Klans of America were convicted of illegal paramilitary training exercises, and leaders of the Identity Movement, which preaches a theology of hatred toward Jews and blacks, were indicted for conspiring to overthrow the government. Federal action has encouraged private lawsuits, including one that bankrupted the United Klans of America. After a black teenager in Mobile, Alabama, was murdered by Klansmen and left hanging from a tree in 1981, the boy's family won a $7 million judgment. To pay damages the Klan had to cede its two-story national headquarters, near Tuscaloosa, Alabama, to the black litigants. Reeling from legal and financial adversity, Klan membership declined from 10,000 in 1981 to less than 5,500 in 1987, the lowest since the early seventies.

Protection of voting rights represents the movement's most unalloyed success, more than doubling black voter registration, to 64 percent, in the seven states covered by the 1965 act. Winning the vote literally changed the complexion of government service in the South. When Congress passed the Voting Rights Act, barely 100 blacks held elective office in the country; by 1989 there were more than 7,200, including 24 congressmen and some 300 mayors. Over 4,800 of these officials served in the South, and nearly every Black Belt county in Alabama had a black sheriff. Mississippi experienced the most radical change, registering 74 percent of its voting-age blacks and leading the nation in the number of elected black officials (646).

Black influence in electoral politics acquired a compelling symbol during the 1980s with the emergence of the Reverend Jesse Jackson of Chicago as a presidential contender. As a young aide to Dr. King from 1966 to 1968, Jackson had stood out for his eloquence, élan, and ambition. In the 1970s Jackson won national acclaim for spurring ghetto youths to excel in school, but his denunciations of American society as racist, capitalist, and imperialist kept him on the fringes of public life. Over the next decade, however, as blacks increasingly protested President Reagan's neglect of minorities and the poor, Jackson began to temper his revolutionary message in hopes of forging a revitalized reform coalition.

Jackson campaigned in the 1984 Democratic presidential primaries, drawing large crowds and intense media coverage with his mixture of evangelical fervor, nimble wit, and self-conscious identification with minority hopes. He spoke of a "Rainbow Coalition" that would transcend racial lines, though his campaign chiefly focused on mobilizing black voter registration and turnout with the aid of Negro churches. This strategy enabled Jackson to win nomination contests in South Carolina, Louisiana, and Washington, D.C., and to finish third in delegates at the Democratic National Convention. Partly offsetting this achievement was Jackson's failure to draw even 5 percent of the white voters, whether because of his race, radical image, or suspect character. (Jews in particular recoiled at Jackson's ties with the Black Muslim Louis Farrakhan, who had branded Judaism a "gutter religion.") Despite these weaknesses Jackson's campaign legitimized Black Power to the American people in a way that Stokely Carmichael and others in the 1960s had vainly tried to do from outside the political mainstream.

In 1988 Jackson hewed closer to the political center and reached well beyond his core supporters, in a second bid for the Democratic presidential nomination. The now seasoned candidate trimmed his radical rhetoric, conciliated many who had thought him opportunistic and divisive, and emphasized broadly appealing liberal themes of economic opportunity for all citizens. Jackson's approach, which this time afforded him second place among seven competitors, reflected and fostered a new openness toward blacks in the Democratic party and in the nation. An especially prominent landmark of political change was Jackson's Michigan primary victory, with 54 percent of the vote, just twenty years after that state's Democratic contest had gone to the Alabama segregationist George Wallace. The candidate's progress, as in 1984, remained in key respects exceedingly personal, for it did not appreciably change his party's stand on key issues nor dispel racism as a factor in national politics. Still, more than any black leader since Martin Luther King, Jr., Jackson had inspired Americans with the faith —crucial to every reform movement— that the decisive state of America's democratic odyssey lay just ahead.

* * *

Despite unsettling parallels with the aftermath of Reconstruction, the modern civil rights movement should prove better able to resist the undoing of black gains. A salient difference is the greater reluctance in recent times to risk convulsing society by spurning the ideal of equality. Blacks during Reconstruction had exerted relatively minor influence over the white leadership that instituted—and then abandoned—measures for racial justice. By contrast blacks a century later shook whole cities with mass demonstrations, demanded and secured sweeping changes in federal law, and reshaped the political agenda of two strong-minded chief executives. These protests brought a new respect for Afro-Americans, breaking forever the comfortable myth that blacks were content with a biracial society and proving that they had the rare courage needed to challenge it.

New currents in world affairs have reinforced the consensus to guarantee black civil rights. During the late nineteenth century Americans were largely indifferent to the nonwhite world except for the growing possibilities of colonizing or otherwise controlling it. The European nations that most influenced this country were themselves indulging in imperialism based on racial as well as national interests. Global pressures today are vastly different. Competition for the support of nonwhite nations and the near-universal ostracism of South Africa, which asserts a racist ideology, require American society to pay at least nominal homage to racial equality.

Pluralism is also more firmly rooted in American values than ever before. The black revolution stimulated others, including women, homosexuals, Hispanics, native Americans, and Asians, who frequently modeled their actions on the values and tactics popularized by Martin Luther King, Jr. Each emerging movement, while pursuing a discrete agenda, has bolstered the principle that government must guarantee equal rights and opportunities to all citizens.

Racism lost more than legal standing with the triumph of civil rights campaigns; it lost social standing. Even the Daughters of the American Revolution, an organization known for its racially exclusive character, apologized in 1982 for having spurned the singer Marian Anderson over four decades earlier. The DAR's president general, a native of Beulah, Mississippi, invited Anderson to perform at the organization's ninety-first convention in Constitution Hall. The eighty-year-old singer was by then too frail to attend, but the black soprano Leontyne Price, who treated the DAR to a concert ending with "The Battle Hymn of the Republic," assured her interracial audience that Anderson was "here in spirit."

The deepening interest in racial harmony has encouraged recognition of the black experience as central to American history. The 1977 television drama "Roots," which engaged audiences in the trauma of racial slavery and the struggle for freedom, became the most widely viewed special series in the history of the medium. Six years later Congress created a holiday to honor Martin Luther King, Jr., and by extension the civil rights movement he symbolized. Such a tribute had eluded Thomas Jefferson, Andrew Jackson, both Roosevelts, and other giants of American history. President Reagan, who had originally opposed enacting a holiday for King as an unwise "ethnic" precedent, signed the popular bill into law while standing alongside King's widow, Coretta.

*   *   *

In the South, as in the rest of the nation, few whites seriously contemplate returning to the state of race relations before 1960. This outlook differs strikingly from Southern intransigence after Reconstruction and reflects the disparate ways in which the two eras of racial change occurred. Reconstruction came as a sudden, violently imposed upheaval in Southern race relations that virtually nothing in the region's history had prepared it to accept. The civil rights movement instead advanced nonviolently, secured small gains over decades, and fostered progress from within the region. The campaigns that ended legalized segregation in the sixties marked the culmination of this gradual change. Many white Southerners had by then reconciled themselves to reforms that seemed inevitable and even, per-haps, beneficial.

Freed from the albatross of defend-ing Jim Crow at the expense of national respect and regional peace, Southerners could focus on tasks of economic and so-cial modernization. Mississippi's leading journal, the *Jackson Clarion-Ledger*, offered a glimpse into this revolution in priori-ties. After the March on Washington in 1963, a front-page story reported that the capital was "clean again with Negro trash removed." Twenty years later the paper won a Pulitzer Prize in public serve for exposing the need for fuller desegrega-tion and better funding of public schools.

Southern memories of black protests have mellowed to the point where both races treat them as parts of their history to be proud of. Montgomery motorists now drive down the Martin Luther King, Jr. Expressway, and the Dexter Baptist Church, where King was pastor, has be-come a national landmark. The prison cell King occupied in Birmingham is set aside as a library for inmates, his "Letter from a Birmingham Jail" framed on the wall. In Georgia's capitol a portrait of King hangs near a bust of Alexander Stephens, the Confederate vice-president. One elderly black tour guide, assigned to interpret these landmarks of the past, ignored the bust of Stephens, and beamed, "Here is Nobel prize winner Martin Luther King, Jr. He was born and bred right here in Atlanta on Auburn Avenue."

Political calculation has sealed this acceptance of racial change. Over a quiet bourbon and branch water in his Senate office, Mississippi's arch-segregationist James Eastland confided, "When [blacks] get the vote, I won't be talking this way anymore." Later Eastland was among the many officials who jettisoned their tested appeals to prejudice, learned to pronounce "Negro" in place of more casual epithets, and prefaced the names of newly valued black constituents with the once forbidden appellation "Mister."

Even the past master of race baiting, Alabama's George Wallace, was struck color-blind on the road to Montgomery in his 1982 gubernatorial campaign. Wal-lace, who like most politicians believed above all in winning elections today, to-morrow, and forever, spent much of his hard-fought contest kissing black babies and humbly supplicating their parents' support, assuring them of his reborn atti-tudes on race matters. (He won the cam-paign with the aid of a forgiving black electorate and welcomed several blacks to positions in his cabinet.) Whatever Wallace's deepest sentiments, his actions were a striking testament to the legacy of the civil rights protests that he once vowed to crush but that instead have left an indelible imprint on the nation's moral landscape.

* * *

The full impact of civil rights campaigns has yet to be felt. The movement could not wholly sweep away old Jim Crow hierarchies, but rather superimposed new patterns of behavior on a still race-conscious society. Cities like Selma, Alabama, where black activists battled white supremacists in the 1960s, today reflect two eras of race relations at once, giving no final sign of which will prevail.

Segregated neighborhoods persist in Selma, along with segregated social patterns. The Selma Country Club has no black members and until 1983 would not allow a black dance band inside. Elks Club members attend separate white and black chapters. Nearly a thousand white students attend two private academies founded with the express purpose of excluding blacks. Racial lines run through the city's economy: the overall jobless rate in Selma in 1985 was 16 percent but nearly twice as high for blacks as for whites. And in politics, residents tend to make racial choices for public office. The black community leader Frederick Reese won 40 percent of the mayoral vote in 1984 but only a handful of white supporters; Joseph Smitherman received 10 to 15 percent of the black vote but stayed in office with nearly 100 percent of the white vote.

Yet race relations in Selma have noticeably changed since the city's landmark civil rights demonstrations in 1965. The onetime "moderate segregationist" Smitherman began to tend an image as a facilitator of black mobility. In 1984 Smitherman observed proudly that 40 percent of the police force was black, including the assistant chief, several lieutenants, captains, and key department heads. The city's personnel board had three blacks and two whites, the eight-person library board was evenly composed of blacks and whites, and the school board had five blacks to four whites. Asphalt pavement, which had often stopped short of black neighborhoods, now stretched for miles through-out the town, covering over dirt roads and, with them, an era of flagrant neglect of black residents.

Perhaps most important to Selma's blacks and many whites, the movement reduced ignorance, fear, and hate. The black lawyer and civil rights activist J. L. Chestnut remarked in 1985, on the twentieth anniversary of his city's civil rights marches, that new attitudes were taking root: "My children don't think of white children as devils, and I don't think white children see my kids as watermelon-eating, tap-dancing idiots. If there is hope, it is in the fact that children in Selma today don't have to carry the baggage that Joe Smitherman and J. L. Chestnut carry. And that means they will never be scared the way we used to be scared." Teenagers at Selma's integrated public high school knew about the events of "Bloody Sunday" but viewed them as a mystery from another time. "Kids today, they're used to the way things are," explained Karyn Reddick, a black student. "Try as you can, you can't believe that white people once treated black people that way. It seems like something that happened long, long ago."

NO

Tom Wicker

TRAGIC FAILURE: RACIAL INTEGRATION IN AMERICA

INTRODUCTION

Sharply conflicting white and black reactions to the O. J. Simpson verdict [not guilty of murder] dramatized the tragic fact that neither civil war in the nineteenth century nor the civil rights movement in the twentieth has brought racial equality, much less racial amity, to America.

I believe they can be reached only in the hearts of the people; wars will never achieve either, nor narrow legalities. Perhaps nothing can. Derrick Bell has written that African-Americans, despite surface changes in society, continue to be "the faces at the bottom of the well," the faces upon which whites, no matter how deprived themselves, can look down in the sure and comforting knowledge that at least *they* aren't black.

Having spent the first thirty-four years of my life in what was then the segregated South and the last thirty-five in what's only legally an integrated nation—and not always that—I believe the problem is not least that those black faces in the well are *reassuring* to most whites and *vital* to the self-esteem of the many disadvantaged among us, few of whom really want those faces to disappear.

The continuing separation of whites and blacks into hostile and unequal classes, however, is a fundamental cause of the political deadlock, economic inequity, and social rancor that mark American life. And if "a house divided against itself" could not stand in the era of chattel slavery, can it long endure in today's destructive atmosphere of black disadvantage, white anger, and racial animosity?

Long before O. J. Simpson went on trial, it was obvious that genuine racial equality—despite laws and legal decisions—had not been achieved in America. The high proportion of African-American[1] males in U.S. prisons and the low economic status of more than half the black population were evidence enough for anyone willing to see it, but few were. Even as the Simpson trial unfolded, white resentment erupted over affirmative action—an effort to overcome black disadvantages that's now widely seen, despite little evidence, as reverse racism.

When a Los Angeles jury brought in the Simpson verdict, the hard truth finally was too visible to be ignored. Whites denounced what they saw as black racial prejudice by a predominantly black jury in favor of a black hero despite the evidence. African-Americans, on the other hand, hailed black jurors for a courageous stand against white racial prejudice and constitutionally impermissible evidence provided by the racist Los Angeles police.

Throughout the long trial, "the white position [that Simpson was guilty] was treated as the rational, normal, acceptable one, David Shaw of the *Los Angeles Times* said on October 25, 1995, in a panel discussion of media coverage of the Freedom Forum. "The black perception [that Simpson was not guilty] was treated as irrational."

It's almost irrelevant the black or white judgment might be more nearly correct. In my view, what mattered was the demonstration that whites and blacks, though living in the same America, see themselves in different worlds. Similarly conflicting views were evident in the responses of African-American journalists and their mostly white supervisors to a survey question of whether U.S. press organizations are "committed to retaining and promoting black journalists." Of the white supervisors, 94 percent believed newspapers and broadcasters were so committed; 67 percent of the black (mostly middle-class) journalists thought not. Both worked in the same newsrooms; neither saw the same world of work.

The Simpson trial and verdict were followed immediately by the so-called "Million-Man March," in which at least hundreds of thousands of orderly African-American males demonstrated peacefully on the Mall in Washington in October 1995. Despite a demagogic speech by Louis Farrakhan of the Nation of Islam, the marchers espoused what white Americans, watching on television, could readily recognize as middle-class values—thus confounding the recent white view of black men as lawless and shiftless, as well as conveying the message that African-Americans still are far from equal citizenship in a supposedly integrated nation.

The march emphasized the strong growth of the black middle class in the last three decades—to perhaps 40 percent of the African-American population. Even that growth has not banished the faces from the bottom of the well, any more than it has produced real racial equality. Middle-class African-Americans testify copiously to the indignities and embarrassments they still suffer from the white assumption of black inferiority, black income and wealth still are far below white levels, housing remains largely segregated by race, and *all* African-Americans tend to be judged by the unacceptable behavior of the worst off among them.

I consider it the saddest racial development of the last quarter century that as the black middle class expanded, the urban underclass grew even faster. The scary and undisciplined behavior of that largely black underclass—those African-Americans who for lack of jobs and hope and discipline turned in the seventies and eighties to crime and welfare and drugs and were sent to prison in droves—was seen (often graphically, on television) by frightened whites as the behavior of African-Americans generally.

In one panicked and self-destructive result, whites turned against social welfare programs designed to benefit the white as well as the black poor—hence society generally. Worse, African-Americans once seen as bravely facing the police dogs and cattle prods of Bull Connor in the name of freedom came to be regarded, instead, as irresponsible muggers, drug dealers, addicts, rapists, and welfare queens.

The same period exposed the failure of the African-American political empowerment that white and black civil rights leaders of the sixties had hoped would be the remedy for black disadvantages. One of them, Dr. Kenneth Clark, sadly conceded in 1993 that greater numbers of black elected officials had been "unable to increase justice and humanity for those who have been forgotten in the inner cities."

Thirty-five years of failing integration have convinced me that economic as well as political empowerment is needed if African-American disadvantages—particularly those of the underclass—are to be overcome. Only when the faces at the bottom of the well achieve generally higher economic status might they—as well as those talented and energetic blacks in the middle class—reach genuine equality in the hearts of whites, and only through economic gains for all might the threatening underclass become a more constructive element in a more amicable American life.

Such an economic transformation will not be easily or soon accomplished, and it probably never will be if the task is left to today's major political parties. Neither any longer even talks of such ambitious goals; both are less concerned with the truly disadvantaged than with the numerically dominant white middle class, with its plaints about an unfair tax burden and unfair preferences for blacks. The Republicans offer a new home to white defectors from a Democratic party the defectors regard as too partial to blacks, and the supposedly "liberal" Democrats, alarmed by the loss of white votes, pay scant attention to the interests of African-Americans, whose allegiance causes the white defections.

In their own interest, therefore, but also in that of a racially torn nation, blacks should turn away from the Democrats to form a new party dedicated to economic equality through economic growth for whites and blacks alike. Such a new party could build upon predicted demographic change that in the next century will bring today's minority groups into rough numerical equality with non-Hispanic whites. It might even win the support of those millions of despairing Americans who now take no part in the politics of a prosperous nation they believe ruled by the affluent and for the affluent.

The new party might never win the presidency, but in the historical tradition of third parties, it could have profound effect upon the other two and upon society generally. That's why I've suggested in this book that such a radically conceived party might also have the potential to do what our old, familiar politics-as-usual never can: "To achieve real democracy—to change American life by attacking its inequities—perhaps to save us from ourselves."

THE END OF INTEGRATION

Integration is like Prohibition. If the people don't want it, a whole army can't enforce it.

—Paul Johnson,
governor of Mississippi

The sweeping conservative victory in the elections of 1994 returned control of Congress to Republicans, repudiated what was left of liberal government, and dramatized the tragic failure of racial integration in America.

Race, as it always is in a modern American election, was the underlying issue. In the autumn of 1994 that issue was a prime determinant of the outcome, as white voters everywhere expressed unmistakable yearning for a lost time, before "they" forced themselves into the nation's consciousness.

White animosity toward and fear of African-Americans—seen largely as criminals and welfare cheats—gave emotional edge and added energy to the election's ostensible issues, and the campaign was fought out in code words and symbolism that disclosed rather than disguised its racial character:

- Fierce denunciations of crime and welfare, in white eyes the most prominent products of the black underclass
- Withering blasts at liberals and liberalism as the "social engineers" behind the "big government" that tried to force racial integration and brought higher taxes
- Diatribes against "spending" and "the redistribution of wealth" to the poor, a euphemism for social programs believed primarily to aid African-Americans
- Loud promises to extend the death penalty, from which African-Americans suffer proportionally far more than whites
- Overwrought demands for a return to "family values" (a term of many meanings, one of which is the sexual restraint that blacks are supposed by whites to disdain)

Anyone who might have misunderstood what had happened in the 1994 elections should have been set straight on January 23, 1995. That day, in the ornate hearing room of the House Rules Committee, the victorious Republicans removed a portrait of former Representative Claude Pepper of Florida, a renowned white liberal Democrat. That was understandable, but the new Republican committee chairman, Gerald Solomon of New York, had ordered the Pepper portrait replaced by that of *another Democrat*, the late Howard Smith of Virginia, a last-ditch segregationist and in his many years as Rules Committee chairman one of the most powerful opponents of the civil rights legislation of the sixties.

Blacks clearly believed race was the principal issue in the campaign; the reason, said Robert Smith, a professor of political science at San Francisco State University, was "absolute disgust" with the campaign among blacks of all walks.

"It took us black people so long to get the vote," T. J. Smith of Philadelphia told Richard Berke of *The New York Times* in 1994. "Now they're making us not want to vote" by neglecting black interests. Chris Williams, a Philadelphia ironworker, agreed: "Why do they talk about just building jails? Why don't they talk about building schools?"

The returns, if anything, left African-Americans feeling even more frustrated. Black turnout—perhaps fueled by fear —more than doubled nationally, over the 1990 midterm elections, with black voters going heavily Democratic; yet the Republicans won in a landslide and not a single Republican incumbent was defeated. Clearly, *white* voters had turned to the Republicans.

Fifty-one percent of the whites, moreover, who had responded to an election-year survey by the Times Mirror Center for the People and the Press said openly that they believed "equal rights" had been pushed too far—an increase of nine percentage points since 1992.

California, the nation's most populous state, voted by an overwhelming margin for Proposition 187, a ballot initiative designed to deprive illegal immigrants—mostly Latinos in California—of education, health, and welfare benefits. Governor Pete Wilson, whose reelection made him seem at the time a strong contender for the Republican presidential nomination, derived substantial political profit from his support for this initiative.

California's approval of Prop 187, which Democratic candidates for governor and senator opposed, may well have been symbolic of the 1994 elections as a whole. It was not an "anti-black" measure, nor was it an anti-black election *by definition.* The vote favoring Prop 187, however, clearly reflected the angry and vengeful or at least resentful racial attitudes many white Americans had developed since the high-water mark of the civil rights movement in the sixties. The entire election reflected such white attitudes.

* * *

If those attitudes reached a political peak in 1994, they had been a long time in the making. Racial integration in America had been failing for years, even though legal segregation in the southern states was ended in the sixties. The elections of 1994 only dramatized a fact that had long existed.

By that year integration had failed nationally because too few white Americans wanted it or were willing to sacrifice for it. Integration had failed too because whites' sterotypical view of blacks had been re-shaped by the violence, idleness, and drug reliance of the urban black underclass. And the kind of political empowerment integration brought to blacks had proved unable to provide most African-Americans the economic and social gains needed for acceptance in white America.

The angry and fearful white reaction to undisciplined ghetto behavior also blinded whites to the concurrent growth of a substantial black middle class. Perhaps worse, that reaction had undermined white support for economic and social programs beneficial not only to the black poor but to millions of impoverished whites as well.

In actual practice, as a result of all this, integration had not been the policy of either Republican or Democratic administrations since the accession of Ronald Reagan to the presidency in 1981. In the decade before that, integration had been pursued only halfheartedly; zeal for enforcement of equal rights in education, housing, and employment had declined as antagonism to African-Americans rose.

Crime, though its victims as well as its perpetrators often were black, and welfare, widely considered a dole and an aid to shiftless blacks' supposed instinct to spawn, had long been favored targets of public and political anger.

Now the primary national approach to the ills of the urban underclass, endorsed in the polling booths of 1994, is to imprison poor blacks—an expensive, ineffective, misdirected, and self-destructive course sustained by white fear, politicians' posturing, and the sensationalism of the white press. More executions, mostly of blacks, an equally punitive and ill-considered response to crimes that already have been committed, are promised in response to the conservative landslide of 1994. Early in 1995 New York's new Republican governor, George Pataki, signed a death penalty law after nearly a quarter century of vetoes by the Democratic governors Hugh Carey and Mario Cuomo.

The inner city does teem with crime, idleness, and anger, spilling dangerously outward. Black family disintegration and welfare dependence are serious concerns. But for better or for worse, the American community necessarily *includes* the black community—African-Americans, some Latinos, many from the Caribbean. The Census Bureau predicts the black community will grow far larger. Its exclusion in anything like a democratic or humane manner would be impossible and would not solve the nation's most pressing problems; rather it would worsen some old problems and create many new ones.

Glaring economic inequities and class distinctions abound, among *both* blacks and whites. Technological or administrative competence, a prerequisite in today's economy, is seldom within the reach of poor and ill-educated Americans, of whom there are more and more of both races. Millions of whites and blacks are out of any kind of work, in the city and on the farm, and more will be in a newly competitive and technological era, with even profitable corporations laying off workers by the thousands. Manufacturing wages have declined for all. The real gap between rich and poor is widening. Unemployment, which strikes blacks first and worst, also hits whites hard—yet is fostered by a government too fearful of inflation to push economic growth strenuously and by a "lean and mean" business sector in which cost cutting has become the new panacea for all problems.

A seventh of the nation lives in poverty: more than forty million people, by no means all of them black, and including more than a fifth of all American children. Families of all races are disintegrating. The economy, measured against population growth and expected living standards, is not adequately expanding. Demographic changes predicted by the Census Bureau for the next fifty years will be of incalculable effect.

What the brash conservatives who triumphed in 1994 may be able to do about any of these troublesome truths remains, at this writing, largely to be seen. But the end of integration more or less subtly marked by their victory will not remove or diminish those ills, each of which, in large part or small, is linked to or affected by race, the continuing, the cancerous, the unconfronted American dilemma.

* * *

In the fifties and the first half of the sixties, owing mostly to effective black demonstrations and demands, the shameful institutions of legally established racial segregation in the South at last were abolished. But this shining hour for the civil rights movement proved to be brief and limited.

In the late sixties and the seventies, efforts to broaden integration into a national, not just a southern, reality caused anxiety and anger in the nonsouthern white majority. Outside the old Confederacy, integration came to be seen as moving too fast and going too far—faster and farther than most whites in the rest of the nation had expected or wanted.

A "backlash" of white resistance to civil rights quickly gathered momentum, importantly furthered by the presidential campaigns of Governor George Wallace of Alabama. The long national retreat from integration was under way within a year or two after its greatest triumphs.

Such a turnabout had hardly seemed possible in the period when antisegregation laws were being passed—slowly but, as it seemed, inevitably—by Congress under pressure from the Eisenhower, Kennedy, and Johnson administrations and over die-hard southern opposition. Even, however, in the Goldwater debacle of 1964—the most smashing Democratic and liberal presidential victory since Franklin Roosevelt's in 1936—the Republicans had carried four southern states.

The old Solid South had been shattered, a development that did not surprise the victorious President Lyndon Johnson, a southerner himself. The night Congress passed the massive Civil Rights Act of 1964, proposed by President Kennedy and pushed through by Johnson, a young White House aide named Bill Moyers called the president to congratulate him on the success of the legislation.

"Bill," Johnson replied, "I think we Democrats just lost the South for the rest of my life."

Inasmuch as LBJ died in 1972, it turned out to be for considerably longer than that. In 1994, thirty years later, the Democratic share of the vote in House races in the South dropped to 13.4 percent of eligible voters.

To most observers in 1964—including Tom Wicker, a *New York Times* political reporter—the southern defections had seemed relatively unimportant. After all, LBJ had defeated Goldwater by 486 to 52 in the electoral college. The Republicans had carried only one state (Goldwater's Arizona) outside the South, had lost 38 seats in the House and retained only

140, their lowest total since 1936. They also had lost 2 Senate seats and held only 32, no more than they had had in 1940. Republican defeats in state and local elections had been so severe as to cause frequent laments that the GOP was no longer an effective national party.

Only two years later, in a vigorous 1966 campaign led by Richard M. Nixon (out of office since 1961 but obviously on the road back), Republicans picked up forty-seven House seats, three in the Senate, and eight governorships, most significantly in California, where the political newcomer and old movie star Ronald Reagan first won political office. The Republican comeback was marked by a superb organizing and fundraising effort in the wake of Goldwater's defeat and by Nixon's leadership. But it benefited above all from *the Democratic party's and Johnson's racial liberalism.*

The president and his party had pushed through the Civil Rights Act of 1964, guaranteeing equal access to public facilities and banning racial discrimination in the workplace. They had achieved the Voting Rights Act of 1965, putting the federal government behind blacks' right to vote. Johnson himself had proclaimed to Congress the battle cry of Martin Luther King and his followers: "We shall overcome!" LBJ and John F. Kennedy rather reluctantly before him had identified their party more closely with African-Americans than any president since Lincoln.

Three decades later, in his 1995 inaugural speech as the new Republican Speaker of the House, Newt Gingrich—magnanimously praising the opposition, or so it appeared—noted that Democrats had been "the greatest leaders in fighting for an integrated America." He added pointedly: "It was the liberal wing of the Democratic party that ended segregation."

These honeyed words, intentionally or not, were political poison. Voters had shown in 1994 and earlier that they were well aware, and not favorably, of the Democrats' racial record. It had been apparent for years that this record was a political liability not just in the South but with the nation's white majority.

In early 1964, the year of Goldwater's defeat, a Gallup poll had found that 72 percent of nonsouthern whites believed the Johnson administration's pace toward civil rights was "about right" or even too slow. But as civil rights legislation began to touch life *outside* the South, although it had been expected generally that only the old Confederacy would be much affected, nonsouthern whites began to fear for property values, job security, local government, neighborhood cohesion—for the old, inherited, comfortable (for them) order of things.

By 1966 opinion surveys were showing a startling reversal: Three quarters of white voters thought blacks were moving ahead too fast, demanding and "being given" too much, at the expense of whites. As white backlash mounted, polls the next year suggested that "the number one concern" of most respondents was fear that black gains would damage the well-being of whites. And as the decade continued, blacks rioting in the cities—fearfully or angrily watched by a nation becoming addicted to television —and blacks raising clenched fists in the black power salute seemed not only threatening but ungrateful for white "concessions" (as whites tended to see changes in the old racial order).

The black separatist and "black is beautiful" movements, the anti-integrationist rhetoric of Malcolm X, the militant stance

and demands of organizations like the Black Panthers and the Student Nonviolent Coordinating Committee (SNCC) all stirred white animosity and anxiety. So did aggressive African-Americans like H. Rap Brown, Stokely Carmichael, Huey Newton, and Bobby Seale. The student and anti-Vietnam demonstrations were assumed by many whites to be a predictable consequence of black protests. Crime was increasing, much of it perpetrated by poor blacks, with television dramatizing it in the living room.

In 1967, as a result of the urban riots, President Johnson appointed a bipartisan commission, chaired by Governor Otto Kerner of Illinois, to look into the riots' causes. After extensive inquiry the Kerner Commission dismissed the notion that integration was proceeding too swiftly. Its report contended instead that despite the apparent success of the civil rights movement, black disadvantages still were so overwhelming that "our nation is moving toward two societies, one black, one white—separate but unequal."

Many prominent Americans, white and black, shared and approved this view, but many others resented it. Hadn't enough already been done for blacks? Even Lyndon Johnson, with a presidential election impending and the nation alarmed at what many believed to be insurrection in the cities, disliked the commission's conclusion and might have disavowed it if he could have. The backlash was not reversed; the riots undoubtedly heightened it.

Thus in 1968 fear and resentment of African-Americans underlay the "law and order" issue loudly demagogued by George Wallace and more subtly exploited by Richard Nixon in the "southern strategy" by which he narrowly won the presidency. The national loss of confidence in "Johnson's war" in Vietnam and destructive divisions within the party hurt the Democrats. But primarily, I believe, it was white racial anxieties that brought disaster to the party of Kennedy and Johnson only four years after its greatest victory. And the black community's impressive gains were becoming the cause of alarming losses of white support for Democrats.

Wallace campaigned widely and effectively, using code words and flamboyant oratory to stimulate white fears and to castigate the federal government. He finished a relatively distant third in the 1968 election, receiving votes from Democrats deserting the old civil rights advocate Hubert Humphrey and from Republicans who preferred Wallace's tough talk to Nixon's subtler appeal to white sentiment. In retrospect, however, Wallace's campaign was one of the most consequential of the postwar years. It effectively moved the country to the right, making racial fears seem more legitimate and paving the way for Ronald Reagan to win the presidency twelve years later.

Nixon's election and Wallace's campaign in 1968 sped along the national retreat from integration (though the courts forced President Nixon to push southern school desegregation in 1970). During the seventies affirmative action and "busing" were widely resented, even in Boston, once the seat of abolitionism. Low-income whites who could not afford private schools for their children and who felt their job security threatened by new competition from minority groups and women were especially alienated.

The Democrats and the integration they had pushed and supported were blamed for these perceived threats to the established order. Twenty-four years of Republican and conservative ascendancy, broken only briefly and feebly by Jimmy Carter's single presidential term (1977–81),[2] followed the election of 1968 with near inevitability.

During the seventies escalating fears of busing, affirmative action, and neighborhood breakdown caused many whites to see integration not as laudable national policy but as "racism in reverse." The deterioration of cities and the increase in crime and violence were largely blamed on blacks. This development of the newly visible underclass, moreover, sharpened white fear and anger.

Whites continued to look down at the black "faces at the bottom of society's well," those "magical faces" of which Derrick Bell has written that "[e]ven the poorest whites, those who must live their lives only a few levels above, gain their self-esteem by gazing down at us." Those black faces had always been there, viewed merely with contempt and complacency by some, with bitter relief by the poor, the disadvantaged, the despised, who had little of value but their white skins. Despite civil rights laws, surely those "faces at the bottom of the well" always would be there.

Their absence would announce to whites not just the end of segregation in the South but the arrival of an all but unimaginable new world, making life less comfortable for some whites, nearly unbearable for others. And those black faces imposed a double imperative on whites: Not only must they be kept at the bottom of the well, but those who would bring them to the top, or nearer to it, must be feared, castigated, opposed.

And then came Reagan.

* * *

On August 3, 1980, looking virile and businesslike, he spoke in shirtsleeves to a cheering crowd of about ten thousand people, nearly all white, at the Neshoba County Fairgrounds near Philadelphia, Mississippi.

"I believe in states' rights," Reagan declared that day in the well-modulated voice that was to become so familiar to Americans. The Republican presidential nominee then promised a restoration to the states and to local governments of "the power that properly belongs to them."

Fresh from his Republican National Convention victory at Detroit, Ronald Reagan was making the first formal appearance of his presidential campaign, and his choice of a site for that opening appearance was powerfully symbolic: Philadelphia, Mississippi, was the place where three volunteer civil rights workers in the Mississippi Summer Project of 1964, two Jews and a black—Andrew Goodman, Michael Schwerner, and James Chaney—had been murdered. The sheriff and deputy sheriff of Neshoba County had been charged with these crimes. Most of the county's white population, by its silence, had been either complicit or oblivious.

No presidential candidate before Reagan had visited remote Neshoba County, in a state that had been the last stronghold of resistance to blacks' civil rights. Reagan was there because a Mississippi member of Congress, Trent Lott (now the [Senate majority leader]), had assured him that a personal visit to the state would carry it for him against President Carter.

The candidate might not fully have grasped the significance of Philadelphia,

as later he would not understand the opposition to his visit to the Bitburg Cemetery in Germany, where members of the Nazi SS were buried. But if Reagan didn't know about Philadelphia, Mississippi, he should have. It could not conceivably have been a routine campaign stop. One week after the bodies of Goodman, Schwerner, and Chaney had been discovered buried in a nearby earthen dam in 1964, Governor Paul Johnson—without a word of sympathy for the dead youths or their families—had told a crowd of six thousand at the Neshoba County fair that no Mississippian, including state officials, had any obligation to obey the Civil Rights Act of 1964.

"Integration," Johnson declaimed, "is like Prohibition. If the people don't want it, a whole army can't enforce it."

In 1964 that was the voice of last-ditch resistance, soon to be overwhelmed by events. But by 1980, as Ronald Reagan stood where the governor had stood, looking out upon much the same sea of white faces, it was possible to see Paul Johnson as a national prophet, no longer as a southern relic. Reagan's mere appearance at Philadelphia—unthinkable for a major-party presidential candidate even a few years earlier—was evidence that times had changed, radically. And when the candidate chose to open his champaign where Schwerner, Chaney, and Goodman had made the last sacrifice to rabid segregationist resistance, he sent the nation a message many Americans *wanted* to hear. That message was far more powerful and far more convincing than the deceptive plausibility with which Reagan was later to call for a "color-blind society" and insist that he was "heart and soul in favor of the things that have been done in the name of civil rights and desegregation. . . ."

Reagan's actual policies exposed those words as lip service, and anyway, much of the nation was watching what he did—visiting Philadelphia, Mississippi, for instance—rather than listening to what he said. Even before his speech at Philadelphia, Reagan had openly opposed the Civil Rights Act of 1964, the Voting Rights Act of 1965, the Open Housing Act of 1968 and in numerous other ways had demonstrated his fundamental opposition to the *fact*, if not the concept, of integration. And by the time he sought the presidency—nearly winning the Republican nomination in 1976, taking it easily in 1980—neither his clear anti-integration record nor even his appearance in Mississippi was a political liability. It was, in fact, largely *because* of these that Ronald Reagan was elected to the White House.

Reagan did not single-handedly and from his own convictions turn the nation against integration. Rather a national reversal had begun not long after the civil rights triumphs of the sixties and his own entry into public life in California. In those years, as outlined above, national reluctance—neither confined to the South nor always most pronounced there—moved steadily toward opposition to integration. That movement owed more to crime, the underclass, busing, affirmative action, and *fear* (as much of the unknown as of any observable phenomena) than to the words or deeds of any one politician, even George Wallace. Reagan benefited politically from a greatly changed public mood even as he contributed to that mood.

Once he was in the Oval Office, moreover, the anti–civil rights record

Reagan accumulated was so lengthy and substantial that he could not have compiled it without the acquiescence and support of white Americans. "From Philadelphia to the Bitburg cemetery to the veto on sanctions against South Africa," Jesse Jackson observed toward the end of the Reagan years, "it's one unbroken ideological line."

That was true enough, but it was also true that Reagan had read accurately a public mood of disenchantment with racial integration. If even a beloved president thought blacks were being "given too much," as his actions (if not always his words) suggested, then surely ordinary Americans could think so too.

With tacit support from a popular president, it became respectable for whites to express loudly their misgivings about integration and to act on their fearful or hostile instincts about black neighbors or employees or schoolmates or job competitors. Those misgivings were many and fierce, those instincts had been frequently offended; so all too many white Americans were grateful that Reagan seemed to share their views. They took full advantage of what seemed to be approval from the top.

NOTES

1. The author is aware that not all black Americans approve of the designation "African-American," or consider it accurate. The term is used interchangeably with "black" throughout this [selection] and no disrespect is intended in either case.

2. Carter's narrow victory over Gerald Ford derived mostly from reaction against the Watergate scandal of the Nixon years and Ford's pardon of Nixon himself. Without those counterbalancing factors, the Democrats might well have lost the close election of 1976 too, owing to the party's racial record and Carter's relatively liberal stance.

POSTSCRIPT

Did the Civil Rights Movement Improve Race Relations in the United States?

Regardless of how one assesses the civil rights movement, there can be little doubt that the struggle for equality produced an important legacy. First, the movement had a critical impact on the civil rights struggles of groups other than African Americans. Women's demands for equality, the American Indian movement, and gay rights protests have all employed activities and strategies inherited from the civil rights movement. Second, there is an obvious tie between the forms of civil disobedience advocated by African American leaders and those carried out in protests against U.S. involvement in Southeast Asia. In fact, antiwar activists have linked continuing racism at home with their perception of American racism abroad. Third, as both Weisbrot and Wicker point out, the civil rights movement inadvertently produced a serious white backlash, based on the notion that majority rights were being overwhelmed by the will of a minority of the nation's citizens, which stymied further advances toward full equality.

The literature on the civil rights movement is extensive. August Meier, Elliott Rudwick, and Francis L. Broderick, eds., *Black Protest Thought in the Twentieth Century*, 2d ed. (Bobbs-Merrill, 1971) presents a collection of documents that places the activities of the 1950s and 1960s in a larger framework. The reflections of many of the participants of the movement are included in Howell Raines, *My Soul Is Rested: The Story of the Civil Rights Movement in the Deep South* (G. P. Putnam, 1977). Students should also consult Aldon D. Morris, *The Origins of the Civil Rights Movement: Black Communities Organizing for Change* (Free Press, 1984).

August Meier's contemporary assessment "On the Role of Martin Luther King," *Crisis* (1965) in many ways remains the most insightful analysis of King's leadership. More detailed studies include David L. Lewis, *King: A Critical Biography* (Praeger, 1970); Stephen B. Oates, *Let the Trumpet Sound: The Life of Martin Luther King, Jr.* (Harper & Row, 1982); David J. Garrow's Pulitzer Prize–winning *Bearing the Cross: Martin Luther King, Jr., and the Southern Christian Leadership Conference* (William Morrow, 1986); and Adam Fairclough, *To Redeem the Soul of America: The Southern Christian Leadership Conference and Martin Luther King, Jr.* (University of Georgia Press, 1987). Taylor Branch's *Parting the Waters: America in the King Years, 1954–63* (Simon & Schuster, 1988) is interesting. For King's own assessment of his campaigns and the movement in general, see *Stride Toward Freedom: The Montgomery Story* (Harper & Brothers, 1958); *Why We Can't Wait* (Signet, 1964); and *Where Do We Go from Here: Chaos or Community?* (Harper & Row, 1967).

The black nationalist critique of King and the nonviolent direct action campaign is effectively presented in Malcolm X (with Alex Haley), *The Autobiography of Malcolm X* (Grove Press, 1964) and Peter Goldman, *The Death and Life of Malcolm X* (Harper & Row, 1974). Recent interest in Malcolm X is reflected not only in Spike Lee's 1992 motion picture *X* but also in Bruce Perry, *Malcolm: The Life of a Man Who Changed Black America* (Station Hill, 1991). James H. Cone's *Martin and Malcolm and America: A Dream or a Nightmare* (Orbis, 1991) is a valuable analysis that emphasizes the convergence of these two leaders' ideas.

For an understanding of two prominent civil rights organizations, see August Meier and Elliott Rudwick, *CORE: A Study in the Civil Rights Movement, 1942–1968* (Oxford University Press, 1973) and Clayborne Carson, *In Struggle: SNCC and the Black Awakening of the 1960s* (Harvard University Press, 1981). William H. Chafe, in *Civilities and Civil Rights: Greensboro, North Carolina, and the Black Struggle for Freedom* (Oxford University Press, 1980), evaluates the impact of the movement on race relations in a single city. Seth Cagin and Philip Dray, *We Are Not Afraid: The Story of Goodman, Schwerner, and Chaney and the Civil Rights Campaign for Mississippi* (Macmillan, 1988); John Dittmer, *Local People: The Struggle for Civil Rights in Mississippi* (University of Illinois Press, 1994); and Charles M. Payne, *I've Got the Light of Freedom: The Organizing Tradition and the Mississippi Freedom Struggle* (University of California Press, 1995) relive the terror and heroic efforts connected with the civil rights campaigns in the Magnolia State. Finally, the texture of the civil rights movement is captured brilliantly in Henry Hampton's documentary series *Eyes on the Prize*.

A critical assessment of the legacy of the civil rights movement is presented in two books by political scientist Robert C. Smith: *We Have No Leaders: African Americans in the Post–Civil Rights Era* (State University of New York Press, 1994) and *Racism in the Post–Civil Rights Era: Now You See It, Now You Don't* (State University of New York Press, 1996).

ISSUE 15

Did the Antiwar Movement Prolong War in Vietnam?

YES: Adam Garfinkle, from *Telltale Hearts: The Origins and Impact of the Vietnam Antiwar Movement* (St. Martin's Press, 1995)

NO: Melvin Small, from *Johnson, Nixon, and the Doves* (Rutgers University Press, 1988)

ISSUE SUMMARY

YES: Author and editor Adam Garfinkle argues that the antiwar movement had little or no effect on major policy decisions about Vietnam during the presidencies of Lyndon Johnson and Richard Nixon. Paradoxically, the movement may have contributed to a patriotic backlash that helped Johnson and Nixon to continue the war.

NO: Professor of history Melvin Small argues that the antiwar movement —especially the October 1967 march on the Pentagon and the October 1969 moratorium—had a significant impact on the Vietnam War policies of Johnson and Nixon.

At the end of World War II, imperialism was coming to a close in Asia. Japan's defeat spelled the end of its control over China, Korea, and the countries of Southeast Asia. Attempts by the European nations to reestablish their empires were doomed. Anti-imperialist movements emerged all over Asia and Africa, often producing chaos.

The United States faced a dilemma. America was a nation conceived in revolution and was sympathetic to the struggles of Third World nations. But the United States was afraid that many of the revolutionary leaders were Communists who would place their countries under the control of the expanding empire of the Soviet Union. By the late 1940s the Truman administration decided that it was necessary to stop the spread of communism. The policy that resulted was known as containment.

Vietnam provided a test of the containment doctrine in Asia. Vietnam had been a French protectorate from 1885 until Japan took control of it during World War II. Shortly before the war ended, the Japanese gave Vietnam its independence, but the French were determined to reestablish their influence in the area. Conflicts emerged between the French-led nationalist forces of South Vietnam and the Communist-dominated provisional government of the Democratic Republic of Vietnam (DRV), which was established in Hanoi in August 1945. Ho Chi Minh was the president of the DRV. An avowed Communist since the 1920s, Ho had also become the major nationalist figure in Vietnam. As the leader of the anti-imperialist movement against French and Japanese colonialism for over 30 years, Ho managed to tie together the communist and nationalist movements in Vietnam.

A full-scale war broke out in 1946 between the communist government of North Vietnam and the French-dominated country of South Vietnam. After the Communists defeated the French at the battle of Dien Bien Phu in May 1954, the latter decided to pull out. At the Geneva Conference that summer, Vietnam was divided at the 17th parallel, pending elections.

The United States became directly involved in Vietnam after the French withdrew. In 1955 the Republican president Dwight D. Eisenhower refused to recognize the Geneva Accord but supported the establishment of the South Vietnamese government. Its leader, Ngo Dinh Diem, an authoritarian Catholic, was more popular with U.S. politicians than with the Buddhist peasants of South Vietnam, who resented his oppressive rule. In 1956 Diem, with U.S. approval, refused to hold elections, which would have provided a unified government for Vietnam in accordance with the Geneva Agreement. The Communists in the north responded by again taking up the armed struggle. The war continued for another 19 years.

Both President Eisenhower and his successor, John F. Kennedy, supported the overthrow of the Diem regime in October 1963 and hoped that the successor government would establish an alternative to communism. It did not work. Kennedy himself was assassinated three weeks later. His successor, Lyndon B. Johnson, changed the character of American policy in Vietnam by escalating the air war and increasing the number of ground forces from 21,000 in 1965 to a full fighting force of 525,000 at its peak in 1968.

The next president, Richard Nixon, adopted a new policy of "Vietnamization" of the war. Military aid to South Vietnam was increased to ensure the defeat of the Communists. At the same time, American troops were gradually withdrawn from Vietnam. South Vietnamese president Thieu recognized the weakness of his own position without the support of U.S. troops. He reluctantly signed the Paris Accords in January 1973. Once U.S. soldiers were withdrawn, Thieu's regime was doomed. In the spring of 1975 a full-scale war broke out and the South Vietnamese government collapsed.

What effect did antiwar demonstrators have on the policies of the Johnson and Nixon administrations? In the following selections, Adam Garfinkle argues that the demonstrators had no effect on the escalations undertaken by Johnson and the Vietnamization of the war carried out by Nixon. He asserts that the protestors were disliked by most Americans and that they created patriotic support for the presidents' foreign policies. Melvin Small maintains that the march on the Pentagon in October 1967 and the nationwide local mobilizations in October 1969 caused both presidents to alter their policies in Vietnam.

YES

Adam Garfinkle

TRUTHS AND CONSEQUENCES

SOUTHEAST ASIA: HOW MUCH DID THE MOVEMENT MATTER?

To evaluate the effect of the antiwar movement on the prosecution of the war and its final outcome is difficult business. We can sum up our argument as follows: To the modest extent that the antiwar movement ever worked to limit U.S. involvement in Vietnam, it did so *before* the election of Lyndon Johnson and *after* the election of Richard Nixon, particularly after U.S. ground troops had been withdrawn and U.S. prisoners of war returned in early 1973. In between, and particularly in the period between 1965 and 1970—and possibly up to the 1972 election—the movement achieved nothing concrete according to its own measure and probably helped the sitting administrations to manage the broadest segments of American public opinion into relative quiescence. Its counterproductive impact may have been modest—as modest as its limiting impact before and after this core period—but that was its direction.

It is clear that the Johnson administration was *self-restrained* from sharp escalation, not restrained because of public opinion, which was more hawkish than the administration much of the time, or because of the antiwar movement, which was marginal to the decision-making process throughout. Antiwar demonstrations mounted and populated by radicals stifled at least as much if not more nonradical dissent against the war than they stimulated. Most Americans, while concerned about a war seemingly without end or prospect of clearcut victory, were more prepared to suffer in silence than to associate themselves with lurid leftists and yelping Yippies.

And when the Johnson administration changed course in March 1968, it did so through a calculation of various costs and benefits in which the antiwar movement counted as only one of several factors and certainly not as a major one. Nor can the changed views of the Wise Men, as they revisited the problem in February and March of that year, be ascribed to the antiwar movement in any simple way. Their changed views appear to have been predicated not only on erroneous assumptions about public opinion after the Tet offensive, but also on account of a confluence of other, more fundamental factors than what they referred to euphemistically as divisions in the nation. Even then, to the Wise Men, those divisions probably meant divisions in establishment opinion, division among Democratic politicians and opinion leaders, not the dissent represented by radicals in the streets.

The antiwar movement succeeded eventually in limiting U.S. military involvement only to the extent that antiwar sentiment became reliberalized through the Democratic Party and its post-1969 Moratorium youth contingent. At that point, only after the fizzled incandescence of the New Left in the 1968–69 period, the movement affected marginally the timing and perhaps the tone of the decision to negotiate withdrawal, and this was done in consort with the Congress —hardly an extra-parliamentary phenomenon over all. The movement was not responsible for the overthrow of policy itself; that rested first with Lyndon Johnson's decision to change U.S. policy aims and then with Richard Nixon's decision to limit them further in deference to broader foreign and domestic policy goals.

We mustn't forget, too, that while the movement moved back toward and into the Democratic Party between 1970 and 1974, that party never had a chance to freely pursue its own plans for withdrawal from Vietnam. This is because the Republicans won the White House in the 1968 election. In other words, another layer, or filter—a Republican White House—interposed itself between the flow of antiwar sentiment into mainstream politics and actual executive branch decisions about the war. President Nixon did shape his administration's diplomatic and military policies over Vietnam to what he thought domestic political traffic would bear, but that isn't the same as claiming that the movement had a direct restraining influ-

ence on administration policy. Rather, the deradicalized movement merged with growing broad public antiwar sentiment, which pushed the Democrats, and the Democrats pushed the Republicans, who, as practicing politicians, were already looking toward the next midterm and presidential elections. Such dynamics describe what radical movement activists used to refer to derisively as "working through the system." It is hardly heroic, and hardly the stuff of which many antiwar radicals were proud then and are still proud of today.

As antiwar sentiment became more firmly ensconced in the Congress, it contributed to the cutoff of U.S. aid to South Vietnam, undermined Saigon's confidence, and contributed to its fall to the Communist regime in Hanoi. This might not have happened had the Nixon administration taken a different approach to the Paris Accords and to foreign policy priorities generally. That is to say: The White House made the essential decision to disengage using the Paris Accords as a means to create a "decent interval." It was a decision not to find out if Vietnamization would work if it took 10 to 12 years instead of 2 or 3. There was nothing inevitable about this decision, but, with a new global foreign policy to unfurl and an election to win in 1972, Richard Nixon made it. To blame the Congress entirely for the fall of South Vietnam is unfair. To blame—or credit— the antiwar movement isn't justified in the least.

The antiwar movement neither lost the war nor caused the subsequent bloodbath in Southeast Asia. In the broadest sense, the war was lost because the American ship of state itself had lost its bearings. The expansion of containment to Asia and its post-Korean War militarization merged with a rapidly expanding economic base to produce a level of American hubris that was bound to send its ship of state onto the rocks sooner or later. However morally motivated, the U.S. commitment to Vietnam was strategically unsound; thus, even had the war been won the costs might well have exceeded any strategic benefits. But the war was not won because U.S. administrative, diplomatic, and especially military strategies failed. In other words, even beyond a flawed decision to commit itself, which flowed from the lack of a realistic strategy for containing polycentric Communism in the geostrategic peripheries of the Cold War, the Vietnam War was lost by some combination of the U.S. military's inability to adapt to politico-military counterinsurgency warfare, ill-advised micromanagement of the war by Pentagon civilians, and maladroit meddling in South Vietnam's stygian political system. None of these sources of American defeat was set in motion or significantly worsened either by antiwar activism or by fear of it in Washington.

What happened to the Vietnamese and Cambodian people happened because the war was lost, but, again, the antiwar movement did not play a major role in that. The only way to argue otherwise is to assume that the movement bolstered Hanoi's morale to a decisive degree as it contemplated the "correlation of forces." No doubt the antiwar movement did boost morale in Hanoi to some degree —how could it not?—but no evidence suggests it was decisive.

Even if we assume the war was unwinnable, it still does not follow that the antiwar movement can take credit for driving that point home. The Wise Men and their bureaucratic allies made their decisions after the Tet offensive in light of their own sense of limits. After all, by March 1968 the United States had already gone beyond its self-imposed restrictions and still not won, and it had to contemplate the possibility of causing still greater damage to American life and squandering still more of its treasure without victory. Such a specter was quite sufficient to generate a change of view; it required no help from the street.

About the essential decision to fight in Vietnam, the antiwar movement was right but for the wrong reasons. The war's sources had nothing to do with the sinister face of corporate capitalism, but the war *was* a mistake. The Johnson administration *was* pursuing policies that, even though well-intended, were incoherent and unwise. Public dissent against those policies was a reasonable response to such unwisdom. There is, after all, nothing sinister about protesting either a futile war or the steely hubris of a government that cannot recognize or admit that it has erred.

The antiwar movement was not responsible for the basic flow of American government judgments about Vietnam, and what minor influence it did have tended to reinforce policy stasis during the Johnson period and to quicken modestly the reduction of military activity during the Nixon period. How does this affect common arguments about the merit, the guilt, and the responsibility that the antiwar movement should bear for what happened in Southeast Asia after 1975?

Few can doubt that a horrific bloodbath took place in Southeast Asia after 1975, and that millions of people who suddenly wanted desperately to escape their homeland did so for good reason. Doves have tended to argue that the antiwar movement saved American lives but did not sacrifice Asian ones because the war was unwinnable, and what was going to happen was going to happen eventually anyway. American participation in the war made what happened worse, they claim, especially in Cambodia, but it never could have made anything better. Most hawks have claimed the reverse, blaming what happened directly on the loss of the war, and the loss of the war on the antiwar movement and other related maladies on the home front. What are we to make of these judgments in light of the analysis brought here?

One way to answer this question is to divide our thinking into consideration of intentions and consequences. Judging intentions alone is often fruitless because the world rarely abets the simple transformation of intentions, whether good or evil, into intended consequences. Judging consequences alone, however, can suggest the premise that history proclaims its own meaning—that what happened was meant to happen—but it doesn't.

What goes for the antiwar movement goes for the war itself. Even if we discount the impact of the movement, it is still no simple matter to determine how much of what happened in Southeast Asia after 1975 was the fault of the United States. Would South Vietnam have survived without American intervention in 1964–65? If not, did all the United States achieve amount to a delay of a decade? Was that worth 58,000 American lives? Would Cambodia have been spared Pol Pot and then a Vietnamese occupation had the Nixon administration not bombed and invaded the country? Or doesn't it follow instead that a quicker Communist victory in Vietnam would have brought the Khmer Rouge to power sooner rather than later? So in consideration of

intentions and consequences it is best to consider those of the antiwar movement and the government it opposed together.

As to intentions, the great majority of those active in the antiwar movement clearly felt themselves to be patriotic Americans. The movement cannot be fairly characterized as having been made up of primarily individuals who were self-hating, psychologically aberrant, or sociopathic. Acts of self-sacrifice, powerful idealism, and a deep love of country characterized the antiwar movement at least in part throughout its existence.

The U.S. government was also well-intended. It wished to stop Communism because it believed it to be wrong, and it wanted to help the Vietnamese achieve self-determination because it believed that to be right. There was no hidden agenda of economic exploitation, of seeking bases in order to wage aggressive war against China, of fighting mainly to generate profits for a military-industrial complex.

But good intentions are not always useful measures for judgment because everyone except the pathologically ill is well-intended at least on an abstract level. When parts of the antiwar movement came to believe that love for country required destroying all existing social structures and norms, it adopted the same dubious logic (dubiously) attributed to a U.S. military commander who said that a certain Vietnamese village had to be destroyed in order to be saved. When the Johnson administration went to war, it did almost everything wrong, from undermining the Saigon government instead of building it up to pushing peasants and intellectuals both into the arms of the Vietcong instead of the other way around. Instead of being flexible enough to recognize error, the U.S. military pursued its counterproductive behavior to a virtual point of no return, politically if not literally, on the battlefield. So much for good intentions.

When one speaks of consequences, on the other hand, the first thing to remember is that ethics is a serious discipline. Several popular but blithe judgments that have been made about Vietnam slide off the low end of the logic scale. Some have argued, for example, that the war effort was worth it, despite the loss of South Vietnam, because it bought a decade's worth of time for the rest of Southeast Asia to mobilize and develop, and for ASEAN (the Association of Southeast Asian Nations) to consolidate. Is this really what 58,000 Americans died for?

Others have argued that since Communism is dead anyway, and since Vietnam is a basket case, it proves that even bothering to stop Communism in Southeast Asia was a stupid thing to do in the first place. Mickey Kaus of *The New Republic* argued that the best case against Communism in the area is Vietnam's economic failure, a case that never could have been made had the United States won the war: "Vietnam may even (in the long run) be better off for the Communists' victory. In power they discredited themselves in a way that never would have been possible if they'd remained a Philippine-like guerrilla opposition."

This is a worthwhile line of reasoning if only because it makes nonsense of Frances Fitzgerald's prophecies about the "cleansing effects" of the Vietnamese revolution. The only thing that the Vietnamese revolution cleansed, or should have cleansed, was the foolish idea that Third World revolutions are cleansing. But Kaus never mentions costs: the re-education camps; the boat people who left, risking or giving their lives in the process; and the millions living in deepening poverty and fear under Hanoi's iron fist since 1975. Is scoring a rarefied debating point about Asian Communism worth it to those who have paid the price? Too bad Kaus never bothered to ask them.

Clearly, justifying the war post hoc on the basis of "results" that were neither primary nor explicit is not very compelling. Neither is justifying opposition to the war based on information no one could possibly have had at the time; obviously, it isn't much of an achievement to conclude that the war was unwinnable after one already knows the outcome. Just because something is hard to do—such as bringing ethics to bear on a war after the fact—is no reason to be satisfied with arguments like these.

Moral judgment is always a problem but always a necessity. So I make mine: Both the government and the antiwar movement were well-intentioned, and both failed to translate good intentions into good consequences. The same can probably be said for both South and North Vietnamese leaders. Simply put, what happened both here and in Southeast Asia is that the mistakes of the powerful overwhelmed the mistakes of the weak. Is it so, as Nietzsche said, that "the errors of great men are venerable because they are more fruitful than the truths of little men"? No, they are only more horrible. The antiwar movement never came close to doing the sort of harm that the failed policies of the U.S. government did. Unfortunately, it seems fairly clear that neither movement nor government did anybody in Vietnam any good at all....

THE POLITICS OF MEMORY: BEYOND FAITH AND REASON

The telltale heart beats loudest within the breasts of those who were there at the creation of the antiwar movement and who lived through its intense, unstuck times. This is the font of the politics of memory, elusive and unfathomable, yet indelible and ineradicable. The movement's consequences for the Vietnam generation, and through it for America itself, have been felt already for a decade or more. They can never be wholly undone. As [Nicholas] Lemann [born in 1954] and so many others have come to realize:

> Everything is pretty much the same on the surface. Underneath, everything is different. We have no center. Our parents did.... People like me assumed the [American] enterprise was not noble, rebelled against it for a time, and then joined it, not out of the sincere belief of our parents, but because there was no other choice. That's why today, although we're better educated than they were, we vote less. It's why... we feel no loyalty to our employers. It's why marriage and children scare us.... When that is the way you are, how do you conduct your life?

It's a tough question.

Whether the revolt of the 1960s, excesses and all, helped move America back to its original spiritual career remains to be seen. Even most 1960s apologists seem unaware of what it is that the youth revolt of the 1960s was trying to teach us. It needs to teach us this: The centrality of value, as communicated and sacralized within the most deeply rooted of family processes, is the core of any healthy society. Without it, we are lost. It comes down to knowing the difference between right and wrong and being able to teach this to our children with sincerity and confidence.

The fact that this issue was raised by the tumult of the 1960s, even if inchoately, is what redeems the entire epoch if nothing else does. This key point, too, has a way of suggesting whether and if the ideas of the 1960s are still meaningful. It is a simple thing really: If the problems that evoked the 1960s have been solved, then the ideas lose force and interest. "Ideas perish from inanition far more frequently than as a result of being refuted by argument," said Isaiah Berlin, because the problems they were designed to confront are no longer pressing. "Philosophy comes from the collision of ideas which create problems. Life changes, so do the ideas, so do the collisions."

But the cultural critique made in the 1960s has not gone away; the strong attraction to the 1960s is *not* mere nostalgia. The French have a phrase that may explain this attraction: *jolie laide*. This literally translates as "good-looking ugly woman." What it means is a woman who is somehow attractive despite not being conventionally pretty. This phrase well describes the 1960s. The reason so many remain fascinated with these difficult and even embarrassing times is that the deeper issues that gave rise to the revolt are with us still. We have not solved the riddle of how to live meaningful and happy lives beyond the ages of both faith and reason. Until we do, the 1960s and other molten times like them will tantalize us with visions of a better world, even amid the miseries of generational warfare and the inevitable anxieties of social change.

NO

Melvin Small

JOHNSON, NIXON, AND THE DOVES

As I was leaving Leonard Garment's office after an interview, he asked me whether I thought antiwar dissenters had affected the decision makers. I replied that I did not know yet, as my research was incomplete. "But surely," the lawyer responded, "you must have a theory of the case."

At that time, midway through my research, I was pursuing many theories. Among the most plausible were that the movement (1) exerted pressures directly on Johnson and Nixon that contributed to their deescalation policies; (2) exerted pressures indirectly by turning the public against the war; (3) encouraged the North Vietnamese to fight on long enough to the point that Americans demanded a withdrawal from Southeast Asia; (4) influenced American political and military strategies, since Johnson and Nixon were convinced that Hanoi counted on the movement; (5) retarded the growth of general antiwar sentiment because the public perceived the protesters as unpatriotic; and (6) combinations of these theories.

Although I still cannot answer Garment's question categorically, it is clear to me now that the antiwar movement and antiwar criticism in the media and Congress had a significant impact on the Vietnam policies of both Johnson and Nixon. At two key points at least—October 1967 and October 1969—mass demonstrations affected American foreign policy. The March on the Pentagon shocked many in the Johnson administration and produced the public relations campaign that contributed to public shock after Tet. The Moratorium helped to convince Nixon that Americans would not accept the savage blows envisaged in Operation Duck Hook. On many other occasions, involving such issues as bombing pauses, diplomatic and military initiatives, and major speeches, antiwar activities and dissent were important factors for the decision makers. Even more dramatically, the movement played a role in Lyndon Johnson's decisions not to seek a second term and to wind down the war and played a major, if latent, role in restraining Richard Nixon from reescalating. In addition, many of the Watergate crimes were related to Nixon's attempt to crush the movement. Thus, the movement played an indirect role in the first resignation of a president in American history.

The extent of the impact of the movement on decision makers cannot be gauged through an empirical approach. The most ingenious attempt, which correlated policy and opinion changes with mass demonstrations, came up with inconclusive and unconvincing findings. The historian must rely instead on traditional tools to flesh out the often impressionistic evidence that allows one to make educated guesses about policymaking.

It is never easy to determine the motivations behind any public policy. The motivations behind foreign policies are even more difficult to determine than the motivations behind domestic policies, if only because officials try to obscure the role of sordid domestic politics when they defend national security. Irrespective of the stated and attributed rationales for foreign policies, one can identify the factors that attracted the attention of the decision makers as they considered their options. Archival and published records reveal the external events that worried them enough to be taken into account as they decided what and when to bomb in Vietnam, how many soldiers to call up or send home, and what sorts of diplomatic initiatives to undertake. Further, one can assess the importance of the antiwar movement to Washington by the energies expended in monitoring and suppressing its activities. If, as the key figures often said, the movement had no impact on their foreign policies, why was it that they spent so much of their time and attention on it?

Even those who downplay the importance of the movement concede that public opinion was a crucial variable in the construction of Vietnam policies. It is in their links to public opinion that the movement and antiwar critics exercised their most profound influence on those policies. To be sure, throughout the terms of both presidents, public opinion polls revealed considerable support for whatever the military did in Vietnam. On the other hand, in both administrations, support for escalation tended to decrease as the war dragged on and as first Johnson and then Nixon proved incapable of terminating it with dispatch.

Antiwar activities helped convince more and more Americans to oppose the war, or at least begin to feel uncomfortable about the nation's involvement in Vietnam. At times, some of their activities, as framed by sensation-seeking media, may have produced a patriotic backlash. Overall, however, the movement eroded support for Johnson and Nixon, especially among college students at the best universities, their parents, and members of the attentive and informed public. Some groups of people in the United States count for more than others. The loss of Yale and the *New York Times* to Johnson and even Nixon meant more than the retention of support from state colleges in Texas and the Scripps-Howard chain of newspapers. Through their constant and often publicized attacks, experts in the movement, the media, and on the campuses helped to destroy the knee-jerk notion that "they in Washington know." This was a very important development. For the first time since 1945, major reference figures in the bipartisan establishment began to speak out against an American cold war policy and led many citizens to question the judgment and wisdom of their presidents.

From the start, it was clear that the longer the war went on, the more likely Americans would tire of their increasingly costly involvement. If the United States could not win, in the absence of a strong initial and sustained commitment to wait out the patient and dedicated enemy in Vietnam, pressures for withdrawal had to increase over time. Dean Rusk, who sees opposition rising at home because of Tet and other policy failures, irrespective of previous criticism from the antiwar movement, emphasizes this approach.

Yet that previous criticism had to be important for several reasons. First, movement activities and elite opposition in the media helped to keep the war "on the front burner" from 1965 through 1971. With the war an object of almost constant attention, presidents found it difficult to pursue military policies that the public would find objectionable. In addition, the critics presented arguments and information that provided a framework for those who did not know how to articulate their general opposition to what was becoming an endless war. The existence of any opposition helped to reinforce other opposition. Senator [Wayne] Morse's lonely stand against the war in 1964 encouraged some citizens in their opposition, as did Senator [J. William] Fulbright's hearings in early 1966, which had been encouraged by the rising opposition on elite campuses during the previous year. That opposition was legitimized to some degree when congressmen read its letters and petitions into the *Congressional Record*.

The movement's impact on the public and on the administration was enhanced by the way the antiwar argument was presented. As one critic of the movement has argued, those who opposed the war stole the moral issue from the administration early on. That issue, simplistic and naive from a Realpolitik perspective, was understood more easily than the incompetently presented limited war argument. The moral argument,

with the bombing and destruction of peasant society as its cornerstone, was echoed in Western Europe as well as in neutral nations. As the war continued, the argument received "disproportionate media attention," according to Walt Rostow.

The antiwar movement plus the course of events affected the intellectual and opinion-making community, which in turn encouraged the activists and weakened the administration. Much of the nation's intellectual elite was associated with the prestigious universities where mass protests began and were nurtured. Both Johnson and Nixon blamed pied-piper professors on those campuses, more than students, for their problems there.

Whether their animosity was properly targeted, Johnson and Nixon should have expected the criticism from those opinion leaders. Irving Kristol contends that "no modern nation ever constructed a foreign policy acceptable to its intellectuals." Perhaps, but American intellectuals were not especially dovish in 1964 and 1965. By 1970, however, according to one survey, intellectuals were overwhelmingly antiwar, with more than two-thirds changing their views during the preceding years. Their favorite journals, the *New York Times*, the *New Yorker*, and the *New York Review of Books*, influenced them, and the journals, in turn, were influenced by many of the intellectuals themselves.

The alienation of the American intellectual elite did not affect the policymakers directly, in part because there was little contact between that elite and the Oval Office. That was to be expected. At the same time, the desertion of the intellectuals had an indirect impact on government officials. In a trickle-down effect, Democratic party leaders, as well as those members of the public who took their lead from favorite writers and professors, were influenced by the desertion from the cold war foreign policy consensus of many liberal intellectuals. "Trickle down" is even too vague a term to describe the relationship between intellectual discontent and the rise of the Kennedy opposition faction within the party after 1965.

Kristol may have been correct about intellectuals generally disapproving of a nation's foreign policy, especially a policy that appears to be amoral or immoral, but it is the extent of that disapproval and the passion with which it was held that is important on the Vietnam issue. It is difficult for a democracy to operate effectively in the international sphere without the support of its intellectual leadership.

It is also clear that the disaffection of intellectuals and elite college students affected establishment types outside of government who feared for the future of their country. Respected leaders such as Dean Acheson and Clark Clifford, who worried about the establishment in the next generation, ultimately urged the administration to cut its losses before the country fell apart.

Antiwar protests, among others, in a period that witnessed unprecedented rowdy demonstrations, took a physical and emotional toll on the occupants of the White House. Neither Johnson nor Nixon could tolerate criticism, even when they expected it from the media or from liberals. Both were subjected to the most extensive and abusive criticism of any twentieth-century president. On occasion, they and their advisers went to great lengths to avoid the demonstrators, who nevertheless managed to appear almost every time the presidents stepped out of the White House. Johnson, in particular, was irritated by the incessant public manifestations of displeasure with his policies and that irritation may have been a background variable in his decision to leave Washington for the peace of his ranch.

Both Johnson and Nixon developed offensives against their critics, especially in the movement, which included the mobilization of the CIA and FBI to monitor and harass them. Both claimed that such activities were not a product of their own concern with demonstrations but their fear that Hanoi would misinterpret them. Further, both believed that some, if not most, of the antiwar movement was foreign inspired and financed; the government had to devote considerable energies to defend the country against subversion.

On the latter charge, they were mistaken. The intelligence agencies concluded in report after report that foreign influences in the antiwar movement were marginal. On the other hand, their major contention that the movement and all of its manifestations encouraged Hanoi is no doubt true. The key question, and an imponderable one at that, is whether that encouragement prolonged the war.

Without a strong antiwar movement that limited the administration's abilities to pursue a tougher military policy, goes the prolongation argument, the North Vietnamese would have accepted a half a loaf and the war would have ended much sooner. The antiwar movement here is linked to the general development of antiwar attitudes among the public.

The contest for the public's support between the government and its opponents was an important element in the making of Vietnam policy. For example, when Richard Nixon committed Washington to a Vietnamization program, domestic opinion was one "crucial variable." Vietnamization would convince the public that the war was not endless; the American commitment would decrease gradually. Domestic support would be maintained that would convince the North Vietnamese not to count on the American people to force Nixon's negotiating hand. There was a "logical flaw" in this position. If Vietnamization cooled dovish fervor in the United States, it also revealed the light at the end of the tunnel for Hanoi. Why negotiate when the last American soldier would depart Vietnam in the foreseeable future?

Moreover, the prolongation-of-the-war argument deemphasizes the commitment of Hanoi to fight on virtually forever for its goal of an independent communist Vietnam. Further, one of the major reasons Johnson and Nixon did not use tougher tactics was their fear that the Russians and Chinese might be compelled to intervene to rescue their socialist ally.

The ability to employ tougher military tactics was not just crippled by an alert antiwar movement. It is likely that the population in general, with or without the leadership of antiwar critics, would not have countenanced the bombing of the dikes in the North or the use or threatened use of tactical nuclear weapons. Americans would not have needed the movement to express their strong displeasure over the employment of such drastic means in a limited war. Here, the administrations caused their own problems. By never explaining in a convincing fashion why the war was so important, Johnson and Nixon found it impossible to escalate in a manner that would only be justified in a full-scale war vital to America's very survival. Johnson kept a low rhetorical profile in the years from 1965 through 1967, in

part to avoid encouraging the growth of the antiwar movement. We have come full circle. Although only strong presidential leadership and a declaration of national emergency would have given the presidents the backing to employ tougher tactics, one of the reasons they eschewed that approach was the fear of arousing the antiwar movement.

It is true that once Nixon talked and acted tougher in 1972, the communists accepted less than the whole loaf at the bargaining table. Whether that would have been the case before détente neutralized the Soviet Union, as well as before the destruction and the disbanding of the antiwar movement, is a difficult question.

Irrespective of the validity of the argument that the movement prolonged the war by encouraging Hanoi, Johnson and Nixon *believed* that the North Vietnamese counted on American opinion, influenced by the movement, as one of its main allies. Both administrations considered this alleged factor as they constructed their political and military strategies. Here, then, is irrefutable evidence of the impact of the movement on policymaking during the war, if only indirect impact.

Some critics ignore the movement and opinion and point to the media, where dissenters and dissenting commentators turned the nation around on the war. Unfair to both Johnson and Nixon, the media allegedly created the movement and undermined both administrations. George Christian thinks the press was lost by 1967. Hubert Humphrey saw the media in 1968, the crucial year of decision, as "viscerally and intellectually" anti-Johnson. In a similar vein, Edith Efron described television network news on Vietnam in the fall of 1969 as reflecting an antiadministration bias. Finally, the media were undoubtedly important in the popular understanding of Tet.

Former antiwar leader and sociologist Todd Gitlin, who does not agree with such criticism, nevertheless points out that movement ideas and activities were publicized by the media. One of his old colleagues, David Dellinger, has written that the movement had three explicit targets—the government, the public, and the activists themselves. Especially in the early days, when the public and government were not listening, media attention provided gratification for the foot soldiers who continued to turn out for the demonstrations. As the movement picked up steam, the media helped to legitimize dissent.

For the most part, however, experts do not agree with the theory of an "oppositional" media. In a study comparable to but more sophisticated than Efron's, Daniel Hallin concluded that at least as far as the *New York Times* and television news were concerned, both administrations received more than a fair break from the media. Another expert, Herbert Gans, demonstrated how, early in the war, Lyndon Johnson dominated the airwaves. Even when critical reports came in from the field through 1967, editors in New York and elsewhere either did not print them or toned them down.

Presidents' views dominate the media until major reference figures from the establishment begin to disagree with them and appear in such numbers that the media are forced to cover their criticism. Both Johnson and Nixon began with overwhelming support in the media, which declined over time. Their slowly developing criticism was legitimate and generally without malice. The presidents' failing and controversial policies, as well as their own growing antag-

onism to the media, led to an entirely understandable decrease in media support. Johnson, for example, blamed the media for creating the credibility gap, when in fact it was his invention.

Even the Tet argument used by the media critics can be turned around to support the notion that the press and television were more than fair to Johnson. One reason for widespread public concern over Tet was the failure of the media to prepare the nation for such an event because it accepted so uncritically the light-at-the-end-of-the-tunnel pronouncements from Washington.

The relationships between the media, the movement, public opinion, and foreign policy are complicated. They are far too complicated to blame the media for the decline of support over time for the Johnson and Nixon policies.

* * *

The antiwar movement succeeded in capturing the attention of Johnson and Nixon and affecting their policies in Vietnam. One of the important lessons one can learn from studies such as this is that government officials do not always behave the way they should according to the neat academic models of opinion formation and policymaking. Johnson and Nixon simply did not behave rationally on many occasions when they confronted media criticism and antiwar demonstrations. Surprisingly thin-skinned for professional politicians, they overreacted to criticism in unpredictable and unstructured manners. One never knew when a few demonstrators in front of the White House, or a speech on a college campus, or an editorial in the *Washington Post* might set off one or the other, even at times when they enjoyed the support of the vast majority of their constituents.

It might well be that there is less to learn here than one might suspect. Johnson and Nixon were unusual residents of the Oval Office. Both were among the most volatile, unstable, and maybe even pathological of recent presidents. Comparing their behavior and personalities to those of Roosevelt, Truman, Eisenhower, Kennedy, Ford, Carter, and Reagan, one must be leery about generalizing from Johnson and Nixon to all presidents.

Yet, as I was told time and again by such experienced presidential counselors and observers as Bryce Harlow, George Reedy, and Jack Valenti, much of the time, *all* presidents are just like everyone else. They react to criticism and challenges, even from a minority of their constituents, quite often from the gut and not from the brain. What this means is that those who exercise their rights as citizens to gather, protest, and petition in comparatively small numbers have more of an impact on their leaders than one would expect. Such a conclusion might help to sustain others who question present and future foreign policies.

POSTSCRIPT

Did the Antiwar Movement Prolong War in Vietnam?

Garfinkle believes that the antiwar demonstrations had no effect on the decisions made by the Johnson and Nixon administrations with regard to Vietnam. Public opinion polls taken at the time buttress Garfinkle's argument that the demonstrations created a patriotic backlash among middle- and working-class Americans, which ironically gave both presidents more room to maneuver in Vietnam. Elsewhere Garfinkle has argued that the backlash against the protesters contributed to the conservative realignment in politics in the 1980s dominated by the Republican presidencies of Ronald Reagan and George Bush and the congressional realignment of 1994.

Small argues that the antiwar protesters stole the moral argument from Presidents Johnson and Nixon as the war dragged on into an endless series of combat skirmishes and aerial bombardments. As the death toll grew, mass demonstrations against the war were mounted, initially at the Pentagon in October 1967, then spreading across the country.

Garfinkle and Small use different types of research in evaluating the antiwar movement. Garfinkle employs public opinion surveys to demonstrate the hostility that the general mass of Americans felt toward the antiwar protesters. Small relies on the historians' "traditional tools"—memoirs, oral interviews, official documents, diaries, and letters in archival collections—"to flesh out the often impressionistic evidence that allows one to make educated guesses about policy making." Both accounts are flawed because they are unclear in their definitions of public opinion.

The literature on the antiwar movement is sizeable and continues to grow. Both Small's *Johnson, Nixon and the Doves* and Garfinkle's *Telltale Hearts* should be read in their entirety. Garfinkle's volume contains a comprehensive and up-to-date bibliography of current and contemporary books and magazine and newspaper articles. David W. Levy offers a concise assessment in *The Debate Over Vietnam* (1991), which is part of The American Movement series published by the Johns Hopkins University Press. Two solidly researched and extensively narrated books sympathetic to the protesters are Charles DeBenedetti and Charles Chatfield, *An American Ordeal: The Antiwar Movement of the Vietnam Era* (Syracuse University Press, 1990) and Tom Wells, *The War Within: America's Battle Over Vietnam* (University of California Press, 1994). Melvin Small and William D. Hoover have edited a series of articles exploring various components of the antiwar movement in *Give Peace a Chance* (Syracuse University Press, 1992).

ISSUE 16

Will History Forgive Richard Nixon?

YES: Joan Hoff-Wilson, from "Richard M. Nixon: The Corporate Presidency," in Fred I. Greenstein, ed., *Leadership in the Modern Presidency* (Harvard University Press, 1988)

NO: Stanley I. Kutler, from "Et Tu, Bob?" *The Nation* (August 22/29, 1994)

ISSUE SUMMARY

YES: According to professor of history Joan Hoff-Wilson, the Nixon presidency reorganized the executive branch and portions of the federal bureaucracy and implemented domestic reforms in civil rights, welfare, and economic planning, despite its limited foreign policy successes and the Watergate scandal.

NO: Professor and political commentator Stanley I. Kutler argues that President Nixon was a crass, cynical, narrow-minded politician who unnecessarily prolonged the Vietnam War to ensure his reelection and implemented domestic reforms only when he could outflank his liberal opponents.

In late April 1994 former president Richard M. Nixon, age 81, died in a coma in a hospital in New York City. Twenty years before, Nixon became the only U.S. president forced to resign from office.

Richard Milhous Nixon was born in Yorba Linda in Orange County, California, on January 9, 1913, the second of five children. When he was nine his family moved to Whittier, California. His mother encouraged him to attend the local Quaker school, Whittier College, where he excelled at student politics and debating. He earned a tuition-paid scholarship to Duke University Law School and graduated third out of a class of twenty-five in 1937. He returned to Whittier and for several years worked with the town's oldest law firm.

Nixon had hopes of joining a bigger law firm, but World War II intervened. He worked in the tire rationing section for the Office of Price Administration in Washington, D.C., before joining the navy as a lieutenant, junior grade, where he served in a Naval Transport Unit in the South Pacific for the duration of the war. Before his discharge from active duty, Republicans asked him to run for a seat in California's 12th congressional district in the House of Representatives. He won the primary and defeated Jerry Vorhees, a nationally known, New Deal Democratic incumbent, in the general election of 1946. In that year the Republicans gained control of Congress for the first time since 1930.

During Nixon's campaign against Vorhees, he accused Vorhees of accepting money from a communist-dominated political action committee. This tactic, known as "red-baiting," was effective in the late 1940s and early 1950s because the American public had become frightened of the communist menace. In 1950 Nixon utilized similar tactics in running for the U.S. Senate against Congresswoman Helen Gahagan Douglas. He won easily.

Young, energetic, a vigorous campaign orator, and a senator from the second largest state in the Union with impeccable anticommunist credentials, Nixon was chosen by liberal Republicans to become General Dwight Eisenhower's running mate in the 1952 presidential election. In the election Eisenhower and Nixon overwhelmed the Democrats. Nixon became the second-youngest vice president in U.S. history and actively used the office to further his political ambitions.

The 1960 presidential campaign was one of the closest in modern times. Nixon, who was considered young for high political office at that time, lost to an even younger Democratic senator from Massachusetts, John F. Kennedy. Out of 68 million votes cast, less than 113,000 votes separated the two candidates.

In 1962 Nixon was persuaded to seek the governorship of California on the premise that he needed a power boost to keep his presidential hopes alive for 1964. Apparently, Nixon was out of touch with state politics. Governor Pat Brown defeated him by 300,000 votes.

Nixon then left for New York City and became a partner with a big-time Wall Street legal firm. He continued to speak at Republican dinners, and he supported Barry Goldwater of Arizona for the presidency in 1964. After Goldwater's decisive defeat by Lyndon B. Johnson, Nixon's political fortunes revived yet again. In March 1968 Johnson announced he was not going to run again for the presidency. Nixon took advantage of the opening and won the Republican nomination.

During the 1968 presidential campaign Nixon positioned himself between Democratic vice president Hubert Humphrey, the liberal defender of the Great Society programs, and the conservative, law-and-order third-party challenger Governor George Wallace of Alabama. Nixon stressed a more moderate brand of law and order and stated that he had a secret plan to end the war in Vietnam. He barely edged Humphrey in the popular vote, but Nixon received 301 electoral votes to 191 for Humphrey. Wallace received nearly 10 million popular votes and 46 electoral college votes.

This background brings us to Nixon's presidency. Was Nixon an effective president? In the first selection Professor Joan Hoff-Wilson argues that Nixon achieved a number of domestic policy successes in the areas of civil rights, welfare, economic planning, and in the reorganization of the executive branch and some federal agencies. Professor Stanley I. Kutler maintains that President Nixon was a crass, cynical, narrow-minded bigot who implemented policy changes for strictly political reasons.

YES

Joan Hoff-Wilson

RICHARD M. NIXON:
THE CORPORATE PRESIDENCY

Richard Milhous Nixon became president of the United States at a critical juncture in American history. Following World War II there was a general agreement between popular and elite opinion on two things: the effectiveness of most New Deal domestic policies and the necessity of most Cold War foreign policies. During the 1960s, however, these two crucial postwar consensual constructs began to break down; and the war in Indochina, with its disruptive impact on the nation's political economy, hastened their disintegration. By 1968 the traditional bipartisan, Cold War approach to the conduct of foreign affairs had been seriously undermined. Similarly, the "bigger and better" New Deal approach to the modern welfare state had reached a point of diminishing returns, even among liberals.

In 1968, when Richard Nixon finally captured the highest office in the land, he inherited not only Lyndon Johnson's Vietnam war but also LBJ's Great Society. This transfer of power occurred at the very moment when both endeavors had lost substantial support among the public at large and, most important, among a significant number of the elite group of decision makers and leaders of opinion across the country. On previous occasions when such a breakdown had occurred within policy- and opinion-making circles—before the Civil and Spanish American Wars and in the early years of the Great Depression—domestic or foreign upheavals had followed. Beginning in the 1960s the country experienced a similar series of failed presidents reminiscent of those in the unstable 1840s and 1850s, 1890s, and 1920s.

In various ways all the presidents in these transitional periods failed as crisis managers, often because they refused to take risks. Nixon, in contrast, "[couldn't] understand people who won't take risks." His proclivity for risk taking was not emphasized by scholars, journalists, and psychologists until after he was forced to resign as president. "I am not necessarily a respecter of the status quo," Nixon told Stuart Alsop in 1958; "I am a chance taker." Although this statement was made primarily in reference to foreign affairs, Nixon's entire political career has been characterized by a series of personal and professional crises and risky political policies. It is therefore not surprising that as president he rationalized many of his major foreign and domestic initiatives as crises (or at least as intolerable impasses) that could be resolved only by dramatic and sometimes drastic measures.

A breakdown in either the foreign or domestic policy consensus offers both opportunity and danger to any incumbent president. Nixon had more opportunity for risk-taking changes at home and abroad during his first administration than he would have had if elected in 1960 because of the disruptive impact of war and domestic reforms during the intervening eight years. Also, he inherited a wartime presidency, with all its temporarily enhanced extralegal powers. Although the Cold War in general has permanently increased the potential for constitutional violations by presidents, only those in the midst of a full-scale war (whether declared or undeclared) have exercised with impunity what Garry Wills has called "semi-constitutional" actions. Although Nixon was a wartime president for all but twenty months of his five and one-half years in office, he found that impunity for constitutional violations was not automatically accorded a president engaged in an undeclared, unsatisfying, and seemingly endless war. In fact, he is not usually even thought of, or referred to, as a wartime president.

Periods of war and reform have usually alternated in the United States, but in the 1960s they burgeoned simultaneously, hastening the breakdown of consensus that was so evident by the time of the 1968 election. This unusual situation transformed Nixon's largely unexamined and rather commonplace management views into more rigid and controversial ones. It also reinforced his natural predilection to bring about change through executive fiat. Thus a historical accident accounts in part for many of Nixon's unilateral administrative actions during his first term and for the events leading to his disgrace and resignation during his second.

The first few months in the Oval Office are often intoxicating, and a new president can use them in a variety of ways. But during the socioeconomic confusion and conflict of the late 1960s and early 1970s, some of the newly appointed Republican policy managers (generalists) and the frustrated holdover Democratic policy specialists (experts) in the bureaucracy unexpectedly came together and began to consider dramatic policy changes at home and abroad. Complex interactions between these very different groups produced several significant shifts in domestic and foreign affairs during the spring and summer of 1969. A radical welfare plan and dramatic foreign policy initiatives took shape.

The country had elected only one other Republican president since the onset of FDR's reform administrations thirty-six years earlier. Consequently, Nixon faced not only unprecedented opportunities for changing domestic policy as a result of the breakdown in the New Deal consensus, but also the traditional problems of presidential governance, exacerbated in this instance by bureaucratic pockets of resistance from an unusual number of holdover Democrats. Such resistance was not new, but its magnitude was particularly threatening to a distrusted (and distrustful) Republican president who did not control either house of Congress. Nixon's organizational recommendations for containing the bureaucracy disturbed his political opponents and the liberal press as much as, if not more than, their doubts about the motivation behind many of his substantive and innovative suggestions on other domestic issues such as welfare and the environment.

Because much of the press and both houses of Congress were suspicious of him, Nixon naturally viewed administrative action as one way of obtaining significant domestic reform. Moreover, some of his initial accomplishments in administratively redirecting U.S. foreign policy ultimately led him to rely more on administrative actions at home than he might have otherwise. In any case, this approach drew criticism from those who already distrusted his policies and priorities. Nixon's covert and overt expansion and prolongation of the war during this period reinforced existing suspicions about his personality and political ethics. In this sense, liberal paranoia about his domestic programs fueled Nixon's paranoia about liberal opposition to the war, and vice versa. By 1972, Nixon's success in effecting structural and substantive change in foreign policy through the exercise of unilateral executive power increasingly led him to think that he could use the same preemptive administrative approach to resolve remaining domestic problems, especially following his landslide electoral victory....

FOREIGN POLICY SCORECARD

It was clearly in Nixon's psychic and political self-interest to end the war in Vietnam as soon as possible. Although he came to office committed to negotiate a quick settlement, he ended up prolonging the conflict. As a result, he could never build the domestic consensus he needed to continue the escalated air and ground war (even with dramatically reduced U.S. troop involvement) and to ensure passage of some of his domestic programs. For Nixon (and Kissinger) Vietnam became a symbol of influence in the Third World that, in turn, was but one part of their geopolitical approach to international relations. Thus the war in Southeast Asia had to be settled as soon as possible so as not to endanger other elements of Nixonian diplomatic and domestic policy.

Instead, the president allowed his secretary of state to become egocentrically involved in secret negotiations with the North Vietnamese from August 4, 1969, to January 25, 1972 (when they were made public). As a result, the terms finally reached in 1973 were only marginally better than those rejected in 1969. The advantage gained from Hanoi's agreement to allow President Nguyen Van Thieu to remain in power in return for allowing North Vietnamese troops to remain in South Vietnam can hardly offset the additional loss of twenty thousand American lives during this three-year-period—especially given the inherent weaknesses of the Saigon government by 1973. On the tenth anniversary of the peace treaty ending the war in Vietnam, Nixon admitted to me that "Kissinger believed more in the power of negotiation than I did." He also said that he "would not have temporized as long" with the negotiating process had he not been "needlessly" concerned with what the Soviets and Chinese might think if the United States pulled out of Vietnam precipitately. Because Nixon saw no way in 1969 to end the war quickly except through overt massive bombing attacks, which the public demonstrated in 1970 and 1971 it would not tolerate, there was neither peace nor honor in Vietnam by the time that war was finally concluded on January 27, 1973; and in the interim he made matters worse by secretly bombing Cambodia.

The delayed ending to the war in Vietnam not only cast a shadow on all Nixon's other foreign policy efforts but also established secrecy, wiretapping, and capricious personal diplomacy as standard operational procedures in the conduct of foreign policy that ultimately carried over into domestic affairs. Despite often duplicitous and arbitrary actions, even Nixon's strongest critics often credit him with an unusual number of foreign policy successes.

Although fewer of his foreign policy decisions were reached in a crisis atmosphere than his domestic ones, Nixon's diplomatic legacy is weaker than he and many others have maintained. For example, the pursuit of "peace and honor" in Vietnam failed; his Middle Eastern policy because of Kissinger's shuttling ended up more show than substance; his Third World policy (outside of Vietnam and attempts to undermine the government of Allende in Chile) were nearly nonexistent; détente with the USSR soon foundered under his successors; and the Nixon Doctrine has not prevented use of U.S. troops abroad. Only rapprochement with China remains untarnished by time because it laid the foundation for recognition, even though he failed to achieve a "two China" policy in the United Nations. This summary is not meant to discredit Richard Nixon as a foreign policy expert both during and after his presidency. It is a reminder that the lasting and positive results of his diplomacy may be fading faster than some aspects of his domestic policies.

OUTFLANKING LIBERALS ON DOMESTIC REFORM

Presidents traditionally achieve their domestic objectives through legislation, appeals in the mass media, and administrative actions. During his first administration Nixon offered Congress extensive domestic legislation, most of which aimed at redistributing federal power away from Congress and the bureaucracy. When he encountered difficulty obtaining passage of these programs, he resorted more and more to reform by administrative fiat, especially at the beginning of his second term. All Nixonian domestic reforms were rhetorically linked under the rubric of the New Federalism. Most competed for attention with his well-known interest in foreign affairs. Most involved a degree of the boldness he thought necessary for a successful presidency. Most increased federal regulation of nondistributive public policies. Most were made possible in part because he was a wartime Republican president who took advantage of acting in the Disraeli tradition of enlightened conservatism. Most offended liberals (as well as many conservatives), especially when it came to implementing certain controversial policies with legislation. Many were also undertaken in a crisis atmosphere, which on occasion was manufactured by individual members of Nixon's staff to ensure his attention and action.

In some instances, as political scientist Paul J. Halpern has noted, Nixon's longstanding liberal opponents in Congress "never even bothered to get the facts straight" about these legislative and administrative innovations; the very people who, according to Daniel Moynihan, formed the "natural constituency" for most of Nixon's domestic policies refused to support his programs. It may well have been that many liberals simply could not believe that Nixon would ever do the right thing except for the wrong reason. Thus they seldom took the time to try to determine whether any of his efforts to make the 1970s a decade of reform were legitimate, however politically motivated. Additionally, such partisan opposition made Nixon all the more willing to reorganize the executive branch of government with or without congressional approval.

My own interviews with Nixon and his own (and others') recent attempts to rehabilitate his reputation indicate that Nixon thinks he will outlive the obloquy of Watergate because of his foreign policy initiatives—not because of his domestic policies. Ultimately, however, domestic reform and his attempts at comprehensive reorganization of the executive branch may become the standard by which the Nixon presidency is judged.

Environmental Policy

Although Nixon's aides cite his environmental legislation as one of his major domestic achievements, it was not high on his personal list of federal priorities, despite polls showing its growing importance as a national issue. White House central files released in 1986 clearly reveal that John Ehrlichman was initially instrumental in shaping the president's views on environmental matters and conveying a sense of crisis about them. Most ideas were filtered through him to Nixon. In fact Ehrlichman, whose particular expertise was in land-use policies, has been described by one forest conservation specialist as "the most effective environmentalist since Gifford Pinchot." Ehrlichman and John Whitaker put Nixon ahead of Congress on environmental issues, especially with respect to his use of the permit authority in the Refuse Act of 1899 to begin to clean up water supplies before Congress passed any "comprehensive water pollution enforcement plan."

"Just keep me out of trouble on environmental issues," Nixon reportedly told Ehrlichman. This proved impossible because Congress ignored Nixon's recommended ceilings when it finally passed (over his veto) the Federal Water Pollution Control Act amendments of 1972. Both Ehrlichman and Whitaker agreed then and later that it was "budget-busting" legislation designed to embarrass the president on a popular issue in an election year. Statistics later showed that the money appropriated could not be spent fast enough to achieve the legislation's stated goals. The actual annual expenditures in the first years after passage approximated those originally proposed by Nixon's staff.

Revamping Welfare

Throughout the 1968 presidential campaign Nixon's own views on welfare remained highly unfocused. But once in the Oval Office he set an unexpectedly fast pace on the issue. On January 15, 1969, he demanded an investigation by top aides into a newspaper allegation of corruption in New York City's Human Resources Administration. Nixon's extraordinary welfare legislation originated in a very circuitous fashion with two low-level Democratic holdovers from the Johnson administration, Worth Bateman and James Lyday. These two bureaucrats fortuitously exercised more influence on Robert Finch, Nixon's first secretary of health, education and welfare, than they had been able to on John W. Gardner and Wilbur J. Cohn, Johnson's two appointees. Finch was primarily responsible for obtaining Nixon's approval of what eventually became known as the Family Assistance Program (FAP).

If FAP had succeeded in Congress it would have changed the emphasis of

American welfare from providing services to providing income; thus it would have replaced the Aid to Families with Dependent Children (AFDC) program, whose payments varied widely from state to state. FAP called for anywhere from $1,600 (initially proposed in 1969) to $2,500 (proposed in 1971) for a family of four. States were expected to supplement this amount, and in addition all able-bodied heads of recipient families (except mothers with preschool children) would be required to "accept work or training." However, if a parent refused to accept work or training, only his or her payment would be withheld. In essence, FAP unconditionally guaranteed children an annual income and would have tripled the number of children then being aided by AFDC.

A fundamental switch from services to income payments proved to be too much for congressional liberals and conservatives alike, and they formed a strange alliance to vote it down. Ironically, FAP's final defeat in the Senate led to some very impressive examples of incremental legislation that might not have been passed had it not been for the original boldness of FAP. For example, Supplementary Security Income, approved on October 17, 1972, constituted a guaranteed annual income for the aged, blind, and disabled.

The demise of FAP also led Nixon to support uniform application of the food stamp program across the United States, better health insurance programs for low-income families, and an automatic cost-of-living adjustment for Social Security recipients to help them cope with inflation. In every budget for which his administration was responsible—that is, from fiscal 1971 through fiscal 1975—spending on all human resource programs exceeded spending for defense for the first time since World War II. A sevenfold increase in funding for social services under Nixon made him (not Johnson) the "last of the big spenders" on domestic programs.

Reluctant Civil Rights Achievements

Perhaps the domestic area in which Watergate has most dimmed or skewed our memories of the Nixon years is civil rights. We naturally tend to remember that during his presidency Nixon deliberately violated the civil rights of some of those who opposed his policies or were suspected of leaking information. Nixon has always correctly denied that he was a conservative on civil rights, and indeed his record on this issue, as on so many others, reveals as much political expediency as it does philosophical commitment. By 1968 there was strong southern support for his candidacy. Consequently, during his campaign he implied that if elected he would slow down enforcement of federal school desegregation policies.

Enforcement had already been painfully sluggish since the 1954 *Brown v. Board of Education* decision. By 1968 only 20 percent of black children in the South attended predominantly white schools, and none of this progress had occurred under Eisenhower or Kennedy. Moreover, the most dramatic improvement under Johnson's administration did not take place until 1968, because HEW deadlines for desegregating southern schools had been postponed four times since the passage of the 1964 Civil Rights Act. By the spring of 1968, however, a few lower court rulings, and finally the Supreme Court decision in *Green v. Board of Education*, no longer allowed any president the luxury of arguing that freedom-of-choice plans were adequate for rooting out racial discrimination, or that de facto segregation caused by residential patterns was not as unconstitutional as *de jure* segregation brought about by state or local laws.

Despite the real national crisis that existed over school desegregation, Nixon was not prepared to go beyond what he thought the decision in *Brown* had mandated, because he believed that de facto segregation could not be ended through busing or cutting off funds from school districts. Nine days after Nixon's inauguration, his administration had to decide whether to honor an HEW-initiated cutoff of funds to five southern school districts, originally scheduled to take place in the fall of 1968 but delayed until January 29, 1969. On that day Secretary Finch confirmed the cutoff but also announced that the school districts could claim funds retroactively if they complied with HEW guidelines within sixty days. This offer represented a change from the most recent set of HEW guidelines, developed in March 1968, which Johnson had never formally endorsed by signing.

At the heart of the debate over various HEW guidelines in the last half of the 1960s were two issues: whether the intent of the Civil Rights Act of 1964 had been simply to provide freedom of choice or actually to compel integration in schools; and whether freedom-of-choice agreements negotiated by HEW or lawsuits brought by the Department of Justice were the most effective ways of achieving desegregation. Under the Johnson administration the HEW approach, based on bringing recalcitrant school districts into compliance by cutting off federal funding, had prevailed. Nixon, on the other hand, argued in his First Inaugural that the "laws have caught up with our consciences" and insisted that it was now necessary "to give life to what is in the law." Accordingly, he changed the emphasis in the enforcement of school desegregation from HEW compliance agreements to Justice Department actions—a legal procedure that proved very controversial in 1969 and 1970, but one that is standard now.

Nixon has been justifiably criticized by civil rights advocates for employing delaying tactics in the South, and particularly for not endorsing busing to enforce school desegregation in the North after the April 20, 1971, Supreme Court decision in *Swann v. Charlotte-Mecklenburg Board of Education.* Despite the bitter battle in Congress and between Congress and the executive branch after *Swann,* the Nixon administration's statistical record on school desegregation is impressive. In 1968, 68 percent of all black children in the South and 40 percent in the nation as a whole attended all-black schools. By the end of 1972, 8 percent of southern black children attended all-black schools, and a little less than 12 percent nationwide. A comparison of budget outlays is equally revealing. President Nixon spent $911 million on civil rights activities, including $75 million for civil rights enforcement in fiscal 1969. The Nixon administration's budget for fiscal 1973 called for $2.6 billion in total civil rights outlays, of which $602 million was earmarked for enforcement through a substantially strengthened Equal Employment Opportunity Commission. Nixon supported the civil rights goals of American Indians and women with less reluctance than he did school desegregation because these groups did not pose a major political problem for him and he had no similar legal reservations about how the law should be applied to them.

MIXING ECONOMICS
AND POLITICS

Nixon spent an inordinate amount of time on domestic and foreign economic matters. Nowhere did he appear to reverse himself more on views he had held before becoming president (or at least on views others attributed to him), and nowhere was his aprincipled pragmatism more evident. Nixon's failure to obtain more revenue through tax reform legislation in 1969, together with rising unemployment and inflation rates in 1970, precipitated an effort (in response to a perceived crisis) to balance U.S. domestic concerns through wage and price controls and international ones through devaluation of the dollar. This vehicle was the New Economic Policy, dramatically announced on August 15, 1971, at the end of a secret Camp David meeting with sixteen economic advisers. Largely as a result of Treasury Secretary Connally's influence, Nixon agreed that if foreign countries continued to demand ever-increasing amounts of gold for the U.S. dollars they held, the United States would go off the gold standard but would at the same time impose wage and price controls to curb inflation. The NEP perfectly reflected the "grand gesture" Connally thought the president should make on economic problems, and the August 15 television broadcast dramatized economic issues that most Americans, seldom anticipating long-range consequences, found boring.

When he was not trying to preempt Congress on regulatory issues, Nixon proposed deregulation based on free-market assumptions that were more traditionally in keeping with conservative Republicanism. The administration ended the draft in the name of economic freedom and recommended deregulation of the production of food crops, tariff and other barriers to international trade, and interest rates paid by various financial institutions. Except for wage and price controls and the devaluation of the dollar, none of these actions was justified in the name of crisis management. In general, however, political considerations made Nixon more liberal on domestic economic matters, confounding both his supporters and his opponents.

Nixon attributes his interest in international economics to the encouragement of John Foster Dulles and his desire as vice-president in the 1950s to create a Foreign Economic Council. Failing in this, he has said that his travels abroad in the 1950s only confirmed his belief that foreign leaders understood economics better than did American leaders, and he was determined to remedy this situation as president. Nixon faced two obstacles in this effort: Kissinger (because "international economics was not Henry's bag"), and State Department officials who saw "economic policy as government to government," which limited their diplomatic view of the world and made them so suspicious or cynical (or both) about the private sector that they refused to promote international commerce to the degree that Nixon thought they should. "Unlike the ignoramuses I encountered among economic officers at various embassies in the 1950s and 1960s," Nixon told me, "I wanted to bring economics to the foreign service."

Because of Nixon's own interest in and knowledge of international trade, he attempted as president to rationalize the formulation of foreign economic policy. After 1962, when he was out of public office and practicing law in New York, he had specialized in international economics and multinational corporations —definitely not Henry Kissinger's areas of expertise. In part because they were not a "team" on foreign economic policy and in part because Nixon bypassed the NSC almost entirely in formulating his New Economic Policy, Nixon relied not on his national security adviser but on other free-thinking outsiders when formulating foreign economic policy.

Next to John Connally, Nixon was most impressed with the economic views of Peter G. Peterson, who, after starting out in 1971 as a White House adviser on international economic affairs, became secretary of commerce in January 1972. Although Connally and Peterson appeared to agree on such early foreign economic initiatives as the NEP and the "get tough" policy toward Third World countries that nationalized U.S. companies abroad, as secretary of commerce Peterson ultimately proved much more sophisticated and sensitive than the secretary of the treasury about the United States' changed economic role in the world. In a December 27, 1971, position paper defending Nixon's NEP, Peterson remarked that the new global situation in which the United States found itself demanded "shared leadership, shared responsibility, and shared burdens... The reform of the international monetary system," he said, must fully recognize and be solidly rooted in "the growing reality of a genuinely interdependent and increasingly competitive world economy whose goal is mutual, shared prosperity —not artificial, temporary advantage." At no point did Peterson believe, as Connally apparently did, that "the simple realignment of exchange rates" would adequately address the economic realignment problems facing the international economy.

In 1971 Nixon succeeded in establishing an entirely new cabinet-level Council on International Economic Policy (CIEP), headed by Peterson. This was not so much a reorganization of functions as it was an alternative to fill an existing void in the federal structure and to provide "clear top-level focus on international economic issues and to achieve consistency between international and domestic economic policy." For a variety of reasons—not the least of which was Kissinger's general lack of interest in, and disdain for, the unglamorous aspects of international economics—the CIEP faltered and finally failed after Nixon left office. Its demise seems to have been hastened by Kissinger's recommendation to the Congressional Commission on Organization of Foreign Policy that it be eliminated, despite the fact that others, including Peterson, testified on its behalf. The CIEP was subsequently merged with the Office of the Special Trade Representative.

* * *

Even with Nixon's impressive foreign and domestic record, it cannot be said that he would have succeeded as a managerial or administrative president had Watergate not occurred. Entrenched federal bureaucracies are not easily controlled or divested of power even with the best policy-oriented management strategies. That his foreign policy management seems more successful is also no surprise: diplomatic bureaucracies are smaller, more responsive, and easier to control than their domestic counterparts. Moreover, public concern (except for Vietnam) remained minimal as usual, and individual presidential foreign policy initiatives are more likely to be remembered and to appear effective than domestic ones. Nonetheless, the real importance of Nixon's presidency may well come to rest not on Watergate or foreign policy, but on his attempts to restructure the executive branch along functional lines, to bring order to the federal bureaucracy, and to achieve lasting domestic reform. The degree to which those Nixonian administrative tactics that were legal and ethical (and most of them were) became consciously or unconsciously the model for his successors in the Oval Office will determine his final place in history.

Although Nixon's corporate presidency remains publicly discredited, much of it has been privately preserved. Perhaps this is an indication that in exceptional cases presidential effectiveness can transcend popular (and scholarly) disapproval. What Nixon lacked in charisma and honesty, he may in the long run make up for with his phoenixlike ability to survive disaster. Nixon has repeatedly said: "No politician is dead until he admits it." It is perhaps an ironic commentary on the state of the modern presidency that Richard Nixon's management style and substantive foreign and domestic achievements look better and better when compared with those of his immediate successors in the Oval Office.

NO

Stanley I. Kutler

ET TU, BOB?

There is nothing quite like H.R. Haldeman's diaries, published recently during the official period of mourning for Richard Nixon. They are repulsive almost beyond belief, yet therein lies their importance. Ostensibly designed to record the doings of a great man, they devastate Nixon's reputation. Truly Haldeman has proved Mark Antony's observation that the good that men do is buried with their bones; the evil they do lives long after them. The diaries appeared three weeks after Nixon's death as a nearly 700-page book, unveiled first on a two-part *Nightline* program, which predictably focused on Nixon's racial and ethnic slurs. Soon thereafter came the CD-ROM, which included a "complete" version of the diaries (60 percent more material than in the book) and some added attractions, including "home" movies (developed at government expense), photos, bios of key and bit players and an amazing apologia in the form of an unsent 40,000-plus-word letter to James Neal, who prosecuted Haldeman. Like Antony, Haldeman had motives other than praising Caesar.

The diaries reflect two men in an "intense one-on-one relationship," men who were not, according to Haldeman's widow, personal friends. Since Nixon had few close friends, this means very little. The two often dined alone on the presidential yacht and then went to the President's sitting room to chat. The President would drink his '57 Lafite-Rothschild and serve Haldeman the California "Beaulieu Vineyard stuff." And Haldeman would have to read aloud Nixon's *Who's Who* entry. Maybe he was supposed to savor that instead.

The tapes revealed Nixon's shabbiness; the diaries underline his shallowness. The recurring themes of the diaries are simple: getting re-elected, getting even. Nixon was consumed with P.R., constantly prodding Haldeman on how to spin stories, how to protect his image and, almost comically, how to deny that the President was interested in such things. Haldeman, the old advertising executive, usually relished the game, yet he must have found it tiresome as well. P.R., he noted, "would work a lot better if he would quit worrying . . . and just be President." Impossible; for Nixon it was all.

Altogether, the picture is not pretty. It is mostly warts and little face, and certainly not the one Nixon had in mind as he took his leave. Shortly after

Haldeman died last fall, Nixon asked Haldeman's family to delay publication, ostensibly so as not to interfere with the promotion of his own book. What a hoot it would have been if Nixon, appearing on the *Today* show, had had to confront some of the juicier items from his trusted aide's diaries. In any event, Haldeman said that he hoped his book—which fleshes out and expands the daily notes that have been available for some time—would "once and for all" put the Nixon years into perspective. It certainly helps, but probably not as he intended.

Nixon always knew that Haldeman's diaries were potential dynamite. Archibald Cox subpoenaed the files on May 25, 1973, but the President had taken control of the diaries and put them with his papers, which eventually went to the National Archives (over his protests, to be sure). In 1980, Haldeman cut a deal with the Archives, deeding the diaries to the public (meaning he always intended for them to be seen, contrary to *Nightline*'s and his wife's assertions) in exchange for the Archives' agreement to keep them closed for a decade, later extended for several more years. Haldeman then promptly filed suit against the government, claiming (falsely) that he had been unlawfully deprived of access to his property in the intervening years. But the court refused to get involved "in the niceties of Fifth Amendment doctrine" since the case revolved around one question: Why did Haldeman leave his diaries in the White House when he was dismissed on April 30, 1973?

The government nailed Haldeman when it introduced Oval Office conversations for May 2 and 9, 1973 (Haldeman had "left" the White House but he returned—to listen to tapes!), in which Nixon and Haldeman typically concocted a scenario for future spin. In brief, Nixon would claim the materials as his own and cloak them with executive privilege: "Your notes belong to the President," Nixon told him. Haldeman finished the thought: "And fortunately, they're ... in your possession; they're not in mine." In those days, we had few illusions about Nixon and his aide. District Judge John Garrett Penn said that Haldeman could have avoided the dispute had he claimed the diaries as his own at the outset, or had he made photocopies when he viewed the materials. The conflict, the judge ruled, was entirely Haldeman's fault. "He could have obviated this entire conflict; he chose another route solely for his own protection, and should not now be given a forum to complain that he did not choose wisely." He may not have chosen wisely as far as Nixon is concerned—but Haldeman will do well by his heirs.

* * *

Most reactions to the diaries have concentrated on long-familiar Nixon slanders of Jews and blacks. The reluctance to confront the policy and institutional concerns of the diaries is somewhat understandable, for if the mainstream media honestly surveyed this material, they would impeach themselves for their insipid attempts to peddle revisionist views of Nixon in the wake of his death. The diaries clearly reveal the President's extraordinary cynicism, as well as his lack of knowledge of both domestic and foreign policy. No single work so effectively exposes Nixon as a mean, petty, vindictive, insecure—even incompetent—man, and all this from one who professed to admire him; from a man Nixon even said he "loved." Could it have been intentional?

Haldeman himself spent the past two decades portraying himself as a selfless, self-effacing, dedicated servant to the President. But the myth of Haldeman as Stevens the butler in *Remains of the Day* —just a passive vessel for Nixon's commands—is misleading. Haldeman was an old-fashioned Southern California reactionary, weaned on his family's nativist and patriotic views and supported by a plumbing fortune. Nixon correctly perceived him as a "son-of-a-bitch" and used him as a "Lord High Executioner."

Unintentionally, I would guess, Haldeman has provided us with wonderful comic moments. After the Thomas Eagleton nomination fiasco in 1972, Spiro Agnew, either with inspired wit or sheer meanness, asked Dr. Joyce Brothers to second his own nomination—as if to receive psychological certification of his sanity. Nixon issued a presidential order directing Agnew to rescind the invitation. Then there are Great Moments of Protocol: Who would ride in the President's golf cart, Bob Hope or Frank Sinatra? Finally, Nixon wanted a White House reception to honor Duke Ellington and told Haldeman to invite other jazz notables, including Guy Lombardo. "Oh well," the knowing Haldeman sighed.

Haldeman's diaries show that he spent either hours or "all day" with the President. Sometimes Haldeman recorded Nixon's thoughts on substantive policy such as China or the settlement of the Vietnam War. But usually the subjects were relentlessly repetitive, as were the homilies that Nixon dispensed. And yet Haldeman faithfully recorded and preserved the President's words. During the 1972 campaign, Haldeman and John Ehrlichman spent inordinate amounts of time listening to the President repeatedly go over matters such as his prospects in every state, who would be dismissed, who would be moved and how enemies would be punished. Apparently even "two of the finest public servants," as Nixon characterized them when he dismissed them, could not abide the monotony of it all without sarcasm. "Why did he buzz me?" Haldeman asked Ehrlichman in a note written during one of the President's soliloquies. Like a schoolchild answering a passed message, Ehrlichman sketched several answers:

"He had an itchy finger."

"Also there was a chair unoccupied."

"Also he has been talking about not just reordering the chaos, and he would like you to understand that point."

Supposedly, Nixon wanted someone to keep the "routine baloney" away from him; it "bores and annoys him," Haldeman noted. Yet Haldeman often wearily complained about the tedium, as when he noted that the "P had the morning clear, unfortunately, and called me...for over four hours as he wandered through odds and ends...."

Aside from the President's behavior, the most significant revelations surround Henry Kissinger. From the outset, Nixon and Haldeman recognized Kissinger as a devious, emotionally unstable person. The President saw him as a rival for public acclaim, ever anxious to magnify himself for the contemporary and historical record. Nixon did not entirely trust Kissinger's briefings. Most surprising, however, was Haldeman's intimate involvement in the management of foreign policy as the President regularly shared his thoughts and views on Kissinger with his Chief of Staff.

In the pathology of the Nixon White House, perhaps the sickest subject involved what Haldeman repeatedly called the "K-Rogers flap," which he blamed equally on Kissinger's "unbelievable ego" and Secretary of State William Rogers's pique. We long have understood Kissinger's pre-inaugural coup that enabled him and Nixon to bypass the State Department bureaucracy; yet what Kissinger wanted was the place for himself. Haldeman relentlessly portrays Kissinger as a mercurial, temperamental infant, constantly concerned with his standing and status; Nixon considered Kissinger "obsessed beyond reason" with Rogers.

Nixon and Kissinger appear more as adversaries than as allies. In November 1972, miffed at Kissinger's media attempts to grab the lion's share of credit for the China opening, Nixon instructed Haldeman to tell Kissinger that he had tapes of their conversations! Nixon warned Haldeman that *Time* might "needle us [and] go for K as the Man of the Year, which would be very bad, so we should try to swing that around a different way." Students of Vietnam policy have an interesting task in sorting out responsibility for the protracted peace negotiations. Kissinger expressed to Haldeman his fear that Nixon wanted to "bug out" and not carry through on long-term negotiations. Kissinger well knew that message would get back to Nixon and steel him against any appearances of being "soft."

Haldeman's diaries substantially confirm the criticism of Kissinger's detractors, especially Seymour Hersh's biting analysis of the Nixon-Kissinger foreign policies in *The Price of Power*. Appearance was often substituted for substance, and at times, as in the SALT negotiations, Kissinger seemed entirely out of his element. What then does this say

of the President of the United States —who similarly was unconcerned with substance and seemed most bent on preventing Kissinger from getting too much praise? Certainly, Adm. Elmo Zumwalt had it right when he said that two words did not apply to the Vietnam peace accords: peace and honor. Kissinger's frantic search for a Shanghai Communiqué in 1972 would have bordered on the comic had it not been so fraught with obsequiousness toward his new friends and cynicism toward Nixon's longtime Taiwanese patrons.

Everything had a political calculus. In December 1970, Nixon, Kissinger and Haldeman considered a Vietnam trip the next spring in which the President would make "the basic end of the war announcement." Kissinger objected, saying that if we pulled out in 1971 there could be trouble (ostensibly for the Thieu regime) that the Administration would have to answer for in the 1972 elections. Kissinger urged Nixon to commit only to withdrawing all troops by the end of 1972. Another year of casualties seemed a fair exchange for the President's electoral security.

Billy Graham's choicer remarks about Jews and their "total domination of the media" have been prominently reported. Let's take Graham at his word and agree that some of his best friends are Jews. In the guise of God's messenger, Graham was a Nixon political operative, dutifully reporting back to the White House on what Lyndon Johnson had said about George McGovern, George Wallace's intentions on resuming his presidential bid in 1972, Graham's efforts to calm down Martha Mitchell, plans to organize Christian youth for Nixon, his advice to Johnny Carson to be a little biased in Nixon's favor if he wanted to be helpful and the Shah of Iran's remark that the President's re-election had saved civilization. When Nixon's tapes were first revealed in April 1974, a chastened Graham complained about Nixon's "situational ethics" and lamented that he had been "used." Used once, used again, he could not resist the limelight of preaching at Nixon's funeral.

* * *

John Ehrlichman has maintained that Nixon would be remembered as the great domestic policy President of the twentieth century. (Guess who was Nixon's domestic adviser?) That notion, too, is a chapter in the current drive for revisionism. Well, it won't wash, unless one accepts the view that whatever was accomplished happened in spite of Richard Nixon. His Administration publicly advocated policies that the President clearly didn't believe in. Consider:

- School desegregation: Haldeman noted that Nixon was "really concerned ... and feels we have to take some leadership to try to reverse Court decisions that have forced integration too far, too fast." Nixon told Attorney General John Mitchell to keep filing cases until they got a reversal. Nixon proposed getting a right-wing demagogue into some tough race and have him campaign against integration—and he "might even win." He fired Leon Panetta, then a mid-level Health, Education and Welfare functionary, who was doing too much in behalf of school desegregation. (Panetta wouldn't quit, so Nixon announced his "resignation.")

- "[Nixon] was very upset that he had been led to approve the IRS ruling about no tax exemption for private schools, feels it will make no votes anywhere and will badly hurt private schools...."

- "About Family Assistance Plan, [President] wants to be sure it's killed by Democrats and that we make big play for it, but don't let it pass, can't afford it."

- "On welfare, we have to support HR 1 until the election. Afterward, we should not send it back to Congress." "On HR 1 there's some concern that if we hang too tight on the passage of it, that it may actually pass and defeat our Machiavellian plot. Our Congressional tactic overall has got to be to screw things up."

- "He's very much concerned about handling of the drug situation; wants the whole thing taken out of HEW. He makes the point that they're all on drugs there anyway."

- Nixon agreed to continue an I.B.M. antitrust action but urged Haldeman "to make something out of it so we can get credit for attacking business."

- "The P was also very upset about the DDT decision. Ruckleshaus has announced a ban on it. He [Nixon] thinks we should get this whole environment thing out of E and [John] Whitaker's hands because they believe in it, and you can't have an advocate dismantle something he believes in. He also wanted [Fred] Malek to check on who Ruckleshaus has on his staff in terms of left-wing liberals."

- Nixon "made the point that he feels deeply troubled that he's getting sucked in too much on welfare and environment and consumerism."

Liberals cringed in 1968 when Nixon promised to appoint judges who would favor the "peace forces" as opposed to the "criminal forces." Nixon, of course, like all Presidents, sought appointments to mirror his (and his constituency's) wishes. After the Senate rejected his nomination of G. Harrold Carswell for the Supreme Court in 1970, Nixon briefly flirted with nominating Senator Robert Byrd, knowing the Senate would be unlikely to reject one of its own. When Hugo Black resigned from the Court in 1971, Nixon, feverishly backed by Pat Buchanan, pushed for Virginia Congressman Richard Poff, once an ardent backer of segregation. Nixon happily recognized that this would only roil the waters again. Poff had the good sense to withdraw, whereupon Nixon raised Byrd's name again. Why not? Byrd was a former Klansman and "more reactionary than [George] Wallace," Nixon said, obviously relishing a chance to embarrass the Senate.

Following this, Nixon warmed to Mitchell's inspired concoction of nonentities: Herschel Friday (a fellow bond lawyer) and Mildred Lilley, an obscure local California judge who was meant only to be a sacrificial lamb. "The theory on the woman is that the ABA is not going to approve her, and therefore, he'll let her pass and blame them for it," Haldeman wrote. (This was the same American Bar Association committee that had endorsed the unqualified Carswell, Haldeman failed to note.) Nixon wanted Lewis Powell, but for the other open seat the White House tendered an offer to Senator Howard Baker, who called in his answer half an hour too late and was displaced by William Rehnquist in a coup led by Richard Moore, friend and aide to John Mitchell. A rare moment as the President caught Haldeman by surprise.

Everyone seemed happy, Nixon said, except his wife, who had been campaign-ing for a woman. That is the only time Haldeman recorded the President taking Mrs. Nixon seriously. The diaries are filled with Nixon and Haldeman's shared disdain for the First Lady; for example, Nixon could spare but a few moments for her 60th birthday party and then he hid out in his office.

* * *

Almost from the day that Nixon assumed office, he was off and running for 1972. Teddy Kennedy preoccupied him; in 1969, Nixon and his staff saw the battle over the antiballistic missile as the opening salvo of the 1972 campaign against Kennedy. Even after Chappaquiddick, Nixon seriously believed that Kennedy was a threat. He instigated Ehrlichman's own investigation of the incident and repeatedly told Haldeman that they couldn't let the public forget Chappaquiddick. He encouraged Charles Colson, who had agents follow Kennedy in Paris and photograph him with various women.

Vietnam was small potatoes compared with the amount of time the President and his aide plotted strategy and dirty tricks against political enemies. The Boys of '72 knew their way around this territory without much help. In Nixon's 1962 gubernatorial campaign, they had established a bogus Democratic committee to mail cards to registered Democrats expressing concern for the party under Pat Brown. A Republican judge convicted them of campaign law violations and held that the plan had been "reviewed, amended and finally approved by Mr. Nixon personally," and that Haldeman similarly "approved the plan and the project."

In July 1969, Nixon directed Haldeman to establish a "dirty tricks" unit with the likes of Pat Buchanan and Lyn Nofziger. "Hardball politics," Haldeman later called it. Nixon regularly urged that the I.R.S. investigate Democratic contributors and celebrity supporters. He also wanted a review of the tax returns of all Democratic candidates "and start harassment of them, as they have done of us." He wanted full field investigations of Clark Clifford and other doves; he ordered mailings describing Edmund Muskie's liberal views to be sent throughout the South; and one basic line of his Watergate counteroffensive was to expose Democratic Party chairman Larry O'Brien's tax problems and his allegedly unsavory list of clients.

Alas, Haldeman has little new to offer on Watergate. He claims that the diaries are unexpurgated and complete on this score. That may be stretching the truth. The Watergate section contains long, discursive comments about the activities of many principals, but they are merely summaries Haldeman compiled from contemporary documents and his own choice memories. The entries focus on the complicity of just about everyone but H.R. Haldeman. When read together with the lengthy letter that Haldeman allegedly wrote (and did not send) in 1978 to the prosecutor, the implication is that he and Nixon were guilty only of a "political containment"—he was no party to a conspiracy to obstruct justice and he committed no perjury. He knew that the burglars had been given "hush money," but he insisted it was not a cover-up. It is a little late in the day for such a defense; furthermore, his own words demolish it.

The diaries expand on the finger-pointing that emerged from the tape revelations twenty years ago. Now we clearly see how Nixon, Haldeman and

Ehrlichman sought to make Mitchell their fall guy, and how they coddled John Dean for so long to keep him in camp. In the letter to prosecutor James Neal, Haldeman turned from Mitchell to establish the outlines of a Dean conspiracy theory, one that has become fashionable among the former President's men in recent years.

From the outset, Haldeman knew the significance of the Watergate break-in. The day after, he called it "the big flap over the weekend," and he immediately knew that the Committee to Re-elect the President was involved. If so, that meant the White House, for John Mitchell and Jeb Magruder reported directly to Haldeman and his aides on campaign activity. Eventually, the True Campaign Chairman—the President himself—knew what happened there. Two days later, Haldeman reported that Nixon "was somewhat interested" in the events. Interested enough that we have eighteen and a half minutes of deliberately erased tape. Later that same day, June 20, Haldeman noted that Watergate "obviously bothered" Nixon and they discussed it "in considerable detail." But he gives us none.

Haldeman is fudging here. Tapes released two years ago, which cover Watergate conversations for June 1972—we previously had only the notorious "smoking gun" tape of June 23—reveal extensive conversations, beginning with the first attempt to concoct a containment or cover-up scenario on June 20. (Once again, the media missed this story as they made much ado about Nixon's remark that Liddy was "a little nuts.") Using the C.I.A. to thwart the F.B.I. was not a one-time occurrence on June 23; the two men repeatedly tried to stifle the investigation under the cover of national security, even after C.I.A. Director Richard Helms ended his cooperation. In these tapes, Haldeman seems to sense the futility of their efforts: "We got a lid on it and it may not stay on," he told the President on June 28. For nearly a year—not just in his last month as Chief of Staff—Haldeman knew that Watergate was trouble.

Significantly, Haldeman omits any mention of the President's offer of cash to him and Ehrlichman in April 1973 —after Ehrlichman ominously said, "I gotta start answering questions." When the President asked if they could use cash, Haldeman reacted with a blend of fury and sarcasm. "That compounds the problem," he said. "That really does." For good reason, Nixon needed their silence. But the President's insensitivity knew no bounds. After he announced Haldeman's resignation, he asked his departing aide to check out reaction to the speech. Probably for the only time, Haldeman refused a direct request. But in fact, he spent several more months listening to tapes to prepare for Nixon's defense.

The thousands of hours of taped conversations that Nixon fought so long to suppress will eventually be made public. Does anyone believe they will exonerate him or enhance his historical reputation? In the meantime, Haldeman's diaries take the lid off the Oval Office for the first four years of Nixon's presidency. What he has shown beyond dispute is that the Nixon of the Watergate years—furtive, manipulative and petty; often weak, sometimes comic and, above all, dishonest—was consistent with the behavior patterns of the earlier years. No Old Nixon; no New Nixon: There was one and only one.

POSTSCRIPT

Will History Forgive Richard Nixon?

Professor Joan Hoff-Wilson is one of the few professional historians to render a positive evaluation of President Nixon. She places him in the context of the late 1960s and early 1970s, when support for big government, New Deal, Great Society programs had dimmed and the bipartisan, anticommunist foreign policy consensus has been shattered by the Vietnam War. She gives him high marks for vertically restructuring the executive branch of the government and for attempting a similar reorganization in the federal bureaucracy.

Unlike most defenders of Nixon, Hoff-Wilson considers Nixon's greatest achievements to be domestic. Though he was a conservative, the welfare state grew during his presidency. In the area of civil rights, between 1968 and 1972, affirmative action programs were implemented, and schools with all black children in the southern states declined from 68 percent to 8 percent. Even on such Democratic staples as welfare, the environment, and economic planning, Nixon had outflanked the liberals.

Hoff-Wilson has fleshed out her ideas in much greater detail in *Nixon Reconsidered* (Basic Books, 1994). British conservative cabinet minister and historian Jonathan Aitken has also written a favorable and more panoramic view of the former president entitled *Nixon: A Life* (Regnery Gateway, 1993).

Historian Stephen E. Ambrose's three-volume biography *Nixon* (Simon & Schuster, 1987, 1989, 1991) also substantiates Hoff-Wilson's emphasis on Nixon's domestic successes. Ambrose's evaluation is even more remarkable because he was a liberal historian who campaigned for George McGovern in 1972 and had to be talked into writing a Nixon biography by his publisher. In domestic policy, Ambrose told *The Washington Post* on November 26, 1989, Nixon "was proposing things in '73 and '74 he couldn't even make the front pages with—national health insurance for all, a greatly expanded student loan operation, and energy and environmental programs." With regard to foreign policy, both Ambrose and Aitken disagree with Hoff-Wilson; they consider Nixon's foreign policy substantial and far-sighted. In the second volume of his biography, *Nixon: The Triumph of a Politician, 1962–1972* (Simon & Schuster, 1989), Ambrose concludes that the president was "without peer in foreign relations where 'profound pragmatic' vision endowed him with the potential to become a great world statesman."

Professor Kutler accepts none of the revisionists' premises. In *The Wars of Watergate: The Last Crisis of Richard Nixon* (Alfred A. Knopf, 1990), Kutler focuses on both the negative side of Nixon's personality and his abuse of presidential power. In his review of *The Haldeman Diaries*, Kutler finds further substantiation for his view that Nixon was a narrow-minded, bigoted, self-calculating individual who took no action in his career that was not politically motivated. Unlike other writers who saw a "new" Nixon emerge as president, Kutler maintains that there was only one Nixon—a man possessed with a "corrosive hatred that decisively shaped" his behavior and career.

Neither Ambrose nor Kutler accept the view that Nixon was a corporate executive who reorganized government to enhance decision making. Both would agree that Nixon loved intrigue, conspiracies, and surprise. At the same time Kutler argues that Nixon went much further than any of his predecessors in abusing presidential power by siccing the Internal Revenue Service (IRS) on potential enemies, impounding funds so that the Democrat-controlled Congress couldn't implement its legislative programs, and finally covering up and lying for over two years about the Watergate scandal.

Clearly, historians will be disputing the Nixon legacy for a long time. Two works have tried to place Richard Nixon within the context of his times. Liberal historian Herbert S. Parmet, the first to gain access to Nixon's prepresidential papers, has published *Richard Nixon and His America* (Little, Brown, 1990). Less thoroughly researched in primary sources but more insightful is *New York Times* reporter Tom Wicker's *One of Us: Richard Nixon and the American Dream* (Random House, 1991).

In order to gain a real feel for the Nixon years, you should consult contemporary or primary accounts. Nixon himself orchestrated his own rehabilitation in *RN: The Memoirs of Richard Nixon* (Grosset & Dunlop, 1978); *The Real War* (Warner Books, 1980); *Real Peace* (Little, Brown, 1984); *No More Vietnams* (Arbor House, 1985); and *In the Arena: A Memoir of Victory, Defeat and Renewal* (Simon & Schuster, 1990). Nixon's own accounts should be compared with former national security adviser Henry Kissinger's memoirs *White House Years* (Little, Brown, 1979). *The Haldeman Diaries: Inside the Nixon White House* (Putnam, 1994), which is the subject of Kutler's review essay, is essential for any undertaking of Nixon. Haldeman's account fleshes out the daily tensions of life in the Nixon White House and adds important details to the Nixon and Kissinger accounts. Other primary accounts include *The Nixon Presidency: Twenty-Two Intimate Perspectives of Richard M. Nixon*, vol. 6, in the series *Portraits of American Presidents* (University Press of America, 1987), which contains a series of discussions with former officials of the Nixon administration conducted by the White Burkett Miller Center for the Study of Public Affairs at the University of Virginia.

Two of the best review essays on the new historiography about our 37th president are "Theodore Draper: Nixon, Haldeman, and History," *The New York Review of Books* (July 14, 1994) and Sidney Blumenthal, "The Longest Campaign," *The New Yorker* (August 8, 1994).

On the Internet, see http://205.185.3.2/presidents/ea/bios/37 pnixo.html, which contains biographical information on Nixon, and http://netspace.net.au/~malcolm/wgate.htm, which provides extensive information on the Watergate scandal.

ISSUE 17

Were the 1980s a Decade of Greed?

YES: Kevin Phillips, from *The Politics of Rich and Poor: Wealth and the American Electorate in the Reagan Aftermath* (Random House, 1990)

NO: Alan Reynolds, from "Upstarts and Downstarts," *National Review* (August 31, 1992)

ISSUE SUMMARY

YES: Political analyst Kevin Phillips argues that President Ronald Reagan's tax reform bills in the 1980s widened the income gap by decreasing the tax burden on the rich and increasing the taxes paid by the middle-income and poor classes.

NO: Conservative economist Alan Reynolds asserts that all income groups experienced significant gains in income during the 1980s.

In 1939, after six years of the New Deal, unemployment remained at an unacceptably high rate of 17 percent. World War II bailed America out of the Great Depression. When 20 million workers entered the armed forces, married American women, along with African American and Hispanic males and females, filled the void in the higher-paying factory jobs. Everyone not only made money but poured it into war bonds and traditional savings accounts. Government and business cemented their relationship with "cost plus" profits for the defense industries.

By the end of 1945 Americans had stashed away $134 billion in cash, savings accounts, and government securities. This pent-up demand meant there would be no depression akin to the end of World War I or the 1930s. Following initial shortages before industry completed its conversion to peacetime production, Americans engaged in the greatest spending spree in the country's history. Liberals and conservatives from both political parties had developed a consensus on foreign and domestic policies. Cold war liberals accepted an anticommunist and interventionist foreign policy, which used Marshall plan money to successfully rebuild the economic foundations of Western Europe and foreign aid to develop capitalist economies in southeast Asia and Japan. Conservatives reconciled themselves to the development of the welfare state that the New Dealers created. These conservatives reluctantly accepted the idea implied in the Employment Act of 1946—that government had become the manager of the economy.

The president's Council of Economic Advisers was comprised of Keynesians, who believed that government spending could increase employment even if it meant that budget deficits would be temporarily created. For nearly 25 years they used fiscal and monetary tools to manipulate the economy so that inflation would remain low while employment would reach close to its maximum capacity.

Around 1968 the consensus surrounding domestic and foreign policy broke down for three reasons: (1) the Vietnam embroglio; (2) the oil crises of 1974 and 1979; and (3) the decline of the smokestack industries.

Lyndon Johnson had his presidency ruined by the Vietnam War. He believed that he could escalate the war and his Great Society programs at the same time. His successor, Richard Nixon, attempted to solve the Vietnam dilemma by bringing the American boys home and letting Asians fights Asians. The process of withdrawal was slow and costly. So were many of the Great Society programs, such as Social Security, Aid to Dependent Children, environmental legislation, and school desegregation, which Nixon continued to uphold. In August 1971 Nixon acknowledged that he had become a Keynesian when he imposed a 90-day wage and price control freeze and took the international dollar off the gold standard and allowed it to float. With these bold moves Nixon hoped to stop the dollar from declining in value. He was also faced with a recession that included both high unemployment and high inflation. "Stagflation" resulted, leading to the demise of Keynesian economics.

In early 1974, shortly before Nixon was forced to resign from office, the major oil-producing nations of the world—primarily in the Middle East—agreed to curb oil production and raise oil prices. The OPEC cartel, protesting the pro-Israeli policies of the Western nations, brought these countries to their knees. In the United States gasoline went from $0.40 to $2.00 per gallon in a matter of days. In the early 1980s President Jimmy Carter implored the nation to conserve energy, but he appeared helpless as the unemployment rate approached double digits and as the Federal Reserve Board raised interest rates to 18 percent in a desperate attempt to stem inflation.

The Reagan administration introduced a new economic philosophy—supply-side economics. Its proponents, led by economists Martin Anderson and Arthur Laffer, believed that if taxes are cut and spending on frivolous social programs is reduced—even while military spending increases—businesses will use the excess money to expand. More jobs will result, consumers will increase spending, and the multiplying effect will be a period of sustained growth and prosperity. Did it work?

In the following selections, Kevin Phillips argues that President Ronald Reagan's tax reform bills in the 1980s lessened the tax burden on the rich, while the upper-middle, middle, and poor classes had a higher effective tax burden because more of their incomes went toward regressive social security and sales taxes. Conservative economist Alan Reynolds maintains that all groups benefited from Reagan's tax reduction program, the economic recession of 1981–1982 notwithstanding.

YES   Kevin Phillips

TAX-BRACKET REDUCTION: THE CENTERPIECE OF THE REAGAN ERA

The reduction or elimination of federal income taxes had been a goal of all three major U.S. capitalist periods, but were ... a personal preoccupation for Ronald Reagan, whose antipathy toward income taxes dated back to World War II, when a top rate of 91 percent made it foolish to work beyond a certain point. Under Reagan, the top personal tax bracket would drop from 70 percent to 28 percent in just seven years. In 1987 the Congressional Budget Office (CBO) showed just who was getting the cream from these reductions: the top 1 to 5 percent of the population.

In 1861 a Republican administration and Congress imposed the first U.S. income tax to finance the Civil War. After two wartime increases, the federal levy was terminated in 1872, abetting the mushrooming fortunes of the Astors, Carnegies, Morgans and Rockefellers.

Later, as postwar laissez-faire collapsed into populism and progressivism, public doubts about excessive wealth resurged, and with them came income tax pressures. In 1894, after the prior year's unnerving stock market panic, Congress passed a tax of 2 percent on incomes over four thousand dollars, which the U.S. Supreme Court declared unconstitutional in 1895. A constitutional amendment solved the problem in 1913. As Europe marched to war in 1914, joined by the United States in 1917, the demand for income tax revenue soon repeated itself. Levies climbed quickly, and by 1920, the top rate was 73 percent.

As a result, postwar federal revenues exceeded peacetime needs and discouraged peacetime enterprise. When the Harding administration took office in 1921, tax rates were quickly reduced, in four stages, to a top bracket of just 25 percent in 1925. As Reaganite theorists would recall six decades later, cutting income taxes amidst gathering commercial prosperity helped create the boom of the 1920s. The prime beneficiaries were the top 5 percent of Americans, people who rode the cutting edge of the new technology of autos, radios and the like, emerging service industries (including new practices like advertising and consumer finance), a booming stock market and unprecedented real estate development. As federal taxation eased, especially on the upper brackets, disposable income soared for the rich—and with it conspicuous consumption and financial speculation.

By the crash of 1929, striking changes had occurred in the distribution of both taxes *and* wealth. The bottom-earning 80 percent of the population, never much affected, had been cut off the income tax rolls entirely. As a result, the top 1 percent of taxpayers were paying about two thirds of what the Treasury took in. Even so, because the top rate had fallen from 73 percent to 25 percent, federal taxation was taking less and less of booming upper-bracket incomes and stock profits. By contrast, many farmers and miners, and some workers, hurt by slumping commodity prices, found themselves with lower real purchasing power than they had enjoyed in the placid decade before World War I. Tax policy was not the only source of upward redistribution, but it contributed greatly to the polarization of U.S. wealth and the inequality of income, which peaked between 1927 and 1929.

But Democrats, soon back in control of Congress and then the White House, preferred to afflict rather than nurture concentrated wealth. Now the direction of redistribution moved *downward*. To achieve that, the top tax rate reached 63 percent by 1932, 79 percent by 1936 and soared to 91 percent during World War II, the incentiveless bracket that so offended Ronald Reagan and his Hollywood friends. Ninety-one percent remained the nominal top rate until 1964, when it fell in two stages to 77 percent and then 70 percent.

If not for the war in Vietnam, there might have been further cuts in the late sixties, but the war was costly, sustaining a high rate structure and even requiring a surtax from 1968 to 1970. More perversely, wartime outlays generated an inflation that lifted more and more middle-class citizens into what had long been *upper-class* brackets. So by the late 1970s, with the war over but with inflation still intensifying, cyclical demand for tax reduction gathered momentum. After nearly fifty years, proposals for deep rate reductions were back on the national agenda. Though Republican politicians aroused little interest in the Kemp-Roth tax cuts in 1978, this lack of support was only temporary.

Over the next two years, a new conservative outlook took shape in Washington, entrenched in 1980 by Reagan's election. The 1981 Economic Recovery Tax Act, passed by a surprisingly willing Congress, offered far more than relief for middle-class bracket creep. Supply-side proponents of individual rate cuts and business-organization lobbyists for capital formation and corporate depreciation allowances shared a half-trillion-dollar victory.[1] For the first time since the New Deal, federal tax policy was fundamentally rearranging its class, sector and income-group loyalties.

Corporate tax rates were reduced and depreciation benefits greatly liberalized. By 1983 the percentage of federal tax receipts represented by corporate income tax revenues would drop to an all-time low of 6.2 percent, down from 32.1 percent in 1952 and 12.5 percent in 1980. For individuals the 1981 act cut taxes across the board—by 5 percent in 1981, then 10 percent in 1982 and another 10 percent in 1983. Another highly significant change trimmed the top bracket from 70 percent to 50 percent. Taxation of *earned* income had been capped at a 50 percent top rate since 1972. Now the same treatment would be extended to *unearned* income, an enormous boon to the small percentage of the population deriving most of its income from rents and interest. Meanwhile, the top rate on capital gains was effectively cut to 20 percent, having earlier been dropped from 49 percent to 28 percent by the Steiger Amendment reductions of 1978. Conservative tax-reduction supporters predicted a surge in savings, venture capitalism and entrepreneurialism. Liberal economists, disheartened, prophesied more inflation and mounting inequality. Both predictions only half proved out. The savings rate didn't grow, and neither did inflation, but enterprise *and* inequality did—an old story.

Critics of emerging income polarization would eventually cite the increasingly benign treatment between 1978 and 1981 of property income (interest, dividends and rents) and capital gains, a benefit that flowed mostly to a small stratum of taxpayers. According to a 1983 Federal Reserve Board survey, families in the top 2 percent owned 30 percent of all liquid assets (from checking accounts to money market funds), 50 percent of the corporate stocks held by individuals, some 39 percent of corporate and government bonds and 71 percent of tax-exempt municipals. And applying a broader measurement of upper-income status, the wealthiest 10 percent owned 51 percent of liquid assets, 72 percent of corporate stocks, 70 percent of bonds and 86 percent of tax-exempts.

The inflation of the late 1970s and then subsequent post-1981 disinflation would affect different economic strata in different ways. At first, under inflation, blue-collar wages stagnated, at least in real terms, but a fair percentage of reasonably well off property owners benefited from increased bank CD interest rates, real estate values, precious metals, jewelry, art and rents. When disinflation took over in 1981–82, the big benefit shifted to the more truly rich. Real interest rates soared, and as that happened, upper-bracket holders of financial assets —mostly stocks and bonds—chalked up the greatest gains. Data compiled by the Economic Policy Institute in 1988 spelled out the much larger 1978–86 gain in property income (up 116.5 percent) compared with wage, salary and other labor income (up 66.6 percent). Lightened levies on capital gain and property income, coming just around the time when those categories were climbing, helped fuel upper-bracket wealth and capital accumulation more or less as conservative tax strategists and entrepreneurial theorists had hoped.

The second big redistributive spur was Washington's decision to let Social Security tax rates climb upward from 6.05 percent in 1978 to 6.70 percent in 1982–83, 7.05 percent in 1985 and 7.51 percent in 1988–89—a schedule originally voted in 1977 under Carter—while income tax rates were coming down. By 1987, however, Maine Democratic senator George Mitchell complained that "as a result, there has been a shift of about $80 billion in annual revenue collections from the progressive income tax to the regressive payroll tax. The Social Security tax increase in 1977 cannot be attributed to the current administration. But the response in the 1980s—to make up for a tax increase disproportionately burdening lower-income households with a tax cut disproportionately benefiting higher-income households—*can* be laid to the policies of this administration." Mitchell was hardly overstating the new reliance on Social Security. Between 1980 and 1988, the FICA tax on $40,000-a-year incomes doubled from $1,500 to nearly $3,000. The portion of total annual federal tax receipts represented by Social Security rose from 31 percent to 36 percent while income tax contributions dropped from 47 percent to under 45 percent. Table 1 shows the consequent 1977–88 realignment of effective tax rates for different groups.

After his reelection in 1984, Reagan moved to replicate the full reduction of the Harding-Coolidge era and succeeded in doing so when the 1986 tax reform cut top individual rates from 70 percent in 1981 to just 28 percent as of 1988 —effectively matching the 1921–25 reduction from 73 percent to 25 percent. Democrats were largely uncritical; as we have seen, their acquiescence in such reversals is typical of capitalist heydays.

Taxpayers would not feel the final effects of the 1986 tax reductions until April 1989, and 1988 tax distribution data couldn't be officially analyzed for several years thereafter, well past the president's departure from office. Yet the debate over who had gained and lost under Reagan intensified. Reaganites and their critics both had a substantial case. Supply-siders and other advocates of bracket reduction could show that the upper-tier rate cuts had not increased the *proportion* of taxes paid by the poor and middle classes. During the Reagan years the percentage of total federal income tax payments made by the top 1 percent of taxpayers actually rose, climbing from 18.05 percent in 1981 to 19.93 percent in 1983, 21.9 percent in 1985 and 26.1 percent in 1986. And this could have been predicted. As we have seen, their share of national income was increasing by similar proportions. When wealth concentrates at the top of the pyramid, lower rates *do* bring larger receipts than the higher rates of the preconcentration period. Coolidge-era precedents, invoked by supply-siders from the first, had been

even more lopsided. Because the upper-bracket rate cuts of the 1920s also removed most lower- and lower-middle-income families from the rolls, the percentage of total taxes paid by the top 1 percent actually climbed from 43 percent in 1921 to 69 percent in 1926. Early supporters of a tax rollback—not least Coolidge—were quick to boast of this, and assigned credit to the rate cuts. The same boasts were made in the 1980s.

The statistical deception, of course, was that the increased ratios of total tax payments by high-income persons were not an increased burden. Overzealous supply-siders were way too insistent that Reagan's tax policy "soaked the rich," promoted "economic justice," and that "the Reagan years have been, contrary to the conventional wisdom, an age of benevolent Robin Hoodism." Claims that the tax cuts had helped promote prosperity under Coolidge and Reagan were plausible, although more plausibly these cuts *overlapped* rather than caused the two capitalist heydays. That the rich were "soaked" during the 1980s was, however, untrue, as anyone walking down Rodeo Drive could see. It was precisely such exaggerations that undermined supply-sider credibility.

Under Reagan, as under Coolidge, the clear evidence is that the net tax burden on rich Americans as a percentage of their total income *shrank* substantially because of the sweeping rate cuts. The surge in actual tax payments was the result of higher upper-bracket incomes. To measure the benefits, imagine a businessman who had made $333,000 in salary, dividends and capital gains in 1980, and paid $120,000 in federal income taxes. As prosperity returned in 1983, his income climbed to $500,000. Yet with the applicable rates reduced, he might well have paid, say,

Table 1

Shifts in Effective Federal Tax Rates by Population Income Decile, 1977–88

Decile	1977	1984	1988	Percentage Point Change in Effective Rate (1977–84)	(1977–88)
First	8.0%	10.5%	9.6%	+2.5%	+1.6
Second	8.7	8.5	8.3	– .2	– .4
Third	12.0	13.2	13.3	+1.2	+1.3
Fourth	16.2	16.3	16.8	+ .1	+ .6
Fifth	19.1	18.5	19.2	– .6	+ .1
Sixth	21.0	20.1	20.9	– .9	– .1
Seventh	23.0	21.5	22.3	–1.5	– .7
Eighth	23.6	23.0	23.6	– .6	±0
Ninth	24.5	23.8	24.7	– .7	+ .2
Tenth	26.7	23.6	25.0	–3.1	–1.7
Top 5%	27.5	23.3	24.9	–4.2	–2.6
Top 1%	30.9	23.1	24.9	–7.8	–6.0

Source: Congressional Budget Office, *The Changing Distribution of Federal Taxes: 1975–1990*, October, 1987, Table 8, p. 48. (Corporate income tax allocated to labor income.) The 1988 figures were estimates.

$150,000 in taxes, *more actual payment*, of course, but *less relative burden*. That many blue-collar and middle-class Americans had lost their jobs in 1981–82 (when unemployment briefly neared 11 percent) also helps explain why the top 1 percent of 1983 taxpayers—disproportionate beneficiaries of a surging stock market—wound up shouldering a higher portion of the overall federal income tax burden. They were gaining while the bottom half of the population was losing. "Soaked" is hardly the term to describe what happened to millionaires paying out lower percentages of sharply rising incomes.

In 1987, to plot the rearrangement of effective *overall* tax rates, the economists at the Congressional Budget Office took *all* federal taxes—individual income, Social Security, corporate income and excise—and calculated the change in their combined impact on different income strata after 1977. Families below the top decile, disproportionately burdened by Social Security and excise increases and rewarded less by any income tax reductions, wound up paying *higher* effective rates. The richest families, meanwhile, paid lower rates, largely because of the sharp reduction applicable to nonsalary income (capital gains, interest, dividends and rents).

These shifts go a long way to explain both the surge in consumption *and* the rising inequality of income. America's richest 5 percent (and richest 1 percent, in particular) were the tax policy's new beneficiaries. Nor did the CBO's 1988 projections anticipate a significant reversal from the 1986 tax reform, with its unusual combination of further rate reductions (down to a 28 percent top bracket) partly balanced by elimination of credits and deductions. Effective tax rates for 1988 *would* fall slightly for the bottom 20 percent relative to 1984, the CBO found, but not by enough to restore 1977's lower combined-impact levels. Middle and upper groups, in turn, would find their effective rates slightly higher in 1988 than in 1984. For these brackets, a part of the 1981 cut was recaptured. As Table 1 notes, however, the *overall* net effect of the 1977–88 tax changes would be different for *middle-class* versus *top-tier* taxpayers. For Mr. and Mrs. Middle America, the changes during Reagan's second term had the effect of canceling out the minor benefits of 1977–84 reductions. Escalating Social Security rates were a principal culprit. *Upper-echelon taxpayers alone were projected to benefit from a large net reduction in effective overall federal tax rates for the entire 1977–88 period.*

Some of the anomalies of the redesigned tax burden were extraordinary, not least the "bubble" that imposed a marginal income tax rate of 33 percent on family incomes of $70,000 to $155,000 in contrast to the 28 percent rate that applied above these levels. In 1988 a $90,000-a-year family with two husband-and-wife breadwinners making $45,000 each found itself in a 40.5 percent marginal federal tax bracket—a 33 percent income tax rate plus a 7.5 percent Social Security levy—in contrast to the 28 percent marginal rate of a millionaire or billionaire.

Policy at the federal level wasn't unique. During 1988 a collateral thesis began to emerge that state-level tax changes during the 1980s were also aggravating the trend to inequality. Citizens for Tax Justice, a group financed by labor unions and various liberal organizations, calculated that rising state sales taxes were falling disproportionately on poor families. And a 1988 study contended that half the states with income taxes had made them less fair for many low- and middle-income residents in 1986–87. The 1986 federal revisions required modification of state tax laws. The complaint was that those modifications were biased. Critics, however, lacked the documentation rapidly proliferating on the federal level, and in any event, *federal fiscal policy was the main issue.*

The irony was that Democratic election-year presidential politicking did not recognize that importance. Opinion polls in April 1988—tax time—revealed public skepticism of tax reform, its fairness and its wisdom. Yet [Democratic candidate Michael S.] Dukakis avoided the subject. Upper-bracket increases were rejected at the Democratic National Convention. Tax issues were ignored in 1988 as they had been in 1928.

What was also ignored—perhaps because of its complexity—were the data, contrary to widespread belief, showing that non–Social Security taxes for all Americans as a percentage of GNP had been significantly cut during the 1980s. Conservative insistence that the overall federal tax burden hadn't been reduced was deceptive. Certain revenue ratios *did* decline. Between 1 and 2 percent of GNP that had been gathered in taxes for *general* public sector purposes under Eisenhower and Nixon—some $40 billion to $80 billion a year in 1988 dollars—was routed back to the private sector under Reagan, enlarging the federal budget deficit, and thereby affecting federal spending and interest rate outlays, also with redistributive effects. It was true, as Table 2 shows, that *total* federal tax receipts remained roughly constant as a percentage of Gross National Product, but Social Security receipts were rising sharply, disguising a relative decline in *other* revenues, reducing Washington's ability to fund non–Social Security programs from schools to highways.

Table 2
Total Federal Receipts/Outlays as a Percentage of GNP

Fiscal Year	Total Social Security Receipts	Total Non–Social Security Receipts	Total Receipts	Total Outlays
1945	1.6%	19.7%	21.3%	43.6%
1960	2.9	15.4	18.3	18.2
1970	4.5	15.0	19.5	19.8
1980	5.9	13.5	19.4	22.2
1981	6.1	14.0	20.1	22.7
1982	6.4	13.3	19.7	23.7
1983	6.3	11.8	18.1	24.3
1984	6.5	11.5	18.0	23.1
1985	6.7	11.9	18.6	23.9
1986	6.8	11.6	18.4	23.7
1987	6.8	12.5	19.3	22.6
1988	7.0	12.0	19.0	22.3

Other postwar Republican administrations had not sought this kind of fundamental reversal in government's role. Under Eisenhower, on average, non–Social Security federal receipts—principally from personal income, corporate income and excise taxes—had represented 15 percent of GNP, enabling the government to run without deficits. By the late 1960s federal deficits were a fact of fiscal life. Ironically, bracket creep in the late 1970s was perversely helpful —non–Social Security receipts expanded to 14 percent of GNP, reducing deficits again, compared with mid-decade figures.

But the 1981 tax cuts, along with rising military outlays, tight Federal Reserve Board policy and the cost of the 1981–82 recession, sent the federal deficit soaring to 5 to 6 percent of GNP, the highest peacetime levels since the Depression. Non–Social Security revenues in the range of 12 percent of GNP simply were not enough to run the U.S. government in the late 1980s, no matter what the stimulus of tax cuts might be. Part of the slack was made up by money borrowed at home and abroad at high cost. But how long could this go on? Tax relief and incentive economics meant not only income polarization but a frightening buildup of debt.

By 1989, the question was no longer whether tax policy would have to change, but when, how much—and to whose benefit?

NOTES

1. That was the estimated cost of the 1981 tax cuts over the next five years.

NO

Alan Reynolds

UPSTARTS AND DOWNSTARTS

The economic policies presided over by Ronald Reagan were stunningly successful—except to informed opinion, as represented by the academy and the major media. The principal charge against Reagan has become almost a chant: The rich got richer, the poor got poorer, and the middle class was squeezed out of existence.

A key player in the campaign to popularize this view has been Sylvia Nasar of the *New York Times*, who relied on statistics concocted by Paul Krugman of MIT, who, in turn, garbled some already disreputable estimates from the Congressional Budget Office (CBO).

The purpose of the crusade was obvious. Mr. Krugman has been advocating that we somehow double tax collections from those earning over $200,000, so as to greatly increase federal spending. Miss Nasar openly boasted about "supplying fresh ammunition for those... searching for new ways to raise government revenue." Governor Clinton immediately seized upon the Krugman–Nasar statistics as the rationale for his economic plan to tax us into prosperity.

Since the question is what happened in the 1980s, after the Carter Administration, it makes no sense to begin with 1977, as Mr. Krugman and Miss Nasar do, or with 1973, as the Children's Defense Fund does. Real incomes fell sharply during the runaway inflations of 1974–75 and 1979–80. Median real income among black families, for example, fell 15 per cent from 1973 to 1980, then rose 16 per cent from 1982 to 1990.

[Table 1] shows the actual real income of households by fifths of the income distribution, for the most commonly cited years. There is no question that *all* income groups experienced significant income gains from 1980 to 1989, despite the 1981–82 recession, and were still well ahead of 1980 even in the 1990 slump. For all U.S. households, the mean average of real income rose by 15.2 per cent from 1980 to 1989 (from $33,409 to $38,493, in 1990 dollars), compared with a 0.8 per cent *decline* from 1970 to 1980.

This table shows that the "income gap" did not widen merely between the bottom fifth and any "top" group, but also between the bottom fifth and the next highest fifth, the middle fifth, and so on.

A common complaint about these figures is that they exclude capital gains, and therefore understate income at the top. However, the figures also exclude *taxes*. Average income taxes and payroll taxes among the top fifth of households amounted to $24,322 in 1990, according to the Census Bureau, but capital gains among the top fifth were only $14,972. To add the capital gains and not subtract the taxes, as some CBO figures do, is indefensible. Indeed, all CBO estimates of income gains are useless, because they include an estimate of capital gains based on a sample of tax returns. Since lower tax rates on capital gains after 1977 induced more people to sell assets more often, the CBO wrongly records this as increased income. It also ignores all capital losses above the deductible $3,000, and fails to adjust capital gains for inflation.

THE MIDDLE-CLASS BOOM

One thing that we know with 100 per cent certainty is that *most* Americans— far more than half—did very well during the long and strong economic expansion from 1982 to 1989. In those fat years, real after-tax income per person rose by 15.5 per cent, and real *median* income of families, before taxes, went up 12.5 per cent. That means half of all families had gains *larger* than 12.5 per cent, while many below the median also had income gains, though not as large. Many families had to have gained even more than 12.5 per cent, since the more familiar *mean* average rose 16.8 per cent from 1982 to 1989. Even if we begin with 1980, rather than 1982, median income was up 8 per cent by 1989, and mean income by 14.9 per cent. And even if we end this comparison with the slump of 1990, median family income was still up 5.9 per cent from 1980, and mean income was up 12 per cent.

In *U.S. News & World Report* (March 23, 1992), Paul Krugman claimed that "the income of a few very well-off families soared. This raised average family income—but *most* families didn't share in the good times" (emphasis added). Mr. Krugman apparently does not understand what a rising median income means.

The whole idea of dividing people into arbitrary fifths by income ignores the enormous mobility of people in and out of these categories. What was most unusual about the Eighties, though, was that the number moving *up* far exceeded the number moving *down*. A Treasury Department study of 14,351 taxpayers shows that 86 per cent of those in the lowest fifth in 1979, and 60 per cent in the second fifth, had moved up into a higher income category by 1988. Among those in the middle income group, 47 per cent moved up, while fewer than 20 per cent moved down. Indeed, many more families moved up than down in every income group except the top 1 per cent, where 53 per cent fell into a lower category. Similar research by Isabel Sawhill and Mark Condon of the Urban Institute found that real incomes of those who started out in the bottom fifth in 1977 had risen 77 per cent by 1986— more than 15 times as fast as those who started in the top fifth. Miss Sawhill and Mr. Condon concluded that "the rich got a little richer and the poor got much richer."

This remarkable upward mobility is the sole cause of "The Incredible Shrinking Middle Class," featured in the May 1992 issue of *American Demographics*. Measured in constant 1990 dollars, the

Table 1

Average Household Income (In 1990 Dollars)

	Lowest Fifth	Second Fifth	Third Fifth	Fourth Fifth	Highest Fifth	Top 5%
1990	7,195	18,030	29,781	44,901	87,137	138,756
1989	7,372	18,341	30,488	46,177	90,150	145,651
1980	6,836	17,015	28,077	41,364	73,752	110,213
1977	7,193	17,715	29,287	42,911	76,522	117,023

Source: Bureau of the Census, *Money Income of Households, Families & Persons: 1990*, p. 202.

percentage of families earning between $15,000 and $50,000 fell by 5 points, from about 58 per cent to 53 per cent. This is what is meant by a "shrinking" middle class. We know they didn't disappear into poverty, because the percentage of families earning less than $15,000 (in 1990 dollars), dropped a bit, from 17.5 per cent in 1980 to 16.9 per cent in 1990. What instead happened is that the percentage earning more than $50,000, in constant dollars, *rose* by 5 points—from less than 25 per cent to nearly 31 per cent. Several million families "vanished" from the middle class by earning much more money!

It is not possible to reconcile the increase in median incomes with the often-repeated claim that low-wage service jobs ("McJobs") expanded at the expense of high-wage manufacturing jobs. Actually, there were millions more jobs in sectors where wages were rising most briskly, which meant competitive export industries but also services. From 1980 to 1991, average hourly earnings rose by 6.8 per cent a year in services, compared with only 4.8 per cent in manufacturing. The percentage of working-age Americans with jobs, which had never before the 1980s been nearly as high as 60 per cent, rose to 63 per cent by 1989.

THE MYTH OF LOW-WAGE JOBS

An editorial in *Business Week* (May 25) claimed that, "according to a just-released Census Bureau study, the number of working poor rose dramatically from 1979 to 1990." This is completely false. In fact, the report shows that the percentage of low-income workers who are in poverty *fell* dramatically. Among husbands with such low-income jobs, for example, 35.7 per cent were members of poor families in 1979, but only 21.4 per cent in 1990.

Low incomes, in this report, were defined as "less than the poverty level for a four-person family" ($12,195 a year in 1990). Yet very few people with entry-level or part-time jobs are trying to support a family of four. Husbands now account for only a fifth of such low-income jobs, which are instead increasingly held by young singles and by dependent children living with their parents. Wives had 34 per cent of such jobs in 1979, but fewer than 28 per cent in 1990. That reflects the impressive fact that the median income of women rose by 31 per cent in real terms from 1979 to 1990.

It is true that the absolute *number* of low-income jobs increased in all categories, but that increase was not nearly as large as the increase in medium- and high-income jobs. All that the rise in low-income jobs really shows is that students living with their parents and young singles found it much easier to find acceptable work. The only reason fewer young people had low-income jobs back in the glorious Seventies is a larger percentage of them had no jobs at all! Only 51.4 per cent of single males had full-time jobs in 1974, but 61.8 per cent did by 1989. Young people always start out with low earnings, if they get a chance to start out at all.

In his... book, *Head to Head*, Lester Thurow writes that "between 1973 and 1990, real hourly wages for non-supervisory workers... fell 12 per cent, and real weekly wages fell 18 per cent." Yet these averages include part-time workers, which is why *average* wages appeared to be only $355 a week in 1991, even though half of all full-time workers (the *median*) earned more than $430 a week. Because many more students and young mothers were able to find part-time jobs in the Eighties, that diluted both the weekly and the hourly "average" wage. It most definitely did not mean that the wages of the "average worker" went down, but rather that otherwise unemployed part-time and entry-level workers were able to raise their wages above zero. The increase in part-time jobs also does not mean that families are poorer; rather, they are richer. Out of 19.3 million part-time workers in 1991, only 1.2 million were family heads, and only 10 per cent said they were unable to find full-time work.

THE RICH WORK HARDER

Although the vast majority clearly had large income gains in the Eighties, Mr. Krugman and Miss Nasar nonetheless assert that those at the top had even larger gains, and that this is something that ought to provoke resentment or envy. Yet the figures they offer to make this point are grossly misleading. Moreover, the whole static routine of slicing up income into fifths is bound to show the highest percentage increases in average (mean) incomes among the "top" 20 per cent or 1 per cent. *That is because for top groups alone, any and all increases in income are included in the average, rather than in movement to a higher group.*

In his *U.S. News* article, Krugman first claimed that CBO figures show that "Ronald Reagan's tax cuts" boosted after-tax income of the top 1 per cent "by a whopping 102 per cent." That figure, though, is based on a "tax simulation model" which estimates "adjusted" incomes as a multiple of the poverty level. The top 1 per cent supposedly earned less than 22 times the poverty level in 1980, but 44 times the poverty level in 1989—hence the gain of 102 per cent. Yet this is a purely relative measure of affluence, not an absolute gain in real income. As more and more families rose further and further above the unchanged "poverty line" in the Eighties, thus lifting the income needed to be in the "top 1 per cent," the CBO technique had to show a "widening gap."

Furthermore, the share of federal income tax paid by the top 1 per cent soared from 18.2 per cent in 1981 to 28 per cent in 1988, though it slipped to 25.4 per cent in 1990. Indeed, this unexpected revenue from the rich was used to double personal exemptions and triple the earned-income tax credit, which was of enormous benefit to the working poor.

By the time Mr. Krugman's alleged 102 per cent gain at the top had reached the

New York Times, it had shrunk to 60 per cent. However, the CBO wrote a memo disowning this estimate too, noting that "of the total rise in aggregate income... about one-fourth went to families in the top 1 per cent." By fiddling with "adjusted" data, the CBO managed to get that share of the top 1 per cent up to one-third. Whether a fourth or a third, these estimates still begin with 1977, not 1980. Between 1977 and 1980, the CBO shows real incomes falling by 6.6 per cent for the poorest fifth. The top 5 per cent fared *relatively* well before 1980, because everybody else suffered an outright drop in real income.

Even if the Krugman–Nasar figures had been remotely accurate, the whole exercise is conceptually flawed. In every income group except the top, many families can move up from one group to another with little or no effect on the average income of those remaining in the lower group. Above-average increases in income among those in the lower groups simply move them into a higher fifth, rather than raising the average income of the fifth they used to be in. Only the top income groups have no ceiling, as those in such a group cannot possibly move into any higher group. A rap star's first hit record may lift his income from the lowest fifth to the top 1 per cent, with no perceptible effect on the average income of the lowest fifth. But two hit records in the next year would raise the total amount of income counted in the top 1 per cent, and thus raise the average for that category.

Nobody knows exactly how much income is needed to be counted among the top 1 per cent, because the Census Bureau keeps track only of the top 5 per cent. Census officials argue that apparent changes in the small sample used to estimate a "top 1 per cent" may largely reflect differences in the degree of dishonest reporting. When marginal tax rates fell from 70 per cent to 28 per cent, for example, more people told the truth about what they earned, so "the rich" *appeared* to earn much more.

One thing we do know, though, is that the minimum amount of income needed to be included among the top 1 per cent has to have risen quite sharply since 1980, because of the huge increase in the percentage of families earning more than $50,000, or $100,000. This increased proportion of families with higher incomes pushed up the income ceilings on all middle and higher income groups, and thus raised the floor defining the highest income groups.

While $200,000 may have been enough to make the top 1 per cent in 1980, a family might need over $300,000 to be in that category a decade later. Clearly, any average of all the income above $300,000 is going to yield a much bigger number than an average of income above $200,000. The CBO thus estimates that average pre-tax income among the top 1 per cent rose from $343,610 in 1980 to $566,674 in 1992. But this 65 per cent increase in the average does *not* mean that those specific families that were in the top 1 per cent in 1980 typically experienced a 65 per cent increase in real income. It simply means that the standards for belonging to this exclusive club have gone way up. That is because millions more couples are earning higher incomes today than in 1980, not because only a tiny fraction are earning 65 per cent more.

Sylvia Nasar totally misreported the CBO's complaints with her first article, and audaciously quoted her own discredited assertions in a later *New York Times* piece (April 21). This front-page editorial changed the subject—from income to wealth. It claimed a "Federal Reserve" study had found that the wealthiest 1 per cent had 37 per cent of all net worth in 1989, up from 31 per cent in 1983. Paul Krugman, writing in the *Wall Street Journal*, likewise cited this "careful study by the Federal Reserve." Yet the cited figures are from a mere *footnote* in a rough "working paper" produced by one of hundreds of Fed economists Arthur Kennickell, along with a statistician from the IRS, Louise Woodburn. It comes with a clear warning that "opinions in this paper... in no way reflect the views of... the Federal Reserve System."

At that, all of the gain of the top 1 per cent was supposedly at the expense of others within the top 10 per cent, not the middle class or poor. In any case, the figures are little more than a guess. The authors acknowledge that they "cannot offer a formal statistical test of the significance of the change."

"The 1983 and 1989 sample designs and the weights developed are quite different," they write. "The effect of this difference is unknown." Their estimated range of error does not account for "error attributable to imputation or to other data problems." Yet it is nonetheless within that range of error for the share of net worth held by the top 1 per cent to have risen imperceptibly, from 34.5 to 34.6 per cent. This is why Kennickell and Woodburn say their estimates merely "suggest that there may have been an increase in the share of wealth held by this top group in 1989." Or maybe not.

The actual, official Federal Reserve study tells a quite different story. It shows that real net worth rose by 28 per cent among 40 per cent of families earning between $20,000 and $50,000, but by only 6.6 per cent for the top 20 per cent,

earning more than $50,000. Since this huge increase in net worth among those with modest incomes means their assets grew much faster than their debts, this also puts to rest the myth that the Eighties was built upon "a mountain of debt." It was, instead, built upon a mountain of assets, particularly small businesses.

CHILDREN WITHOUT FATHERS

What about the poor? There is no question that there has been a stubbornly large increase of people with very low incomes. However, annual "money income" turns out to be a surprisingly bad measure of ability to buy goods and services. In 1988, average consumer spending among, the lowest fifth of the population was $10,893 a year—more than double their apparent income of $4,942. That huge gap occurs partly because annual incomes are highly variable in many occupations, and many people have temporary spells of low income, due to illness or job loss. People can and do draw upon savings during periods when their income dips below normal.

Another reason why those in the bottom fifth are able to spend twice their earnings is that many in-kind government transfers (such as food stamps) are not counted as "money income." Census surveys also acknowledge that a fourth of the cash income from welfare and pensions is unreported. And, of course, very little income from illegal activities is reported. In CBO figures, incomes of low-income families are further understated by counting singles as separate families, as though young people stopped getting checks from home the minute they get their first apartment.

Despite such flaws in measured income, nearly all of the income differences between the bottom fifth and the top fifth can nonetheless be explained by the number of people per family with full-time jobs, their age, and their schooling. Among household heads in the lowest fifth, for example, only 21 per cent worked full-time all year in 1990, and half had no job all year. In the top fifth, by contrast, the average number of full-time workers was more than two.

The May 25 *Business Week* editorial noted that "the percentage of Americans below the poverty line rose from 11.7 per cent in 1979 to 13.5 per cent in 1990." Yet this poverty rate is exaggerated, because it is based on an obsolete consumer price index that mismeasured housing inflation before 1983. Using the corrected inflation measure, the poverty rate was 11.5 per cent in 1980 and 11.4 in 1989, before rising to 12.1 per cent in 1990. That 12.1 per cent figure, though, is only one of 14 different Census Bureau measures of poverty, and not the most credible. Like income for the "bottom fifth," the usual measure of poverty excludes many in-kind transfer payments, as well as cash from the earned-income tax credit. By instead including such benefits, and also subtracting taxes, the Census Bureau brings the actual poverty rate down to 9.5 per cent for 1990, or to 8.5 per cent if homeownership is considered (those who own homes need less cash because they don't pay rent).

Even by the conventional measure, the poverty rate among married-couple families dropped slightly, from 5.2 per cent in 1980 to 4.9 per cent in 1990, and poverty rates among those above age 65 have fallen quite substantially. On the other hand, among female household heads with children under the age of 18 and "no husband present," poverty rose from 37.1 per cent in 1979 to 39.9 per cent in 1980, and then to 41.6 per cent by 1990.

The poverty rate among fatherless families, then, is slightly higher now than it was in the previous decade, and is lower if these young women work. (Among female householders with children under the age of 6, the poverty rate among those with jobs dropped from 20.2 per cent in 1979 to 17.9 per cent in 1989, and the percentage of such mothers who worked full-time rose from 24.9 to 30.6 per cent.) But there are so many more female-headed households, and so few of these women work, that the net effect is nonetheless to keep the overall poverty rate from falling. The number of female-headed households with children under age 18 rose from 5.8 million in 1979 to 7.2 million in 1989. In too many cases, these mothers are so young that child-labor laws would not allow them to work in any case.

In March 1991, the average money income of female-headed families with children was only $17,500, and most of that money (plus food stamps, housing allowance, and Medicaid) came from taxpayers. For married couples who both worked full-time, average income was $55,700 before taxes—about enough to put the *average* two-earner family in the top fifth. Taxing hardworking two-earner families to subsidize broken, no-earner families can only discourage the former, encourage the latter, and thus exacerbate the problems it pretends to solve.

To summarize what actually happened in the 1980s, the "middle class," and the vast majority by any measure, unquestionably experienced substantial gains in real income and wealth. With millions more families earning much higher incomes, it required much higher incomes to make it into the top 5 per cent or top 1 per cent, which largely accounts for the illusion that such "top" groups experienced disproportionate gains. The rising tide lifted at least 90 per cent of all boats. About 9 to 12 per cent continued to be poor, but this group increasingly consisted of female-headed households with young children. More and better jobs cannot help those who do not work, improved investment opportunities cannot help those who do not save, and increased incomes cannot help families whose fathers refuse to support their own children.

POSTSCRIPT

Were the 1980s a Decade of Greed?

Phillips is a well-known political analyst who, at the age of 29, predicted that the Republican Party would become the country's major party in the 1970s and 1980s. He contended that blue-collar, urban Catholics and traditional, southern whites would flee the Democratic Party, which became associated with the counterculture values of the 1960s. *The Emerging Republican Majority* (Arlington House, 1969) became the bible of the Nixon administration and paved the way for the southern strategy used to reelect Nixon and his successors, Reagan and Bush.

A self-proclaimed conservative populist, Phillips became disillusioned with the policies of the Reagan administration, whose tax bills in 1981 and 1986 favored the economic interests of the wealthy classes over the middle and poorer classes, drastically widening the income gap between the rich and the rest of the American people.

Reynolds, a well-known conservative economist with the Hudson Institute, disagrees with the conventional wisdom that the 1980s primarily benefited the wealthy classes at the expense of everyone else. Marshaling an array of figures compiled at the Census Bureau, Reynolds finds that incomes rose for all classes, including the poor.

Historians will debate the meaning of the 1980s for a long time. Support for Phillips's view comes from Frederick Strobel, a former senior business economist at the Federal Reserve Bank of Atlanta, in *Upward Dreams, Downward Mobility: The Economic Decline of the American Middle Class* (Rowman & Littlefield, 1993). The reasons that Strobel gives for the economic decline include an increased supply of workers (baby boomers, housewives, and immigrants), a decline in union membership, a strong dollar, and an open import dollar that destroyed many U.S. manufacturing jobs, corporate merger mania, declining government jobs, energy inflation, high interest rates, and the corporate escape from federal, state, and local taxes.

Unexpected criticism also comes from President Reagan's own director of the Office of Management and Budget, David A. Stockman. His *Triumph of Politics: Why the Revolution Failed* (Harper & Row, 1986) details the "idealogical hubris" that surrounded Reagan's advisers, who, in conjunction with a spendthrift Congress beholden to outside interest groups, ran up massive budget deficits by implementing a theory known as supply-side economics. More critical from the left are a series of academic articles in *Understanding America's Economic Decline* edited by Michael A. Bernstein and David E. Adler (Cambridge University Press, 1994).

CONTRIBUTORS
TO THIS VOLUME

EDITORS

LARRY MADARAS is a professor of history and political science at Howard Community College in Columbia, Maryland. He received a B.A. from the College of the Holy Cross in 1959 and an M.A. and a Ph.D. from New York University in 1961 and 1964, respectively. He has also taught at Spring Hill College, the University of South Alabama, and the University of Maryland at College Park. He has been a Fulbright Fellow and has held two fellowships from the National Endowment for the Humanities. He is the author of dozens of journal articles and book reviews.

JAMES M. SoRELLE is chair and professor of history at Baylor University in Waco, Texas. He received a B.A. and an M.A. from the University of Houston in 1972 and 1974, respectively, and a Ph.D. from Kent State University in 1980. In addition to introductory courses in American history, he teaches upper-level sections in African American, urban, and late-nineteenth- and twentieth-century U.S. history. His scholarly articles have appeared in *Houston Review, Southwestern Historical Quarterly,* and *Black Dixie: Essays in Afro-Texan History and Culture in Houston* (Texas A&M University Press, 1992), edited by Howard Beeth and Cary D. Wintz. He has also contributed entries to *The Handbook of Texas, The Oxford Companion to Politics of the World,* and *Encyclopedia of the Confederacy.*

STAFF

David Dean   List Manager
David Brackley   Developmental Editor
Ava Suntoke   Developmental Editor
Tammy Ward   Administrative Assistant
Brenda S. Filley   Production Manager
Juliana Arbo   Typesetting Supervisor
Diane Barker   Proofreader
Lara Johnson   Graphics
Richard Tietjen   Publishing Systems Manager

AUTHORS

RICHARD M. ABRAMS is a professor of history at the University of California, Berkeley, where he has been teaching since 1961. He has been a Fulbright professor in both London and Moscow and has taught and lectured in many countries throughout the world, including China, Austria, Norway, Italy, Japan, Germany, and Australia. He has published numerous articles in history, business, and law journals, and he is the editor of *The Shaping of Twentieth Century America: Interpretative Essays* (Little, Brown, 1965) and the author of *The Burdens of Progress* (Scott, Foresman, 1978).

BARTON J. BERNSTEIN is a professor of history at Stanford University in Stanford, California, and cochair of the International Relations Program and the International Studies Program. He has edited several works on the Truman administration and the atomic bomb, and he is the author of *Hiroshima and Nagasaki Reconsidered: The Atomic Bombings of Japan and the Origins of the Cold War, 1941–1945* (General Learning Press, 1975).

GARY DEAN BEST is a professor of history at the University of Hawaii in Hilo, Hawaii. He is a former fellow of the American Historical Association and of the National Endowment for the Humanities, and he was a Fulbright Scholar in Japan from 1974 to 1975. His publications include *The Nickel and Dime Decade: American Popular Culture During the 1930s* (Praeger, 1993).

ROGER BILES is a professor in and chair of the history department at East Carolina University in Greenville, North Carolina. He is the author of *The South and the New Deal* (University Press of Kentucky, 1994)

and *Richard J. Daly: Politics, Race, and the Governing of Chicago* (Northern Illinois Press, 1995).

ALEXANDER B. CALLOW, JR., is a professor emeritus of history at the University of California, Santa Barbara. He is the editor of such books as *The City Boss in America: An Interpretive Reader* (Oxford University Press, 1976) and *American Urban History: An Interpretive Reader,* 3rd ed. (Oxford University Press, 1982).

ALFRED D. CHANDLER, JR., is the Straus Professor Emeritus of Business History at the Harvard Business School. He has reconceptualized the field of business history with such books as his Pulitzer Prize–winning *The Visible Hand: The Managerial Revolution to American Business* (Harvard University Press, 1977). He is also the author of *Scale and Scope: The Dynamics of Industrial Capitalism* (Harvard University Press, 1990), which won the Association of American Publishers Award, and coauthor, with Thomas K. McCraw and Richard S. Tedlow, of *Management: Past and Present: Casebook on the History of American Business* (South-Western College Publishers, 1996).

ROBERT A. DIVINE is a professor of history at the University of Texas at Austin. He has written several books, including *Eisenhower and the Cold War* (Oxford University Press, 1981) and *Since 1945: Politics and Diplomacy in Recent American History,* 3rd ed. (Alfred A. Knopf, 1985).

MELVYN DUBOFSKY is the Distinguished Professor of History and Sociology at the State University of New York at Binghamton. Since 1978 he has been a State University of New York Faculty Exchange Scholar, and he is a member of the Organization of Americans and the American Historical Association. He received his Ph.D. from the University of Rochester in 1960. He is the author of *The State and Labor in Modern America* (University of North Carolina Press, 1994).

ERIC FONER is the DeWitt Clinton Professor of History at Columbia University in New York City. He is the author of several books and articles on the Civil War and Reconstruction eras, including *Free Soil, Free Labor, Free Men: The Ideology of the Republican Party Before the Civil War* (Oxford University Press, 1970) and *Nothing but Freedom: Emancipation and Its Legacy* (Louisiana State University Press, 1983). He is also the author of *Freedom's Lawmakers: A Directory of Black Officeholders During Reconstruction* (Oxford University Press, 1993). He received a Ph.D. in history from Columbia University in 1969.

ADAM GARFINKLE is executive editor at *The National Interest* and a resident scholar at the Foreign Policy Research Institute in Philadelphia. He is also the author of several books, including *Politics and Society in Modern Israel: Myths and Realities* (M. E. Sharpe, 1997).

OSCAR HANDLIN is the Carl M. Loeb Professor of History at Harvard University in Cambridge, Massachusetts, where he has been teaching since 1941. A Pulitzer Prize–winning historian, he has written or edited more than 100 books, including *Liberty in Expansion* (Harper & Row, 1989), which he coauthored with Lilian Handlin, and *The Distortion of America*, 2d ed. (Transaction Publishers, 1996).

LOUIS R. HARLAN is a Distinguished Professor of History Emeritus at the University of Maryland in College Park, Maryland. His publications include *Separate and Unequal: Public School Campaigns and Racism in the Southern Seaboard States, 1901–1915* (University of North Carolina Press, 1958) and *Booker T. Washington: The Wizard of Tuskegee* (Oxford University Press, 1983), which won the 1984 Pulitzer Prize for biography, the Bancroft Prize, and the Beveridge Prize.

LEO HERSHKOWITZ is a professor of history at Queens College, City University of New York.

JOAN HOFF-WILSON is a professor of history at Indiana University in Bloomington, Indiana, and coeditor of the *Journal of Women's History*. She is a specialist in twentieth-century American foreign policy and politics and in the legal status of American women. She has received numerous awards, including the Berkshire Conference of Women Historians' Article Prize and the Stuart L. Bernath Prize for the best book on American diplomacy. She has published several books, including *Herbert Hoover: The Forgotten Progressive* (Little, Brown, 1975) and *Without Precedent: The Life and Career of Eleanor Roosevelt* (Indiana University Press, 1984), coedited with Marjorie Lightman.

RICHARD HOFSTADTER (1916–1970) was a professor of history at Columbia University and the greatest American historian of the post–World War II generation. His book *The American Political Tradition and the Men Who Made It* (Alfred A. Knopf, 1948) is considered a classic.

HENRY KISSINGER, a distinguished scholar, diplomat, and writer, was the secretary of state to Presidents Richard Nixon and Gerald Ford. He has published two volumes of memoirs from those years, *The White House Years* (Little,

Brown, 1979) and *Years of Upheaval* (Little, Brown, 1982).

STANLEY I. KUTLER is the E. Gordon Fox Professor of American Institutions at the University of Wisconsin–Madison and editor of *Reviews in American History*. He is the author of *The Wars of Watergate: The Last Crisis of Richard Nixon* (Alfred A. Knopf, 1990) and the editor of *American Retrospectives: Historians on Historians* (Johns Hopkins University Press, 1995).

WILLIAM E. LEUCHTENBURG is the William Rand Kennan Professor of History at the University of North Carolina at Chapel Hill and a former president of the American Historical Association and of the Organization of American Historians. He received his Ph.D. from Columbia University. His publications include *Franklin D. Roosevelt and the New Deal, 1932–1940* (Harper & Row, 1963), which won the Bancroft Prize and the Francis Parkman Prize, and *In the Shadow of FDR: From Harry Truman to Bill Clinton*, 2d ed. (Cornell University Press, 1993).

ARTHUR S. LINK is a professor of history at Princeton University. He is a coeditor of the Woodrow Wilson papers and the author of the definitive multivolume biography of President Wilson.

ROBERT JAMES MADDOX is a professor of American history at Pennsylvania State University. He received his Ph.D. from Rutgers University in 1964. He is the editor of *Annual Editions: American History, Volume I, Pre-Colonial Through Reconstruction* and *Annual Editions: American History, Volume II, Reconstruction Through the Present* (Dushkin/McGraw-Hill).

RICHARD L. McCORMICK is president of the University of Washington in Seattle, Washington. Prior to that he served as provost and vice chancellor for academic affairs at the University of North Carolina at Chapel Hill. He received his Ph.D. in history from Yale University in 1976. He is the author of *The Party Period and Public Policy: American Politics from the Age of Jackson to the Progressive Era* (Oxford University Press, 1986).

DOUGLAS T. MILLER is the Distinguished Professor of History at Michigan State University in East Lansing, Michigan. He is the author of 10 books, including *On Our Own: Americans in the Sixties* (D. C. Heath, 1996).

MARION NOWAK is a journalist living in Chicago, Illinois.

WALTER T. K. NUGENT is the Andrew V. Tackes Professor of History at the University of Notre Dame in Notre Dame, Indiana. He received his Ph.D. from the University of Chicago in 1961. He is the author of several books, including *Crossings: Transatlantic Population Movements, 1870–1914* (Indiana University Press, 1992) and the forthcoming *Into the West: A History of Its People*.

KEVIN PHILLIPS is editor and publisher of *The American Political Report*. He is the author of several books on politics and government, including *Arrogant Capital: Washington, Wall Street, and the Frustration of American Politics* (Little, Brown, 1994).

ALAN REYNOLDS is a senior fellow and director of economic research at the Hudson Institute in Indianapolis. He is also the research director with the National Commission on Economic Growth and Tax Reform and the economics editor of *National Review*.

ARTHUR M. SCHLESINGER, JR., is the Albert Schweitzer Professor Emeritus of the Humanities at the City University of New York and the author of prize-winning books on Presidents Andrew Jackson, Franklin Roosevelt, and John F. Kennedy. His publications include *The Cycles of American History* (Houghton Mifflin, 1986) and *History of American Life* (Simon & Schuster, 1996). He is also trustee emeritus of the Twentieth Century Fund.

DAVID A. SHANNON is the author of *Twentieth Century America*, 4th ed. (Rand McNally, 1977) and the editor of *Southern Business: The Decades Ahead* (MacMillan, 1981).

MELVIN SMALL is a professor of history at Wayne State University in Detroit, Michigan. He has written several books, including *Covering Dissent: The Media and the Anti-Vietnam War Movement* (Rutgers University Press, 1994) and *Democracy and Diplomacy: The Impact of Domestic Politics on U.S. Foreign Policy, 1789–1994* (Johns Hopkins University Press, 1996).

DONALD SPIVEY is a professor in and chair of the history department at the University of Miami. He received his Ph.D. from the University of California, Davis, in 1976. He is the editor of *Sport in America: New Historical Perspectives* (Greenwood Press, 1985) and the author of *The Politics of Miseducation: The Booker Washington Institute of Liberia, 1929–1984* (University Press of Kentucky, 1986).

KENNETH M. STAMPP is the Morrison Professor Emeritus of History at the University of California, Berkeley. He has written numerous books on southern history, slavery, and the Civil War, including *And the War Came: The North and the Secession Crisis, 1860–1861* (Louisiana University Press, 1970), *The Peculiar Institution: Slavery in the Ante-Bellum South* (Vintage Books, 1989), and *America in 1857: A Nation on the Brink* (Oxford University Press, 1990). He is also the general editor of *Records of Ante-Bellum Southern Plantations from the Revolution Through the Civil War* (University Publications of America, 1985).

ATHAN THEOHARIS is a professor of history at Marquette University in Milwaukee, Wisconsin. He is a noted historian of the FBI files and records. He is a member of the Academy of Political Science and the Organization of American Historians. He has written several books, including *J. Edgar Hoover, Sex, and Crime: An Historical Antidote* (Ivan R. Dee, 1995). He received his Ph.D. from the University of Chicago.

JOHN TIPPLE is a professor of history at California State University, Los Angeles.

RUDOLPH J. VECOLI is director of the University of Minnesota Immigration and History Research Center in St. Paul, Minnesota. He is also vice president of the executive council of the Immigration History Society and a member of the council of the American Italian Historical Association.

ROBERT WEISBROT is a professor of history at Colby College in Waterville, Maine. He is also on the advisory committee for the African-American studies program at Colby. He is the author of *From the Founding of the Southern Christian*

Leadership Conference to the Assassination of Malcolm X (1957–65) (Chelsea House, 1994).

TOM WICKER, one-time chief of the Washington bureau of *The New York Times,* was a political columnist for *The New York Times* for 25 years, until he retired in 1991. His publications include *A Time to Die: The Attica Prison Revolt* (University of Nebraska Press, 1994) and *One of Us: The Age of Richard Nixon and the American Dream* (Random House, 1995).

INDEX